Reading and Writing for Civic Literacy

The Critical Citizen's Guide to Argumentative Rhetoric

Brief Edition

Donald Lazere

Paradigm Publishers
Boulder • London

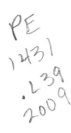
Copyright © 2009 Paradigm Publishers

Published in the Cultural Politics and the Promise of Democracy Series, Henry A. Giroux, Series Editor

Published in the United States by Paradigm Publishers, 3360 Mitchell Lane Suite E, Boulder, CO 80301 USA. Paradigm Publishers is the trade name of Birkenkamp & Company, LLC, Dean Birkenkamp, President and Publisher.

Library of Congress Cataloging-in-Publication Data

Lazere, Donald.
    Reading and writing for civic literacy : the critical citizen's guide to argumentative rhetoric / Donald Lazere.—Brief Ed.
        p. cm.
    Includes bibliographical references and index.
    ISBN 978-1-59451-709-9 (acid-free paper)—ISBN 978-1-59451-710-5 (pbk. : acid-free paper)
    1. Persuasion (Rhetoric) 2. Citizenship—United States. 3. Civil society—United States. 4. Critical thinking—United States. 5. English language—United States—Rhetoric. I. Title.
    PE1431.L393 2009
    808'.00973—dc22

                                                                                                    2008050599

Printed and bound in the United States of America on acid free paper that meets the standards of the American National Standard for Permanence of Paper for Printed Library Materials.

Designed and Typeset by Straight Creek Bookmakers

  13 12 11 10 09 1 2 3 4 5

Contents in Brief

Contents

Part III: Elements of Argumentative Rhetoric

Part IV: Thinking Critically About the Rhetoric of Politics and Mass Media

Preface for Teachers (and Curious Students) to the Brief Edition

The original edition of *Reading and Writing for Civic Literacy* is a composition and rhetoric text with readings that addresses the need for college students to develop critical reading, writing, and thinking skills for self-defense amid the arguments that inundate them in American public discourse, especially as filtered through the mass media. Within the format of a textbook, mainly for the second term of first-year English or a more advanced composition course, it presents an original theory of argumentative rhetoric, an ideological framework for understanding public controversies, and a practical method for analyzing them. This new brief edition maintains these original attributes but is about one-third shorter.

Why publish a brief edition? I guess my eyes were bigger than my stomach in the original edition, in which my appetite to be comprehensive resulted in a bulk that many teachers—including myself—found impossible to digest in a one-semester course. As one of the more generous teacher responses put it, it was "just too much of a good thing." Abridgment has also enabled the book's price to be reduced, so as to be more affordable for students—although even in the original edition, Paradigm Publishers admirably kept the price well below that of comparable texts by more commercial, bottom line–obsessed publishers.

The primary means for shortening has been the reduction of readings by about half. Vestiges of some removed readings remain in references to them and quotations, with citations so readers can search for the originals. Some chapters have been eliminated, or combined and condensed. Also, the following sections have been moved to the book's website (http://www .paradigmpublishers.com/Books/BookDetail.aspx?productID=208952): the sample student research paper, Steve Brouwer's full article "If We Decided to Tax the Rich," the glossary of critical thinking and rhetorical terms, and the works cited. I hope this new brief edition will satisfy the needs of those who want a shorter, less expensive book for classes, but the longer original edition continues to be available for those who use the book for the entire year or who have found a way to squeeze a lot of material into a single semester course.

BACKGROUND TO THE TEXT

The approach to argument here is based on the principles of "critical thinking"—a term that has all too often been used as a vague, catchall concept in textbooks but that I use with specific reference to the definitions developed by specialists in the discipline over the past two decades. In brief, this conception of critical thinking avoids technical terminology, complicated theoretical schemas, and elaborate classification of types of arguments, all of which have limited practical use outside of artificial classroom assignments. Instead, it emphasizes commonsense reasoning about familiar controversies in everyday life, along with analysis of cultural influences and psychological dispositions that lead to open-minded or closed-minded reasoning.

In contrast to the many textbooks whose primary aim is for students to generate papers based on their own ideas and arguments, the main focus here is on writing papers that demonstrate understanding and critical evaluation of arguments in sources from books, newspapers, magazines, speeches, student writing, and elsewhere. The justification for this is that in my own and many other teachers' experiences, most college students can begin to express themselves effectively about public controversies only after they have acquired a base of factual, historical, and current knowledge about them (what E. D. Hirsch calls "cultural literacy"). They further need to have studied a diversity of sources on them, learning to analyze the ideological positions and rhetorical patterns of opposing sources.

Many of the examples presented for analysis in the text and readings focus on issues in current political economy that impinge directly on students' present and future lives, such as the growing gap between the wealthy and the middle class and the poor; concentration of corporate ownership and political influence; the global economy and sweatshop labor; the decline in recent decades of job prospects and real income for most workers; the escalating cost of college education and reduction of financial aid; inequities in tax and wage policy; and crime and welfare among the poor versus the rich. These issues are presented through opposing viewpoints in readings from conservative, liberal, libertarian, and leftist authors, with glosses analyzing rhetorical aspects of the points of opposition and prompting student debates on them.

In contrast to the common textbook approach to logical fallacies that assumes they result only from unintentional lapses in reasoning, the book confronts the hard truth that real-life arguments frequently are tainted by deliberate deception, political partisanship and polemics, special pleading, double standards, conflicts of interest, "hype," and other forms of propaganda or outright lying. Moreover, it alerts students to sources of biased arguments including political "spin doctors," public relations agencies, lobbies, and partisan foundations and think tanks that sponsor journalism or research.

Thus the book assumes that college students are capable of dealing with public disputes in which the truth is often fiendishly difficult to determine, even for the most knowledgeable analysts. However, political and economic issues are not addressed at the same level or in the same manner as they would be in social science courses. They are addressed, rather, at the level of campaign speeches, news and entertainment media, op-ed columns, general-circulation journals of opinion, and other realms of public discourse to which everyone is exposed every day. The political vocabulary and information covered here are no more specialized than what every citizen in a democracy should be expected to know.

PRELUDE TO THE BRIEF EDITION

There is often a great deal of pressure on textbook authors by the more commercial presses to bring out frequent new editions with extensive changes to be "up to date." This pressure is often motivated less by valid concern for replacing out-of-date readings and references than by arbitrary price increases by the corporate-conglomerate publishers who have acquired a near-monopoly on the business (Paradigm being a brave holdout of independence). Another motive is a reaction to the transformation of the used-textbook business from an individual, local enterprise into a branch of other nationwide corporations, which buy up virtually all used copies after the first year of sale, through databases, then sell them to campus bookstores, so that few new copies are sold, while neither the publisher nor author receive any income on used copies. The end result is that many changes in new editions really serve little value except to raise the price and beat the used-book market for profits.

My choice of readings and references in the original edition was calculated to include examples that were prototypes of particular points in rhetoric and critical thinking, so that they would not quickly date even when the particular points of reference might become unknown to younger readers. I have held to that principle in this edition, bringing in new readings and contemporary references only when they truly improved on previous ones and incorporated pertinent recent information. Some reviewers, for example, singled out Holly Miller's 1985 "Bunker Hunt's Greatest Investment," in chapter 12 of this edition, as being too dated. But I have kept it because it has been a favorite of mine and of students, a classic of its kind in exemplifying the kind of journalistic "puff piece" that sentimentalizes the virtues of rich people and cosmeticizes their vices, while also exemplifying perennial lines of opposing arguments between liberals and conservatives about those virtues and vices—a central topic in chapters 13, 16, and 17.

NEW TO THE BRIEF EDITION

- Is one-third shorter than the original edition to make it more affordable for students and easier for teachers to cover in a semester or quarter.
- Adds new readings on current topics, including the 2008 presidential election and debates related to it on the growing inequality of wealth distribution, the root causes of the recent financial crisis, and the rising cost of college education. A model student term paper analyzes the rhetoric of Barack Obama and John McCain on these topics.
- Provides a sharper focus on analyzing statistical doublespeak, the rhetoric of opposing ideologies, and bias in media and education.
- Streamlines the table of contents, combining topics that naturally relate such as culture and stereotyping, and special interests and propaganda.

As in the original edition, the conceptual heart of the text continues to be chapter 13, "Thinking Critically About Political Rhetoric." Its discussion of denotation and connotation in political language, definitions of various party and ideological positions—along a worldwide and nationwide spectrum—and predictable patterns of political rhetoric is foreshadowed throughout much of the earlier sections. Some reviewers have suggested moving this chapter nearer the beginning. This would have obvious advantages, but I think it would have the disadvantage of suggesting that the book was entirely about political rhetoric. I do believe that it is essential to apply principles of rhetoric and critical thinking to politics, and that this application warrants much more emphasis than in most other textbooks, but I also believe that there are many other important dimensions and applications of rhetoric and critical thinking that precede and perhaps transcend politics; thus my decision, at least for this edition, to keep that chapter about two-thirds of the way through. Certainly, though, teachers whose courses focus centrally on politics might well assign that chapter, and perhaps the following one, "Thinking Critically about Mass Media," toward the beginning. In any case, I welcome suggestions from teachers and students about changing this and other organizational choices in future editions.

LOOKING AHEAD

This edition went to press shortly before the 2008 presidential and congressional elections, when John McCain and Barack Obama were neck-and-neck running for president, and Congress was predicted to go heavily Democratic. The many political references throughout the book focus on the period from President Ronald Reagan's election in 1980 through President George W. Bush's last term, although references to McCain's and Obama's positions on some central issues in the book have been incorporated. Obviously, a new administration will bring with it new examples of principles of rhetoric and critical thinking. It is also foreseeable that the election of 2008 might mark not just a new presidential and congressional regime but a dramatic shift in the dominant issues and rhetorical clashes of the past three decades. So it will be up to students, teachers, and other readers to apply their rhetorical skills and BS detectors to a new era. I invite them to pass along their insights to me for inclusion in the *next* edition.

Donald Lazere

Acknowledgments

This book is the culmination of a long career in teaching, scholarship, and journalism. Consequently, the list of people to whom I owe thanks, professionally or personally, stretches back through several decades. These begin with Charles Muscatine and Marlene Griffith, whose classic *The Borzoi College Reader* was the first textbook I ever taught from, in the Department of Rhetoric at Berkeley, and which was so formative in my thinking that I tell Chuck and Marlene that this book could be called "Child of *Borzoi Reader.*" I have long admired (and taught) two other textbooks, to the extent of that imitation which is the sincerest form of flattery: Ray Kytle's *Clear Thinking for Composition,* which I expressly credit throughout the book for several of my key concepts, and *Logic and Contemporary Rhetoric: The Use of Reason in Everyday Life,* by my friends Howard Kahane and Nancy Cavender, who since Howard's death has taken over authorship of the book that this one resembles most in scope and authorial tone (though their book is mainly in the discipline of philosophy while mine is in English). Ira Shor's and Henry Giroux's great books on teaching, beginning with Ira's *Critical Teaching and Everyday Life* and Henry's *Theory and Resistance in Education,* have been equally inspiring. Hugh Rank's several works developing his "Intensify-Downplay Schema" are the main source for my "Semantic Calculator for Bias in Rhetoric" and other variations on playing up and downplaying in argumentation. Gerald Graff's notion of "teaching the conflicts" is probably the strongest influence, and my long-running friendship with and professional encouragement by Jerry and Cathy Birkenstein-Graff have been priceless.

The administration and English department at California Polytechnic State University, San Luis Obispo, provided generous support and esprit de corps through the many years in which this book evolved out of my class assignments in both composition and literature courses. Since my retirement from Poly, the English department at the University of Tennessee, Knoxville, has graciously provided me with the opportunity to keep teaching and keep in touch with the lively pulse of a new generation of students.

Many of the ideas in this book developed and were tested over several summer sessions of the International Conference on Critical Thinking and Moral Critique at Sonoma State University, sponsored by the Center for Critical Thinking there, whose resident genius is Richard Paul. My distinctive concept of critical thinking was fostered by Richard and many of the distinguished faculty members from around this country and the world who made those conferences so exciting.

Other steadfast friends and colleagues through the years, several of whom read all or part of this manuscript in draft, include Alan Hausman, Sandra Gilbert, Stephen Parks, Lori Schor, Richard Ohmann, Ben Bagdikian, Mary Jo Reiff, Nina Gregg, Doug Gamble, Karen Fitts, and the late Alan France. My brother Arthur Lazere chipped in with computing expertise. Invaluable student assistance was provided by Jennifer Trainor (now a distinguished colleague at the University of Santa Clara), Glen Starkey, Kim Gottschall, and Kaitlin Madigan.

I am immeasurably grateful to Paradigm Publishers, which had the faith and integrity to publish this book without the dumbing down and depoliticizing demanded these days by the corporate conglomerates that have come to monopolize the textbook industry and whose sole concern with the bottom line has become part of the problem of mass culture that textbooks ought to be combating. The Paradigm team that got the book into publication with amazing speed and care included Dean Birkenkamp, Mike Peirce, Dianne Ewing, Cheryl Hoffman, Lisa Molinelli, Jason Potter, Alison Sullenberger, and for the second edition, Melanie Stafford and Ann Hopman, Sara Planck of Matrix Productions, and proofreader Diane Jones.

Above all, thanks to my patient partner through the years of agonies and ecstasies in writing and revising this book: my wife, Janet M. Atwill, the love of my life and an awe-inspiring scholar of classical rhetoric.

Chapter 13 was developed from "Teaching the Political Conflicts: A Rhetorical Schema," in *College Composition and Communication,* May 1992.

Part I

Introduction

CHAPTER 1

An Appeal to Students

Resolved, that the National Council of Teachers of English support the efforts of English and related subjects to train students in a new literacy encompassing not only the decoding of print but the critical reading, listening, viewing, and thinking skills necessary to enable students to cope with the sophisticated persuasion techniques found in political statements, advertising, entertainment, and news.

—Resolution Passed in 1975

I believe in the development of a critical, skeptical, humorous habit of mind—in the development of a liberally educated consciousness, a sensitivity to nuances and unstated implications, an ability to read between the lines and to hear undertones and overtones—both for the sake of political and social enlightenment and for the sake of our personal enlightenment and pleasure as individuals. I am a teacher of literature and of writing because I believe that precision, clarity, beauty and force in the use of language, and appreciative perception of these qualities in the language of others, not only make us harder to fool but are good things in themselves; since in a free society we are not only citizens but also individuals. I believe that the more sensitively we perceive things the more fully we can live and the less likely we are to be imposed on by advertisers, politicians and other Saviors.

—J. Mitchell Morse, The Irrelevant English Teacher

ENGLISH AS A SURVIVAL SKILL

This is a textbook primarily for the second term of first-year English or a more advanced composition course emphasizing argumentative rhetoric, the research paper, and writing from sources. It is also a survival guide for self-defense against manipulation by politicians, the media, teachers, and assorted propagandists. Our culture places huge value on physical fitness and self-defense. Newspapers and television are filled every day with ads for building muscles, working off fat, and martial arts. There are not many ads for building our mental muscles, reducing the fat in our brain, or defending ourselves in argumentation. Isn't it

3

equally important to be able to fight back against those trying to take verbal and intellectual advantage of us?

A bizarre feature of American public discourse in the early twenty-first century has been a parade of best-selling nonfiction books with titles like *Treason: Liberal Treachery from the Cold War to the War on Terrorism* and *Slander: Liberal Lies about the American Right* (Ann Coulter), *Deliver Us from Evil: Defeating Terrorism, Despotism, and Liberalism* (Sean Hannity), *Bias: A CBS Insider Explores How the Media Distort the News* (Bernard Goldberg, excerpted here in chapter 14), *Weapons of Mass Distortion: The Coming Meltdown of the Liberal Media* (Brent Bozell), *What Liberal Media? The Truth about Bias and the News* (Eric Alterman), *Stupid White Men: And Other Sorry Excuses for the State of the Nation!* (Michael Moore), *Lies and the Lying Liars Who Tell Them: A Fair and Balanced Look at the Right* (Al Franken), *Big Lies: The Right-Wing Propaganda Machine and How It Distorts the Truth* (Joe Conason), *Blinded by the Right: The Conscience of an Ex-Conservative* and *The Republican Noise Machine: Right-Wing Media and How It Corrupts Democracy* (David Brock). In such books as well as on competing talk-radio networks and cable channels, liberals (including Alterman, Moore, Franken, Conason, and Brock) and conservatives (including Coulter, Hannity, Goldberg, and Bozell), Democrats and Republicans shrilly accuse the other side of diabolically deceptive, monopolistic control of American politics, media, culture, and education, while portraying their own side as powerless, persecuted, and wholly virtuous. What are we to make of this dizzying, vicious circle of accusation? How can we possibly tell who in fact is telling the truth and who is lying? Among the aims of this book is to approach these questions through the systematic application to them of principles of critical thinking and argumentative **rhetoric*** (defined as the study of elements and patterns of persuasion—both scrupulous and unscrupulous ones, though popular usage tends to equate rhetoric solely with the latter).

Most argumentation textbooks cover a very wide variety of subjects, in the hope of providing something for everybody, but with the unfortunate consequence that their diffuseness and lack of continuity reproduce the fragmented thought patterns in most other realms of American public discourse, which impede the coherent, **synthesizing** mental activity necessary to critical thinking. So *Reading and Writing for Civic Literacy* mainly concentrates on rhetorical approaches to some of our most pressing current political and social controversies—especially issues related to the widening wealth gap in America and the financial pressures it puts on most citizens, including college students—in the length and depth necessary to develop coherent understanding of them, through studying them **cumulatively** and **recursively**, and to follow and write extended lines of argument about them.

Politics Is Interested in *You*

Uh-oh! At the first mention of the word "politics," many students start groaning, "I'm just not interested in politics." As a plea to persuade you not to turn off right here, let me argue that "politics" doesn't just refer to dry matters of the branches of government, the structure of parties and electoral processes, and such. Many Americans believe their life and work are wholly personal matters and under their own control, and thus they can ignore what happens in the public sphere; to the extent they are aware of larger national or international forces, they believe that those forces are beyond their understanding or control, hence not worth thinking about. You may not think you are interested in politics; however, politics is interested in *you*.

Americans were especially shocked by the events of September 11, 2001, because many had little or no knowledge of the Al Qaeda terrorist organization, the location of Afghani-

---

*Words in **boldface** throughout the book refer to key terms in rhetoric and critical thinking that will be defined in subsequent chapters and can usually be located through the index. The boldfacing also provides a model for how you might incorporate these terms into your own writing.

stan and Iraq where we were soon plunged into war, or the long-term political conflicts in the Middle East and Central Asia that were necessary background for full understanding of these events. Among the reactions to the attacks was a widespread recognition that this was a wake-up call for Americans to make much more effort to educate themselves about historical and current events throughout the world, especially those in which America's government, military, and corporations are directly involved and in which the consequences of that involvement can change any of our personal lives. (See Martha Nussbaum's "Can Patriotism Be Compassionate?" in chapter 3). When the United States invaded Iraq in 2003, tens of thousands of young men and women in the armed services, many of whom had entered the military mainly for its vocational or educational opportunities, found themselves fighting in a distant part of the world for a cause they knew little about, other than what they had been indoctrinated in by their commanding officers, and in a foreign culture about whose language, religion, and customs they knew even less. At this writing, in mid-2008, the United States is facing increasing resistance to its invasion and occupation of Iraq; the toll of American troops' death is rising, amid calls for a larger military force there. The possibility that many more college students and other young men and women will be pressured to join the military, perhaps even through a draft, has suddenly brought the war in distant Iraq closer to home and caused previously indifferent students to engage in the public disputes over whether the administration of George W. Bush deceived us in its justifications for the war. All these issues surrounding the terrorist attacks on September 11, 2001, and Iraq are "politics."

Shortly after teaching an American literature survey course at the University of Tennessee in spring 2004 in which we had briefly discussed the Iraq war in relation to Henry David Thoreau's essay "Civil Disobedience," I received the following e-mail from a student in the class:

> I just wanted to tell you that I have gotten much more into politics since I started your class and feel that it has become more important to me now that I am getting older. The events in Iraq over the last few months have disturbed me very much in relation to the prisoner abuse and the beheadings. In addition, one of my closest friends from high school was killed in Iraq over the weekend and his death has very much disturbed me since I was so close to him. He was a U.S. Marine stationed and killed in Fallujah, and now I have another good friend who is being sent back to Iraq in the next few weeks. Now, I feel like all of this mess in Iraq was pointless and I am frustrated that my friend laid down his life for a fiasco. I finally feel like the whole situation in Iraq has become very real to me after his death. It is very scary when people mention the possibility of a draft after a tragedy like this. I only wish we could have talked more about this in your class during the past semester.

Politics further includes controversies about MONEY, a subject that interests *everyone*. We live today in a political economy in which personal concerns like the cost of living, availability of jobs, access to and cost of health care, tax policy, placement of and return on our investments (especially retirement pensions) are determined by national and international forces that we cannot afford to ignore. The concentration of corporate ownership in recent decades, the growing gap in the distribution of income, power, and taxation between the rich and the middle class and poor, and between big business and small, individual businesses—all of these directly influence everyone's daily life. Your ability to find a job in the location of your choice, and at the salary of your choice, may be determined by corporate mergers, downsizing, bankruptcies (like those of Enron and WorldCom in the early years of this century), automation, or movement of industries globally into cheap labor markets. Your family business or farm may be subject to a corporate takeover or at least be affected by fluctuations in international stock and monetary markets, competition from companies that have moved to Third World countries with lower operating costs, or other forces in the global economy. As a character in the film *Network* (excerpted in chapter 8) puts it, "We are no longer an industrialized society; we aren't even a post-industrial or technological society. We are now a corporate society, a corporate world, a corporate universe."

You are certainly concerned about the quality of secondary education that you have received, how adequately it has been financed through the taxes your parents or you pay for it and other public services, and how fair the distribution of the tax burden is on different income levels. You are concerned about the increasingly high cost of college tuition, textbooks, and housing; how much financial aid is available to you and at what cost; what part-time jobs are available to you as a student, how much they pay; and—above all—what your occupational and financial prospects are after you graduate. (On this topic, see Adolph Reed's article "Majoring in Debt" in this chapter.) But how are public policies on all these matters determined, and by whom? Not by impersonal, uncontrollable forces like the weather. They are mostly controlled by human agents, by struggles for dominance between opposing political parties and ideologies (an **ideology** is a system of political concepts, such as liberalism and conservatism, or of economic concepts like capitalism and socialism), between interests representing corporate management versus those of employees, between the public sector (government employees, schools and colleges, and other nonprofit organizations) and the private, for-profit sector (corporations and small businesses, professions like law and medicine), between supporters of a planned economy and of the free market, and so on. Whether you ever become conscious of it or not, you have the choice either to become aware of the workings of all these forces and to attempt actively to influence them, or to go through a life controlled by them without your ever understanding or exerting any influence on them.

In the first edition of this book, the model student research paper in chapter 17, which was written at the University of Tennessee, was prompted by a financial crisis in Tennessee in 2002 in which large deficits in state spending resulted from the refusal of voters and legislators to enact an income tax in a state whose overall tax rates are among the lowest in the country. Because the budget debate remained deadlocked beyond the deadline for the coming fiscal year, the state government was shut down for part of a week, half the state employees were temporarily "furloughed" (a **euphemism** for laid off), the university's summer term was curtailed (leaving some students unable to graduate as planned), campus staff and services were reduced, and yet another in an annual series of tuition increases was implemented. These events woke students up to the political forces controlling the conditions of their education and motivated many of them to join lobbying efforts on behalf of the university community at the state capitol in Nashville, in opposition to well-financed anti-tax lobbies that had prevailed in the legislature for years. In this lobbying campaign students found a quite meaningful real-life application of rhetorical skills acquired in academic study.

The author of this paper became further interested in researching the ideological views underlying the debates over flat-rate sales taxes versus progressive income taxes, a subject that has been a major source of controversy between conservatives and liberals from the presidency of Ronald Reagan to that of George W. Bush. The student found that debates over the success or failure of "Reaganomics" in the 1980s were directly pertinent to the present state of the economy in the United States and in Tennessee. (That paper has been replaced by one on Obama and McCain's debates, online at http://www.paradigmpublishers.com /Books/BookDetail.aspx?productID=208952.)

Beyond controversies over political economy, other issues like environmentalism, feminism, racism, affirmative action, abortion, gun control, and capital punishment are sometimes perceived as political, but it is often far from clear in public disputes over them that they all involve a dimension of **partisan** politics, along liberal versus conservative or left versus right ideological lines, though not always Democratic versus Republican party lines—as will be explained in chapter 13. Indeed, a **predictable pattern of political rhetoric** is for those arguing about such issues to conceal the partisan nature of their arguments under a guise of nonpartisanship. Of course, not all public arguments fall into left versus right oppositions—but a lot *do,* and the failure of many citizens to perceive the nature of these oppositions can leave them without adequate understanding of the issues.

Who Makes the Rules?

The Free Speech Movement at the University of California, Berkeley, in 1964, was set off in part by many students' frustration over the feeling that college education had become a process just to turn them into cogs in the machinery of business, professions, or government. The movement's most eloquent leader, twenty-two-year-old Mario Savio, asserted about the university:

> The best among the people who enter must for four years wander aimlessly much of the time questioning why they are on campus at all, doubting whether there is any point in what they are doing, and looking toward a very bleak existence afterward in a game in which all of the rules have been made up—rules which we can not really amend.... The "futures" and "careers" for which American students now prepare are for the most part intellectual and moral wastelands. This chrome-plated consumers' paradise would have us grow up to be well-behaved children.

(See Savio's speech, "An End to History," later in this chapter.) Do you too perhaps have the feeling that you are being educated to play a game, vocationally and politically, in which someone else has made all the rules? This textbook attempts to present a beginning toward the kind of knowledge and critical skills you need, first, to learn the language of those who make the rules and, ultimately, to become an active participant in making them.

This kind of knowledge and critical skills begins with the value of opening your mind and broadening your perspective on the beliefs with which you were brought up. One way of doing that is to try to look at your beliefs in a new way: in regard to any belief that you are convinced is based on facts or the truth, ask yourself how you came to believe it is true. In other words, what is your **viewpoint** on it, and how did you acquire that viewpoint? From what sources did you get the belief—your family, teachers, peers, church, political leaders, news, entertainment, and advertising media? Others? Where did *those* sources get their beliefs? What might be the limitations or biases in your knowledge, and in that of your sources? Those sources' views are often colored by conscious or unconscious **ethnocentrism**, self-interest, and ideological biases, to say nothing of outright **hype**, **propaganda**, and deception on occasion. So we need to develop a critical perspective on *them* to evaluate their reliability. In contrast, then, to the common textbook approach that assumes faulty arguments result only from unintentional lapses in reasoning, this book confronts the hard truth that real-life arguments frequently contain deliberate deception, **special pleading**, partisanship, propaganda, and out-and-out lying, as well as ideological biases that may be conscious or unconscious.

Some students and teachers will react against this orientation by complaining that it is too "negative," with all the emphasis on detecting and defending against deceptive, fallacious arguments. If you react this way, I urge you to ask yourself two questions as you are reading: Is this "negative" approach *realistic* in relation to the state of American public discourse? And does it enable you to be a more critical and active participant in that discourse? An article titled "You're on Your Own," by Daniel Kadlec, which appeared in *Time* (January 28, 2002) after the collapse of Enron Corporation and its accounting firm, Arthur Andersen, presented an unusually frank acknowledgment—especially in a magazine that has long been a booster of American free enterprise:

> We are now responsible for so many decisions requiring so much homework that many of us feel helpless and paralyzed. The risks of inaction or unwise action are rising, even as many of the professionals on whom we would like to rely for guidance are proving untrustworthy and

> even corrupt.... We now know we can't trust stock analysts and financial planners, who often
> get paid more for selling us shaky stocks and mutual funds than for selling us solid ones....
> The Enron scandal has shown us or perhaps reminded us that when money is involved, we
> are truly on our own. (24–25)

Finally, try to keep in mind that the purpose of training yourself to spot fallacious arguments
is not to cynically dismiss each side in every dispute as equally fallacious but to be able to
distinguish invalid arguments from valid ones, liars from truth tellers—so as to inspire you
to give your wholehearted support to the truth tellers.

Another response to the charge of negative thinking is that the prevailing emphasis in
American society and education on "positive thinking" and "feeling good about yourself" can
sometimes serve the function of ostrichlike **sentimentality** and **denial** of the gravity of our
national problems. This point was addressed in an op-ed (an opinion column on the page
opposite the editors' own editorials) by Michael Kinsley in the *Los Angeles Times* (June 22,
2004, online edition), following the death of President Ronald Reagan, titled "The Trouble
with Optimism." Kinsley wrote:

> Thanks to Reagan, optimism is now considered an essential ingredient of any presidential
> candidate's public self-presentation.... Could there be an emptier claim made on behalf of
> someone hoping to lead the United States of America than to say that he is "optimistic"?
> Optimism may or may not be part of the American character, but it is pretty insufficient as
> either a campaign promise or a governing principle.... If forced to choose between a leader
> whose vision is clouded by optimism and one clouded by pessimism, there is a good case that
> pessimism is the more prudent choice. Another name for pessimism is a tragic sensibility. It
> is a vivid awareness that things can go wrong, and often have done so. An optimist thinks he
> can pop over to Iraq, knock Saddam Hussein off his perch, establish democracy throughout
> the Middle East and be home for dinner. A pessimist knows better.

While in most other democracies students are immersed in public controversies and
instruction in debating them from an early age, much of American culture and education
tends to shelter high school and even college students from such controversies, thereby trying to keep them in the mentality of adolescence rather than leading them toward thinking
and acting like adults. Remember Mario Savio's words, "This chrome-plated consumers'
paradise would have us grow up to be well-behaved children." Even adults are treated like
children by many public "leaders." In a controversial article in the *New Yorker* after 9/11,
author Susan Sontag described the Bush administration's over-simplified statements after
9/11 as "a campaign to infantilize the public." In William Safire's book *Before the Fall,* about
his experiences as a speechwriter in the Nixon White House, President Richard Nixon is
quoted as saying, "The average American is just like the child in the family" (649), and, "We
sophisticates can listen to a speech for a half hour, but after ten minutes, the average guy
wants a beer" (315). When Howard Jarvis, sponsor of Proposition 13, the influential 1978
tax-cutting ballot initiative in California, was asked why he spent all his advertising money
on TV and radio rather than newspapers, he replied, "People who decide elections today
don't read" (quoted in *Los Angeles Times,* Feb. 10, 1980, pt. 2, p. l).

To provide a few exemplary **anecdotes** from my own experience, in my younger years
when I was working as a copy-writing trainee at one of the world's largest advertising agencies, on Madison Avenue in New York, I was assigned to suggest a campaign for the latest
model of a brand-name refrigerator. The account executive explained to me, "There's really
no difference between this year's model and last year's, but we have to keep putting out a
new model every year to hype up profits, and the average housewife is too stupid to know
the difference." I worked as a public relations agent (a euphemism for propagandist) for
wealthy individuals and corporations, making them look like saints, especially in "damage
control" after they had been caught in misbehavior. I also worked in public relations for Dick

Clark's *American Bandstand,* and backstage at the telecasts, I overheard the adult managers of teenage singing stars snickering contemptuously at their clients' and their audiences' "moronic pimple music." After several years at such jobs, I became ashamed of being an agent of this kind of manipulation (albeit a well-paid one) and decided to go to graduate school in English and prepare instead to teach students how to defend themselves against manipulation. My long years of teaching and writing this book are based on the conviction that the average housewife, or the average American voter, or the average college student is not "too stupid to know the difference," provided that he or she receives the encouragement and resources to think critically.

The subject of infantilization illustrates a rhetorical term, **self-fulfilling prophecy**, which refers to a situation in which because people are induced to believe something is true, it becomes true; this is a variant on another term, **vicious circle**, in which an **effect** of some **cause** itself reinforces that cause, creating a loop that is difficult to break. In this case, if authorities treat people like children, many will act like children. After all, it's so much easier to be a child than an adult. Who doesn't prefer candy to vegetables, junk food to a nutritious diet, the teacher who gives you an easy A to one who makes you work hard for it? Everything in my teaching experience, however, has indicated that although many students at the conscious level prefer everything to be made simple and painless for them, deep down they understand that junk-food education does not help them grow and insults their intelligence. So this book attempts to break the vicious circle of infantilization by assuming that college-age students want to deal with adult realities and complexities, especially concerning the socioeconomic issues emphasized here, frustrating as they may be. (Older students who have had more hard experience of the world will not need to have this point labored.)

Go to the Mall Instead?

Back to the "negative" attitude toward politics and public discourse in this book, it would be hard to outdo the fear and loathing that many American students and adults alike already feel toward politics. The widespread attitude is, "Politicians are all a bunch of crooks, and politics has gotten so complex and corrupt that it's a waste of time even to think about it. Leave it to the professionals." On the surface, this attitude appears perfectly sensible. When you plunge into the kinds of disputes aired in the readings throughout this book and find that on virtually every issue not only Democrats and Republicans or liberals and conservatives but also libertarians and radical leftists (or socialists) present diametrically opposed versions of the truth, each persuasively argued and supported by impressive evidence, a natural reaction is to throw your hands in the air, despair of ever knowing whom you can believe, and go to the beach or mall instead. Moreover, many Americans are kept so busy just scrambling to get the necessary credentials in school to get a job, and then working at that job while worrying about being able to pay their bills from one month to the next, that they feel they cannot spare the time to take courses about public affairs or inform themselves about what is going on politically, to vote, or to take part in political organizations and activities.

Consider, though, that this reaction is another vicious circle, playing right into the hands of the crooks and the **special interests** that spend a great deal of money and effort trying to obscure the truth. If enough ordinary citizens give up on pursuing the truth and participating in the political process, it will guarantee that the deceitful, corrupt "professionals," with no one keeping tabs on them, become ever more corrupt and win by default. As the freed slave and abolitionist leader Frederick Douglass put it on the brink of the Civil War in 1857, "Find out just what people will submit to, and you have found out the exact amount of injustice and wrong which will be imposed upon them. . . . The limits of tyrants are prescribed by the endurance of those whom they oppress" (quoted in Wolfgang Mieder, *"No Struggle, No Progress": Frederick Douglass and His Proverbial Rhetoric* 31).

The most famous commentary on the principles being developed here is George Orwell's 1946 essay "Politics and the English Language," in which Orwell observes:

> Now, it is clear that the decline of a language must ultimately have political and economic causes; it is not due simply to the bad influence of this or that individual writer. But an effect can become a cause, reinforcing the original cause and producing the same effect in an intensified form, and so on indefinitely. A man may take to drink because he feels himself to be a failure, and then fail all the more completely because he drinks. It is rather the same thing that is happening to the English language. It becomes ugly and inaccurate because our thoughts are foolish, but the slovenliness of our language makes it easier for us to have foolish thoughts. The point is that the process is reversible. Modern English, especially written English, is full of bad habits which spread by imitation and which can be avoided if one is willing to take the necessary trouble. If one gets rid of these habits one can think more clearly, and to think clearly is a necessary first step toward political regeneration. (249)

Orwell is discussing another vicious circle here, using the **analogy** of the drunkard: the clarity of our language is eroded by political and economic causes that prevail partly because they numb clear thinking about them, and unclear thinking leads to unclear language; but our unclear language itself then becomes a cause for unclear thinking—and for further political decay (some examples that Orwell presents will be cited in later chapters). Similar vicious circles have been described here: if you treat people like children, they are likely to behave like children; the more that Americans believe politics is hopelessly corrupt and obscure, the more corrupt and obscure it *will* be; and as students are forced by financial and social pressures to specialize in occupational majors at the expense of general education, they deprive themselves of precisely the kind of education they need to understand the causes of those pressures and to launch an organized movement against them. However, Orwell continues, the circle of corrupt politics-thought-language might be broken by our starting to clarify our language. Orwell insists that he is not talking about proper grammar or usage, which are incidental, but about forming words and ideas that accurately correspond to external reality, or "language as an instrument for expressing and not for concealing or preventing thought" (259).

Similarly, perhaps a starting point for American students and citizens to break the vicious circles they are caught in is to develop the critical vocabulary and rhetorical concepts enabling them to understand ideas like vicious circle. The thesis of this book, then, is that a framework of rhetorical terms and concepts like those identified by bold-facing throughout this chapter and subsequently can provide us with a beginning point for becoming more critical and active citizens, the weapons we need to defend ourselves against infantilization.

Without buying into conspiracy theories, it seems reasonable to conjecture that the tendencies in American politics, media, and education toward keeping people in childlike ignorance, deemphasizing the importance of civic education, and presenting political issues in a superficial, incoherent manner are perpetuated because they serve, directly or indirectly, the interests of those who benefit from maintaining the present hierarchies of power. What is certain is that the pervasiveness and elaborate engineering of both political and commercial propaganda in our time far exceed that in any past period of history, and that the level of American public rhetoric—mainly under the influence of televised and talk-radio political news (especially on twenty-four-hour-a-day cable networks), debates, and advertising—has been declining steadily toward ever shorter and more irrational "sound bites." The professional consultants who developed the rapid-fire "top-forty-stories" format for local newscasts justified it by claiming, "People who watch television the most are unread, uneducated, untraveled and unable to concentrate on single subjects more than a minute or two" (*San Francisco Examiner and Chronicle,* March 16, 1975, 14).

Political party organizations and government administrations employ television performance consultants and "spin doctors," often from advertising or public relations agencies accustomed to using market research to sell products, who calculate their messages not for their truth-value but for whether they will be "bought" by the largest, least informed segment of the public. So social policies and even wars are now sold like soap flakes (see the readings in chapter 15), and prime qualifications for public office are telegenic good looks and acting ability (including the ability to lie convincingly), rather than wisdom and honesty. This situation, in both politics and "entertainment" forms like talk radio, is inevitably a breeding ground for the **demagogue**, a public figure who manipulates the ignorance and prejudices of the masses for his or her own power or profit. (The very fact that so few American students or citizens know the meaning of the word *demagogue* increases their vulnerability to demagogy.)

These destructive influences on public discourse are very likely among both the leading causes and effects of the facts confirmed by many recent reports on literacy in the United States, along with books and articles by both conservative and liberal social commentators, indicating an alarmingly low level of interest and knowledge in young Americans of precisely those areas of education—including basic knowledge of history, economics, political science, and sociology—that are most necessary for them to exert democratic control over the forces influencing their lives. Deficiencies in a base of factual knowledge about social science and in critical thinking proficiency in evaluating that knowledge cut across nearly all social segments of American high school and college students. Since the voting age was lowered from twenty-one to eighteen in 1973 (a concession, it should be noted, to the student and anti–Vietnam War protests of the sixties), the lowest rate of voting has been precisely in the eighteen-to-twenty-one-year-old bracket, and the United States now has the lowest rate of voting of any democracy in the world. According to an article in the *Boston Globe* (February 15, 1999), "Each year of the past five, the annual survey of national freshman attitudes conducted by the University of California at Los Angeles has hit a new record low with students who say it is important to keep up with political affairs. At 26 percent this year, it was down from 58 percent when the survey was first done in 1966." (More recent studies, however, have shown a resurgence of student and other youthful interest in politics, especially in the 2006 midterm and 2008 presidential elections, with particular enthusiasm among the young in support of Barack Obama.)

None of this bad news is meant to **imply** that your generation of students is "dumb." It would be a foolhardy **overgeneralization** to suggest that a whole generation was born intellectually deficient. The more valid generalization would be that this generation, by and large, is inadequately educated and informed about politics, through little fault of its own. (To place the fault on *the students* is an example of the **causal fallacy** of **blaming the victim**.) My experience with students tells me that their indifference toward politics is largely the product of the skimpy amount and poor quality of the political education they have received; students avoid political issues largely because their education has provided little help in understanding them—and, as noted earlier, that understanding is made all the more difficult because the discourse of American politics, media, and even education tends to approach political issues incoherently and superficially, without providing any explanatory overview of opposing ideologies or viewpoints that would help provide a context for full understanding. I believe most students are perfectly capable of understanding and taking an interest in political issues if those issues are explained in a comprehensible, step-by-step manner and within a coherent framework of ideological concepts, as this book attempts to do.

The Role of English Studies

Educators and students at every level and in every pertinent academic discipline face a vital challenge to reorient our schools toward enabling young Americans to become more informed and active citizens. But what distinctive role can English studies, and composition courses in particular, play in achieving this goal, and what is the difference between their orientation and that of political science or other social sciences? English studies can apply basic reading and research skills (including an introduction to locating and evaluating sources of information on public affairs, in periodicals, books, and reports), the critical insights of literature and literary theory, the analytic tools of logic, argumentative rhetoric, and general semantics to education for critical citizenship—and more specifically to the "new literacy" described in the National Council of Teachers of English resolution cited at the head of this chapter.

Of course, it would not be helpful to pitch this book at a level far above the heads of what first- or second-year college students are prepared to understand. It attempts to start at a level comprehensible to most lower-division college students and—on the assumption that they are willing and able to stretch their cognitive and emotional capacities—to move from there toward more sophistication and the ability to engage in public controversies at the level of liberally educated adults. The book culminates cumulatively in part V, in which everything before is synthesized into a suggested process for writing a critical research paper on the subject "Rhetoric and the Wealth Gap," which includes parts of papers by students who have gone through this process in my own courses.

Moreover, issues are analyzed in this book at the level at which they are addressed, not in social science scholarship, but in political speeches, news and entertainment media, op-ed columns, general-circulation journals of opinion, and other realms of public discourse to which everyone is exposed every day. The political vocabulary and information covered here are no more specialized than what every citizen in a democracy should be expected to know, even before taking a college argumentative and research writing course. Nevertheless, in sections dealing with political rhetoric, especially chapter 13, elementary definitions and explanations of political concepts are provided for those students who need them, and they may benefit from jumping ahead to read that chapter first and returning to it for reference throughout the book.

Indeed, one of the main points stressed in this book is the difference in levels of rhetoric between public and scholarly treatments of political issues, and the need for students to take courses in more specialized disciplines to gain deeper knowledge of these issues. Students *can* learn in argumentative writing classes, though, to develop a more complex and comprehensive rhetorical understanding of political events and ideologies than that provided by politicians and mass media—or, for that matter, by most social science courses, which usually emphasize factual exposition or theory at the expense of rhetorical analysis.

Avoiding Political Correctness

Finally, an approach like mine can invite the danger of being turned into an indoctrination to the instructor's personal political ideology, or into an excuse for teaching political science instead of rhetoric and writing. This concern has certainly been warranted by the tendency of some "politically correct" teachers (usually liberal or leftist, though there are also cases of conservative political correctness) to assume that all students and colleagues agree—or *should* agree—with their particular view. So one of my main efforts has been to avoid turning this book and the kind of course it is intended for into indoctrination into any particular ideological position. My method involves addressing as an explicit topic for rhetorical study the issues of political subjectivity, partisanship, and bias in sources of information, including teachers and authors of textbooks—including this one. The principle is that any writer or reader addressing controversial issues will almost inevitably have a subjective, **partisan viewpoint** (that is, a viewpoint siding with a particular party or ideology). There is nothing wrong with having such a viewpoint; indeed, a clear-cut expression of a particular partisan viewpoint can be a rhetorical virtue in enabling you to understand what that viewpoint stands for, particularly if the expression is relatively unbiased and supported through sound argumentation. Our aims should simply be to learn to identify and understand what the viewpoint of any given source is, so that we can weigh its rhetorical quality against that of opposing viewpoints.

In the same way, we need to learn to recognize our own ideological viewpoint, and possible biases, as readers and writers, and certainly as teachers. I do not believe that teachers or textbook writers should coyly hide their viewpoint, as they often do, but that they should honestly identify it and present it, not as "the truth" or "the facts" but as one viewpoint among others, needing to be scrutinized for its own biases and fairly evaluated against opposing ones. Thus, although total objectivity may never be attainable, dealing honestly with our own subjectivity may be the best way to approximate objectivity. This principle obliges me to come out from the hiding place of authorial anonymity and pretended objectivity that is the convention in textbooks and to speak as "I" from time to time throughout the book, especially in addressing issues where it is most difficult for anyone to present an objective, impartial analysis. On several such issues I provide a "Reader Advisory" alerting you to my possible biases. The intention of this method, then, is to guarantee that students will not be indoctrinated into my own or any teacher's or writer's ideology, but rather that the scope of students' own critical thinking, reading, and writing capacities will be broadened so as to empower them to make their own autonomous judgments on opposing ideological positions in general and on specific issues. It is exactly this intention that justifies introducing political issues in writing courses, within a *rhetorical* framework quite different from anything you are apt to encounter in political science or any other courses. All this may sound terribly **abstract** to you right now, but it will be **concretized** throughout the body of the book.

CRITICAL EDUCATION IN HISTORICAL PERSPECTIVE

> Their critical approach to value choices does not put the humanities at odds with the traditional social mission of American schools—preparing students for citizenship by teaching the democratic values that have shaped the American heritage. For learning to be critical does not imply disloyalty to traditional values. Indeed, questioning, debate, and dissent are central to our heritage. They leaven the stable values of citizenship—charity, tolerance, and goodwill—that enoble the American definition of civic virtue.
>
> —*Rockefeller Foundation Commission on the Humanities,*
> The Humanities in American Life *(1980)*

The academic study of writing, and particularly argumentative writing, in modern times derives primarily from two historical sources: rhetoric and literature, both of which have been closely related to philosophy and other traditional fields of humanistic study. In ancient Greece and Rome, argumentative rhetoric formed the center of general, or liberal, education, and the central purpose of rhetorical education was preparation for active involvement in civic affairs. (The availability of such education was limited, to be sure, mainly to white males and also excluded slaves and the lower classes.) The germinal text in rhetorical education, the *Rhetoric* of Aristotle, written in the fourth century BC, focuses first and foremost on political rhetoric. Aristotle took a largely pragmatic, "how to" approach to its skills and devices. Aristotle's teacher Plato, by contrast, viewed purely pragmatic rhetoric as unscrupulous, associating it with the school of the Sophists—hence the modern terms *sophistry* and *sophistic* as synonymous with deceptive rhetoric: "making the weaker argument appear the stronger," as Socrates, the hero of Plato's dialogues, described the Sophists' method (*Apology* 35).

Socrates and Plato viewed authentic rhetoric as the embodiment in speech of the philosophical search for truth and justice. Socrates himself was brought to trial, however, under charges of undermining the authority of the state and under false accusation by jealous rivals of teaching his students deceptively clever rhetoric in the manner of the Sophists. He began his defense, recorded in Plato's *Apology,* by declaring, "I shall prove that I am not a clever speaker in any way at all—unless, indeed, by a clever speaker they mean someone who speaks the truth" (21). He continued by urging the judges, "Never mind the manner of my speech—it may be superior or it may be inferior to the usual manner. Give your whole attention to the question, whether what I say is just or not? That is what is required of a good judge, as speaking the truth is required of a good orator" (350).

The concept of education in rhetoric for critical citizenship was also essential in the origins of the United States, with the significant innovation that this kind of education was deemed necessary and proper for all citizens, not just the social elite. (Here again, of course, the democratic ideal of education fell short in practice, as women, African Americans, Native Americans, and others were excluded, and continued to be well into the twentieth century, and the ideal of equal access to liberal education has still not been realized.) The study of public rhetoric was assumed by the eighteenth-century founders to be at the heart of secondary and higher education, and active involvement in civic debates by the entire populace was considered the essence of American democracy. One of the defining statements of this period was the essay "What Is An American?" (1782) by J. Hector St. John de Crèvecoeur, a Frenchman who emigrated to the New World shortly before the Revolution. About typical Americans, he wrote, "As citizens it is easy to imagine that they will carefully read the newspapers, enter into every political disquisition, freely blame or censure governors and others" (46).

Thomas Jefferson was the founder of free public education in America and of the first public college, the University of Virginia. He expressed his concept of the primary value of public education in a famous 1813 letter to John Adams disputing Adams's belief that America should maintain a hereditary aristocracy as a ruling elite. Jefferson described the model for education that he had proposed in Virginia:

> To establish in every ward a free school for reading, writing and common arithmetic; to provide for the annual selection of the best subjects from these schools, who might receive, at the public expense, a higher degree of education at a district school, and from these district schools to select a certain number of the most promising subjects, to be completed at a university, where all the useful sciences [subjects of study in general] should be taught. Worth and genius would thus have been sought out from every condition of life, and completely prepared by education for defeating the competition of wealth and birth for public trusts....
>
> This ... would have raised the mass of the people to the high ground of moral respectability necessary to their own safety, and to orderly government; and would have completed the great object of qualifying them to select the veritable aristoi [aristocrats], for the trusts of government, to the exclusion of the pseudalists [the pseudo-aristocracy of inherited privilege]. ("The Natural Aristocrat," 1308)

Intellectuals as Dissenters

From ancient times to the present, a long line of writers and scholars in the fields of rhetoric and philosophy, as well as many literary artists, has been inspired by Socrates' mission of fidelity to the language of truth and justice in public life, often against the grain of public opinion and official authority. The quotation at the beginning of this chapter from J. Mitchell Morse aptly captures the respect for qualities like "precision, clarity, beauty and force in the use of language" that commit, or ought to commit, writers and students of both rhetoric and literature to "political and social enlightenment." Dedicated artists, writers, and scholars tend to be nonconformists, to resist going into more "practical" occupations in order to devote their lives to the search for wisdom and truth, serving in effect as society's voice of conscience. Thus the English poet of the nineteenth-century romantic age Percy Bysshe Shelley wrote in his "Defense of Poetry," "Poets are the unacknowledged legislators of mankind"; *Newsweek* writer David Gates makes an **allusion** to Shelley's line in "The Voices of Dissent" in this chapter.

Ralph Waldo Emerson's 1837 speech "The American Scholar" remains the classic American reaffirmation of the responsibility of the man or woman of letters (unfortunately, only "the man" in Emerson's dated usage, which includes other terms that strike us now as sexist) to speak truth to power, for "there can be no scholar without the heroic mind" (94). "It becomes him to feel all confidence in himself, and to defer never to the popular cry" (102).

> It is a shame to him if his tranquillity, amid dangerous times, arise from the presumption that like children and women, his is a protected class; or if he seek a temporary peace by the diversion of his thoughts from politics or vexed questions, hiding his head like an ostrich in the flowering bushes, peeping into microscopes, and turning rhymes, as a boy whistles to keep his courage up. So is the danger a danger still; so is the fear worse. Manlike let him turn and face it.... What deafness, what stone-blind custom, what overgrown error you behold, is there only by sufferance,—by your sufferance [allowing it]. See it to be a lie, and you have already dealt it its mortal blow. (104–105)

Although Emerson insists on scholars' and artists' responsibility to confront political issues, he adds that their manner of doing so must provide wiser, deeper, longer-range consideration than politicians or news media themselves exercise:

> The office of the scholar is to cheer, to raise, and to guide men by showing them facts amidst appearances. He plies the slow, unhonored, and unpaid task of observation.... The world of any moment is the merest appearance. Some great decorum, some fetish of a government, some ephemeral trade, or war, or man, is cried up by half of mankind and cried down by the other half, as if all depended on this particular up or down. The odds are that the whole question is not worth the poorest thought which the scholar has lost in listening to the controversy. Let him not quit his belief that a popgun is a popgun, though the ancient and honorable of the earth affirm it to be the crack of doom. In silence, in steadiness, in severe abstraction, let him hold by himself; add observation to observation; patient of neglect, patient of reproach, and bide his own time,—happy enough if he can satisfy himself alone that this day he has seen something truly....
> If the single man plant himself indomitably on his instincts, and there abide, the huge world will come round to him. (102–103, 115)

Higher education in both composition and literature, then, has the unique, Emersonian mission of bringing to bear on current events the longer view, the synthesizing vision needed to counteract the hurriedness, atomization, and ideological hodgepodge that debase our public discourse as well as our over-departmentalized curricula and overspecialized scholarship. As Emerson's disciple Henry David Thoreau advised: "Read not the Times [the name of a newspaper]. Read the Eternities" ("Life without Principle," 437). "The world of any moment is the merest appearance." Think, for example, about how the American public and media rushed to accept the appearances presented by the Bush administration in 2002–2003 for going to war in Iraq, and how quickly those appearances changed within a year. (They undoubtedly will have changed again, in unpredictable ways, by the time you read this.)

Emerson's Platonic belief that social falsehood, injustice, and fragmentation should be offensive to men and women of letters' sense of linguistic and literary wholeness has been echoed by many subsequent writers in the United States and elsewhere throughout the world, including Ernest Hemingway, who reputedly replied to the question of what makes a good writer, "Every good writer has a built-in BS detector." As recently as September 2001, the same idea was reaffirmed in an article titled "The Public Role of Writers and Intellectuals," by Edward Said, a prominent professor of literature at Columbia University and activist for the Palestinian cause in the Middle East: "At the dawn of the twenty-first century, the writer has taken on more and more of the intellectual's adversarial attributes in such activities as speaking the truth to power, being a witness to persecution and suffering, and supplying a dissenting voice in conflicts with authority" (*Nation,* September 27, 2001, 27). The *Newsweek* article on page 25, "The Voices of Dissent," presents a similar account of the tradition of writers as dissenters from the political and social mainstream, indicating why writers like the three discussed there, Susan Sontag, Arundhati Roy, and Barbara Kingsolver—along with teachers and students of writing—tend to be political liberals, in the sense of critically questioning the social status quo. And that is why there are constant culture wars between writers, scholars, and other intellectuals, versus conservatives, who accuse them of being unpatriotic, "moral relativists," a destructive "adversary culture," and perpetrators of their own, "politically correct" status quo in their own realms of power, including university humanities departments. The antagonism between American conservatives and liberal intellectuals has resulted over the past three decades in the sponsorship by conservative political and corporate leaders of what they term a "counter-intelligentsia" based in the media, foundations, and research institutes—the source of many of the readings by conservatives that are counterposed to liberal ones throughout this book.

The modern term *intellectual,* as Said uses it, is broadly used to refer to the class of people who seek to emulate the critical mind-set discussed above of rhetoricians and philosophers, literary and other artists, scholars, and responsible journalists. Unfortunately, although most of the founders of the United States were among the leading intellectuals of their time, since the mid–nineteenth century the word *intellectual* has taken on a negative **connotation** in this country that it does not have in most other societies. (The actual historical behavior of intellectuals has sometimes, alas, provided sound reasons for that connotation.) And although most students do not go to college with the purpose of becoming intellectuals, intellectual culture nevertheless remains synonymous with humanistic education, and your exposure to college education should, ideally, provide you basic acquaintance with and respect for the positive aspects of that culture, which can serve you as a survival tool applicable to your everyday life as your personal "BS detector."

Topics for Discussion and Writing

1. What are the primary aims of learning, writing, and argumentation as they are developed in chapter 1? Do they differ from those you are accustomed to being taught in school? In what way?

2. Write a paper weighing the pros and cons of these aims—in terms of their personal value to you—in comparison to the aims pursued in other courses you have taken, and in relation to the more "practical" or occupational aims of a college education.

3. Write a paper summarizing the various aspects of the distinctive role of English studies in fostering critical citizenship that this chapter develops, using quotations from several of the cited sources for support, and evaluating the persuasiveness of the argument made here that this is an English textbook, not one for political science.

4. Today many Americans believe that the primary goal of education is to enable one to become wealthy. In the excerpt from Jefferson's essay "The Natural Aristocrat," exactly what is he suggesting as the proper role of education in relation to wealth; that is, does he say that education should enable one to get rich,

or what? (Some students carelessly misread the sentence beginning, "Worth and genius ..." as saying that education will prepare those of worth to defeat the highly born in competition for wealth, but the competition Jefferson refers to is for "public trusts," or "the trusts of government"—that is, those to whom government is best entrusted.) Why do you suppose American attitudes have changed so much from Jefferson's? Do some research on the history of American education in this regard.

5. In the passage quoted from Emerson's essay "The American Scholar," you may have been struck negatively by his assumption that the scholar is a "he" and by the phrases "like children and women, his is a protected class," "as a boy whistles to keep his courage up," and "Manlike let him turn and face it." In your opinion, to what extent do these sexist phrasings, which largely reflect the **culturally conditioned assumptions** and limitations of Emerson's time, detract from the validity of the ideas he is expressing here? Support your opinion.

6. What connotation does the noun "intellectual" have for you? What is your reaction to the suggestion here that the purpose of a general education should be to make you, to some extent, an intellectual?

An End to History

Mario Savio

Humanity, December 1964

Last summer I went to Mississippi to join the struggle there for civil rights. This fall I am engaged in another phase of the same struggle, this time in Berkeley. The two battlefields may seem quite different to some observers, but this is not the case. This same rights are at stake in both places—the right to participate as citizens in [a] democratic society and to struggle against the same enemy. In Mississippi, an autocratic and powerful minority rules, through organized violence, to suppress the vast, virtually powerless, majority. In California, the privileged minority manipulates the University bureaucracy to suppress the students' political expression. That "respectable" bureaucracy masks the *financial plutocrats:* that impersonal bureaucracy is the efficient enemy in a "Brave New World."

In our free speech fight at the University of California, we have come up against what may emerge as the greatest problem of our nation—depersonalized, unresponsive bureaucracy. We have encountered the organized status quo in Mississippi, but it is the same in Berkeley. Here in Berkeley we find it impossible usually to meet with anyone but secretaries. Beyond that, we find functionaries who cannot make policy but can only hide behind the rules. We have discovered total lack of response on the part of the true policy makers. To grasp a situation which is truly Kafkaesque, it is necessary to understand the bureaucratic mentality. And we have learned quite a bit about it this fall, more outside the classroom than in.

As bureaucrat, an administrator believes that nothing new happens. He occupies an a-historical point of view. In September, to get the attention of this bureaucracy which had issued arbitrary edicts suppressing student political expression and refused to discuss its action, we held a sit-in on the campus. We sat around a police car and kept it immobilized for over thirty-two hours. At last, the administrative bureaucracy agreed to negotiate. But instead, on the following Monday, we discovered that a committee had been appointed, in accordance with usual regulations, to resolve the dispute. Our attempt to convince any of the administrators that an event had occurred, that something new had happened, failed. They saw this simply as something to be handled by normal University procedures.

The same is true of all bureaucracies. They begin as tools—means to certain legitimate goals—and they end up feeding their own existence. The conception that bureaucrats have is that history has in fact come to an end. No events can occur, now that the Second World War is over, which can change American society substantially. We proceed by standard procedures as we are.

The most crucial problems facing the United States today are the problem of automation and the problem of racial injustice. Most people who will be put out of jobs by machines will not accept an end to events, this historical plateau, as the point beyond which no change occurs. Negroes will not accept an end to history here. All of us must refuse to accept history's final judgment that in America there is no place in society for people whose skins are dark. On campus students are not about to accept it as fact that the University has ceased evolving and is in its final state of perfection, that students and faculty are respectively raw material and employees, or that the University is to be autocratically run by unresponsive bureaucrats.

Here is the real contradiction: The bureaucrats hold history as ended. As a result significant parts of the population both on campus and off are dispossessed, and these dispossessed are not about to accept this a-historical point of view. It is out of this that the conflict has occurred with the University bureaucracy and will continue to occur until that bureaucracy becomes responsive or until it is clear that the University can not function.

The things we are asking for in our civil rights protests have a deceptively quaint ring. We are asking for the due process of law. We are asking for our actions to be judged by committees of our peers. We are asking that regulations ought to be considered as arrived at legitimately only from the consensus of the governed. These phrases are all pretty old, but they are not being taken seriously in America today, nor are they being taken seriously on the Berkeley campus.

I have just come from a meeting with the Dean of Students. She notified us that she was aware of certain violations of University regulations by certain organizations. University Friends of SNCC [Student Nonviolent Coordinating Committee], which I represent, was one of these. We tried to draw from her some statement on these great principles—consent of the governed, jury of one's peers, due process. The best she could do was to evade or to present the administration party line. It is very hard to make any contact with the human being who is behind these organizations.

The university is the place where people begin seriously to question the conditions of their existence and raise the issue of whether they can be committed to the society they have been born into. After a long period of apathy during the fifties, students have begun not only to question, but, having arrived at answers, to act on those answers. This is part of a growing understanding among many people in America that history has not ended, that a better society is possible, and that it is worth dying for.

This free speech fight points up a fascinating aspect of contemporary campus life. Students are permitted to talk all they want so long as their speech has no consequences.

One conception of the university, suggested by a classical Christian formulation, is that it be in the world but not of the world. The conception of Clark Kerr by contrast is that the university is part and parcel of this particular stage in the history of American society; it stands to serve the needs of American industry; it is a factory that turns out a certain product needed by industry or government. Because speech does often have consequences which might alter this perversion of higher education, the university must put itself in a position of censorship. It can permit two kinds of speech: speech which encourages continuation of the status quo, and speech which advocates changes in it so radical as to be irrelevant in the foreseeable future. Someone may advocate radical change in all aspects of American society, and this I am sure he can do with impunity. But if someone advocates sit-ins to bring about changes in discriminatory hiring practices, this can not be permitted because it goes against the status quo of which the university is a part. And that is how the fight began here.

The administration of the Berkeley campus has admitted that external, extra-legal groups have pressured the University not to permit students on campus to organize picket lines, not to permit on campus any speech with consequences. And the bureaucracy went along. Speech with consequences, speech in the area of civil rights, speech which some might regard as illegal, must stop.

Many students here at the University, many people in society, are wandering aimlessly about. Strangers in their own lives, there is no place for them. They are people who have not learned to compromise, who for example have come to the University to learn to question, to grow, to learn—all the standard things that sound like clichés because no one takes them seriously. And they find at one point or another that for them to become part of society, to become lawyers, ministers, business men, or people in government, very often they must compromise those principles which were most dear to them. They must suppress the most creative impulses that they have; this is a prior condition for being part of the system. The university is well structured, well tooled, to turn out people with all the sharp edges worn off—the well-rounded person. The university is well equipped to produce that sort of person, and this means that the best among the people who enter must for four years wander aimlessly much of the time questioning why they are on campus at all, doubting whether there is any point in what they are doing, and looking toward a very bleak existence afterward in a game in which all of the rules have been made up—rules which one can not really amend.

It is a bleak scene, but it is all a lot of us have to look forward to. Society provides no challenge. American society in the standard conception it has of itself is simply no longer exciting. The most exciting things going on in America today are movements to change America. America is becoming ever more the utopia of sterilized, automated contentment. The "futures" and "careers" for which American students now prepare are for the most part intellectual and moral wastelands. This chrome-plated consumers' paradise would have us grow up to be well-behaved children. But an important minority of men and women coming to the front today have shown that they will die rather than be standardized, replaceable, and irrelevant.

Majoring in Debt

Adolph L. Reed Jr.

Progressive, January 2004

This column condenses material from "Why Political Scientists Should Support Free Public Higher Education," by Preston H. Smith II and Sharon Szymanski," at http://freehighered.org.

Higher education is a basic social good. As such, it should be available to all, without cost, who meet admission standards. The federal government, as the guarantor of social rights, should bear primary responsibility for providing free college for all.

This proposal isn't prohibitively costly; the total bill for all students currently enrolled in public institutions is under $27 billion, less than one-third of what George W. Bush is spending on Iraq this year. Closing recently opened corporate tax loopholes would also more than meet the program's cost, even if enrollments doubled as a result of eliminating tuition as a constraint.

Moreover, this program isn't pie in the sky. It has a clear precedent in living memory. The GI Bill paid full tuition and fees, as well as a living-wage stipend, for nearly eight million returning World War II veterans. We've done it before, we can do it again, and this time for everyone.

The crisis in public education is intensifying. As almost every state reels from the effects of recession and tax cuts, legislatures slash funding for higher education, the largest discretionary item in most state budgets. Colleges respond with hefty tuition increases, reduced financial assistance, and new fees. These measures put an extra burden on the average family, whose net worth has declined over the last two years for the first time in half a century.

Increased tuition, coupled with dwindling financial aid, is a significant problem for millions of families. According to the College Board, over the last decade, average tuition and fees at public four-year colleges increased 40 percent, and last year alone it increased by 14 percent. Community colleges increased tuition by a similar percentage last year.

Financial aid is not picking up the slack. Three decades ago, the financial aid system, with Pell grants as the backbone, guaranteed access to public colleges for primarily low- and moderate-income students. Millions of Americans earned college degrees as a result. In 1975, the maximum Pell grant covered 84 percent of costs at a four-year public college. Now, the grant covers only 42 percent of costs at four-year public colleges and only 16 percent of costs at four-year private colleges.

Meanwhile, colleges are shifting away from grants and toward loans. A decade ago, 50 percent of student aid was in the form of grants and 47 percent was in the form of loans. Today, grants are down to 39 percent of total aid; loans have increased to 54 percent.

What's worse, many of these loans are irrespective of need. In 1992, Washington decided to further help out the wealthier by making unsubsidized loans available to all students, changing the definition of need, and increasing the limits for subsidized loans. Now unsubsidized loans, although the most expensive, account for more than half of all federal loan monies.

In a bureaucratic maneuver, the Bush Administration recently changed the federal needs formula that determines how much of a family's income is really discretionary—and therefore fair game for covering college costs. A report by the Congressional Research Service states that the new financial formula will reduce Pell grants by $270 million, disqualify 84,000 students from receiving any Pell grants, and reduce the amount of Pell grants for hundreds of thousands more students.

Skyrocketing tuition and reliance on interest-carrying loans force some students to forgo college altogether, while others drop out or delay graduation.

By reducing tuition subsidies, public colleges violate their mandates to individuals and to society to provide a quality education to all who qualify. Many universities are retreating from their commitments to provide low-cost education for state residents, as they shift the balance of admissions more toward out-of-state applicants who pay substantially higher tuition. State schools have traditionally been the ladders to good jobs for students from working families. Soon, only the wealthiest will be able to afford the best public colleges and universities.

In fact, the Congressional Advisory Committee on Student Financial Assistance reports that by the end of this decade as many as 4.4 million college-qualified high school graduates will be unable to enroll in a four-year college, and two million will not go to college at all because they can't afford it.

Many students who do go to college have to work long hours, which adversely affects their education. A whopping 53 percent of low-income freshmen who work more than thirty-five hours per week drop out and do not receive a degree. Contrast this with low-income freshmen who work fewer hours: Of those who work one-to-fourteen hours per week, only 20 percent do not receive a degree, according to the Congressional Advisory Committee on Student Financial Assistance.

Those who graduate carry an enormous debt. The majority of students (64 percent) graduate with an average debt of almost $17,000, up significantly from $8,200 in 1989. Faced with repaying huge loans, students often reconsider their career plans. Our society suffers if students abandon lower paying occupations in teaching, social services, and health care in order to seek courses of study that lead to higher income jobs that speed loan repayment.

Budget cuts and tuition increases ripple throughout the academic community. They result in more hiring freezes and early retirements among full time faculty. Poorly paid and overworked contingent instructors replace them, classrooms become more crowded, and students have fewer courses to choose from.

Another widespread effect of budget cuts is to make public institutions more private, as they seek to supplement their loss of public monies with private gifts. This fits right in with the Bush Administration's agenda to privatize public services. And it will only make the promise of education for all more remote.

These days, many young people see the military as their only way to get an education. But Uncle Sam uses a bait and switch. The offer "Join the Army and earn up to $50,000 for college" does not often pan out. Almost 66 percent of recruits never get any college funding from the military (although they have paid into the college fund), and many who do qualify end up getting far less than $50,000.

To receive any education benefit from the Montgomery GI Bill and the Army College Fund or Navy Fund, enlistees must contribute $100 per month for the first twelve months of their tour. Even if recruits change their minds about attending college, the military will not cancel the monthly payment or refund the accumulated $1,200. The military bestows benefits only on those who receive a fully honorable discharge; "general" discharges and those "under honorable conditions" mean no college benefits.

To be eligible for the $50,000 benefit, enlistees must qualify (and only one in twenty enlistees do) for the Army or Navy College Fund by scoring in the top half of the military entry tests and enlisting in specific military occupations, typically unpopular jobs that have no transferable skills in the civilian job market. To receive the maximum amount, the military requires graduation with a four-year degree, achieved only by 15 percent of those who qualify. However, the majority of enlistees attend two-year schools and therefore can receive only a maximum of $7,788.

It's time for us now to demand that the federal government guarantee access to higher education, just as it does for K-12. This is the norm in nearly all other industrialized countries and even much of the impoverished Third World. Today, the intensifying crisis of affordability provides a perfect opportunity to insist on the principle of higher education as a basic right.

This issue resonates widely, and you can hear it finally in the Democratic Presidential race. John Edwards was the first Presidential candidate to address this issue. More than year ago, he proposed a program that would pay all tuition costs for the first year for every student meeting academic standards.

John Kerry also has drawn attention to the crisis and has called for substantial increases in the Pell grant program.

Dennis Kucinich has made free college education for all a central plank in his campaign, and the other candidates have indicated their general support for the view that the federal government should have a responsibility to ensure access.

Most recently, Howard Dean unveiled an elaborate proposal that combines loan subsidies, tax credits, and grants with requirements of work and public service to offer tuition relief to many, if not most, students.

[Editor's note: In his 2008 presidential campaign, Barack Obama said, "We need to put a college education within reach of every American. That's the best investment we can make in our future. I'll create a new and fully refundable tax credit worth $4,000 for tuition and fees every year, which will cover two-thirds of the tuition at the average public college or university. I'll also simplify the financial aid application process so that we don't have a million students who aren't applying for aid because it's too difficult. I will start by eliminating the current student aid form altogether—we'll use tax data instead." See http://www.barackobama.com/issues/pdf/CollegeAffordabilityFactSheet.pdf.*]*

But a crucial limitation of most of the Democratic Presidential candidates' proposals is that they don't boldly assert access to higher education as a right.

Universities themselves are responding. The University of North Carolina at Chapel Hill recently announced a plan to cover the full costs of education for poor students without forcing them to take on loans. Students will have to work in state and federal work-study programs at a manageable ten-to-twelve hours per week.

However, it is a mistake to imagine that states can shoulder this burden on their own. Because of the budget crisis, Georgia, for instance, may discontinue its decade-old scholarship program for all students who maintain a B average.

The Debs-Jones-Douglass Institute, a non-profit educational organization associated with the Labor Party, is building a national campaign to make higher education a right, available to everyone meeting admission standards and without regard to cost and ability to pay. The campaign calls for the federal government to pay all tuition and fees for all students attending two-year and four-year public colleges and universities. Period.

Early response to the campaign has underscored how great a concern the cost of higher education is with students and their families. The campaign for Free Higher Education already has been adopted by dozens of union bodies and other organizations, including large faculty and staff unions in Massachusetts, New Jersey, New York, and California, as well as the state federations of labor in Oregon and South Carolina.

We can generate a vibrant, exciting national movement around it on campuses, at workplaces, and in communities around the country.

This is an issue that can be won.

Where's the Misery?

Rich Lowry

National Review Online, June 29, 2004

"George Bush is pricing thousands of young people right out of the American dream," John Kerry said in April 2004. According to Kerry's campaign, "Rising tuitions often mean that students have to drop out and others cannot afford to come." The campaign touted a 13.4-percent tuition increase by Ohio State

University for the 2004–2005 school year as yet more evidence of Bush's depredations against aspiring college students.

Put aside the fact that George Bush doesn't himself set the tuition at any universities. The entire premise of this line of Kerry attack is still mistaken. Almost no one pays official tuition rates, and college tuition has become more affordable in recent years, not less. A report in *USA Today* found that the amount students pay public universities has fallen by a third since 1998. "In fact," according to the paper, "today's students have enjoyed the greatest improvement in college affordability since the GI Bill provided benefits for returning World War II veterans."

One would think that this constitutes what the Kerry campaign welcomes only through gritted teeth—good news. At public universities, students are paying roughly 27 percent of the official tuition price. Students pay more at private schools, but private tuition actually paid has gone up only 7 percent during the past five years, less than the 20 percent rise in the official price.

It is positively raining college aid, meaning students are in a tight competition with the elderly over who can be more pampered by government. Georgia began a program in 1993 to pay full tuition to state universities for students who had a B average in high school. Thirteen states have created similar programs. Eight new federal tuition tax breaks have been created since 1997. Total federal and state financial aid hit a record $49 billion in 2003, according to *USA Today*.

The game for universities is obvious— hike official tuition rates ever higher. Then everyone thinks students cannot afford college and plies them with more aid, which ends up lining the pockets of the schools. It's one of the great scams of our time, and Kerry has been happy to play along by hyping nominal tuition increases and promising yet more aid. He is the dream candidate of greedy college administrators.

The problem isn't that students hungry for knowledge are being frozen out from college, but the opposite. Marginal students take their generous aid and go to colleges that don't teach them. Eighty percent of universities aren't selective, e.g. more or less happy to accept anyone who shows up with a check. Only 37 percent of first-time freshmen graduate in four years, and only 60 percent graduate in six years. Universities are happy to take money from unprepared students and fail them right back out, or dumb down their standards to stay on the government-aid gravy train.

Meanwhile, Kerry's jury-rigged misery index needs another adjustment. "Soaring tuition costs," as the Kerry campaign puts it, shouldn't cut it anymore as scare rhetoric. Well, there is always the price of gas, another component of Kerry's index. But it has dropped a little and might well fall further with the end of summer. So, Mr. Kerry, where's the misery?

Young America Foundation's Homepage (http://www.yaf.org)

Young America's Foundation is committed to ensuring that increasing numbers of young Americans understand and are inspired by the ideas of individual freedom, a strong national defense, free enterprise, and traditional values.

As the principal outreach organization of the Conservative Movement, the Foundation introduces thousands of American youth to these principles. We accomplish our mission by providing essential conferences, seminars, educational materials, internships and speakers to young people across the country....

Campus Lectures

Young America's Foundation broadened its promotion of conservative ideas on campus when it expanded the campus lecture program. Before the Foundation grew its *breakthrough lecture program,* other organizations focused on sponsoring conservative professors and intellectuals. These individuals espoused conservative ideas as effectively as anyone, but they were not reaching sufficient numbers of students to have a significant impact. The Foundation introduced the idea of using conservative speakers with national reputations as a means to ensure a large audience. These are speakers that students, the local community, and even professors want to hear. They are policy makers, celebrities, and newsmakers, rather than obscure professors. The large audiences these speakers generate show the campus communities that students are eager to hear conservative ideas. The left has embarrassed itself through negative reactions to our lectures through the years. Student radicals burned Bibles outside Pat Buchanan's lecture at Syracuse University, a couple staged a "gay kiss-in" during Ralph Reed's lecture at Northwestern University, and radical feminists disrupted a Star Parker lecture with an obnoxious skit in front of the stage. Many breakthrough lectures have occurred at campuses throughout the country. More than a million students have attended a live Young America's Foundation lecture over the years, and millions more have seen our speakers on C-SPAN. In 1992, Gulf War hero Norman Schwarzkopf addressed over 3,000 cheering students at Chapman University in California. William F. Buckley, Jr. addressed over 1,700 students at the University of North Carolina, Chapel Hill in 1993 after a controversial appearance by Jesse Jackson. William F. Buckley, Jr. noted the importance of the Foundation's lecture program when he said, "On the matter of your lecture series, these are experiences of infinite importance. As recently as last night, a 42-year-old affluent influential conservative told an audience of 400 people that his orientation came from hearing such a talk (yes, by me) at Cornell when he was a sophomore. So I do hope that your important Foundation will be able to continue to support such appearances in the years ahead."...

Activism

Young America's Foundation has taught students how to share conservative ideas with their peers and defended students' rights since its inception. The Foundation stands up for students wishing to defend their country through the Reserve Officer Train-

ing Corps (ROTC), who have long had their rights challenged and stripped by administrators at many campuses. A more recent battle has been to defend students' rights to meet with military recruiters on college campuses. As students become young activists, they often face similar difficulties in organization, event planning, and in responding to attacks from the Left. For that reason, Young America's Foundation developed the *Conservative Guide to Campus Activism*, a book with activism advice from the leading activists and tacticians of the Conservative Movement. The first edition was released in the early 1990's, and the second edition was released in 2005. The most recent version features breakthrough advice on the secrets of activism from the leading tacticians of the Conservative Movement including Ann Coulter, David Horowitz, Michelle Malkin, Bay Buchanan, and others. A new activism publication of Young America's Foundation is the *Campus Conservative Battleplan*. The *Battleplan* is a thematic, month-by-month guide jammed-packed with activism ideas from August to May. The book encourages students to become involved with the Foundation's theme projects including *Freedom Week*, an initiative that celebrates the fall of the Berlin Wall and the toppling of communism by honoring the U.S. military. Another activism project is the *9/11: Never Forget* project where students are encouraged to properly remember the victims of 9/11 with a flag memorial and other activities on their campuses.

Resources

Over a million conservative posters have been distributed to students nationwide since 1969. Students, professors, and alumni proudly share conservative ideas with their peers when they display our conservative posters. Early posters targeted topics ranging from reverse discrimination through race-based admissions policies, to the false claims made by reactionary environmentalists, to documenting the rise in the standard of living under the Reagan presidency. More recently, posters have featured conservative heroes such as Ronald Reagan, Ann Coulter, and Friedrich Hayek, as well as themes such as "I Love Capitalism" and the importance of reading conservative books. Outstanding student activists who host lectures, attend conferences, and make a difference on their campus are rewarded by Young America's Foundation's Club 100 activist rewards program. Any student earning over 100 points in an academic year qualifies for an all expense paid trip to the Reagan Ranch where he or she will experience life as Ronald Reagan did—riding horses and living in ranch-like accommodations.

National Journalism Center

The National Journalism Center (NJC) was founded by M. Stanton Evans in 1977 and became part of Young America's Foundation in 2002. A unique venture in journalism education, NJC is devoted to accuracy, balance, and comprehension of the issues. The program, held three times per year, trains scores of students in the skills of press work while they are assigned an internship at a cooperating media location. The NJC has placed interns at more than 50 outside outlets, including ABC, *Newsweek*, CNN, *New Republic*, C-SPAN, *National Journal*, BBC, *Nation's Business*, Fox News, *Roll Call*, Black Entertainment Television, *The Hill*, UPI, *The City Paper*, Larry King Live, and *Washingtonian*. Over 1,400 students have graduated from the NJC's 12-week program. NJC alumni have written more than 100 books, many of which developed from projects while in the program. Prominent alumni include authors Ann Coulter, *Wall Street Journal* columnist John Fund, and Reagan scholar Steven Hayward. It is estimated that at least 900 other alumni have gone on to work in the media. Among the outlets where NJC graduates have worked after graduation are the *New York Times*, *Washington Post*, *USA Today*, and *Wall Street Journal*; ABC, CBS, NBC, Fox, PBS, NPR, CNN, C-SPAN, *Time*, and *Newsweek*. NJC students receive rigorous journalism training outside their internship. Speakers from the world of public policy and the media, many of whom are alumni of the program, regularly address participants. As in all other facets of our training, the stress in these discussions is on the practice of the trade, not academic theory. Past speakers have included Brian Lamb of C-SPAN, syndicated columnist Robert Novak, *National Review* Editor and NJC Board of Directors member Rich Lowry, Tony Snow of Fox News Channel, and many others.

The Voices of Dissent

David Gates

Newsweek, November 19, 2001

Despite Shelley's old wheeze about poets being the unacknowledged legislators of the world, writers don't have a great track record when it comes to politics. For every savvy Chaucer[1] (a career diplomat) or Vaclav Havel,[2] there seem to be a dozen Allen Ginsbergs[3] trying to levitate the Pentagon. Most writers are dissenters by nature—and dissent, by definition, implies an orthodoxy that's getting its way. The hell of it is, history often proves dissenting writers weren't crazy. Now, had Robert Lowell[4] rather than Robert McNamara been LBJ's secretary of Defense . . . oh well.

Since September 11, political dissent has seemed a decadent luxury, rather than a democratic necessity. The new united-we-stand orthodoxy holds that we're all engaged in a war of unquestionable good against inexplicable evil—that, in fact, the attempt to understand the enemy's perception of us is disloyal—and that bombing Afghanistan, approved by 90 percent of Americans, is both morally and practically justified. These assumptions are worth questioning, if only for prudential reasons. But our official opposition party has signed on; so have most of the world's leaders. And again, the writers won't get with the program. John le Carré and Alan Gurganus have written to critique the war and the United States' arrogance; Alice Walker has been ridiculed for saying the only "punishment" that will work on Osama bin Laden is love. (Didn't this ring a bell with the Bible-reading Christians around the president?) But the most audible voices have been those of Susan Sontag and Barbara Kingsolver, and the Indian novelist Arundhati Roy.

Sontag, the essayist and author of the National Book Award–winning "In America: A Novel," drew a bizarrely fierce reaction for a 473–word New Yorker piece. She called the president "robotic" (mild by pre–September 11 rules), said the attacks were motivated by "specific American alliances and actions" (it must have been something), deemed courage "morally neutral" (ask a GI who fought the SS) and broadly hinted that high-altitude bombing was more cowardly than flying airplanes into buildings (inflammatory, but arguable). But her main point was that the government was talking down to us. "They consider their task to be ... confidence-building and grief management. Politics, the politics of a democracy—which entails disagreement, which promotes candor—has been replaced by psychotherapy." For this, she was called a "traitor" and a "moral idiot." On ABC's "Nightline," Sontag expressed astonishment; she thinks the bombing is a bad idea, but she's no pacifist, believes there can be no compromise with Islamist extremism—"and, no, I don't think we have brought this upon ourselves, which is of course a view that has been attributed to me."

Sontag denied that the bombing of Afghanistan is morally equivalent to the attack on the World Trade Center; but Roy, author of "The God of Small Things," believes it is. "Each innocent person that is killed must be added to, not set off against, the grisly toll of civilians who died in New York and Washington," Roy wrote in London's Guardian. Her belletristic[5] analysis of bin Laden as "the American president's dark doppelgänger"[6] crosses over into Sillyville. But her image of America is something we should take seriously: "Its merciless economic agenda ... has munched the economics of poor countries like a cloud of locusts." But for Americans, Roy's strongest argument against the war may be the practical one. "Operation Enduring Freedom is ostensibly being fought to uphold the American Way of life. It will probably end up undermining it completely. It will spawn more anger and terror across the world. For ordinary people in America, it will mean lives lived in a climate of sickening uncertainty: will my child be safe in school? ... Will my love come home tonight?"

Both Sontag and Roy declined requests for an interview. But Kingsolver—whom another writer in these pages[7] has called "mindless"—was glad to talk. "Well, I'm babbling," the author of "The Poisonwood Bible" said after summarizing the essay she'd just sent to her agent about FDR's "Four Freedoms" speech. "You haven't even asked me a question." What got my colleague up on his hind legs was a line from a San Francisco Chronicle op-ed piece suggesting that the flag has come to stand for "intimidation, censorship, violence, bigotry, sexism, homophobia, and shoving the Constitution through a paper shredder. Whom are we calling terrorists here?" But Kingsolver was simply talking about the hard right's co-opting of patriotic symbolism: "My patriotic duty is to recapture my flag from the men now waving it in the name of jingoism and censorship."

Ever since September 11, Kingsolver has been pouring out editorials and essays. Her dissent, like Roy's, is both moral and practical. "If our goal is to reduce the number of people in the world who would like to kill us," she says, "this is not the way to go about it." She resents having her patriotism impugned. "I'm speaking out because I'm a patriot," she says. "Because I love my country and I want it to do the right thing." And she also resents being told—as she has been lately—that she should stick to writing novels. "It's a nasty slapdown that's been used against those of us, particularly Arundhati Roy, who have spoken out," Kingsolver says. "As if the fact of our being novelists disqualified us for any other sort of speech. I can't make any sense of that. Words are my tools. Words are what I have to offer."

Notes

1. Geoffrey Chaucer, fourteenth-century author of *The Canterbury Tales.*
2. Vaclav Havel, Czechoslovakian playwright who was imprisoned for writing and speaking against Soviet domination of his country in the 1980s, then became its president after the fall of Communism.
3. Allen Ginsberg, American poet who led a mock-serious ceremony in Washington in the late 1960s attempting to end the Vietnam War by causing the Pentagon building to levitate.
4. Robert Lowell, another prominent American poet who was an outspoken opponent of the Vietnam War.
5. Belletristic. Literary. From a French term for literature, *les belles lettres,* literally "beautiful letters."
6. *"Doppelgänger."* German, "double."
7. David Anson, in *Newsweek.*

Topics for Discussion and Writing

1. Discuss with classmates and express your opinions (with concrete support) about the continuing validity today of the following statements in Savio's speech:
   a. "The most crucial problems facing the United States today are the problem of automation and the problem of racial injustice." [The problem of automation refers to the dwindling availability of jobs because of automated services, in factory production as well as in kinds of work like automated bank tellers and telephone response lines.]
   b. "The university is the place where people begin seriously to question the conditions of their existence and raise the issue of whether they can be committed to the society they have been born into."
   c. "Many students here at the University, many people in society, are wandering aimlessly about. Strangers in their own lives, there is no place for them. . . . [They are] looking toward a very bleak existence afterward in a game in which all of the rules have been made up—rules which we can not really amend."
   d. "The university is well structured, well tooled, to turn out people with all the sharp edges worn off—the well-rounded person." (Explain Savio's use of **irony** here.)
   e. "The 'futures' and 'careers' for which American students now prepare are for the most part intellectual and moral wastelands. This chrome-plated consumers' paradise would have us grow up to be well-behaved children."
2. Savio characterizes the university administration as a bureaucracy. Write about any experiences you have had with bureaucracy at your college or university that would confirm or contradict his account. Have you and your schoolmates discovered any effective means of getting satisfaction in dealing with such bureaucracies?
3. Write a paper tracing the continuity of ideas in the citations from Crèvecoeur, Jefferson, and Emerson, and the readings by Savio and Reed. What similar concern is expressed in Jefferson's comments on the power of the wealthy and Savio's on "the financial plutocrats"? (See the definition of *plutocracy* in chapter 13.) Savio was referring to the regents of the University of California, political

appointments by the governor consisting primarily of conservative executives of the largest corporations in California, who pressured the University of California's president Clark Kerr to crack down on student activism in the civil rights movement and other off-campus liberal political causes. You might want to do some research on the Free Speech Movement at Berkeley or of the civil rights movement in the fifties and sixties.

4. Reed's "Majoring in Debt" condenses, in journalistic form, a much longer and more fully documented article at http://freehhighered.org (in which you can find sources for his data) by two of his colleagues in the Campaign for Free Higher Education. That article, written by professors and reprinted from the journal of the American Political Science Association, is a good example of the scholarly level of writing, discussed in chapter 5 as a better source of information for college writing than journalism. Reed is also a Political Science professor, at the University of Pennsylvania, but he is writing for a non-academic audience here. Singly or in discussion groups, compare "Majoring in Debt" with your own situation regarding the cost of college, student loans and other financial aid, and the need to work at outside jobs to get through college. If the conclusion is in agreement with Reed, discuss ways in which this issue might become a platform for student activism and draft a resolution for legislative action at the state and national level. Discuss possible tactics with your student government leaders. Compare the positions on college costs and financial aid of the Republican and Democratic parties and their leaders, nationally and in your state. Write letters to, or interview, your national and state senators and representatives, candidates for office, and political party committees to voice your concern and ask them if they would support a program of legislative action. Write opinion columns for your campus or community newspaper and local TV and radio stations. Or contact the organization Reed discusses in the concluding section, the Debs-Jones-Douglass Institute, about its campaign for free higher education.

5. Reed's main **premise** is, "Higher Education is a basic social good. As such, it should be available to all, without cost, who meet admission standards. The federal government . . . should bear primary responsibility for providing free college to all." By "social good" he presumably means a benefit to society, not just to individual students. This assertion expresses a viewpoint that is politically to the left of Democratic Party liberals on the issue (the article appeared in the leftist *Progressive* magazine, and Reed says the Campaign for Free Higher Education is a project of the leftist Labor Party). This viewpoint clearly runs contrary to established American policies. On what ideological grounds would conservatives oppose it? (See the points of opposition between conservatives and liberals or leftists in chapter 13.) An editorial on the same topic as Reed's article, titled "Public Colleges, Broken Promises," in the *New York Times,* May 5, 2002, p. 14, said, "Once seen as a benefit to society as a whole, a college education is now viewed as a boon to an individual, who should be forced to pay for it." The editorial, like Reed, disagrees with this current view. Discuss and write about whether society or the individual should bear the primary financial responsibility for college, and why. Liberals in general argue that public money spent on education is one of the best investments a society can make, producing financial returns far exceeding the investment, and that the American economy is currently suffering from an insufficient number of college graduates. Can you find conservative **refutations** of this argument? Does Rich Lowry address it? Do some research on the financial costs and benefits of public spending on colleges and universities for communities

and the nation, as well as for corporate and other employers and beneficiaries of university research, and on the financial productivity of college graduates versus high school graduates. In most other democracies, higher education at the best universities remains free or costs relatively little. The Scandinavian countries even pay all college students a salary; do research on their justification for this and what the socioeconomic consequences are.

6. Rich Lowry is editor of *National Review*, one of the most influential conservative journals of opinion. His and Reed's columns are a classic case of diametric opposition between liberal and conservative **polemicists**, particularly in **causal analysis**, the topic of chapter 11. (See chapters 13 and 16 for general lines of ideological oppositions between conservatives and liberals in relation to socioeconomic issues, and discuss how they apply here.) Apply to both the Semantic Calculator for Bias in Rhetoric in chapter 4 to determine what points each is **playing up** and **downplaying**. Make parallel lists of their assertions about the causes of rising college costs and other points of opposition, evaluate their supporting evidence and citation of sources, and do some research to establish which is more credible. (The *USA Today* article that Lowry cites was "Tuition Burden Falls by a Third," by Dennis Cauchon, June 28, 2004.) When Lowry says, "Total federal and state financial aid hit a record $49 billion in 2003, according to *USA Today*," can you **infer** that this includes loans? If so, how does Reed's data about the shift from grants to high-cost loans reflect on Lowry **downplaying** this point? As a student, how do you react to the **tone** of Lowry's statements like, "It's positively raining college aid, meaning students are in a tight competition with the elderly over who can be more pampered by government"? See Richard Vedder, "The Real Costs of Federal Aid to Higher Education," http://www .heritage.org/Research/Education/hl984.cfm, a Heritage Foundation study, for a conservative scholarly counterpart to Smith and Szymanski's "Why Political Scientists Should Support Free Public Higher Education."

7. Another obvious conservative **rebuttal** to Reed is that his proposal would be exorbitantly expensive, necessitating large tax increases. What sources for financing it does he recommend, and how persuasive is his case for claiming they would not necessitate tax increases for individuals? (Research his claim about "recently opened corporate tax loopholes," in, for example, Paul Krugman's *The Great Unraveling: Losing Our Way in the New Century.*) Debate the pros and cons of his **implication** that tax money would be better spent on education than on war in Iraq. He further supports his case with an **analogy** with the GI Bill of Rights after World War II. Debate the soundness of this analogy, and research the history of the GI Bill. He also makes an analogy with the federal government guaranteeing access to primary and secondary education. Evaluate this analogy by the criteria in the section on analogies in chapter 9.

8. Young America's Foundation is one of several conservative campus organizations that were founded to counteract the liberal student activism of the sixties, represented by Savio. (These organizations and the corporate foundations that fund them will be discussed further in chapters 9 and 13.) In their viewpoint, they are the dissenters against liberal and leftist domination of campus life. From their self-description, why and how can you **infer** that they would disagree with Savio's defense of student activism for civil rights and for more of a voice in college administration, or with Reed's call for activism to counter the rising cost of college? (Note that Rich Lowry is affiliated with YAF.) Other recent arenas for liberal student activism include protests against the use of sweatshop labor by

American corporations abroad (particularly in the production of college-branded products sold in campus stores), and demonstrations for environmental protection and for "living wage" campaigns for blue-collar campus employees. (See David Moberg, "Students Stand Up for Workers' Rights," *In These Times*, May 27, 2002.) Do further research on YAF's and other conservative groups' positions on these issues. Do some **primary research**, singly or in teams of students, on what organizations and forms of conservative and liberal activism are currently represented on your own and neighboring campuses or communities. Interview representatives of these organizations, as well as students, faculty, and administrators, to get a diversity of opinions for and against them.

9. Several **semantic** issues (the topic of chapter 4) are involved in Gates's "The Voices of Dissent." Gates cites essayist Susan Sontag's comments on the subjectivity of the words *courage* and *cowardly*. Her point is that our **ethnocentrism** inclines us to apply positive words selectively to our own side and negative ones to our enemies, without considering that they too may be courageous and patriotic, even if we believe their causes are evil. (This is presumably what Gates means about the German elite SS combat troops in World War II.) She also suggests that American officials have a **double standard** in characterizing suicide bombers as "cowardly" while that word might more accurately apply to "those who kill from beyond the range of retaliation, high in the sky," as in American bombing of Iraq or Afghanistan. How would you reply to these arguments?

10. Further semantic dispute surrounds the word *patriotism*. In his book *Why We Fight,* a conservative response to 9/11, William J. Bennett says of "those in our institutions of higher learning" and other intellectuals that "those who are *un-patriotic* are those who are, culturally, the most influential" (141). He explicitly includes Barbara Kingsolver in this group. On the other side, Kingsolver insists, "'My patriotic duty is to recapture my flag from the men now waving it in the name of jingoism and censorship.'" (**Jingoism** is a nineteenth-century term meaning flag-waving manipulation of the masses by politicians or the media into unthinking support of a war that might not be just.) How would you make the distinction between jingoism and authentic appeal to patriotism, and how can we make that distinction in a particular case like the wars on Afghanistan and Iraq? Look up a couple of dictionary definitions of *patriotism* and see if you can reconcile Bennett's and Kingsolver's apparently different definitions. Regarding censorship, American government censorship of media during the wars in Afghanistan and Iraq is a good topic for research and debate, especially with the historical perspective of what has become known about it by the time you read this.

11. Roy is quoted as saying, "Each innocent person that is killed [by American forces in Afghanistan] must be added to, not set off against, the grisly toll of victims who died in New York and Washington." What moral or practical arguments in support of and against this position can you think of? Does the quotation support Gates's claim that Roy believes "the bombing of Afghanistan is morally equivalent to the attack on the World Trade Center" and Bennett's criticism of those who "have wondered whether America is really better than its enemies around the world"? Did those who argued that our killing of an equivalent number of Afghani or Iraqi civilians was a way of "getting even" commit the fallacy of **two wrongs make a right**?

12. In Gates's account, both Roy and Kingsolver follow a line of argument exemplifying one of the critical thinking skills outlined in chapter 3, "The ability to

predict probable consequences of an event or series of events." Roy says the war against Afghanistan "will spawn more anger and terror across the world." Kingsolver is quoted as saying, "If our goal is to reduce the number of people in the world who would like to kill us, this is not the way to go about it." Defenders of America's invasion of Afghanistan argued that civilian casualties were a necessary evil in the cause of tracking down Al Qaeda leaders and overthrowing the repressive Taliban government. At the time you are reading this, how accurate do these opposing predictions of consequences look? Apply the same question to the similar debates about America's war on Iraq in 2003.

13. Kingsolver responds to critics who say writers like her, Roy, and Sontag should stick to writing novels by saying, "As if the fact of our being novelists disqualified us for any other sort of speech." Do you think being a novelist *qualifies* one as an authority on political subjects, or is this an example of the fallacy of **transfer of authority**? A novel is fictional or imaginative, as opposed to factual writing. The novels of these three writers, however, do deal with political topics. To what extent does their authority to speak on real political issues depend on how well-informed, well-written, and true to life their fictional treatment of political issues is? You might read their novels—such as Sontag's *In America: A Novel*, Roy's *The God of Small Things*, and Kingsolver's *The Poisonwood Bible*—as well as their more extensive, nonfiction political writings (such as Roy's book of essays *An Ordinary Person's Guide to Empire*) in search of answers to these questions.

CHAPTER 2

What Is an Argument? What Is a Good Argument?

In everyday life, an argument usually means any kind of disagreement—who should clean up the room, did one member of a couple do what the other accused him or her of, and so on. Such arguments often end in screaming matches of "Did not!" "Did too!" Although many public arguments often unfortunately consist of similar screaming matches such as *Crossfire* and political attack ads, it is sometimes possible for personal arguments to be resolved on a more reasoned level, while we as critical citizens should always demand the same of public arguments. Thus the meaning of argumentation in responsible speaking or writing is not simply the expression of an opinion or attitude—though many people are confused on this point—but reasoned *support* for an opinion. To put it another way, when someone expresses a controversial opinion or assertion of truth, the critical citizen asks "*Why* is that true? How do you know that? What reasons or evidence do you have to support it?" If the person expressing the opinion can answer these questions with supporting reasons, she will be making an argument.

Writers of letters to the editor, for example, often simply sound off without any real arguments. Here is one responding to an excerpt in the *San Francisco Chronicle* from a book, *The End of Racism,* by Dinesh D'Souza, a prominent conservative:

> *The Chronicle* has done the public a service by allowing D'Souza's hopelessly twisted rhetoric to besmirch its pages. This allows more thinking citizens to become aware of D'Souza, the right wing's current lawn jockey, as a grand manipulator of fact and logic, in the spirit of Hitler's *Mein Kampf.*
>
> Hopefully, as word spreads about this demagoguery, this will allow more thinking folks to rationally discriminate his message to its rightful place on the trash heap.

The letter is filled with **name-calling**, along with **guilt by association** with Hitler, but fails to provide any evidence that the name-calling is warranted. Furthermore, while the pure expression of an opinion like this one about D'Souza is calculated to win unquestioning agreement from those in our own party and to antagonize those in the opposing party, an effective spoken or written argument intends to *persuade* those who disagree with us to come around to our position, through a process of reasoning, which in this case might consist

32

of quoting "hopelessly twisted rhetoric" in passages from D'Souza's book, then providing evidence that they are unfactual and illogical.

WHAT IS A *GOOD* ARGUMENT?

The word *good* here is unfortunately vague and subjective. We are all inclined to judge any argument that agrees with our biases a good one, and any that disagrees a bad one, regardless of its substantive merits. Nevertheless, let us try to define some more-or-less objective criteria.

A Good Argument Is Well Supported

The means of supporting an argument in a written argument (say, a student paper) include (1) evidence from the writer's personal experiences, examples, anecdotes, reasoned analysis, or common knowledge (truths that are generally acknowledged without significant dispute), (2) **primary research** conducted by the writer (interviews, polls, study of data, experiments, etc.), and, most frequently, (3) **secondary research** (presenting facts, figures, and lines of argument put forth by reputable scholars, journalists, research institutes, or officials, mainly published in periodicals and books, whom you cite in your text, introduced by phrases like "According to Author X," "Author X presents evidence that" or "As Author X argues"). Many of the analyses of arguments in the readings throughout this book focus on disagreements about the quality of opposing sides' supporting evidence.

Of course, it is impractical to provide evidence supporting every assertion you speak or write, and one rhetorical challenge that every writer (including myself throughout this book) faces with every sentence is calculating which assertions of fact or opinion your readers are likely to accept without support and which ones some readers are likely to demand support for in order to be persuaded of their truth. In conversation, when the speaker makes an assertion that the listener disputes, the listener will *ask* the speaker for support, but when you are writing, without immediate feedback from the audience, you need to imagine your readers' response. Thus, developing your consciousness of writing for an **audience** consists largely of this calculation of what the exact mind-set is of your readers, so that you can anticipate what assertions you need to support.

A Good Argument Distinguishes Facts from Opinions, Takes Care to Verify Facts, and Expresses Informed Opinions

The distinction between fact and opinion may seem like a simple one, but it is the source of constant, fierce disagreements in public rhetoric, even—or *especially*—among the most knowledgeable scholars, journalists, and politicians. In many of the courses you take, you learn facts that have been verified beyond much reasonable dispute—$2 \times 2 = 4$, water freezes at 32 degrees Fahrenheit, the Declaration of Independence was signed in 1776, and so on. But when it comes to issues like why the American Revolution took place or exactly what the political beliefs of the Founding Fathers were, there is wide disagreement among historians over the facts. In such issues, and nearly always in more contemporary public controversies, what is involved is actually differing viewpoints on, opinions about, or interpretations of the facts. Confusion arises, however, when people feel certain that they know the facts rather than simply having a **viewpoint** on the facts that may be faulty.

In writing arguments yourself or evaluating other writers' arguments, then, you need first to distinguish between arguments that are phrased as statements of fact and those phrased as statements of opinion. If you write, "George W. Bush was the best president in American history" or "George W. Bush was the worst president in American history," you really mean your opinion is that this is a fact, so you should preface the assertion by a phrase like "In my opinion." For practical purposes, however, making the distinction between statements of fact and opinion is less important than establishing the quality of *support* for assertions, whichever way they are worded; in either case you need to present *evidence* about Bush in comparison to his predecessors.

Verifying Facts. Scholarly writing, by either professors or students, along with responsible journalism and book publishing, is distinguished from the flood of information emitted by mass media, political propaganda, and barroom argumentation by scrupulous attention to getting facts right. "Responsible" newspapers, magazines, and book publishers hire professional fact-checkers who go to great lengths to verify that any "facts" published are accurate. Unfortunately, fact-checking has been a casualty of the rise of 24/7 cable news networks, talk radio, and trash-talking political books, which typically do not employ fact-checkers and are concerned little or not at all with distinguishing facts from rumors.

Informed versus Uninformed Opinions. Some college students fall into one of two extreme positions in regard to expressing opinions. At one extreme are those who somewhere in their education were taught never to write in the first person or express opinions in writing or who for other reasons are reluctant to do so. This attitude often seems to derive from instruction in scientific or technical report writing, which is supposed to be objective and in which the writer's personality and opinions would be irrelevant. In many other forms of writing, however, the expression of the writer's personal viewpoint or opinion is perfectly legitimate and valuable. Newspapers and magazines have a page or an entire section devoted to opinion, including editorials (written by the publication's own editorial board), letters to the editor, and opinion columns written by staffers, syndicated columnists, or freelance contributors and commonly published on the "op-ed" page, opposite the editorial page (the shorter papers—say 1,000 words or less—that you write in an argumentative-writing class can be similar in form). Serious journalistic reports in periodicals or books (more like what you will write for term papers or a senior project) also often contain a large degree of opinion, and there are many magazines known as "journals of opinion" that are essential reading for college students and graduates and that provide models of writing throughout this book. The writing of opinion, then, is a perfectly legitimate form; however, you do need to learn the qualities that distinguish an effective expression of opinion from an ineffective one.

At the other extreme from students who are overly shy about expressing their opinions are those students—and many older citizens—who have a know-it-all attitude, or **primary certitude**. They are apt to make comments like "It's a free country, and everyone's entitled to their opinions," or "My opinion's as good as anybody else's." Unfortunately, these attitudes are misguided when applied to college studies. It is true that everyone is entitled to express his or her opinions, but it is not true that all opinions about all subjects are equally "good"; an opinion that is educated, or informed, on the subject at issue and well supported, is more worth listening to—and certainly more worth *reading*—than one that is uninformed and poorly supported. The act of writing lends statements permanence and the need for verification more than speaking them usually does. Uninformed or poorly supported statements might slip by in the rush of conversation, but writing freezes them on the page where their weaknesses become visible, especially in rereading.

Know-it-alls are typically unaware that their opinions are not well informed or supported. They are already convinced that their opinions correspond to the facts, or the truth, so that they do not need any support, and they have closed their minds to any evidence to the contrary. In other words, their opinions are *prejudiced*—that is, they have prejudged the issue on insufficient study and evidence, or have expressed a **hasty judgment**. The fault here is not expressing strong or emotional opinions in itself; not every strong opinion is a prejudiced one. An unprejudiced opinion, however adamant or emotional, is one that is justified by the facts of the situation, as verified by evidence, and by the knowledge and broad-mindedness undergirding the speaker's or writer's arguments. The quality of support for any opinion is one of the many judgment calls you need to make in writing your own arguments and evaluating others'.

Another common misunderstanding about opinions is reflected when, in response to some particularly outrageous statement by a public figure, someone comments, "Well, that's just his opinion," as though that is all there is to it. Public figures have a responsibility not to make defamatory statements without adequate support; yet such statements have proliferated in public discourse in recent years, especially under the influence of talk radio and political negative campaigning and attack advertising, where the stakes seem to increase toward ever more inflammatory rhetoric. If you publicly make a defamatory factual allegation about someone, without being able to provide evidence supporting it, you can be sued for slander or defamation of character. The ever-growing frequency of such accusations through the media, and the prohibitive cost of civil lawsuits, however, has made legal action impractical in most cases. As moderator in debate between John McCain and Barack Obama in the 2008 election, Tom Brokaw implied that the Social Security system is about to grow broke. Economist Dean Baker responded, in a blog for *American Prospect,* that unlike an individual or private business, "A government program cannot sue for libel," so "Social Security cannot sue Brokaw even if he deliberately tells explicit lies about its financial health" (www.prospect .org, October 7, 2008). So if we shrug off slanderous rhetoric by saying "Well, that's just her opinion," then we are contributing to a serious debasement of our national discourse.

The increasing tendency for Americans to express strong opinions on public topics about which they are ignorant is the subject of the following article from the *New Yorker.*

"The Intellectual Free Lunch"

Michael Kinsley

New Yorker, February 6, 1995

The weekend before President Clinton's State of the Union Address, the *Wall Street Journal* assembled a focus group of middle-class white males—the demographic group *du jour*—to plumb the depth of their proverbial anger. The results were highly satisfactory. These guys are mad as hell. They're mad at welfare, they're mad at special-interest lobbyists. "But perhaps the subject that produces the most agreement among the group," the *Journal* reports, "is the view that Washington should stop sending money abroad and instead zero in on the domestic front."

A poll released last week by the Program on International Policy Attitudes at the University of Maryland contains similar findings. According to this survey, seventy-five per cent of Americans believe that the United States spends "too much" on foreign aid, and sixty-four per cent want foreign-aid spending cut. Apparently, a cavalier eleven per cent of Americans think it's fine to spend "too much" on foreign aid. But there is no denying the poll's larger finding that big majorities say they think the tab is too high.

Respondents were also asked, though, how big a share of the federal budget currently goes to foreign aid. The median answer was fifteen per cent; the average answer was eighteen per cent. The correct answer is less than one per cent: the United States government spends about fourteen billion dollars a year on foreign aid (including military assistance), out of a total budget of a trillion and a half. To a question about how much foreign-aid spending would be "appropriate," the median answer was five per cent of the budget. A question about how much would be "too little" produced a median answer of three per cent—more than three times the current level of foreign-aid spending.

To the International Policy folks at the University of Maryland, these results demonstrate "strong support for maintaining foreign aid at current spending levels or higher." That's just their liberal-internationalist spin, of course. You might say with equal justice that the results demonstrate a national wish to see foreign aid cut by two-thirds. It's true that after the pollsters humiliated their subjects with the correct answer to the question about how much (or, rather, how little) the United States spends on foreign aid, only thirty-five per cent of the respondents had the fortitude to say they still wanted to see it cut. But what people will say after being corrected by an authority figure with a clipboard hardly constitutes "strong support."

This poll is less interesting for what it shows about foreign aid than for what it shows about American democracy. It's not just that Americans are scandalously ignorant. It's that they seem to believe they have a democratic right to their ignorance. All over the country—at dinner tables, in focus groups, on call-in radio shows, and, no doubt, occasionally on the floor of Congress—citizens are expressing outrage about how much we spend on foreign aid, without having the faintest idea what that amount is. This is not, surely, a question of being misinformed. No one—not even Rush Limbaugh—is out there spreading the falsehood that we spend fifteen per cent of the federal budget (two hundred and twenty-five billion dollars) on foreign aid. People are forming and expressing passionate views about foreign aid on the basis of no information at all. Or perhaps they think that the amount being spent on foreign aid is a matter of opinion, like everything else.

Populism, in its latest manifestation, celebrates ignorant opinion and undifferentiated rage. As long as you're mad as hell and aren't going to take it anymore, no one will inquire very closely into what, exactly, "it" is and whether you really ought to feel that way. Pandering politicians are partly to blame, to be sure. So is the development christened "hyperdemocracy" by last week's *Time*: the way the communications revolution is eroding representative government by providing instant feedback between voters' whims and politicians' actions. But ubiquitous opinion polls are part of the problem, too.

The typical opinion poll about, say, foreign aid doesn't trouble to ask whether the respondent knows the first thing about the topic being opined upon, and no conventional poll disqualifies an answer on the ground of mere total ignorance. The premise of opinion polling is that people are, and of right ought to be, omni-opinionated—that they should have views on all subjects at all times—and that all such views are equally valid. It's always remarkable how few people say they "aren't sure" about or "don't know" the answer to some pollster's question. ("Never thought about it," "Couldn't care less," and "Let me get back to you on that after I've done some reading" aren't even options.) So, given the prominence of polls in our political culture, it's no surprise that people have come to believe that their opinions on the issues of the day need not be fettered by either facts or reflection.

Add opinions to the list of symptoms of the free-lunch disease that blights American politics. First, in the early nineteen-eighties, came the fiscal free lunch: taxes can be cut without cutting middle-class government benefits. Then, with the end of the Cold War, came the foreign-policy free lunch: America can strut as the world's super power without putting blood or treasure at risk. Now there's the intellectual free lunch: I'm entitled to vociferous opinions on any subject, without having to know, or even think, about it.

All this may sound horribly snooty. But it isn't. It is not the argument that Walter Lippmann made in "Public Opinion," where he advocated relying on elite "bureaus" of wise men to make crucial policy decisions. Lippmann's belief was that modern life had rendered public policy too complex for the average voter. But there is nothing especially complex about the factual question of how much the country spends on foreign aid. It may be too heavy a burden of civic responsibility to expect every citizen— what with work and family and life outside politics—to carry this number around in his or her head. But it is not asking too much to expect a citizen to recognize that he or she needs to know that number, at least roughly, in order to have a valid opinion about whether it is too large or too small. Americans are capable of making informed, reflective decisions on policy questions. But they often seem to be under the impression that they needn't bother.

We need a new form of democratic piety. It shows respect, not contempt, for "the people" to hold them to something approaching the intellectual standard you would apply to yourself or a friend. By contrast, it is contemptuous, not respectful, to excuse "the people" from all demands of intellectual rigor or honesty on the ground that their judgments are wise by definition. We honor our friends by challenging them when we think they're wrong. It shows that we take them seriously. Believers in democracy owe "the people" no less.

*   *   *

Note Kinsley's qualification, or **drawing the line**, that he is not snobbishly saying that the masses of Americans are incapable of having informed opinions; on the contrary, he says, "It is contemptuous, not respectful, to excuse 'the people' from all demands of intellectual rigor or honesty on the ground that their judgments are wise by definition." Also note Kinsley's suggestion that an honest way of responding to such poll questions might be "aren't sure," "don't know," or best of all, "Let me get back to you on that after I've done some reading." This suggestion is especially good advice for college students studying controversial current events. You should never be reluctant to admit that you simply don't know enough about a given subject to have a strong opinion on it, nor should your feelings be hurt at the suggestion that you may be ignorant about it. Being ignorant is not the same thing as being *dumb*. Ignorant simply means not knowing something. Even the most brilliant and well-educated people are ignorant about many subjects, and the more honest ones cheerfully admit it. After all, aren't you in college taking courses because you want to overcome your ignorance about the subjects of those courses?

Learning to understand the difference between educated and uneducated, or ignorant, opinions on public issues is in large part what college study is about. College study, that is, not just in vocational or preprofessional education, but in liberal or general education, which forms the entirety of traditional college education and remains the core of required courses even in most vocationally oriented colleges because it is vitally important for every citizen to understand this difference. This is not to claim that every college graduate has learned to form educated, unprejudiced opinions; some have not, but they have missed what they should have learned in this regard. Nor is this to claim that no one who is not a college graduate is capable of forming educated opinions; many people who have never gone to college, and who may even have dropped out of high school, develop educated opinions through their own mental initiative. The autobiography of Frederick Douglass is a classic story of a nineteenth-century slave's self-education, against the rigid opposition of his owners, into a powerfully persuasive writer and speaker. Mark Twain is another example; he left school at twelve but educated himself, beginning with his work as an apprentice typesetter at a newspaper, to the point where he became one of the best-read and wisest people of his time.

A Good Argument Is Cogently Reasoned

Scholars of rhetoric, philosophy, and formal logic split hairs disagreeing about the correct terminology for the elements and structures in reasoning and the criteria for evaluating its quality. Much of this terminology, along with extensive elaborations of formal logic, is not essential for coping with the kinds of arguments we are commonly exposed to in everyday discourse. For the purposes of this book, then, a few simple terms are sufficient to begin with, though they will be refined somewhat further in subsequent sections, especially chapter 11. Arguments are constructed in just a few standard expository sequences. In one sequence, an **assertion** of either opinion or fact, also sometimes called a **claim**, is followed by various kinds of support for it, with phrasing like "because," "for the following reasons," "on the basis of the evidence that," or "for example." (This would be the form of the D'Souza letter if it had supported the assertion about D'Souza's "hopelessly twisted logic" by presenting and analyzing examples of them after making the initial claim.) In another sequence, a series of items of evidence leads to, or supports, a **conclusion** or **inference**, which is introduced by phrases like, "therefore," "thus," or "it follows that." (The D'Souza letter could take this form if the writer began with a series of examples of D'Souza's manipulations of fact and logic, then drew the conclusion from them that his logic is hopelessly twisted.)

These two sequences are simply variants in expository order for making the same argument. There are also two important *categories* of argumentative reasoning, **induction** and **deduction**, both of which can be incorporated in either of these expository sequences. Induction marshals **empirical** evidence (based on systematic observation or experiment), data (facts and figures), or specific examples either to support an assertion or to lead to a conclusion or inference. (An oddity of common usage is the expression "I deduce that," which in fact means "I induce," as in "I induce from all these antique cars on this road that they are probably going to, or from, a car show.") There are many forms of inductive reasoning, including *reasoning by analogy* (for example, Republicans might argue that the Democratic presidential candidate is very similar to Democratic presidential candidates of the past, so we should expect similar policies if that candidate is elected); *causal reasoning,* where typically we use correlations between two events or kinds of events and other reasons as supporting evidence for claims that one event caused the other; *hypothesis testing,* where the predictions from a hypothesis that turn out to be correct are used as supporting evidence for the correctness of the hypothesis; and *argument to the best explanation,* where there are competing explanations or theories and one explanation is chosen because it explains the evidence more accurately and straightforwardly than its competitors and/or it explains a wider range of evidence.

In each of these kinds of inductive argument, although the supporting reasons, if correct, don't exactly guarantee the assertion they are used to support (you could still hypothesize alternative assertions as being correct), they still provide solid grounds for accepting the assertion. When the reasons or evidence do not adequately support the conclusion drawn from them, this kind of **non sequitur** ("It does not follow") is, especially in blatant cases, called an **inductive leap**.

Deductive reasoning is based historically on the **syllogism** in classical logic, in which two **premises** lead inescapably to a conclusion, as in the standard example, "All humans are mortal. Socrates is a human. Therefore, Socrates is mortal." (A syllogism can also take the form "If all humans are mortal, and Socrates is a human, then Socrates is mortal.") A common variant is the **enthymeme**, in which one of the premises is **implied** or **hidden**, not explicitly stated: "Socrates is a human; therefore, Socrates is mortal." The D'Souza letter could have been written as an enthymeme, something like: "D'Souza manipulates facts and logic; therefore, he is not a credible source." Here the implicit premise is "Anyone who manipulates facts and logic is not a credible source," a premise that doesn't really need to be made explicit because it is self-evident.

The next question is when a sequence of inductive or deductive reasoning adds up to a *good* argument. Actually, logicians, mainly in the discipline of philosophy, use an array of more specifically definable terms than *good,* such as *valid, sound, strong,* and *cogent.* Some logicians use *valid* to refer only to the internal logic of a deductive argument—whether the conclusion follows inescapably from the premises, regardless of the adequacy of support for the premises—so that rules this word out for broader use. Let's try instead to use *sound* here, then, just to judge the logic of an argument. Most broadly, in inductive reasoning, a sound argument is one in which the evidence presented is accurate and adequate to support the initial assertion or claim, or to justify the conclusion or inference reached from the evidence. In deductive reasoning, a sound argument is one in which (1) the evidence supporting the premises is accurate and adequate, and (2) the conclusion follows from the premises.

One theoretical difference between induction and deduction is that the truth of the conclusions reached through induction typically has only a greater or lesser degree of *probability* or empirical verifiability, whereas the truth of deductive conclusions, if they are soundly reasoned, is *certain.* When I observe the string of antique cars on the highway, the inference that they are going to or from a car show is pretty probable, though it is not certain. I *could* verify the inference empirically by following the cars to their destination or asking their drivers, in which case the inference would be correct for all practical purposes. On the other hand, in a syllogism like the one about Socrates, the conclusion has the certainty of a mathematical proof: all humans belong to the class or set of mortals; Socrates belongs to the class or set of humans; therefore, the conclusion that Socrates is mortal is inescapable. In common practice, however, deductive arguments—even if they are internally *valid*—are only as good as their premises, which must be arrived at and evaluated by the same criteria as inductive assertions. So the weakness in many deductive arguments lies in the disputability of their explicit or implicit premises.

A common form of deductive non sequitur results from an enthymeme containing a hidden premise, like the D'Souza example above, but one that is more disputable than in that example. The hidden premise is assumed by the writer or speaker to be true, but if it is in fact disputable, then the conclusion drawn from the explicit premise is disputable too. For example, in Mario Savio's speech "An End to History" in chapter 1, Savio asserts that the student protesters were simply asking to be treated, in the governance of the university as well as in the larger society, as citizens entitled to "due process of law" and regulations arrived at through the consent of the governed. This argument can be recast as an enthymeme:

> *Premise:* Citizens of American democracy are entitled to constitutional rights.
> *Conclusion:* Students are entitled to constitutional rights within the university.

The hidden premise here is that the university is a democratic institution, within which students are entitled to all the same rights citizens have in the broader society. But this premise was in fact disputed by the University of California (UC) administrators and other critics of the Free Speech Movement, who argued that the administration and faculty must have certain kinds of authority over students that differentiate this relationship from that between a democratic government and its citizens. Savio's argument would have been stronger, then, if he had addressed this objection and indicated where to draw the line in granting students more legitimate democratic rights, without this position being vulnerable to being pushed to extremes, such as claiming that students have the same right to teach courses as professors.

A Good Argument Is Relevant, Consistent, and Free of Fallacies

All your arguments should be directly relevant to the issue in dispute, avoiding fallacies of irrelevance like **evading the issue**, **ad hominem**, **straw man**, and **red herring**; a good argument is often distinguished by its ingenuity in calling attention to a particularly relevant, salient point. It might be worth your time now to read ahead to chapters 10 and 11 to familiarize yourself with the definitions of the other most common logical and rhetorical fallacies, which are referred to all through the intermediate chapters. In addition, all your arguments must be consistent with one another, without contradictions or **shifting ground**.

A Good Argument Is Well Balanced, Fair-Minded, and Qualified

You should evenhandedly acknowledge the strong and weak points of both sides and reach a conclusion that balances them judiciously. If you are arguing for one side in a dispute, you must show that you understand the central arguments on the opposing side and can summarize them in a manner that opponents would accept (avoiding straw-man distortion of the opposition), in order for your **rebuttal** or **refutation** of the opposing position to be effective. (See chapter 6 for further aids here.)

Academic argumentation is, or should be, characterized by a certain modesty of tone and wording, an avoidance of primary certitude, **hasty conclusions**, and **overgeneralization**. Academic writers tend to use nonabsolute phrases like "tend to." Instead of saying, "Author X commits the ad hominem fallacy in attacking the motives of her opponents," they say, "Author X might be committing," or they pose questions instead of making assertions: "Might Author X be committing ... ?" In concluding your papers you should be similarly cautious. The kind of wording to aim for is something like, "I have not yet studied this subject in enough breadth and depth to come to an absolute conclusion about who is right. However, on the basis of the limited number of sources I have studied, I conclude that side X has made the better case."

A Good Argument Effectively Refutes Opposing Arguments

All of these aspects of argument, and of support for them, are incorporated in another key element in many arguments, rebuttal or refutation, in which the writer or speaker does not just present her or his own argument but responds to (rebuts) or shows the unsoundness of (refutes) someone else's line of argument, often that of an opponent. An effective refutation typically criticizes the argument under analysis by accurately pointing out weaknesses on one or more of the above points: that it is *not* factually accurate, well informed, well reasoned, relevant, consistent, well balanced, fair-minded, or qualified, or it commits specific logical fallacies. (See further discussion of refutation in chapter 9.)

An effective refutation must speak *directly* to an opposing argument. Often writers or speakers will claim to be refuting the opposition, but rather than doing so directly, will simply make another argument supporting their own side. This is a form of the fallacy of **irrelevance** through evading the issue.

ANALYSIS, SYNTHESIS, AND JUDGMENTS

This bare-bones account of the traits of sound arguments is only the first step toward understanding of good argumentative writing or speech. Most argumentation is not limited to a single line of reasoning but consists of more than one argument, built into an extended line of argument and integrated with other elements including exposition (the part of any kind of writing or speaking that summarizes whatever background information is needed, often incorporating narration and description), analysis and synthesis, style and tone, and moral or value judgments. Each of these elements can be more or less well executed.

Extended arguments incorporate various modes of **analysis**, a process that can consist of identifying and interpreting key issues and elements in them; of establishing relationships between events or facts (frequently through **analogy**, **equation**, or comparison and contrast); of breaking a subject down into components and defining, grouping, or ordering them; or of making reasoned moral or evaluative judgments of ideas, arguments, or actions. For example, this chapter analyzes the concept of good argumentation through definition, division into components, and criteria for evaluative judgment. Every discipline employs its own distinctive modes of analysis. Those in the natural and applied sciences are mostly beyond the scope of this book. The social sciences, which provide source material for several of the political controversies studied in this book, employ analysis of statistical and socioeconomic data and social psychology. However, most of the topics and readings throughout this book emphasize modes of analysis that are distinctive to humanistic studies, including rhetorical analysis (incorporating analysis of logical soundness), semantic analysis (see chapter 4), causal analysis (see chapter 13), and historical analysis. (For a model of an extended, analytical line of argument, with marginal notes on its development, see "A Historical-Causal Analysis of 'The White Problem,'" later in this chapter.) English studies further emphasize stylistic analysis and critical analysis—the modes of reviews of and commentaries on books, films, music in concerts or recordings, and other cultural events. These analyses typically begin with a summary or abstract of the work and then go into interpretation and evaluation from a variety of critical perspectives, aesthetic and/or ideological.

Synthesis involves cumulatively connecting or assembling data or arguments (including those previously analyzed) into an extended line of argument, leading to a conclusion. A typical argumentative sequence might look like this:

1. Summary exposition of the situation
2. Analysis of the situation through one or more of the above modes
3. Synthesis of the analysis into a moral or value judgment
4. Conclusion (or **peroration**, in classical rhetoric), often with an exhortation or call for action to support a policy that the argument has shown to be desirable, or to change one that is undesirable, morally wrong, or socially unjust

Consider, for example, Mario Savio's speech "An End to History" in chapter 1. Savio's brief exposition begins with a *summary* of then recent events in the civil rights movement in Mississippi and the Free Speech Movement at Berkeley, which he relates to one another through an *analogy* or *equation* supported by the evidence of several points of similarity. He then *defines* the bureaucratic mentality, particularly in university administrators, as it functions to dehumanize students and to block challenges to the social status quo. He gives the *examples* of the students protesting denial of free speech on campus and being unable to meet with anyone but secretaries and of the administration appointing a committee instead of directly negotiating the protesters' grievances with them. He next *identifies* the relevant larger social issues of the time, racial injustice and automation, and the unwillingness of governing bureaucracies to address the human needs of African Americans, workers, and students who are being treated as "raw material."

Savio then *asserts* that the protesters are simply asking to be treated, in the university as well as in the larger society, not as "well-behaved children" but as citizens entitled to due process of law. (As noted above, his reasoning perhaps falters here, in his unqualified equation of the university with civic society.) He next *contrasts* two views of the university: "the place where people begin seriously to question the conditions of their existence and raise the issue of whether they can be committed to the society they have been born into," as opposed to UC president Clark Kerr's view of it as "a factory that turns out a certain product needed by industry or government." (You might read Kerr's memoirs, *The Gold and the Blue,* to contrast his viewpoint on these issues with Savio's.) In a *causal analysis,* Savio argues that as a result of the conflict between these different conceptions, "the best among the people who enter must for four years wander aimlessly much of the time questioning why they are on campus at all" and "[look] toward a very bleak existence afterward in a game in which all of the rules have been made up—rules which one can not really amend." Savio's concluding paragraph reiterates his *moral judgment* against "the utopia of sterilized, automated contentment" and tacitly *exhorts* students: "But an important minority of men and women coming to the front today have shown that they will die rather than be standardized, replaceable, and irrelevant."

STYLE AND TONE, ELOQUENCE AND MORAL FORCE

Aristotle's handbook, *Rhetoric* (Greek, fourth century BC), defined three key elements in argument: **logos**, which translates as logic or reasoning; **pathos**, or **emotional appeal**; and **ethos**, which concerns the **tone**, or moral or intellectual character, that speakers or writers project, as well as the kind of identity they establish with their listeners or readers. The Greek word *ethos* is the root of the English word *ethics,* so we can extend the meaning of ethos to include the ethical dimension in argument, including the previously mentioned moral judgments and the quality of support for them, as well as the forcefulness of the emotion and language supporting the judgment or action being advocated, which when most successful deserve the description of *eloquence.* Emotional appeal is, of course, an ambiguous quality, as often used for deplorable purposes as for noble ones (the uses and abuses of emotional appeal are the subject of chapter 12); the word *eloquence,* however, is usually reserved for language that is both emotionally moving and on a high moral plane, such as Lincoln's Gettysburg Address or Martin Luther King's "I Have a Dream" speech. Eloquence also is distinguished by memorably articulate, ingenious, and apt language—as the eighteenth-century English poet Alexander Pope put it, in what is itself a famously eloquent phrase, "What oft was thought, but ne'er so well expressed." So an outstanding writing **style**, such as characterizes enduring works of literature, contributes to eloquence. Conversely, poor writing detracts from the force of an argument. The writer of the letter about Dinesh D'Souza says, "Hopefully, as word spreads about this demagoguery, this will allow more thinking folks to rationally discriminate his message to its rightful place on the trash heap." The repetition of "this" is awkward, the word "discriminate" is misused (in place of something like "relegate" or "deposit"), and "rationally" is superfluous, as is the clichéd **metaphor** of "the trash heap." Essentially the whole sentence adds nothing substantial to what has already been said.

Elements of style and tone will be defined more fully in chapters 4 and 9, but for now, let us just look at how the combination of emotional appeal and forceful style contributes to the ethos and eloquence of Savio's "An End to History." Savio at the outset invokes the moral and emotional authority of the civil rights movement, at a time when many activists in the South had recently been murdered, beaten, or imprisoned. His broader description of many young people's sense of alienation from the social and educational institutions in post–World War II America struck a chord of emotional identification, not only with his immediate audience of students at Berkeley, but also with others throughout the country and world. (He was articulating a prominent theme of many social and cultural critics of the late 1950s and 1960s, such as Paul Goodman in his 1961 book *Growing Up Absurd* and Tom Hayden, the principal author of the Students for a Democratic Society's 1962 manifesto, *The Port Huron Statement.*) When my students read this speech today, many are moved by its continuing timeliness. Stylistically, this almost extemporaneous speech was quite literary in its use of **allusions**, **figures of speech**, and poetic techniques like the rhythm and alliteration (repetition of consonants) in the description of America in the metaphor "this *ch*rome-plated *c*onsumer's *p*aradise." There are allusions to Franz Kafka's novels about mysterious bureaucracies, Aldous Huxley's futuristic novel *Brave New World,* and the American Declaration of Independence and Constitution in "due process of law," "committees of our peers," and "consensus of the governed."

At the heart of the speech is an **extended metaphor** developing the theme of automation by comparing the university to a factory, as in the punning image, "The university is well structured, well tooled, to turn out people with all the sharp edges worn off—the well-rounded person." Soon after this, Savio delivered another speech protesting disciplinary actions taken by the university against him and other Free Speech Movement leaders in contravention of assurances that their grievances would be negotiated without punitive action. (This speech was captured on film in the documentary *Berkeley in the Sixties.*) Here Savio continued to develop the factory metaphor and used a classical oratorical technique of rhythmically repeating phrases and adding items incrementally in them, to build toward a climax:

> If this is a firm, and if the Board of Regents are the board of directors, and if President Kerr in fact is the manager, then I'll tell you something—the faculty are the workers, and we're the raw material. But we're a bunch of raw material that ... don't mean to be made into any product, don't mean to end up being bought by some clients of the university, be they the government, be they industry, be they organized labor—be they anyone. We're human beings!

Savio's peroration exhorted his audience:

> There's a time when the operation of the machine becomes so odious, makes you so sick at heart, that you can't take part, you can't even passively take part, and you've got to put your bodies upon the gears, and upon the wheels, upon the levers, upon all the apparatus, and you've got to make it stop, and you've got to indicate to the people who own the machine that until you are free, the machine will be prevented from working at all.

In this sentence Savio was probably alluding consciously to one of the most influential argumentative essays ever written, Henry David Thoreau's 1849 "Civil Disobedience." In this essay, also originally a speech, Thoreau protested slavery and the American acquisition of Texas as a slave state through the Mexican-American War. He said, "If the injustice ... is of such a nature that it requires you to be the agent of injustice to another, then, I say, break the law. Let your life be a counter friction to stop the machine" (1798). Savio's speech prompted a sit-in at the administration building by some eight hundred students that indeed prevented the machine of the university from working at all for several days and eventually precipitated the administration's acceptance of the students' demands for restoration of free speech.

CONCLUSION

The extensive analysis of Savio's speech here is merely intended to indicate how many elements can contribute to good argumentative writing, beyond just logical soundness, which is a necessary element, to be sure, but not sufficient in itself. Savio, speaking in immediate response to a distinctive, highly emotional public situation, managed to draw from a wide base of historical, political, and literary knowledge, as well as his personal experiences in the civil rights and Free Speech movements, in synthesizing an argument that was both soundly constructed (though not above possible critical disagreements) and memorably eloquent in emotion and style.

There is not, however, any fixed formula, like a computer program, that you can follow to produce good argumentative writing for any occasion. Some student readers of this book, especially older ones, might presently be engaged in comparable public activities that require argumentative writing or speaking, on their campus, in their community, or elsewhere, but many are probably not, though they may well be sooner or later. While this chapter and the rest of the book provide some broad guidelines for engaging in such arguments, that is not the central aim. (If that is what you need immediately, there are several good texts addressing that need, such as Linda Flower, *Problem-Solving Strategies for Writing in College and Community,* Harcourt-Brace, 1998; and Thomas Dean, *Writing Partnerships: Service Learning in Composition,* NCTE, 2000.) The aim of this book, rather, is to enable you, as a critical citizen, to understand what distinguishes good from poor arguments in sources that you encounter in reading, watching, and listening to public discourse, and to write papers incorporating that understanding both in your own rhetorical practices and in your analyses of sources and arguments.

Toward this aim, there follows an invention guide, or **heuristic** (a prompt list), both for analyzing arguments made by your sources and for checking over arguments you make on your own, which synthesizes the major and rhetorical and critical thinking issues raised throughout this book. (Several dimensions of these issues—psychological, semantic, social, and political—will be addressed more systematically in chapter 3 and throughout parts II, III, and IV.) Obviously, not every point here will be pertinent to every subject, but the guide provides a broad "menu" from which to select the most pertinent sections. In incorporating these questions into your writing, you should try to adjust the wording to your own natural style rather than sounding like you're just parroting them word for word.

RHETORIC: A CHECKLIST FOR ANALYZING YOUR OWN AND OTHERS' ARGUMENTS

1. When you are expressing your views on a subject, ask yourself how extensive your knowledge of it is, what the sources of that knowledge are, and what restrictions there might be in your vantage point. When you are studying a writer on the subject (or when she cites a source on it), try to figure out what her qualifications are on this particular subject. Is the newspaper, magazine, Web site, book publisher, or research institute he is writing for (or citing) a reputable one? What is its ideological viewpoint?

2. Are you, as reader or writer (or is the author), indulging in **rationalization**, or wishful thinking—believing something merely because it is what you *want* to believe? In other words, are you distinguishing what is personally advantageous or disadvantageous from what you would objectively consider just or unjust?

3. Are the actions of the author, or those she is supporting, consistent with their professed position, or are they saying one thing while doing another? (This is one form of **compartmentalization**, the other most common one being internal inconsistencies in the author's arguments.)

4. Are all of the data ("facts") or quotations correct? Are any data used misleadingly or any quotes taken out of context?

5. Semantic issues: Does she make it clear, either by explicit definition or by context, in exactly what sense she is using any controversial or ambiguous words? In other words, is she using vague, **unconcretized abstractions**, or is she concretizing her abstractions? Are there any evasive **euphemisms** (i.e., "clean" words that obscure a "dirty" truth)?

6. Are the **generalizations** and assertions of opinion—especially those that are disputable or central to the argument—adequately qualified and supported by reasoning, evidence, or examples? In your own writing, if you haven't been able to provide this support, it may be a good idea not to make these assertions.

7. Is there any unjustifiable (i.e., not supported by adequate evidence) emotional appeal through empty "conditioned response" words (or **"cleans" and "dirties"**), name-calling, straw man, or innuendo?

8. Are the limits of the position defined, or are they vulnerable to being pushed to absurd logical consequences (reduction to absurdity)? In other words, does the author indicate where to draw the line?

9. Are all of the analogies (saying two situations are similar) and equations (saying two situations are the same) valid?

10. Does the author honestly acknowledge the opposition, fairly balancing all the evidence and arguments of one side against those of the other, giving each side's arguments accurate weight and evaluating them in accurate proportion to each other? Or does she dishonestly **stack the deck** through using a **double standard** or **selective vision**? That is, is she using **half-truths**, leaving out arguments or suppressing facts that might contradict her arguments? Are there faults on her side that correspond to the faults she has pointed out in the opposing position?

11. Are there any faulty **causal analyses**? Does the author view any actions as causes that may really be effects or reactions? Does he use any post hoc reasoning—that is, when he asserts that something has happened because of something else, might it be true that the second event happened irrespective of, or even in spite of, the first? Has he reduced a probable multiplicity of causes to one (reductionism)? When he argues that a course of action has been unsuccessful because it has been carried too far, might the opposite be true—that it has been unsuccessful because it has not been carried far enough (or vice versa)?

12. Does the argument contain other logical fallacies, especially evading the issue, non sequiturs (conclusions that don't follow logically from the arguments preceding them, or two statements that seem to be related but aren't), **either-or thinking**, false dilemmas, or false dichotomies?

13. Theory versus practice: Are the theoretical proposals practicable or the abstract principles consistent with empirical (verifiable) facts and probabilities, and are they based on adequate firsthand witness to the situation in question?

Topics for Discussion and Writing

1. Choose an issue that you are concerned about on your campus, in your community, in the nation, or in the world and write a speech or article about it, following this model (see chapter 4 for further writing guidelines):
   a. Summary exposition of the situation
   b. Analysis of the situation through one or more of the modes discussed above
   c. Synthesis of the analysis into a moral or value judgment
   d. Conclusion, with an exhortation or call for action to support a policy that the argument has shown to be desirable, or to change one that is undesirable, morally wrong, or socially unjust

2. Analyze any of the readings throughout this book in terms of (1) the logical cogency of individual arguments in it, (2) the quality of its supporting evidence, (3) its overall expository and argumentative organization, (4) the effectiveness of its rebuttals to opposing positions, (5) its style and tone, (6) the quality of its moral judgments and force.

3. In an article titled "The Age of Irony?" in *Journal of Advanced Composition* (Fall 2002), Susan Searls Giroux writes:

> The consequences of [conservatives'] concerted attack on progressive taxa-
> tion, social welfare [publicly funded services in general, such as education and
> Social Security], and a living wage have been that . . . the pay gap between
> top executives and production workers grew from 42:1 in 1980 to a stagger-
> ing 419:1 in 1998 (excluding the value of stock options), according to *Business
> Week*'s "Forty-ninth Annual Executive Pay Survey." The same report notes
> that "Had the typical worker's pay risen in tandem with executive pay, the
> average production worker would now earn $110,000 a year and the minimum
> wage would be $22.08" instead of the current wage of $5.15. And how does
> this wage figure in terms of yearly salary? A 40-hour week at $5.15 per hour
> "nets a pre-tax annual income of $10,300, or about $6,355 below the official
> 1998 poverty line for a family of four." In contrast to these poverty wages, "the
> average large company chief executive was paid $10.6 million, a 36 percent jump
> over 1997." (971)

Students were assigned to write their responses to these data, as present or
future possible workers. (Grammatical note: in Latin, *datum* is a singular noun,
though it is rarely used in English; the more common *data* is plural.) Here are
two responses. Evaluate their relevance to Giroux's assertions in terms of direct
refutations of her specific data.

> Student A: "The wealth gap is increasing every day, but is that all bad? I
> think not. Giroux's article outlines how the rich are getting richer and the poor
> are getting poorer, but is comparing a minimum wage worker to a big chief
> executive fair? This is like comparing diamonds to rocks."
>
> Student B: "For many years there has been a wealth gap in America, but
> it looks as though there is not really a way to fix this gap. Raising taxes is not
> the answer. People should be able to work and reap the benefits of their hard
> work. Corporate executives work hard and deserve every dollar they earn.
> Most poor people dropped out of school along the way and in return for their
> lack of motivation have lived in poverty. I don't care for the fact that my tax-
> payer money goes towards welfare to support them."

4. Giroux's data here form part of an inductive argument. What are some reasonable
   inferences or **conclusions** that could be drawn from these figures, in terms of
   implications for the future if the discrepancy between workers and executives
   continues to widen at the same rate? What economic or moral **judgments**
   could reasonably be based on them? For related arguments that do make such
   inferences and judgments, see Adolph Reed's "Majoring in Debt" in chapter 1
   and all of chapter 16.

5. The following are two deductively structured arguments in recent debates over
   the First Amendment to the Constitution and separation of church and state.

   a. In an op-ed column in the *Los Angeles Times* titled "In God We Trust . . .
      Let's Affirm It in Laws" (February 6, 1983), Pat Robertson, then head of the
      Christian Coalition, one of the largest evangelical Christian organizations in
      America, argued for reversing the Supreme Court's 1962 decision against
      prayer in public schools. This was his conclusion:

      > According to the Gallup Poll, 94% of the American people believe in God. Without
      > question, those who believe must give the 6% who do not believe the freedom
      > to speak, write, broadcast and disagree. But I do not think that the believing
      > majority has an obligation to the disbelieving minority to dismantle our public
      > affirmation of faith in God. Nor do we owe this 6% minority an absolute veto
      > over a constitutional amendment . . . that would restore our freedom to address
      > Almighty God in our schools and public places.

Robertson argues from the premise that 94% of the public believe in God to the conclusion that we should amend the Constitution to restore prayer in schools. There are at least a couple of hidden premises implicit in this enthymeme; identify them and evaluate their logical soundness and implications for the conclusion. Is Robertson's **ad populum** argument relevant to the constitutionality of prayer in school? Robertson is a political conservative and influential figure in the Republican Party (he once ran for the Republican nomination to be president). Conservatives generally express a belief in individual liberties against infringement on them by government (especially the federal, as opposed to state, government), strict adherence to the Constitution, and opposition to rash or drastic change. Is there an inconsistency between these professed beliefs and Robertson's call here for a constitutional amendment, or the more recent conservative campaign for a constitutional amendment banning homosexual marriage?

b. More recently, Erwin Chemerinsky, a liberal professor of law and political science at the University of Southern California, wrote an op-ed in the *Los Angeles Times* titled "Next Time, Court Should Rule 'Under God' Out of Pledge" (June 17, 2004), in which he argued:

> As a matter of First Amendment law, the Pledge of Allegiance case should be easy. For more than 40 years, the Supreme Court has held that government-sponsored religious activity is not allowed in public school classrooms. The words "under God" are inherently religious. . . .
>
> But every day, children feel pressure to say "under God" in public school classrooms. Such government-sponsored religion is a clear violation of the establishment clause [in the First Amendment].

Here we see, in classic deductive form, two explicit premises leading to a conclusion. What are the two premises? Does the conclusion follow logically from them? Conservative disagreement with this line of argument would most likely focus, not on the internal logic of the argument, but on a **semantic** issue in the first premise concerning the phrase "government-sponsored religious activity." The First Amendment states that "Congress shall make no law respecting an establishment of religion, or prohibiting the free exercise thereof." Chemerinsky implies that "establishment of religion" is equated with any government-sponsored religious activity. However, the exact meaning of "establishment of religion" is the major source of disagreement on this issue. As a research-paper topic, study some opposed views on it by legal scholars or historians.

6. In another view on the issue of separation of church and state, a public address by Roane County, Tennessee, high school principal Jody McLoud, delivered before a football game in 2003, was circulated on the Internet (http://www.deceptioninthechurch.com/roanecounty/html). McLoud said:

> It has always been the custom at Roane County High School football games to say a prayer and play the National Anthem to honor God and Country. Due to a recent ruling by the Supreme Court, I am told that saying a prayer is a violation of Federal Case Law. As I understand the law at this time, I can use this public facility to approve of sexual perversion and call it an alternate lifestyle, and if someone is offended, that's OK. I can use it to condone sexual promiscuity by dispensing condoms and calling it safe sex. If someone is offended, that's OK. I can even use this public facility to present the merits of killing an unborn baby as a viable means of birth control. If someone is offended, no problem. I can designate a school day as earth day and involve students in activities to

> religiously worship and praise the goddess, mother earth, and call it ecology. I can use literature, videos and presentations in the classroom that depict people with strong, traditional, Christian convictions as simple minded and ignorant and call it enlightenment. However, if anyone uses this facility to honor God and ask Him to bless this event with safety and good sportsmanship, Federal Case Law is violated. This appears to be at best, inconsistent and at worst, diabolical. Apparently, we are to be tolerant of everything and anyone except God and His Commandments.

Argue the pros and cons of McLoud's analogy between permitted and nonpermitted activities here, the soundness of his assertion that it is *inconsistent* to bar prayer at football games, and the legitimacy, in relation to the First Amendment, of a public high school principal making a public statement like this.

7. As supplements to "A Historical-Causal Analysis of 'The White Problem'," read Jonathan Kozol's "Other People's Children" and William J. Bennett's "Crisis in American Education" in chapter 11 (also see the topics for discussion and writing on them in that chapter). What evidence or reasoning do each of these present either in support or refutation of the arguments in "A Historical-Causal Analysis"? Which side's arguments more effectively refute the other side's? Write a paper or prepare a debate presentation synthesizing these readings, along with additional sources, fair-mindedly acknowledging the strongest arguments on both sides, then judging which side makes the better case on balance.

8. Summarize and evaluate the implicit line of argument and rhetorical techniques in the following "Mallard Fillmore" cartoon. On what issues is the cartoon's viewpoint conservative, by the terms of the "Guide to Political Terms and Positions" in chapter 13? ("Congresspersons who won't vote for vouchers" refers to liberals who oppose tax credits for parents whose children go to private schools.) In the second panel, to whom do you think "us" refers? Discuss this as a possible example of the "What do you mean, 'we'?" fallacy in chapter 10.

9. In the 2004 presidential election campaign, John Kerry's wife, Teresa Heinz Kerry, made a speech appealing for more civility in politics, with particular criticism of the "un-American" attack mode of some conservative politicians and media. When she was aggressively questioned on the speech by a conservative newspaper editor, she told him, "Shove it." Of what rhetorical fault might this be considered an example?

A Historical-Causal Analysis of "The White Problem"

White Americans used to talk about "the Negro problem," but during the 1960s, writers like James Baldwin argued that this very phrase indicated the kind of **doublethink** mentality that obscured the fact that what we have always had in this country is "the White problem," and that the kind of **rationalizations** that whites have concocted amount to mass delusion.

Introduction: Thesis statement

The most common white rationalizations are the following: "Slavery and discrimination against blacks were all in the past. Why do they keep complaining now, when they have all the advantages?" "My family never had slaves, and I don't discriminate, so why should I feel guilty or responsible?" "Other immigrant groups have come to this country and overcome adversity. Why haven't the blacks?" And, "Blacks have a high rate of crime and immorality, which causes legitimate fears and disapproval by whites."

Summary of positions to be refuted

A historical perspective on this problem begins with the question, "When did the past end, and the present begin" (William Faulkner wrote, with specific reference to the persistent after-effects of slavery in the South, "The past isn't dead, it isn't even past.") Specifically, since exactly what date has discrimination against blacks been a thing of the past? Let us look at the chain of **historical causation**.

Transition to main body

Many immigrant groups have endured vicious prejudices, but none have suffered as African Americans have from legally authorized, systematic persecution, from this country's beginnings, one generation after another, down to the present. The first black slaves were brought to this country in 1617—three years before the Pilgrims landed at Plymouth Rock—in the Jamestown, Virginia, colony. The last slaves were imported in 1808, and few blacks ever "immigrated" here voluntarily before the twentieth century. That means most African Americans' families have been in this country far longer than most white Americans', as well as most immigrant groups'. (So much for comments like, "Why don't they go back to Africa if they don't like it here?") This is one of many points on which the **analogy** between African Americans and other ethnic groups, other than Native Americans, is inaccurate. What is the heritage of black Americans from the nearly 400 years their ancestors have been here?

Main Body: Introduction to refutation of analogy with immigrant groups

Transition to hist. evidence

Blacks were kidnapped and brought here from Africa in chains on ships under subhuman conditions in which hundreds of thousands died en route. They were stripped of their own language, religion, and culture—even their names. Families were broken up as husbands, wives and children were sold as separate chattel. They were deliberately kept illiterate as a means to keep them from gaining any possible means of enlightenment about their situation or of communication with others in insurrection, and—as Frederick Douglass reports in his autobiography—they were encouraged to get drunk and party on off hours to let off the steam that might otherwise lead to revolt.

Historical evidence

Most ethnic groups immigrating from other countries have been able to maintain their family ties, cultural traditions, and access to education. As they arrived, many stayed in contact with and received aid from kinspeople in the old country or from those already established here. By the time slavery was

Development of refutation of analogy with immigrant groups

abolished, however, blacks had been cut off from their African roots for some two hundred fifty years, the continuity of their families and cultural heritage destroyed and their access to education deliberately blocked. As Alex Haley's *Roots* and other recent studies have shown, many throughout the period of slavery and subsequently struggled against all odds to maintain their family ties and traditions; nevertheless, African Americans have always had to live with the burden of being aliens in their "own" country and with the absence of a sense of belonging anywhere.

Economic analysis

Whites tend to think of slavery (if they think about it seriously at all) as a moral or social institution, but it was always first and foremost an *economic* institution. Slavery was an immensely profitable *business,* both in the slave trade and in the fruits of slave labor, which in the 17th and 18th centuries produced huge returns in capital investment for Southern plantation owners. As James Baldwin observed ironically in *The Fire Next Time,* white Americans pride themselves on the myth that the prosperity of this country was created through rugged individualism and the puritan work ethic—God rewarded those who work hard; but in the South, black slaves did all the work and a handful of white plantation owners got all the rewards. Some recent historians have argued that this country's prosperity was due *primarily* to slave labor. Certainly, some of the country's greatest fortunes were amassed by slaveowners, and some of their descendants today are still living off those fortunes. What have the descendants of their slaves gotten out of their ancestors' centuries of hard work?

Trans. to chain of causation

Step One: Immediate aftermath of abolition

Slavery was abolished in 1861 and the Civil War ended in 1865. Many people who have not studied this history seem to assume that abolition marked the end of African Americans' grievances, and that ever since, white America has shown good will in helping blacks gain equality. But have you ever thought about how Southern slaveowners, white workers, and others who benefitted economically from slavery must have reacted to abolition? Do you suppose most of them opened their arms lovingly to welcome freed slaves as equal citizens? Here were some eight million workers, one-third of the population of the South, who had been providing unpaid labor for two hundred fifty years, now competing for wages with whites in the poorest part of the country. Many whites obviously perceived that their interests lay in keeping blacks in conditions as close to slavery as the law now permitted. Following abolition, the federal government promised each freed slave family "forty acres and a mule" to start homesteading, but this legislation was killed in Congress by Southerners and Northern industrial interests motivated by maintaining a cheap labor pool. The hundred years following the Civil War saw the rise of the Ku Klux Klan, mass lynchings, segregation in social life and education (with "separate but equal" a **rationalization** for inferior schools), and "Jim Crow" laws denying Southern blacks voting and other civil rights.

Step Two: Hundred subsequent years of segregation

Further development of refutation of immigrant analogy

So, while the many waves of immigrants from other countries have been enabled to gain a foothold and eventual advancement here, blacks have been more or less systematically kept at the bottom of the social ladder, providing a permanent "underclass" socially and economically, and humiliated by the fact that each newly arrived ethnic group has been allowed to step over them in social assimilation. (Perhaps the most **analogous** group to blacks in this respect has been Mexican and other Latin American farm and domestic workers, who have suffered comparably deliberate economic exploitation.)

Step Three: Migration to North and its consequences.

Under the conditions of continuing oppression in the South, millions of Southern blacks understandably migrated North to seek better opportunities, in wave after wave from the early twentieth century to the 1980s—constituting the largest migration in American history, according to Nicholas Lemann's *The Promised Land: The Great Black Migration and How It Changed America,* a powerfully written history of this period. Lemann recounts that as blacks arrived in Northern cities, white residents, fearful of loss of their property value, resorted to the same kind of hate crimes blacks thought they had left in the South, including Ku Klux Klan terrorism, lynchings, riots culminating in beatings and house-burnings. (The frustrations of blacks too erupted periodically in rioting, most recently in Los Angeles after the Rodney King trial.) As blacks moved into urban neighborhoods, white residents and businesses moved out to the suburbs, taking with them jobs and the base of property-tax and corporate-tax income needed for the support of neighborhood schools, police, hospitals, street repair, and other essential community services. "Restrictive covenants," clauses in deeds to houses and apartment buildings restricting their sale or residence in them to whites (and in many cases Christians), were legal and widespread throughout the North well into the 1950s, before they were declared unconstitutional; many figures who are still prominent in American politics and public life bought and sold houses with such covenants. Thus, in Northern housing and schools, there has been segregation in fact (*de facto*) if not by law (*de jure*), as in the South, with a low tax base guaranteeing deprivation in education and other formative influences that perpetuated economic disadvantages generation after generation.

Discrimination not only in housing and education but in employment, insurance, legal justice, medical care, and the cost of commodities further contributed to the cycle of poverty in Northern ghettos. The lack of good jobs and the resulting despair led many residents to turn to crime, drugs, alcoholism, and prostitution, with dealing in drugs, liquor, weapons, and sex becoming among the few relatively prosperous work options. Contrary to common **stereotypes**, however, the majority of ghetto residents have managed to maintain high moral standards; many also managed to work their way into middle-class status, at which point most understandably moved up out of the ghetto, inadvertently contributing to segregation along class as well as racial lines.

In one of the many vicious circles here, all these conditions in turn discouraged large employers from investing in inner cities. These conditions steadily worsened throughout the twentieth century, the latest turn for the worst coming since the 1960s, when large manufacturers have relocated from inner cities and other American sites into Third World locations providing even cheaper labor. Jonathan Kozol's 1991 book *Savage Inequalities* succinctly describes the **causal** sequence in the Lawndale section of Chicago:

> Between 1960 and 1970, as the last white families left the neighborhood, North Lawndale lost three quarters of its businesses, one quarter of its jobs. In the next ten years, 80 percent of the remaining jobs in manufacturing were lost.
>
> "People carry a lot of crosses here," says Reverend Jim Wolff, who directs a mission church not far from one of the deserted factories. "God's beautiful people live here in the midst of hell."
>
> As the factories have moved out, he says, the street gangs have moved in. Driving with me past a sprawling red brick complex that was once the world headquarters of Sears, Roebuck, he speaks of the increasing economic isolation of the neighborhood: "Sears is gone, International Harvester is gone. Western Electric has moved out. The Vice Lords, the Disciples and the Latin Kings have, in a sense, replaced them. (42)

The whole peculiar history of crime and sexuality between whites and blacks is another element differentiating African Americans from any other ethnic or

---

Sidebar annotations:

First consequence: White reactions

Step Four: Flight of jobs and tax base; segregation in northern housing and schools

Step Five: Other conditions leading to vicious circles

Step Six: Relocation of manufacturing abroad since 1960s

Whites' double standard and confusion of cause and effect in thinking about black criminality

immigrant group in America. Throughout and long after the slavery period, until the 1960s, virtually any white man was free to murder or rob any black, to rape or force into being a prostitute or mistress any black woman, without taking responsibility for the resulting babies; indeed, white men were encouraged to father children by black women because any such children were defined by law as black, providing more slave labor or, after abolition, cheap labor. (Blacks themselves were tacitly encouraged to have illegitimate children among themselves for the same economic benefits to whites.) Consequently, this country is filled with the descendants of mixed race parentage—making the whole concept of a "white" and a "black" race in America largely a fabrication.

Yet, white America has always applied **compartmentalized thinking** and a **double standard** toward crimes by blacks against whites versus those by whites against blacks. Above all, in spite of the countless instances of white men raping black women with impunity, a black man raping, or even being perceived as making advances to, a white woman was always the ultimate taboo, the most frequent incitement to lynching; fears of the purity of white blood being polluted by black insemination of white women was the foremost obsession of racists. Knowledge of this history was necessary to understand the possible **implications** of the broadcast in George Bush's 1988 presidential campaign of a TV commercial criticizing Bush's opponent, Governor Michael Dukakis of Massachusetts for having allowed a weekend furlough to Willy Horton, an imprisoned rapist, during which he raped and murdered a woman. Horton was black, the woman white; nothing was said of this in the commercial and Bush's defenders said the incident was not racist because Horton was guilty of the crime. The **between-the-lines** issue, however, was whether the commercial was playing subconsciously on the entrenched white double standard on rape, and whether the Bush campaign would have chosen to make an issue of the case if the rapist had been white and his victim black.

Consider in the larger historical perspective the most frequent allegations against blacks today—they have high rates of illiteracy, crime, alcohol or drug abuse, and illegitimate births. To whatever extent such allegations are grounded in fact (and this is highly disputed ground), doesn't it seem likely that these present day conditions are the predictable consequence of nearly four hundred years of the conditions forced on American blacks, and that those consequences are unlikely to disappear within a few decades of blacks' attainment of equal legal rights in the 1960s? However, precisely because many American whites have not learned to think in terms of historical **cause and effect**, they **decontextualize** the present behavior of a deviant minority of blacks and see it as a cause of social problems rather than an **effect** or **reaction**. This does not excuse any such misbehavior or absolve individuals from responsibility; it simply indicates that the problem must be approached in broad social and historical terms beyond individual cases.

Now, if you follow this entire chain of causation over nearly four hundred years, it becomes apparent that "the past is not even past," that today's racial problems are inseparable from this unbroken chain of causation; it also becomes apparent that, from beginning to end, African Americans on the whole have not been responsible or to blame for any of the injustices that have blighted their lives generation after generation (although as individuals they have coped with the **effects** of these injustices with varying degrees of personal responsibility). Their bewilderment was summed up by a brilliant **metaphor** in the title of a song written in the 1940s by Fats Waller: "What Did I Do To Be So Black and Blue?"

[margin note:] Avoiding implication that blacks are absolved from individual responsibility

[margin note:] Summary of arguments to this point

[margin note:] White hatred of blacks as blaming the victim,

What explanation can there be, then for the hatred that so many whites have vented on blacks throughout the centuries? This would seem to be a classic case of **blaming the victim**. Baldwin's *The Fire Next Time* explores the psychology of this mind-set, in the mix of willful ignorance, **ethnocentrism**, and **rationalization** that have led whites to be "the slightly mad victims of their own brainwashing" (137). Baldwin sees whites as being in a state of psychological **denial** of the truth of the crimes whites have committed against blacks throughout American history, and of **projection** of those crimes into **stereotypes** of blacks as the criminal class. He says that although many whites in the past and present have sincerely wanted to enable blacks to attain equality, many others have been driven by fear that if blacks gained economic, political, and sexual equality, they would want to "get even" and take revenge on whites for all the past crimes; rather than admit that they are unwilling to see blacks gain equality—or at least to give up any of their own advantages, as necessitated by policies like affirmative action and welfare—they rationalize that blacks are themselves to blame for failing to "pull themselves up."

One of the more recent varieties of this "brainwashing," in Baldwin's view, is many whites' belief that the attainment of civil rights and increased opportunities by blacks since the 1950s has resulted out of the goodness of white America's heart; he argues, on the contrary, that whites have given ground only when they have been forced to by the pressures of the civil rights movement, the influence of newly independent African and other Third-World nations, the economic obsolescence of segregated society, and—above all—by the fear instilled since the mid-sixties by highly destructive ghetto riots and the Black Power movement.

Now throughout this entire tragic sequence of events from the Emancipation Proclamation to the present, most of the damage done to blacks has probably not resulted from the ill will of individual whites, but from a series of social consequences that has followed inevitably from the throwing of millions into the labor market and civic life without adequate accommodation by American society for their assimilation. For generation after generation, down to your own, with no adequate corrective policies by the society at large, individual whites have been able to say, "It isn't my fault. I never owned slaves or discriminated." This kind of statement, though justified to a point, reflects a typical American tendency to reduce every problem to personal attitudes, while ignoring the responsibility we each have for the collective political and economic policies that have perpetuated racism and that would need to be changed in order finally to end it. This attitude also disregards the historical truth that the sins of the fathers are visited on the children, and that present generations might have to make sacrifices or suffer injustices to redress injustices done by previous generations.

Young whites have come into the world at the latest stage in this inheritance of evasion and are likely to see only the current *consequences,* not the *causes.* Policies like welfare and affirmative action, insofar as they have been intended to aid blacks, have been designed as minimal efforts to deal with these consequences, not with their causes at the roots; nevertheless, it is unlikely that most of those who loudly denounce affirmative action and welfare have much understanding of the historical causes justifying these policies, or any more effective solutions to suggest for repairing the continuing damage done by the causes.

rationalization, projection

Conclusion: Fallacy of whites reducing racial problems to personal attitudes, while ignoring responsibility for political and economic policies and present consequences of past injustices

Necessity of addressing *causes* of conditions of which welfare and affirmative action are *consequences.*

CHAPTER 3

Definitions and Criteria of Critical Thinking

This chapter will briefly explain the scholarly background for the content of subsequent chapters and the sequence in which they are organized. Around 1980 American educators began to identify critical thinking as a subject that needed increased, explicit emphasis in our high schools and colleges, and as an essential element in civic literacy. The Rockefeller Foundation's Commission on the Humanities reported in 1980, "The humanities lead beyond 'functional' literacy and basic skills to critical judgment and discrimination, enabling citizens to view political issues from an informed perspective. . . . Educational policy makers at all levels should define critical thinking as a basic skill and recognize the value of the humanities for developing it" (*The Humanities in American Life,* 12, 22).

Also in 1980, Chancellor Glenn Dumke announced the requirement of formal instruction in critical thinking throughout the nineteen California State University campuses, serving some three hundred thousand students. The announcement read:

> Instruction in critical thinking is to be designed to achieve an understanding of the relationship of language to logic, which should lead to the ability to analyze, criticize, and advocate ideas, to reason inductively and deductively, and to reach factual or judgmental conclusions based on sound inferences drawn from unambiguous statements of knowledge or belief. The minimal competence to be expected at the successful conclusion of instruction in critical thinking should be the ability to distinguish fact from judgment, belief from knowledge, and skills in elementary inductive and deductive processes, including an understanding of the formal and informal fallacies of language and thought.

Similar requirements were soon adopted by community colleges and secondary schools throughout California and elsewhere. Here is the list of "basic critical thinking skills" in the California State Department of Education's Model Curriculum for Grades 8–12 in 1984.

1. *Compare similarities and differences*
   The ability to compare similarities and differences among two or more objects, living things, ideas, events, or situations at the same or different points in time. Implies the ability to organize information into defined categories.
2. *Identify central issues or problems*
   The ability to identify the main idea or point of a passage, argument, or political cartoon, for example. At the higher levels, students are expected to identify central issues in complex political arguments. Implies ability to identify major components of an argument, such as reasons and conclusions.
3. *Distinguish fact from opinion*
   The ability to determine the difference between observation and inference.
4. *Recognize stereotypes and clichés*
   The ability to identify fixed or conventional notions about a person, group, or idea.
5. *Recognize bias, emotional factors, propaganda, and semantic slanting*
   The ability to identify partialities and prejudices in written and graphic materials. Includes the ability to determine credibility of sources (gauge reliability, expertise, and objectivity).
6. *Recognize different value orientations and different ideologies*
   The ability to recognize different value orientations and ideologies.
7. *Determine which information is relevant*
   The ability to make distinctions between verifiable and unverifiable, relevant and nonrelevant, and essential and incidental information.
8. *Recognize the adequacy of data*
   The ability to decide whether the information provided is sufficient in terms of quality and quantity to justify a conclusion, decision, generalization, or plausible hypothesis.
9. *Check consistency*
   The ability to determine whether given statements or symbols are consistent. For example, the ability to determine whether the different points or issues in a political argument have logical connections or agree with the central issue.
10. *Formulate appropriate questions*
    The ability to formulate appropriate and thought-provoking questions that will lead to a deeper and clearer understanding of the issues at hand.

11. *Predict probable consequences*
    The ability to predict probable consequences of an event or series of events.
12. *Identify unstated assumptions*
    The ability to identify what is taken for granted, though not explicitly stated, in an argument.

Some scholars make a distinction between critical thinking *skills,* related formally or informally to traditional logic, and *dispositions* that foster or impede critical thinking within the broader context of psychological, cultural, social, and political influences. Dispositions that foster critical thinking, also studied throughout part II (partly from the perspective of semantics, especially in chapter 9), include the development of skepticism, open-mindedness, autonomous thought, and reciprocity (psychologist Jean Piaget's term for the ability to empathize with other individuals, social groups, nationalities, ideologies, etc.). Dispositions that act as impediments to critical thinking include **culturally conditioned assumptions, egocentrism** and **ethnocentrism, authoritarianism, rationalization, compartmentalization, stereotyping, prejudice,** and **defense mechanisms**. These positive and negative dispositions will be surveyed in the following chapters.

CRITICAL THINKING AND CULTURAL LITERACY

Much debate in academic circles has centered on the relative importance of learning critical thinking skills versus factual knowledge related to specific disciplines like history, social science, or the natural sciences. This debate seems to me a classic **either-or fallacy**, since common sense dictates that both are indispensable and inseparable in practice. The leading recent advocate of increased emphasis on factual knowledge in American education, E. D. Hirsch, in his controversial 1987 book *Cultural Literacy: What Every American Needs to Know,* agrees:

> The old prejudice that facts deaden the minds of children has a long history in the nineteenth and twentieth centuries and includes not just the disciples of Rousseau and Dewey but also Charles Dickens who, in the figure of Mr. Gradgrind in *Hard Times,* satirized the teaching of mere facts. But it isn't facts that deaden the minds of young children, who are storing facts in their minds every day with astonishing voracity. It is incoherence—our failure to ensure that a pattern of shared, vividly taught, and socially enabling knowledge will emerge from our instruction.
>
> The polarization of educationists into facts-people versus skills-people has no basis in reason. Facts and skills are inseparable. There is no insurmountable reason why those who advocate the teaching of higher order skills and those who advocate the teaching of common traditional content should not join forces. (133)

Hirsch and many other authorities concur that historical facts are foremost among the fields of knowledge essential for critical thinking—*not* for the purpose of rote memorization of dates and names, but for the purpose of reasoning back and forth between the past, present, and future, of being able to understand present conditions in comparison and contrast to past conditions and in a sequence of causal analysis explaining how conditions have evolved to their present state. As *The Humanities in American Life* puts it:

> The humanities do not impose any single set of normative values, whether moral, social, or aesthetic; rather, as a record of the ideals that have guided men and women in the past, they give historical perspective. Students made sensitive to what it might be like to live in a different time, place, or culture can make value choices without automatically assuming that contemporary reality has no precedent, or that quick scientific or humanistic prescriptions can remedy every problem. The humanities bring to life the ideal of cultural pluralism by expanding the number of perspectives from which questions of value may be viewed, by

enlarging young people's social and historical consciousness, and by activating an imaginative critical spirit. (30)

And, on the relation of English courses to history and other humanistic disciplines:

> High schools should concentrate on an articulated sequence of courses in English, history, and foreign languages. Courses in these disciplines should not divorce skills and methods from knowledge of content and cultural context.... English courses need to emphasize the connections between expression, logic, and the critical use of textual and historical evidence. (44)

"The critical use of textual and historical evidence" is the subject of large portions of *Reading and Writing for Civic Literacy,* since the most important part of inductive argumentation is learning to provide persuasive evidence in support of your opinions or assertions, and since that evidence must frequently be drawn from historical sources.

The most important link between critical thinking and cultural literacy is the vocabulary of words denoting mental operations, rhetorical terms, and factual knowledge that constantly expands over the course of our education and varied life experience. In *Errors and Expectations: A Guide for the Teacher of Basic Writing* (1977), Mina Shaughnessy, a pioneer scholar in the learning challenges to students in college writing courses, summed up the kinds of words that college students are being introduced to and that constitute what she termed "the vocabulary of general literacy," though she might equally well have referred to the vocabulary of "critical thinking," "cultural literacy," or "academic discourse":

1. Words that allude to events, places, and people that are assumed to be commonly, if but vaguely, known (Gandhi, the French Revolution, the Nile, etc.).
2. Words that serve as formal equivalents to concepts already familiar to the student in different words (as *atheist* is the equivalent to "someone who doesn't believe in God").
3. Words that serve to identify complex historical movements (Renaissance, Marxism, evolution, etc.).
4. Words that, although part of the nomenclature of certain fields, are also used in the wider culture with variant meanings (in literature, for example, such terms as *fiction, drama,* or *novel*).
5. Words that are intended to initiate highly specific academic activities (*define, compare, generalize, document, illustrate, prove, summarize, interpret,* etc.).
6. Words that are used in deliberately ambiguous ways in order to enrich or refine meaning (*irony, figures of speech,* etc.).
7. Words that articulate relationships such as addition, negation, condition, or causation (*moreover, therefore, however,* etc.).
8. Words that represent Latin- or Greek-based synonyms for familiar words (i.e., *initiate* or *commence* for *begin*) and that tend to give an academic flavor to the writing and speech of teachers. (217)

MAKING CONNECTIONS

> To the young mind, every thing is individual, stands by itself. By and by, it finds how to join two things, and see in them one nature, then [to join] three, then three thousand....
> —*Ralph Waldo Emerson, "The American Scholar"*

Scholars in developmental psychology, sociolinguistics, and composition theory have identified other critical thinking skills that distinguish advanced stages in reading, writing, and reasoning (sometimes termed "higher-order thinking"). These include the abilities to retain and apply material previously studied and to sustain an extended line of argument in reading, writing, and speaking, incorporating **recursive** and **cumulative thinking** (the abilities to refer back to previously covered material and to build on that material in developing stages in an argument); see, for an example of an extended argument, "A Historical-Causal Analysis of 'The White Problem'" in chapter 2.

These skills and others further contribute to the abilities to make connections between diverse experiences, ideas, and subjects studied, through **analysis** and **synthesis**, which were introduced in chapter 2. The most important analytic and synthetic skills (again illustrated in many of the readings and exercises throughout this book) include the abilities to reason back and forth between (and connect) the concrete and the abstract; between the personal and the impersonal; between the literal and the figurative, the explicit and the implicit ("reading between the lines"); between the actual and the hypothetical or between what presently exists and conceivable alternatives; between the past, present, and future; and between causes and effects. Other skills include the abilities to understand (within personal, historical, and political contexts) multiple levels of meaning or points of view and to recognize irony, paradox, and ambiguity in disparities between what is said and meant, between appearance and reality (especially between what people say and what they do), and between intentions and results.

On a negative note, some critics of contemporary American society and culture make the case that many individuals' development of analytic and synthetic skills—indeed their capacity to make connections between events and ideas at all—has actually been impaired by the atomizing "sound bites" and low reasoning level of mass political discourse and media and that, in a **vicious circle**, the diminished level of the public's reasoning skills is pandered to by politicians and media "giving the people what they want," a point further developed in chapter 16. As sociologist Stanley Aronowitz puts it in "Mass Culture and the Eclipse of Reason: The Implications for Pedagogy":

> Research suggests a correlation of television watching (and consumption of mass culture in general) to a tendency toward literalness in thought.... Put succinctly, children of all social classes ... seem unable to penetrate beyond the surfaces of things to reach down to those aspects of the object that may not be visible to the senses.... The problem of abstraction becomes a major barrier to analysis because students seem enslaved to the concrete. Finally, teachers notice that many have trouble making connections between two objects or sets of concepts that are not related to each other in an obvious manner.... The critical project of learning involves understanding that things are often not what they seem to be and that abstract concepts such as "society," "capitalism," "history," and other categories not available to the senses are nonetheless real. This whole critical project now seems in eclipse. (282–283)

DIALOGUE IN CRITICAL THINKING AND LITERATURE

> Only by art can we get outside ourselves, know what another sees of his universe, which is not the same as ours and the different views of which would otherwise have remained unknown to us as those there may be on the moon.
>
> —*Marcel Proust,* Remembrance of Things Past:
> The Past Recaptured

Plato's works about Socrates, written in fourth-century-BC Greece and among the greatest influences on the whole history of Western philosophy, rhetoric, and literature, are in the form of dramatic dialogues between Socrates and other characters. In these dialogues, the truth is pursued through dialogic (or dialectical) exchange and refinement of positions, as opposed to a monologue by one author or character. As we will see in chapter 6, the crucial role of dialogue in current models of critical thinking is apparent in the use of methods like **Rogerian argument** and "Believers and Doubters," which help us to get outside our own egos and empathize with others' viewpoints. The dialogic dimension of critical thinking is also incorporated throughout this textbook, in my drawing attention to my own subjective viewpoint and periodically inviting challenges to it from opposing ones, as well as in the pairing of readings that directly or indirectly oppose one another on a point-by-point basis.

The emphasis on dialogue in critical thinking scholarship coincides with a long tradition in creative literature from Plato onward. Indeed, it might be said that every work of literature or art engages the reader in dialogue and making a compassionate connection with an alien viewpoint, as expressed in the quotation here from French novelist Marcel Proust's multivolume masterpiece *Remembrance of Things Past*. (It is also implicit in Emerson's "American Scholar" and Whitman's "Noiseless, Patient Spider" that the intellectual connections made by the scientist, scholar, and poet also serve to connect all human beings in compassion.) For Albert Camus, the French Nobel Prize–winning author, this concept of literature as dialogue formed the link between his career as a writer of fiction and drama and his commitments as a political journalist and activist. In an essay titled "Neither Victims nor Executioners," written in 1946 in the wreckage of World War II and at the beginning of the Cold War, he called for a new "civilization of dialogue" between individuals of all countries that would transcend the contrived, deadly hatreds and propagandistic language of nationalistic rivalry: "What is necessary to defend is dialogue and universal communication between men. Servitude, injustice, and falsehood are the scourges that shatter that communication and forbid that dialogue" (18). Elsewhere he writes:

> The mutual understanding and communication discovered by rebellion can survive only in the free exchange of conversation. Every ambiguity, every misunderstanding, leads to death; clear language and simple words are the only salvation from this death. The climax of every tragedy lies in the deafness of its heroes. Plato is right and not Moses and Nietzsche. [References to Moses handing down the Ten Commandments from the mountaintop and to Nietzsche's monologic *Thus Spake Zarathustra*.] Dialogue on the level of mankind is less costly than the gospel preached by totalitarian regimes in the form of a monologue dictated from the top of a lonely mountain. On the stage as in reality, the monologue precedes death. (*The Rebel*, 283–284)

The reading later in this chapter, "Can Patriotism Be Compassionate?" by Martha Nussbaum, a classics scholar, is a good example of the applicability of these themes in classical humanism to our thinking about current issues like the events following September 11, 2001.

RECURSIVENESS, CUMULATIVENESS, AND LEVELS OF MEANING

Writing, the clearest demonstration of the power of analytical and sequential thinking, seems increasingly to be an alien form to many of our young, even to those who may be regarded as extremely intelligent.... The electronic information environment, with television at its center, is fundamentally hostile to conceptual, segmented, linear modes of expression; thus, both writing and speech must lose some of their power. Language is, by its nature, slow-moving, hierarchical, logical, and continuous. Whether writing or speaking, one must maintain a fixed point of view and a continuity of content; one must move to higher or lower levels of abstraction; one must follow to a greater or lesser degree rules of syntax and logic.... Every word contains the possibility of multiple meanings and therefore of multiple ideas.... The young in particular are experiencing an acute inability to make connections, and some have given up trying. The TV curriculum, we must remember, stresses the fragmented and discrete

nature of events, and indeed is structurally unable to organize them
into coherent themes or principles.
—*Neil Postman,* Teaching as a Conserving Activity *(1979)*

The word *recursiveness* is related to the *cursor* of a computer, and similarly refers to moving
forward and back. In reading others' texts and writing your own, it involves the process of
rereading as many times as necessary to decode the author's full, complex meaning (or to
encode your own), to follow the development of theme or thesis and of the reasoning (or
lack thereof). Good writing requires such rereading and holds up, or even appears better,
under many rereadings, but poor writing falls apart thematically, stylistically, or logically
under closer scrutiny. In your own writing, the counterpart to rereading is *revision* (*re-vision*).
About this process, Orville Schell, a distinguished journalist and dean of the Graduate School
of Journalism at Berkeley, writes:

> Nine-tenths of good journalism is writing a piece over and over until you get it right. I would
> love to teach a course in which each student writes one article and spends the whole semester
> editing it over and over, which is maybe not something you can always do in the real world
> but which builds an awareness that good writing is not a question of getting it right the first
> time, it's a question of sticking with it until you can get it to sing. (*San Francisco Examiner,*
> June 16, 1996, B-9)

Cumulativeness refers to the continuous building and retention by the writer or reader
of knowledge (**cultural literacy**), ideas, and reasoning throughout a particular work, and
from that work to future ones. The entire process of general education, from kindergarten
to graduate school and beyond, depends on this steady accumulation. But many cultural
forces today impede any such accumulation. Postman, Aronowitz, and other cultural critics
consider the atomized discourse of television and politics foremost among these forces, but
the structures of education itself in many ways work against cognitive accumulation. Maybe
you have been lucky in the schools you have attended, but for many students, high school
and college education consists of what I call "jumping through hoops." How accurately does
this correspond to your experience of schooling?

You're taking four or more courses each term, few of which have much continuity with the
others or with ones you've taken earlier or will take later. Many individual courses are structured
as a sketchy sequence of modular units with little sense of building on what has been learned
previously. Assignments and tests cover only the current unit, and you have been conditioned
into the attitude that studying consists of cramming for each day's assignment and then forgetting
it to go on to the next one. So even when class discussion is lively, it is hard to retain enough
from last week's or yesterday's to continue it today. And with all the pressure put on "getting
the grade," short-term efforts to do so naturally take precedence over motivation to truly learn.
So education is reduced to a sequence of jumping through hoops, doing no more than what is
needed to finish each day's assignment, to pass the exam, to get the grade, to get the diploma,
to get the job—with the result that in the end you are apt to have retained little of what you
have studied at all. This textbook is structured in a way that attempts to provide an antidote to
these negative cognitive influences and to model the process of cumulative learning, within the
discipline of English or rhetoric, and in application to critical citizenship.

In approaching serious academic studies, it is necessary not only to read or write recursively and cumulatively, on a linear or horizontal plane, so to speak, but also to stop
frequently to process **levels of meaning**—varieties of information stacked or compressed
"vertically" in a text, through rhetorical and stylistic techniques that will be defined and
described (recursively and cumulatively!) in subsequent sections.

These three processes are summed up in the diagram in figure 3.1.

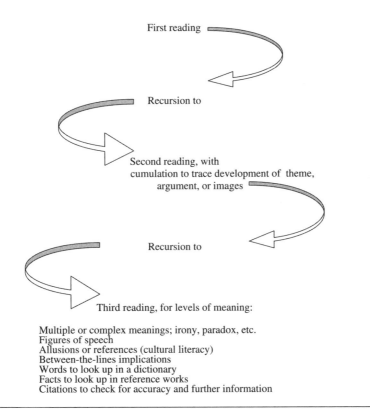

First reading

Recursion to

Second reading, with
cumulation to trace development of theme,
argument, or images

Recursion to

Third reading, for levels of meaning:

Multiple or complex meanings; irony, paradox, etc.
Figures of speech
Allusions or references (cultural literacy)
Between-the-lines implications
Words to look up in a dictionary
Facts to look up in reference works
Citations to check for accuracy and further information

Figure 3.1

DRAWING THE LINE AND ESTABLISHING PROPORTION

Another important facet of critical thinking to emphasize near the outset of our studies here has to do with item 8 in "Rhetoric: A Checklist for Analyzing Your Own and Others' Arguments" in chapter 2: "Are the limits of the position defined or are they vulnerable to being pushed to absurd logical consequences (**reduction to absurdity**)? In other words, does [the author] indicate where to **draw the line**?" One of the most frequent fallacies committed by argumentative writers is first setting two positions in opposition to each other and then siding absolutely with one, without qualifications or recognition of sensible limits beyond which that position would no longer be viable. A similar fallacy is to reject an extreme position on one side then to lurch to the **equal and opposite extreme** on the other.

A good example of this problem comes up in the discussion of the model student paper in chapter 5 about "the beauty myth." One of Christina Hoff Sommers's arguments against Naomi Wolf is that "Stressing the importance of diet and fitness can hardly be considered as an insidious attempt by the male establishment to disempower women." One of the students in the discussion argues that Sommers is attacking a **straw man** version of Wolf's position, since Wolf never denies the importance of fitness and attractiveness—*to a point.* Her case is that the beauty industry has pushed these values to an unhealthy extreme, in anorexic models of beauty and an overload in marketing of beauty products. Both Wolf and Sommers, then, need to draw the line on exactly what degree of fitness and attractiveness is healthy and what degree is unhealthy, and you as a critical reader need to evaluate how effectively each does so.

The same principle is central to arguments about the increasing inequality of incomes and wealth between the rich and the middle class and poor over the past few decades in the United States, a topic explored in part V of this book. One student writes, "It's a good thing that Bill Gates's wealth more than doubled last year from $18 billion to $39 billion. The more successful Microsoft is, the more employees they will need and the more taxes it and its employees will be paying. When corporations are successful, they give back to the people as dictated by the trickle-down theory." This assertion **evades the issue** of the logical consequences of the effect on American society of the accumulation of a constantly larger percentage of national wealth and power in the hands of a few individuals and corporations—consequences that have prompted antimonopoly legislation against Microsoft. In other words, this student fails to draw the line on a possible point at which the compounding of Gates's and Microsoft's wealth would be socially counterproductive. So the position could be reduced to absurdity by an opponent imagining an America totally owned by Gates!

At the other extreme, a second student writes, "It's criminal that someone like Bill Gates is allowed to gain wealth beyond the net worth of several of the world's countries. His billions should be confiscated through taxes and used toward eliminating poverty in the United States and the rest of the world." This student fails to draw the line on exactly what kind and degree of income equalization would be feasible and just, without going to the opposite extreme of the total equalization of income imposed by dictatorial governments under communism. The aim of good argumentation, then, should be to apply a sense of proportion and limits in delineating an exact degree of validity in any position argued for, following Aristotle's principles of "the golden mean" and "nothing in excess."

AVOIDING OVERSIMPLIFICATION AND RECOGNIZING COMPLEXITY

Most logical fallacies, psychological blocks to critical thinking, and forms of bias—for example, stereotypes and prejudices, causal reductionism, and either-or thinking—are variants of one master fallacy: **oversimplification**. Oversimplification is the essence of election campaign oratory and ads, advertising, talk radio and TV programs, and propaganda in general. Aldous Huxley's futuristic novel *Brave New World* (1932) described a totally managed society in which the citizens are kept in blissful ignorance and pacified through bland oversimplifications. In Huxley's later book *Brave New World Revisited* (1958), a chapter titled "Propaganda under a Dictatorship," described more sinister uses of oversimplification after Huxley's observation of Nazi and Communist totalitarianism and the simplistic propaganda on all sides in World War II, along with the proliferation of commercial propaganda in postwar democracies. Huxley quotes Adolf Hitler's formulas for manipulating the uneducated masses: "All effective propaganda must be confined to a few bare necessities and then must be expressed in a few stereotyped formulas." These formulas must be constantly repeated, for "only constant repetition will finally succeed in imprinting an idea upon the memory of a crowd." . . . The demagogic propagandist must therefore be consistently dogmatic. All his statements are made without qualification. There are no grays in his picture of the world; everything is either diabolically black or celestially white. In Hitler's words, the propagandist should adopt "a systematically one-sided attitude towards every problem that has to be dealt with. He must never admit that he might be wrong or that people with a different point of view might be even partially right" (36).

Huxley adds, "Unlike the masses, intellectuals have a taste for rationality and an interest in facts. Their critical habit of mind makes them resistant to the kind of propaganda that works so well on the majority. . . . Intellectuals are the kind of people who demand evidence and are shocked by logical inconsistencies and fallacies. They regard over-simplification as the original sin of the mind and have no use for the slogans, the unqualified assertions and sweeping generalizations which are the propagandist's stock in trade" (35–36).

Unfortunately for his case, Huxley himself falls into oversimplified, black-and-white thinking in his absolute opposition between the thinking of intellectuals and that of "the masses." While historical evidence supports much of what Huxley says, there have also been numerous cases of intellectuals becoming ardent supporters of fascist and communist dictatorships as well as of other undemocratic regimes that offered them a taste of power. And many members of the unintellectual masses have heroically resisted dictatorships throughout the world. Nevertheless, the case can be made that intellectuals who have been corrupted by power have betrayed the independent-mindedness that ought to be intrinsic to the intellectual mind.

Oversimplified rhetoric has unfortunately pervaded American public discourse as a characteristic of politics and mass media aimed at appealing to the lowest common denominator of critical thinking skills. A 1994 article by David Osborne in *Mother Jones* magazine about Congressman Newt Gingrich described a speech Gingrich gave to a group of Republican activists:

> "The number one fact about the news media," he told them, "is they love fights." For months, he explained, he had been giving "organized, systematic, researched, one-hour lectures. Did CBS rush in and ask if they could tape one of my one-hour lectures? No. But the minute Tip O'Neill attacked me, he and I got 90 seconds at the close of all three network news shows. You have to give them confrontations." (24)

Another comment in *Mother Jones* about this speech by Gingrich, by historian Dan T. Carter, adds, "And they had to be confrontations in a bipolar political system of good and evil, right and wrong. The greatest hope for political victory was to replace the traditional give-and-take of American politics with a 'battlefield' between godly Republicans and the 'secular anti-religious view of the left' embodied in the Democrats" (24). An article by Alison Mitchell in the *New York Times* (March 31, 1996), titled "Now, It's the Rhetorical Presidency," described how President Bill Clinton's advisers discouraged him from making long speeches that were "too chock full of ideas for the age of sound bites" (E2).

Just as most modes of fallacies are varieties of oversimplification, most modes of critical thinking are varieties of complex thought. "Higher-order thinking" necessitates developing beyond a literal-minded mentality that absorbs only what appears on the surface of things; it is related to an understanding of multiple **viewpoints**, **irony**, and the difference between **literal** and **figurative language** and other **levels of meaning**. The following commentary appeared in a 1995 opinion column in the *Chronicle of Higher Education,* titled "Good Art Asks Tough Questions," by Beeb Salzer, a drama professor. Salzer is defending the social value of art, in the face of attempts to eliminate the National Endowment for the Arts and other widespread criticisms of the arts.

> Artists are almost always dissidents, which makes them an essential ingredient in a democracy that claims to tolerate difference. Artists' approach to life is the opposite of that of politicians. Politicians are required to provide answers; artists ask questions. Politicians must always appear to be certain; artists steep themselves in ambiguity, in the unknown. Herein lies the conflict between those in power and artists.
>
> Certainty is always comforting, particularly in the midst of the current societal dislocations caused by the changing economy, demographics, and continuous technological advances. People search for the security of truths that can explain the jumble of disconnected forces governing their lives. Some of us seek simple answers to complex problems, finding solace in believing in far-fetched conspiracy theories, extraterrestrial beings, cults, or bizarre religious philosophies. Such gullible people are the natural prey of mirror-faced politicians, whose only ideology is power....
>
> Brought up on half-hour sitcoms, students must be shown that complex problems rarely have simple answers. First, they must learn to use reason to examine their emotional and intuitive reactions. (Painters do this all the time. After a creative burst of energy, they stand

back, look critically at what they have done, make corrections, and then repeat the process.) Then, students must learn how to recognize complexity and paradox as necessary, not only in the arts but in every other discipline as well.

Even in the sciences, which laymen think are awash in provable facts, scientists are constantly dealing with paradoxical events, complex systems, and the difficulty of explaining counterintuitive theories—to the public as well as to other scientists. It is not possible to adequately describe our existence without appreciating complexity and paradox. (B2)

"Complexity and paradox," along with multiple viewpoints and levels of meaning, were key characteristics of the movement of literary modernism in the twentieth century, especially in the novels of writers like Marcel Proust, Virginia Woolf, James Joyce, and William Faulkner. One of the defining works of modernism was Proust's seven-volume novel *Remembrance of Things Past* (1913–1927). We earlier quoted Proust's summation, "Only by art can we get outside ourselves, know what another sees of his universe, which is not the same as ours and the different views of which would otherwise have remained unknown to us as those there may be on the moon." Art enables us not only to perceive other people's views of the universe but also to perceive the shifts in our *own* viewpoints as time passes and we change locations in space and in our relations with other people. Proust's novel is like a massive dramatization of Emerson's comment "The world of any moment is the merest appearance." In the first volume, *Swann's Way,* the fictional narrator, largely modeled on Proust himself, remembers a significant experience from his childhood. He has been accustomed to seeing, from the stable viewpoint of his home, a particular configuration of three church spires in the distance. But one day, in a ride in a horse-drawn carriage around the countryside, "I caught sight of the twin steeples of Martinville, on which the setting sun was at play, while the movement of the carriage and the windings of the road seemed to keep them continually changing their positions; and then of a third steeple, that of Vieuxvicq, which although separated from them by a hill and a valley, and rising from rather higher ground in the distance, appeared none the less to be standing by their side" (258).

This passage presents a rich example of literary **symbolism** in its levels of implicit meaning, which further compound the already complex ideas about what psychologists call "cognitive mapping" prompted by the visual impressions that the narrator reflects on—the illusion that the steeples are moving rather than the carriage he is in. As we read further in *Remembrance of Things Past,* we gradually realize that the narrator's perception of his shifting points of view on the three spires through his movement in space, and of the simultaneous changes in lighting on the spires in time as the sun sets, serves as a symbol for the instability of personal perceptions that is dramatized throughout the seven volumes. The narrator's viewpoint on his family members and other people he knows is constantly shifting (1) as he grows older and gains a different perspective on them, (2) as he gets other people's perspectives on his acquaintances that sharply differ from his own, and (3) as all the other people change with age and with shifts in social status. Proust's spires serve a similar symbolic purpose to Henry David Thoreau's images of a stream of water to symbolize life's flux and false "surface" appearances in the "Where I Lived and What I Lived For" chapter of *Walden,* to be discussed in chapter 4, and both passages illustrate the power of the human intellect and language to get outside our momentary impressions and immersion in the ceaseless flow of experience, to connect diffuse perceptions, and to **synthesize** them into an articulate, stable structure of meaning on the written page.

READING BETWEEN THE LINES

In the passage cited at the beginning of this book, from J. Mitchell Morse's book *The Irrelevant English Teacher,* Morse says, "I believe in ... a sensitivity to nuances and unstated implications, an ability to read between the lines and to hear undertones and overtones—both for the sake of political and social enlightenment and for the sake of our personal enlightenment and pleasure as individuals." This kind of sensitivity is essential to becoming a critical reader, writer, and thinker.

In personal relations, too, with growing experience we learn to "read between the lines," to send and receive coded messages, in every kind of situation. Consider the rituals of courtship. One student spots another, interesting-looking one in the college cafeteria and politely asks if the seat next to the other is free. Permission to sit is given, which also presents an opening for conversation (after an obligatory interlude in which each pretends to be engrossed in lunch). One of the first things each has done is check out the other's ring finger: no engagement or wedding ring signals possible singleness. Small talk begins, on the usual everyday topics, but gradually, by indirection, sounding out backgrounds, attitudes, tastes, and acquaintances in common. At any point, the two may discover a basic incompatibility, or one will drop in a reference to "my boyfriend" or "my fiancée," and one will find an excuse for an exit with a routine "Well, it's been nice meeting you." If all verbal signals are "go," however, and body language is favorable, the conversation leads to something like, "Are you involved with anybody?" If not, then it's, "Would you like to go out with me sometime?" Short of the hoped-for unconditional "Yes," a degree of reluctance may be signaled by a response like "I'm pretty busy evenings, but we could meet for coffee." (A dinner or other evening date symbolizes possible romantic consequences; a daytime date symbolizes unwillingness to consider those consequences, at least immediately.) And throughout this whole sequence, each has been dancing along a fine line, trying to come across as friendly without seeming aggressive or desperate, as confident and wanting to make a good impression without seeming conceited, and so on.

Most of us learn then, simply through life experience, to "read" the subtexts in personal encounters like this. Decoding discourses outside of our personal experiences, however, comes less naturally. Coming to appreciate literature is one of the best routes toward developing the sensitivity to nuances Morse describes, because of the mental initiative good literature demands from the reader. The following passage from Alice Walker's novel *The Color Purple* takes place in a general store in the rural South early in the twentieth century. The narrator, Celie, a poor young black woman, is watching an exchange between another black woman and the white clerk.

> He say, Girl you want that cloth or not? We got other customers sides you.
>   She say, yes sir. I want five yards, please sir.
>   He snatch the cloth and thump down the bolt. He don't measure. When he think he got five yard he tare it off. That be a dollar and thirty cent, he say. You need thread?
>   She say, Naw suh.
>   He say, You can't sew thout thread. He pick up a spool and hold it against the cloth. That look like it bout the right color. Don't you think.
>   She say, Yessuh.
>   He start to whistle. Take two dollars. Give her a quarter back. He look at me. You want something gal?
>   I say, Naw Suh. (15)

No further comment is made on this exchange in the book, and the uncritical reader is likely to skim over it without registering anything more than the surface events. With a little **recursiveness**, though, much more comes into focus. The clerk has obviously shortchanged the customer, since the cloth costs $1.30 but he only returns a quarter from $2.00; the spool of thread probably would not have cost more than a few cents at that time. The error of some 40 cents would have meant a serious loss in the poorest part of the country and at the preinflation value of a dollar. Celie's expression apparently signals to the clerk that she has caught on, which is why he looks at her and silently dares her to say something.

He probably thinks either that both she and the customer are too dumb to know the difference or that if they do, they will be too intimidated to complain, which is more likely the truth. So the episode dramatizes, in a small way, the helplessness of southern blacks, before the civil rights movement in the late 1950s, to protest against being cheated by whites—a common occurrence, as shown on a larger scale in other sequences of the novel, in which blacks who do protest are cruelly punished.

IRONY AND PARADOX

> From this same sheet of paper on which he has just written the sentence against an adulterer, the judge steals a piece for a love letter to his colleague's wife.... This is the way men behave. We let laws and precepts go their way, we keep to another.... Human wisdom never yet came up to the duties that it had prescribed for itself, and if it had come up to them, it would prescribe itself others beyond which it would ever aspire and pretend, so hostile to consistency is our human condition.
>
> —*Michel de Montaigne (1533–1592)*, Essays (493–495)

> "Ideals are good, but people are sometimes not so good. You must try to look up at the big picture."
>
> Yossarian rejected the advice with a skeptical shake of his head. "When I look up, I see people cashing in. I don't see heaven or saints or angels. I see people cashing in on every decent human impulse and every human tragedy."
>
> —*Joseph Heller,* Catch-22 (1961), 455

The very concept of irony is a complex one, defying simple definitions. Most argumentative uses of irony in writing or speaking involve drawing attention to a discrepancy, disparity, or opposition: between appearance and reality, or between what certain people preach and what they practice, between what is expected or intended and what results, between what we want and what we get, between apparent opposites that converge or reverse roles, and so on. And irony is often used by skillful writers to criticize an internal inconsistency, **compartmentalization**, or **double standard** in an opponent's position. Irony as a technique of written or spoken **style**, then, is used to point out that what you see is often *not* what you get. In this sense irony is sometimes defined as a form of figurative language—in opposition to literal language and related to **metaphor**, **simile**, **hyperbole**, **understatement**, and so on—referring to a statement whose meaning is not a direct, single one but the expression of a duality of some kind that the reader or listener must work to decode. In a broader sense, we speak of *an ironic sense of life,* referring to a mind-set that appreciates the ironies that pervade every kind of experience; that mind-set is essential to critical thinking, reading, and writing.

The most familiar form of irony, verbal, is a technique of spoken or written style, signifying a particular **tone**, often verging on **sarcasm** and consisting of saying the opposite of what you mean, as in, "You're really smart"—meaning, "You're really dumb." *Socratic irony* and *Socratic ignorance* are terms associated with the hero of Plato's dialogues, who, as we have seen in *The Apology,* is always going to the "wise men" of his time claiming to be ignorant and humbly asking them to explain something he doesn't understand, with the purpose of exposing their false pretensions.

All of us, even children, have learned to hear an ironic or sarcastic tone of voice in speaking, but it takes experience in critical reading to become attuned to catching it in print. So college teachers frequently tell anecdotes about students who, for example, read literally—and are horrified by—Jonathan Swift's essay "A Modest Proposal," in which Swift protests England's imposition of starvation on the Irish in the early eighteenth century by proposing, with tongue in cheek, that Irish children be sold and boiled for food. Several of the topics for exercises throughout this book are prefaced by "Irony Alert," indicating ironic passages in readings that students sometimes misread literally.

One of the most frequent themes in classic literature is the irony of appearance versus reality. Things and people are not always what they appear to be. In Shakespeare's *Hamlet* (1604), Hamlet discovers that his uncle Claudius has murdered his own brother, the king of Denmark and Hamlet's father, to gain the throne and marry Hamlet's mother; yet everyone grovels before Claudius in his court, where he presents a benevolent, smiling face. Hamlet cries in despair, "That one may smile, and smile, and be a villain" (1.5.109).

Religion is another realm in which some people's false pretenses have always been a source of irony in literature and life. "Woe unto you, scribes, Pharisees, hypocrites," Jesus Christ said of the priests who made a great show of preaching and praying in the temple but who did not practice what they preached (Matthew 23:13). The majority of religious leaders are undoubtedly sincere, but any ideal can be corrupted and exploited by hypocrites, and religion is especially vulnerable because so many believers are reluctant to recognize that an outward appearance of piety might be a fraud. Indeed, ostentatious display of piety tends toward a form of pride, and as the Bible says, pride goeth before a fall (Proverbs 16:18). Montaigne drily comments on "those venerable souls exalted by the ardor of devotion and religion to a constant and conscientious meditation on divine things, who ... disdain to apply themselves to our beggarly, fleeting, and ambiguous comforts.... Between ourselves, these are things that I have always seen to be in remarkable agreement: supercelestial thoughts and subterranean conduct" (601). Montaigne's three volumes of essays conclude, "So it is no use for us to mount on stilts, for on stilts we must still walk with our own legs. And on the loftiest throne in the world we are still sitting on our own behind" (602).

Similarly, nearly every year brings a new example of politicians who try to create a self-righteous public image but who fall victim to Montaigne's axiom of "supercelestial thoughts and subterranean conduct." As vice president to Richard Nixon after 1968, Spiro Agnew made a speech accusing intellectual Democratic critics of the Nixon administration of being "the elite ... the raised-eyebrow cynics, the pampered egotists who sneer at honesty, thrift, hard work, prudence, common decency, and self-denial" (quoted in Nobile, *Intellectual Skywriting* 5). In 1973 Agnew was indicted for taking bribes and evading income taxes as governor of Maryland and as vice president. He pleaded no contest and resigned.

Not only are things often not what they seem, they sometimes turn out to be the exact opposite, as when super-macho movie stars or gay-bashing politicians and preachers are revealed to be gay. Conversely, ideological extremes also tend to converge or mirror their opposites. Extreme left-wing ideologies like communism and right-wing ones like fascism have more commonalities than differences. (See the definitions of these terms in chapter 13.) Likewise, in the American culture wars of recent decades, **polemicists** on the right and left often sound like they are mimicking exactly the rhetorical excesses they denounce in their opponents.. All this confirms the ancient Greek ideal of "nothing in excess" and the wisdom of aiming for the golden mean or the sensible limit, or **drawing the line**, without falling into the **fallacy** of the equal and opposite extreme.

In public policies, social scientists speak of an ironic "law of unintended consequences." So conservatives argue that liberal government welfare policies may inadvertently perpetuate poverty and dependency, or that affirmative action may intensify the racial or sexual divisiveness it is intended to overcome. Conservatives' use of this line of argument is weakened, however, when they apply it with **selective vision**, failing to acknowledge instances when it also might apply to conservative policies. One of the greatest controversies in recent years concerned whether President George W. Bush's war on Iraq reduced the danger of terrorism, by attacking it at one of its alleged sources, or *increased* it, by placing Americans in direct range of Middle Eastern terrorists and by actually breeding more terrorists than before out of Muslims' anger over the U.S. invasion and occupation of one of their countries and abuses like the Abu Ghraib prison scandal. Along this line, James Rosen, in the McClatchy Newspapers, wrote:

> Before the war in Iraq, Bush and senior administration officials made controversial claims of ties between Saddam and al-Qaida. Some note the irony that the war itself has helped create that reality, as the Baathist regime teams up with foreign Islamic militants to attack Americans.
> "Terrorism didn't exist in Iraq before," French Foreign Minister Dominique de Villepin told Le Monde newspaper. "Today, it is one of the world's principal sources of world terrorism." (*Knoxville News Sentinel*, March 23, 2004, A2)

A paradox is yet another variety of irony, a statement that seems to be self-contradictory yet has a rational explanation, in the manner of a riddle. The paradoxical nature of life and social problems is reflected in creative writers' frequent use of paradox as a stylistic technique or figure of speech. One of the most influential pieces of argumentative and literary writing in our time, James Baldwin's book-length essay *The Fire Next Time* (1963), is a study of the multiple paradoxes (or "conundrums," to use Baldwin's term) in the relations between whites and blacks throughout American history and culture. Baldwin's book was published at the height of the civil rights movement and came out of the late 1950s when legal segregation in the South, de facto segregation in the North, and denial of African Americans' legal rights were still generally accepted. (Indeed, the book was among the forces that contributed to the advances in racial attitudes up to the present.) Whites at that time were accustomed to viewing blacks from the white **viewpoint**, but Baldwin turned the camera around to show whites what they looked like in blacks' eyes, with all of their collective delusions of moral and biological superiority, their failure to recognize that "the Negro problem" is really "the White problem." In an introductory letter to his young nephew, he describes in paradoxical form whites' willful ignorance of the historical and then-present truths of white crimes against blacks: "They have destroyed and are destroying hundreds of thousands of lives and do not know it and do not want to know it" (5). And, "It is the innocence that constitutes the crime" (6). After sarcastically reiterating several times whites' "innocence" as a **euphemism** for their ignorance, he uses an ironic reversal in dispelling liberal whites' notion that blacks merely want to be "accepted" by whites and "integrated" into white society—in its contemporary state of delusions. Instead, he poses two more paradoxes to his nephew: "You must accept them and accept them with love" (8) and "We cannot be free until they are free" (10). We **infer** the answer to these conundrums to be that whites are slaves to their own ignorance and illusions. "And if the word *integration* means anything, this is what it means: that we, with love, will force our brothers to see themselves as they are and to cease fleeing from reality and begin to change it" (9–10). In other words, he was not saying that blacks should have meekly accepted the segregationist status quo, or that they should have only sought integration under the terms of whites' continuing illusions of superiority, but that true integration could only occur once whites were forced to recognize blacks' full equality and to redress past injustice.

My Dungeon Shook: Letter to My Nephew on the Hundredth Birthday of the Emancipation

James Baldwin

From *The Fire Next Time,* Dial Press, 1963; Vintage Books, 1992

Dear James:

I have begun this letter five times and torn it up five times. I keep seeing your face, which is also the face of your father and my brother. Like him, you are tough, dark, vulnerable, moody—with a very definite tendency to sound truculent because you want no one to think you are soft. You may be like your grandfather in this, I don't know, but certainly both you and your father resemble him very much physically. Well, he is dead, he never saw you, and he had a terrible life; he was defeated long before he died because, at the bottom of his heart, he really believed what white people said about him. This is one of the reasons that he became so holy. I am sure that your father has told you something about all that. Neither you nor your father exhibit any tendency towards holiness: you really *are* of another era, part of what happened when the Negro left the land and came into what the late E. Franklin Frazier called "the cities of destruction." You can only be destroyed by believing that you really are what the white world calls a *nigger.* I tell you this because I love you, and please don't you ever forget it.

I have known both of you all your lives, have carried your Daddy in my arms and on my shoulders, kissed and spanked him and watched him learn to walk. I don't know if you've known anybody from that far back; if you've loved anybody that long, first as an infant, then as a child, then as a man, you gain a strange perspective on time and human pain and effort. Other people cannot see what I see whenever I look into your father's face, for behind your father's face as it is today are all those other faces which were his. Let him laugh and I see a cellar your father does not remember and a house he does not remember and I hear in his present laughter his laughter as a child. Let him curse and I remember him falling down the cellar steps, and howling, and I remember, with pain, his tears, which my hand or your grandmother's so easily wiped away. But no one's hand can wipe away those tears he sheds invisibly today, which one hears in his laughter and in his speech and in his songs. I know what the world has done to my brother and how narrowly he has survived it. And I know, which is much worse, and this is the crime of which I accuse my country and my countrymen, and for which neither I nor time nor history will ever forgive them, that they have destroyed and are destroying hundreds of thousands of lives and do not know it and do not want to know it. One can be, indeed one must strive to become, tough and philosophical concerning destruction and death, for this is what most of mankind has been best at since we have heard of man. (But remember: *most* of mankind is not *all* of mankind.) But it is not permissible that the authors of devastation should also be innocent. It is the innocence which constitutes the crime.

Now, my dear namesake, these innocent and well-meaning people, your countrymen, have caused you to be born under conditions not very far removed from those described for us by Charles Dickens in the London of more than a hundred years ago. (I hear the chorus of the innocents screaming, "No! This is not true! How *bitter* you are!"—but I am writing this letter to *you,* to try to tell you something about how to handle *them,* for most of them do not yet really know that you exist. I *know* the conditions under which you were born, for I was there. Your countrymen were *not* there, and haven't made it yet. Your grandmother was also there, and no one has ever accused her of being bitter. I suggest that the innocents check with her. She isn't hard to find. Your countrymen don't know that *she* exists, either, though she has been working for them all their lives.)

Well, you were born, here you came, something like fourteen years ago; and though your father and mother and grandmother, looking about the streets through which they were carrying you, staring at the walls into which they brought you, had every reason to be heavyhearted, yet they were not, for here you were, Big James, named for me—you were a big baby. I was not—here you were: to be loved. To be loved, baby, hard, at once, and forever, to strengthen you against the loveless world. Remember that: I know how black it looks today, for you. It looked bad that day, too, yes, we were trembling. We have not stopped trembling yet, but if we had not loved each other none of us would have survived. And now you must survive because we love you, and for the sake of your children and your children's children.

This innocent country set you down in a ghetto in which, in fact, it intended that you should perish. Let me spell out precisely what I mean by that, for the heart of the matter is here, and the root of my dispute with my country. You were born where you were born and faced the future that you faced because you were black and *for no other reason.* The limits of your ambition were, thus, expected to be set forever. You were born into a society which spelled out with brutal clarity, and in as many ways as possible, that you were a worthless human being. You were not expected to aspire to excellence: you were expected to make peace with mediocrity. Wherever you have turned, James, in your short time on this earth, you have been told where you could go and what you could do (and *how* you could do it) and where you could live and whom you could marry. I know your countrymen do not agree with me about this, and I hear them saying, "You exaggerate." They do not know

Harlem, and I do. So do you. Take no one's word for anything, including mine—but trust your experience. Know whence you came. If you know whence you came, there is really no limit to where you can go. The details and symbols of your life have been deliberately constructed to make you believe what white people say about you. Please try to remember that what they believe, as well as what they do and cause you to endure, does not testify to your inferiority but to their inhumanity and fear. Please try to be clear, dear James, through the storm which rages about your youthful head today, about the reality which lies behind the words *acceptance* and *integration.* There is no reason for you to try to become like white people and there is no basis whatever for their impertinent assumption that *they* must accept *you.* The really terrible thing, old buddy, is that *you* must accept *them.* And I mean that very seriously. You must accept them and accept them with love. For these innocent people have no other hope. They are, in effect, still trapped in a history which they do not understand; and until they understand it, they cannot be released from it. They have had to believe for many years, and for innumerable reasons, that black men are inferior to white men. Many of them, indeed, know better, but, as you will discover, people find it very difficult to act on what they know. To act is to be committed, and to be committed is to be in danger. In this case, the danger, in the minds of most white Americans, is the loss of their identity. Try to imagine how you would feel if you woke up one morning to find the sun shining and all the stars aflame. You would be frightened because it is out of the order of nature. Any upheaval in the universe is terrifying because it so profoundly attacks one's sense of one's own reality. Well, the black man has functioned in the white man's world as a fixed star, as an immovable pillar: and as he moves out of his place, heaven and earth are shaken to their foundations. You, don't be afraid. I said that it was intended that you should perish in the ghetto, perish by never being allowed to go behind the white man's definitions, by never being allowed to spell your proper name. You have, and many of us have, defeated this intention; and, by a terrible law, a terrible paradox, those innocents who believed that your imprisonment made them safe are losing their grasp of reality. But these men are your brothers—your lost, younger brothers. And if the word *integration* means anything, this is what it means: that we, with love, shall force our brothers to see themselves as they are, to cease fleeing from reality and begin to change it. For this is your home, my friend, do not be driven from it; great men have done great things here, and will again, and we can make America what America must become. It will be hard, James, but you come from sturdy, peasant stock, men who picked cotton and dammed rivers and built railroads, and, in the teeth of the most terrifying odds, achieved an unassailable and monumental dignity. You come from a long line of great poets, some of the greatest poets since Homer. One of them said, *The very time I thought I was lost, My dungeon shook and my chains fell off.*

You know, and I know, that the country is celebrating one hundred years of freedom one hundred years too soon. We cannot be free until they are free. God bless you, James, and Godspeed.

Your uncle,

James

Topics for Discussion and Writing

1. On the basis of the lists of critical thinking skills and dispositions here, think back on courses you have taken through high school and college. Which of them promoted these skills and dispositions, and how? Which of them fit the later description of just "jumping through hoops"? From which set have you retained more useful knowledge?

2. The quotations here from Stanley Aronowitz and Neil Postman suggest destructive effects on thinking and learning that result from growing up on television and other electronic media. Do these analyses strike you as accurate? Has the critical thinking involved in college study presented you with a difficult adjustment from a TV-oriented mind-set? How much TV do you watch in college compared to high school?

3. Discuss a work of literature (or another work of art such as a movie, song, painting, or sculpture) that has caused you to "decenter" from your accustomed ethnocentric viewpoint and enabled you to identify more compassionately with a viewpoint with which you were previously unfamiliar or unsympathetic.

4. Find examples of arguments where the author either does or does not do a good job of "drawing the line."

5. Can you remember having a "Proustian moment," in which you experienced a startling, sudden shift in a previously fixed perspective in time, space (say, in a landscape or urban vista, an auto route, or a house in which the décor or arrangement of furniture has changed), or your knowledge of other people? Think, for example, about how your impression of the professor and fellow students in a class has changed from the beginning of a semester to its end.

6. On the basis of the description of the meeting between two students, describe a similar personal conversation you have had that has required reading between the lines.

7. Think of recent personal experiences or public events that illustrate some of the forms of irony described here.

8. At the moment of history when you read this, does it look like President Bush's war on Iraq did more to reduce or to increase the incidence and magnitude of world terrorism?

9. When *The Fire Next Time* was published in 1963, many whites reacted with **defense mechanisms** denying the truth of Baldwin's arguments or their personal responsibility for racism, even though he was not accusing most whites of active racism but rather of "not knowing" and "not wanting to know" the facts of past and present racism, to avoid pushing for government action to end segregation, denial of civil rights, and other forms of discrimination. Many white readers still react defensively reading Baldwin today. If you are white and you do, try to gain some objective distance on why you react this way and consider whether your reaction can be reasonably defended or whether it might involve **denial** of your own "innocence," in the sense of ignorance of the historical facts behind Baldwin's arguments and those in "A Historical-Causal Analysis of 'The White Problem'," in chapter 2, or of present conditions like those described in Jonathan Kozol's "Other People's Children" in chapter 11.

10. Baldwin's **tone** in this passage is a very interesting subject for rhetorical analysis. Do you think he was primarily addressing an audience of black or white readers? Whites are clearly "them" or "the other" here; Baldwin is highly sarcastic toward them, and many readers infer that he hated them. Yet he was obviously trying to appeal to their conscience and exhort them "to see themselves as they are, to cease fleeing from reality and begin to change it." And what is the effect of his calling them "our brothers" here? Read the rest of the book with an eye to Baldwin's complex shifts of tone in his attitude toward whites.

A Noiseless Patient Spider

Walt Whitman

From *Leaves of Grass*, 1868

> A noiseless patient spider,
> I mark'd where on a little promontory it stood isolated,
> Mark'd how to explore the vacant vast surrounding,
> It launch'd forth filament, filament, filament, out of itself,
> Ever unreeling them, ever tirelessly speeding them.
>
> And you O my soul where you stand,
> Surrounded, detached in measureless oceans of space,
> Ceaselessly musing, venturing, throwing, seeking the spheres to connect them,
> Till the bridge you will need be form'd, till the ductile anchor hold,
> Till the gossamer thread you fling catch somewhere, O my soul.

Topics for Discussion and Writing

Whitman was a mid-nineteenth-century American disciple of Emerson, and this poem embodies ideas similar to those in the passage quoted above from "The American Scholar," "To the young mind, every thing is individual, stands by itself . . . ." The first five-line stanza is a **literal**, almost scientific description of the spider building a web. The second stanza uses **figurative language** (**symbolic analogy** through verbal substitution of one word for another) to connect the spider and Whitman's own "soul" or mind, which is similarly isolated in the universe yet (metaphorically) is ceaselessly "seeking the [celestial] spheres to connect them." We can **infer** that "seeking the spheres to connect them" means something like Emerson's description of the scientific mind making connections between diverse aspects of nature, and/or suggests the transcendentalist quest to connect life on earth with a higher, spiritual reality symbolized by the spheres—which Emerson similarly describes as "this web of God." Metaphors like this do not appear only in poetry but are common in everyday life—for example, the World Wide Web.

Whitman, like Emerson, merges the scientific imagination with the poetic through his use of metaphors like "spheres," "bridge," "anchor," and "thread" to describe the activities of his mind, so he is not only writing a poem about a spider but is implicitly writing a poem about the symbolic web of connective language and ideas that constitute poetry. Whitman's poem "Song of Myself," which opens the collection *Leaves of Grass,* begins:

> I celebrate myself, and sing myself,
> And what I assume you shall assume,
> For every atom belonging to me as good belongs to you. (885)

The theme runs throughout *Leaves of Grass* that Whitman's poems connect his "solitary self" with his readers and all humans. In this light, it seems likely that "A Noiseless, Patient Spider" has a further **level of meaning** on which it is a statement about how poetry creates a web of communication linking the solitary poet with other humans. Like "The American Scholar," then, Whitman's poem condenses many aspects of critical thinking into a few words through the resources of literary language.

Discuss the plausibility of this interpretation of the poem, along with other possible levels of meaning you might find in it.

Can Patriotism Be Compassionate?

Martha Nussbaum

Nation, December 17, 2001

In the aftermath of September 11, we have all experienced strong emotions for our country: fear, outrage, grief, astonishment. Our media portray the disaster as a tragedy that has happened to our nation, and that is how we very naturally see it. So too the ensuing war: It is called "America's New War," and most news reports focus on the meaning of events for us and our nation. We think these events are important because they concern us—not just human lives, but American lives. In one way, the crisis has expanded our imaginations. We find ourselves feeling sympathy for many people who did not even cross our minds before: New York firefighters, that gay rugby player who helped bring down the fourth plane, bereaved families of so many national and ethnic origins. We even sometimes notice with a new attention the lives of Arab-Americans among us, or feel sympathy for a Sikh taxi driver who complains about customers who tell him to go home to "his country," even though he came to the United States as a political refugee from Punjab. Sometimes our compassion even crosses that biggest line of all, the national boundary. Events have led many Americans to sympathize with the women and girls of Afghanistan, for example, in a way that many feminists had been trying to get people to do for a long time, without success.

All too often, however, our imaginations remain oriented to the local; indeed, this orientation is implicit in the unusual level of our alarm. The world has come to a stop in a way that it never has for Americans when disaster has befallen human beings in other places. Floods, earthquakes, cyclones—and the daily deaths of thousands from preventable malnutrition and disease—none of these typically make the American world come to a standstill, none elicit a tremendous outpouring of grief and compassion. The plight of innocent civilians in the current war evokes a similarly uneven and flickering response.

And worse: Our sense that the "us" is all that matters can easily flip over into a demonizing of an imagined "them," a group of outsiders who are imagined as enemies of the invulnerability and the pride of the all-important "us." Just as parents' compassion for their own children can all too easily slide into an attitude that promotes the defeat of other people's children, so too with patriotism: Compassion for our fellow Americans can all too easily slide over into an attitude that wants America to come out on top, defeating or subordinating other peoples or nations. Anger at the terrorists themselves is perfectly appropriate; so is the attempt to bring them to justice. But "us versus them" thinking doesn't always stay focused on the original issue; it too easily becomes a general call for American supremacy, the humiliation of "the other."

One vivid example of this slide took place at a baseball game I went to at Chicago's Comiskey Park, the first game played there after September 11—and a game against the Yankees, so there was a heightened awareness of the situation of New York and its people. Things began well, with a moving ceremony commemorating the firefighters who had lost their lives and honoring local firefighters who had gone to New York afterward to help out. There was even a lot of cheering when the Yankees took the field, a highly unusual transcendence of local attachments. But as the game went on and the beer flowed, one heard, increasingly, "U-S-A, U-S-A," echoing the chant from the 1980 Olympic hockey match in which the United States defeated Russia. This chant seemed to express a wish for America to defeat, abase, humiliate its enemies. Indeed, it soon became a general way of expressing the desire to crush one's enemies, whoever they were. When the umpire made a bad call that went against the Sox, the same group in the stands turned to him, chanting "U-S-A." In other words, anyone who crosses us is evil, and should be crushed. It's not surprising that Stoic philosopher and Roman emperor Marcus Aurelius, trying to educate himself to have an equal respect for all human beings, reported that his first lesson was "not to be a fan of the Greens or Blues at the races, or the light-armed or heavy-armed gladiators at the Circus."

Compassion is an emotion rooted, probably, in our biological heritage. (Although biologists once portrayed animal behavior as egoistic, primatologists by now recognize the existence of altruistic emotion in apes, and it may exist in other species as well.) But this history does not mean that compassion is devoid of thought. In fact, as Aristotle argued long ago, human compassion standardly requires three thoughts: that a serious bad thing has happened to someone else; that this bad event was not (or not entirely) the person's own fault; and that we ourselves are vulnerable in similar ways. Thus compassion forms a psychological link between our own self-interest and the reality of another person's good or ill. For that reason it is a morally valuable emotion—when it gets things right. Often, however, the thoughts involved in the emotion, and therefore the emotion itself, go astray, failing to link people at a distance to one's own current possibilities and vulnerabilities. (Rousseau said that kings don't feel compassion for their subjects because they count on never being human, subject to the vicissitudes of life.) Sometimes, too, compassion goes wrong by getting the seriousness of the bad event wrong: Sometimes, for example, we just don't take very seriously the hunger and illness of people who are distant from us. These errors are likely to be built into the nature of compassion as it develops in childhood and then adulthood: We form intense attachments to the local first, and only gradually learn to have compassion for people who are outside our own immediate circle. For many Americans, that expansion of moral concern stops at the national boundary.

Most of us are brought up to believe that all human beings have equal worth. At least the world's major religions and most secular philosophies tell us so. But our emotions don't believe it. We mourn for those we know, not for those we don't know. And most of us feel deep emotions about America, emotions we don't feel about India or Russia or Rwanda. In and of itself, this narrowness of our emotional lives is probably acceptable and maybe even good. We need to build outward from meanings we understand, or else our moral life would be empty of urgency. Aristotle long ago said, plausibly, that the citizens in Plato's ideal city, asked to care for all citizens equally, would actually care for none, since care is learned in small groups with their more intense attachments. Reading Marcus Aurelius bears this out: The project of weaning his imagination from its intense erotic attachments to the familial and the local gradually turns into the rather alarming project of weaning his heart from deep investment in the world. He finds that the only way to be utterly evenhanded is to cultivate a kind of death within life, seeing all people as distant and shadowlike, "vain images in a procession." If we want our life with others to contain strong passions—for justice in a world of injustice, for aid in a world where many go without what they need—we would do well to begin, at least, with our familiar strong emotions toward family, city and country. But concern should not stop with these local attachments.

Americans, unfortunately, are prone to such emotional narrowness. So are all people, but because of the power and geographical size of America, isolationism has particularly strong roots here. When at least some others were finding ways to rescue the Jews during the Holocaust, America's inactivity and general lack of concern were culpable, especially in proportion to American power. It took Pearl Harbor to get us even to come to the aid of our allies. When genocide was afoot in Rwanda, our own sense of self-sufficiency and invulnerability stopped us from imagining the Rwandans as people who might be us; we were therefore culpably inactive toward them. So too in the present situation. Sometimes we see a very laudable recognition of the interconnectedness of all peoples, and of the fact that we must join forces with people in all nations to defeat terrorists and bring them to justice. At other times, however, we see simplifying slogans ("America Fights Back") that portray the situation in terms of a good "us" crusading against an evil "them"—failing to acknowledge, for instance, that people in all nations have strong reasons to oppose terrorism, and that the fight has many active allies.

Such simplistic thinking is morally wrong, because it encourages us to ignore the impact of our actions on innocent civilians and to focus too little on the all-important project of humanitarian relief. It is also counterproductive. We now understand, or ought to, that if we had thought more about support for the educational and humanitarian infrastructure of Pakistan, for example, funding good local nongovernmental organizations there the way several European nations have done in India, young people in Pakistan might possibly have been educated in a climate of respect for religious pluralism, the equality of women and other values that we rightly prize instead of having fundamentalist *madrassahs* as their only educational option. Our policy in South Asia has exhibited for many years a gross failure of imagination and sympathy; we basically thought in terms of cold war values, ignoring the real lives of people to whose prospects our actions could make a great difference. Such crude thinking is morally obtuse; it is also badly calculated to advance any good cause we wish to embrace, in a world where all human lives are increasingly interdependent.

Compassion begins with the local. But if our moral natures and our emotional natures are to live in any sort of harmony, we must find devices through which to extend our strong emotions—and our ability to imagine the situation of others—to the world of human life as a whole. Since compassion contains thought, it can be educated. We can take this disaster as occasion for narrowing our focus, distrusting the rest of the world and feeling solidarity with Americans alone. Or we can take it as an occasion for expansion of our ethical horizons. Seeing how vulnerable our great country is, we can learn something about the vulnerability that all human beings share, about what it is like for distant others to lose those they love to a disaster not of their own making, whether it is hunger or flood or war.

Because human beings find the meaning of life in attachments that are local, we should not ask of people that they renounce patriotism, any more than we now ask them to renounce the love of their parents and children. But we typically do ask parents not to try to humiliate or thwart other people's children, and we work (at least sometimes) for schools that develop the abilities of all children, that try to make it possible for everyone to support themselves and find rewarding work. So too with the world: We may love our own nation most, but we should also strive for a world in which the capacities of human beings will not be blighted by hunger or misogyny or lack of education—or by being in the vicinity of a war one has not caused. We should therefore demand an education that does what it can to encourage the understanding of human predicaments—and also to teach children to recognize the many obstacles to that pursuit, the many pitfalls of the self-centered imagination as it tries to be just. There are hopeful signs in the present situation, particularly in attempts to educate the American public about Islam, about the histories of Afghanistan and Pakistan, and about the situation and attitudes of Arab-Americans in this country. But we need to make sure these educational efforts are consistent and systematic, not just fear-motivated responses to an immediate crisis.

Our media and our systems of education have long given us far too little information about lives outside our borders, stunting our moral imaginations. The situation of America's women and its racial, ethnic and sexual minorities has to some extent worked its way into curricula at various levels, and into our popular media. We have done less well with parts of the world that are unfamiliar. This is not surprising, because such teaching requires a lot of investment in new curricular initiatives, and such television programming requires a certain temporary inattention to the competition for ratings. But we now know that we live in a complex, interconnected world, and we know our own ignorance. As Socrates said, this is at least the beginning of progress. At this time of national crisis we can renew our commitment to the equal worth of humanity, demanding media, and schools, that nourish and expand our imaginations by presenting non-American lives as deep, rich and compassion-worthy. "Thus from our weakness," said Rousseau of such an education, "our fragile happiness is born." Or, at least, it might be born.

Topics for Discussion and Writing

1. What aspects of critical thinking surveyed in this chapter are most prominently applied in Nussbaum's article?
2. What is the conflict between patriotism and compassion in the title? What arguments does Nussbaum present that the two often are in conflict, and how

persuasive are her reasons for trying to overcome the conflict? Is it realistic to expect us to have the same concern for the suffering of people in distant countries that we have for Americans, or is this just "bleeding-heart liberalism?" Does Nussbaum present convincing arguments that it is in our practical interests to develop such concern? To what extent did the terrorist acts of September 11, 2001, make you more aware that events in those distant countries, and American policies there, can have a direct influence on our lives?

3. You may find Nussbaum's line of argument somewhat hard to follow. It might help to try to outline it. Can you find an introduction, main body, and conclusion? Is there a single, explicit or implicit thesis statement, or is her thesis more complex than that?

4. How effective for her thesis are her **anecdotes** about the baseball game and the 1980 Olympics? Might it be a fallacy of **false analogy** or **false equation** for us to act as though our attitude toward sports events should be similar to that toward international or military conflicts, or as though different countries' sports teams really represent their nation as a political entity? Look for examples in political and media discourse of war being described in sports metaphors, and think about how they affect our perceptions of the realities of war. In chapter 4, one criterion given for whether a figure of speech is effective or not is whether it makes the reality it describes more concrete and immediate, or more abstract and distant. For example, before the war on Iraq in 2003, Central Intelligence Agency director George Tenet reportedly told President George W. Bush that finding weapons of mass destruction in Iraq would be "a slam dunk." What were some of the ways this basketball metaphor oversimplified the realities?

6. "Our media and our systems of education have long given us far too little information about lives outside our borders, stunting our moral imaginations." If you think this is true, why do you think it is, and in what ways can you imagine the media and schools doing a better job here?

7. As a scholar of classics, Nussbaum alludes to the ancient Greek philosophers Socrates (specifically to "The Apology," discussed here in chapters 1 and 6) and Aristotle, the Roman emperor Marcus Aurelius, and to the eighteenth-century French philosopher Jean-Jacques Rousseau. What relevance does she find in each of their ideas for Americans today, and how effective do you think the **allusions** are?

CHAPTER 4

Semantics in Rhetoric and Critical Thinking

Semantics is the field of linguistic studies that deals with language as meaning and communication. The International Society for General Semantics, a scholarly organization that came to prominence in the 1940s, was devoted to a philosophy of semantics best known through a classic textbook, *Language in Thought and Action,* by S. I. Hayakawa. The organization, now called Institute of General Semantics, is still active, publishing a quarterly magazine, *Etc.* The principles of general semantics encompass the complex relationships diagrammed in figure 4.1, between the external world, human thought, language, and communication.

The common phrase "a semantic misunderstanding" refers to the breakdowns of understanding and expression that frequently occur at each stage of these relationships. Humans perceive the external world through sense impressions that, through a mysterious yet almost instinctive process, get translated into ideas and then into the vocabulary and syntax (order within and between sentences) of language. External reality, however, is infinitely complex, and the human mind and language are at best imperfect instruments, so there can never be a complete or precise correspondence between that reality and its transformation into the symbols of thought and language. Hence, one key slogan of general semantics is "The map is not the territory"—that is, maps and other symbols, visual or linguistic, can only be partial replicas of the original.

This first stage of breakdown is compounded at each further stage: putting ideas into language presents a constant struggle to say exactly what we mean, as does communicating our ideas to other people. Such communication is impeded by the cultural, physical, psychological, and semantic filters through which each of us receives messages from others. So virtually every idea, every act of speaking or writing, every communication should be thought of as provisional, subject to revision and further development, possibly to be followed by an "etc."—hence the title of IGS's magazine. The practical implication of these

External world ◄──────► Thought ◄──────► Language ◄──────► Communication

Figure 4.1. Semantics: A Summary

points for you as a student is to suggest a **tone** of "thoughtful uncertainty" (see chapter 6) in whatever you say or write in academic studies and life in general.

The imperfection of the pictures of reality we carry in our thoughts and language has been infinitely compounded in our age of mass communication by the proliferation of images of the world conveyed in print media, films, radio, and above all television. "Reality is Silly Putty" was a facetious slogan in the 1960s, and the lines between news, drama, advertising, and publicity have been increasingly blurred by all-devouring media and their recombinations of an increasingly plastic reality: infotainment, infomercials, and docudramas in the style of Oliver Stone's *JFK* and *Nixon,* in which history is irresponsibly fictionalized to propagandize for the producer's political line—in Stone's case, a liberal one.

DENOTATION AND CONNOTATION

Both the **denotation** and the **connotation** of words are key elements in argumentation and critical thinking. Denotation is close in meaning to *definition;* definition is what a word means in general, while its denotation is the particular object it refers to. A chair may be defined as "a piece of furniture, usually with four legs, designed for one person to sit on." "This chair" denotes a particular embodiment of this definition. Some words, however, not only define or denote an object but also carry a connotation, an attitude or emotion toward the object. "Draft evader," "draft dodger," and "draft resister" all denote the same object, but "draft evader" is relatively neutral or denotative, while "draft dodger" has a negative connotation and "draft resister" has a positive connotation.

DEFINITION AND DENOTATION IN ARGUMENT

A central issue in the impeachment of President Bill Clinton involved Clinton's denial of having had sex with Monica Lewinsky; he turned out to be hedging on the literal definition of "having sex." In response to another question under oath, he responded, "That depends on what your definition of 'is' is." As we see in many issues throughout this book, particularly the political issues surveyed in chapter 13, the heart of disagreements is very often differing definitions of terms; if opponents are operating with a different understanding of disputed terms, if they have different "semantic filters," they can reach no common ground. Describing someone as "pro-abortion" or "anti-abortion" neutrally denotes a position on the issue. But "prochoice" and "prolife" denote the same positions in a way that defines abortion in **partisan** terms, either the terms of women's control over their bodies or the terms of a fetus's right to be born. *Homosexual* is a neutral term, *gay* a positive one, and numerous derogatory expressions denote homosexuality in negative terms. On an issue like legalizing homosexual marriage, its defenders try to define the issue as one of "equal rights," while opponents try to define it as "special privileges." Likewise with "affirmative action" versus "reverse discrimination." In polls asking whether people favor "attempts to remedy discrimination against nonwhites," the majority answer yes; but when the same people are asked whether they favor "racial preferences," the majority say no.

A news report by Stanley Meisler in the *Los Angeles Times,* headlined "Women's Conference Bogs Down in Semantics" (September 1, 1995, A25), describes a dispute at the United Nations Fourth World Conference on Women, in Beijing, China, between liberal and conservative delegates over which word, *sex* or *gender,* should be used in conference reports:

> Feminists argue the word *sex* differentiates men and women only by biological makeup; the word *gender,* they say, focuses on the differences between men and women that are set down by societies....

Using the word *sex* instead of *gender,* according to the feminists, misses the point of why women have fewer rights than men in most societies.

But conservatives claim that feminists are using the word *gender* as a subterfuge to cover a host of activities that the right wing objects to, such as lesbianism or bisexuality.

Events related to the terrorist attacks of September 11, 2001, have raised many semantic issues, beginning with their widespread abbreviation into "9/11." Soon after the attacks, the Bush administration labeled its response a "war on terrorism." Throughout history, the enemy in a war has been the government of another country. Al Qaeda, however, was not a government but a terrorist organization with cells in many countries, and with support stemming in part from the historical grievances of Arabs and Muslims internationally against the United States and Europe. These semantic complications made the waging of conventional war against Afghanistan and especially Iraq (whose support of Al Qaeda and links to 9/11 were disputed by many investigators) of questionable effectiveness. The U.S. war in Iraq raised several more issues of semantic labeling. Was it a "liberation," an "invasion," or an "occupation"? The enemy in Iraq was presumably Saddam Hussein and his supporters. But after they were overthrown, a problem arose in how to label the different forces who then fought against the American presence, whose political and religious identity was diverse; thus they began to be termed vaguely "insurgents" or "militants." A report by Richard T. Cooper in the *Los Angeles Times* (June 26, 2004, online edition, 1) headlined "Semantics Skirmish on 9/11 Report" discussed the Bush administration's disagreement with the wording of the conclusion of a bipartisan commission investigating 9/11 asserting that Saddam Hussein's contacts with Al Qaeda "do not appear to have resulted in a collaborative relationship." On the same point, Michael Isikoff remarked in *Newsweek* (July 5, 2004, 6), perhaps with a wink to President Clinton's semantic evasions about Monica Lewinsky, "It all depends on what your definition of a relationship is." And a *New York Times* op-ed by Adam Hochschild titled "What's in a Word? Torture" (May 23, 2004, News of the Week, 11), which addressed the prisoner abuse scandal at Abu Ghraib prison in Iraq, quoted Secretary of Defense Donald Rumsfeld saying, "What has been charged so far is abuse, which I believe technically is different from torture.... I'm not going to address the 'torture' word."

All of these examples illustrate an important axiom: *Whoever defines the terms wins the argument, or at least gains the upper hand.* For two analyses of this point in terms of semantic "framing," see the readings by George Lakoff and Thomas Sowell at the end of this chapter.

CONNOTATION IN ARGUMENT: "CLEANS" AND "DIRTIES"

Semanticists use various terms to describe the use of words with positive versus negative connotations: "God terms and Devil terms," "purr words and snarl words," and my favorites, "**'cleans'** and **'dirties.'**" In argumentation, we constantly apply a semantic **double standard** to apply clean words to our side and dirty ones to the other. You need to become aware when others—or you yourself—are doing this, and verify whether they are justifying their positive and negative judgments or whether they are just emotive. In a televised election debate, the Republican candidate referred to "labor bosses" but "the business community," while the Democrat referred to "business fat cats" but "labor leaders." Unfortunately, the moderator did not catch them in their double standards and press them to justify their loaded judgments of the two groups.

During the Gulf War in 1991, the United States employed a missile named the Patriot, while Iraq used one called (in U.S. media) the Scud. What is the difference between a Patriot and a Scud? Mainly semantic. "Patriot" might seem a curious **personification** (to use a literary term) of a weapon of destruction, if you think about it, but the name obviously was chosen for its positive, humanizing connotation, compounded by all the emotional appeal associated with patriotism. "Scud," on the other hand, has neither denotative or **metaphorical** meaning—it is an acronym of the four words of its technical name in English—but it ingeniously embodies several negative connotations by association, like "scum," "crud," "dud," "mud." It might be argued that the Patriot was a defensive weapon, hence it did serve the patriotic function of shooting down attacking missiles. This is a reasonable argument, but the United States also happened to have an offensive nuclear warhead missile called the Peacekeeper. The main point is that any country will predictably give its own weapons— whether defensive or offensive—positive names and its opponents' weapons negative ones. Most likely, the Iraqis' names for the two missiles had the opposite connotations from ours. This manipulation of words by politicians and media in our society and most others is a powerful force in **cultural conditioning** into nationalistic **ethnocentrism**. Indeed, semantic ethnocentrism regarding patriotism runs so deep that it is hard to imagine that our "enemies" in any war are *also* patriots in their own eyes. Being able to make this kind of leap of imagination, however, marks an important step beyond the psychological block of ethnocentrism toward being an open-minded, critical thinker. (Also see "The Rhetoric of War" in chapter 12.)

Connotative language is the most frequent form of **emotional appeal** in rhetoric, and it must be evaluated by the same criteria as other forms (see chapter 12). That is, it can be quite legitimate if the passion and eloquence that emotion adds to an argument are supported by sound reasoning, evidence, and truth with respect to concrete realities. But an argument usually becomes weakened the further it moves away from denotative to connotative language, from concrete realities to **unconcretized abstractions**, and the more it depends on swaying the audience's emotions with highly charged words alone. Much **demagogic** argumentation consists of connotative **slanting** and **stereotyping** labels—heavy use of cleans and dirties to create denotatively empty "good guys versus bad guys" **oversimplifications**, **false dichotomies**, and double standards: sentimentality toward our side, **name-calling**, and fear and loathing toward the other.

People are frequently swayed in their opinions simply by differing connotations in writers' or speakers' selection of words. An article titled "The Vocabulary of Votes" in the *New York Times Magazine* (March 26, 1995) describes how political consultant Frank Luntz tests public reactions to different word choices that denote the same reality:

> While 62 percent favor sending the children of abusive welfare mothers to "orphanages," 72 percent favor sending them to "foster homes."... If you ask Americans whether they are "overregulated," Luntz contends that a majority will say they are. But if you ask them whether Federal regulations are "excessive," the number who agree drops off. And if you ask whether the regulations "hurt people," the number falls even further. (46)

An editorial in the *San Francisco Examiner* titled "The Power of Words" (August 4, 1996) tells how "a judge in Sacramento was obliged to become a semanticist in a crucial dispute over how state voter pamphlets should describe Proposition 209," the so-called California Civil Rights Initiative, whose title, according to opponents, exploited the "clean" connotation of "civil rights" to fool voters into voting for a measure that repealed affirmative action policies guaranteeing civil rights to minorities and women. The immediate dispute was over the following wording:

> "To prohibit state and local governments from discriminating against or providing preferential treatment in public contracting, employment and education on the basis of race, sex, ethnicity or national origin."

Misleading and unfair, said opponents. They cite polls that suggest the public is generally opposed to "preference" but likely to support "affirmative action" programs aimed at past patterns of discrimination in hiring, education, and contracts. (B10)

An explicit "how-to" manual for controlling connotation was found in the memo from Newt Gingrich to Republican candidates in 1995, via Gingrich's political action committee GOPAC, as reported in *Extra! Update,* a newsletter of the leftist Fairness and Accuracy in Reporting:

As you know, one of the key points in the GOPAC tapes is that "language matters." In the video "We Are a Majority," Language is listed as a key mechanism of control used by a majority party, along with Agenda, Rules, Attitude and Learning. As the tapes have been used in training sessions across the country and mailed to candidates, we have heard a plaintive plea: "I wish I could speak like Newt."

That takes years of practice. But we believe that you could have a significant impact on your campaign and the way you communicate if we help a little. That is why we have created this list of words and phrases.

This list is prepared so that you might have a directory of words to use in writing literature and mail, in preparing speeches, and in producing electronic media. The words and phrases are powerful. Read them. Memorize as many as possible. And remember that, like any tool, these words will not help if they are not used. . . .

CONTRASTING WORDS

Often we search hard for words to help us define our opponents. Sometimes we are hesitant to use contrast. Remember that creating a difference helps you. These are powerful words that can create a clear and easily understood contrast. Apply these to the opponent, their record, proposals and their party.

decay . . . failure (fail) . . . collapse (ing) . . . deeper . . . crisis . . . urgent(cy) . . . destructive . . . destroy . . . sick . . . pathetic . . . lie . . . liberal . . . they/them . . . unionized bureaucracy . . . "compassion" is not enough . . . betray . . . consequences . . . limit(s) . . . shallow . . . traitors . . . sensationalists . . .

endanger . . . coercion . . . hypocrisy . . . radical . . . threaten . . . devour . . . waste . . . corruption . . . incompetent . . . permissive attitudes . . . destructive . . . impose . . . self-serving . . . greed . . . ideological . . . insecure . . . anti (issue): flag, family, child, jobs . . . pessimistic . . . excuses . . . intolerant . . .

stagnation . . . welfare . . . corrupt . . . selfish . . . insensitive . . . status quo . . . mandate(s) . . . taxes . . . spend(ing) . . . shame . . . disgrace . . . punish (poor . . .) . . . bizarre . . . cynicism . . . cheat . . . steal . . . abuse of power . . . machine . . . bosses . . . obsolete . . . criminal rights . . . red tape . . . patronage

OPTIMISTIC POSITIVE GOVERNING WORDS

Use the list below to help define your campaign and your vision of public service. These words can help give extra power to your message. In addition, these words help develop the positive side of the contrast you should create with your opponent, giving your community something to vote for!

share . . . change . . . opportunity . . . legacy . . . challenge . . . control . . . truth . . . moral . . . courage . . . reform . . . prosperity . . . crusade . . . movement . . . children . . . family . . . debate . . . compete . . . active(ly) . . . we/us/our . . . candid(ly) . . . humane . . . pristine . . . provide . . .

liberty . . . commitment . . . principle(d) . . . unique . . . duty . . . precious . . . premise . . . care(ing) . . . tough . . . listen . . . learn . . . help . . . lead . . . vision . . . success . . . empower(ment) . . . citizen . . . activist . . . mobilize . . . conflict . . . light . . . dream . . . freedom . . .

peace . . . rights . . . pioneer . . . proud/pride . . . building . . . preserve . . . pro-(issue): flag, children, environment . . . reform . . . workfare . . . eliminate good-time in prison . . . strength

... choice/choose ... fair ... protect ... confident ... incentive ... hard work ... initiative ... common sense ... passionate

A prominent application of Gingrich's semantic guidelines for GOPAC appeared in all the "clean" words in titles of provisions in the congressional Republicans' 1994 Contract with America. The Job Creation and Enhancement Act had nothing to do directly with creating or enhancing jobs; it reduced the capital gains tax. The Common Sense Legal Reforms Act, described by its sponsors as placing "reasonable limits on punitive damages and reform of product liability laws to stem the endless tide of litigation," reduced the possibility of successful legal action against corporations for securities frauds such as those in the savings-and-loan scandals, as well as for the manufacture and sale of defective parts or for hazardous workplace conditions and environmental destruction. The Personal Responsibility Act prohibited welfare to minor mothers, denied increased Aid to Families with Dependent Children (AFDC) for additional children on welfare, enacted a two-years-and-out provision with work requirements, and in a provision "to help combat illiteracy" and "provide incentives to complete high school," enabled states to reduce AFDC payments to young mothers who have not completed high school; none of these clauses included provisions for creating jobs or job training to compensate for reduced welfare benefits.

One other provision in the Personal Responsibility Act, a proposal to cap spending in future years on the established free school lunch program for poor children, provoked a heated semantic controversy. Democrats charged that the proposal cut funding, while Republicans countered that it actually increased funding over the previous level. The facts were that it did indeed increase funding, but at a lower rate in future years than that mandated in the existing law, a rate that would lag behind school population growth, inflation, and so on. Critics said that the Republicans attempted to cover up the negative growth rate, so that their claim of an increase amounted to a **half-truth**. Thus the proposal could be defined as either a "cut"—a **dirty**—or an "increase"—a **clean**—according to whoever got to control the semantic agenda. Some commentators at the time pointed out **ironically** that when Democrats in earlier years had tried to slow the rate of military spending, they had similarly tried to **euphemize** what might be an unpopular act by saying they were increasing spending, while the Republicans charged that it was a cut.

The Republicans won the 1994 congressional election largely on the glittering euphemistic appeal of the Contract with America, yet subsequent surveys showed that few voters were at all familiar with its specific provisions, and when they were informed of the details, most opposed them.

EUPHEMISM

Euphemism is the substitution of a "clean" word for a "dirty" reality. Many common euphemisms are harmless, if somewhat squeamish, conventions, such as "pass away" instead of "die," or "restroom" instead of "toilet." But euphemisms are also frequently used in public discourse to deceive or to obscure issues. Writing during the period of World War II in "Politics and the English Language" (1946), George Orwell said:

> In our time, political speech and writing are largely the defense of the indefensible. Things like the continuance of British rule in India, the Russian purges and deportations, the dropping of the atom bombs on Japan, can indeed be defended, but only by arguments which are too brutal for most people to face, and which do not square with the professed aims of political parties. Thus political language has to consist largely of euphemism, question-begging and sheer cloudy vagueness. Defenseless villages are bombarded from the air, the inhabitants driven out into the countryside, the cattle machine-gunned, the huts set on fire with incendiary bullets:

this is called *pacification*. [The same euphemism was later used by the U.S. government in the Vietnam War.—.]. . . .

    A mass of Latin words falls upon the facts like soft snow, blurring the outlines and covering up all the details. (256)

Similarly dehumanizing uses of euphemisms are constants in every society and age. About the trend of massive firings from corporations in the 1980s and 1990s, *New York Times* columnist Bob Herbert wrote:

The euphemism of choice for the corporate chopping block is downsizing, but variations abound. John Thomas, a 59–year-old AT&T employee, was told on Tuesday that his job was "not going forward." . . .

    Other workers are discontinued, involuntarily severed, surplussed. There are men and women at AT&T who actually talk about living in a "surplus universe."

    There are special leaves, separations, rebalances, bumpings and, one of my favorites, cascade bumpings. (Jan. 19, 1996, A15)

Euphemism is often resorted to in politics to conceal a destructive policy by giving it a "clean" name with positive associations. Everybody likes "reforms" and "relief," but be sure to read the fine print when you hear a bill described as "welfare reform," "tax reform," or "tax relief" (see Lakoff's "Framing the Issues"). Likewise, be wary of the appeal of "free," as in "the North American Free Trade Agreement" (NAFTA), or "fair," as in "fair trade" and "The Fair Tax." A prominent semantic issue in the late 2000s involved whether the American government's interrogative methods in prisons at Guantanamo Bay and Abu Ghraib constituted "torture" or "enhanced interrogation," and other hedges on exactly what defines torture. Likewise, "extraordinary rendition" during the Iraq War was code for the government's policy of handing over detainees to friendly foreign governments who could torture prisoners without American legal restraints.

ABSTRACT AND CONCRETE LANGUAGE

Semanticists refer to a "ladder of abstraction," or a scale of words from very concrete to very abstract. The most concrete are words that denote physical objects, like *the tree* or *a chair.* The most abstract are those describing ideas, beliefs, values, or moral judgments, like *justice, patriotic, liberty, honor, good, evil, family values, "American"* and *"un-American,"* and all the ideological -isms like *conservatism* and *liberalism.* Developmental psychologists have also identified what they term concrete and abstract modes of thinking or cognition. Children's early speech and thought are almost solely concrete, being limited to their physical surroundings and sensations. But as their experience and learning expand, they come to understand concepts that are abstract or outside their immediate experience. Adults who have not fully developed the capacity to understand abstractions, and whose language or thought remains almost *solely* concrete, are restricted in their ability to conceptualize or empathize with people, events, and ideas outside their firsthand experience. Hence they tend to have an ethnocentric or parochial viewpoint that inclines them toward prejudice against both people and ideas that are foreign to them. Also remember Stanley Aronowitz's speculation in chapter 3 about the cognitive effects of TV and other mass media: "The problem of abstraction becomes a major barrier to analysis because students seem enslaved to the concrete. . . . The critical project of learning involves understanding that things are often not what they seem to be and that abstract concepts such as 'society,' 'capitalism,' 'history,' and other categories not available to the senses are nonetheless real. This whole critical project now seems in eclipse."

    That is not to say, however, that abstract thinking is always preferable to concrete in adults. At the **equal and opposite extreme** from people who have trouble grasping abstractions are those whose language and thought are so abstract that they are disconnected from concrete realities. Concrete thinking is conducive to clarity, immediacy, and sensuous and vivid **imagery**, as opposed to the danger in abstractions of impersonality, evasiveness, and (in Orwell's words) "sheer, cloudy vagueness." So the ideal mental state to strive for as a critical thinker is to have the ability to connect and move back and forth between the concrete and the abstract, between your own, firsthand experience and the experience of those whose viewpoints differ from yours, and between your personal perceptions and larger, distant realities.

UNCONCRETIZED ABSTRACTIONS

The denotation of abstract words like *freedom, patriotic, conservative* and *liberal* is not readily apparent if they are not explicitly defined; there is a great deal of disagreement over their definitions, so differing implicit definitions of them are frequently the cause of arguments. When you speak or write about abstract ideas, then, you should be able to ground them in concrete specifics, using phrases like "for example" or "for instance," or employing description, narration, dialogue, or vivid images and figures of speech. Another danger in unconcretized abstractions is that, while they are often vague in denotative meaning, they are apt to be strongly loaded connotatively, evoking "clean" or "dirty" conditioned responses. Moreover, abstractions with "clean" connotations are often used euphemistically. In the same vein as Orwell's "Politics and the English Language," Albert Camus, addressing an audience of Catholic clergy shortly after World War II, in a talk titled "The Unbeliever and Christians," appealed for believers and nonbelievers like himself to join together in opposing the euphemizing of mass murder by all the world powers in that new age of total war: "What the world expects of Christians is that Christians should speak out loud and clear, and that they should voice their condemnation in such a way that never a doubt, never the slightest doubt, could rise in the heart of the simplest man. That they should get away from abstraction and confront the blood-stained face history has taken on today" (*Resistance, Rebellion, and Death*, 71).

LITERAL AND FIGURATIVE LANGUAGE

The words *figurative* and *figure*, as in *figure of speech*, are synonymous with *symbolic*. This synonym is ambiguous, however, because semantically, all words merely **symbolize** the object they denote—"the map is not the territory." We say that words like *Hollywood* and *Washington* literally designate those cities, or visualize an image of them, but of course, the names aren't *literally* literal—they're just collections of spoken sounds and written scrawls. We accept them as relatively literal symbols, though, compared to figures of speech—which *Hollywood* and *Washington* also happen to be when they symbolize the movie industry and the national government, respectively. These are examples of the figure known as **metonymy**, the symbolic substitution of a part for a whole or of a location for what is located there. We can say that literal words are one symbolic step removed from the objects they denote, while figures are two steps removed. They work by an extension of the literal meaning to a symbolic one, in metonymies like these, or by an **analogy** symbolically substituting one object or image for another, as in metaphor ("You're a turkey"), **simile** ("Like a rolling stone") or **personification** ("That golf course ate me up"). (*Image* refers to a picture evoked by a word; an image can be either literal or figurative.)

As forms of analogy, figures of speech in argumentation need to be evaluated by the same criteria (see chapter 9): in a good analogy or figure, the two terms compared have more important similarities than differences; the reality described is made clearer and more concrete (rather than fuzzier and vaguer); and the emotions evoked connotatively are appropriate to the situation. The lead sentence in a *New York Times* report (national edition, June 23, 1996, A1) on a series of arson fires in black churches in 1996 uses a simile: "The flames rise into the sky like malignant ghosts from the South's past, evoking some of the most racially charged images in the nation's history." The analogy between flames and malignant ghosts is both visually vivid and historically apt, evoking the history of lynch-mob burnings of southern blacks or their property.

An op-ed column about the Clinton administration Whitewater scandals by William Safire, also in the *New York Times* (June 24, 1996, A11), begins, "A cancer has been growing on the Clinton Presidency." A later sentence extends the metaphor: "As the scandal metastasizes, we are beginning to get some idea of its scope and seriousness." The metaphor is vivid and appropriate to the notion that a relatively minor misdoing in the White House might grow out of control, through attempts to obstruct justice by covering it up, to the point of destroying the presidency. Safire's metaphor also acquires additional **levels of meaning** through its allusion to similar phrasing used by President Richard Nixon's attorney John Dean in warning Nixon about the growing Watergate scandal in 1972, and through Safire's assumption that his readers remember he was a speechwriter for Nixon at the time of Watergate and understand that he is taking relish, **between the lines**, in payback against a Democratic president. Coincidentally, the metaphor of cancer also appeared on the same date in a letter to the editor in the *San Francisco Chronicle,* concerning a convicted killer in California: "Should he receive the death sentence, it will be the same as a surgical removal of a cancerous growth." Here, however, the metaphor is strong on evoking fear and hatred but weak in clarification. What is the logical point of comparison between a criminal and a cancer? To remove him from society and prevent him from committing further crimes? Life imprisonment without possibility of parole could do that. To remove an evil influence that might encourage other killers—that is, to deter others? Most criminological evidence fails to show that executions deter anyone. In short, the equation of a human being with a spreading disease introduces so many possible significant differences that it only produces logical confusion.

LITERAL AND FIGURATIVE LANGUAGE IN LITERATURE

The use of figurative language for imaginative purposes, as opposed to argumentative ones, is a defining characteristic of creative literature, especially poetry, including song lyrics. (In many literary cases, though, the imaginative and argumentative functions work together, as in the section from Thoreau's *Walden* discussed below.) Sometimes it serves for pure humor and the delight of an ingenious verbal association, as in a song sung by Uncle Dave Macon, a star of the Grand Ole Opry in the 1930s, describing a man with a long beard in the simile: "Look at that hair all around his mouth, / Like he swallowed a mule and left the tail a-hangin' out."

Creative writers' use of figurative language to create multiple levels of meaning and complexity of thought and argument can be illustrated with one of the best-known passages in American literature, the climax of Henry David Thoreau's chapter "Where I Lived, and What I Lived For," in his book of essays *Walden, Or Life in the Woods* (1854). The thematic and figurative development in this passage is a perfect example of the process of cumulation and recursiveness in reading and writing discussed in chapter 3. Thoreau is explaining why he left the society of Concord, Massachusetts, to live by himself self-sufficiently in the woods near Walden Pond. He wanted to escape urban, industrial society's illusions, conformity, rush, and absorption in trivial busywork, so as to "spend one day as deliberately as Nature, and not be thrown off the track by every nutshell and mosquito's wing that falls on the rails" (87). The thesis sentence in the passage is, "I perceive that we inhabitants of New England live this mean life that we do because our vision does not penetrate the surface of things." "The surface of things" suggests the surface of water, which both distorts the reality beneath it through refraction and gives a false sense of fixity, or "illusory foundations," while it is in constant flux. This metaphor is developed by several comparisons of daily routine and conformity with water images like, "Why should we knock under and go with the stream?" (87). (The stream metaphor is presumably inspired by Thoreau's literal presence by a tributary of Walden Pond.) He further extends the stream metaphor to contrast the "mud and slush of opinion, prejudice, and tradition" to the "hard bottom" spiritual, intellectual, and poetic realities of life that Thoreau believed in as part of the Platonic idealism underlying transcendentalist philosophy.

The development of these metaphors through several paragraphs culminates: "Time is but the stream I go a-fishing in. I drink at it; but while I drink I see the sandy bottom and detect how shallow it is. Its thin current slides away, but eternity remains. I would drink deeper; fish in the sky, whose bottom is pebbly with stars." Here the literal stream becomes a metaphor for time, in the sense of the here-and-now and of surface illusions as opposed to eternal truths. Thoreau, who frequently turns puns into metaphors, does so here with "current," connoting both shallow appearances in space and "current events" in time. Even the bottom of the stream is shallow and shifting, which is to say that the physical world and current events are ultimately an illusion. Thoreau then brilliantly turns the image of the stream's pebbled, sandy bottom upside down and transforms it into an image of the sky, "pebbly with stars," symbolizing Heaven or God, infinite space opposed to the finite measures of the physical world, and eternal time as opposed to the transitory stream of life on earth. (Compare with Whitman's image of his soul "seeking the spheres to connect them" in "A Noiseless Patient Spider.") All of these symbolic connections are created by the active exercise of Thoreau's poetic imagination or intellect. His mind has first visually associated the pebbles at the bottom of a stream with the stars in the sky, then translated these sense images into thought and words (literal, metaphorical, and symbolic), then transcribed those words on the written page, to be communicated to his readers. And all this poetic mental activity has developed his argumentative theme of opposition to social conformity—in issues like majority support of slavery and the Mexican-American War in his essay "Civil Disobedience"—and habitual "sleepwalking" through life.

This passage is one of the best illustrations of the aesthetic theory of the American transcendentalist writers like Thoreau, Whitman, Ralph Waldo Emerson, and Margaret Fuller, for whom metaphor is the essence of poetry in its power to create connections between the physical world and the intellectual or spiritual world. Poets have a special calling as visionaries of these connections and translators of them into metaphorical language. A remarkably similar conception of poetry is expressed by the contemporary American writer Gloria Anzaldua in her book *Borderlands/La Frontera: The New Mestiza* (1987), in which she views her marginal identity between Latino, Indian, and Anglo culture as a vital source of poetic connections. In a chapter titled "Tlilli, Tlapalli: The Path of the Red and Black Ink," she writes:

> For the ancient Aztecs, *tlilli, tlapalli, la tinta negra y roja de sus codices* (the black and red ink painted on codices [pictographic sacred documents]) were the colors symbolizing *escritura y sabiduría* (writing and wisdom). They believed that through metaphor and symbol, by means of poetry and truth, communication with the Divine could be attained.
>
> … An image is a bridge between evoked emotion and conscious knowledge; words are the cables that hold up the bridge. Images are more direct, more immediate than words, and closer to the unconscious. Picture language precedes thinking in words; the metaphorical mind precedes analytical consciousness. (33–34)

SUMMARY: APPLYING SEMANTIC ANALYSIS

A. Abstract versus concrete language
   1. Criticize examples where the author fails to concretize abstractions.
   2. Praise examples where the author concretizes abstractions or describes a situation effectively through concrete language that exposes the vagueness of abstract accounts.
B. Criticize use of passive voice to evade responsibility ("Mistakes were made").
C. Point out examples where opposing sides use different definitions or interpretations of controversial words (e.g., *freedom, patriotism*).
D. Criticize examples where sources assume that a word (e.g., *patriotism, peace, America*) is absolutely and always admirable, without recognizing limitations.
E. Connotative language
   1. Criticize examples where sources arbitrarily use "clean" words to describe their own side, or "dirties" to describe the other, without support.
   2. Criticize examples of the use of euphemism to gloss over an unpleasant reality.
F. Figurative language
   1. Praise effective figures of speech; explain why they are effective.
   2. Criticize ineffective figures; explain why they are ineffective.

A SEMANTIC CALCULATOR FOR BIAS IN RHETORIC

This is a guide that you can apply in writing papers about sources, with respect both to those sources' biases and to your own as a writer.

1. What is the author's vantage point, in terms of social class, wealth, occupation, gender, ethnic group, political ideology, educational level, age, and so on? Is that vantage point apt to color her/his attitudes on the issue under discussion? Does she/he have anything personally to gain from the position she/he is arguing for, any **conflicts of interest** or other reasons for special pleading? (See chapter 17.)
2. What organized financial, political, ethnic, or other interests are backing the advocated position? What groups or **special interests** stand to profit financially, politically, or otherwise from it? In the Latin phrase, cui bono, "Who benefits?" (See chapter 17.)
3. Once you have determined the author's vantage point and/or the special interests being favored, look for signs of ethnocentrism, **rationalization or wishful thinking**, **sentimentality**, **one-sidedness**, **selective vision**, or a **double standard**. (See chapter 8.)
4. Look for the following forms of **setting the agenda** and stacking the deck reflecting the biases in number 3:
   a. **Playing up**
      (1) arguments favorable to one's own side
      (2) arguments unfavorable to the other side
      (3) the other side's wealth, power, extremism, misdeeds ("a widespread pattern of abuses"), or unity ("a vast conspiracy," "a tightly coordinated machine")
   b. **Downplaying** (or suppressing altogether)
      (1) arguments unfavorable to one's own side
      (2) arguments favorable to the other side
      (3) one's own side's power, wealth, extremism, misdeeds ("a small number of isolated instances," "a few rotten apples"), or unity ("an uncoordinated collection of diverse, grassroots groups")
   c. Applying "clean" words (ones with positive connotations) to one's own side, without support

Applying "dirty" words (ones with negative connotations) to the other side, without support

d. Assuming that the representatives of one's own side are trustworthy, truthful, and have no selfish motives, while assuming the opposite of the other side's representatives ("They're only in it for money or publicity")

e. Giving credit to one's own side for positive events

f. Blaming the other side for negative events

This calculator can be usefully applied to all of the opposed readings from conservative versus liberal or leftist sources in this book, as well as to all your daily intake of information in the public sphere. It indicates the ways in which we all are inclined, intentionally or unintentionally, to react—often with anger and exaggeration—to our opponents' perceived faults and exercises of power, while ignoring our own side's comparable ones. Of course, emphasizing our side's "good" and the other side's "bad" is a perfectly legitimate part of argumentation, so long as it is done honestly, accurately, with sufficient support, and with a sense of proportion. But good-faith efforts at doing so need to be distinguished from the bad-faith ones of propagandists who stack the deck by deliberately, dishonestly using semantic slanting to present a simplistic opposition between "good guys" and "bad guys," or the efforts of sincere but closed-minded **ideologues** who resort to the techniques in a knee-jerk conditioned reaction to every public event. In any given case, differential semantic descriptions might serve to make an accurate, supportable judgment on the relative merits of opposing camps—or they might not; it's for you to judge.

If you don't find blatant signs of the above biases, and if you judge that the emotional language is supported by adequate evidence, that's a good indication that the writer is a credible one. If there *are* many such signs, that's an indication that the writer is not a credible source. However, finding signs of the above biases does not in itself prove that the writer's arguments are fallacious. Don't fall into the **ad hominem** ("to the man") fallacy—evading the issue by attacking the character or motives of the writer or speaker without refuting the substance of the argument itself. What the writer says may or may not be factual, regardless of the semantic biases. *The point is not to let yourself be swayed by emotive words alone, especially when you are inclined to wishful thinking on one side of the subject yourself. When you find these biases in other writers, or in yourself, that is a sign that you need to be extra careful to check the facts with a variety of other sources and to find out what the arguments are on the other side of the issue.*

When Words Cheapen Life

Mary Ann Glendon

New York Times, Tuesday, January 10, 1995

After months of relative calm in the abortion debate, the shootings in Brookline, Mass., on Dec. 30 have unleashed yet another volley of bitter recriminations between activists. A Planned Parenthood newspaper ad with the heading "Words Kill" blamed pro-life rhetoric for the deaths of two clinic receptionists.

This charge deserves to be taken seriously, for how we name things determines to a great extent how we think, feel and act regarding them. Words can kill, but it's not so simple as pro-choice leaders would have it. Words kill by creating a climate where life is cheap: they can stifle the inner voice that reminds us that evil can never be overcome by evil. From abortion rights to euthanasia to indifference to the plight of the poor, the road has been paved with soothing words chosen to harmonize conscience with convenience.

Consider how brutal regimes of chattel slavery and apartheid were legitimated by the notion that blacks weren't fully human. The Supreme Court endorsed that view in 1857 when Dred Scott came before the Court as a man, only to be dismissed as a piece of property.

In Roe v. Wade, the Court again made a fateful semantic choice. By refusing to acknowledge the developing fetus as either human or alive, it entered into complicity with advocates' deceptive phrases like "clump of tissue" and "product of conception." Even those who would distinguish between the born and the unborn should be nervous when the state dissembles about the definition of life.

In the two decades after it handed down its decision, the Court foreclosed most opportunities for influencing abortion law through legislative politics. Courts have also sanctioned the use of injunctions, buffer zones and organized crime statutes to keep pro-life demonstrators away from clinics. The danger of such measures was summed up last week by the pro-choice civil rights lawyer Harvey Silvergate, who said that if such techniques had been used against civil rights protesters in the 60's "you can be assured there would have been a lot more violence."

Now, Planned Parenthood seeks to silence even "verbal attacks" against abortion rights. What it really wants is to suppress the pro-life movement's insistence—so hurtful to the clinic business—that abortion destroys developing life. To banish opponents of abortion and their deeply held beliefs from public life, however, would be unwise and undemocratic.

This is not to claim that the language of dehumanization alone has been responsible for increasing violence and waning compassion in these troubled United States. Or that Government approval of abortion has been the only factor promoting acceptance of brutal quick fixes for a range of social problems. But how can the pro-choice movement's rhetoric fail to promote a coarsening of spirit, a deadening of conscience and a disregard for the humanity of one's opponents—as well as for those who seem to us to be less than full-fledged "persons"?

That's why the late Walker Percy, physician and novelist, deplored "the chronic misuse of words" to disguise what takes place during abortion. It is, an ominous sign, as artists are often the first to realize, when a society begins to manipulate the concept of humanity.

In the wake of the Brookline tragedies, are there any words of hope? Perhaps. The Massachusetts news media have begun to cover those services that make the pro-life movement more than just anti-abortion—financial aid to single mothers, shelters for mothers and children with AIDS, parenthood classes. This has put into focus the common task to which the overwhelmingly female rank-and-file of both movements have always been committed: building a culture that is respectful of women, supportive of child-raising families and protective of the weak and vulnerable.

Framing the Issues: UC Berkeley Professor George Lakoff Tells How Conservatives Use Language to Dominate Politics

University of California, Berkeley, News Center

October 7, 2003

BERKELEY—With Republicans controlling the Senate, the House, and the White House and enjoying a large margin of victory for California Governor-elect Arnold

Schwarzenegger, it's clear that the Democratic Party is in crisis. George Lakoff, a UC Berkeley professor of linguistics and cognitive science, thinks he knows why. Conservatives have spent decades defining their ideas, carefully choosing the language with which to present them, and building an infrastructure to communicate them, says Lakoff.

The work has paid off; by dictating the terms of national debate, conservatives have put progressives firmly on the defensive.

In 2000 Lakoff and seven other faculty members from Berkeley and UC Davis joined together to found the Rockridge Institute, one of the few progressive think tanks in existence in the U.S. The institute offers its expertise and research on a nonpartisan basis to help progressives understand how best to get their messages across. The Richard & Rhoda Goldman Distinguished Professor in the College of Letters & Science, Lakoff is the author of "Moral Politics: How Liberals and Conservatives Think," first published in 1997 and reissued in 2002, as well as several other books on how language affects our lives.

In a long conversation over coffee at the Free Speech Movement Café, he told the NewsCenter's Bonnie Azab Powell why the Democrats "just don't get it," why Schwarzenegger won the recall election, and why conservatives will continue to define the issues up for debate for the foreseeable future.

Why was the Rockridge Institute created, and how do you define its purpose?

I got tired of cursing the newspaper every morning. I got tired of seeing what was going wrong and not being able to do anything about it.

The background for Rockridge is that conservatives, especially conservative think tanks, have framed virtually every issue from their perspective. They have put a huge amount of money into creating the language for their worldview and getting it out there. Progressives have done virtually nothing. Even the new Center for American Progress, the think tank that John Podesta [former chief of staff for the Clinton administration] is setting up, is not dedicated to this at all. I asked Podesta who was going to do the Center's framing. He

got a blank look, thought for a second and then said, "You!" Which meant they haven't thought about it at all. And that's the problem. Liberals don't get it. They don't understand what it is they have to be doing.

Rockridge's job is to reframe public debate, to create balance from a progressive perspective. It's one thing to analyze language and thought, it's another thing to create it. That's what we're about. It's a matter of asking "What are the central ideas of progressive thought from a moral perspective?"

Language always comes with what is called "framing." Every word is defined relative to a conceptual framework. If you have something like "revolt," that implies a population that is being ruled unfairly, or assumes it is being ruled unfairly, and that they are throwing off their rulers, which would be considered a good thing. That's a frame.

If you then add the word "voter" in front of "revolt," you get a metaphorical meaning saying that the voters are the oppressed people, the governor is the oppressive ruler, that they have ousted him and this is a good thing and all things are good now. All of that comes up when you see a headline like "voter revolt"—something that most people read and never notice. But these things can be affected by reporters and very often, by the campaign people themselves.

Here's another example of how powerful framing is. In Arnold Schwarzenegger's acceptance speech, he said, "When the people win, politics as usual loses." What's that about? Well, he knows that he's going to face a Democratic legislature, so what he has done is frame himself and also Republican politicians as the people, while framing Democratic politicians as political as usual—in advance. The Democratic legislators won't know what hit them. They're automatically framed as enemies of the people.

Why do conservatives appear to be so much better at framing?

Because they've put billions of dollars into it. Over the last 30 years their think tanks have made a heavy investment in ideas and in language. In 1970, [Supreme Court Justice] Lewis Powell wrote a fateful memo to the National Chamber of Commerce saying that all of our best students are becoming anti-business because of the Vietnam War, and that we needed to do something about it. Powell's agenda included getting wealthy conservatives to set up professorships, setting up institutes on and off campus where intellectuals would write books from a conservative business perspective, and setting up think tanks. He outlined the whole thing in 1970. They set up the Heritage Foundation in 1973, and the Manhattan Institute after that. [There are many others, including the American Enterprise Institute and the Hoover Institute at Stanford, which date from the 1940s.]

And now, as the *New York Times Magazine* quoted Paul Weyrich, who started the Heritage Foundation, they have 1,500 conservative radio talk show hosts. They have a huge, very good operation, and they understand their own moral system. They understand what unites conservatives, and they understand how to talk about it, and they are constantly updating their research on how best to express their ideas.

Why haven't progressives done the same thing?

There's a systematic reason for that. You can see it in the way that conservative foundations and progressive foundations work. Conservative foundations give large block grants year after year to their think tanks. They say, "Here's several million dollars, do what you need to do." And basically, they build infrastructure, they build TV studios, hire intellectuals, set aside money to buy a lot of books to get them on the best-seller lists, hire research assistants for their intellectuals so they do well on TV, and hire agents to put them on TV. They do all of that. Why? Because the conservative moral system, which I analyzed in "Moral Politics," has as its highest value preserving and defending the "strict father" system itself. And that means building infrastructure. As businessmen, they know how to do this very well.

Meanwhile, liberals' conceptual system of the "nurturant parent" has as its highest value helping individuals who need help. The progressive foundations and donors give their money to a variety of grassroots organizations. They say, "We're giving you $25,000, but don't waste a penny of it. Make sure it all goes to the cause, don't use it for administration, communication, infrastructure, or career development." So there's actually a structural reason built into the worldviews that explains why conservatives have done better.

Back up for a second and explain what you mean by the strict father and nurturant parent frameworks.

Well, the progressive worldview is modeled on a nurturant parent family. Briefly, it assumes that the world is basically good and can be made better and that one must work toward that. Children are born good; parents can make them better. Nurturing involves empathy, and the responsibility to take care of oneself and others for whom we are responsible. On a larger scale, specific policies follow, such as governmental protection in the form of a social safety net and government regulation, universal education (to ensure competence, fairness), civil liberties and equal treatment (fairness and freedom), accountability (derived from trust), public service (from responsibility), open government (from open communication), and the promotion of an economy that benefits all and functions to promote these values, which are traditional progressive values in American politics.

The conservative worldview, the strict father model, assumes that the world is dangerous and difficult and that children are born bad and must be made good. The strict father is the moral authority who supports and defends the family, tells his wife what to do, and teaches his kids right from wrong. The only way to do that is through painful discipline—physical punishment that by adulthood will become internal discipline. The good people are the disciplined people. Once grown, the self-reliant, disciplined children are on their own. Those children who remain dependent (who were spoiled, overly willful, or recalcitrant) should be forced to undergo further discipline or be cut free with no support to face the discipline of the outside world.

So, project this onto the nation and you see that to the right wing, the good citizens are the disciplined ones—those who have already become wealthy or at least self-reliant—and those who are on the way. Social programs, meanwhile, "spoil" people by giving them things they haven't earned and keeping them dependent. The government is there only to protect the nation, maintain order, administer justice (punishment), and to provide for the promotion and orderly conduct of business. In this way, disciplined people become self-reliant. Wealth is a measure of discipline. Taxes beyond the minimum needed for such government take away from the good, disciplined people rewards that they have earned and spend it on those who have not earned it.

From that framework, I can see why Schwarzenegger appealed to conservatives.

Exactly. In the strict father model, the big thing is discipline and moral authority, and punishment for those who do something wrong. That comes out very clearly in the Bush administration's foreign and domestic policy. With Schwarzenegger, it's in his movies: most of the characters that he plays exemplify that moral system. He didn't have to say a word! He just had to stand up there, and he represents Mr. Discipline. He knows what's right and wrong, and he's going to take it to the people. He's not going to ask permission, or have a discussion, he's going to do what needs to be done, using force and authority. His very persona represents what conservatives are about.

You've written a lot about "tax relief" as a frame. How does it work?

The phrase "Tax relief" began coming out of the White House starting on the very day of Bush's inauguration. It got picked up by the newspapers as if it were a neutral term, which it is not. First, you have the frame for "relief." For there to be relief, there has to be an affliction, an afflicted party, somebody who administers the relief, and an act in which you are relieved of the affliction. The reliever is the hero, and anybody who tries to stop them is the bad guy intent on keeping the affliction going. So, add "tax" to "relief" and you get a metaphor that taxation is an affliction, and anybody against relieving this affliction is a villain.

"Tax relief" has even been picked up by the Democrats. I was asked by the Democratic Caucus in their tax meetings to talk to them, and I told them about the problems of using tax relief. The candidates were on the road. Soon after, Joe Lieberman still used the phrase tax relief in a press conference. You see the Democrats shooting themselves in the foot.

So what should they be calling it?

It's not just about what you call it, if it's the same "it." There's actually a whole other way to think about it. Taxes are what you pay to be an American, to live in a civilized society that is democratic and offers opportunity, and where there's an infrastructure that has been paid for by previous taxpayers. This is a huge infrastructure. The highway system, the Internet, the TV system, the public education system, the power grid, the system for training scientists—vast amounts of infrastructure that we all use, which has to be maintained and paid for. Taxes are your dues—you pay your dues to be an American. In addition, the wealthiest Americans use that infrastructure more than anyone else, and they use parts of it that other people don't. The federal justice system, for example, is nine-tenths devoted to corporate law. The Securities and Exchange Commission and all the apparatus of the Commerce Department are mainly used by the wealthy. And we're all paying for it.

So taxes could be framed as an issue of patriotism.

It is an issue of patriotism! Are you paying your dues, or are you trying to get something for free at the expense of your country? It's about being a member. People pay a membership fee to join a country club, for which they get to use the swimming pool and the golf course. But they didn't pay for them in their membership. They were built and paid for by other people and by this collectivity. It's the same thing with our country—the country as country club, being a member of a remarkable nation. But what would it take to make the discussion about that? Every Democratic senator and all of their aides and every candidate would have to learn how to talk about it that way. There would have to be a manual. Republicans have one.

They have a guy named Frank Luntz, who puts out a 500-page manual every year that goes issue by issue on what the logic of the position is from the Republican side, what the other guys' logic is, how to attack it, and what language to use.

What are some other examples of issues that progressives should try to reframe?

There are too many examples, that's the problem. The so-called energy crisis in California should have been called Grand Theft. It was theft, it was the result of deregulation by Pete Wilson, and Davis should have said so from the beginning.

Or take gay marriage, which the right has made a rallying topic. Surveys have been done that say Americans are overwhelmingly against gay marriage. Well, the same surveys show that they also overwhelmingly object to discrimination against gays. These seem to be opposite facts, but they're not. "Marriage" is about sex. When you say "gay marriage," it becomes about gay sex, and approving of gay marriage becomes implicitly about approving of gay sex. And while a lot of Americans don't approve of gay sex, that doesn't mean they want to discriminate against gay people. Perfectly rational position. Framed in that way, the issue of gay marriage will get a lot of negative reaction. But what if you make the issue "freedom to marry," or even better, "the right to marry"? That's a whole different story. Very few people would say they did not support the right to marry whom you choose. But the polls don't ask that question, because the right wing has framed that issue.

Do any of the Democratic Presidential candidates grasp the importance of framing?

None. They don't get it at all. But they're in a funny position. The framing changes that have to be made are long-term changes. The conservatives understood this in 1973. By 1980 they had a candidate, Ronald Reagan, who could take all this stuff and run with it. The progressives don't have a candidate now who understands these things and can talk about them. And in order for a candidate to be able to talk about them, the ideas have to be out there. You have to be able to reference them in a sound bite. Other people have to put these ideas into the public domain, not politicians. The question is, How do you get these ideas out there? There are all kinds of ways, and one of the things the Rockridge Institute is looking at is talking to advocacy groups, which could do this very well. They have more of a budget, they're spread all over the place, and they have access to the media.

Right now the Democratic Party is into marketing. They pick a number of issues like prescription drugs and Social Security and ask which ones sell best across the spectrum, and they run on those issues. They have no moral perspective, no general values, no identity. People vote their identity, they don't just vote on the issues, and Democrats don't understand that. Look at Schwarzenegger, who says nothing about the issues. The Democrats ask, How could anyone vote for this guy? They did because he put forth an identity. Voters knew who he is.

Look Behind Statistics for Changing Definitions

Thomas Sowell

Knoxville News-Sentinel, July 6, 2002

One of the latest in the seemingly endless rounds of alarming statistics is that one out of 12 American children has some form of disability. With all the things that are supposedly getting worse, you have to wonder how our life expectancy keeps increasing.

A cynic might even wonder if the increasing availability of money from the government has anything to do with the increasing number of "problems" that need to be "solved" by government programs.

One way of telling whether a given statistic is a fact or an artifact is to ask whether the definition used fits the thing that is being defined. Buried in the news story about the children with disabilities is the fact that the definition of "disability" has been expanding over the years.

A child who is likely to be diagnosed as autistic today might not have been some years ago, yet that is seldom mentioned in alarming statistics about the escalating number of cases of autism. As the author of a couple of books about late-talking children, I hear regularly from parents who tell me that they are being asked to allow their children to be labeled autistic in order to get either the government or their insurance company to pay for speech therapy.

It is amazing that, with something as serious—indeed, catastrophic—as autism, statistics are thrown around without mentioning the variation in what is being diagnosed as autism. In something much less serious, such as sales receipts at Wal-Mart, a comparison of how much money was taken in this year compared to last year will almost certainly make a distinction between sales receipts at the same stores as last year vs. sales receipts that include new stores opened since last year.

In other words, they notify you of changing definitions behind the numbers. Otherwise, the statistics could mean almost anything. If it is important enough to do this for Wal-Mart sales, it certainly ought to be important enough to do it for autism.

Regardless of whether the old or the new criterion for autism is better, they are different criteria. Statistics should tell us whether or by how much autism has risen by any consistent standard. Moreover, those who diagnose autism range from highly trained specialists to people who never set foot in a medical school.

Another set of statistics whose definition is at least questionable are statistics about the incomes of high school dropouts vs. those who have more education. Since most high school dropouts resume their education at some later time, are these statistics really counting all—or even most—dropouts? Or just the minority of dropouts who never enter a classroom again?

Although I dropped out of high school more than half a century ago and still do not have a high school diploma, I do have a couple of postgraduate degrees. Is my income counted when they add up the incomes of dropouts? Not bloody likely.

This is not just a fine point. All sorts of efforts are being made to prevent kids from dropping out of high school, as if dropping out means the end of their education. Since it usually means only an interruption, leading eventually to a resumption of their education after some experience in the real world, the urgency of preventing them from encountering the real world is by no means obvious. They may be more serious students afterwards.

One of the most brazen uses of statistics which do not fit the definition was in a much-praised book that attempted to show that black students admitted to colleges under affirmative action do just fine. The book was titled "The Shape of the River," written by William Bowen and Derek Bok, former presidents of Princeton and Harvard, respectively.

Although this book is crammed full of statistics, not one of those statistics is about black students admitted under affirmative action. Black students admitted under the same standards as white students are lumped together with black students admitted under lower standards. Yet, from this the authors conclude that affirmative action is a good thing—to the applause of those who apparently wanted to see that conclusion more than they wanted to see meaningful statistics.

Advocates of campaign finance reform often speak of the corrupting influence of money. But they seldom include the corrupting influence of the government's money on what statistical "facts" are fed to the public.

Topics for Discussion and Writing

1. Apply "Applying Semantic Analysis" to a current speech by a government official, a talk-radio broadcast, TV commentary, or op-ed column.
2. Look for examples of good figures of speech in some of your favorite song lyrics and in a day's conversations, courses, or media news and entertainment.
3. Glendon's "When Words Cheapen Life" addresses an emotionally charged, highly partisan subject. Do you find her tone relatively evenhanded? Does she come down clearly on one side of the issue, or is she simply criticizing semantic excesses and double standards on both sides? Role-play a defender of abortion **refuting** her arguments by **playing up** the euphemisms and other dehumanizing language used by opponents to obscure the realities of pregnancy by rape, illegal abortions, and other justifications for legal abortion.
4. Lakoff in "Framing the Issues" talks about issues on which conservatives control the semantic framing of certain issues, while Sowell in "Look Behind Statistics for Changing Definitions" does the same about liberal framing of other issues. Discuss the way in which each of them is himself framing a frame, or **setting the agenda**, for what issues are played up and **downplayed** in American public discourse. Do you find either more persuasive, or might they both be equally right?

CHAPTER 5

Writing Argumentative Papers

There are many varieties of argumentative writing, and no single, simple formula for organization or style. Every writing assignment presents unique challenges in rhetorical strategies. The length of an assignment dictates much about its writing; a letter to the editor of 200 words; a paper or op-ed column of 1,000 words, or three or four printed, double-spaced pages; a term paper of 2,500–4,500 words, ten or fifteen pages; a senior thesis of thirty or forty pages; a report or book of one hundred or more pages—each of these calls for a different mode of development and degree of detail in summary, supporting evidence, rebuttal, and so on. Your writing for courses will obviously also vary according to each instructor's specifications in topics and form.

Try to forget whatever you may have heard from writing teachers who approach writing as a strictly formulaic process—the five-paragraph essay, the funnel-shaped essay, and so on. Those are formulas for dull writing, the kind that no one other than a teacher would want to read. In real life, people write arguments because they are compelled to express themselves and communicate their ideas about an issue they feel strongly about; the form of what they write is determined by rhetorical decisions about the most effective organization and tone for persuading others to agree with what they have to say. So you need first and foremost to design whatever you write to interest readers in the originality, intelligence, and energy of what you have to say, not to bore them with a paper that looks like you are just going through the motions of an assignment.

Argumentative essays usually take one of two broad forms: either making an argument of your own or summarizing, analyzing, and evaluating the arguments of sources. These two are not entirely distinct, of course, since in making your own arguments you often need to cite sources for support, while analyzing and evaluating others' arguments is apt to entail making your own judgments on the issues. The first form works best for topics that are well within your own realm of experience and prior knowledge. This book (and the kind of course it is keyed to) emphasizes the second form because it approaches argumentative writing as a means of analyzing, evaluating, and synthesizing information acquired from sources in college courses and from your independent reading, listening to, and viewing of communication media.

There is no fixed formula for argumentative writing, and there is a wide variety of topics and rhetoric strategies to challenge your ingenuity, but there *are* some general, step-by-step *procedures* that most proficient writers employ. Again, for the kinds of papers that you will write in college courses, most of which are based on a designated topic, readings, or research assignment, something like the following is the process, in three broad stages: prewriting, writing, and postwriting.

PREWRITING

Reading and Research

The prewriting stage begins with reading and research. Take lots of notes by highlighting passages and making marginal comments in books and articles and keying notes in your notebook to page references. At this stage, you also need to bring to bear on the subject your whole previous storehouse of cultural literacy, everything you remember or have books and notes on from previous studies, along with your own life experience.

Brainstorming, Freewriting, Small-Group Discussions

You may have used these techniques for generating ideas in previous writing courses that emphasized personal expression and an open choice of topics. Brainstorming involves random jotting down of ideas and beginning to group them to develop an outline. Freewriting is spontaneous written expression of these ideas, before you start to edit, narrow down, or organize them; it is a good way to avoid getting stuck on where to begin writing. Discussions with groups of students, friends, or teachers are valuable for feedback at every stage of the writing process, particularly for getting viewpoints that differ from, or are opposed to, your own; this is the best way to become aware of how you need to modify your arguments to persuade someone who doesn't already agree with them.

Brainstorming and freewriting must take a different, more limited, form in argumentative writing based on responding to source readings on an assigned topic than in purely personal writing in which you have a free choice of subjects and what to say about them. In argumentative writing, you may find it useful to apply these techniques after you have done your initial reading, research, and note taking, or in response to "Rhetoric: A Checklist for Analyzing Your Own and Others' Arguments" in chapter 2.

WRITING

Narrowing Down

This is a crucial part of every writing assignment. You need to calculate carefully how many topics and sources you can cover, and how much you can say about them, in the time and space available. You will rarely be able to use all the ideas, sources, and notes you have generated in preparing for the paper, so avoid the temptation to toss in everything you've considered using, as that will make the paper seem too diffuse and shallow. In general, your rhetorical choice in writing papers is either to include a large number of sources and topics, which might result in broad but superficial coverage, or to cover a smaller number in more depth. *Usually* it is more effective to cover a smaller number in greater length and depth, without giving the impression that you have narrowed the range so much that you do not address central issues or exclude arguments and sources that might refute those you include.

Writers for publication are constantly subjected to brutal cutting of passages dear to their hearts by nasty editors. In fact most writing can benefit from rigorous cutting of repetitions, redundancies, and irrelevancies, and you should act as your own nasty editor. Always select what you judge to be the most important, interesting points and your own best rhetorical analyses; prune the rest to avoid being graded down for padding.

Outlining

Some teachers and students of writing approach outlining as simply a formulaic, constricting grid arbitrarily imposed on a paper. In fact, however, outlining is a central, organic stage of the writing process, essential to work out the continuity and cohesion, or "flow," of ideas in nearly every form of writing from a love letter to a dissertation. When I ask students who turn in papers that seem to go off in every direction, with unrelated jumps from one section to another and illogically reasoned, non sequitur ideas, whether they outlined, they invariably answer no.

Organic outlining begins with gathering your notes first into a broad outline, then into increasingly more detailed and better organized outlines, trying out different sequences and different degrees of narrowing down topics and sources for the most effective economy and continuity within the number of pages assigned. Believe me, this is the hardest stage for all writers, including professional journalists and scholars—it's all downhill once you have the detailed outline to the point where you sense that the pieces fit together right. See the outline of opposing arguments on wealth and poverty in chapter 16 for a sample "menu" of possible lines of argument, from which you might select a limited number; one or two of these topics could make a 1,000-word paper, four or five a 4,000–7,000-word term paper.

Here is a generic broad outline for the basic sections of the kind of argumentative paper emphasized here:

I. Introduction: Briefly identify the issues and opposing positions, along with your own previous viewpoint on them.
II. Main body
   1. Summarize opposing viewpoints of sources and their lines of argument. (Note: it is vital when you are summarizing a source or line of argument that you do so objectively, without injecting your own approval or disapproval, either explicitly or implicitly through tone [e.g., sarcasm] or snide comments. Rhetorically, you need to show the reader that you are capable of approaching the opposing arguments evenhandedly and open-mindedly.)
   2. Analyze and evaluate the reasoning and evidence on opposing sides. (Apply the rhetoric and semantic checklists here.) Bring in source authors' or your own rebuttals of fallacious arguments on one side or both and give possible counter-rebuttals. In this section as in 1, you may summarize all of one side's arguments and then the other's, then follow this section with all of each side's rebuttals, or you may develop one argument and its counterargument or rebuttal at a time, then move on to the next. Use trial and error to see which approach works best for any particular paper.
   3. Support your analyses and evaluations of lines of argument through citations of sources written by reputable scholars, journalists, or officials, possibly supplemented by primary research (interviews, surveys, experiments, etc.), as well as your own experiences, anecdotes, and reasoning.
III. Conclusion: Offer your balanced judgment on the strong and weak points on opposing sides and indicate which side you think makes the better case, and why.

Drafting and Revising

The next stage is to create a first draft, then a second draft, a third, fourth, and so on, revising and polishing for clarity, conciseness, and continuity until you get it just right. (It has been truly said that every piece of writing is infinitely improvable.) There is, again, no formula here, only a process of trial and error, cutting and pasting, to test what "works" best. Word processing is a godsend to writers, since you can write and store any number of drafts to compare and merge. It's a good idea to get feedback from friends and teachers at any step in this process, to get a second opinion on what works and what doesn't.

Attributing Opinions to Sources

The most frequent form of support in college argumentative papers is the citation of sources. In using citations it is essential to understand the principle of attribution and the value of using formulations like "according to" and "in X's opinion" (this is what journalists call "sourcing"). Suppose you write, "Barack Obama as president wil raise everyone's taxes." This is an assertion of fact that demands evidence in its support. (You could preface your assertion by saying "In my opinion," but if you present no evidence to support that opinion, it isn't going to persuade anybody.) On the other hand, if you write, "According to John McCain, Barack Obama as president . . . ," it is easy to verify the fact that McCain said this, through his Web page or other sources, and then the burden of proof for the statement's truth is on McCain, not you. A handy principle to learn, to avoid getting graded down for writing unsupported assertions, is to prune your own opinions from your papers and substitute a summary of the opinions of your sources. Of course, the mere fact that a source asserts an opinion does not make it any more valid in itself than your own unsupported opinion. To be sure, the opinion of an expert on the subject carries more weight than that of a novice, but experts too need to support their opinions, and you need to evaluate their support.

Phrasing your arguments mainly as summaries of opposing sides' arguments also enables you to reach a conclusion that is adequately qualified but not completely wishy-washy—for example, by phrasing the issue of whether Obama would raise taxes on everyone not as your own opinion, but as your reasoned evaluation of McCain's support for the claim that Obama would.

Continuity, Transitions, Connections

The effective "flow" of a paper depends on continuity, the skill of leading readers smoothly from one sentence, paragraph, or section to the next, without leaving them puzzling over how you got from here to there. Transitional phrases, including conjunctive adverbs (those grammatically joining two ideas) are useful tools here: "as a result," "for example," "however," "consequently," "nevertheless." Here is part of the main body of a student paper summarizing the case that American economic policies in the late 1970s and 1980s increased the gap between the rich, the middle class, and the poor. The previous paragraph ended with data about the growing gap in individual income and wealth during this period. This paragraph, which begins with a transitional sentence, will develop the argument by showing some of the consequences for public policies and institutions:

> More importantly than the growing gap in personal wealth, these policies had destructive consequences for institutions like public schools that serve the needs of the poor and middle class more than those of the rich, who can afford to send their children to private schools. For example, in California, the funding cuts resulting from the passage of Proposition 13, the 1978 initiative putting a lid on property taxes, led to

the decline of the state to forty-third nationally in education spending; according to a column by Brent Staples in *The New York Times* in 1998, California now spends about $30,000 less per classroom per year than the national average.

Another important element of continuity, which reflects a key critical thinking skill, is being able to connect two ideas, sets of data, or sources to support the same point. Elsewhere in the paper quoted above, the student connects two sources that make complementary points:

> A letter to *The New York Times* criticizing high-priced "skyboxes" in a new, tax-subsidized sports stadium, argues, "New York's taxpayers will be paying twice for those seats—once when they are constructed and a second time when they are occupied," because they are frequently purchased for clients by businesses who then write off the entire evening from their taxes as a business deduction. How do such outrageous policies come about? An answer is suggested, concerning a host of similar subsidies for the rich on the national level, by Donald Barlett and James Steele in their book *America: What Went Wrong?*: "For this, you can thank the people in Washington—a succession of Congress and presidents, administrators and regulators, Democrats and Republicans, who write the government rule book, the accumulation of laws and regulations that provide the framework for the country's economy. As might be expected, some people profit handsomely from the rule books."

More About Introductions and Conclusions

Student writers often get stuck in starting to write a paper because they think that they have to have decided exactly what they are going to say from beginning to end. Here is a professional tip for overcoming writer's block in introductions: there is no law saying that you have to write a paper in linear progression from introduction through main body to conclusion; no one but you will know what sequence led you to the final version. When you have gathered your notes and made a broad outline, there will probably be some points that you're more ready to write about than others; simply start writing whatever section you're most ready for, then work backward and forward from there adding others. In any case, don't even try to write the introduction before you have completed the main body. Once you know what you will be saying, you can calibrate the introduction to lead most economically into the main body.

The exact nature of introductions and conclusions will vary according to the length of the paper. In a long paper, say, twenty pages or more, and especially in a book-length manuscript, it may be worthwhile to use the introduction to outline the points you will be making, and to use the conclusion to summarize them, helping the reader synthesize a complex, extended line of argument. In a paper of ten pages or less, this kind of summary may be redundant. Many students seem to have had English teachers who instructed them to preview in the introduction everything they are going to say, then to repeat it again in the conclusion. This is another recipe for dullness, as is the kind of vague, generalizing introduction that begins something like, "Throughout history, people have disagreed about the distribution of wealth in society" and the equally platitudinous kind of conclusion that goes, "Everybody has his own opinion about ...."

If you have been taught to write this kind of introduction and conclusion, please try to forget it and instead keep these principles in mind: *never labor the obvious, and never repeat points except for needed clarification.* Do not tell your readers anything that they probably know and agree with already; do not make any generalizations beyond the level of the specific issues you are addressing. In the introduction to any paper of ten pages or less, lead readers as quickly and directly as possible to your specific topic and thesis, with only the minimum of background information to enable them to follow your argument. In your conclusion, do not repeat anything you have said previously, unless it needs special emphasis, but add something new by way of a judgment on the ideas and sources you have presented, such as a balance of the strong and weak points you have found in the opposing sides. The many newspaper and magazine op-ed columns, running 700–900 words, throughout this book provide good models of introductions and conclusions that get in and out of the subject in a rapid, lively manner.

It often *is* a good idea, however, to grab the reader's interest at the beginning and to end on an original note in the conclusion by interjecting a personal touch, in an observation (possibly humorous if the subject warrants it), an anecdote, an experience, or a pertinent allusion to or quotation from a song, movie, fictional work, poem, TV show, or the like.

POSTWRITING

Proofreading and Polishing

If worrying about sentence and paragraph structure, spelling, punctuation, and grammar distracts you from the content of your writing, don't even think about them until you have finished a semifinal draft. Then tighten up your sentences, paragraphs, and transitions and proofread several times, very carefully, first sentence by sentence, then continuously through the entire paper to get a sense of it as a whole. Print out the paper and spread the pages out so you can see as many as possible at once; doing this will help you catch unnecessary repetitions, identify things you may have left out, and devise possible improvements in organization.

This is the time to use your dictionary and grammar book or whatever checklists your instructor has provided. Some students erroneously believe that the better a writer you are, the less you need to use the dictionary and other reference books. Just the opposite is true. Most professional journalists and other writers keep their reference books close at hand and check them several times every day, using the dictionary both for spelling and for meaning. Another error that recent students have fallen into is to believe that the computer's spelling and grammar checks provide a substitute for learning rules of spelling and grammar. Spelling and grammar form part of the complex, organic system of a written language (as opposed to a spoken dialect, such as black English, whose rules, though internally consistent and functional, follow a different system from those of standard written English), and you need to learn them in order to develop a grasp of the system as a whole.

Only after you have used your own knowledge and looked up every possible error you see in reference materials should you use your computer's spell check and grammar check to catch points you overlooked. Do not rely on computer checks, because they miss as much as they catch, and— lacking a human sense of variable contexts—will sometimes misadvise you.

Reading Aloud

Here is another pointer that can dramatically improve your writing. Get in the habit of reading aloud everything you write. Read it several times over, so that it sounds as much as possible like your natural speaking voice; read as you are composing each sentence, then read the entire paper as though you were presenting it before an audience. Doing this is guaranteed to improve your sentence rhythms and structure, to enable you to catch words accidentally left out or put in, and to help you spot gross misspellings, since spelling in general corresponds to the sound of spoken words.

Table 5.1. Levels of Education of Audiences and Credibility in Sources of Information That Might Be Used as Research Resources

	Books	Periodicals
High School	Best-sellers, checkout stands	Most mass circulation newspapers and magazines
College	Serious journalistic books, government documents	Journals of opinion: *NY Times, LA Times, Washington Post, Washington Times, Wall Street Journal* & their book reviews
	Guides: *Books in Print* Library of Congress Catalog Online subject indexes	Guide: *Reader's Guide to Periodical Literature;* Infotrack
Scholarly and Professional	University press books Government and research institute reports	Scholarly, professional journals Guides: Indexes and abstracts, *New York Review; Chronicle of Higher Education*

LOCATING AND EVALUATING SOURCES

Table 5.1 indicates three broad levels of possible sources of information for the kind of critical writing you will be doing for college courses. The levels refer to presumed levels of education in target audiences: high school graduate or below, college student or graduate, and scholarly and professional.

High School Level

Most mass-circulation newspapers, magazines (tabloids, *Readers Digest, People,* and so on), and nonfiction books on current events, such as those you find at checkout stands, seek to maximize profits by appealing to the widest possible audience, which they calculate to be at a tenth-grade or lower level of reading ability and attention span; most commercial television and radio programs aim at an even lower level. Such media tend to be of dubious credibility because they operate under the pressure of speedy production, sensationalistic appeal, oversimplification of issues to fit abbreviated spaces or "sound bites," and skimpy documentation, so they are not always scrupulous about checking the accuracy of what they print or broadcast. The history of these media over the past century in America includes moguls like William Randolph Hearst, Joseph Pulitzer, and Henry Luce (founder of *Time, Life,* and *Fortune*), who competed in irresponsible sensationalism and use of their media to advance their own political agendas (usually conservative) and business interests. Since the 1950s, many of these media have become more responsible, hiring professionally educated editors and writers and becoming somewhat more concerned with factuality—but the remnants of the earlier age are still widespread.

This is not to say that you should avoid these sources or should never cite them in college papers. They can be quite useful for suggesting topics for further study, lines of argument, and particular viewpoints (found especially in opinion sections). You just need to be wary of accepting their factual assertions without question and try to verify them through more reliable sources.

College Level

The most frequent kind of sources for college papers is to be found in media at the next higher level of literacy and credibility—close to that of college students and graduates with a grounding in general education—in periodicals, the contemporary weekly newsmagazines

Time, Newsweek, and *US News and World Report,* as well as newspapers that have national circulation and influence—most prominently the *New York Times,* the *Washington Post,* the *Wall Street Journal,* the *Washington Times,* the *Los Angeles Times,* the *Christian Science Monitor,* and a few others in large metropolitan centers. These publications hire fact-checkers and are committed to factual accuracy, in principle though not always in practice.

These newspapers also publish daily book reviews and full Sunday book-review supplements on new fiction and nonfiction books. Their reviews of books on current events, history, and other topics studied in general education courses should be regular reading for college students and graduates. Most serious readers read a lot more reviews than actual books, and reading reviews is an excellent way to build your general store of knowledge; a review also can tell you at a glance whether the book is likely to be useful for your current studies, and you might want to cite reviewers' comments and passages they quote or paraphrase from the book itself.

In magazines, the comparable level—a step above that of the newsweeklies—is what are termed "journals of opinion," several of which are included in chapter 13, appendix 1; these are weeklies, biweeklies, monthlies, or quarterlies that generally express, more openly than do most newspapers and newsmagazines, the viewpoint of owners, editors, and their target audiences, who usually are highly educated, and of writers. The writers are generally at a higher level of professionalism than in the mass media and are expected to base their stories on verifiable research; scholars often also write for these journals, adapting their academic studies for a broader readership. Most of the journals operate at a loss, having little and low-revenue advertising and small circulation (they are subsidized by wealthy individual owners and by subscribers and donors), but some of them exert a great deal of influence because they are read by well-informed insiders in politics, the professions, and the intellectual and artistic world. Their "back of the book" sections contain authoritative reviews of current books, films, and other arts, and these reviews can be very influential in the reception of these works. The major journals of opinion can be found at better newsstands and bookstores or are available at reasonable cost by subscription; many of them now have Web sites that contain the full text or synopses of recent issues. Most are indexed by subject and title of articles in *Readers' Guide to Periodical Literature* and comparable electronic versions like FirstSearch, CARL, and JSTOR.

The comparable level of books includes those by responsible journalists who scrupulously research and document their reports on current events and who are less concerned with writing sensational best sellers than with the honest pursuit of truth; prepublication excerpts from their books are regularly published in the newsweeklies or journals of opinion. Documentation in such books falls somewhere between that in mass-circulation books and that in scholarly books; they contain varying degrees of "light" or "heavy" footnoting or other means of citing sources. The counterparts at this level in TV and radio are the Public Broadcasting System (PBS), National Public Radio (NPR), Pacifica Radio, and other noncommercial media, along with some commercial "magazine" programs based on investigative reporting like *60 Minutes* and *Nightline.*

Although sources at this level are generally more trustworthy than those in mass commercial media, they cannot be assumed always to be accurate. There are often lapses, and several scandals have occurred in recent years involving writers' faking or bungling their research.

Scholarly and Professional Level

This is the level of books, reports, and periodicals that is essential to in-depth, advanced research papers in undergraduate or graduate courses and dissertations. Most books here are published by university presses, which (at least until recent years, when the larger presses have become more commercial) are not operated as profit-making enterprises but are subsidized by universities for the propagation of research by faculties. They can be expected to contain the most thoroughly conducted and documented research, as can monographs (long articles published in pamphlet form) and book-length reports published by scholarly organizations, research institutes, or government agencies.

In periodicals here, there are many thousands of scholarly and professional journals, on every subject from feedlot management to gay and lesbian studies, which are usually available only in libraries or by subscription (although some are now accessible on the Internet). Articles in these journals are indexed in reference volumes, similar to *Readers' Guide to Periodical Literature,* for each academic discipline and subjects within the discipline; in many cases, there are also companion volumes of abstracts—brief summaries of each article's contents, which can tell you whether the article might be useful to you.

Two periodicals aimed at a readership of professors, graduate students, and other intellectuals—the *New York Review of Books* and the *Chronicle of Higher Education*—are not recommended as regular reading for most college students, but they do contain many articles that can provide excellent source material for college papers. The biweekly *New York Review* carries long reviews that typically survey several books, along with opinion articles and excerpts from forthcoming books on a wide range of current controversies, with solid documentation. It also carries long exchanges of letters to the editor that provide a lively model of intellectual polemics. The weekly *Chronicle* is the major newspaper of the academic world (on both scholarly and institutional matters), and its news reports, opinion columns, and letters are often good sources for student research and argumentative papers.

The only broadcast media on this level, unfortunately, are some university-affiliated local FM radio and public TV stations and C-SPAN on national TV, which regularly broadcasts academic conferences and lectures that can be quite useful for students (see http://C-SPAN.org *for schedules*). Scholarly and professional experts do, however, turn up fairly often as "talking heads" on news and interview programs, especially on public radio and television.

Political Viewpoints in Sources

One more important variable in sources is their explicit or implicit political viewpoint. Please refer to appendix 1, "Political Viewpoints in Sources," in chapter 13 for a survey of these viewpoints in book publishers, general-circulation periodicals, and research institutes or "think tanks." Also see the lists of resources identified by viewpoint in chapter 18.

A MODEL OF THE WRITING PROCESS IN A STUDENT PAPER

The approach outlined in this chapter is illustrated in the following sequence coming out of an assignment to write a paper of about five pages, or 1,200–1,500 words, analyzing the opposing views in the chapters from Naomi Wolf's book *The Beauty Myth* and Christina Hoff Sommers's *Who Stole Feminism?* later in this chapter. (Reading those selections first will help you follow this sequence.)

First Draft

Susan Brooks wrote the following first draft.

MAKE-UP VEILS
Susan Brooks

> "I was in a land where men forced women to hide their facial features, and here in the West it's just the same but they're using make-up veils"
>
> —Andy Partridge, XTC

Feminism is a controversial issue that women have faced in the twentieth century. How extreme is it? Who is to blame? Do women take the blame, or are the media and men to blame? These questions are broad and diverse, and have been addressed by many individuals. It is difficult to determine which author's opinions are to be believed on this subject.

Naomi Wolf, author of *The Beauty Myth: How Images of Beauty Are Used Against Women,* believes that as women shifted from the primary roles of wife, mother and housekeeper, the advertising giants needed to shift their focus from "housework guilt" to "beauty guilt" to sustain their profits. Thus the Beauty Myth was born.

Wolf says that advertising revenues diminished once women joined the workforce. So the media and advertisers figured they had to convince women to spend more money to look beautiful. The advertising giants have created a problem that was non-existent before. Their focus had shifted from maintaining a perfect household to maintaining beauty and youth. "Somehow, somewhere, someone must have figured out that they will buy more things if they are kept in the self-hating, ever failing, hungry and sexually insecure state of being aspiring 'beauties'" (66). Fortunately, younger women are acknowledging the manipulation by the media and are questioning women's responses to such advertising.

Christina Hoff Sommers, author of *Who Stole Feminism?: How Women Have Betrayed Women,* does not agree that women are being manipulated by advertising or by themselves. She believes that there is much more to feminism than just appearances.

A common issue brought up on this subject is the influence advertisers and businesses have on women. It is believed that companies are constantly trying to create a new product desirable by women, which promises them they will be beautiful and fit the stereotype illustrated in the magazines. Millions of dollars are spent on hair styles, make-up, and clothing, and accessories, not to mention the eating disorders that are a health risk. Money is spent on developing newer products or better hairstyles resulting in more consumer spending. Only one side in this scenario is smiling, and that is of the advertising industry. "Today, business wants even more desperately to seduce.... It wants to demolish resistance" (Wolf 79).

Sommers' chapter "The Backlash Myth" refutes the theories of the Beauty Myth. She questions the validity of theories and research studies noted by Wolf and by Susan Faludi. She thinks that Wolf and Faludi are sensationalists with a radical-leftist agenda and an anti-male, anti-capitalist bias, who try to alarm us with exaggerated (and factually inaccurate) accounts of a backlash against women's gains, and she charges that such radical feminists have gained a stranglehold on women's studies programs in universities and elsewhere. Sommers contacted research sources and refutes Wolf's claim that attractive women "compare themselves only to models, not to other women" (Sommers 233). Women possessing the need to be beautiful can't be blamed on just the advertising agencies. "Peer beauty qualified as a more appropriate standard for social comparison than professional beauty" (Sommers 233).

Sommers also does not agree that women are being manipulated by advertising, or that they make themselves unhappy or sick trying to look like fashion models:

> Much of the support Wolf brings for her beauty-myth theory consists of merely labeling an activity insidious rather than showing it to be so—exercising, dieting, and buying Lancome products at the cosmetics counter in Bloomingdale's all come under attack.

> Characterizing Weight Watchers as a cult does not constitute evidence that it is one. In her zeal to construe every effort of American women to lose weight as a symptom of a male-induced anxiety, she overlooks the fact that many people—men as well as women—suffer from obesity and are threatened by diseases that do not affect people who are fit. Stressing the importance of diet and fitness can hardly be considered as an insidious attempt by the male establishment to disempower women. (234)
>
> I definitely agree with Sommers here. What's wrong with wanting to be healthy, well-toned, and attractive looking? And nobody forces me to wear make-up, starve myself, work out or shop til I drop. Although all the research Wolf cites may not support her theory, I do believe that many women in our society are obsessed with youth, beauty, and thinness. But women are not all naïve and many recognize the subtle manipulation by the media that Wolf describes, and are not taken in.

Peer Editing

Susan's draft was then discussed in a peer editing session, in which two classmates, who had been studying the topics and terminology in this chapter and the rest of *Reading and Writing for Civic Literacy,* first read and wrote comments on her paper. One student's notes are reproduced on pages 110–113. A transcript of the discussion follows.

Class Discussion

Lachelle: I think you make some really good points in your paper, Susan. I like the song you quote at the beginning, and the title. But your introductory paragraph is too vague to tell me where you're going in the rest of the paper, and then I have a hard time following your line of argument after that. It doesn't look like you worked from a clear outline.

Susan: You're right, I really wasn't very confident about where I was going, so was just winging it. I'll write an outline before revising it.

Lachelle: For example, you sort of assume the reader is familiar with both Wolf's and Sommers's books, so you make a lot of references to them that no one would understand without looking back over the texts.

Roberto: I agree with Lachelle about that. You jump into the middle of the authors' arguments without taking the audience along with you, and back and forth between the two books. Sometimes I can't figure out when you're expressing your own opinion and when you're attributing an opinion to Wolf or Sommers—and there are a couple spots where you seem to attribute something to Sommers when she's quoting somebody else.

Lachelle: Yeah. What I'd like to see is a fuller summary at the beginning of your paper of Wolf's main arguments and Sommers's rebuttals, then develop it from there.

You could also say something about where the two writers are coming from politically, where there's a pretty clear opposition between Wolf as a liberal and Sommers as a conservative. Don't you sort of need to explain where conservatives and liberals are opposed on feminism?

Susan: OK, I can add that from our class discussion about this.

Roberto: Another point that I thought was unclear was your conclusion paragraph. I can't tell whether you're agreeing with Wolf or Sommers.

Lachelle: Right, your last sentence is sort of wishy-washy: "But women are not all naïve and many recognize the subtle manipulation by the media that Wolf describes, and are not taken in." Is this just your opinion, or can you back it up with evidence? Maybe you could do a survey of women at our college. Even if you're right, though, this seems to take any blame away from the media, and Wolf's main aim is to criticize the media—and the corporations they advertise for—because they spend such a huge amount of money and energy *trying* to manipulate women. Sommers tries to take the corporations and media off the hook.

Susan: I *was* sort of faking it in the conclusion, cause I wasn't really clear on the disagreements between Wolf and Sommers, or where I stood, because I've never thought much about these arguments before.

Roberto: I think a really important point that you could say more about, is when Sommers says Wolf has this conspiracy theory that a bunch of men get together and plan how to hypnotize millions of women into buying beauty products, and then women internalize these images to make themselves miserable. Sommers says Wolf doesn't really have any evidence to prove that this conspiracy exists, and that it insults women's intelligence to imply that they've been turned into robotic "Stepford Wives"—which I agree with.

Susan: Right, I should say more about that, 'cause I agree with Sommers too.

Lachelle: Whoa, hold on a minute. I don't think Sommers presents a fair account of Wolf's case. What Wolf says is, there doesn't *have* to be a conspiracy, in the literal sense. All she says is that corporations always try to maximize their profits, and manufacturers, advertising agencies, and media have done a lot of market research that shows there's megaprofits to be made from keeping women in constant anxiety about their faces, their weight, their clothes, their hair, their age—through comparing themselves to those freakishly thin, gorgeous models that are on every magazine cover and in every commercial. Plus those models are nearly all Caucasian, because the advertisers figure that it's upscale white women who have the most money to spend on beauty products. It's really humiliating to women of color to always see white women set up as the norm. Can anyone deny all this? Or that guys are equally programmed to go after women who look like these ideal beauties? Wolf also says that feminists have opposed the beauty myth in favor of a better-rounded (and less expensive) self-image for women, and so the manufacturers and media have a bias against feminism because it threatens their profits. That's a sensible theory, isn't it? And Wolf supports the theory with research studies that manufacturers and the media themselves have conducted.

Roberto: Yeah, but Sommers nails Wolf with misrepresenting two studies—the one, I think it was at Old Dominion University, and the other one—which you don't talk about, but should—was on the number of women who die from anorexia, where her figures are way off. If Wolf is that sneaky about these cases, it makes you doubt her overall reliability.

Lachelle: OK, I concede that Sommers catches Wolf in getting those two studies wrong, and that really weakens her case. If there were a lot of other inaccuracies in her book, that would totally shoot down her credibility. But she presents a lot more evidence, on much more central issues, so I'd say these two errors could be honest slip-ups and an inadequate sampling of Wolf's credibility, which Sommers uses to evade Wolf's most solid arguments and evidence. It just seems to me from my own experience, and most of the other girls and women I know, that Wolf's basic argument makes sense, that the beauty industry does play on our insecurities because their profits depend on it, so it's a reasonable inference that they've intentionally calculated how to do this. As far as reliability of evidence is concerned, how do we know that *Sommers's* documentation is accurate? Wouldn't we need to check with the source of the Old Dominion study to make sure what she claims is accurate?

Susan: Good point. Maybe I'll say something like that in my revision. Getting back to what Roberto said, though, I agree that women aren't just helpless dupes of the media, with no mind or will of their own to resist the beauty myth if they choose. Nobody forces me to wear make-up or work out or buy brand-name fashions.

Lachelle: But this gets into the whole issue of cultural conditioning. If the media have been trying to program us, from the day we're born, into a certain set of attitudes—say, about looks, weight, or fashions—how can we say for sure that the choices we think we make freely haven't really been conditioned? Sommers never really addresses that argument. For example, look at the increase in eating disorders in girls and women that Wolf discusses. She may have her statistics wrong, but who *doesn't* know at least one girl or woman who is anorexic or bulimic? Isn't it pretty obvious that this was largely the result of conditioning by the media to worship thinness? Or look at the way students all wear brand-name clothes, with their logos prominently displayed—where does everyone get the idea to do that?

Roberto: Yeah, but it isn't just the media that causes us to conform. There's also peer pressure—which is what Sommers said that study at Old Dominion showed.

Lachelle: So what do you think causes the peer pressure? Doesn't it come mainly from the media? That's a perfect example of a vicious circle.

Roberto: Maybe so, but as Sommers says, the main reason people diet and work out is not that they're conforming, but that it makes them healthier. What's wrong with that, or with wanting to look your best? That's true of everyone, men as well as women.

Lachelle: I don't think Wolf disagrees with any of that. Sommers is just attacking a straw man—or straw feminist—if she puts those words in Wolf's mouth. Wolf's point is that these healthy impulses have been pushed to destructive extremes by the beauty industry, just because they have constantly increasing investments, billions of dollars, that depend on hyping the sales of these products. Sommers totally downplays that argument and evades this issue, and I think that may be partly because her own work is subsidized by conservative foundations funded by big corporations, which she says in her own acknowledgments at the beginning of her book.

Roberto: Isn't there pressure on men too to wear brand names, work out and diet so they'll look like Brad Pitt? And don't sports in the media present the same kinds of idols for men that fashion models do for women? Why doesn't Wolf criticize that?

Lachelle: Well, I think Wolf would agree that the media manipulate men as well as women, and she'd say two wrongs don't make a right. But do you really think there's as much emphasis on men's looks as women's in the media? Gimme a break! Look at TV commercials, or the magazine covers at any supermarket check-out stand, and compare the proportion of women's and men's pictures, and whether they're shown for their looks or their accomplishments.

Roberto: That would be a good topic for a research paper project, just to count the number of images of women and men on magazine covers and commercials, and how many are shown for looks versus accomplishments.

Susan: Wow, those are all pretty complicated questions to get into a four- or five-page paper. Maybe I can just raise some of these points briefly at the end, to leave the conclusion sort of open-ended. Anyway, thanks to both of you for your suggestions. This has given me a lot more ideas for topics to talk about and how to pull the paper together. Now I feel like I have more ideas than I can even fit into a five page paper, so I'll have to cut instead of padding!

MAKE-UP VEILS

Susan Brooks

[handwritten: Great title and quote!]

"I was in a land where men forced women to hide their facial features, and here in the West it's just the same but they're using make-up veils"—Andy Partridge, XTC

[handwritten: pretty vague intro ¶. Why not begin with this point in specific reference to Wolf & Sommers]

Feminism is a controversial issue that women have faced in the twentieth century. How extreme is it? *[handwritten: feminism? — for what?]* Who is to blame? Do women take the blame, or are the media and men to blame? *[handwritten: for feminism?]* These questions are broad and diverse, and have been addressed by many individuals. It is difficult to determine which author's opinions are to be believed on this subject.

[handwritten: When did this shift occur?]

Naomi Wolf, author of The Beauty Myth: How Images of Women Are Used Against Women, believes that as women shifted from the primary roles of wife, mother and housekeeper, the advertising giants needed to shift their focus from "housework guilt" to "beauty guilt" to sustain their profits. Thus the Beauty Myth was born.

[handwritten: no ¶?]

[handwritten: Good summary]

Wolf says that advertising revenues diminished once women joined the workforce. So the media and advertisers figured they had to convince women to spend more money to look beautiful. The advertising giants have created a problem that was non-existent before. Their focus had shifted from maintaining a perfect household to maintaining beauty and youth.

2

"Somehow, somewhere, someone must have figured out that they will buy more things if they are kept in the self-hating, ever failing, hungry and sexually insecure state of being aspiring `beauties'" (66).

[handwritten: Save this point for the conclusion]

Fortunately, younger women are acknowledging the manipulation by the media and are questioning women's responses to such advertising.

Christina Hoff Sommers, author of <u>Who Stole Feminism?: How Women Have Betrayed Women</u>, does not agree that women are being manipulated by advertising or by themselves. She believes that <u>there is much more to feminism</u> than just appearances.

Explain that S's book is a response to W's

A common issue <u>brought up on this subject</u> is the influence advertisers and businesses have on women. ~~It is believed~~ Wolf believes that companies are constantly trying to create a new product desirable by women,

by whom?

See next page for comment

You seem to jump from Sommers' book back to Wolf here. And doesn't this repeat the ¶ before the previous one? Why not cut this one and then continue with Sommers? That would give you more space to get into other issues.

which promises them they will be beautiful and fit the stereotype illustrated in the magazines. Millions of dollars are spent on hair styles, make-up, and clothing, and accessories, not to mention the eating disorders that are a health risk. Money is spent on developing newer products or better hairstyles resulting in more consumer spending. Only one side in this scenario is smiling, and that is of the advertising industry. "Today, business wants even more desperately to seduce. . . . It wants to demolish resistance" (Wolf, 79).

3

Sommers' chapter "The Backlash Myth" refutes the theories of the Beauty Myth. She questions the validity of theories and research studies noted by Wolf and by Susan Faludi. She thinks that Wolf and Faludi are sensationalists with a radical-leftist agenda and an anti-male, anti-capitalist bias, who try to alarm us with exaggerated (and factually inaccurate) accounts of a backlash against women's gains, and she charges that such radical feminists have gained a stranglehold on women's studies programs in universities and elsewhere. Sommers contacted research sources and refutes Wolf's claim that attractive women "compare themselves only to

Explain who she is and S's reference to her book Backlash

Good summary

this sentence unclear. Give some details about this research models, not to other women" (Sommers, 233). Women possessing the need to be beautiful can't be blamed on just the advertising agencies. "Peer beauty qualified as a more appropriate standard for social comparison than professional beauty" (Sommers, 233).

your opinion or S's?

S doesn't say this herself. She's quoting someone else. Explain this, and use quotes within quotes " 'Peer... ' "

Sommers also does not agree that women ~~are being manipulated by advertising, or that they~~ make themselves unhappy or sick trying to look like fashion models:

> Much of the support Wolf brings for her beauty-myth theory consists of merely labeling an activity insidious rather than showing it to be so—exercising, dieting, and buying Lancome

4

> products at the cosmetics counter in Bloomingdale's all come under attack. Characterizing Weight Watchers as a cult does not constitute evidence that it is one. In her zeal to construe every effort of American women to lose weight as a symptom of a male-induced anxiety, she overlooks the fact that many people—men as well as women—suffer from obesity and are threatened by diseases that do not affect people who are fit. Stressing the importance of diet and fitness can hardly be considered as an insidious attempt by the male establishment to disempower women. (234)

nice quote

I definitely agree with Sommers here. What's wrong with wanting to be healthy, well-toned, and attractive looking? And nobody forces me to wear make-up, starve myself, work out or shop til I drop. Although all the research Wolf cites may not support her theory, I do believe that many women in our society are obsessed with youth, beauty, and thinness. But women are not all naïve and many

Who are you agreeing with W or S?

```
recognize the subtle manipulation by the media that

Wolf describes, and are not taken in.
```

Don't a lot of us recognize this manipulation but still let ourselves be taken in, and go along with fashions, dieting, etc?

Susan's Outline for Revision

I. Introduction: Difficulty of sorting out the truth in opposing sources, illustrated by Wolf vs. Sommers

II. Main Body
  A. Summary of Wolf's arguments
      1. Changes in marketing after World War II from housekeeping to beauty
      2. Feminism in sixties posed a threat to beauty myth
      3. In backlash against feminism, corporations intensified selling of beauty
      4. Beauty myth handicaps women's equality with men
  B. Sommers
      1. Note political viewpoint of Sommers vs. Wolf: Wolf a liberal Democrat, Sommers says she's also a feminist and not a Republican, but associated with conservative foundations and publisher, and she thinks Wolf's and Susan Faludi's variety of feminism is sensationalistic and dogmatic.
      2. Sommers' rebuttals of Wolf and Faludi
          a. Inaccuracies in their research (S's strongest argument)
              1. Old Dominion study showed women don't compare themselves to media images, as Wolf claims
              2. Wolf confuses number of anorexia sufferers with number of deaths
          b. Sommers says Wolf has conspiracy theory, but Wolf says there's no conspiracy, only a common drive for profits by corporations
          c. Sommers says there's nothing wrong with wanting to be healthy and to look good.
              1. I agree, but W's defenders would say she does too, and is only criticizing excesses, like anorexia
              2. S downplays Wolf's criticisms of the beauty industry and its power to get inside our heads, even when we think we know they're trying to manipulate us. Are we really free to "take it or leave it" when we've been conditioned into the beauty myth every day of our lives?

III. Conclusion
  A. It's a draw between W and S, who are both skillful writers and rhetoricians. More research is needed to judge between the two
  B. Studying this subject has made me question the source of my own attitudes toward beauty, and made me more aware of how much everyone's attitudes are influenced by cultural conditioning and what side they're on politically

Revised Draft

Make-Up Veils (Revision)
Susan Brooks

"I was in a land where men forced women to hide their facial features, and here in the West it's just the same but they're using make-up veils"—Andy Partridge, XTC

In public controversies, it can be very difficult to know who you can believe amid a variety of viewpoints in sources that totally contradict each other. I found this out in reading the book *The Beauty Myth: How Images of Beauty Are Used Against Women,* by Naomi Wolf (published in 1991) and a rebuttal to it in another book, *Who Stole Feminism?: How Women Have Betrayed Women,* by Christina Hoff Sommers, published in 1994, which includes a chapter titled "The Backlash Myth," aimed at Wolf and Susan Faludi, author of *Backlash: The Undeclared War Against American Women.*

Wolf argues that in recent decades the "beauty industry" has tried to brainwash women into living up to totally unrealistic models of cosmetic glamour, thinness, and youth. Wolf's thesis is that up to World War II, marketing, advertising, and media content for women manipulated insecurities about being a good housewife. As modern technology took a lot of the drudgery out of childrearing and housekeeping, manufacturers and the media shifted to beauty products. At the same time, in the sixties, a revival of feminism was fighting for women's equality with men in education and jobs, and feminists rejected the excessive emphasis that the media were putting on beauty. Wolf claims that women's economic equality and the rejection of the beauty myth posed a threat to men in power, while manufacturers, advertisers, and the media (also dominated by men) feared that they would lose billions of dollars in profits if the sales of beauty products declined. So Wolf says there has been a backlash against feminism, which has involved a campaign to convince women that they need to spend ever more money, time, and fretting to make themselves beautiful and thin—on top of working at jobs and being wives and mothers. "Somehow, somewhere, someone must have figured out that they [women] will buy more things if they are kept in the self-hating, ever-failing, hungry, and sexually insecure state of being aspiring 'beauties'" (66). This drain on women's time, money, and psyche creates a handicap for women against men, who are not judged as much on looks and so are able to devote more of their energy to professional achievement, instead of to makingup, dressing up, doing their hair, shopping, and starving themselves.

I found all of Wolf's arguments very persuasive—until I read Sommers' refutation of them. There is an interesting political issue going on "between the lines" in Wolf vs. Sommers. Wolf, a free-lance journalist, is well-known as a feminist, a liberal, and a Democratic Party activist, who has been an advisor to Hillary Clinton (the feminists' heroine!) and Al Gore. Sommers, a philosophy professor at Clark University, does not come out and say she is a conservative. She insists that she too is a feminist, and a member of the Democratic Party, which is more identified with feminist causes than the Republicans, who tend to support more traditional gender roles (128). Her position is more conservative than Wolf's, though, in that she believes women have made great advances in American society, to the point where they are nearly equal to men. She believes some feminists like Wolf and Faludi are sensationalists with a radical-leftist agenda and an anti-male, anti-capitalist bias, who try to alarm us with exaggerated (and factually inaccurate) accounts of a backlash against women's gains, and she charges that such radical feminists have gained tyrannical control over women's studies in universities and elsewhere. Sommers does say in her book's acknowledgments that her research was funded by the Lynne and Harry Bradley Foundation, the Carthage Foundation, and the John M. Olin Foundation, all conservative institutions allied with large corporations and the Republican Party (8)—so she might have a conflict of interest in defending corporations against Wolf's charges—while Wolf's acknowledgments do not indicate that she had any financial sponsors. Sommers' book was published by Simon and Schuster, which does feature a lot of conservative books, while Wolf's was published by Doubleday and Anchor, which aren't identified with any political viewpoint.

Sommers' strongest arguments are the many examples she gives of gross inaccuracies in research by feminists, including Wolf and Faludi. Sommers checked the source of a research study at Old Dominion University, which Wolf claimed showed that women measure themselves more against images of beauty in the media than against their peers, but which Sommers says in fact showed just the opposite (233). Worse yet, according to Sommers, Wolf claimed that about 150,000 American women die of anorexia each year, but when Sommers traced this figure to its alleged source, the American Anorexia and Bulimia Association, she was informed that their figures showed that was the number of *sufferers,* not deaths, which number only somewhere between one hundred and four hundred per year. (Sommers does acknowledge, "The deaths of these young women are a tragedy, certainly" [12].) Sommers says she wrote a letter about this error to Wolf, who promised to correct it in the second edition of her book (Sommers 276). (Wolf must have done this, since I couldn't find the figure in the second edition.) This point really illustrates how important it is for writers to get their facts right. Much of Wolf's documentation and reasoning concerning women's anxieties about their looks, and about eating disorders, seem to be pretty valid (even Sommers acknowledges some of Wolf's basic points), but a few errors like this cast doubt on her credibility and give her political opponents ammunition to discredit everything she says.

Sommers accuses Wolf of having a conspiracy theory that "somewhere in America a group of male 'elders' has sat down to plot ways to perpetuate the subjugation of women" (227). But what Wolf actually says is: "This is not a conspiracy theory; it doesn't have to be" (17). It's just about a common pursuit of profits by many of the world's largest corporations, whose effect is as powerful as a conspiracy.

Sommers further argues:

> Much of the support Wolf brings for her beauty-myth theory consists of merely labeling an activity insidious rather than showing it to be so—exercising, dieting, and buying Lancôme products at the cosmetics counter in Bloomingdale's all come under attack. Characterizing Weight Watchers as a cult does not constitute evidence that it is one. In her zeal to construe every effort of American women to lose weight as a symptom of a male-induced anxiety, she overlooks the fact that many people—men as well as women—suffer from obesity and are threatened by diseases that do not affect people who are fit. Stressing the importance of diet and fitness can hardly be considered as an insidious attempt by the male establishment to disempower women. (234)

I definitely agree with Sommers here. What's wrong with wanting to be healthy, well-toned, and attractive looking? And nobody forces me to wear make-up, starve myself, work out or shop til I drop. Of course, Wolf's defenders might reply that Sommers is attacking a "straw feminist," that Wolf isn't really criticizing a healthy lifestyle or attention to weight and appearance *to a point,* but just criticizing pushing it to an extreme where women who are perfectly healthy and ok-looking are made to feel miserable because they don't match up to Julia Roberts. Don't these media images have a lot to do with the incredible increase in anorexia and bulimia? And Sommers evasively downplays Wolf's sensible theory that manufacturers and the media do have a big investment in constantly selling more beauty products, diet food, gyms and workout equipment, etc.

Wolf's defenders might also question how much we are all really free to "take it or leave it" concerning the images that the media bombard us with. How can I say for sure that the choices I think I make freely haven't been influenced by the media I've been conditioned by every day of my life, or the peer pressures the media create?

I'd call the debate between Wolf and Sommers a draw: both are very skillful writers and rhetoricians, although both let their political partisanship draw them into some fallacious arguments. I'd need to think about and study these arguments a lot more to decide which is right on balance. I do know, though, that studying the pros and cons of this subject has made me question the reasons for my own attitudes about appearance and made me more aware of how much *everyone's* attitudes may be biased by their cultural conditioning and what side they're on politically.

Works Cited

Partridge, Andy (Composer for XTC). "Make-Up Veils." (Recording, no date or place of publication).

Sommers, Christina Hoff. *Who Stole Feminism?: How Women Have Betrayed Women.* New York: Simon & Schuster, 1994.

Wolf, Naomi. *The Beauty Myth: How Images of Beauty Are Used Against Women.* Anchor Books, Revised Edition, 1992.

Topics for Discussion and Writing

Here are the chapters from Naomi Wolf's *The Beauty Myth* and Christina Hoff Sommers's *Who Stole Feminism?* that Susan wrote her paper on. Carry on the debate among yourselves and generate your own papers out of it.

From *The Beauty Myth: How Images of Beauty Are Used Against Women*

Naomi Wolf

Anchor Books, 1992

Preface

It's been a wild year since *The Beauty Myth* was first published in hardcover—a year of

sharp, exhilarated, and sometimes very angry debate about the issues I raised. Before you enter into your own dialogue with the book,

I'd like to lay to rest three fallacies that often got in the way of its actual message.

The first fallacy is that this book is antibeauty. If I could write *The Beauty Myth* again, I'd put the clear conclusion of the argument—that we need to embrace pleasure, choice in adornment, our own real beauty and sexuality, *and* call ourselves feminists—in the first paragraph. There is not a single sentence on a single page in this book that condemns women for the choices that we make about beauty, or suggests that we should not wear makeup if we want to, dress up, or show our bodies. On the contrary: I argue that we deserve the choice to do whatever we want with our faces and bodies without being punished by an ideology that is using attitudes, economic pressure, and even legal judgments regarding women's appearance to undermine us psychologically and politically.

Many such critics—Marcelle Clements in the *New York Times,* for instance, who charged that "My life is complicated and my vision of myself is made up as I go along and it sometimes translates into buying a lipstick or a pair of cowboy boots. Why are you making me feel bad? Give me a break!"; or Betty Friedan, who wrote that "If feminism really meant a war against men—a repudiation of love and beauty and home and children—most women wouldn't want to win it"—seem not to have read it. For I conclude that the enemy is not lipstick, but guilt itself; that we deserve lipstick, if we want it, *and* free speech; we deserve to be sexual *and* serious—or whatever we please; we are entitled to wear cowboy boots to our own revolution. The terrible irony of this frequent misreading of my message is that one damaging aspect of "the beauty myth" as I define it is not makeup—but the disempowering, backlash propaganda that suggests that feminism makes women ugly, or forces women to choose between beauty and liberation. Critics who made this mistake fell victim to the very dynamic of the backlash that I criticize: an antifeminist impulse that invariably seeks—as many TV shows did as well—to pit "The Feminist" against "The Beauty Queen."

A related fallacy is that *The Beauty Myth* objects categorically to images of glamour and beauty in mass culture. Absolutely not.

The harm of these images is not that they exist, but that they proliferate at the expense of most other images and stories of female heroines, role models, villains, eccentrics, buffoons, visionaries, sex goddesses, and pranksters. If the icon of the anorexic fashion model were one flat image out of a full spectrum in which young girls could find a thousand wild and tantalizing visions of possible futures, that icon would not have the power to hurt them; fashion and beauty scenarios would be yet another source of the infinite pleasures and intrigues of life in the female body.

The real issue, if we understand this, is one of censorship and free speech. Beauty advertisers pressure mass culture to populate itself almost entirely with images of the icon; this effectively censors vast pools of American talent. Aspiring actresses, rock singers, writers and TV journalists, comediennes, athletes, and politicians, who might not fit the narrow confines of the icon, are returned to ground by this screening process. American culture is the loser. And we as consumers of mass culture lose out too, as ad pressure forces women's magazines to center readers' anxieties on the scale and the mirror, at the expense of real coverage of the wide world of women.

This double standard for free speech in women's media versus men's is compounded by the double standard for consumer rights. Women deserve real information if we are to make real choices about beauty; but the unspoken loyalty oath advertisers have demanded of editors over the decade of the beauty backlash has brought disastrous consequences.

The charge I made—that mass media aimed at women was not telling the whole truth about the beauty industry because they could not—brought frenzied and hostile denials from editors of magazines on national television. But the evidence keeps growing: The NIH issued a report debunking the dieting industry, the FDA cracked down on cosmetic surgeons for silicone injections, Dow Corning has been accused of concealing evidence of serious medical problems associated with breast implants, and a House Subcommittee is investigating the dangerously unregulated nature of the beauty surgery industry. Women who believed the products and procedures were safe are asking, dismayed, "Why weren't we told?" Again and again, women editors and TV journalists would attack this position and deny ad pressure on the air; but when the lights went down, they would say, "Of course you're right. But I can't say that on camera and keep my job." Women paid the price for this orchestration of silence.

The third fallacy in the debate is that I am constructing a conspiracy theory. As I write in the first chapter: "This is not a conspiracy theory; it doesn't have to be." A backlash against women's advancement does not originate in a smoke-filled room; it is often unconscious and reflexive, like racism. A backlash against feminism that uses an ideology about beauty to keep women down is not an organized conspiracy with maps and pins, but a generalized atmosphere in which men's fears and women's guilt are addressed and elaborated through the culture's images of women, and its messages to women about the relationship between their value and their bodies.

We know that ideals of femininity have sought to control women before: The suffragists of the nineteenth century were faced with the glamorized invalid, and women were driven out of the work force in the 1950s by the glamorized full-time housewife. The beauty myth's backlash image of women does not suddenly appear everywhere in the media as a result of a conspiracy, but as a result of how audience response and mass media interact. Research shows that people will react to those ads, films, and videos that strike their deepest feelings, regardless of whether the images soothe anxiety or provoke it.

Ours is a time when gender roles are contested as never before. At a moment when many women have guilt feelings and uncertainties about their entry into public life, and many men have fears about women's empowerment made all the stronger by the doubled competition during a recession, those images or articles that show women being put, or putting themselves, *back under control* are most likely to get a strong audi-

ence reaction. The savvy editor or marketer knows that a story on the breast implant trend is "sexier" in such a Zeitgeist than a story on the La Leche League; that a series on semistarvation diets is "sexier" than a series on women's health.

A magazine sensitive to the backlash mood does what the *New York Times* did, according to *Working Woman:* For the cover of the Sunday Magazine that profiled Karen Valenstein, one of the first female traders on Wall Street, it chose—out of contact sheets of smiling, pretty shots of this slim blond woman—the one unattractive, unsmiling portrait. This selection was not a conscious effort to portray powerful women in a negative light; but by stirring up women's insecurities while soothing men's fears, this choice simply sold more copies.

The beauty backlash against feminism is no conspiracy, but a million million separate individual reflexes such as that one that coalesce into a national mood weighing women down; the backlash is all the more oppressive because the source of the suffocation is so diffuse as to be almost invisible. The beauty myth is an employer saying to a woman engineer, We can't hire you because you're so pretty you'll keep the men from doing their work. It's a judge ruling that Christine Craft doesn't deserve her job back. It's a journalists' organization ranking Roseanne Barr above Saddam Hussein in a poll for its "Sitting Duck" Awards. It's *Playboy* recruiting from women in the military, women in the Ivy League, women in the Police Department. It's Barbara Walters saying angrily on "20/20" that the charge that there is a double standard for appearance in her profession is "a crock." It's a *People* magazine "health" feature in which a young actress says that she knows it's time to eat when she passes out on the set. It's a male student telling a female classmate that she got a scholarship only because of her looks. It's an anchorwoman losing her job when her laughlines start to show. It's the phrase, "You're too pretty to be a feminist." It's an Alabama judge ruling that he didn't believe Karen Smith had been sexually harassed by her boss because in his opinion the boss's wife was prettier. It's the caption under a newspaper cartoon of Patricia Bowman, the alleged victim in the William Kennedy Smith rape trial: "I liked her better behind the blob." It's congressmen, beaten again this year by a professional women's basketball team, saying, "They're faster. They're younger. And they're prettier." Instead of simply: "They won."

Because I wrote this book as a tribute to women's beauty and power, one of the most difficult parts of the debate was the often angry denial of the problem from women. For a decade, women have had drilled into us the belief that we bear individual responsibility for the social problem of sexism. In such a climate, an analysis that points out just what the pressures on us really are can be upsetting to listen to—precisely because most of us intuit the situation so well.

Those initial impulses of denial are understandable: People most need the mechanism of denial when an intolerable situation has been pointed out to them—but the means for change does not yet exist. Slowly, though, alternatives are becoming imaginable; and as that happens, the response to the message grows steadily warmer. The deep freeze of feminism within the beauty backlash has finally begun to crack and thaw.

The past year not only saw the FDA confront Dow Corning; it also saw Continental service representative Theresa Fischette, fired because she did not wear makeup, fight on national television for her job—and win. American Airlines flight attendants fought discriminatory weight tables—and won. On a hotline staffed by 9 to 5, the working women's organization, looks discrimination surfaced as one of the top three forms of sex discrimination on the job. The Clarence Thomas hearings exposed as a myth the "post-feminist" pretense of a level playing field, and membership in women's organizations jumped. Susan Faludi's *Backlash* added new dimensions as well as validation to my charge that we live in a backlash against women's liberation. *Elle* offered "The shapely, well-fed body of the '90's." A *Glamour* readers' poll showed that women no longer ranked losing weight over success in work or love. And two California cities made appearance discrimination illegal—establishing that

women "don't have to be thin and blonde to do their jobs well."

New evidence came out, adding details to my basic argument: Fashion magazine editors acknowledged at last the existence of the Scitex machine—a computer graphics machine that alters almost every fashion or glamour image we see. Research has found that young women's self-esteem scored measurably lower after they were shown fashion and beauty images than before. And the final piece of the puzzle fell into place: researchers at Wayne State University found that anorexia and bulimia were triggered, in women who had a biochemical predisposition to it, by simple dieting; caloric restriction resulted in biochemical changes in the brain, which addicted women physiologically to anorexia and bulimia.

When asked, What should be done? I've said that it is readers themselves who will write the final chapter of *The Beauty Myth*. And women did so, each one inventing solutions within her own life. Teachers across the country devised anti-anorexia programs for their preadolescent students. College women organized consciousness-raising groups, finding a new introduction to feminism in the discovery that, even if you have reproductive rights, you don't control your body if you cannot eat. Many took up the challenge to dismantle the beauty myth through culture: they made art projects that reimagined the female body and its beauty; they created videos and rap songs, performance art, photography exhibits, and street theater.

For all the controversy surrounding this book, there is one development of the last year that is so heartening that it is like a gift of energy. At the points in *The Beauty Myth* where I addressed my own generation's problematic relationship to feminism, I did so in real darkness. Where were they? Why were they so quiet? A year later, I can say with certainty that I've seen the Third Wave on college campuses and young women's organizations across America, its numbers and commitment swelling every day. A college senior writes in *The Village Voice* about her generation's "Third Wave Feminism"; another student writes in *Ms.*

that "I am not a postfeminist feminist. I am the Third Wave." A national organization of "Third Wave feminists"—updating the feminist agenda for today's young women—has recently been formed. Even William F. Buckley has referred to the Third Wave in the *National Review.*

Finally, in response to the criticism that the beauty myth is not the biggest problem women face today, of course that is true. But the beauty backlash arose specifically to hypnotize women into political paralysis. Therefore, by knowing how to break its spell,

we liberate those occupied territories of our minds and energize ourselves to take up the real fight for women's equality.

As my feminist foremothers taught me, naming a problem has power. Many young women tell me that the connections they were able to make between the beauty myth with its stereotype of "the ugly feminist," and their own fears about calling themselves feminists, allowed them to speak up at last on their own behalf as women. The turbulence of the past year is worth it a thousand times over, when I see it in the light of that gift.

The Backlash Myth

Christina Hoff Sommers

From *Who Stole Feminism?* Simon and Schuster, 1994

Original footnotes and a section have been deleted in this reading.

> When regard for truth has been broken down or even slightly weaned, all things will remain doubtful.—ST. AUGUSTINE

A couple of years ago, American publishing was enlivened by the release of Susan Faludi's *Backlash* and Naomi Wolf's *The Beauty Myth,* two impassioned feminist creeds uncovering and denouncing the schemes that have prevented women from enjoying the fruits of the women's movement. For our purposes, what these books have in common is more interesting and important than what distinguishes them. Both reported a widespread conspiracy against women. In both, the putative conspiracy has the same goal: to prevent today's women from making use of their hard-won freedoms—to punish them, in other words, for liberating themselves. As Ms. Wolf informs us: "After the success of the women's movement's second wave, the beauty myth was perfected to checkmate power at every level in individual women's lives."

Conspiracy theories are always popular, but in this case the authors, writing primarily for middle-class readers, faced a tricky

problem. No reasonable person in this day and age could be expected to believe that somewhere in America a group of male "elders" has sat down to plot ways to perpetuate the subjugation of women. How, then, could they persuade anyone of the existence of a widespread effort to control women for the good of men?

The solution that they hit upon made it possible for them to have their conspiracy while disavowing it. Faludi and Wolf argued that the conspiracy against women is being carried out by malevolent but invisible backlash forces or beauty-myth forces that act in purposeful ways. The forces in question are subtle, powerful, and insidiously efficient, and women are largely unconscious of them. What is more, the primary enforcers of the conspiracy are not a group of sequestered males plotting and planning their next backlash maneuvers: it is women themselves who "internalize" the aims of the backlash, who, unwittingly, do its bidding. In other words, the backlash is Us. Or, as Wolf puts it, "many women internalize Big Brother's eye."

Faludi's scope is wider than Wolf's; she argues that the media and the political system have been co-opted by the backlash, as well:

> The backlash is not a conspiracy, with a council dispatching agents from some central control room, nor are the people who serve its ends often aware of their role; some even consider themselves feminists. For the most part, its workings are encoded and internalized, diffuse and chameleonic ... generated by a culture machine that is always scrounging for a "fresh" angle. Taken as a whole, however, these codes and cajolings, these whispers and threats and myths, move overwhelmingly in one direction: they try to push women back into their "acceptable" roles.

Wolf focuses more narrowly on the "beauty backlash," which pressures women to diet, dress up, make up, and work out in ways that are "destroying women physically and depleting us psychologically." "The beauty backlash against feminism is no conspiracy, but a million separate individual reflexes ... that coalesce into a national mood weighing women down; the backlash is all the more oppressive because the source of the suffocation is so diffuse as to be almost invisible."

Having thus skirted a claim of outright conspiracy, Faludi and Wolf nevertheless freely use the *language* of subterfuge to arouse anger and bitterness. In their systems, the backlash and the beauty myth become malevolent personified forces behind plot after plot against women.

They incite unscrupulous stooges in the media to write articles that make "single and childless women feel like circus freaks." Cosmetics saleswomen are backlash agents, "trained," Wolf says, "with techniques akin to those used by professional cult converters and hypnotists." ...

What the backlash "wants" is clear to both Faludi and Wolf. By the seventies, women had been granted a great deal of equality. The primary aim of the backlash is to retake lost ground, to put women to rout. The subtitle of Faludi's book is *The Undeclared War Against American Women*. *Backlash* itself may be regarded as a feminist counterattack in this supposed war. As Patricia Schroeder noted in a review of the book, women are not "riled up enough," and Faludi "may be able to do what political activists have tried to do for years." Indeed, she and Wolf together succeeded in moving countless women to anger and dismay. ...

Wolf and Faludi tend to portray the "disciplined" and docile women in the grip of the backlash as Stepford wives—helpless, possessed, and robotic. Wolf sometimes speaks of women as victims of "mass hypnosis." "This is not a conspiracy theory," she reminds us. "It doesn't have to be." Faludi explains how the backlash managed to "infiltrate the thoughts of women, broadcasting on these private channels its soundwaves of shame and reproach."

... Faludi and Wolf have appropriated masses of statistics and studies that "consistently show" the workings of the backlash and the beauty myth and their effects on American women. But although their books are massively footnoted, reliable statistical evidence for the backlash hypothesis is in terribly short supply. According to Wolf, "Recent research consistently shows that inside the majority of the West's controlled, attractive, successful working women, there is a secret 'underlife' poisoning our freedom; infused with notions of beauty, it is a dark vein of self-hatred, physical obsessions, terror of aging, and dread of lost control." The research she cites was done in 1983 at Old Dominion University. She claims that the researchers found that attractive women "compare themselves only to models, not to other women," and feel unattractive. This kind of claim is central to Wolf's contention that images of beautiful, willowy women in fashion magazines demoralize real women. In fact, the study she cited suggested the opposite. The Old Dominion researchers compared the self-reports of three groups of college-age women: one group evaluated themselves after looking at photos of fashion models, another group after looking at pictures of unattractive peers, and a third group after looking at pictures of very attractive peers. The researchers were careful not to exaggerate the significance of this small experiment, but they (tentatively) concluded that although reactions to attractive *peers* negatively influenced women's self-evaluation, exposure to the models had no such effect:

> Perhaps in the eyes of most of our subjects, peer beauty qualified as a more appropriate standard for social comparison than professional beauty.... Viewed in a practical sense, our results further suggest that thumbing through popular magazines filled with beautiful models may have little immediate effect on the self-images of most women.

I called the principal author of the study, Thomas Cash, a psychologist at Old Dominion, and asked him what he thought about Ms. Wolf's use of his research. "It had nothing to do with what we found. It made no sense. What I reported was just the opposite of what Wolf claimed.... She grabbed it, ran with it, and got it backward." We have already discussed her sensational disclosure that the beauty backlash is wreaking havoc with young women by leading them into a lethal epidemic of anorexia with annual fatalities of 150,000. The actual fatalities may be as low as 100 per year.

Much of the support Wolf brings for her beauty-myth theory consists of merely labeling an activity insidious rather than showing it to be so—exercising, dieting, and buying Lancôme products at the cosmetics counter in Bloomingdale's all come under attack.... In her zeal to construe every effort of American women to lose weight as a symptom of a male-induced anxiety, she overlooks the fact that many people—men as well as women—suffer from obesity and are threatened by diseases that do not affect people who are fit. Stressing the importance of diet and fitness can hardly be considered as an insidious attempt by the male establishment to disempower women. The desire to achieve greater fitness is perhaps the main motive inspiring both men and women to exercise and to monitor their diets.

Wolf recycled results from every alarmist-advocacy study she could get her hands on. Mary Koss's results on date rape are duly reported: "One in four women respondents had an experience that met the American legal definition of rape or attempted rape." She does not mention that Koss's definition of rape was controversial. She does not tell us that almost half the women Koss classified as victims dated their "rapists" again. Wolf does sometimes point to real problems, such as the overwhelming fear of being "unfeminine," the excessive rate of cosmetic surgery, and the high incidence of domestic violence. But she errs in systematically ascribing them to the same misogynist cause. Good social theorists are painfully aware of the complexity of the phenomena they seek to explain, and honest researchers tend to be suspicious of single-factor explanations, no matter how beguiling.

Part II

Attaining an Open Mind: Overcoming Psychological Obstacles to Critical Thinking

From Cocksure Ignorance to Thoughtful Uncertainty: Viewpoint, Bias, and Fairness— Culturally Conditioned Assumptions and Centrisms

Education is the process of moving from cocksure ignorance to thoughtful uncertainty.

—*Proverb*

The trouble ain't that people are ignorant; it's that they "know" so much that ain't so.

—*Josh Billings (nineteenth-century American humorist)*

Chapter 1 made a case that "[a]ny writer or reader addressing controversial issues will almost inevitably have a subjective, **partisan viewpoint** (that is, a viewpoint siding with a particular party or ideology).... Our aims should simply be to learn to identify and understand what the viewpoint of any given source is, so that we can weigh its rhetorical quality against opposing viewpoints." Is every viewpoint, then, a "biased" one? Yes and no. The word *bias* is an ambiguous one; it is usually, but not necessarily, used with a negative **connotation**. Bias can simply mean a particular subjective viewpoint, which is to say, once again, that all of us inevitably have our own biases resulting from the **ethnocentric** limitations of our experience and temperament, as much as we may try to attain objectivity.

This notion of bias derives from the long philosophical tradition of **skepticism**. *The American Heritage Dictionary* defines *skepticism* as "the philosophical doctrine that absolute knowledge is impossible and that inquiry must be a process of doubting in order to acquire approximate or relative certainty." Skepticism does not necessarily deny that there are objective, external truths but asserts that these truths are often too obscure or complex for any one human being to know *with absolute certainty,* so that our *perceptions* of objective reality are inevitably biased to a large extent by our subjective viewpoint. **Primary certitude** is a psychological term for the mind set of people who are fixed in absolute beliefs so dogmatically, without recognizing their own bias, that they cannot bear to have their beliefs questioned or doubted. Much of the rest of this book develops possible ways to overcome primary certitude and the multiple forces in all of our lives that block objectivity.

A key **paradox** discovered in the course of higher education (or of wide reading and personal experience) is that the more you study subjects of controversy, the less certain you are apt to become that you know the truth about them. A large part of higher education consists of finding out how much you don't know that you previously thought you did, or of "moving from cocksure ignorance to thoughtful uncertainty." The reason for this is that you are constantly seeing more complexities and complications, more differing viewpoints on any given issue. People with less education are likely to be exposed to a narrower range of information and viewpoints, so it is easier for them to feel sure they know the truth and remain fixed in primary certitude. (To be sure, highly educated people can lurch to the **equal and opposite extreme** in being limited to intellectual sources to the exclusion of the realms of hard experience and experiential common sense in which the less educated may be more sophisticated.)

A classic site of skepticism is Plato's dialogues about his teacher Socrates, particularly "The Apology," written in Greece in the fourth century BC. Explaining at his trial the reasons he has antagonized the citizens of Athens to the point of their sentencing him to death, Socrates says that the oracle of Delphi once declared that there is no one wiser than Socrates. Socrates muses:

> I am going to explain to you why I have such an evil name. When I heard the answer, I said to myself, What can the god mean? and what is the interpretation of his riddle? for I know that I have no wisdom, small or great. What then can he mean when he says that I am the wisest of men? And yet he is a god, and cannot lie; that would be against his nature. After long consideration, I at last thought of a method of trying the question. I reflected that if I could only find a man wiser than myself, then I might go to the god with a refutation in my hand. I should say to him, 'Here is a man who is wiser than I am; but you said that I was the wisest.' Accordingly I went to one who had the reputation of wisdom, and observed him—his name I need not mention; he was a politician whom I selected for examination—and the result was as follows: When I began to talk with him, I could not help thinking that he was not really wise, although he was thought wise by many, and wiser still by himself; and thereupon I tried to explain to him that he thought himself wise, but was not really wise; and the consequence was that he hated me, and his enmity was shared by several who were present and heard me. So I left him, saying to myself, as I went away: Well, although I do not suppose that either of us knows anything really beautiful and good, I am better off than he is,—for he knows nothing, and thinks that he knows; I neither know nor think that I know. In this latter particular, then, I seem to have slightly the advantage of him. (353)

Albert Camus, a twentieth-century exponent of skepticism, writes about this passage in Plato, "Socrates, threatened by the death penalty, granted himself no superiority other than this: he did not presume to know what he did not know. The most exemplary life and thought of these centuries ends with a proud acknowledgment of ignorance" (*Lyrical and Critical Essays* 149–150). To be sure, neither Plato, Socrates, nor Camus was a total skeptic; on the contrary, the philosophy of "Platonic idealism" is based on the belief that there *is* a transcendent world of true, logical ideas that can be approximated through painstaking philosophical inquiry, although most humans live in a world of distorted shadows of those ideas and deceive themselves into mistaking the shadows for the reality, as Plato dramatizes in his allegory of the cave in *The Republic*. Socrates' skepticism, then, is directed at those who are locked into primary certitude by their faulty perception of truth. Again, the aim of skepticism is not to cynically belittle all beliefs and values but to rationally distinguish those that are legitimate from those that are false. Elsewhere in "The Apology," Socrates says, "I tell you that no greater good can happen to a man than to discuss human excellence every day and the other matters about which you have heard me arguing and examining myself and others, and that an unexamined life is not worth living" (371). Likewise, an unexamined idea is not worth holding on to.

A contemporary echo of this passage from Plato can be heard in a June 27, 2004, *Los Angeles Times* op-ed column by conservative political scientist Francis Fukuyama. Criticizing the Department of Defense's inadequate understanding of the problems that would face American forces in Iraq after their overthrow of Saddam Hussein in 2003, Fukuyama writes, "The Pentagon, we learned only later, didn't have the capacity to organize things and didn't know what it didn't know."

RELATIVISM AND COMMITMENT

The issues discussed here have been a center of controversy in the American "culture wars" in the past several decades, dividing liberals and conservatives. Conservatives like William J. Bennett and Lynne V. Cheney (respectively Secretary of Education in the administration of Ronald Reagan and head of the National Endowment for the Humanities in the administrations of Reagan and George H. W. Bush) have attacked liberal academics for allegedly substituting "moral relativism" for any belief in objective truth or universal values. In her 1995 book *Telling the Truth: Why Our Culture and Our Country Have Stopped Making Sense— and What We Can Do about It,* Cheney writes:

> In the view of a growing number of academics, the truth was not merely irrelevant, it no longer existed. They had moved far beyond the ideas that have shaped modern scholarship—that we should think of the truth we hold today as tentative and partial, recognizing that it may require rethinking tomorrow in light of new information and insight—to the view that there is no truth. They had leaped beyond the commonsense observation that people's descriptions of reality differ to the conclusion that there is no independent reality and thus no basis for making judgments about truth—or falsity. (15–16)

Whether Cheney's account of what this "growing number of academics" believe is accurate or is a **straw man** misrepresentation is disputable and beyond our concerns here. The particular viewpoint that I am presenting is not the extreme position she criticizes but is closer to what she accepts as "the ideas that have shaped modern scholarship" and "commonsense," as well as the ideas associated with skepticism throughout the history of Western humanistic education. (Cheney defends this history against what she sees as its rejection by advocates of multicultural canon revision, but to my mind this is a **false dilemma**, since the two are not mutually exclusive, as shown throughout this book in the emphasis on continuity between classics of the past and multicultural contemporary views.) To reiterate, I agree with Cheney that objectivity is a worthy goal to strive for, though we can rarely attain it completely. **Paradoxically**, becoming aware of our subjective viewpoint and biases is an essential step toward objectivity. (It is necessary to clarify one's position on such loaded issues beyond any possible misunderstanding, because in culture-war **polemics**, it is common for those on one side to distort the ideas of their opponents to imply **guilt by association** with extreme positions, particularly through the fallacy of **quotation out of context**, pulling a few, extreme-sounding words out of their qualifying context. You might also want to check Cheney's text to make sure I have not quoted *her* out of context!)

A valuable perspective on relativism and skeptical questioning has been provided by psychological researchers such as William Perry and Lawrence Kohlberg, who have studied development in cognition (acquisition of knowledge and learning and reasoning skills) and moral reasoning in college students over the period of a four-year liberal arts education. In Perry's terms, students entering college tend to think in terms of black-and-white *absolutism*. As they are exposed to a diversity of perspectives, they are apt to lurch to the opposite, skeptical extreme of unqualified *relativism,* the attitude that "Everyone has his or her own opinion, and who's to say which one is right?" The ultimate stage in development is *committed relativism,* in which students have learned that, in spite of the complexity and uncertainty of many truths, judgments of truth and falsity, right and wrong, and moral commitments still need to be made, on the basis of the most complete, diverse knowledge presently available to us. (Kohlberg's and Perry's ideas have been questioned on the grounds of gender bias and somewhat modified by Carol Gilligan, their colleague in the Harvard psychology department, in her book *In a Different Voice: Psychological Theory and Women's Development* and in another book by followers of Gilligan, *Women's Ways of Knowing: The Development of Self, Voice, and Mind,* by Mary Field Belenky and others.

BIASED AND UNBIASED VIEWPOINTS: THE ESBYODS PRINCIPLE

The concept of the term "bias" that equates it with a subjective, relative viewpoint is more benign than that which equates it with deliberate slanting and propaganda—often a legitimate equation, to be sure, as we will see throughout this book, especially in relation to the rhetoric of politics, mass media, and scholarship. For now, however, let us only consider how difficult it is to recognize the biases in ourselves and sources of information that support any group we identify with—in contrast to how easy it is for us to recognize biases in other individuals and supporters of other groups.

An inelegant but wise old folk saying goes, "Everyone defecates, but your own doesn't stink." (This, of course, is a euphemized version of the original, but we have a social **taboo** against using the "s" word in media like college textbooks or classrooms, even though it is far from an unfamiliar or shocking term to most college students; I will incorporate the uneuphemized version in an acronym of the first letters of each phrase: the ESBYODS principle.) Here is a test of the ESBYODS principle: Can you remember any instance in which you thought a statement by a politician, a news reporter or commentator, a teacher or textbook was biased when that statement supported *your* side? A large step in the direction of objectivity, then, is learning to avoid applying a double standard toward biases favoring our own side versus those favoring the other. If each of us is captive, in differing degrees, to many subjective biases, the same truth applies to the sources of information from which we derive our beliefs. It is a totem of our society for government officials, journalists, teachers, and scholars to insist on their commitment to the objective pursuit and transmission of truth in the arguments they put forth. This goal may be a worthy one in principle, but in practice those who pay lip service to it often deceive themselves, if not the public, about the extent to which their views are colored by the biases of partisan ideology, gender, race, social class, age, and so on. A large body of scholarship in the humanities and social sciences since the 1960s has documented countless instances in which such claims to objectivity or disinterestedness have been belied in the practice of government, journalism, and education.

The point here, once again, is not to breed cynical rejection of everything you read and hear but simply to alert you as a critical reader and listener to be somewhat skeptical about excessive claims to objectivity in your sources of information and to suggest that such sources of information are in fact more credible when they are out front in admitting to their own subjective viewpoint, possible biases, and inclination to **special pleading** (see chapter 15). By doing so, writers and speakers can replace the pretense of total objectivity with the more realistic principle of presenting a viewpoint that they acknowledge as subjective and perhaps biased, and that consequently takes extra care to be *fair-minded* in presentation of viewpoints differing from, or opposed to, their own. That is to say, conscientious writers and speakers will bend over backward to present views they themselves do not endorse in a manner acceptable to their advocates—fully, accurately, and sympathetically. Even though the writer or speaker might then go on to voice disagreements or **refutations** of those views, they will be more credible because they have demonstrated that they are responding to an accurate version of an opposing position, not a straw-man account of it. Even in heatedly polemical arguments, it is possible to present opponents' positions fairly; guidelines for doing so will be outlined in "Ground Rules for Polemicists" in chapter 9. Your written and spoken arguments will be far more effective if as a student you make the same efforts to acknowledge your own subjective viewpoint and possible biases and to summarize arguments with which you might disagree in a full, accurate, and sympathetic manner, prior to attempting to refute them.

In other words, every writer or speaker has subjective opinions and viewpoints, but not all opinions or viewpoints are equally biased, in the negative sense of *prejudiced*. Your aim as a critical thinker and writer should not be to avoid expressing opinions but to express opinions that will impress your readers as educated, unprejudiced, and fair, by the criteria surveyed in chapter 2.

To clarify an essential point for this entire book: There is no reason to suppose that all sides have equally strong arguments on every issue. On any given issue, members of one camp might have overwhelming reasoning and evidence on their side, and members of the other might be lying through their teeth. Neither open-mindedness, fairness, nor objectivity obliges you to give a side with few strong arguments and many weak ones more credit than it deserves or "equal time" with one that has many strong arguments and few weak ones. (In fact, a predictable rhetorical tactic of those with lame arguments on their side is to complain that their position has not been accorded equal time or respect, that it is the victim of "prejudice.")

In the student paper in chapter 5, the author concluded that there was about an equal balance of strong and weak points in the opposing arguments by Naomi Wolf and Christina Hoff Sommers. In that particular case, this conclusion was warranted by the preceding analysis, but you should not necessarily take it as a model for every paper you write. In general, you should avoid the generic, wishy-washy, evasive conclusion, "Everybody has his or her own viewpoint, and who is to judge which is right and which is wrong?" *You* are to judge! If you judge one side's arguments to be weak, you are simply obliged to *summarize* them objectively, without either distorting or commenting negatively about them, but then you are also obliged to point out their weaknesses. The judgment about which are the stronger or weaker arguments is, of course, to some extent a subjective one; the point is for you to provide adequate support for that judgment—support that, in your mind and in that of your readers or listeners, gives a fair account of arguments in the process of pointing out their weaknesses.

ACKNOWLEDGE YOUR OWN AND OPPOSING VIEWPOINTS

In acknowledging your own subjective biases, in college papers and discussions you should not be expected to reveal details of your personal life or beliefs that you consider private; still, you should be able to indicate your background in terms broad enough that you don't consider them intrusive. For example, a student might begin a paper on affirmative action:

> As an African-American woman who has seen many beneficial effects of affirmative action for minorities and women from disadvantaged backgrounds, I am of course inclined to spring to the defense when affirmative action is attacked. This being my bias, I will now try to summarize the argument against affirmative action the way its opponents see it.

Or another might write:

> I am a middle-class white male, so I guess I'm against affirmative action mainly because I see it discriminating against me and those I identify most closely with. Nevertheless, I will make my best effort to make the case in favor of affirmative action, and then will look at how well my objections to it hold up against that case.

The principles developed here about learning to recognize your own subjective biases and those of sources you write about can be extended to one of the most important keys to effective argumentative writing and speaking: *Always acknowledge, and speak to as sympathetically as fairness requires, the position opposed to yours.* You will never persuade anyone who doesn't already agree with you if you **stack the deck** by presenting only arguments in support of your own position, while ignoring or distorting arguments on the other side. *Imagine a reader or listener who not only disagrees with your position but whose ethnocentric mindset is quite different from your own, then calculate everything you say to win that person over to your position, through showing that you understand her position, anticipating her arguments, and respectfully explaining to her why yours are more reasonable.*

ROGERIAN ARGUMENT, BELIEVERS AND DOUBTERS

Scholars of composition have come up with various techniques to generate argumentative writing that stretches students' minds beyond their own customary viewpoint. One of the most popular is called **Rogerian argument**, based on the ideas of Carl Rogers, a psychologist affiliated with the International Society for General Semantics. Rogerian argument grew out of a technique that Rogers used both in personal psychotherapy for couples and for organizational or group psychology. The idea was that conflict is frequently based on semantic or psychological misunderstandings and inability to empathize with someone else's viewpoint when it clashes with your own. (The Swiss child psychologist Jean Piaget expressed a similar notion in theorizing that the healthiest development of reasoning in children consists of a progression from *egocentrism* and *ethnocentrism* [or, in Piaget's term, *sociocentrism*] to *reciprocity,* or empathy.) In Rogers's technique patients are asked to address those with whom they are in conflict in a manner that assures them that the speaker fully understands and empathizes with their viewpoint; in other words, one person must present the other's position in a way that the latter accepts as accurate. The speaker next acknowledges points on the other side that he or she finds valid and then tries respectfully to explain where and why he or she differs. This method thus avoids an antagonistic atmosphere in arguments, as well as straw-man misrepresentation of an opponent's ideas.

Rogerian argument works better in face-to-face arguments than written ones, but it is an excellent way to air opposing positions on assigned writing topics in class discussion prior to writing. When writing the paper, you can then translate the classroom dialogue into the section summarizing the opposing positions, thereby assuring that you are presenting both sides fairly.

Believers and Doubters is a similar method devised by composition theorist Peter Elbow in his 1973 book *Writing without Teachers;* it is most helpful in the prewriting stage. The technique consists of your first reading a source on one side of an issue and writing an account of it in the most sympathetic way you can, thinking of additional arguments and evidence in support of the author's position—and then switching to write an account that disagrees with it, using whatever arguments and evidence you can find in rebuttal. You can then draw from both accounts in balancing the source's strengths and weaknesses in your final version.

You can use either Rogerian argument or Believers and Doubters to generate the sections in your paper fair-mindedly summarizing and evaluating the strong and weak points of opposing sources. Do not, however, use either of them to get you off the hook of making the final judgment that one side's arguments are much stronger than the other's, if that is the case!

CULTURALLY CONDITIONED ASSUMPTIONS AND CENTRISMS

In his textbook *Clear Thinking for Composition,* Ray Kytle introduces this subject in better words than I could devise:

> We are, to a large degree, creatures of our particular age. We grow up in a certain "climate of opinion." And this climate of opinion determines the form of many of our *attitudes* and *values.*... Because we live in a particular country, in a particular part of the world, in a particular age, because we were raised in a particular class and educated in a particular educational system by teachers who were also in many ways the product of their culture, *we possess a large collection of attitudes and values whose accuracy, truth, or merit we have probably never questioned.*
>
> These attitudes and values can be called *assumptions* because we *assume* them to be accurate. We don't question them; we probably don't even see them as open to question. (47–49)

Kytle's list of factors in our cultural conditioning—"a particular country ... [historical] age ... class ... educational system"—can be expanded to include our particular family, peers and age group, race, gender, geographical region, religion, political ideology and party, and so on. Each of these factors and others tend to impose their own filters on our perception of the world. Your critical thinking and writing should include acknowledgment of your own cultural conditioning, and an effective line of argument can be to point out the cultural biases in sources you are studying.

TOTEMS AND TABOOS

We go through life taking for granted any number of beliefs, customs, norms, habits, routines, and tastes as the way things are, always have been, and ought to be, in both small matters and large ones, local matters and global ones. Some of these may be perfectly reasonable and practical, but others may be wholly arbitrary—that is, they don't have any logical reason for being but are conformed to, blindly worshiped as **totems** or shunned as **taboos**. A cartoon by Dedini in the *New Yorker* shows a large group of middle-aged men sitting, fully dressed, in armchairs on a beach. A young boy has asked a question to one of them, his father, who replies, "Generations of our people have sat by the sea, my son. When you are older and have sat by the sea, you will understand." The point humorously made in the cartoon is that people often follow the same customs generation after generation for no other reason than circular reasoning—this is the way we've always done it. Some arbitrary customs last for centuries and cross different cultures; others are specific to one locality or subculture and may change drastically over time, even in our own lifetime, and yet as long as they remain in force (even in the short life span of fashions and fads), they can exact conformity as rigidly as if they were eternal commandments.

The human tendency to conform without question to established traditions, right or wrong, and to the present status quo is a strong force for social and political conservatism. To be sure, there is often wisdom in the instinct, as Shakespeare's Hamlet says, to "rather bear those ills we have/Than fly to others that we know not of" (3.1.56). However, it is a prime test of the critical thinking ability of **drawing the line** to judge when to be critically wary of uncertain changes and when to be willing to question past conventions and the present powers that be. The terms **appeal to the past or tradition** or **resistance to change** might be defined as the logical fallacy of arguing for a policy only because it has been followed in the past, is a tradition in one's culture, or has been established as the status quo, regardless of its possible outdatedness. This line was used to justify slavery in the South for centuries before its abolition and segregation of blacks for another century afterwards, and used similarly to oppose women's and gay rights because they transgressed traditional roles. A similar line argues that because in the past there has been a large degree of opportunity to get ahead economically and socially in the United States; this is still true and always will be—in disregard of possible changes in economic realities over recent decades.

A ruling by a San Francisco judge that the words "under God" in the Pledge of Allegiance were unconstitutional provoked a storm of outrage by politicians of both parties from President George W. Bush on down. Many people's angry reaction seemed to assume that these words were embedded in the Constitution or the Declaration of Independence, but several commentators pointed out that they dated only from 1954 and were motivated by Cold War competition with "godless Communism." A further historical **irony** was that the original pledge, without reference to God, was written in 1892 by a minister who believed Jesus was a socialist. Critics also argued that phrases like "under God" and "In God We Trust" are only expressions of **religiosity**, a public pose of devout religious belief without any substantial commitment to practice that belief. In other words, it is a totem for all American politicians to pay **lip service** to religious belief—even though many of them fail to practice what they preach in their public or personal life, and some of them probably do not even believe in God—and it is taboo for any of them to express **skepticism** about religious belief or the dubious constitutionality of these references to God, vague and politically motivated as they may be.

Think about the arbitrariness of many of our culture's other customs. Our mass media reproduce habits that would seem quite bizarre in other times and places, such as artificially engineered laugh tracks on situation comedies; do viewers at home really laugh when they are electronically coached to? Or the custom of everyone in advertisements constantly wearing a big smile, whether they are selling workout equipment, tires, or laxatives (in addition, of course, to their all being young, slender, and beautiful, as though these envied qualities will carry over to the product by association). Even the custom of smiling in photographs or painted portraits is a mid-twentieth-century innovation; previously, a rather serious, dignified expression was the norm. Then there is the assumption that used to dominate radio and TV newscasts or commentary that a deep, reassuring—and usually male—tone of voice carries more authority than a higher-pitched male or female one would (this is a form of the fallacy of **argument to authority**). Broadcast reporter Cokie Roberts says, in defense of affirmative action, that when she was starting out, "I was told, 'We will not hire women to deliver the news. Their voices are not authoritative. We won't hire women as writers. Men would have to work for them and we can't have that'" (Richard Reeves, "The Best and

Worst in the National Heart," *San Francisco Examiner,* May 10, 1995, A26). Now, however, the cultural conditioning has shifted so that on cable news networks news is broadcast not by professional journalists but by anchors of both sexes who are young, chirpy, and look like fashion models, and there is little apparent concern for their journalistic credentials.

Another bizarre cultural convention perpetuated by mass media is that our lives should constantly be filled with music or noise. Music through the ages until the twentieth century had two uses: to be listened to with all one's attention, or to be danced to. Only recently, with the advanced development of radio and recordings, has the concept of purely "background music," to be absorbed while we are doing something else, been conceivable. But what exactly is the point of background music not of our choosing—especially when we are forced to listen to it while shopping, eating, riding an elevator, or on telephone "hold"—except as a kind of chewing gum for the ears? It is often used in parties, bars, or restaurants, as a presumed accompaniment to conversation, but then why is it played so loudly that any conversation has to be shouted over it? In bars, it is common for two or more television sets to be showing different sports events, at top volume, while at the same time recorded music is blaring; even professional sports events are interrupted with loud music and visual spectacles. The assumption seems to be that people desire to be bombarded constantly with noise and visual stimuli. Is this true of you or anyone you know?

Gender roles are one of the most powerful fields of cultural conditioning. But these roles have been challenged by feminists in recent years with criticisms, for example, of boys being socialized into aggression through GI Joe, toy guns, and muscle building, while girls are socialized into concern with looks and grooming with Barbie dolls and nurturing through playing nurse. How different might adult roles be if these modes of childhood conditioning were changed, and how much have they been changing in your lifetime? Gender conditioning continues in adult roles and identities. Consider that men typically wear pants with pockets in which they carry keys, coins, and billfolds with identification cards and paper money. Social psychologists might observe that these are symbols of power and that the proximity in which they are worn to the physical symbols of masculinity serves to reinforce the sense of male empowerment. Most women's clothes, however, do not have pockets, mainly because the fashion industry has decreed that they are "unfeminine." So women are bodily separated from their symbols of identity, which must be carried in a purse that can easily be lost or stolen and whose cavernous depths must constantly be searched for keys, money, and ID.

Or consider dress codes. In the 1950s, short hair was the norm for American males; late in that decade and into the sixties, long hair became a **symbol** of nonconformity, and long hair could get you killed in some parts of the country. Little by little, the custom changed, and today long hair has become, if not the norm, at least acceptable in most parts of the country and walks of life. If you are a male college student interviewing for a job, you are probably expected to wear a suit and tie to the interview. (If you are a woman, you are expected to wear a more "dressy" dress or slacks than you would ordinarily wear.) Nowadays, once you get the job, you might never need to wear a jacket and tie to work; still, you must go through the ritual, as must those who are interviewing you. The reasons are obscure—having partly to do with vestiges of earlier decades when dress was more formal and even college students were required to wear a tie to school. Historically, ties originated as an item of sartorial, individually tailored elegance in the upper classes, but by the early twentieth century mass-produced ties had become more a uniform of the middle class, a symbol of "white-collar" status as opposed to "blue-collar," manual workers. Although many men find ties and shirts buttoned at the neck uncomfortable, and they have become far less common with the relaxation of cultural formalities, especially since the 1960s, it is still generally the rule that the higher a man's professional status is, the more likely he is to wear a tie.

Women are even more captive to culturally conditioned styles in clothing and physical appearance than men—beginning with the greater expectations of beauty in women than in men.

(See Naomi Wolf's "The Beauty Myth" in chapter 5.) In most periods before the mid-twentieth century, the norm of female beauty in Western culture was plump by today's standards, yet today women undergo enormous self-deprivation and social pressure to become unnaturally slender. A boyish figure with small breasts was fashionable in the 1920s, and today's idealized combination of large, but upright, breasts on an otherwise slender torso is both a historical novelty and a physical rarity. Likewise, before the twentieth century, pale skin was considered the norm of beauty, as it was associated with the sheltered upper classes; suntan was associated with peasants, and hence was shunned by the fashionable. Suntan became a mark of beauty and prestige in our time as outdoor life and sports became fashionable. Ironically, in spite of the history of doctrines of white supremacy in America, whites go to great lengths to make their skin look like that of darker races. Now that excessive exposure to sun has become recognized as a cause of skin cancer, suntanning is declining in fashionability again.

In dress codes, throughout history women have suffered everything from bound feet in China to high-heeled shoes, which damage feet and restrict the ability to walk or run, to corsets, girdles, bustles, and multiple layers of petticoats in the West. And think about how arbitrary the custom of women disguising their natural appearance with makeup is, even though it has been accepted as the norm for centuries in Western and other societies. In some past periods, such as the European Renaissance, men (at least in the fashionable classes) wore makeup too. The deceptiveness of women's makeup was a favorite topic in Renaissance rhetorical exercises; the poet John Donne (1573–1631) wrote a tongue-in-cheek argumentative essay titled "That Women Ought to Paint," and Shakespeare's Hamlet railed against the custom in venting his grievances against women to Ophelia: "I have heard of your paintings too, well enough. God hath given you one face, and you make yourselves another" (3.1.141–143) Of course, this might be considered a typical case of **blaming the victim**, since women have generally worn makeup because it pleases men.

ETHNOCENTRISM

Ethnocentrism is the mentality of "Ours is best" or "We're number one," or in my inelegant acronym, "ESBYODS." The term refers literally to seeing life solely from the perspective of one ethnic group, but it extends to many other factors in socialization discussed throughout this book. Painful as it is for us to admit it, those beliefs are sometimes misinformed, mistaken, or prejudiced, even though they may have been passed down from generation to generation as what is termed *received* or *conventional wisdom*. Because we are dependent on our family and immediate peers throughout childhood for nurturing and learning, we need to accept as the truth most of what they tell us. In later childhood and adolescence, however, most of us little by little become aware of the limitations in their knowledge and wisdom, and we develop the ability to think independently. This process often accelerates dramatically when we go away to college, leading typically to quarrels between students questioning their parents' authority and parents reacting defensively against that questioning. These quarrels can be very traumatic, but they are a necessary part of growing up for the children and of letting go for the parents. After all, there is no logical reason to suppose that our parents are especially well informed and wise about every issue *simply because they are our parents*. We all want to think the best about our families and friends, and it is hard to admit that Aunt Edith is an alcoholic or that Cousin George's business practices are crooked. Even Hitler's mother probably would have **rationalized**, "All those things they say about Adolf can't be true. He was always a good boy—he wouldn't hurt a fly."

Of course, ethnocentrism serves a positive role in enabling us to take justifiable pride in ourselves and whatever groups we belong to, and many of its forms are quite worthwhile. But ethnocentrism throughout history has also been a major cause of wars and social divisiveness;

BABY'S FIRST WORDS

think of the perpetual conflicts among the Bosnians, Serbs, and other ethnic groups comprising the former Yugoslavia. Propagandists, office seekers, advertisers, and other self-serving rhetoricians specialize in manipulating appeals to varieties of ethnocentrism like jingoism (blind patriotism in support of war), religious dogmatism, boosterism (contrived business-community or school "spirit"), and racial, class, or sexual prejudice. The nouns **demagogue** and **demagogy** (or **demagoguery**) refer precisely to a politician or other public figure who makes **emotional appeals** to such forms of ethnocentrism for self-advancing aims, while pretending to be a **populist**—a member or true representative of the common people. **The plain folks fallacy** consists of exactly this false pretense by a member of the **elite** to be a spokesperson for populism, or concern for the well-being of "the little guy."

Two words synonymous with ethnocentrism are *parochialism* and *provincialism*. *Parochialism* derives from *parish*, a small church district; so a parochial-minded or provincial person is one who literally never ventures outside a small, isolated area or who, by **metaphoric** extension, goes through life with a narrow-minded perspective. Liberal education is essentially the process of growing out of our provincial narrow-mindedness, multiplying the different perspectives from which we can view issues. In her 1938 essay "Three Guineas," English writer Virginia Woolf described being asked what kind of freedom would advance the fight against fascism and its allies racism, colonialism, and sexism. She replied: "Freedom from unreal loyalties.... You must rid yourself of pride of nationality in the first place; also of religious pride, college pride, family pride, sex pride and those unreal loyalties that spring from them" (quoted in Margo Jefferson, "Unreal Loyalties," *New York Times Book Review,* April 13, 2003, p. 31). This is not to say that education obliges us to disown our native culture; we can maintain our loyalty and reaffirm what is valuable in it, while becoming able to evaluate it in a broader perspective and to "switch codes," as linguists say, from our own culture to others and back.

Gaining perspective on our own ethnocentrism enables us to view with amusement some of the **hyperboles** of parochialism. A little nightclub in San Luis Obispo, California, advertises itself as "The World Famous Dark Room." "The World Series" includes a rather small portion of the actual world and is ignored in most other countries—though many countries are equally fanatic about soccer championships. Every high school in every small town in America vaunts its sports teams as "number one." In Illinois, the Big Game is Illinois versus

Northwestern, but in New England everyone knows it's Harvard versus Yale, in Northern California it's Stanford versus Berkeley, in Southern California it's UCLA versus USC, in the Southeast it's Tennessee versus Alabama, and so on.

In politics and religion, members of every sect or party tend to cluster together and confirm one another's ethnocentric certainties. In Orange County, California, conservatives gather in bars to proclaim, "Rush is right—isn't it awful about those welfare swindlers and the bleeding-heart liberals who coddle them—along with those feminazis and commie intellectuals and environmental wackos," while everyone chants, "Right! Right!" Meanwhile, five hundred miles to the north, leftists are gathered in Berkeley cafés reading *The Nation* and lamenting, "Isn't it awful about those corporate crooks and racist cops and fascist talk show hosts," while everyone chants, "Right! Right!" Both groups are like planets in separate galaxies, circling endlessly in their own orbits without ever having their assumptions challenged by communicating with anyone who thinks differently. Learning to "decenter" from our need to believe our group is best or right is a lifelong, painful struggle, but an essential one in intellectual and emotional growth.

Likewise, in personal relations each of us is compelled to believe that he or she is right and the other person wrong in any conflict—think about the amazingly different accounts you've heard from the opposing parties after a marriage or love affair has broken up. As the nineteenth-century Scottish poet Robert Burns wrote, "Oh wad some Power the giftie gie us/To see oursels as ithers see us!"

In normal child development, aided by education and other experiences like travel, we grow beyond ethnocentrism to a greater or lesser degree, toward what child psychologist Jean Piaget termed "reciprocity," becoming able to recognize the possible validity of others' viewpoints. This is not to **imply** that your previous beliefs, or those of your family or community, are necessarily wrong. The point is that as an educated person you should not just go through life maintaining any belief automatically, never holding it up to critical examination. If a belief is valid, it should stand up under that critical examination; you should be able to defend it rationally against opposing beliefs, and if you can do so, then it will be a far more secure belief than one that is held blindly and irrationally. By the same token, if that belief does not hold up against opposing ones, then you should be willing to change your mind about it. If you approach your studies with the attitude of "My mind's made up; don't try to change it with the facts," you're wasting your own and your teachers' time in college.

AMERICAN ETHNOCENTRISM

Battle over Patriotism Curriculum

Larry Rohter

New York Times, May 15, 1994

Like other generations who went through the public schools in this small town an hour's drive north of Orlando, students at Tavres Middle School are taught to take pride in American citizenship and heritage. The school's athletic teams are even nicknamed the Patriots, and the school colors are red, white and blue.

But the fundamentalist Christians who dominate the Lake County school board say that is not enough. As part of a policy approved this week by a vote of 3 to 2, teachers will be required to teach the county's 22,526 students that American culture, values and political institutions are inherently "superior to other foreign or historic cultures."

Members of the local teachers union and citizens groups are protesting the measure, which they say is jingoistic and probably illegal. They have filed an appeal to the state Department of Education, and a court challenge appears likely.

"People don't understand the purpose and the point of this," said Keith Mullins, chairman of People for Mainstream Values, a local political action committee formed in response to the religious right's rise to power here. "We are already teaching our children to love and honor our country, so why spend all this time and money talking about something we are already doing? We've become sort of a laughingstock."

The new policy, conceived as a response to the state's multicultural education policy, is the handiwork of the board's chairman, Pat Hart, who describes herself as a patriot, a Christian and a Republican. She said it was fine that students learn about other nations, as required by the state's multicultural education curriculum, so long as they were also taught that the United States was "unquestionably superior" to any other society in all of human history.

Mrs. Hart said she drafted the policy statement, which also requires teachers to promote "strong family values" and "an appreciation of our American heritage and culture," to insure that students never forget that "we are the best of the best."

Mrs. Hart, whose own children are enrolled in private religious schools, acknowledges that she has never set foot outside the United States, speaks no foreign languages and has no academic training in comparative culture, religion or government.

"I don't need to visit other countries to know that America is the best country in the world," she said. "Thousands of people risk life and limb every day to come to America because they know this is the land of the free."

The controversy over multicultural education in this central Florida county, a blend of 160,000 people living in Orlando bedroom suburbs, small towns, retiree trailer parks and farms, follows nearly two years of acrimony over issues like sex education and government aid.

Mrs. Hart was elected four years ago in a contest that attracted few voters. She was joined in 1992 by two other religious conservatives who, like her, espouse the views of Pat Robertson's Christian Coalition. With their support, she became board chairman.

One board member, Judy Pearson, said, "We need to reinforce that we should be teaching America first." Otherwise, she said, young people, "if they felt our land was inferior or equal to others, would have no motivation to go to war and defend our country."

Ms. Pearson, who is a member of both the Christian Coalition and the equally conservative Citizens for Excellence in Education, said she thought it was evident that "our form of government is superior to other nations because it has survived when others have fallen."

Phyllis Patten, one of two board members who voted against the measure, said such views were simplistic and undemocratic. "These are people with no experience and no education," she said of her fundamentalist colleagues. "You've got three people sitting on that board with high school educations who want to wrap the Bible and the flag around themselves, who don't believe in public education and are trying to undermine the system."

Mrs. Hart, whose seat is up for election this year, originally ran on a tax-efficiency platform, emphasizing her religious agenda only after narrowly winning election.

In one early action that stirred controversy here, the revamped board rejected Federal money intended for Head Start programs for disadvantaged children. Mrs. Hart or her allies have also sought to severely limit sex education, to mandate creationism in the science curriculum and to limit some reading material in schools, primarily children's books by Shel Silverstein.

The state government, which has the authority to suspend state aid or take the issue to court, has so far taken no action against the school board. But the Education Commissioner, Doug Jamerson, quickly condemned the new policy, which he and other officials said was clearly at odds with state requirements.

"American culture is made up of many different cultures from around the world," Mr. Jamerson said. "To say American culture is superior to all others calls into question the rich history and significant contributions of all other nations and cultures whose influence helped shape this country."

Mrs. Hart dismissed the importance of the controversy, saying "everything is be-

ing blown out of proportion by a radical teacher's union." And Mrs. Pearson said, "If we are already teaching these things, then there should be no opposition to this, and no problem, should there?"

Steven Farrell, one of the social studies teachers who will be required to teach the new curriculum, said they were not quite sure what the board wanted them to do. "We need clearer definitions," said Mr. Farrell, who teaches American history. "We regard American culture as very diverse, and we're not sure what values they see as American culture."

*   *   *

The story goes that an American lands for the first time in a European country, and upon seeing a sign saying Foreigners This Way, exclaims, "But *you're* the foreigners." Nationalistic ethnocentrism is common to most countries. (Piaget studied the attitudes of children in Switzerland—a tiny country surrounded by France, Italy, and Germany—toward their own and neighboring countries, finding that the younger ones consistently believed "Switzerland is best." As they got older, they tended to outgrow this "sociocentrism" and recognize that "everyone thinks his own is best.") However, ethnocentrism is a distinctive problem in the United States, for several reasons. We have always been more insulated than most major countries geographically and culturally. Because of the conditions of our country's founding and development, it has been regarded throughout the world as a unique land of democracy, opportunity, and even virtue. Over the course of the twentieth century, the United States became the largest economic and military power in the world. During nearly half a century of Cold War with the Soviet Union and its Communist allies, when it appeared necessary for Americans to side with one or another of the two world superpowers, there was little question that the United States represented the superior alternative. However, this hard choice resulted in a certain amount of **oversimplification**, and valid criticisms of this country were often stifled because they were perceived to give aid and comfort to the enemy, giving rise to **either-or fallacies** like "America: Love It or Leave It" and "If you don't like it here, why don't you go to Russia"—as though there were no other democratic countries in the world. Even the common use of the word *America* as a synonym for the United States reflects our ethnocentric exclusion of Canada, Mexico, and Central and South America.

The danger implicit in our country's fortunate situation is an inclination toward smugness if not arrogance, toward **defense mechanisms** against admitting that we have social problems or that we are not necessarily and always number one in every way, and that we might have something to learn from other democratic countries' different ways of doing things. In the preceding article, "Battle over Patriotism Curriculum," a Florida school board head is quoted as insisting that children be taught "that the United States was 'unquestionably superior' to any other society in human history." She then is quoted as saying that refugees come to America "because they know this is the land of the free." This might be viewed as an example of **compartmentalization** if we consider that one of the central American freedoms is that of speech and thought—including the freedom to question America's "unquestionable" superiority or to learn about other countries that also welcome refugees.

In response to reports in 2004 about the sadistic abuse of prisoners by American military personnel at Abu Ghraib prison in Iraq, President George W. Bush declared, "Their treatment does not reflect the nature of the American people. That's not the way we do things in America.... I also want to remind people that those few people who did do that do not reflect the nature of men and women we've sent overseas" (*Pittsburgh Post-Gazette,* May 1, 2004, p. 1). Think about the level of **generalization** and **semantic abstraction** (see chapters 4 and 7) in these ethnocentric appeals, which represent an extreme form of what is sometimes called "American exceptionalism," the belief that the United States has been historically exempt from the faults that have plagued every other country through history. Can anyone accurately make such sweeping statements about the "nature" of everyone in a country or its armed forces? Minimal knowledge of our history confirms that Americans, while relatively more civilized than many peoples through history, have been far from free of sadistic violence against Native Americans, African Americans (both during and for a hundred years after slavery), women, immigrants, labor organizers, homosexuals, and other victimized groups. Violent "frontier justice" dominated the settling of the West, and our modern rates of crime and imprisonment are among the highest in the world. Is there a town anywhere in the United States—like anywhere else—that doesn't have its hoodlums, bullies, bigots, and corrupt officials? Our officials **sentimentalize** the nature of war and military service, which in America, as everywhere, sometimes attracts those whose violent inclinations might make them criminals in civilian life. Soldiers are necessarily indoctrinated to kill and to dehumanize the enemy. It is arguable that the occurrence of atrocity killings, torture, rape, and pillaging by American forces in wars is not vastly less frequent or vicious than what has always taken place in wars everywhere—e.g., the massacre of hundreds of civilians in the village of My Lai and elsewhere in the Vietnam War, and similar numbers of peasants and church workers in Central America massacred in the 1980s by militias supported by the U.S. government. In fact, among the rationalizations used to excuse such events, including those in Iraq, was that they are **common practice**, the kind of thing that happens in every war, or that there are always "a few bad apples," or that they weren't so different from athletes' roughhousing or fraternity hazing, practices that have in fact often gotten out of hand and resulted in deaths.

No country has ever remained the leading world power for more than a few centuries, and America's lease on prosperity and power is not necessarily granted in perpetuity. A sobering perspective on contemporary America is provided in Andrew Shapiro's book *We're Number One: Where America Stands—and Falls—in the New World Order,* a two-hundred-page catalog of the many areas in which we rank number one in the *least* desirable traits compared to other industrial democracies. We have, for example, the highest ratings in crime and violence, extremes of wealth and poverty, the gap between employers and workers, cost of college education, and environmental destruction and the lowest ratings in health and health care, status of women, participation in elections, and aspects of education such as funding of public schools, teacher salaries, amount of homework and days in school, and proficiency in math and science, geography, and foreign languages. Likewise, according to Steve Brouwer's *Sharing the Pie: A Citizen's Guide to Wealth and Power in America*, excerpted in chapter 13, the United States ranks far behind most contemporary industrial democracies in unionization of workers, minimum wage levels, length of work week, and vacation time.

Many Americans have a strong tendency toward rationalization, **denial**, and other defense mechanisms in reacting against critiques like Shapiro's by dismissing them as motivated by "anti-American prejudice." Such critiques might be motivated simply by the desire to see our country face its problems realistically, and we need to look at such commentaries with a cool head, evaluating them as objectively and open-mindedly as possible, solely on the grounds of the evidence supporting them, not on whether or not they make us feel good about our country. Remember, Adolf Hitler did a wonderful job of making Germans feel good about their country too—to the point of fostering illusions about "Deutschland über Alles" (Germany Over All) that led to their destruction.

QUESTIONING CAPITALISM

The American economy is primarily based on capitalism, or free enterprise. There is a classic semantic problem of **denotation** and **connotation** here: *capitalism* has a negative **connotation** in many people's minds, though not everyone's; *free enterprise* is a somewhat **euphemistic** substitute preferred by advocates because of the positive connotation associated with *freedom*. Both words, however, denote an economic system in which most businesses and industries are owned by private corporations and run on the principle of investment for profit. Our culturally conditioned assumptions perpetuate the premises of that system, frequently without consciousness or questioning. One of those premises, which is in fact disputable, is that a free enterprise economy is synonymous with *political* freedom and democracy; for the contrary opinion held by leftists, see "Conservatives, Liberals, Socialists, Libertarians" in chapter 13 and Robert Jensen's "Anti-Capitalism in Five Minutes or Less" here.

The current equation of corporate capitalism with political democracy did not prevail in earlier American history. Contemporary defenders of corporate society often invoke the eighteenth-century "founding fathers" as sources for the belief that free enterprise, industrial capitalism, and private property are intrinsic to "the American way of life." However, such invocations commit the logical fallacy of **equivocation**, a shift in definition of words away from the one appropriate to the context in question. When writers like Thomas Jefferson, Benjamin Franklin, and J. Hector St. John de Crèvecoeur praised free enterprise, they meant

individual farms or trades, not the modern usage of corporate enterprise free from government regulation. When they lauded "industry," they meant individual industriousness, not corporate industries. Crèvecoeur emphasized in "What Is An American," "Here there are . . . no great manufacturers employing thousands, no great refinements of luxury. . . . We are all animated with the spirit of an industry which is unfettered and unrestrained, because each person works for himself" (40–41). And by private property, they meant ownership of one's own house, farm, or trade, not private ownership, through stocks, of large corporations, as in contemporary usage.

In fact, Jefferson wrote in 1816, "I hope we shall crush in its infancy the aristocracy of our monied corporations which dare already to challenge our government to a trial of strength, and bid defiance to the laws of our country." (Quoted in Lawrence Goodwyn, *The Populist Movement* [New York: Oxford University Press, 1978], frontispiece.) Jim Hightower and Phillip Frazer write in the *Hightower Newsletter* (April 2003):

> From the start, the corporate structure was the exact opposite of democracy, and its single-minded pursuit of private gain was at odds with the public good. The founders knew that this anti-democracy bomb had to be tightly controlled, so the state charters authorizing each corporation to exist served as rigorous watchdogs for the public interest. To get a charter, a corporation:
>
> - Had to have a public purpose, from building canals to providing education (Harvard University, for example, was the first U.S. corporation). If it failed to perform its public purpose, the corporation was dissolved.
> - Was limited in what business it could pursue, was not allowed to buy other corporations, and could amass only a certain level of capital.
> - Faced term limits, with its charter usually expiring after 15 or 20 years, requiring it to seek renewal.
> - Had to treat farmers, small businesses, and other suppliers fairly and responsibly.
> - Was strictly prohibited from engaging in lobbying or political campaigns.

Jefferson, James Madison, and others actually wanted an eleventh amendment in the Bill of Rights. As described by Thom Hartmann in his book about the rise of corporate dominance, *Unequal Protection:* "Jefferson kept pushing for a law, written into the Constitution as an amendment, that would prevent companies from growing so large that they could dominate entire industries or have the power to influence the people's government." Referring to "artificial aristocracies," Jefferson pushed for a formal declaration of "freedom of commerce against monopolies." The chief reason that this was not included in our constitutional protections is that other founders felt it was simply unnecessary, since corporate power was so universally condemned at the time and was considered to be held in check by the vigilant state-chartering process.

If only they had heeded Jefferson's warnings that the corporation is an incorrigible beast that will not—cannot—restrain itself, and perpetually seeks to expand its reach, wealth, and power beyond whatever limits society draws! While the people continued to favor strict restraints, by the time of the Civil War, corporate fiefdoms were growing with industrialization, and the war itself fueled these new empires with rich government war contracts. This rise did not go unnoticed. . . . Abraham Lincoln was appalled by the brazenness of corporate war profiteers. J. P. Morgan, for example (hailed today as an icon of corporate meritocracy), bought 5,000 defective rifles for $3.50 each from a U.S. Army arsenal, then resold them to a Union field general for $22 each and skipped off with his war profits, while the rifles exploded in the hands of the soldiers who carried them. In an 1864 letter to his friend Col. William Elkins, Lincoln wrote: "I see in the near future a crisis approaching that unnerves me and causes me to tremble for the safety of my country. As a result of the war, corporations have been enthroned and an era of corruption in high places will follow, and the money power of the country will endeavor to prolong its reign by working upon the prejudices of the people until all wealth is aggregated in a few hands and the Republic is destroyed."

Like all social systems, then, ours has its irrational or unjust aspects, arguably contrary to political freedom and democracy, to which our conditioning tends to blind us. Nor is this conditioning wholly accidental or impersonal. Those who have benefited the most from free enterprise, large corporations and wealthy individuals, quite naturally have a personal stake (or **interest**, in the sense of "self-interest" or "a special-interest group") in selling the public on the virtues of this economic system, and they spend billions of dollars every year in the effort to do so, and to influence political policies in their own favor (see the readings in chapter 15). The additional facts that news, entertainment, and other communications media—such as computer hardware, software, and Internet providers—are among the industries mostly owned by corporations and operated for profit in America and that they also serve as media for corporate advertising and public relations mean that those media form part of the whole system of what can be termed—without a negative connotation—capitalistic propaganda, in the sense of that word meaning "the propagation of a particular ideology." (Defenders of capitalistic ownership of media, of course, deny that those media are dominated by capitalist ideology; see chapter 14.)

Of even more immediate concern to you as a student, if you plan eventually to work for a corporation, is the fact that employers have the power to hire and fire. Employees (or students as future employees) have a strong tendency to rationalize their necessary compliance with this power by tailoring their beliefs to match those of corporations—one of the most widespread forms of **authoritarianism**.

One of the premises of this book is that courses in critical thinking have a responsibility to examine the assumptions of free enterprise, as a counterbalance to corporate cultural conditioning, propaganda, and power; thus, many of the readings address the pros and cons of these assumptions. To the extent that corporate interests can be identified as *conservative,* then many if not most teachers and scholars, especially in higher education, can be identified as *liberal* in raising views that critically examine free enterprise. (See chapter 13 for further refinement of these definitions.) It would be a false inference and an **either-or fallacy**, however, to deduce that teachers who criticize free enterprise therefore must advocate socialism or other leftist alternatives. They may or may not, but they see their primary mission simply to be enabling students to get beyond the ethnocentric assumptions of our culture that restrict critical thinking.

On the other hand, in a case of the **equal and opposite extreme**, conservatives often accuse college teachers of having a liberal, leftist, socialist, or even Communist bias and of imposing that bias propagandistically through attitudes recently labeled political correctness. Another line of argument that conservatives take is that teachers themselves form part of a "new class" of public employees, professionals, and intellectuals with its own, opposing set of culturally conditioned assumptions; because members of this class themselves as rivals to capitalists, their criticisms of free enterprise may be propaganda for themselves as a **special interest** group (see chapter 15, and David Horowitz's article "The Intellectual Class War" in chapter 13). Whatever the truth may be in this particular opposition of **viewpoints**, the approach of this book is simply to alert you to the predictable patterns of rhetoric that you should learn to look for in opposing sides on public controversies. Once you understand whose ideological viewpoint you are getting and what their argumentative moves are likely to be, you can then judge whether they are presenting their viewpoint in a biased or unbiased way.

Arguments on the pros and cons of capitalism and corporations are emphasized throughout this book, but for now a few examples will serve to indicate some of the self-contradictory aspects of free enterprise that we normally accept as rational. (Again, this is not to imply an "anti-free-enterprise" or, worse yet, "anti-American" viewpoint; any alternative system, real or hypothetical, is likely to have comparable self-contradictions, and these arguments simply need to be weighed in proportion to the positive aspects of free enterprise that you are likely to have heard more about.) If and when you are in a position to invest some money (or even put some in a checking or savings account or retirement pension), it is natural, under the logic of the capitalist system, for you to want to gain the maximum return on your capital; indeed the entire system is predicated on the competition of corporations and investment firms to return maximum profits to investors. But this very aspect of the system sometimes dictates corporate policies that are harmful to the public good, so that every investor develops a possible special interest, or a stake, in policies that they might personally oppose or that might harm them. The tobacco industry and the manufacture and sale of handguns, assault weapons, and war armaments in this country and internationally (where they have frequently been turned against Americans) are examples of industries where many investors' profits depend on the sale of products that much of the public has recognized as socially harmful. (See "Confessions of a Tobacco Lobbyist" in chapter 15.)

Higher profits for your corporate employer might be attained at the cost of lower wages for you, or even the loss of your job if the company downsizes or relocates to Third World countries where workers can be paid slave wages. Relocation also permits products like sports shoes to be sold at a lower price than if they were made in the United States, so what you save as a consumer buying sweatshop-produced goods may cost you as a worker. If you have money invested in energy stocks, you profit from high gas prices and reduction of environmental regulation, even though as a driver you may scream about the price at the pump or about air pollution from auto emissions. Maximizing profits can lead to businesses cutting corners on environmental protection, marketing products bad for health and nutrition, and maintaining unsafe workplaces.

Deliberate waste and "planned obsolescence" have become standard practices for hyping corporate profits. Stockings used to be manufactured to last and were mended when holes finally developed; now they spring holes after a few wearings and no one knows how to mend them. Cloth handkerchiefs, which were laundered when soiled, have been replaced by disposable tissues. Billions of plastic water bottles have replaced tap water around the world and cluttered the landscape, although recent research has indicated that bottled water may be no healthier; and most bottled drinks used to come in glass bottles that could be reused. We have been conditioned to buy food from American supermarkets in a plethora of little plastic bags, used once and thrown in the trash, although in most other countries people shop with their own fabric bags, which last for years. (This has recently become a trend in America—a good example of how culturally conditioned assumptions do eventually change.) Buying products on the Internet is a great convenience, but it can drive local merchants out of business and increases traffic for personal delivery. All of these practices contribute enormously not only to traffic jams and trash disposal problems (styrofoam and most packing "peanuts" aren't even recyclable), but to our excessive consumption of oil in manufacturing and transportation of products, and to further air pollution and other causes of global warming. To be sure, Communist countries like China have even worse environmental policies, and those of some (though not all) social democracies (see chapter 13) are little better than America's.

It is true that a growing number of companies have pledged to subordinate maximizing profits to socially responsible policies. Isn't it also true, however, that many investors have little or no awareness of the policies of companies in which they invest and perhaps would rather not know about irresponsible policies, as long as the profits are rolling in?

American society's norms of, and emphasis on, female beauty are largely taken for granted. However, in the reading in chapter 5 from Naomi Wolf's book *The Beauty Myth,* Wolf argues that these norms have been engineered and maintained mainly for the purposes of maximizing profits for "the $33-billion-a-year diet industry, the $20-billion cosmetics industry, the $300-million cosmetic surgery industry, and the $7-billion pornography industry" (17). Manufacturers of beauty and diet products conduct psychological depth research on what insecurities in women can be manipulated and then use the results to saturate print, broadcast, and film media with images and ads playing on these insecurities:

> Why is it never said that the really crucial function that women serve as aspiring beauties is *to buy more things for the body?* Somehow, somewhere, someone must have figured out that they will buy more things if they are kept in the self-hating, ever-failing, hungry, and sexually insecure state of being aspiring 'beauties.' (67)

In a final example of the more irrational aspects of capitalism, a headline in the *New York Times* (July 6, 1996) reads, "Signs of Unexpected Growth Send Markets Tumbling." The story, by Floyd Norris, reports that Wall Street "reacted with alarm to the disclosure that a lot more Americans were working than had been anticipated. The report renews concern that the Federal Reserve would soon tighten credit," thereby causing inflation (Y17). In a satirical column titled "Those Vital Paupers," in the *New York Times*, Russell Baker used verbal **irony** to comment humorously on this self-contradiction in relation to the Clinton administration's cutbacks in welfare benefits and attempts to move welfare recipients into jobs. "There is probably no solution to the welfare problem. It is the inescapable product of an economic system with which the powers that be are quite content.... Attacking the problem at its root would mean admitting that it is rooted in the structure of American capitalism." Baker explained, "The health of the American economy obviously depends on keeping a percentage of the workforce unemployed. The Federal Reserve System sees to this by constantly raising interest rates to prevent the economy from 'overheating.'" In addition, full employment and a surplus of available jobs would mean that workers can command higher wages. So a degree of unemployment—"Something around 5 percent seems to be just about right"—is desirable both to enable employers to pay lower wages and to prevent the inflation resulting from workers having more money to spend, thus causing consumer prices to rise. Thus Baker concludes that unemployed welfare recipients are beneficial to the economy, so that we should be grateful to them rather than despising them or pretending to oblige them to find nonexistent jobs.

The headline of an op-ed in the *New York Times* (June 30, 2002, online edition) by Kurt Eichenwald asks, "Could Capitalists Actually Bring Down Capitalism?" In the wake of recent corporate scandals, Eichenwald asks, "Could the short-time, self-rewarding mentality of a handful of capitalists truly destroy capitalism? Bring on hundreds of bankruptcies, force banks under, end the giving of loans? Destroy America as we know it?" These are the kinds of questions traditionally raised by Marxists and other socialists who believe that capitalism sows the seeds of its own destruction through its erratic cycles of boom and bust, financial "bubbles" and their bursting, such as we have seen over the first decade of the twenty-first century, and which have worsened since Eichenwald's article in 2002. Eichenwald's answer, though, reveals that he is a liberal capitalist, not a socialist (see the distinction in chapter 13): "Not very likely. The system has a built-in corrective factor, which kicks in when abuses go too far. Harm to investor confidence harms the market, which harms the ability of corporations to raise the capital they need to grow and be profitable. Eventually, the capitalists' desire to get investor confidence back wins the day."

PHALLOCENTRISM

Some feminist theorists have identified male "phallocentrism" or "patriarchy" (paternal rule) as a source of many of the world's evils and have advocated counterbalancing or replacing it with "gynocentrism," ways of being, doing, and communicating that are more cooperative and collective than competitive and individualistic, more nurturing and intuitive than autonomous and pragmatic. Two influential recent books along these lines are psychologist Carol Gilligan's *In a Different Voice: Psychological Theory and Women's Development,* and *Women's Ways of Knowing: The Development of Self, Voice, and Mind,* by Mary Field Belenky, Blythe McVicker Clinchy, Nancy Rule Goldberger, and Jill Mattuck Tarule. Gilligan and Belenky et al. modify and supplement the paradigms of cognitive development in the work of Piaget, William Perry, and Lawrence Kohlberg with the hypothesis that young women's cognitive development differs in important aspects from that of the young men studied exclusively by Perry and Kohlberg.

Some applications of feminist psychological theory have gone to the **equal and opposite extreme** in setting up an absolute opposition between male and female psychology, in favoring the latter unconditionally, and in throwing out the entire notion of stages of cognitive development for its alleged male bias. The most profound contribution that feminist approaches like Gilligan's and Belenky's have had, however, is in their more moderate versions, by simply pointing out the many ways in which biases in favor of men's assumed superiority and blind spots toward women's sensibility in society and in scholarship have resulted in neglect of the "feminine" side in each of us and in social values. See the excerpt from Virginia Woolf's book *A Room of One's Own* later in this chapter for Woolf's powerful description of the psychology behind the **culturally conditioned assumption** of male superiority throughout the ages.

OTHER CENTRISMS

Other kinds of "-centrism" have been the subject of heated debate in the "culture wars" of recent years. Multiculturalists have challenged the dominance of "Eurocentrism" in American and other Western cultures. Some African-American scholars have developed an entire competing philosophy of "Afrocentrism," emphasizing the centrality of contributions to civilization by black peoples over the ages, and in a few cases going to the **equal and opposite extreme** by inverting the claims of white supremacists to assert the biological superiority of the black race.

A little-known humorous essay by Benjamin Franklin, "Remarks Concerning the Savages of North America," written in 1784, skeptically satirizes the ethnocentrism of white Christians' sense of moral and religious superiority over Native Americans during the colonial period. In one of Franklin's **anecdotes**, "A Swedish Minister, having assembled the chiefs of the Susquehanah Indians, made a Sermon to them, acquainting them with the principal historical Facts on which our Religion is founded; such as the Fall of our first parents by eating an Apple, the coming of Christ to repair the Mischief, his Miracles and Suffering, etc. When he had finished, an Indian Orator stood up to thank him. 'What you have told us,' says he, 'is all very good. It is indeed bad to eat Apples. It is better to make them all into Cider.'" The Indian then tells some of his tribe's beliefs.

> The good Missionary, disgusted with this idle Tale, said, "What I delivered to you were sacred Truths; but what you tell me is mere Fable, Fiction, and Falsehood." The Indian, offended, reply'd, "My brother, it seems your Friends have not done you Justice in your Education; they have not well instructed you in the Rules of common Civility. You saw that we, who understand and practice those Rules, believ'd all your stories; why do you refuse to believe ours?"

Franklin's piece, though tongue-in-cheek, indicates that the belief in what many conservatives scorn as "moral relativism" in recognizing the worthiness of other cultures in comparison to our own was not the invention of twentieth-century academics but derives from a tradition dating back at least to the eighteenth-century secular intellectual movement called the Enlightenment, of which Franklin, Jefferson, and other "founders" were prominent advocates.

Many writers in the skeptical tradition have satirized not only the follies of ethnocentrism but also those of the human race as a whole, in its often excessive pretensions to superiority over the rest of nature and our "anthropocentric" (or, more commonly, "anthropomorphic")

THE FAR SIDE® By GARY LARSON

"That was incredible. No fur, claws, horns, antlers, or nothin' ... just soft and pink."

tendency to view animals, the earth, and the universe through human lenses. Reversal of our anthropomorphic perspective is the most common theme in Gary Larson's "Far Side" cartoons, which look at humans from the viewpoint of animals or extraterrestrials. Satirists in earlier centuries have taken similar views. In book 4 of *Gulliver's Travels* (1726) by Jonathan Swift, the hero finds himself in the land of the Houyhnhnms, horselike creatures whose intelligence and virtues far exceed those of humans, while their slaves—filthy, malicious, monkeylike creatures called Yahoos—are gradually revealed to symbolize the human race.

Mark Twain's essay "The Lowest Animal," written around 1905, applies Twain's inimitable humorous style to a devastatingly "decentering" reversal of the conventional belief that the "moral sense" elevates humans above the animals. Twain puns on Charles Darwin's theory that humans are descended through evolution from animals, in describing the results of his studies, which contradict Darwin's account of the ascent of humans from "'the lower animals' (so called)." Twain writes: "It now seems plain to me that that theory ought to be vacated in favor of a new and truer one, this new and truer one to be named the *Descent* of Man from the Higher Animals."

> The higher animals engage in individual fights, but never in organized masses. Man is the only animal that deals in that atrocity of atrocities, War. He is the only one that gathers his brethren about him and goes forth in cold blood and with calm pulse to exterminate his kind. He is

the only animal that for sordid wages will march out, as the Hessians did in our Revolution, and as the boyish Prince Napoleon did in the Zulu war, and help to slaughter strangers of his own species who have done him no harm and with whom he has no quarrel. . . .

Man is the only Patriot. He sets himself apart in his own country, under his own flag, and sneers at the other nations, and keeps multitudinous uniformed assassins on hand at heavy expense to grab slices of other people's countries, and to keep *them* from grabbing slices of *his*. And in the intervals between campaigns he washes the blood off his hands and works for "the universal brotherhood of man"—with his mouth.

Man is the Religious Animal. He is the only Religious Animal. He is the only animal that has the True Religion—several of them. He is the only animal that loves his neighbor as himself, and cuts his throat if his theology isn't straight. He has made a graveyard of the globe in trying his honest best to smooth his brother's path to happiness and heaven. (225–226)

From *A Room of One's Own*

Virginia Woolf

Harcourt, 1929

Life for both sexes ... is arduous, difficult, perpetual struggle. It calls for gigantic courage and strength. More than anything, perhaps, creatures of illusion as we are, it calls for confidence in oneself. Without self-confidence we are as babes in the cradle. And how can we generate this imponderable quality, which is yet so invaluable, most quickly? By thinking that other people are inferior to oneself. By feeling that one has some innate superiority—it may be wealth, or rank, a straight nose, or the portrait of a grandfather by Romney—for there is no end to the pathetic devices of the human imagination—over other people. Hence the enormous importance to a patriarch who has to conquer, who has to rule, of feeling that great numbers of people, half the human race indeed, are by nature inferior to himself. . . . Women have served all these centuries as looking-glasses possessing the magic and delicious power of reflecting the figure of man at twice its natural size. . . . That serves to explain in part the necessity that women so often are to men. And it serves to explain how restless they are under her criticism; how impossible it is for her to say to them this book is bad, this picture is feeble, or whatever it may be, without giving far more pain and rousing far more anger than a man would do who gave the same criticism. For if she begins to tell the truth, the figure in the looking-glass shrinks; his fitness for life is diminished. How is he to go on giving judgements, civilizing natives, making laws, writing books, dressing up and speechifying at banquets, unless he can see himself at breakfast and dinner at least twice the size he really is? (34–36).

Anti-Capitalism in Five Minutes or Less

Robert Jensen

CommonDreams.org, April 30, 2007

We know that capitalism is not just the most sensible way to organize an economy but is now the only possible way to organize an economy. We know that dissenters to this conventional wisdom can, and should, be ignored. There's no longer even any need to persecute such heretics; they are obviously irrelevant.

How do we know all this? Because we are told so, relentlessly—typically by those who have the most to gain from such a claim, most notably those in the business world and their functionaries and apologists in the schools, universities, mass media, and mainstream politics. Capitalism is not a choice, but rather simply is, like a state of nature. Maybe not like a state of nature, but the state of nature. To contest capitalism these days is like arguing against the air that we breathe. Arguing against capitalism, we're told, is simply crazy.

We are told, over and over, that capitalism is not just the system we have, but the only system we can ever have. Yet for many, something nags at us about such a claim. Could this really be the only option? We're told we shouldn't even think about such things. But we can't help thinking—is this really the "end of history," in the sense that big thinkers have used that phrase to signal the final victory of global capitalism? If this is the end of history in that sense, we wonder, can the actual end of the planet far behind?

We wonder, we fret, and these thoughts nag at us—for good reason. Capitalism—or, more accurately, the predatory corporate capitalism that defines and dominates our lives—will be our death if we don't escape it. Crucial to progressive politics is finding the language to articulate that reality, not in outdated dogma that alienates but in plain language that resonates with people. We should be searching for ways to explain to co-workers in water-cooler conversations—radical politics in five minutes or less—why we must abandon predatory corporate capitalism. If we don't, we may well be facing the end times, and such an end will bring rupture not rapture.

Here's my shot at the language for this argument.

Capitalism is admittedly an incredibly productive system that has created a flood of goods unlike anything the world has ever seen. It also is a system that is fundamentally (1) inhuman, (2) anti-democratic, and (3) unsustainable. Capitalism has given those of us in the First World lots of stuff (most of it of marginal or questionable value) in exchange for our souls, our hope for progres-sive politics, and the possibility of a decent future for children.

In short, either we change or we die—spiritually, politically, literally.

1. Capitalism is inhuman

There is a theory behind contemporary capitalism. We're told that because we are greedy, self-interested animals, an economic system must reward greedy, self-interested behavior if we are to thrive economically.

Are we greedy and self-interested? Of course. At least I am, sometimes. But we also just as obviously are capable of compassion and selflessness. We certainly can act competitively and aggressively, but we also have the capacity for solidarity and cooperation. In short, human nature is wide-ranging. Our actions are certainly rooted in our nature, but all we really know about that nature is that it is widely variable. In situations where compassion and solidarity are the norm, we tend to act that way. In situations where competitiveness and aggression are rewarded, most people tend toward such behavior.

Why is it that we must choose an economic system that undermines the most decent aspects of our nature and strengthens the most inhuman? Because, we're told, that's just the way people are. What evidence is there of that? Look around, we're told, at how people behave. Everywhere we look, we see greed and the pursuit of self-interest. So, the proof that these greedy, self-interested aspects of our nature are dominant is that, when forced into a system that rewards greed and self-interested behavior, people often act that way. Doesn't that seem just a bit circular?

2. Capitalism is anti-democratic

This one is easy. Capitalism is a wealth-concentrating system. If you concentrate wealth in a society, you concentrate power. Is there any historical example to the contrary?

For all the trappings of formal democracy in the contemporary United States, everyone understands that the wealthy dictate the basic outlines of the public policies that are acceptable to the vast majority of elected officials. People can and do resist, and an occasional politician joins the fight, but such resistance takes extraordinary effort. Those who resist win victories, some of them inspiring, but to date concentrated wealth continues to dominate. Is this any way to run a democracy?

If we understand democracy as a system that gives ordinary people a meaningful way to participate in the formation of public policy, rather than just a role in ratifying decisions made by the powerful, then it's clear that capitalism and democracy are mutually exclusive.

Let's make this concrete. In our system, we believe that regular elections with the one-person/one-vote rule, along with protections for freedom of speech and association, guarantee political equality. When I go to the polls, I have one vote. When Bill Gates goes the polls, he has one vote. Bill and I both can speak freely and associate with others for political purposes. Therefore, as equal citizens in our fine democracy, Bill and I have equal opportunities for political power. Right?

3. Capitalism is unsustainable

This one is even easier. Capitalism is a system based on the idea of unlimited growth. The last time I checked, this is a finite planet. There are only two ways out of this one. Perhaps we will be hopping to a new planet soon. Or perhaps, because we need to figure out ways to cope with these physical limits, we will invent ever-more complex technologies to transcend those limits.

Both those positions are equally delusional. Delusions may bring temporary comfort, but they don't solve problems. They tend, in fact, to cause more problems. Those problems seem to be piling up.

Capitalism is not, of course, the only unsustainable system that humans have devised, but it is the most obviously unsustainable system, and it's the one in which we are stuck. It's the one that we are told is inevitable and natural, like the air.

A tale of two acronyms: TGIF and TINA

Former British Prime Minister Margaret Thatcher's famous response to a question about challenges to capitalism was TINA—

There Is No Alternative. If there is no alternative, anyone who questions capitalism is crazy.

Here's another, more common, acronym about life under a predatory corporate capitalism: TGIF—Thank God It's Friday. It's a phrase that communicates a sad reality for many working in this economy—the jobs we do are not rewarding, not enjoyable, and fundamentally not worth doing. We do them to survive. Then on Friday we go out and get drunk to forget about that reality, hoping we can find something during the weekend that makes it possible on Monday to, in the words of one songwriter, "get up and do it again."

Remember, an economic system doesn't just produce goods. It produces people as well. Our experience of work shapes us. Our experience of consuming those goods shapes us. Increasingly, we are a nation of unhappy people consuming miles of aisles of cheap consumer goods, hoping to dull the pain of unfulfilling work. Is this who we want to be?

We're told TINA in a TGIF world. Doesn't that seem a bit strange? Is there really no alternative to such a world? Of course there is. Anything that is the product of human choices can be chosen differently. We don't need to spell out a new system in all its specifics to realize there always are alternatives. We can encourage the existing institutions that provide a site of resistance (such as labor unions) while we experiment with new forms (such as local cooperatives). But the first step is calling out the system for what it is, without guarantees of what's to come.

Home and abroad

In the First World, we struggle with this alienation and fear. We often don't like the values of the world around us; we often don't like the people we've become; we often are afraid of what's to come of us. But in the First World, most of us eat regularly. That's not the case everywhere. Let's focus not only on the conditions we face within a predatory corporate capitalist system, living in the most affluent country in the history of the world, but also put this in a global context.

Half the world's population lives on less than $2 a day. That's more than 3 billion people. Just over half of the population of sub-Saharan Africa lives on less than $1 a day. That's more than 300 million people.

How about one more statistic: About 500 children in Africa die from poverty-related diseases, and the majority of those deaths could be averted with simple medicines or insecticide-treated nets. That's 500 children—not every year, or every month or every week. That's not 500 children every day. Poverty-related diseases claim the lives of 500 children an hour in Africa.

When we try to hold onto our humanity, statistics like that can make us crazy. But don't get any crazy ideas about changing this system. Remember TINA: There is no alternative to predatory corporate capitalism.

What Is Realistic? What Is Crazy?

One of the common responses I hear when I critique capitalism is, "Well, that may all be true, but we have to be realistic and do what's possible." By that logic, to be realistic is to accept a system that is inhuman, anti-democratic, and unsustainable. To be realistic we are told we must capitulate to a system that steals our souls, enslaves us to concentrated power, and will someday destroy the planet.

But rejecting and resisting a predatory corporate capitalism is not crazy. It is an eminently sane position. Holding onto our humanity is not crazy. Defending democracy is not crazy. And struggling for a sustainable future is not crazy.

What is truly crazy is falling for the con that an inhuman, anti-democratic, and unsustainable system—one that leaves half the world's people in abject poverty—is all that there is, all that there ever can be, all that there ever will be.

If that were true, then soon there will be nothing left, for anyone.

I do not believe it is realistic to accept such a fate. If that's being realistic, I'll take crazy any day of the week.

Topics for Discussion and Writing

1. Discuss the form of skepticism that "does not deny that there are objective, external truths, but asserts that these truths are often too obscure or complex for any one human being to know *with absolute certainty*, so that our *perceptions* of objective reality are inevitably colored to a large extent by our subjective viewpoint. . . . Objectivity is a worthy goal to strive for, though we can rarely attain it completely. Paradoxically, becoming aware of our subjective viewpoint and biases is an essential step toward objectivity." What examples or evidence can you present in support of this position, and what ones against it? Which people whom you know or know of might disagree with it, and why?

2. "Primary certitude is a psychological term for the mind-set of people who are fixed in absolute beliefs so dogmatically that they cannot bear to have those beliefs questioned or doubted." Write a description of someone you know who is captive to primary certitude on some particular subject.

3. "Can you remember any instance in which you thought a statement by a politician, a news reporter or commentator, a teacher or textbook was biased when that statement supported *your* side?" Can you? The next time you hear or read such a statement, try to think of ways in which it might in fact be biased.

4. Find examples of the ESBYODS principle in (a) your own personal relationships and those of others you know, and (b) current public arguments.

5. Apply Rogerian argument or Doubters and Believers, in class discussion or individual writing, to any of the opposed sources in the readings for this book, such as those on the beauty myth in chapter 5.

6. Write or role-play in class discussion an imagined version of a Rogerian argument between leading Republicans and Democrats, or between the opponents on *Crossfire*-style TV talk programs.

7. Discuss and write notes on some culturally conditioned assumptions, totems and taboos, that strike you as artificial and questionable.

8. Think of one example, from your own experience or knowledge, of a case in which ethnocentrism has served a socially beneficial function and one in which it has served a harmful one.

9. Think of a recent, specific example in America of a public figure indulging in what you consider **demagogy** or the **plain folks** fallacy in appealing to the mass audience's ethnocentrism. Think of another example of someone authentically speaking as a populist. Support your judgments with evidence.

10. What do you think Mrs. Hart, the school board chair in Larry Rohter's "Battle over Patriotism Curriculum," might say in **rebuttal** to the unfavorable statistics about the United States in Shapiro's *We're Number One*, Brouwer's *Sharing the Pie*, or Jensen's "Anti-Capitalism"?

11. Stage a class debate between defenders of corporate capitalism as the traditional "American way of life" and the account of the founders' anticorporate views documented by Hightower and Frazer in the excerpts in this chapter.

12. How seriously do you think Russell Baker's humorous argument can be taken that welfare recipients are "vital paupers," serving to keep employment rates, wages, and inflation low? How defensible a **refutation** is this of conservatives' belief that people are unemployed or on welfare mainly because of lack of motivation or skills? It might similarly be argued that in a capitalist economy, a large number of low-wage workers are required to do necessary but undesirable jobs, so that people with relatively privileged jobs would not necessarily want everyone to have equal educational or employment opportunity because it might increase competition and raise prices. True or false?

13. Individually or collectively, do some research on organizations dedicated to reducing environmental waste and destruction or to investing responsibly.

14. Conservatives often accuse liberal Democrats of being anti-capitalistic, but isn't it in fact a **taboo** for any Democratic leader to come out openly rejecting capitalism as Jensen does in, "Anti-Capitalism"? (Barack Obama repeatedly says, "I believe in capitalism," before criticizing some aspect of it that needs reform.) Jensen, professor of journalism at the University of Texas, Austin, challenges our culturally conditioned assumption that TINA—"there is no alternative" to capitalism, but admits that expressing views like his gets one dismissed in America as crazy. Indeed, in American mass media this position is typically labeled as "extremist," "fanatical," or only held by "the loony left." Debate with classmates what if anything you find in his article that merits these labels, or that is not worthy of widespread public consideration. (Why don't I "balance" this article with one defending capitalism? Aren't we saturated in the assumptions of capitalism every day, usually without any views balanced against *them*?) See chapter 13 for further arguments about differences between liberal Democrats and socialists and about the pros and cons of capitalism versus democratic socialism—which Jensen clearly identifies with, against what he argues are the undemocratic systems of both capitalism and "the outdated dogma" of Communism.

15. How accurate in the contemporary United States is Woolf's portrait of the importance to the powerful male "who has to conquer, who has to rule, of feeling

that great numbers of people, half the human race indeed, are by nature inferior to himself," and the corollary that "women have served all these centuries as looking-glasses possessing the magic and delicious power of reflecting the figure of man at twice its natural size"?

16. Woolf asks, "How is he to go on ... civilizing natives ... unless he can see himself at breakfast and dinner at least twice the size he really is?" Woolf was a harsh critic of British colonialism. With that knowledge we can **infer** or **read between the lines** that she meant "civilizing natives" as **irony**. There is also an echo in this line of Jonathan Swift's *Gulliver's Travels,* in which Swift, two centuries before Woolf, discussed English and European conquest of distant lands "by Divine Right" (the belief that all actions of kings were approved by God):

Ships are sent with the first opportunity; the natives driven out or destroyed, their princes tortured to discover their gold; a free license given to all acts of inhumanity and lust; the earth reeking with the blood of its inhabitants; and this execrable crew of butchers employed in so pious an expedition is a *modern colony* sent to convert and civilize an idolatrous and barbaric people. (237)

Who is Swift suggesting are the real "idolatrous and barbaric people" and who are the civilized ones? Compare his use of irony on this subject with Woolf's, as well as with Franklin's in "Remarks Concerning the Savages of North America" and Twain's in "The Lowest Animal."

CHAPTER 7

Overgeneralization, Stereotyping, and Prejudice

Inadequately qualified generalizations, or **overgeneralizations**, are probably the most common and often the most offensive variety of logical fallacy, especially in the forms of **stereotyping** and **prejudice**. Almost all oral or written communications, and particularly arguments, involve frequent generalizations. (The last two sentences just made some.) Generalizations are central elements of argumentation, then, and perfectly legitimate, when they are adequately qualified. Critical thinkers and writers must constantly **draw the line** about the degree to which they can accurately generalize without lapsing into overgeneralization; they must regularly decide what is the highest acceptable level of generalization, from the following ladders of adjectives and adverbs:

all	always
almost all	almost always
most	usually
many	often, frequently
some	sometimes
a few	occasionally
almost no/none	almost never
no/none	never

Good axioms are "Never say never" or "Almost never say never," and "Never say all/always" or "almost never say all/always." Even when you say or write "most," listeners or readers are apt to expect you to provide evidence. Both "Most welfare recipients cannot find a good-paying job no matter how hard they try" and "Most welfare recipients could find a good job if they tried" call for documentation through citing **empirical** studies, with statistics and percentage points verifying that the statement is true of a majority of those studied. "Many" is not as likely to require evidence, and "some" is even safer—though in the preceding two sentences, the use of these safer adjectives is still likely to be met with a demand for statistics. (Specific percentages in general are preferable to any of these degrees of generalization.) So always (there he goes again!) bring your generalizations down to the safest level, and be careful to use further qualifying phrases like "listeners or readers *are apt to* expect you to provide evidence," and "Cautious writers *tend to* qualify their generalizations."

Try to keep in mind, then, first, that not all generalizations are overgeneralizations or stereotypes and, second, that stereotypes are not always prejudiced and that some may be accurate to a degree. Indeed, some people do act in a stereotypical manner, unintentionally or even intentionally, in an effort to conform to a certain image. There are students, unfortunately, who do come across as computer nerds, dumb jocks, sorority queens, and so on, although it is a pleasant surprise when one shows that such a first impression is deceptive. African Americans derisively refer to "Uncle Toms," blacks who act in just the stereotyped servile manner that pleases racist whites. Stereotyping can also be a two-edged sword, as when certain people, in stereotyping others unfairly, become a stereotype themselves, an Archie Bunker–like bundle of prejudices. Among the sources you read or listen to, criticize those that are guilty of stereotyping without adequate support, but praise those that provide supported criticisms of stereotyping in their opponents.

When you read an author or listen to a speaker, watch carefully for the qualifications and degrees in their generalizations and be fair-minded toward sources. Beware of a common form of **false inference** in which the reader or listener (often emotionally involved in the issue) assumes that the writer or speaker has overgeneralized when in fact she or he has not done so.

PREJUDICE

Prejudice is an extremely touchy subject to discuss today. Many people insist they aren't prejudiced and get indignant at any suggestion that they might be. Even the most virtuous of us, however, are bound to have some prejudices, and the best we can do is acknowledge and do our best to overcome them. Throughout human history most cultures have been steeped in prejudices. In the United States, until a few decades ago, prejudices were blatantly displayed toward African Americans and many other ethnic and racial groups as well as women and homosexuals. Prejudices were not only accepted as **culturally conditioned assumptions** but as the basis for jokes, comedy routines, and face-to-face taunting, extending even to handicapped, obese, or homely people. Movements like those for civil rights and women's and gay liberation put opposition to prejudice on the national agenda; consequently, the cultural norms have shifted significantly, especially among younger people, and most Americans regard this shift as an advance toward a more humane society.

Nowadays, it is no longer as common to hear people express outright bigotry, to declare, "I hate ——s," or to make stereotypical overgeneralizations about all members of a group. This is not to say, however, that prejudice no longer exists. In the 1980s and 1990s, the United States and other countries saw a resurgence of prejudice in the growth of white supremacist and neo-Nazi groups, and even college campuses, ideally bastions of tolerance, became the sites of widespread incidents of racist and homophobic hate speech and occasional violence.

In many cases, however, people have simply learned to be more guarded in expressing their prejudices, to restrict them to special settings, such as white male enclaves like bars, clubs, and sports events. Golf is my game, and I am continually embarrassed in playing at public courses by "the guys" assuming everyone wants to listen to jokes based on the crudest ethnic and sexual stereotypes. Or people will speak in certain codes; they will say, for example, "I'm not prejudiced, but …"—and then go on to express highly prejudiced opinions. (This is a nice example of that form of **compartmentalization** I've termed **I won't, but I will**.) Or they will denounce welfare recipients and high illegitimacy rates without explicitly associating them with African Americans, although it is implicit that they are the group being referred to, or they will complain about illegal immigration, when they are thinking specifically of Mexicans or Central Americans.

Moreover, prejudice doesn't always consist of blatant bigotry but may take more subtle forms. It comes out in people's readiness to jump to **hasty conclusions** or to overgeneralize about some groups. After the U.S. government building in Oklahoma City was bombed by Timothy McVeigh in 1995, many American mass media, politicians, and citizens immediately assumed that the perpetrators were Arabs or Muslims—groups stereotypically associated with terrorism. Similarly, prejudice comes out in considering every individual in one group as responsible for, or **guilty by association** with, its worst members. This kind of prejudice was evident in several violent acts against innocent American Muslims after the Oklahoma City bombing and again after September 11, 2001, when this kind of irrationality extended to hate acts against dark-skinned Americans or citizens from a variety of national origins and religions, including some East Indian Hindus. Prejudice comes out in an ethnocentric **double standard**—the ESBYODS principle—when we exact a higher degree of morality from some other group than from our own, in **selective vision** when we get angry at that group for something that doesn't bother us in our own, in **playing up** or exaggerating that group's wealth, power, or privileges while **downplaying** or understating our own in comparison.

For example, Jews are often negatively stereotyped as being "pushy" because their culture has a long tradition of encouraging industriousness and high professional achievement—qualities that are generally praised in the majority culture. Anti-Semitism similarly involves a faulty **causal analysis** attributing Jews' high achievement level in many professions to a conspiracy or favoritism by those in power toward their own—an explanation that is likely to be a resentful **rationalization** for the more plausible explanation, that the achievement level results mainly from the same tradition of socialization of children to be achievers, and that Jews probably favor their own no more and no less than any other group when given the opportunity.

What prejudice isn't. Another point of confusion concerning prejudice is that, in accordance with the ESBYODS principle in chapter 6, we all are inclined to label any viewpoint opposed to our own as "prejudiced." Keep in mind, however, this point from chapter 2, "An unprejudiced opinion, however adamant or emotional, is one that is justified by the facts of the situation, as verified by evidence." So it is a form of **ad hominem** fallacy to dismiss an argument that is disagreeable to you by saying the author is prejudiced, rather than judging the argument on its own merits.

CLASS PREJUDICE

One of the most common and universal forms of prejudice is that toward people in social classes below one's own. Gordon Allport, a Harvard psychologist associated with the philosophy of general semantics, discusses this form in his book *The Nature of Prejudice,* first published in 1954:

> Now young children early learn the facts of caste and class. In one experiment, both white and Negro children in kindergarten and in the first and second grades were given different types of doll clothing and houses, and asked to assign them to dolls representing Negro and white men and women. A great majority of the children of both races gave the white doll good clothes and housing, and the Negro doll poor clothes and housing.... One little girl, five years of age, cried when she saw the Negro family next door moving away. "Now," she wailed, "there is no one that we are better than."

At a somewhat older age, children are inclined to ascribe all sorts of virtues to upper-class individuals and all sorts of defects to members of the lower classes. An experiment with fifth- and-sixth-grade children, for example, asked them to give the names of schoolmates whom they considered "clean," "dirty," "good-looking," "not good-looking," "always having a good time," and the like. For every desirable quality the children of higher social classes in the school were given high ratings. Children from lower social classes were given lower ratings. It seems that the youngsters were not able to perceive their classmates as individuals, but only as representatives of class. To them children from the upper classes seem to be good-in-general; from the lower classes, bad-in-general. Since these fifth and sixth graders are "thinking ill without sufficient warrant" we conclude that they are manifesting class prejudice. (322)

As these experiments indicate, we seem much more inclined to be prejudiced against those below us on the socioeconomic scale than against those above us. The diagram in figure 7.1 suggests the hypothesis that people in the middle class tend to have a **double standard** toward the rich and poor.

In a paper on the morality of the rich and poor, a student writes, "Many of those in poverty are perfectly able to work, yet still don't. I personally have seen people sitting on curbs with signs saying, 'Will work for food.' What makes me so mad is that right behind them there is a fast food restaurant with a sign in the window claiming that they were now hiring. You cannot tell me that these people have not lost their incentive to make something of themselves." And, a few pages later: "Conservatives feel that the rich have been unnecessarily stereotyped. Granted, there are the few who take advantage of their wealth through corporate crimes such as embezzlement, racketeering, income tax evasion, and insider trading. However, I feel that these crimes are a small minority of those in the highest tax bracket of wealth. Many wealthy people are a benefit to our society and should not be penalized by being stereotyped."

Authoritarianism
Sentimentality
Positive stereotypes and
    generalizations
"Clean" words
Rationalizations excusing their
    privileges and misdeeds

Middle-class
ethnocentric attitudes

Prejudice
Negative stereotpyes and
    generalizations
"Dirty" words
Rationalizations for dumping on
    them (blaming the victim)

Figure 7.1. Middle-Class Ethnocentric Attitudes

Note this student's quickness to generalize about the "many" unvirtuous poor, versus the "few" unvirtuous rich and the "many" who are a benefit to society—without any data indicating the relevant percentages in both groups or other support beyond "I feel" and the one example of the people with the "Will work for food" sign. (Do employers hire the first person who walks in the door, without checking their physical condition, qualifications and references? See Stephanie Salter's "An Unexpected Education at St. Anthony's" here for a first-hand account of the circumstances of street people.) Also note the **selective vision** in the student's complaint about the rich being stereotyped, with no comparable recognition of stereotyping about the poor, in which the paper itself might be considered to indulge.

We in the middle class are strongly conditioned to be prejudiced in favor of the rich. After all, many, many people would like to be rich, but almost no one wants to be poor. The rich have power over us, as employers and otherwise, while we have power over the poor and are apt to resent the threats they pose to us through crime, begging, or dependence on government aid. The rich tend to be surrounded with people eager to serve them, gain a piece of the pie, and eventually join their ranks. Think *The Apprentice*—wasn't that program basically a shrine to Donald Trump's power to hire and fire?

In fact, the case can be made that there is as much crime and misconduct at the top of any society as at the bottom—although this tends to be a **taboo** subject for widespread public discussion in America. Think about it. To begin with, isn't it plausible that the larger the amount of money available, the more likely it is to attract greedy or dishonest people? What's more, we are more likely to encounter poor people "up close and personal," and to see their misconduct, than very rich people, who live out of our immediate sight and whose business and personal lives are largely beyond critical scrutiny or accountability. The effects of their misconduct might harm us more in the long run than street crime, but its immediate effects are not likely to be visible.

When I was working in celebrity journalism and public relations in New York in the 1960's, my job included making the rounds of the most expensive restaurants and nightclubs, centers of the "lifestyle of the rich and famous." What I saw was not only celebrities, but lesser-known billionaire playboys, executives, publicists, and lobbyists of top corporations, spending hundreds of dollars (thousands in today's terms) in partying nightly. Virtually all this spending was on company expense accounts, deducted from taxes as "business expenses." The businesspeople often were "entertaining" (often a **euphemism** for bribing) clients, government officials (Democrats and Republicans alike), journalists and media personalities. As they indulged in the most expensive alcohol, drugs, and prostitutes, the attitude I heard frequently expressed was contempt for "middle class morality" and the "suckers" like my family back in Iowa who idolize the rich while decrying their taxes being wasted on welfare swindlers. This is my first-hand evidence. Does it indicate a prejudice against the rich?

In the readings at the end of this chapter, Donald Barlett and James Steele recount some of the excesses of expense account spending that, along with speculative investment in "junk bonds," contributed to the collapse of the savings and loan industry in the 1980s and the need for taxpayers to "pay for a bailout expected to cost more than $1.5 billion." A similar pattern repeated itself in the late 2000s in the meltdown of the banking and mortgage industries precipitated by their speculation in risky, subprime mortgages, with the government stepping in to bailout the biggest loan companies. Business reporter Russell Mokhiber edits the online journal *Multinational Monitor*, which compiles an annual list of the "Ten Worst Corporations," inspired by the FBI's "Ten Most Wanted Criminals." In "Corporations: Underworld, USA" (*In These Times*, April 1, 1996), Mokhiber wrote, "The FBI reports burglary and robbery combined cost the nation about $4 billion in 1995. In contrast, white-collar fraud, generally committed by intelligent people of means—such as doctors, lawyers, accountants and businessmen—alone costs an estimated 50 times as much—$200 billion a year." Mokhiber argues that those at the bottom of society can hardly be expected to respect law and order when those at the top set such a poor example, and that these lost billions deprive the government of possible means for preventing poverty and crime at the bottom. "Corporate welfare" is an **ironic** term for government subsidies and "earmarks" to "needy corporations," such as those in Lisa Hoffman's reading here, "Dozens of Billionaires Receive Ag Handouts." This practice has been denounced by critics on both the political left and right, such as prominent libertarian conservative Stephen Moore, who reports, "The Cato Institute [a leading libertarian think tank] calculates that Congress finances more than 125 programs that subsidize private businesses at a net cost of about $85 billion per year. Add tax breaks, and the price tag exceeds $100 billion a year—or half the annual Federal deficit" (*New York Times*, April 5, 1995). Corporate welfare, along with other **special interest** legislation and occasional outright bribery of legislators, most often is initiated by corporations lobbying for favoritism—not by the government forcing money into the hands of its beneficiaries. Pulitzer Prize–winning *New York Times* reporter David Cay Johnston, who describes himself as a moderate conservative, has published one book titled *Perfectly Legal: The Covert Campaign to Rig Our Tax System to Benefit the Super-Rich—and Cheat Everybody Else*, and another, *Free Lunch: How the Wealthiest Americans Enrich Themselves at Government Expense (and Stick You With the Bill)*.

A parade of corporate criminals in the 2000s included figures like Dennis Koslowski of Worldcom, who staged a million-dollar toga-themed birthday party for himself in Rome on the company's expense account shortly before it went bankrupt. Enron, one of the country's largest and most politically influential corporations in the energy business, was guilty of causing electrical outages and jacking up prices in California by creating artificial shortages. In collusion with the Arthur Andersen accounting firm, Enron fabricated fictitious subsidiaries to boost the value of its stock, justifying multimillion-dollar executive salaries. When they received warnings of whistleblowers about to go public, the top executives, without notifying anyone below them, sold their stock at a vast profit, just before the stock plummeted and the company went bankrupt, causing the ruin of small stockholders and employees who had been encouraged to invest in the company pension plan. When CEO Kenneth Lay died shortly after his conviction, a court ruled that his estate could not be held responsible for compensating those he had defrauded.

In 2006 Washington corporate lobbyist Jack Abramoff pleaded guilty to a cluster of charges of multimillion dollar frauds, bribes to members to Congress, and tax evasion, and is now in prison. According to CNN, evidence in his trial included "thousands of e-mails in which he describes influence-peddling and explains what lawmakers were doing in exchange for the money he was putting into their campaign coffers." Typical was Republican Representative Bob Ney, who received from Abramoff "a 'lavish' golf trip to Scotland, tickets to sporting events and other entertainment, meals at Abramoff's 'upscale' Washington restaurant, and campaign contributions to the representative and his political action committee in exchange for a series of actions by that representative." Abramoff and his partner Michael Scanlon, former press secretary to House Majority Leader Tom DeLay, lobbied and were public relations agents for several Indian tribes seeking favorable legislation for their gambling casinos. "Abramoff and others would cause clients to falsely believe that some of the fees charged were being used for specific purposes, when the money was being used for their own personal benefit." For example, "Abramoff persuaded a Louisiana tribe to pay nearly $30.5 million for 'grass roots work' to a Scanlon company, which, in turn, kicked back nearly $11.4 million to Abramoff." According to an e-mail obtained by a Senate committee, Abramoff made a fortune from the tribes while privately mocking tribal leaders as "monkeys" and "morons." In partnership with former Christian Coalition leader Ralph Reed, Abramoff formed a non-profit organization of religious conservatives through which they solicited millions from members, ostensibly to lobby against the establishment of gambling casinos, but in reality used to lobby for one tribe's casinos over others. (Reed and contributors like

James Dobson, head of Focus on the Family, denied that they knew the contributions were misused.) Ney was convicted of taking bribes and resigned his seat. Scanlon was convicted of fraud. DeLay, a long-time close associate of Abramoff and beneficiary of his favors, resigned his House seat in 2006 under pressure from fellow Republicans over a long list of corruption charges, although he has maintained his innocence in his book *No Retreat, No Surrender*. The *Washington Post* quoted Abramoff saying, "I can't imagine there's anything I did that other lobbyists didn't do and aren't doing today." (Sources: "Lobbyist Admits Kickbacks, Influence Peddling," *CNN Online*, January 3, 2006; "Unraveling Abramoff," *Washington Post*, June 26, 2007; "Abramoff's Evangelical Soldiers," *The Nation Online*, February 2, 2006.)

Republican Representative Randall "Duke" Cunningham was convicted of receiving $2.4 million dollars from weapons manufacturers for favoritism in military contracts for the Iraq War. Democratic Representative William Jefferson was convicted of receiving $400,000 in bribes, also from military contractors. In none of these cases or many other prominent recent ones implicating both Republicans and Democrats in Congress, were lobbyists working for, or politicians bribed by, welfare recipients or minimum wage workers—who have no organization or money or expense accounts to hire lobbyists and make campaign contributions—nor even by unions, including teachers' unions, although lobbying and occasional bribery and fraud by union leaders do occur too. (See *Fortune*'s list of top lobbies in chapter 15, and a report in the *Los Angeles Times*, August 9, 2008, about officials of the Service Employees International Union defrauding their members of hundreds of thousands of dollars in dues.)

When students read accounts like these of misconduct by the wealthy and corporations, they may be inclined to say their authors are over-generalizing by implying that all rich people and corporate executives are crooks. Conservative **polemicists** especially are apt to say, "Sure, there are a few rotten apples in every barrel, but they're the exception to the rule. Intellectuals and the media always play up all the bad things rich people and corporate executives do, but why don't they give equal time to all the good things and to the rich people who work hard for their money, who are civic-minded and charitable?" These reactions in turn might sometimes involve an element of over-reaction, **false inference**, and **defense mechanism** in our tendency to jump to the defense of those who are in positions of authority and whom we would like to emulate. After all, rich people do not really need defending by those in the middle class; they can do it themselves quite adequately through owning media and hiring public relations and advertising agencies, lobbyists, and corporate lawyers, as surveyed in chapter 15. For an example of many media's willingness to provide a cosmetic gloss on corporate criminals, see Holly Miller's "Bunker Hunt's Greatest Investment" in chapter 12.

None of these authors do imply that all rich people or corporations are crooks, nor do they need to do so to make their case. The appropriate level of generalization here is a complicated matter and needs to be carefully qualified. Obviously, *some* wealth is made or compounded through honest, hard work, but some isn't. *Some* wealthy people are public-spirited, scrupulous, and innocent of the above kinds of abuses of power—but others aren't. The real issues, which need to be studied through scholarly research, critical thinking, and debate, are these: How can we determine whether the positive things rich people do, individually or collectively, outweigh the negative ones, or vice versa? (Consider Bunker Hunt's charitable activities and ardent Christianity weighed against his multimillion-dollar fraud and income-tax evasion in silver trading.) If some rich people are scrupulous and some aren't, what is to prevent those who aren't from prevailing over those who are? How many rotten apples does it take to spoil the barrel? Has corporate misconduct increased over recent decades, and if so, why? (Liberal sources, like Barlett and Steele here, make the case that the excessive power of wealthy people and corporations over government since the 1980s has resulted in many kinds of legislation, especially relaxation of regulatory standards, that have opened the gates for abuses like the S & L, Enron, and subprime mortgage crisis, farm subsidies to billionaires, bribery of government officials, and runaway executive incomes.)

These questions are compounded by the fact that much activity of the wealthy, especially their influence on government, takes place beyond public scrutiny and the awareness of most citizens, especially in the United States where the mass of people are notoriously uninformed about politics and economics. What reason (beyond the authoritarian mentality analyzed in chapter 8) do you have to blindly believe in the trustworthiness of those at that level of power? On the contrary, is there any reason to trust ANYONE not to rob us blind if we allow them invisible, unlimited, unregulated power? So the bottom-line question about generalizations here is this: Are crime and unscrupulous behavior among the rich and corporations widespread *enough* to warrant restoration of increased government regulation and other restraints on runaway wealth like raising taxes on the rich and corporations, and to warrant increased critical scrutiny by the media, education, scholarly research, and every citizen? These difficult questions will be pursued throughout the subsequent chapters of this book. Is simply studying them open-mindedly, as a subject for debate, a sign of "prejudice against the rich"?

Particularly in relation to media, whenever a news medium reports a story or commentary unfavorable to the rich or corporations, it is a predictable pattern of conservatives' rhetoric for them to scream about "anti-business bias." Consider, though, that with few exceptions (like PBS and C-SPAN) news and entertainment media *are* businesses—integral parts of the largest multinational corporations—which derive their profits from the advertising of other corporations. Many of their owners and top executives (as well as "star" journalists and performers) are among the wealthiest Americans. How likely are they to be biased against their own class instead of in favor of it? Is it possible that any negative coverage of corporations and the rich is the bare minimum that the media need to meet in order to maintain credibility? Might the negative coverage be **tokenism**, just the tip of the iceberg of corporate corruption that is suppressed in most corporate media? This is the case made by critics like Mokhiber, Barlett and Steele, Noam Chomsky and Edward Herman (see chapter 14), and consumer-advocacy groups like Public Citizen and Ralph Nader's Citizenworks and Public Interest Research Groups. From their viewpoint, it is the corporate media that are biased, in favor of their own class ethnocentrism, so these critics see their role simply as providing some counterweight to *that* bias. Some college courses and textbooks like this one are similarly devoted to presenting "the other side" from what students are apt to hear every day from the corporate media and from their business-oriented courses. (To be sure, the issue of media bias is more complicated than this. Some media are obviously more critical of corporations and the rich than others, for reasons having to do with their audiences and other factors that will be explored more in chapter 14.)

REVERSE PREJUDICE

In recent years, many claims have been made, mainly by political conservatives, that liberals sincerely attempting to overcome prejudice have sometimes failed to **draw the line** and have thus produced reverse prejudice or discrimination (terms that have most often been used to describe affirmative action). This would be a case of the fallacy of the **equal and opposite extreme**. Certainly, some members of groups that have been the victims of prejudice in the past retaliate in an equally prejudiced way against all members of the group that has oppressed them, or against some other group; some Israeli Jews, for example, might have re-channeled past prejudices against them into prejudice toward Palestinians. In the early 1960s, the leader of the Nation of Islam (or Black Muslims), Elijah Muhammad, preached that all white people are devils—an extreme position that led prominent African Americans like Malcolm X and James Baldwin to dissociate themselves from the Black Muslims. The leader of the Nation of Islam in the 1990s, Louis Farrakhan, also alienated many people with anti-Semitic statements. Some extreme advocates of Afrocentrism stereotype blacks as "sun people" and whites as "ice people," or claim that all whites are genetically deficient in skin coloring. Likewise, some (though not most) feminists stereotype all men as rapists and abusers; others, overreacting against past negative stereotypes of women as emotional creatures incapable of reason, have uncritically celebrated emotionality and "women's intuition," rejecting rationality and reasoned argument altogether as mere male-centered biases—although with what might be considered compartmentalized thinking, they use reasoned argument to argue against rationality.

Another controversy since the nineties has involved "political correctness," or "PC," on college campuses and elsewhere. The claim was that groups that had previously been discriminated against in American society and education, including minorities, women, homosexuals, and socialists, were now imposing their viewpoints on students and faculties in a prejudicial way. PC was to some extent a classic case of the invention by the media of a **semantic** label that grossly overgeneralized about and **oversimplified** a large diversity of issues and incidents. The controversy also, either at its origins or quickly thereafter, became a political football, with the charges of PC being launched mainly by conservatives and supported by leaders of the Republican Party, and with leftists denying the accuracy of many alleged incidents and launching countercharges that conservatives had imposed *their* PC dogmas and used the anti-PC crusade as a strategy to silence liberals and leftists altogether. (Some liberals lined up with the conservatives, and some sided with the leftists.) As difficult as it was to evaluate which charges were accurate and which weren't, most responsible liberals and leftists agreed with conservatives that enough of these charges were accurate to conclude that PC in at least some cases was indeed another real form of reverse prejudice.

We have established a consensus, then, that reverse prejudice is a reality. The rhetorical dimensions of the issue are highly complex, however. Let's say that you are an old-fashioned racist, but you see that it is no longer socially acceptable to speak or act accordingly. You hear all the talk about reverse discrimination, and from it you get the idea that if you are deprived of your "right" to discriminate against minorities or to benefit from social advantages solely on the basis of your class, race, or sex, that amounts to discrimination against *you.* This is the mind-set satirized in Joseph Heller's novel *Catch-22* in the character of General Dreedle, who considers himself persecuted because he's not allowed to have anyone under his command shot at his whim. It is a difficult moral, legal, and rhetorical issue of drawing the line to decide just how tolerant we should be of those who are intolerant. A student kicked out of a university for yelling drunken slurs against minorities and homosexuals may have a legitimate legal case in his defense, but should he be praised as a heroic, victimized defender of free speech? And are white males who consider themselves persecuted perhaps indulging in the same victimology they ridicule in minorities and feminists?

It is also likely that some people who really are prejudiced will rationalize that anyone who claims legitimately to be discriminated against is just "whining." They will overgeneralize that most claims of discrimination are phony and will greet with "megadittos" every such charge by conservative authority figures like Rush Limbaugh—without thoughtfully weighing the facts in every particular case. And certainly anyone demonstrates a lack of proportion and a double standard who gets more angry at the relatively recent and lesser instances of reverse prejudice by minorities or women than they ever have or will at the more numerous and graver instances of prejudice against those groups. There is little dispute that such prejudice has been the historical rule and reverse prejudice a very recent exception to the rule—in causal terms a *reaction* to a prior *action,* or long series of actions. This is not to condone or rationalize reverse prejudice but only to recognize that one must judge it in proportion to that series of prior actions, without falling into the fallacies of

argument from the exception or selective vision in judging the reaction in isolation from the action that provoked it. In terms of discrimination between whites and blacks or men and women, "Who started it?" is a legitimate rhetorical consideration, as is, of course, "Two wrongs don't make a right."

An Unexpected Education at St. Anthony's

Stephanie Salter

San Francisco Examiner, January 18, 1994

Privileged children of the middle class, they went into their two-week stint at St. Anthony's Dining Room expecting the stereotypes: hostile and violent drug addicts, filthy and shameless street people, able-bodied men and women who like being parasites on society.

Instead: "We've become realists, and it's scary.... The reality is that those people (at St. Anthony's) and the other thousands like them *are* like you and us. The overwhelming majority are people who have been beaten by some bad odds—family abuse, mental illness, alcoholism, catastrophic illness, old age or were just unemployed one month too many and had no one to help out."

The above is from a copy of a letter written by six St. Ignatius College Prep students and their teacher. The original letter went to a columnist for another Bay Area newspaper in response to an essay about the unattractive "realities" of San Francisco's homeless.

Too bad the other paper chose not to print the letter. These S.I. kids not only understand poverty and homelessness, their letter pointedly demonstrates what happens when the comfortable do as Mother Teresa suggests:

"Come and see."

For the record, the students are Aram Bloom, Lisa Devitt, Beth Horan, Tom Fregoso, Jenjie Pineda and Anne Warren. Their teacher is Mary Ahlbach, a 40-year-old native San Franciscan who teaches English and theology.

Ahlbach is one of those Catholics who doesn't just talk Christianity but tries to put its essence—love thy neighbor as thyself—into action in daily life. As part of an S.I. peace and justice program called "Immersion," which was created by history teacher Kathy Purcell, Ahlbach and her students spent two weeks this past summer working every day at St. Anthony's in the Tenderloin.

No one emerged unchanged.

"You have to stand behind the counter and hand out 2,000 trays of food as fast as the kitchen can dish them out," wrote the students. "You have to walk up and down the jammed tables and bus the used trays of the handicapped and elderly. Try and stop to talk to a few of these individuals or families and hear their stories.

"It takes a while to see the shame they carry right beneath their survival-toughened surface ... Stay a bit longer to talk to those who work there ... the elderly who have volunteered for five or 10 years, the young, those who have experienced homelessness, and those, by luck, or fate or fortitude, who never will."

According to Ahlbach, the students spent most of their first week at St. Anthony's in one of two, intense emotional states: anger or depression.

"They kept saying, 'We can't *treat* people this way,'" she said.

Priorities were radically reordered. Perspectives were turned inside out. As the students put it in their letter.

"How many people would stop for a dog, hungry and sick, lying in the bottom of the emptied fountain in front of City Hall, as we witnessed a man, a human being, last Tuesday?"

Rather than scapegoat and blame the people they got to know, the St. Ignatius students know exactly where to place the blame.

"We, as a society that calls itself civilized, have rationalized so well and so convincingly this shame of denying human beings the dignity and self-worth of employment or the basic right to be cared for if they are ill or old," they wrote.

"We are madly rushing to circle the wagons and separate ourselves as far as possible from these people, not because their plight is a sham but because their plight is so utterly beyond our capacity or willingness to comprehend, let alone solve.

"Somewhere in the past 10 years, we've walked over that one-too-many person lying in the street, and we had to escape—intelligently arguing the obvious reasons we need to do this in order not to face the reality of our inhumane and unjust policies and attitudes toward the poor."

With the help of some of the veteran volunteers at St. Anthony's said Ahlbach, the students learned a lesson that is necessary for anyone who wants to work for social change and survive: Anger must be channeled into action, and helplessness is fought by thinking and working small—with individuals, not the whole world.

Perhaps most important, by serving the poor, seeing their faces, hearing their stories—by recognizing their human value—the six S.I. students learned something that far too many adults have yet to understand.

Contrary to an increasingly popular tendency to blame the poor, criminalize the homeless and obsess on ferreting out "fraud" in a mean and despicable system of social welfare, the students learned:

"The bottom line has to be: We who have our lives, through whatever reasons, intact, need to help those who don't put theirs back together again. If a few take advantage of that, then so be it."

Life on the Expense Account

Donald Barlett and James Steele

From *America: What Went Wrong? Dismantling the Middle Class*, Andrews McNeely, 1992

Meet Thomas Spiegel. He is the former chairman and chief executive officer of Columbia Savings & Loan Association, a Beverly Hills-based thrift that the *New York Times* described in February 1989 as an institution that "has been extremely successful investing in junk bonds and other ventures." Spiegel is a major fund-raiser and financial supporter of political candidates, Democrats and Republicans alike. He and his family live in a six-bedroom Beverly Hills home—complete with swimming pool, tennis court and entertainment pavilion—that could be purchased for about $10 million.

Spiegel thrived at Columbia during the 1980s, a time when the executive branch of the federal government loosened regulatory oversight of the savings and loan industry. Working with his friend and business associate Michael Milken, whose Drexel Burnham Lambert, Inc. office was just down the street in Beverly Hills, Spiegel used depositors' federally insured savings to buy a portfolio of junk bonds, the high-risk debt instruments that promised to pay big dividends.

Columbia's profits soared. Earnings jumped from $44.1 million in 1984 to $122.3 million in 1985 and $193.5 million in 1986, before trailing off to $119.3 million in 1987 and $85 million in 1988.

Spiegel's compensation for those years averaged slightly under $100,000 a week.

He spent $2,000 for a French wine-tasting course, $3,000 a night for hotel suites on the French Riviera, $19,775 for cashmere throws and comforters, $8,600 for towels and $91,000 for a collection of guns—Uzis, Magnums, Sakos, Berettas, Sig Sauers.

Not unusual outlays, you might think, for someone who collected a multimillion-dollar yearly salary. Only in this case, according to a much-belated federal audit, it was Columbia—the savings and loan—not Spiegel, that picked up the tab.

There is, to be sure, nothing new about lavish corporate expense accounts. The practice of converting personal living expenses to a deduction on a company or business tax return has been around as long as the income tax. It is a practice that Congress has been unable to curb. But in the 1980s, corporate tax write-offs for personal executive expenses as well as overall corporate excesses—from gold-plated plumbing fixtures in the private office to family wedding receptions in Paris and London—reached epidemic proportions.

The reasons varied. Among them:

- The pace of corporate restructuring brought on by Wall Street created a climate in which once-unacceptable practices became acceptable, indeed, were even chronicled on radio and television, in newspapers and magazines.
- In a monumental change in the rules, Congress deregulated the savings and loan industry, in effect opening the doors to the vaults of the nation's savings institutions, while at the same time discouraging meaningful audits or crackdowns when irregularities were detected.
- The Internal Revenue Service lacks the staffing and time to conduct the intense audits of companies that would uncover such abuses. And even if the resources were available, an impenetrable tax code places too many other demands on the agency.

All this made possible a Tom Spiegel—and an army of other corporate executives who lived high on their expense accounts. Federal auditors eventually found that Spiegel used Columbia funds to pay for trips to Europe, to buy luxury condominiums in Columbia's name in the United States and to purchase expensive aircraft. From 1987 to 1989, for example, Spiegel made at least four trips to Europe at Columbia's expense, the auditors reported, staying at the best hotels and running up large bills.

They included, the report said "$7,446 for a hotel and room service bill for three nights in the Berkeley Hotel in London . . . for Spiegel and his wife . . . in November 1988" and "$6,066 for a hotel and room service bill for three nights in the Hotel Plaza Athenee in Paris . . . in July 1989."

The Spiegels' most expensive stay was in July 1989 at the Hotel du Cap on the French Riviera, where the family ran up a $16,519 bill in five days. And when they weren't flying to Europe, the Spiegels spent time at luxury condominiums, acquired at a cost of $1.9 million, at Jackson Hole, Wyoming; Indian Wells, California; and Park City, Utah.

To make all this travel easier, Spiegel arranged for Columbia, a savings and loan that had no offices outside of California, to buy corporate aircraft, including a Gulfstream IV equipped with a kitchen and lounge. Federal auditors now say that Columbia paid $2.4 million "for use of corporate aircraft in commercial flights for the personal travel for Spiegel, his immediate family and other persons accompanying Spiegel." Columbia wrote off those expenses on its tax returns, thereby transferring the cost of the Spiegel lifestyle to you, the taxpayer.

The Federal Office of Thrift Supervision has filed a complaint against Spiegel, seeking to recover at least $19 million in Columbia funds that it claims he misspent. Spiegel's lawyer, Dennis Perluss, said Spiegel is contesting the charges.

"All of the uses that are at issue in terms of the planes and the condominiums were for legitimate business purposes," Perluss said.

But you are paying for more than Spiegel's lifestyle. You are also going to be picking up the tab for his management of Columbia. After heady earnings in the mid-1980s, Columbia lost twice as much money in 1989 and 1990—a total of $1.4 billion—as it had made in the previous twenty years added together. Federal regulators seized Columbia in January 1991. Taxpayers will pay for a bailout expected to cost more than $1.5 billion.

That final figure depends, in part, on how much the government collects for the sale of the corporate headquarters on Wilshire Boulevard in Beverly Hills. When construction started, it was expected to cost $17 million. By the time work was finished, after Spiegel had made the last of his design changes— "the highest possible grade of limestone and marble, stainless steel floors and ceiling tiles, leather wall coverings"—the cost had soared to $55 million.

It could have been even higher, except that one of Spiegel's ambitious plans never was translated into bricks and mortar. According to federal auditors, he had wanted to include in the building "a large multi-level gymnasium and 'survival chamber' bathrooms with bulletproof glass and an independent air and food supply."

Just who Spiegel thought might attack the bathrooms of a Beverly Hills savings and loan is unclear.

Dozens of Billionaires Receive Ag Handouts

Lisa Hoffman

From Scripps Howard News Service, November 17, 2007

More than 50 American billionaires have received government farm handouts in recent years from a program created to help struggling small farmers survive.

In just two years, between 2003 and 2005, at least 56 of the richest people in the country have pocketed taxpayer-funded federal agriculture subsidies totaling more than $2 million, according to a Scripps Howard News Service analysis of a newly released U.S. Department of Agriculture database.

Included in that roster are banker-philanthropist David Rockefeller Sr.; five members of Wal-Mart founder Sam Walton's family; hotel czar William Barron Hilton; Microsoft co-creator Paul Allen; and nine members of the Pritzker clan of Hyatt Hotel fame.

Like them, most of the other billionaires either made or inherited their fortunes in ways unrelated to agricultural pursuits.

Instead, they qualified for the payments through their investments or other holdings or via conservation programs that pay landowners to keep their acreage fallow to protect wildlife or curb runoff. Estee Lauder cosmetics heir Leonard Lauder, for instance, received about $4,000 via his 5 percent interest in an Idaho organic dairy farm.

Until now, the names of most of these notables, and more than 350,000 other individual beneficiaries, had never been publicly listed. Previously, only payments to agribusinesses or other firms—without a list of those who made money from their ownership percentage or investments in those entities—were released.

In a computer analysis of the 64 million records in the new, massive database, Scripps compared the names listed there with the *Forbes* magazine roster of America's 400 billionaires and found nearly five dozen matches.

That number surprised even those who have criticized the government for allowing farm funds to fatten the wallets of the wealthy. "That makes the case," said Brian Riedle, a senior budget analyst at the Heritage Foundation, a conservative think tank in Washington.

The Senate began digging into the $283 billion farm bill Nov. 5, wrestling with ways to curb the amount of subsidies pocketed by the rich. Some of those recipients can be found in the Senate itself, where at least six of the 100 lawmakers have themselves received five-figure-or-higher farm subsidy checks.

Earlier this year, the House took its own stab at limiting subsidies to the well-off, but experts say its measure, like the Senate's efforts so far, leaves loopholes large enough to drive a tractor through. For that and other reasons, the White House has threatened to veto any bill that it sees as too generous.

According to the Scripps analysis, the most generous billionaire subsidy in the 2003–2005 span—a total of $306,627.09—went to Whitney MacMillan, heir to the Cargill agribusiness dynasty. *Forbes* estimated his fortune to be about $1.2 billion.

The Pritzker family—which besides Hyatt Hotels also owns Royal Caribbean Cruise Lines and commands a collective worth of at least $22 billion—took in $273,461.57 in subsidies. Among their holdings: cattle and horse ranches in California and Wisconsin, along with timber interests in Louisiana, Illinois and elsewhere.

Oil heir and avid outdoorsman Lee Marshall Bass of Fort Worth, Texas, who is estimated to command a $3 billion fortune, collected nearly $250,000. Also in the upper ranks was oil-and-gas kingpin Tom Ward, who received subsidies totaling $135,710.98 for his investments in Kansas and Texas farms and feedlots. Ward's estimated wealth is $1.6 billion.

That billionaires are getting paid by a program—created during the Great Depression—intended to help small farmers stay on the land is the best evidence that wholesale changes are needed, critics said.

"It is not within the nation's values to tax waitresses and welders to subsidize multimillionaires," Heritage analyst Riedle said.

Whether the Senate will close the loopholes—and whether those limits would survive a House-Senate committee that crafts the final bill—is unknown. Senate agriculture committee chairman Tom Harkin, D-Iowa, says reform is a matter of "basic fairness."

"It is also a matter of recognizing that (the Agriculture Department) should not pay out hundreds of thousands of dollars—or even well over a million dollars in cases—to billionaires," Harkin said. "These are payments we can't afford, going to people who don't need them."

Senators Who Get Agriculture Handouts

* Sen. Jon Tester, D-Mont.: $304,000 in federal farm aid since 1995.
* Sen. Charles Grassley, R-Iowa: $283,000 in government subsidies for his family farm between 1995 and 2005; son Robin received nearly $654,000 during the same time.
* Sen. Sam Brownback, R-Kan.: Since 1995, about $50,000 in subsidies; Brownback's father and brother have received $605,000 over the same time.
* Sen. Gordon Smith, R-Ore.: Collected about $47,000 in subsidies since 1995.
* Sen. Richard Lugar, R-Ind.: Received about $18,000 in subsidies since 1995.
* Sen. Blanche Lincoln, D-Ark.: Listed on the Agriculture Department database using her maiden name, Blanche Lambert, has collected about $11,000 in subsidies for her portion of a farm since 1995.
* Sen. Max Baucus, D-Mont.: Baucus does not appear on the Agriculture database as having personally received subsidies, but close family members have collected more than $230,000 since 1995, according to the records.

Wal-Mart: Rise of the Goliath

Liza Featherstone

Multinational Monitor, January–February 2005

Back in 1980, when *Multinational Monitor* was founded, Wal-Mart operated in only 11 states, with fewer than 300 stores and just over 21,000 employees. The company had no stores overseas. Its annual sales were $1 billion.

Today, Wal-Mart is a Goliath of previously unimaginable girth. Its sales totaled $256.3 billion in the fiscal year ending in January 2004. There are more than 3,600 Wal-Mart stores in the United States, including general merchandise stores, Supercenters, and a membership warehouse chain called Sam's Club, named after company founder Sam Walton. With more than 1.3 million workers in the United States, Wal-Mart is the nation's largest private employer. Wal-Mart has stores in every state in the union, and by March 2004, nearly 2,600 U.S. towns and cities had at least one Wal-Mart or Sam's Club.

Topping the Fortune 500 for the past three years, Wal-Mart is the world's largest corporation. More than twice the size of its largest U.S. competitor, Home Depot, it dominates the retail sector overwhelmingly. Wal-Mart is also the most profitable company in the world, announcing a profit of $27 billion in mid-2004.

From having almost no presence in Washington, D.C. in the 1980s, Wal-Mart is now a formidable corporate lobbyist and a top corporate contributor to political campaigns. . . .

Overseas, Wal-Mart operates more than 1,570 stores, in Mexico, Puerto Rico, the United Kingdom, Canada, Argentina, Brazil, China, South Korea and Germany. Every week, around the world, more than 138 million people shop at Wal-Mart.

Wal-Mart has completely transformed the retail industry with a single-minded focus on giving the customer the lowest possible price. . . . Keeping prices low entails keeping wages down. The average sales clerk at Wal-Mart makes just $8.50 an hour; even working full-time, that wage would, if the worker was the sole breadwinner, leave a family of three $1,000 below the federal poverty line. Workers at Wal-Mart must also pay more than a third of their own health insurance premium—as a result, many choose to go without. Many depend, too, on publicly funded health care plans, as well as food stamps and other forms of welfare.

Last year, in California, Democratic Assembly Member Sally Leiber announced that her staff had uncovered documents that Wal-Mart had given to its employees explicitly telling them how to apply for public assistance. Wal-Mart has denied this, but the documents speak for themselves.

Welfare is quite clearly a part of the company's business model (especially jarring considering that the company gives more than 80 percent of its corporate campaign contributions to Republicans, who would love to do away with the social safety net altogether). According to a recent University of California-Berkeley study, Wal-Mart costs California taxpayers about $86 million a year in public assistance to employees. A Georgia study found that one in four Wal-Mart workers in that state had a child enrolled in Peachcare, the state's healthcare program for impoverished kids. When we stand in the checkout line at Wal-Mart, we may notice how much money we're saving, but we rarely consider that we may be paying, quite literally, in other ways. The public costs don't show up on the receipt.

Wal-Mart's success has had a devastating impact on competitors—driving countless small businesses to close their doors, pushing large chains like K-Mart and Toys R Us into bankruptcy and forcing down wages and employee benefits throughout the retail sector. It depresses employee compensation not only because other retailers face competitive pressure from Wal-Mart, but because it provides a model of business success. As former Wal-Mart worker Linda Gruen—now an organizer with the UFCW (United Food and Commercial Workers)—puts it, other companies "see what Wal-Mart gets away with." Observing how profitable Wal-Mart is, they of course seek to do the same.

Wal-Mart's economic impact, however, reaches far beyond the retail industry. The company also drives down wages in other sectors worldwide, by ruthlessly demanding the lowest possible price from suppliers.

According to several experts interviewed for a recent PBS "Frontline" special, Wal-Mart is one of the key forces driving the outsourcing of U.S. jobs to Asia—as only countries with the lowest-cost labor can meet the low prices the company demands.

In fact, if Wal-Mart were a country, it would be China's fifth largest export market. Wal-Mart sells 10 percent of all goods imported to the United States from China, where independent trade unions are illegal and it is notoriously difficult to monitor factory conditions. (In March 2004, the company announced that it would, for the first time, hold its board of directors meeting in China, where the company operates 35 stores, with 18,000 employees.) But Wal-Mart makes the conditions much worse than they need to be, pressuring factory bosses to cut their prices, so those bosses have no choice but to make employees work longer hours for lower pay.

To keep compensation so low, and supply chains so "flexible," Wal-Mart has had to keep unions out of its stores, something it has done quite effectively. The story of unions' struggle to organize Wal-Mart takes place in a context of organized labor's declining numbers and diminishing political power, especially in the private sector, where only 8 percent of workers are now unionized. Unions rightly view organizing Wal-Mart as a struggle for their survival: the success of such a deeply anti-labor company is a powerful symbol of their own powerlessness. To unionize it would completely transform organized labor's currently dismal position in the United States. "Wal-Mart is the juggernaut," says one organizer. So far, however, the attempt to organize Wal-Mart has, in the United States, been a total failure.

That's one thing that hasn't changed since *Multinational Monitor*'s founding. At that time, the Teamsters were trying to organize the company's distribution centers, an effort that lost momentum due in part to company founder Sam Walton's zealous willingness to break the law in order to defeat the union, even firing pro-union workers, as Wal-Mart has been doing ever since.

Beginning in the late 1980s, UFCW began to realize that Wal-Mart's rapid growth and competitiveness posed an urgent threat to its members' jobs. The first Supercenter opened in 1988, in Washington, Missouri.

Wal-Mart had historically been concentrated in "right-to-work" states in the South, but as it grew, it encroached upon more traditionally unionized western and Northeastern regions. Despite the obvious threat, the union effort was half-hearted until the late 1990s, when supermarkets began losing market share to Wal-Mart and it became painfully obvious that Wal-Mart threatened the UFCW's very survival.

Even then, the union has been unable to fight Wal-Mart on its own. Devoting insubstantial resources to the organizing campaign (only 2 percent of its national budget), the UFCW is constantly stymied by Wal-Mart's limitless resources to hire union-busters and, equally significantly, fight court challenges to its violations of organizing rights.

In the United States, only one group of Wal-Mart employees has successfully organized. In February 2000, 10 meat cutters in a Jacksonville, Texas Wal-Mart voted 7 to 3 to unionize their tiny bargaining unit. Two weeks later, Wal-Mart abruptly eliminated the butchers' jobs by switching to prepackaged meat and assigning the butchers to other departments, effectively abolishing the only union shop on its North American premises. After more than three years, in June 2003, a federal labor judge ruled this move illegal, and ordered Wal-Mart to restore the department and recognize the butchers' bargaining unit. Wal-Mart has appealed that decision, but of course, most of the original butchers have left the company, so whatever the outcome, Wal-Mart wins. That incident typifies the way in which for Wal-Mart going to court for violating labor laws is simply part of the cost of doing business (and not a very big one).

In early 2004, after striking for months, grocery workers in California were forced to accept a vastly reduced health plan, as supermarkets, anticipating competition from new Wal-Mart Supercenters throughout the state, began refusing to compromise with the union. They're not alone. Supermarkets all over the country have been lowering wages and decimating workers' health plans. Says Russ Davis of Massachusetts Jobs With Justice, who has worked closely with grocery workers in the Northeast who are struggling to maintain their standard of living, "It's all about Wal-Mart."

Susan Phillips, vice president of the UFCW and head of its Working Women's department, agrees. For any private-sector union in the United States today, she says, "anytime you go into negotiations, it's like there's this invisible 800-pound gorilla sitting in the room at the bargaining table." As long as Wal-Mart workers remain unorganized, that gorilla will continue to set the agenda.

Labor may be waking up. The AFL-CIO has recently announced a campaign to fight Wal-Mart and the "Wal-Martization" of U.S. jobs, and Andy Stern of the Service Employees International Union (SEIU) has proposed financing it by allocating $25 million of the AFL-CIO's royalties from purchases on its Union Plus credit card—appropriately enough, since at least 30 percent of purchases on that credit card are made at Wal-Mart. It's unclear still what this campaign will look like, and what institutional forms it will take, but at least the labor movement—and not just the UFCW—is finally having a conversation about what to do about the Wal-Mart problem.

Communities—often working closely with unions—have had far more success fighting Wal-Mart than labor has had in organizing it, preventing at least 13 Wal-Mart Supercenters from opening in 2004. Labor and community groups in Chicago prevented Wal-Mart from opening a store on the city's South Side. Wal-Mart does plan to open a store on the city's West Side, but may yet be thwarted by an ordinance that would force the retailer to pay Chicago workers a living wage. Citizens in Inglewood, California defeated a Wal-Mart Supercenter in a voter referendum. In Hartford, Connecticut, labor and community advocates just won passage of an ordinance protecting their free speech rights on the grounds of the new Wal-Mart Supercenter, which is being built on city property. Similar battles are raging nationwide. The company's growth has been slowing down slightly, and Wal-Mart CEO H. Lee Scott blames some of that slowdown on organized community opposition.

Wal-Mart's critics have also been able to attract more media attention recently—stories in which Wal-Mart appears in a negative light now appear in the papers almost every day. It's essential—and not easy—to figure out how this growing anti-Wal-Mart sentiment in our culture can be strategically deployed to benefit workers and communities. Should the goal be to block Wal-Mart from opening new stores wherever possible, or to force the company to win back the public trust by making more ethical use of its enormous power?

Perhaps, for example, we should demand that since Wal-Mart doesn't want to pay for employees' health insurance, Wal-Mart's highly paid Washington lobbyists should push for national healthcare, which would benefit everybody.

Destroying—or changing—Wal-Mart will require many more local mobilizations, and more coordination between community and labor groups fighting the company. It will also probably require a progressive movement serious about taking power and reining in corporate criminals like Wal-Mart—a movement that is emerging, but still lacks the institutions and structures—including political parties—to wield much national clout. Over the next quarter-century, for such a movement, *Multinational Monitor* will be an invaluable resource. But let's hope that when we celebrate MM's fiftieth anniversary, Wal-Mart—and its many imitators—will be a mere footnote.

Topics for Discussion and Writing

1. In small groups with classmates, then in general class discussion, devise a survey of the attitudes of students at your college toward the morality of poor people versus rich ones, which might indicate individual students' opinions both about what social class they themselves belong to and the extent of generalizations and

stereotypes they are inclined to make about the rich and poor. Refer to figure 7.1, "Middle-Class Ethnocentric Attitudes," as a guide to possible questions. Then implement the survey.

2. Stephanie Salter quotes the high school students working at St. Anthony's homeless shelter writing, "'We, as a society that calls itself civilized, have rationalized so well and so convincingly this shame of denying human beings the dignity and self-worth of employment or the basic right to be cared for if they are ill or old.'" Debate this assertion in class. As a research and writing project, try to volunteer to work in a homeless facility in your locality and report on it.

3. Discuss a popular song, TV series, or movie that either indulges in stereotyping or challenges stereotypes.

4. "Life on the Expense Account" by Donald Barlett and James Steele, Lisa Hoffman's "Dozens of Billionaires," and Liza Featherstone's "Wal-Mart, Rise of the Goliath," present collections of **empirical evidence** that contradict positive generalizations and stereotypes about the morality of the rich and large corporations. How well reasoned and supported are their arguments? How well qualified is their level of generalization? Can it be accurately inferred that they are generalizing about *all* corporations, *most, many,* or what? How would you phrase the most appropriate level of generalization?

5. You might look at the rest of the chapter excerpted from Barlett and Steele, and at their complete book *America: What Went Wrong?*, to get a clearer sense of the **context**. Their central argument is that the policies of the Reagan administration in the 1980s enacting large tax cuts, deregulating industries like savings and loans, and providing other benefits to the wealthy led to abuses on a large enough scale to discredit Reaganomics—a line of argument that has gained increasing currency in light of the drastically increasing wealth gap and corporate scandals in recent years. How persuasive is this one example, and the **causal analysis** of reasons for this corruption, toward that larger argument? (Also see the arguments about Reaganomics in chapters 16 and 17.)

6. Compare the arguments in Lisa Hoffman's "Dozens of Billionaires Receive Ag Handouts" and Joseph Heller's *Catch-22* cited in chapter 8 about the compartmentalized thinking, double standard, and rationalization of those who condemn handouts for the poor but approve of them for wealthy farmers and other corporate recipients of government subsidies. Is this a valid or a false **analogy**? Do some research on the amount that federal and state government spends on welfare versus corporate subsidies, and on recent debates over farm subsidies and congressional "earmarks."

7. Sam Walton is often pointed to as a positive example of the entrepreneur who builds a company up from scratch. However, six of his Wal-Mart heirs are perennially on the *Forbes* list of richest Americans, each with billions and without ever having had to work. To what extent does Featherstone's account of Walton's and the present owners' treatment of employees negate that positive example? Does her evidence support her description of the owners as "corporate criminals"? Look up some defenses of Wal-Mart, and find the DVD *Wal-Mart: The High Cost of Low Prices* (Brave New Films) to evaluate how "fair and balanced" an account it gives of Wal-Mart's critics and defenders.

CHAPTER 8

Authoritarianism and Conformity, Rationalization and Compartmentalization

Authoritarianism is the mental trait of uncritically accepting or obeying anything that someone perceived to be in a position of authority says; it also describes the mentality of political rulers who impose that uncritical acceptance of their authority on those they rule, particularly through an undemocratic government, and it can be the name given to a society with that kind of government. Note that the words *authoritative* and *authoritarian* are not synonymous. To say that someone is authoritative means that he or she is an authority on a particular subject, speaking with authentic expertise on it, so this word has a positive **connotation**, in contrast to the negative connotation implied when a person or society is described as authoritarian. (We might, however, fall into a somewhat authoritarian mind-set if we uncritically assume that whatever an authority says is true simply because the individual is an authority, without our verifying his or her evidence and reasoning.)

Of course, in many cases people in positions of authority—government officials, business executives, religious leaders, military and police officers, professionals, educators, scholars and authors, as well as elder members of our own families and communities—deserve to be respected, and the **equal and opposite extreme** from authoritarianism is falling into knee-jerk, undiscriminating *disrespect* for anyone in authority. (In the ambivalent and paradoxical nature of human psychology, extreme antiauthoritarianism often is not really the opposite of authoritarianism but rather a twisted reflection of it. Thus people who try to assassinate public figures often turn out to be driven by conflicts within their own deep-seated authoritarian mentality.) The golden mean is determining which authorities merit respect on the basis of exercising authority responsibly and which do not, and this is one of the important judgment calls that critical citizenship constantly entails.

If many people are inclined to submit blindly to political or social authorities, many also go through life conforming to the **ethnocentric** customs and attitudes of their families, friends, schoolmates, church, political party, associates at work, and other social groupings. Conformity is an especially ticklish subject to discuss objectively because although most of us are conformists to a greater or lesser extent, few of us want to admit it. Would you or anyone you know admit outright, "I am a conformist"? The subject is doubly ticklish in the United States, where there has long been a **compartmentalization** between our image as a society of rugged individualists and the tendencies toward regimentation that many critics such as Ralph Waldo Emerson and Henry David Thoreau have noted since the mid-nineteenth century. Contrast Jefferson's vision of a public education system that would "raise the mass of people to the high ground of moral respectability necessary to their own safety, and to orderly government" with Emerson's contemptuous reference in "The American Scholar" some twenty-five years later: "Men in the world of to-day are bugs, are spawn, and are called 'the mass' and 'the herd'" (106). In *Walden* (1854) Thoreau famously said, "The mass of men live lives of quiet desperation" (7) and "If a man does not keep pace with his companions, perhaps it is because he hears a different drummer" (295). There is a social **taboo** today against even raising the subject of conformity, so it comes as rather a shock when a journalist like Jennifer Crichton, in an article from *Ms.* magazine, declares (albeit with **hyperbolic** humor), that "American high schools are as notoriously well-organized as totalitarian regimes, complete with secret police, punishment without trial, and banishment" (3).

Social psychologists trace what they term "the authoritarian personality" to childhood socialization in which parents, and especially the father, exert strict, often harsh and unreasonable, authority over their children. In this view, children's unquestioning submission to paternal authority tends to be projected into their adult compliance with religious, social, and political authority. (Compare with George Lakoff's description in chapter 4 of "the strict father model" of society that characterizes conservative ideology.) The term *patriarchy* describes the concept, delineated by Virginia Woolf in the excerpt from *A Room of One's Own* in chapter 6, that our whole social order is based on domination by paternalistic authority and more broadly by the power of men over women; thus the women's liberation movement represented a challenge to the **culturally conditioned assumption** of male dominance. Sylvia Plath's famous 1962 poem "Daddy" fantasized her domineering, German-American father as a Nazi:

> Every woman adores a Fascist,
> The boot in the face, the brute
> Brute heart of a brute like you.

The poem ends:

> There's a stake in your fat black heart
> And the villagers never liked you.
> They are dancing and stamping on you.
> They always *knew* it was you.
> Daddy, daddy, you bastard, I'm through.

This last stanza has been widely interpreted as a rejection, not only of Plath's father, but of patriarchal domination of women in general.

Erich Fromm's 1941 book *Escape from Freedom* is a classic study of the authoritarian social psychology that attracted so many Europeans to fascism—an ultraconservative ideology that combines fanatic nationalism with totalitarian government led by an all-powerful ruler—in the 1930s and that has been a strong tendency even in other modern democracies, including the United States. (See the definition of fascism in chapter 13.) Fromm discusses many individuals' fear of growing out of infantile dependency on their parents, projected into a larger fear of thinking critically and exercising free will as an adult in society. He relates this personal and social fear of freedom to masochistic neurosis:

The annihilation of the individual self and the attempt to overcome thereby the unbearable feeling of powerlessness are only one side of the masochistic strivings. The other side is the attempt to become a part of a bigger and more powerful whole outside of oneself, to submerge and participate in it. This power can be a person, an institution, God, the nation, conscience, or a psychic compulsion. By becoming part of a power which is felt as unshakably strong, eternal, and glamorous, one participates in its strength and glory. One surrenders one's own self and renounces all strength and pride connected with it, one loses one's integrity as an individual and surrenders freedom; but one gains a new security and a new pride in the participation in the power in which one submerges. One gains also security against the torture of doubt. The masochistic person ... is saved from making decisions, saved from the final responsibility for the fate of his self, and thereby saved from the doubt of what decision to make.... These questions are answered by the relationship to the power to which he has attached himself. The meaning of his life and identity of his self are determined by the greater whole into which the self has emerged. (155–156)

Thus, in Fromm's view, "If the individual finds cultural patterns that satisfy these masochistic strivings (like the submission under the 'leader' in Fascist ideology), he gains some security by finding himself united with millions of others who share these feelings" (153). We can see here a key to the recent attraction of various cults for many young Americans. We can also see a key to the tendency after an external threat to a nation like September 11, 2001, for many people to seek security in a president who is a "strict father" figure entrusted to take whatever measures he considers necessary to protect us from foreign and domestic threats. However, many people in this situation also tend not to understand the danger in giving up critical scrutiny of governmental or military authorities, who often in such circumstances historically have manipulated the people's fears to seize total power and crush democracy and civil liberties—Hitler in Germany being the most notorious example.

Fromm's title *Escape from Freedom* **alludes** to the Russian novelist Fyodor Dostoyevsky's chapter "The Grand Inquisitor" in *The Brothers Karamazov* (1880). The Grand Inquisitor, Dostoyevsky's imaginary, sinister prototype of the twentieth-century totalitarian dictator, **rationalizes** his regime's antidemocratic social control as follows: "Man is tormented by no greater anxiety than to find some one quickly to whom he can hand over that gift of freedom with which the ill-fated creature is born" (302).

Oh, we shall persuade them that they will only become free when they renounce their freedom to us and submit to us.... We shall show them that they are weak, that they are only pitiful children, but that childlike happiness is the sweetest of all. They will become timid and will look to us and huddle close to us in fear, as chicks to the hen.... They will tremble impotently before our wrath, their minds will grow fearful, they will be quick to shed tears like women and children, but they will be just as ready at a sign from us to pass to laughter and rejoicing, to happy mirth and childish song. Yes, we shall set them to work, but in their leisure hours we shall make their life like a child's game, with children's songs and innocent dance. (306–307)

Dostoyevsky's dark prophecy has been echoed by many writers opposing the social control exercised by both modern governments and corporations through mass cultural "children's songs and innocent dance," such as in Susan Sontag's description, cited in chapter 1, of the Bush administration's post-9/11 statements as "a campaign to infantilize the public."

The ultimate modern literary depiction of authoritarianism and conformity is George Orwell's futuristic 1949 novel *1984*. The hero, Winston Smith, rebels throughout the novel against a totally regimented society dominated by a perhaps nonexistent ruler called Big Brother. Smith is ultimately captured, tortured, and brainwashed to correct his "deviation" from conformity. On the last page of the book, he finally submits to servitude before a huge televised picture of Big Brother, perceived here as all-wise father:

Forty years it had taken him to learn what kind of smile was hidden beneath the dark mustache. O cruel, needless misunderstanding! O stubborn, self-willed exile from the loving breast! Two gin-soaked tears trickled down the sides of his nose. But it was all right, everything was all right, the struggle was finished. He had won the victory over himself. He loved Big Brother. (197)

A more contemporary version of authoritarian society was presented by the American playwright Paddy Chayefsky in his 1972 screenplay for the film *Network,* which satirically suggests that by the late twentieth century, the major authority in the world has become not governments but multinational corporations. In the film's most famous sequence, a TV anchorman, Howard Beale, goes slightly berserk and starts urging all his audience members to rebel against monopolistic corporate control of television and American society in general, by sticking their heads out of their windows and yelling, "I'm mad as hell and I'm not going to take this any more!" Beale is called into the headquarters of the corporation that owns the network for which he works and is lectured by the CEO, Arthur Jensen, in the following scene updating "The Grand Inquisitor" and *1984:*

From *Network*

Sam Hedrin and Paddy Chayefsky

Random House, 1976

"You have meddled with the primal forces of nature, Mr. Beale, and I won't have it, is that clear? You think you have merely stopped a business deal—that is not the case! The Arabs have taken billions of dollars out of this country, and now they must put it back. It is ebb and flow, tidal gravity, it is ecological balance! You are an old man who thinks in terms of nations and peoples. There are no nations! There are no peoples! There are no Russians. There are no Arabs! There are no third worlds! There is no West! There is only one holistic system of systems, one vast and immane, interwoven, interacting, multi-variate, multinational dominion of dollars! Petrodollars, electrodollars, multidollars, reichsmarks, rubles, Yin, pounds and shekels. It is the international system of currency that determines the totality of life on this planet! That is the natural order of things today! That is the atomic, subatomic and galactic structure of things today! And you have meddled with the primal forces of nature and you will atone! Am I getting through to you, Mr. Beale?"

In the darkness, Howard said, "Amen."

"You get up on your little twenty-one inch screen, Mr. Beale" Jensen resumed, "and howl about America and democracy. There is no America. There is no democracy. There is only IBM and ITT and AT&T and Du Pont, Dow, Union Carbide and Exxon. Those are the nations of the world now. What do you think the Russians talk about in their councils of state—Karl Marx? They pull out their linear programming charts, statistical decision theories and minimize solutions like the good little systems-analysts they are and compute the price-cost probabilities of their transactions and investments just like we do.

"We no longer live in a world of nations and ideologies, Mr. Beale. The world is a college of corporations, inexorably determined by the immutable bylaws of business. The world is a business, Mr. Beale! It has been that way since man crawled out of the slime, and our children, Mr. Beale, will live to see that perfect world without war and famine, oppression and brutality—one vast and ecumenical holding company, for whom all men will work to serve a common profit, in which all men will hold a share of stock, all necessities provided, all anxieties tranquilized, all boredom amused. And I have chosen you to preach this evangel, Mr. Beale."

"Why me?" Howard whispered humbly.

"Because you're on television dummy. Sixty million people watch you every night of the week, Monday through Friday."

Howard slowly rose from the blackness of his seat so that he was lit only by the ethereal diffusion of light shooting out of the rear of the room. He stared at Jensen, spotted on the podium, transfixed.

"I have seen the face of God!" Howard said.

Jensen considered this curious statement for a moment. "You just might be right, Mr. Beale."

That evening, Howard Beale went on the air to preach the corporate cosmology of Arthur Jensen. He seemed sad, resigned, weary.

BEALE: Last night, I got up here and asked you people to stand up and fight for your heritage and you did and it was beautiful. Six million telegrams were received at the White House. The Arab takeover of CCA has been stopped. The people spoke, the people won. It was a radiant eruption of democracy. But I think that was it, fellers. That sort of thing isn't likely to happen again. Because in the bottom of all our terrified souls, we all know that democracy is a dying giant, a sick, sick, dying, decaying political concept, writhing in its final pain. I don't mean the United States is finished as a world power. The United States is the most powerful, the richest, the most advanced country in the world, light-years ahead of any other country. And I don't mean the Communists are going to take over the world. The Communists are deader than we are. What's finished is the idea that this great country is dedicated to the freedom and flourishing of every individual in it. It's the individual that's finished. It's the single, solitary human being who's finished. Because this is no longer a nation of independent individuals. This is a nation of two hundred-odd million, transistorized, deodorized, whiter-than-white, steel-belted bodies, totally unnecessary as human beings and as replaceable as piston rods. . . .

What I'm talking about, of course, is dehumanization. That's a bad word, dehuman-ization, like imperialism, military-industrial complex, big-business. We're all supposed to resist dehumanization. Lord knows, I've been getting up on this program for eight months and that's all I've been yelling about—we must fight the dehumanization of the spirit. I kept yelling all the good words like justice and brotherhood, the dignity of man, compassion, decency and simple human kindness. Well, we all know that's a lot of shit. I mean, just look around you. So the time has come to say: is dehumanization such a bad word? Because good or bad, that's what is so. And we are moving inexorably towards more total dehumanization, drawn by gravitational forces far greater than anything we can comprehend. And not just us, the whole world.

We're just the most advanced country, so we're getting there first. The rest of the world—Russia, China, the undeveloped world—can't wait to catch up to us. It'll be easy for them. They're already dedicated to mass societies. The whole world then is becoming humanoid, creatures that look human but aren't. We are becoming mass-produced, programmed, wired—insensate things useful only to produce and consume other mass-produced things, all of them as unnecessary and useless as we are. Nevertheless, that is the cosmic state of affairs.

Once you've grasped that, once you've understood the total futility and purpose-lessness of human existence, then the whole universe becomes orderly and comprehensive. We are no longer an industrialized society; we aren't even a post-industrial or technological society. We are now a corporate society, a corporate world, a corporate universe. This world is a vast cosmology of small corporations orbiting around larger corporations who, in turn, revolve around giant corporations, and this whole endless, eternal, ultimate cosmology is expressly designed for the production and consumption of useless things. . . . (130–135)

*   *   *

This sequence from *Network* is a good example of **dramatic irony**, through which an author creates a gap between what the characters know or say and the way the audience is expected to interpret it. Here, we are not expected to take Arthur Jensen's "corporate cosmology" as the benevolent model that he is "selling" but to reject it as an antidemocratic nightmare, with Jensen as Big Brother. Nor are we expected to give in to Howard Beale's pessimism at the end but again to say, "We're mad as hell, and we're not going to take this any more!"

Likewise, if many writers, ancient and modern, have warned pessimistically of the dangers of authoritarianism and conformity, many have also depicted heroic models of critical nonconformity and rebellion against authority. In Plato's dialogue *The Apology,* Socrates in his trial declares his willingness to die for defying social conformity: "There is no man who will preserve his life for very long, either in Athens or elsewhere, if he firmly opposes the multitude, and tries to prevent the commission of much injustice and illegality, in the state.... But I thought that I ought to face the danger, with law and justice on my side, rather than join with you in your unjust proposal, from fear of imprisonment or death" (364). Also in ancient Greece, Sophocles' play *Antigone* dramatizes the defiance of a brave woman against the arbitrary authority of the emperor Creon. Shakespeare's Hamlet stands up to the conformity of a court and society that rationalize the dictates of a corrupt, murderous king.

In American literature, some of the most powerful statements against conformity were made shortly before the Civil War by writers associated with the transcendentalist movement, including Ralph Waldo Emerson, Henry David Thoreau, Margaret Fuller, and Frederick Douglass, denouncing the nation's cowardice in refusing to abolish slavery. Thoreau's 1849 essay "Civil Disobedience" (also sometimes titled "Resistance to Civil Government") was written to protest the Mexican-American War, which was waged at least partially with the motive of bringing Texas, whose ruling Anglo slave owners wanted independence from Mexico after that country abolished slavery, into the union to strengthen the proslavery faction in the federal government. With specific reference to the Mexican-American War, Thoreau says:

> A common and natural result of an undue respect for law is, that you may see a file of soldiers, colonel, captain, corporal, privates, powder-monkeys and all, marching in admirable order over hill and dale to the wars, against their wills, aye, against their common sense and consciences, which makes it very steep marching indeed, and produces a palpitation of the heart. They have no doubt that it is a damnable business in which they are concerned; they are all peaceably inclined. Now, what are they? Men at all? or small moveable forts and magazines, at the service of some unscrupulous man in power? (637)

Thoreau refused to pay a poll tax used to finance the war and was sent to prison for one night, an episode he describes and justifies: "I know this well, that if one thousand, if one hundred, if ten men whom I could name,—if ten *honest* men only—aye, if *one* HONEST man in this state of Massachusetts, *ceasing to hold slaves,* were actually to withdraw from this copartnership, and be locked up in the county jail therefore, it would be the abolition of slavery in America. For it matters not how small the beginning may seem to be: what is once done well is done forever" (646). In a broader defense of nonconformity against government authority, Thoreau asks, "Why does it [government] not encourage its citizens to be on the alert to point out its faults.... Why does it always crucify Christ, and excommunicate Copernicus and Luther, and pronounce Washington and Franklin rebels?" (644).

"Civil Disobedience" has been highly influential on subsequent leaders of rebellions like Mahatma Gandhi, Martin Luther King, and Mario Savio. To be sure, the excesses by some elements of the protest movements in the later 1960s provoked a conservative backlash against this variety of nonconformity and a broader questioning of the validity of the whole tradition of antiauthoritarianism. "The sixties" and their "adversary culture" remain fighting words even today, invoked by both sides in the ongoing culture wars four decades later.

To summarize, your challenge as a critical citizen is to judge rationally for yourself in any given situation whether support of authority and majority opinion or criticism of and active opposition to it is warranted, rather than either conforming or rebelling simply because of cultural conditioning or peer pressure.

RATIONALIZATION, COMPARTMENTALIZED THINKING, AND DOUBLE STANDARDS

Psychological blocks like ethnocentrism and authoritarianism typically lead us toward a need to twist logic around to justify whatever actions and ideas support the authority or group we identify with. *Rationalization* is the word for this process of deceiving ourselves into believing what we want to believe or what benefits us personally, at the expense of what we would believe on rational grounds. (Definitions get confusing here because *rationalize* derives from *rational*, but *rationalization* means to convince ourselves that an irrational idea is rational; *to rationalize* is to reason in a way that justifies a predetermined or desired conclusion.) Geoffrey Chaucer succinctly defined rationalization another way: "Making virtue of necessity." Many people go through their whole lives confusing rationalization with reasoning, never understanding that what they firmly believe is rational is really rationalization of whatever serves their own or their group's interests. One common form of rationalization is making excuses and blaming somebody or something else for our own failures: when a student gets a low grade, it's the teacher's fault; when a teacher gets poor student evaluations, it's the students' fault. Another form is "sour grapes," saying we don't really want what we can't get. Still another common form is simple **denial** of unpleasant truths.

Rationalizations in turn lead us into unconscious inconsistencies and self-contradictions, or compartmentalized thinking. In Joe Masteroff's script for the 1966 Broadway musical play *Cabaret*, set during Hitler's rise to power in 1930s Germany, a fervent follower of the Nazis is reading the party newspaper and muttering to his fellow boarders that Jewish capitalists own all the banks, "and they're all Communists too." Someone asks him how the same people can be capitalists and Communists. He pauses a second, then replies ominously, "They're very crafty."

George Orwell's *1984* captures the essence of these mental traps in the concept of **doublethink**, the term devised by the all-powerful ruling party of the future state of Oceania to describe the mental process through which the masses are programmed into rationalizing all of the party's lies, deprivations of rights, and constant changes of policy or of foreign allies and enemies. Doublethink is brilliantly defined in the reading here through the thoughts of the central character, Winston Smith, a government bureaucrat whose job is rewriting history daily to reconcile it with the shifting party line (when historical records are destroyed, they go "down the memory hole," suggesting that the entire capacity for memory of the past can be destroyed). The slogans summing up the compartmentalized thinking of doublethink in *1984* are emblazoned on the facade of the Ministry of Truth (the agency in charge of producing lies, of course): "WAR IS PEACE. FREEDOM IS SLAVERY. IGNORANCE IS STRENGTH" (19).

In Oceania every military defeat is described in official broadcasts as a stunning victory, every reduction in the standard of living as a "glorious" increase. At one point Winston learns that the chocolate ration is to be reduced to twenty grams, but the public announcement describes the change as an *increase*, and "there had even been demonstrations to thank Big Brother for raising the chocolate ration to twenty grams a week" (51–52). Winston's co-workers "swallowed it fanatically, passionately, with a furious desire to track down, denounce, and vaporize anyone who should suggest that last week the ration had been thirty grams." The citizens are regularly stirred up in a collective "Two Minutes Hate" frenzy against whichever other country the government has identified as the enemy of the moment.

In reading *1984* we are apt to feel grateful that we are living in a free society and not in a totalitarian dictatorship like that of the Soviet Union, the immediate model for Orwell's nightmarish vision. But, in spite of the enormous differences between such dictatorships and American society, our reaction might contain an element of compartmentalized thinking and **projection** in our denial of the many ways in which we too conform to the power structure of our own society. Are the rationalizations of the shifting alliances in Orwell's world, for example, so different from our government's and media's changing attitudes toward China, Vietnam, and other Communist countries—demonizing them when they were economic rivals but establishing normal relations with them when they decided to do business with us? The United States was an ally of Saddam Hussein, selling him arms (which he used against his own people), when Iraq was at war with Iran in the 1980s. Michael Moore's film *Fahrenheit 9/11* (which alludes directly to *1984* in exposing the alleged rewriting of history by the Bush administration) includes newsreel footage from that period showing Donald Rumsfeld, who would be the secretary of Defense directing the war against Iraq in 2003, cordially shaking hands with Saddam in Baghdad as an emissary to Iraq in the eighties. Later, in our two wars against Saddam, he was transformed by both Bush presidents and Rumsfeld into a Hitler-like monster (which he may well have been, but no less so in the eighties). We also supported the Taliban and leaders of Al Qaeda when they were resisting the Soviet Union's control of Afghanistan in the eighties; President Ronald Reagan praised them as "freedom fighters"—before they turned the weapons that we provided them against us and became "terrorists."

At the time the Bush administration was persuading the public to support its war on Iraq in 2002–2003, a *Washington Post* poll indicated that 70 percent of Americans believed Iraq played a direct role in 9/11. Another poll found that 44 percent of respondents thought "most" or "some" of the 9/11 hijackers were Iraqi. None were; most were citizens of Saudi Arabia (as was Osama Bin Laden), a country that was a close American ally, with which the Bush family had long-standing ties in the oil business. Fifty-five percent polled believed Saddam Hussein directly supported Al Qaeda. A majority of Americans also believed that weapons of mass destruction had been located in Iraq and that Saddam was about to build a nuclear bomb. Among regular viewers of Fox News, these percentages were even higher (see Susan Gerhard's article "*Outfoxed* Tweaks Rupert Murdoch's Mayhem-isphere" in chapter 14). Several subsequent investigations by Congress and government commissions, however, concluded (at least at the time of this writing) that all of these beliefs were ungrounded. In some cases, the Bush administration denied ever having even made these claims, although critics cited many administration statements **implying** they were true. Was this perhaps a classic case of Orwellian rationalization, wishful thinking by masses of citizens, terrified by 9/11 and desperately wanting to believe that the war against Iraq was both justified and an effective retaliation against the perpetrators of 9/11? Considering the often hate-filled denunciations of the war's critics (including the Dixie Chicks) as unpatriotic or even treasonous and heightened government surveillance under the Patriot Act, mightn't some supporters also have been rationalizing their conformity and unwillingness to be tracked down, denounced, and vaporized?

The issue concerning the Iraq War was not what the facts about Saddam Hussein actually were (which at this writing were still open to dispute and new revelations) but whether people's conformity to the government line might have been yet another example of Orwell's depiction of these tendencies in all humans and all societies, particularly under the conditions of mass **propaganda** in modern democracies as well as dictatorships. Indeed, Orwell objected to the popular reception of *1984* in the West as simply an anti-Communist tract or as a warning against the totalitarian potential in English socialism ("Ingsoc"): "The name suggested in *Nineteen Eighty-Four* is of course Ingsoc, but in practice a wide range of choices is open. In the USA the phrase 'Americanism' or 'hundred per cent Americanism' is suitable and the qualifying adjective is as totalitarian as one could wish" (quoted in Bernard Crick, *George Orwell: A Life*, 566).

Joseph Heller's 1961 novel *Catch-22* applies many of Orwell's concepts to a satire of American society. One character is a master of rationalization and compartmentalization:

> He was a long-limbed farmer, a God-fearing, freedom-loving, law-abiding rugged individualist who held that federal aid to anyone but farmers was creeping socialism. He advocated thrift and hard work and disapproved of loose women who turned him down. His specialty was

alfalfa, and he made a good thing out of not growing any. The government paid him well for every bushel of alfalfa he did not grow. The more alfalfa he did not grow, the more money the government gave him, and he spent every penny he didn't earn on new land to increase the amount of alfalfa he did not produce. (86)

The **double standard** that Heller is satirizing here, of conservatives who stand up for free enterprise yet lobby for government subsidies for their business enterprises, continues to be timely today, as indicated in Lisa Hoffman's "Dozens of Billionaires Receive Ag Handouts" in chapter 7.

The famous title phrase of *Catch-22* refers to an imaginary rule used to force a squadron of American airmen in Europe during World War II to fly an unreasonable number of dangerous combat missions. When the novel's hero Yossarian asks the company doctor if there is any way his stressed friend Orr could get out of such missions, he is assured that the doctor is empowered to ground any flyer who is crazy. There is, however, a catch—"Catch-22": "Anyone who wants to get out of combat duty isn't really crazy. . . . Orr was crazy and could be grounded. All he had to do was ask; and as soon as he did, he would no longer be crazy and would have to fly more missions" (47). Over the course of the novel, however, Catch-22 turns out to be an all-purpose gimmick; those in power invent a different version of it in any situation to rationalize their capricious exercise of authority over those beneath them in the hierarchy in exactly the same manner that Orwell's rulers use doublethink. Most of the characters—including the company chaplain—have learned to deceive themselves into justifications for conforming to the corruptions of the bureaucratic system in which they are caught: "The chaplain had mastered, in a moment of divine intuition, the handy technique of protective rationalization, and he was exhilarated by his discovery. It was miraculous. It was almost no trick at all, he saw, to turn vice into virtue and slander into truth, impotence into abstinence, arrogance into humility, plunder into philanthropy, thievery into honor, blasphemy into wisdom, brutality into patriotism, and sadism into justice. Anybody could do it; it required no brains at all. It merely required no character" (372).

In political disputes, opposing sides constantly resort to rationalization, compartmentalization, and their related fallacies to excuse their side's faults. When Republicans controlled Congress from 1994 to 2006, they were so aggrieved over Democratic filibusters that they tried to impose "the nuclear option"—illegalizing filibusters—but after Democrats gained a majority in 2006, Republicans resorted to a record-setting number of filibusters. When stories first surfaced in 2004 about American abuse of prisoners at Abu Ghraib prison in Iraq, conservatives tended at first to say, "Oh well, it was just a few rotten apples among the rank-and-file troops." But when information came out suggesting that approval for the abuse had come from high government officials, the story shifted to, "Oh well, when you're dealing with terrorists, anything goes." According to *Newsweek* (July 19, 2004, 41–42), many of those abused were petty criminals who had nothing to do with terrorism, and others were not guilty of any crime—so some new variety of rationalization was predictable.

One of the most common forms that compartmentalized thinking and rationalization take is **selective vision**: applying a more demanding standard of morality to the other side than to our own, or blaming the other side for the same faults that we overlook or even praise as virtues on our own. (These are also varieties of **stacking the deck**, and they frequently involve projection of our own faults onto the other side.) It's one of the hardest challenges of critical thinking to get beyond the ESBYODS principle and see the double standards and selective vision that blind us all to faults on our own side that we are so quick to see on the other side.

In virtually every day's news, you can see Republicans and Democrats self-righteously denouncing the other party's politicians for vices of which their own side is just as likely to be guilty. In scandals during Republican presidential administrations, like Watergate or Iran-Contra, Democrats **play up** the gravity of every accusation, while Republicans go into a mode of denial, **downplaying** the importance of the alleged crimes ("It was just a third-rate burglary"), claiming the charges are motivated by political partisanship, and invoking "national security" or "executive privilege" as excuses not to cooperate with the investigation. When Democrats are in office, as in President Bill Clinton's Monica Lewinsky and Whitewater scandals, the roles and rhetoric switch diametrically. When House Republicans tried to impeach Clinton, they were highly self-righteous in their moral condemnation of Clinton's adulterous affairs, yet after the impeachment effort failed, it became public knowledge that several Republicans leading that effort had also committed adultery—some at the very time of the impeachment trial.

On the positive side, pointing out double standards in your opponent's arguments is one of the most effective lines of refutation—that is, if you do not fall into a double standard yourself in so doing! Pointing them out involves a form of argument by **analogy**, showing that "what's sauce for the goose is sauce for the gander."

The quality of the argument, then, depends on the validity of the analogy in the claim that the two situations are indeed comparable in the way the author suggests. (See chapter 9 on analogies.) At the end of this chapter are two opinion columns using double-standard arguments and analogies, one by left-of-liberal Katha Pollitt criticizing conservative opponents of affirmative action and one by conservative Jeff Jacoby criticizing liberal environmentalists.

OTHER DEFENSE MECHANISMS

Psychologists identify further varieties of blocks to open-mindedness stemming from **primary certitude** and rationalization. Two of the most common defense mechanisms are **denial** and **projection**.

When we are confronted with facts or views that threaten our primary certitude, we tend to react by "being in denial," a state of angry, irrational defense of our own closed-minded opinion and refusal to consider any evidence to the contrary. To be sure, not every denial fits the psychological profile of being in denial. There is a big difference between denying the validity of an opposing viewpoint through coolheaded reasoning (even though it may be passionately expressed) and a knee-jerk reaction that is purely emotional and unsupported with evidence and reason.

When we are at fault in relationship to other people but don't want to admit it, a common form of denial is to convince ourselves that it is the others who are at fault and that they are committing the fault against us that we have committed against them, or at least that our bad behavior toward them is a justified reaction against their behavior toward us, that "they started it." (This mentality feeds into the causal fallacy of **blaming the victim**.) Another form that projection often takes is intense anger toward someone who exhibits traits that we have suppressed within ourselves; thus men who are extremely homophobic and who might commit violence against homosexuals may be projecting self-hatred over their own suppressed homosexual tendencies onto an external target.

An excellent analysis of both denial and projection is found in James Baldwin's 1963 book *The Fire Next Time*. Baldwin, expressing an African-American viewpoint on how white Americans' illusions of racial superiority were threatened by the civil rights movement, suggested that whites were in constant denial about four centuries of crimes committed by whites against blacks—beginning with kidnapping and slavery, followed after abolition by unpunished lynching, rape, robbery, segregation, and denial of civil rights. Baldwin said about the truth of this history that many whites "do not know it, and do not want to know it" (15). They suppressed consciousness of reality by rationalizing that blacks preferred to be subordinate and segregated, or by projecting criminality into **stereotypes** of black men as rapists of white women, murderers, thieves, and loafers. To whatever extent these stereotypes had any basis in reality, that reality was judged causally as a sign of blacks' innate criminality, not as an effect of or reaction to centuries of crimes against them. Simultaneously, according to Baldwin, in the white psyche, blacks symbolized an uninhibited sexuality and day-to-day intensity of life that whites denied themselves, so that whites' attitudes were highly compartmentalized: they both looked down on blacks as morally inferior and envied their flamboyant sensuality:

> The white man's unadmitted—and apparently, to him, unspeakable—private fears and longings are projected onto the Negro. The only way he can be released from the Negro's tyrannical power over him is to consent, in effect, to become black himself, to become a part of that suffering and dancing country that he now watches wistfully from the heights of his lonely power and, armed with spiritual traveler's checks, visits surreptitiously [secretly] after dark. (129)

A more recent discussion of projection is found in David Brock's 2002 book *Blinded by the Right: The Conscience of an Ex-Conservative*. Brock confesses that as a highly successful conservative journalist in the 1990s, he was not really an objective reporter but a propagandist for the Republican Party, with little regard for truth. He says that he and other conservative propagandists rationalized their unscrupulousness by the assumption that liberals had a similarly powerful and unscrupulous machine, but he eventually came to realize this was a false assumption: "I unconsciously projected onto the liberals what I knew and saw and learned of the right wing's operations" (114).

From 1984

George Orwell

Harcourt Brace, 1949

For several months during his childhood there had been confused street fighting in London itself, some of which he remembered vividly. But to trace out the history of the whole period, to say who was fighting whom at any given moment, would have been utterly impossible, since no written record, and no spoken word, ever made mention of any other alignment than the existing one. At this moment, for example, in 1984 (if it was 1984), Oceania was at war with Eurasia and in alliance with Eastasia. In no public or private utterance was it ever admitted that the three powers had at any time been grouped along different lines. Actually, as Winston well knew, it was only four years since Oceania had been at war with Eastasia and in alliance with Eurasia. But that was merely a piece of furtive knowledge which he happened to possess because his memory was not satisfactorily under control. Officially

the change of partners had never happened, Oceania was at war with Eurasia: therefore Oceania had always been at war with Eurasia. The enemy of the moment always represented absolute evil, and it followed that any past or future agreement with him was impossible.

The frightening thing, he reflected for the ten thousandth time as he forced his shoulders painfully backward (with hands on hips, they were gyrating their bodies from the waist, an exercise that was supposed to be good for the back muscles)—the frightening thing was that it might all be true. If the Party could thrust its hand into the past and say of this or that event, *it never happened*—that, surely, was more terrifying than mere torture and death.

The Party said that Oceania had never been in alliance with Eurasia. He, Winston Smith, knew that Oceania had been in alliance with Eurasia as short a time as four years ago. But where did that knowledge exist? Only in his own consciousness, which in any case must soon be annihilated. And if all others accepted the lie which the Party imposed—if all records told the same tale— then the lie passed into history and became truth. "Who controls the past," ran the Party slogan, "controls the future: who controls the present controls the past." And yet the past, though of its nature alterable, never had been altered. Whatever was true now was true from everlasting to everlasting. It was quite simple. All that was needed was an unending series of victories over your own memory. "*Reality control*" they called it; in Newspeak, "doublethink."

Winston sank his arms to his sides and slowly refilled his lungs with air. His mind slipped away into the labyrinthine world of doublethink. To know and not to know, to be conscious of complete truthfulness while telling carefully constructed lies, to hold simultaneously two opinions which cancelled out, knowing them to be contradictory and believing in both of them, to use logic against logic, to repudiate morality while laying claim to it, to believe that democracy was impossible and that (the party) was the guardian of democracy, to forget whatever it was necessary to forget, then to draw it back into memory again at the moment when it was needed, and then promptly to forget it again, and above all, to apply the same process to the process itself—that was the ultimate subtlety: consciously to induce unconsciousness, and then, once again, to become unconscious of the fact of hypnosis you had just performed. Even to understand the word "doublethink" involved the use of doublethink.

On the Merits

Katha Pollitt

From *Reasonable Creatures*, Knopf, 1994

The other day my old classmate Allen and I were discussing who would be the next editor in chief of the influential magazine whose staff he had recently joined. I proposed Rosemary, the deputy editor: She had seniority, she was extremely able, she was practically doing the job already. Allen looked at me as if I had suggested sending out a spacecraft for the editor of *The Neptune Gazette*. Come on, he said, you know they'd never give it to a woman. So who do you think it will be? I asked innocently. Well, he replied with a modest blush, actually, me.

This exchange made me think again about one of the more insidious arguments being made in the current onslaught against affirmative action: Advancing women and minorities on the basis of sex and race damages their self-esteem. According to Clarence M. Pendleton, Jr., Reagan-appointed chair of the United States Commission on Civil Rights, those who benefit from social and legal pressures on their behalf know in their hearts that they are unworthy and suffer terribly because they fear, correctly, that they won't measure up. Worse, the women and minorities who would have won the golden prizes anyway—the college acceptance, the job, the promotion—are guilty by association: Everyone thinks they're tokens, even if they're not.

It's an ingenious argument, because it not only appears to demonstrate concern for the same constituency as affirmative action but also makes affirmative action seem by comparison both crude and condescending. What is money, after all, or a job title, compared with the priceless gift of psychological peace? Don't we all need to think we are rewarded on our merits? Yes, indeed, which is why I'm very worried about my friend Allen's peace of mind. If his publisher promotes him over Rosemary because he is a man, won't Allen spend a lot of sleepless nights wondering if the world is snickering at him behind his back?

Not on your life. Allen has been blithely ignoring such threats to his self-esteem for decades.

We both attended Harvard-Radcliffe, for example, at a time when the ratio of male to female students was fixed at five to one. Granted that the pool of female applicants was smaller, the fact remains it was harder for girls to get in. Everyone knew this, but Allen and his friends never saw themselves as having been rounded up to fill an inflated male quota. Nor did they see as tarnished victories their acceptance into the many all-male clubs and activities that flourished in those benighted years—the Signet Society, for instance, where literary Harvard men were served lunch by literary Radcliffe women employed as waitresses—or scorn to go off to Europe on postgraduate fellowships closed to female classmates.

If the self-esteem argument were true, who would get a good night's sleep? After all, we live in a society where all sorts of considerations besides merit are accepted as valid means of choosing candidates. Because elite schools want diversity, it's easier for a student from Montana to get in than one from New York City. Because lawmakers want to reward military service, veterans get lifelong preference for a slew of state and federal jobs. Because political parties want votes, they craft ethnically and geographically balanced tickets.

Some of these nonmerit considerations are rather shady, to say the least. At the Ivy League college where I taught last year, a delicious scandal came to light when an alumnus wrote an outraged letter to the campus newspaper alleging that his son had been passed over for admission in the rush to accept women and blacks. It turned out that although the overall odds of acceptance were one in seven, for the children of alumni they were almost one in two. Many sheepish things were said in defense of this practice: For example, administrators cited the natural desire of the college to create a sense of con-tinuity between the generations, translated by campus cynics as the natural desire of the college to receive large financial contributions from prosperous grads. But I'm still waiting for Mr. Pendleton to acknowledge the existence of alumni-child preferences, let alone express solicitude for the self-esteem of alumni children.

It's a curious thing. As long as we're talking about white men competing with each other, we tacitly acknowledge that we live in a realistic world of a Balzac novel, a world in which we know perfectly well that Harvard C's beat A's from Brooklyn College, in which family connections and a good tennis serve never hurt, and sycophancy, backstabbing and organizational inertia carry the undeserving into top jobs every day of the week. Add women and blacks into the picture, though, and suddenly the scene shifts. Now we're in Plato's Republic, where sternly impartial philosopher-kings award laurels to the deserving after nights of fasting and prayer. Or did, before affirmative action threw its spanner into the meritocratic works.

So how do the beneficiaries of social privilege avoid the dreaded inferiority complex? That's where individual psychology and social myopia come in. On the personal level they live in both worlds at once: *I* slave away in Plato's Republic, while *you* weasel your way down the boulevards of Balzac's Paris. This collective delusion is so culturally approved that people who get the formula backward are considered to be victims of "the impostor syndrome" and in need of psychiatric help.

To transform America into a true meritocracy would be a fascinating experiment in social engineering, but it would make the minor adjustments required for affirmative action look like piano tuning. We'd have to strip the credentials of all male doctors over the age of thirty-five, for instance, since they got into medical school back when a woman had to be Albert Schweitzer in skirts to win a place in the class. Ditto for lawyers, engineers, tenured professors, corporate executives and military officers. The children of the famous would have to change their names. Perhaps it would be too cruel to force the powerful to remain celibate in order to discourage nepotism. But we could certainly make it a criminal offense to marry the boss's daughter, or even to take her out for coffee.

Brave New World or simple justice? Whichever, I'm ready for it, whenever Mr. Pendleton gives the word; even though, as an alumni child, I'll have to turn in my college diploma. Because in the perfect meritocracy that would result, Rosemary would get that job. And Allen? Well, he'd have something even more precious. His self-esteem.

Greens Dodge Links to Unabomber

Jeff Jacoby

San Francisco Chronicle, April 24, 1996

That perfect silence you hear is the environmental movement not being blamed for the crimes of the Unabomber. It is President Clinton not calling a press conference to denounce the purveyors of hate and division on the ecological fringe. It is the Sunday-morning Beltway pundits not accusing environmental activists of inflaming an unstable creep like Theodore Kaczynski, the Unabomber suspect. It is editors in America's great newsrooms not assigning long takeouts on radical groups like Earth First, which blow up logging equipment and demand the blood of environmental "villains"—such as those the Unabomber killed.

There's environmentalism on the mind of the Unabomber. His own writings cite "anarchist and radical environmentalist journals" to justify attacks on the "the industrial-technological system," and he obviously drew his victims from the demonology of green extremists. Two examples:

• At a 1994 Earth First meeting in Missoula, Mont., the public-relations giant Burson-Marsteller was excoriated for supposedly having helped Exxon recover from the Valdez oil spill disaster. Kaczynski attended that meeting. One month later, Thomas Mosser, a former Burson-Marsteller executive, was killed by a bomb mailed to his home. In a letter to the *New York Times,* the Unabomber claimed credit. "Among other misdeeds," he wrote, "Burson-Marsteller (sic) helped Exxon clean up its public image after the Exxon Valdez incident."

• In a 1989 tract called "Live Wild or Die," a group of enviro-nihilists put out an "Eco-(expletive deleted) Hit List." No. 1 on the list was the Timber Association of California. Last year the Unabomber addressed an explosive to the association at its Sacramento headquarters, unaware that it had been renamed the California Forestry Association. Gilbert Murray, the group's president and a father of three, opened the package. He died on the spot.

So isn't it odd that the nation's opinion makers aren't skewering environmentalists for the Unabomber's long trail of death and mayhem?

Isn't it curious that editorial writers and "Nightline" producers aren't hyping Kaczynski's connection to the eco-fanatics? Isn't it strange that we're not being reminded that deadly rhetoric can fuel deadly deeds—that when environmental advocates put timber executives on a "hit list," they are encouraging psychopaths to blow up timber executives?

Well, no, it isn't strange. It would be absurd to blame decent environmentalists for the Unabomber's murders. Just as it would have been absurd to blame decent conservatives for the horror in Oklahoma City. Whoops. Did somebody say . . . "double standard?"

Twelve months ago, when Timothy McVeigh and Terry Nichols were arrested for the bombing in Oklahoma City, it was open season on anything right of center. President Clinton slammed conservative talk show hosts as "promoters of paranoia" who "leave the impression that … violence is acceptable." *Washington Post* pundit David Broder observed, "The bombing shows how dangerous it really is to inflame twisted minds with statements that suggest political opponents are enemies." Even the Republican Party found itself charged with the terrorism in Oklahoma City.

He who says X must say Y. Either Al Gore, Earth First and Greenpeace had a hand in the Unabomber's killings—or Newt Gingrich, the NRA and Rush Limbaugh's radio show didn't cause the carnage in Oklahoma City. *Every* movement has its kooks and degenerates. To blame the left for the crimes of the Unabomber would be shameless. Even as it was shameless to blame the right for the crime in Oklahoma City.

Topics for Discussion and Writing

1. In the following cartoon, what generalization is implicit as a **hidden premise** in the man's connection between his father and the president? What exceptions to the belief that authority figures "must know what they're doing" in recent history can you think of that would provide evidence that it is an **overgeneralization**?

Cobb Weekly Editorial Cartoon 286. Reprinted with permission, Sawyer Press, Los Angeles, California 90046 U.S.A.

2. A student writes: "From what we have read in this course, it appears like a small handful of corporations are in control of just about everything in America, and it's a good thing. The average one of the masses could hardly run his own

life correctly if someone weren't looking after him, or so it seems. These huge corporations are responsible for the economic and social well-being of the nation. Hence it is logical to assume that they know what is best." What line of argument, and possible logical fallacy, is similar here to that in the cartoon in question 1? Would you guess that the student considers herself or himself "the average one of the masses"? If not, do you think she or he considers herself or himself one of those who will "look after" the others as an executive of one of that "small handful of corporations"? Is compartmentalized thinking perhaps evident here? What **evidence** can you think of that might be presented either in support of or in refutation of the unsupported assertions about the average one of the masses and about corporate responsibility?

3. Do you consider yourself a conformist or a nonconformist, or some mix of the two? Support.

4. Write an essay, based on your own high school memories, supporting or refuting Jennifer Crichton's semihumorous description of American high schools as "totalitarian regimes."

5. How applicable to contemporary America do you find the descriptions of an authoritarian society by Dostoyevsky, Fromm, Orwell, and Chayefsky? How plausible do you find the **hypothesis** that our childhood relations with our parents, and particularly our fathers, shape our adult attitudes toward social and political authority? And that many people want to "escape from freedom," to go along with the crowd and submit passively to authority?

6. When Sylvia Plath says, "Every woman adores a fascist," she is obviously using poetic **hyperbole** (deliberate exaggeration for dramatic or humorous effect), rather like Crichton. Do you think there is some truth, though, in the notion that repressive patriarchal cultural conditioning induces some females to seek out males who are domineering father figures? Read the rest of "Daddy" and some of Plath's other poems in the collection *Ariel*. Debate whether you think Plath eloquently expresses the grievances of women against patriarchy, as her defenders say, or is just, as some critics charge, venting her personal neuroses.

7. Thoreau's views on government, laws, and war in "Civil Disobedience" frequently provoke strong disagreement in contemporary readers. Debate Thoreau's condemnation of the fact that soldiers give up their individual conscience and submit blindly to military and governmental authority. On the one hand, it can be argued that such submission is a justifiable part of the military chain of command and discipline needed to fight any war. On the other hand, it can be argued that ignorance of the situation one is in is never a good thing and that blind trust in commanders, by both soldiers and the public, has resulted throughout history in abuses of power and cover-ups of blunders or corruption. Thoreau was not a complete pacifist; indeed, as an abolitionist he strongly supported the Union in the Civil War. Read the complete text of the essay to see if he **draws the line** about when war is justified and when it isn't, or if he was just **inconsistent**.

8. Review Thoreau's sentences "I know this well, that if one thousand, if one hundred, if ten men . . . it would be the abolition of slavery in America. For it matters not how small the beginning may seem to be: what is once done well is done forever." Do you think he is just using **hyperbole** here, or do you see a grain of truth in what he says? For example, Thoreau's eloquent essay and his night in jail for not paying his taxes were not immediate causes of the abolition of slavery, but they are remembered today as a significant chapter in the eventual achievement of abolition.

9. The rhetoric and tactics of civil disobedience advocated by Thoreau and applied by Mario Savio and other leftists in the protest movements of the sixties have more recently been adapted by conservative movements such as militias and antiabortion activists. Write an essay or a dialogue in which you imagine whether or not Thoreau and Mario Savio would agree with the application of their principles to justification of pro-life groups or individuals preventing the normal operation of abortion clinics. Or write one on what you think Savio would say if conservative students shut down the Berkeley campus in protest against the accession of the administration to the demands of the Free Speech Movement.

10. Think of examples of rationalization, compartmentalized thinking, double standards, denial, or projection in current public life or in your own acquaintances. Look for examples in which Democrats and Republicans condemn members of the other party for misdeeds that their own party members have also committed.

11. How strong do you find Katha Pollitt's and Jeff Jacoby's lines of argument using analogies and allegations of double standards against opponents? Pollitt's **tone** is semihumorous, but how serious and persuasive is her argument defending affirmative action?

12. Jacoby holds environmentalists accountable for the actions of the Unabomber, Theodore Kaczynski, who murdered people he considered guilty of environmental destruction, and of other extreme environmentalist groups like Earth First. Is Jacoby committing the fallacy of **guilt by association**, or is his association a defensible one? Kaczynski was in fact a fan of Thoreau's "Civil Disobedience." On the basis of the excerpt from that essay here, or of the full text, would you infer that Thoreau would endorse such extreme and violent forms of protest? Does he indicate where to **draw the line** in avoiding having his beliefs being pushed to such extremes?

Part III

Elements of Argumentative Rhetoric

CHAPTER 9

Some Key Terms in Logic and Argumentation

DEDUCTIVE AND INDUCTIVE ARGUMENTS

This section continues development of the introduction to deduction and induction in chapter 2. To reiterate, theorists of logic and rhetoric going back to Aristotle have distinguished between two basic forms of reasoning or argument, deductive and inductive. Very briefly and broadly, **deduction** involves reaching a **conclusion** (alternately called an **inference**) or supporting a **thesis** or **hypothesis** by reasoning through a logical chain of **premises** (or **assertions**), where, if the chain of reasoning is logically valid, the conclusion or thesis follows from the premises with certainty, as in a mathematical proof—from the postulates that *a* is a subset of *b* and that *b* is a subset of *c,* it follows with logical certainty that *a* is a subset of *c.* (It would not follow logically, however, that *b* is a subset of *a* or that *c* is a subset of either *a* or *b.*) **Induction** involves drawing a conclusion from, or supporting a **claim**, **assertion**, or hypothesis with **empirical** (or **experimental**) **evidence**. In induction, conclusions generally do not follow logically from claims with the mathematical certainty of deduction, but only with a greater or lesser degree of *probability,* as with the example in chapter 2 of the antique cars on the highway: it's a pretty probable hypothesis that they're going to or from a car show, and that hypothesis could be proved with empirical certainty by following them, though this is a different *kind* of proof from a deductive one. Often, the premises in an inductive argument are used to lead not just to a limited conclusion (the cars are going to or from a show) but to a broader **generalization**, an **analogy**, a **causal**, **statistical**, or other variety of analysis like those surveyed in chapter 2, or to a moral or value judgment. A number of these inductive forms are analyzed in depth in other chapters (causal analysis in chapter 11), so they will not be examined here, beyond some general guidelines on analogies and statistical arguments, along with a discussion of accounting for variable factors.

I personally don't think it's worth spending a great deal of time in what you write laboring differences between inductive and deductive reasoning. Most real-life arguments mix elements of deduction and induction, and the main practical value of the distinction is to be able to identify which elements need to be evaluated through deductive means—verifying the internal logic of the argument—and which through inductive means—verifying the evidence and whether it is sufficient to warrant the conclusion. Nor is it especially practical to use a lot of formal logical terms in your writing. It may become useful to you, if you can't quite figure out what's fishy about an argument, to recast it into an **enthymeme** and then a **syllogism**, as in some of the examples below, to see what issue is being evaded. But usually you can figure that out, and write about it, just with common sense and everyday language.

Varieties of Induction

The Use and Misuse of Analogies and Equations.   In an argumentative analogy, the speaker or writer presents us with something that we recognize as true about one situation, then tries to persuade us that another situation is similar, and therefore that the same is true about it. (It might be useful also to use the terms **equation** or **equivalency**, in which it is argued that two situations are not only similar but exactly the same or "morally equivalent." The parallel term to **false analogy**, then, would be **false equation**.) Scholars of rhetoric disagree about the value of analogies in argumentation. Some scholars go to the extreme of claiming that all analogies are false because no two situations in life are exactly alike. A more moderate position is that an analogy is valid if there are more significant similarities between the two situations than differences *on the specific point of comparison*; if the differences can be shown to be greater than the similarities, however, then the analogy is false. Try making this judgment on the set of analogies in the topics for discussion and writing that follows this section, number 4, and in the topics at the end of the chapter.

The Use and Misuse of Statistics.   Statistics are an integral part of many arguments, both in inductive and deductive reasoning. The inductive use involves gathering accurate statistical data through empirical research and drawing conclusions from the data. Deductive reasoning is applied in the logic of interpreting data; opponents might agree on the statistical evidence itself but select and interpret it differently or draw different conclusions from it. Some statistical arguments are so complex that you may need to take a course in economics or statistics to follow them, but those that appear in everyday political rhetoric and mass media ought to be comprehensible to lay readers or listeners with some close attention and commonsense reasoning; if they are not, that may be a sign they are deceptive.

Most of us tend to be easily impressed by statistics, but when confronted with statistics that contradict those supporting our side, we are also inclined to grumble skeptically, "Anybody can prove anything with statistics." Statistics are a key component of political arguments as well as of advertising and public relations campaigns, and as such are subject to all the varieties of rhetorical strategies discussed throughout this book. **Partisan** forces on opposing sides often sponsor statistical research, polls, and surveys in which the deck is stacked to guarantee that the results will support that side. Thus, each side can produce statistical findings that seem irrefutably to support its case, though the other side's opposite findings seem equally impressive. Once again, in any such case, one side's case may in fact be more credible than the other's, so do not give in to cynical despair in thinking you can't believe *anyone*: simply learn to spot partisan statistical studies when you encounter them and to evaluate them as such, wherever possible weighing them against parallel studies, or **rebuttals**, by the other side. And watch out for the **ESBYODS principle**, in the tendency to **rationalize** that the statistics supporting your own side must be right! Extensive analysis of statistical arguments concerning the recent growth of income and wealth inequities in the United States will be central to chapters 16 and 17.

Accounting for All Variables or Factors.   Scientists doing empirical research use terms like "controlling for variables." In testing the effectiveness of a medical drug, for example, they will compare the result of the drug with that of a placebo, a pill containing no medicine, given to patients while telling them it's the real thing, to control for the possible psychological factor of people's tendency to believe they feel better just because they have taken a medication.

Responsible empirical research in the social sciences also entails the attempt to account for all significant variables or factors in drawing a particular conclusion or inference. Failure to do so may lead to a form of **non sequitur** or **hasty conclusion** logical fallacy. In causal analysis, the **reductive fallacy** is the reduction of a probable multiplicity of causes to a single one, neglecting other possible factors. In statistical analysis, similar fallacies often result from failure to recognize factors in a situation—or an interpretation of their significance—other than the ones emphasized, and this failure is sometimes a form of deliberate deception. (In "A Semantic Calculator for Bias in Rhetoric" in chapter 4, this is identified as a frequent mode of downplaying arguments or evidence unfavorable to one's own side or favorable to the other side.) For example, liberal critics of the outsourcing of American jobs to other countries through globalization often argue that it has resulted in a loss of jobs and economic decline here, while they disregard the possibility that globalization has also resulted in financial benefits and job creation here through the import of low-priced foreign products and increased demand for American exports.

In a defense of President George W. Bush's tax cuts, conservative *New York Times* columnist David Brooks writes, "Some outside economists say the cuts created or preserved 1.5 million jobs." Brooks unfortunately fails to identify those economists, their possible political bias, or a source in which their evidence can be looked up. His argument also opens questions about other possible variables. Might other factors have contributed to the job creation (**reductive fallacy**)? What was the quality of most of the jobs created—college-graduate level or flipping hamburgers? How did the job growth in this period compare with previous periods? How much resulted from more than one member of a family being forced to work to keep up with declining wages? Has the amount of revenue following the tax cuts offset the amount of revenue lost to the government through the cuts? Did some of the gains from the cuts for the wealthy go toward investments in companies outsourcing jobs to other countries? Mightn't the lost tax revenue have gone to create about the same number of jobs through government employment? Is public sector employment, financed through taxes, any less valuable to the national economy than private sector employment? (This is a crucial point of difference between political conservatives and liberals or leftists, which is explored further in chapters 13, 16, and 17.)

Varieties of Deduction

Syllogisms. The classic form of deductive reasoning is the syllogism, consisting of two premises and a conclusion drawn from them, as in the classic example presented in chapter 2:

> *First premise:* All humans are mortal
> *Second premise:* Socrates is a human
> *Conclusion:* Socrates is mortal

In this form of syllogism, known as a **categorical syllogism**, one of the premises makes some kind of generalization (*all ... always ... none ... never*), and the other premise states that someone or something belongs to the category in the first, so that the conclusion affirms that the characteristic of the category in the first also applies to the instance of that category in the second. In order for this and other kinds of syllogism to be logically sound, both of the premises must be true (they must be factually accurate and adequately supported), and the conclusion must follow logically (with certainty, inescapably) from both of them. (The fallacy of non sequitur refers to a conclusion that does not follow thus.)

Few deductive arguments about the kind of social issues emphasized in this book have the certainty of mathematical proofs, and establishing their premises often necessitates elements of inductive reasoning. The generalizing premise in a categorical syllogism must be verified through the inductive principles of evaluating generalizations discussed in chapter 7. The second premise may be established through a variety of means—in this case by definition or classification of Socrates as a man, but in other cases by the several varieties of inductive supporting evidence surveyed in chapter 2. In 2008, for example, conservatives argued, "Liberals favor tax-and-spend policies. Barack Obama is a liberal. So Obama favors tax-and-spend policies." In order for this conclusion to be sound, we must empirically verify both the generalization in the first premise about liberals and the categorizing of Obama as a liberal in the second.

The deductive reasoning in syllogisms (especially categorical ones) and enthymemes can also be fallacious in ways related to mathematical sets and subsets, or classes and subclasses, as in circles A, B, and C in figure 9.1. Such circle diagrams, also called **Venn diagrams**, are useful for visualizing this kind of fallacy. In the syllogism concluding that Socrates is a mortal, one might conceivably argue that all cats are also mortal, and then conclude either that all mortals are cats or that Socrates is a cat. One might also reason something like: all humans are mortals (creatures that die); Socrates is a human; therefore, all mortals are human. There are various formal names for this kind of fallacy in which sets and subsets

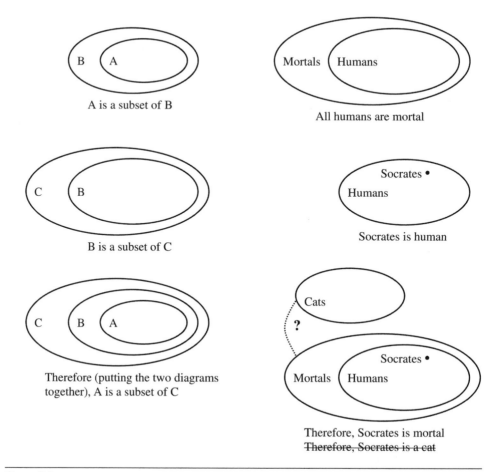

A is a subset of B

All humans are mortal

B is a subset of C

Socrates is human

Therefore (putting the two diagrams together), A is a subset of C

Therefore, Socrates is mortal
~~Therefore, Socrates is a cat~~

Figure 9.1

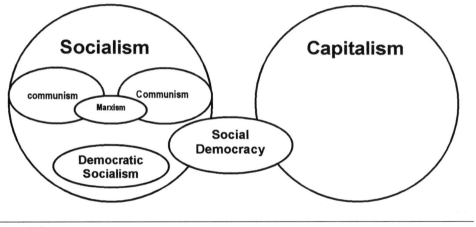

Figure 9.2

are erroneously linked—most commonly **argument from the converse**; that is, it is a false inference to conclude from the fact that all humans are mortal that the converse, all mortals are human, is true.

The circle diagrams in figure 9.2, taken from chapter 13, serve there to reveal a frequent argument from the converse, when people reason from the fact that Communists (governments or members of the Communist Party) are a subset of socialists to the false conclusion that socialists are a subset of Communists, or that all socialists are Communists. Likewise, all Communists are Marxists, but not all Marxists are Communists. The diagrams also clarify the relations among socialism, social democracy, and capitalism defined in chapter 13.

Categorical syllogisms are often interchangeable with another form of deductive argument, called a *conditional argument* (sometimes called a *conditional syllogism,* or in Latin, *modus ponens,* "method of affirming"), such as the following:

> If a person is human, then that person is mortal
> Socrates is human.
> Therefore, Socrates is mortal.

Enthymemes. As noted in chapter 2, few arguments in everyday life are phrased as formal syllogisms or state all of the premises in the nice and tidy forms given above. Instead, deductive arguments most often take the form of an enthymeme, which is a syllogism in which one of the two premises is left unstated and is implied or hidden ("Socrates is a human; therefore, Socrates is mortal"). For a hidden premise to form an implicit part of a valid chain of deductive reasoning, it must be one that, once added explicitly to the original premise, makes the conclusion follow syllogistically. Leaving a premise implicit is a perfectly reasonable, time-saving move if the unstated premise (here, "All humans are mortal") is so obviously true that no one is likely to question it. However, dispute very often arises over such a premise that the arguer assumes to be true but that her or his opponents do not. So one of the most important rhetorical skills that you can develop is learning to spot the disputable hidden premises on which an argument that you hear or read may be based. Such premises are often generalizations, so you should apply to them the usual tests for generalizations studied in chapter 7: see if you can find significant examples that disprove the generalization or empirical evidence refuting it. (In chapter 2, we used the example of Mario Savio's implied assertion that students in the university should have all the same rights as citizens under a democratic government, which is disputable on the empirical grounds that students' rights are generally by agreement subject to limitations.)

In a *Los Angeles Times* article on a California school-voucher initiative in 2000, a supporter of vouchers is quoted as arguing that a voucher redeemed at a private school would be worth $4,000 and that this is $2,000 less than what is normally spent on a child in a public school. Thus, "For every child that redeems a voucher and goes to private school, there's more money left in the system." This argument can be reworded as an enthymeme something like this:

> *Premise:* Vouchers would save schools the difference between the cost of the voucher and what is now spent per student in the public schools.

> *Conclusion:* Therefore, public schools would gain money for every student who leaves with a voucher.

However, an opponent of vouchers refuted this by saying, "The state distributes general fund money to schools based on how many students are enrolled, so funding could drop along with enrollment." With this empirical evidence provided by the opponents, we see that there is a hidden premise in the above enthymeme, which could be recast as a syllogism:

> *Hidden premise:* Per student funding in public schools remains constant if the number of students declines.

> *Premise:* Vouchers would save schools the difference between the cost of the voucher and what is now spent per student in the public schools.

> *Conclusion:* Therefore, public schools would gain money per student for every student who leaves with a voucher.

In this form we can see that the truth of the first premise is disputed, so that even if the second premise is granted to be true, the conclusion does not follow. It is essential to bring premises into the open like this because they often contain what is most disputable in the argument, and hiding them amounts to **begging the question**.

To see how practical arguments combine deductive and inductive elements, consider that disputes over capital punishment often include the assertion "The death penalty deters potential murderers." This argument is an enthymeme whose implicit reasoning goes something like:

> *Premise:* Most normal, rational people would be deterred from committing murder by the fear of execution.

> *Conclusion:* The death penalty is an effective deterrent to murder.

Opponents of capital punishment dispute this reasoning by challenging the hidden premise, that most murderers think the same way that normal, rational people do; many murderers are hardened criminals with low esteem for others' lives or their own, or they are mentally ill, high on drugs or alcohol, or otherwise irrational at the moment of committing murder, so they are unlikely to be deterred by rational calculation of the risk. This deductive line of refutation is then joined to an inductive line, in which abolitionists argue that there is little empirical evidence showing a correlation between enforcement of the death penalty and crime rates. Thus the burden of proof is on defenders to produce enough evidence to the contrary to justify executions (opposition to which is based on several grounds, most prominently the high incidence of judicial error and variability of standards for sentencing in different places and times).

Sometimes, advocates **shift ground** at this point and argue, somewhat facetiously, "Well, at least capital punishment deters the executed criminal from killing again." This argument is, to begin with, based on an **equivocation**, a shifting definition of deterrence. Secondly, it contains a hidden premise: that preventing any criminal from committing further crime is in itself sufficient grounds for execution. This premise can be **reduced to absurdity** by an analogy: executing jaywalkers would also deter them from jaywalking again. If those making the first argument are serious, they need to qualify it by specifying why murder (and presumably only in the first degree) merits "deterrence" through execution and not other crimes. In nineteenth-century America, horse thieves and cattle rustlers were hanged; in Puritan days, sodomy with animals was a capital offense, to say nothing of "witchcraft." Conventional defenses of capital punishment tend similarly to shift ground from one line of deductive argument to another, as each line is refuted: from deterrence (of the individual criminal, or of others), to revenge (an eye for an eye), to protecting society (without consideration of the alternative of life imprisonment without parole), and so forth.

One version of the last argument above—protecting society—is also based on a hypothesis: "Murderers should be executed, because if they are not, they might escape from prison or murder guards and other inmates." Most people would agree that this hypothesis is plausible in principle; however, it assumes the hidden premise that the incidence of escape or murder in prison is unacceptably high. This premise needs to be verified empirically. What does criminological research show about the number of murderers who have escaped or who have murdered within prison? Is it high enough to offset every argument against capital punishment? Does evidence show that it is possible to implement adequate protection against escape or killings in prison?

Topics for Discussion and Writing

1. "I go to the gym every Tuesday and Thursday, and this same woman is always there working out. She must go every day." What other inductive conclusions are possible here?

2. "'Who controls the past,' ran the Party slogan, 'controls the future: who controls the present controls the past.'" (George Orwell, *1984* 25.) What deductive conclusion would follow from these two premises?

3. In *The Way Things Ought to Be*, Rush Limbaugh writes, "The civil rights coalition . . . delivers up to 90 percent of the minority vote to the Democratic candidate for president every presidential election year" (117). Would it be a logical inference that 90 percent of Democratic voters are members of minorities? Draw a Venn diagram to illustrate the fallacy here.

4. Judge whether the following analogies are sound or false, and explain why:

   a. In a letter to the editor of the *New York Times* objecting to the editors' criticism of the Walt Disney Company's decision not to distribute Michael Moore's documentary *Fahrenheit 9/11* in 2004, Disney CEO Michael Eisner wrote: "Your accusations of stifling free expression are misplaced. The First Amendment does not say that The New York Times must print every article presented to it or that the Walt Disney Company must distribute every movie." (Also evaluate this as a **tu quoque** argument, as defined in chapter 10.)

b. Columnist Thomas Sowell writes, "Ironically, those politicians who complain most loudly about the outsourcing of jobs often advocate the outsourcing of the job of making foreign policy and safeguarding American national security to the United Nations or to our allies in Europe."

c. A letter to the editor of the *New York Times* argued:

Since the Littleton, Colo., shooting, we've seen politicians, newscasters, and talk-show hosts all reciting the same nonstop mantra. "America is the most heavily armed society in the world; we have too many guns." It's just not true.

The most heavily armed country in the world is Switzerland.

Its per capita gun ownership greatly exceeds that of the United States and every other country. Switzerland has a small standing army and would therefore call upon the entire citizenry to defend the country.

Yet the Swiss do not experience the United States' level of gun-related crime and school violence. Gee, maybe it has to do with values, morals and culture, not the number of guns.

d. Letter to the editor in the *San Francisco Chronicle*:

So I smoke for 30 years, get cancer, and it's the tobacco company's fault. I use a gun, and it's the gun manufacturer's fault. By following this logic, I can get stoned drunk and run you over with my car, and it's the distillery's and the car manufacturer's fault . . . .

Are any individuals in our society responsible for anything, or is everything someone else's fault?

e. A California ballot proposition in 1998 (which was defeated) would have required labor unions that contributed money to politicians to poll their members and give them the option of receiving their share of dues funding any contribution back in cash if they didn't support it. Opponents argued that by the same principle, corporations contributing to politicians should be required to poll all of their stockholders and give dissenters the same option of getting back a share of their stock.

f. Historian Michael Bellesiles has published research purporting to support the interpretation of the Second Amendment right to bear arms as referring only to militias. Among Bellesiles's arguments (which incidentally have met with strong criticism regarding their empirical accuracy) was that a much smaller percentage of individuals actually owned guns in Colonial times than today. A law professor wrote about Bellesiles's argument in a letter to the editor of *Lingua Franca:* "After all, scholars like Jane Mansbridge and Michael Schudson point out that the percentage of eligible voters participating in town meetings during Colonial times was similarly small. . . . One hopes that Bellesiles would not argue that this low participation rate means that the framers of the Constitution did not believe in a right to vote." Evaluate this analogy, and do some research on criticisms of Bellesiles's research, which have been extensively covered in general-circulation journals and the *Chronicle of Higher Education*.

g. When the scandals over abuse by American forces of prisoners in Abu Ghraib prison in Iraq broke in 2004, the following exchange was aired on Rush Limbaugh's radio program:

CALLER: It was like a college fraternity prank that stacked up naked men.

LIMBAUGH: Exactly. Exactly my point! This is no different than what happens at the Skull and Bones initiation and we're going to ruin people's lives over it and we're going to hamper our military effort, and then we are going to really hammer them because they had a good time. You know, these people are being fired at every day. . . . You ever heard of need to blow some steam off?

IMPLICATIONS AND INFERENCES

Though the two terms are often confused, the speaker or writer *implies,* the listener or reader *infers.* Hidden assertions in enthymemes are one common form of implication in arguments, but there are other forms of implicit arguments: hints, suggestions, and forms with connotations of malicious intention like innuendo and insinuation. Fallacies and misunderstandings occur on both the sending and the receiving side here: the writer or speaker is responsible for avoiding false implications, and the reader or listener is responsible for not making **false inferences**. A student paper analyzing a column by investigative reporter Jack Anderson about accidents in nuclear facilities accurately points out, "Most of Anderson's examples are about mishaps in nuclear weapons testing, but he implies without support that these provide evidence that nuclear *power plants* are unsafe."

Writers also talk about "the implications in So-and-So's position," meaning possible empirical consequences of the position as it is formulated. We talked earlier about the necessity of **drawing the line** in any position you take, indicating its limits to prevent the possibility of its being pushed farther than you would be willing to defend. If you fail to draw that line, then your argument may be subject to reduction to absurdity or charged with leading to a **slippery slope**, rhetorical techniques of pushing an opponent's unqualified position to its extreme logical consequences, in order to show a weakness in it, as in the above example about executing criminals to deter them from repeating their crime.

On the inference side, students—and professional writers as well—frequently go off the track by misunderstanding what a source text means or reading something into it that the author did not imply. **Polemicists** frequently draw false inferences from an opposing source, sometimes unintentionally, sometimes maliciously. The same student who made the sound argument above about Jack Anderson's column, drew the conclusion, "Jack Anderson is opposed to nuclear power, so his arguments are biased." Anderson, however, was not making a blanket argument against nuclear power plants but only urging greater safety measures in them—though his arguments still might have been biased. As frequently happens when we are emotionally involved in a subject, this student's strong pro-nuclear feelings may have led him into a **reaction formation** causing him defensively to jump to an exaggerated conclusion.

SETTING THE AGENDA

In public disputes, opponents not only present opposing arguments on various points at issue but also often attempt to control what issues are and are not addressed to begin with. Each side, in other words, tries to "set the agenda" to **play up** discussion of issues on which its spokespeople think their position is strongest, and to **downplay** or avoid discussion altogether of issues more favorable to the other side. There is not necessarily anything devious about attempting to control the agenda—everyone does it in any argument, and those on one side may be quite justified in believing that their agenda is more important than the other side's and in trying to make theirs prevail for that reason. Ideally, when you do this, you should provide convincing support for why your agenda is more important.

Since about the 1992 presidential election, the Democratic and Republican parties, along with media and scholars that side with one or the other, have been jockeying to control the public agenda. Republicans have played up "the social agenda" on issues including abortion, family values (defined partly in opposition to expansion of homosexual rights), gun control, and affirmations of religion in public life. Democrats, more concerned about the growing gap in income and power between the rich and the middle class and poor, which they argue has resulted partly from the "supply-side" economic policies of President Reagan in the 1980s, have played up "the economic agenda." So when Bill Clinton gained the 1992 Democratic presidential nomination and polls showed that the public was more concerned about economic insecurity than about the social and moral issues being stressed by President George H. W. Bush and the Republicans, Clinton's campaign staff's slogan became "It's the economy, stupid!"

You have probably **inferred** by now that *Reading and Writing for Civic Literacy* has a liberal-to-leftist agenda. If this is true, it is because I decided over the course of writing this book that it would be hypocritical to give the impression that there is an even balance of strong and weak arguments on the liberal and conservative side of every issue addressed here. After being brought up and working for years in a conservative background, I have subsequently been led by several decades of teaching and studying public rhetoric, and of reading widely and deeply in both left and right sources, to what I think is a reasoned conclusion that the democratic (small *d*, not the Democratic Party) left (as opposed to the Communist left—see chapter 13), while far from faultless, more often than not has greater intellectual independence, stronger evidence and reasoning, and social justice on its side than the right, while conservative arguments tend to be less sound logically and more typically tainted by being the product of highly organized and funded **special interests** like corporate lobbies, public relations firms, mass media, foundations, and research institutes. (For documentation on this point, see David Brock, *The Republican Noise Machine.*) Indeed, liberals and Democrats frequently lament that they have failed to build up the kind of networks and funding that conservatives have since the 1970s, and they have recently been trying to counter with think tanks like the Center for American Progress and Air America Radio.

Many of the readings and analyses throughout the book are intended as supporting evidence for my judgment here, and it is up to you as a reader to judge the merits of that evidence. To illustrate, chapter 1 includes two articles on left and liberal student activism past and present (four in the first edition)—by Savio and Reed—but only one on conservative activism, sponsored by Young America's Foundation. My justification was that most progressive groups (except College Democrats) have been organized at students' own initiative. They are not connected to the Democratic Party and stand to the left of it politically. Their only sources of outside support (to my knowledge) are some labor unions and environmental nonprofits, whose own financial resources are extremely limited. The constituencies these students speak for, like the poor, sweatshop workers employed abroad by American corporations, blue-collar campus workers seeking a "living wage," victims of environmental hazards, or students themselves, cannot afford to hire lobbyists and public relations agents to speak for them. Nor is an author like Reed apparently guilty of the suspicious motives and methods in "A Semantic Calculator for Bias in Rhetoric." He is a professor at the University of Pennsylvania, a private Ivy League university, where most students either are wealthy or receive private financial aid to cover the expensive tuition. So he would not seem to have any selfish motives in arguing for free tuition at public universities. Conservative student organizations more often are Republican-aligned and do have outside supporters, mainly wealthy corporate foundations, which in many cases have actually organized the groups. A single patron, billionaire Richard Mellon Scaife, who is one of the most influential financial backers of Republican causes, has through his foundations given some $146 million to conservative campus organizations including the Young America's Foundation (source, *Washington Post,* cited by Eric Alterman in *What Liberal Media?* 250). According to the *Chronicle of Higher Education* (September 14, 2004, A9): "About a dozen national [conservative] organizations—among the largest are Young America's Foundation, the Intercollegiate Studies Institute, and the Leadership Institute—spend some $38 million annually pushing their agendas by bringing speakers to colleges and financing student publications." *Time* magazine's online edition, in an article titled "The Right's New Wing," August 22, 2004, reporting that YAF's annual budget is $13 million, notes:

Today the left can claim no youth organization as powerful as Young America's Foundation, ISI, or the Leadership Institute. One of the biggest young-liberal groups, the Sierra Student Coalition (an arm of the Sierra Club), has a budget of just $350,000 for 150 college chapters.... Last school year, the 38–year-old National Association for Women spent twice the amount it usually does on campus in order to publicize April's feminist march on Washington, but the total, $5,000, was just 4% of Young America's budget.

In a recent book, *The Wrecking Crew: How Conservatives Rule*, Thomas Frank traces the history, back to the 1970s, of how College Republican clubs were turned into a money-making and career-advancing enterprise by national leaders like Karl Rove and future anti-tax crusader Grover Norquist, notorious lobbyist Jack Abramoff, and Christian Coalition official and political consultant Ralph Reed. No comparable critique of College Democrats or other liberal student organizations has come to light at this writing.

At the same time, I have tried my best to abide by my own "ground rules for polemicists," listed below, by presenting conservative arguments in their strongest formulations, voiced by their leading spokespersons and in an accurate, fair-minded account—even when I, or readers, may not find them persuasive. Furthermore, openly admitting this "bias," I cordially invite conservative teachers, students, colleagues, and critics to challenge anything and everything in this book, and I will welcome suggestions for incorporating rebuttals and alternative views in future editions. For example, while my analysis of conservative student organizations **implies** that they may have **conflicts of interest** because of their Republican-aligned and corporate sponsors, their defenders will certainly refute this argument as an example of the **ad hominem** or **guilt by association** fallacies (see chapter 10). David Horowitz's article "The Intellectual Class War" in chapter 13 makes exactly this refutation; he also argues that liberal foundations outspend conservative ones and that corporations are as inclined to support liberal causes as conservative ones (although he does not quite explain why capitalistic corporations would fund their opponents, as a general rule, and he downplays the more overtly conservative financiers like Richard Mellon Scaife, whose foundations fund Horowitz's own enterprises). Horowitz further has argued elsewhere that outside-funded conservative student organizations, such as one he helped organize called Students for Academic Freedom, are simply counteracting the liberal bias of most university faculties, especially in the humanities and social sciences. For more on this topic, see the section "Research Institutes and Foundations ('Think Tanks')" at the end of chapter 13.

Deviousness in agenda setting comes about when those on one side, knowing their position is weak on some issue or set of issues, try to keep it off the agenda by diverting discussion to other, less important issues. This rhetorical move involves **stacking the deck**, **evading the issue**, **distraction**, or invoking a **red herring**. In reading and listening to arguments, then, we need to be alert, not just to what topics are being discussed, but also to significant ones that are *not* being discussed for purposes of evasion. This can be a difficult task without any clues; the best way to find clues is to read sources on the opposing side that may point out what the first side is suppressing. In your own writing, you can then cite those sources for a line of rebuttal to the first side. For example, in chapter 12, in "Bunker Hunt's Greatest Investment," the author, Holly Miller, suppresses any mention of Hunt's fraudulent business activities and spectacular rise and fall in the silver market; you would need to have heard accounts of these activities elsewhere to perceive how Miller is stacking the deck, and then you would need to cite some of these accounts in rebuttal to Miller.

Sometimes you read that a certain writer or speaker has a "hidden agenda." We often encounter hidden agendas in personal relations, as when a couple gets into an argument that is not really about what it seems to be about. Something deeper is obviously bugging one of them, but it may take hours or days of probing, guessing, or dead silence before the real problem comes out. In public argument, a hidden agenda is similar to **special pleading**, in that the person might appear to be presenting issues objectively but is in fact arguing for a partisan position. More specifically, it involves making what appears to be a single, manifest argument, while that argument really is a kind of code for, or opening wedge toward, a larger ideological agenda. For example, conservatives argue that when liberal scholars or journalists advocate more government spending on education, the environment, civil rights, welfare, public broadcasting, or the arts and humanities, or when they advocate more government regulation of business, their hidden agenda is to advance the dominance of their own intellectual class within governmental and nonprofit bureaucracies. [*Reader Advisory*: **Look for possible signs of this hidden agenda throughout** *Reading and Writing for Civic Literacy.*] When such liberals hear this criticism, they retort that conservatives too have a hidden agenda beyond the pros and cons of government spending and regulation, which is to eliminate liberal competition to corporate domination, by cutting public funds for fields that favor liberal constituencies like minorities, labor unions, and the poor, or in which liberals are widely employed and in which they can express their viewpoint, such as education and public broadcasting. (For more systematic accounts of liberal and conservative lines of argument on these issues, see chapters 13, 16, and 17.)

Critics of mass media talk about "the agenda-setting function of the media," referring to the power of the media to determine not only what news stories or dramatic topics are transmitted but also what broad issues come to public attention. The Anita Hill versus Clarence Thomas conflict put sexual harassment on the agenda of the media, which had previously paid little attention to it; likewise for the militia movement before and after the Oklahoma City bombing in 1995. And of course the terrorist attacks on September 11, 2001, put not only terrorism much higher on the national agenda than it had been before, but also American foreign policy in the Middle East and Central Asia. Libertarians and socialists criticize the media for excluding their ideological viewpoint from the agenda of American political discourse, by restricting the range of commentary on current events to Republicans and Democrats.

TONE AND STYLE

Tone is a key term in argumentative rhetoric, as well as in expository writing and literature. It refers to the author's implicit attitude, the tone of voice you "hear" in a piece of writing. Its importance in argumentation lies in the appropriateness and persuasive effectiveness of the tone the author chooses to use. So in your own writing, you always need to be aware of making your tone appropriate and persuasive for the subject at hand. You are apt to alienate readers, for example, if you use a facetious, snide tone in addressing a subject that they are likely to consider a serious one. Likewise, your analysis of sources' arguments should include judging the effectiveness of their tone.

Some of the adjectives applicable to the tone of the various readings throughout this book include *compassionate, fair-minded, evenhanded, calmly and carefully reasoned, (all characteristic of* **Rogerian argument**)*, objective, opinionated, inspirational, sentimental, skeptical, cynical, humorous, ironic, satirical, tongue-in-cheek, sarcastic, facetious, angry, belligerent, accusatory, derisive, strident, shrill, polemical,* and *invective.*

The **style** of a piece of writing, especially in the sense of its level of discourse, is related to its tone. Popular journalistic writing is likely to be more simplified, generalized, and superficial, as well as more polemical, than serious journalism or scholarly writing. Writers using the latter styles, however, often combine serious research and documentation with a polemical tone, as in the readings by Naomi Wolf and Christina Hoff Sommers in chapter 5, Jonathan Kozol and William J. Bennett in chapter 11, Steve Brouwer and David Horowitz in chapter 13, Joel Bleifuss in chapter 15, and several of the authors of readings in chapter 16.

POLEMICS

The American Heritage Dictionary of the English Language defines a polemic as "A controversy or argument, especially one that is a refutation of or an attack upon a specified opinion, doctrine, or the like." The plural form is *polemics,* though it is usually used as a singular noun like *politics* and *economics.* Polemics involves strongly opinionated, often partisan arguments on exactly the kinds of controversies that dominate this book; hence most of the readings here are polemical. Some scholars and teachers of rhetoric place a negative **connotation** on polemics as being opposed to objective or scientific writing. The viewpoint throughout this book, however, is that polemics is a vital part of the subject matter of education and public discourse, and that we simply need to judge polemical arguments on how well they adhere to the principles of responsible rhetoric. To be sure, because a certain level of professional knowledge is prerequisite to writing polemics responsibly, student writers should avoid taking polemical positions on subjects that they have not studied thoroughly; on the other hand, a large part of the intention of this book is to help you evaluate the quality of polemical writing in sources you study.

The negative connotation often attached to polemics derives partly from the false equation of polemics and **invective**, defined by *American Heritage* as a form of argument "characterized by abuse and insult" (see chapter 15 for more on invective.) Polemics sometimes does take the form of invective, but not necessarily. The following rules for fair play in polemics indicate principles that responsible polemicists honor but that writers of invective do not. You should not only attempt to follow these rules in whatever you write but also use them to evaluate the sources about which you are reading and writing.

GROUND RULES FOR POLEMICISTS

1. Do unto your own as you do unto others. Apply the same standards to yourself and your allies that you do to your opponents, in all of the following ways.
2. Identify your own ideological viewpoint and how it might bias your arguments. Having done so, show that you approach opponents' actions and writings with an open mind, not with malice aforethought. Concede the other side's valid arguments—preferably toward the beginning of your critique, not tacked on grudgingly at the end or in inconspicuous subordinate clauses. Acknowledge points on which you agree at least partially and might be able to cooperate.
3. Summarize the other side's case fully and fairly, in an account that they would accept, prior to refuting it. Present it through its most reputable spokespeople and strongest formulations (not through the most outlandish statements of its lunatic fringe), using direct quotes and footnoted sources, not your own, undocumented paraphrases. Allow the most generous interpretation of their statements rather than putting the worst light on them; help them make their arguments stronger when possible.
4. When quoting selected phrases from the other side's texts, accurately summarize the context and tone of the longer passages and full texts in which they appear.
5. When you are repeating a secondhand account of events, say so—do not leave the implication that you were there and are certain of its accuracy. Cite your source and take account of its author's possible biases, especially if the author is your ally.
6. In any account that you use to illustrate the opponents' misbehavior, grant that there may be another side to the story and take pains to find out what it is. If opponents claim they have been misrepresented, give them their say and the benefit of the doubt.
7. Be willing to acknowledge misconduct, errors, and fallacious arguments by your own allies, and try scrupulously to establish an accurate proportion and sense of reciprocity

between them and those you criticize in your opponents. Do not play up the other side's forms of power while denying or downplaying your own side's.

8. Respond forthrightly to opponents' criticisms of your own or your side's previous arguments, without evading key points. Admit it when they make criticisms you cannot refute.

9. Do not substitute ridicule or name-calling for reasoned argument and substantive evidence.

Vouchers, Choice: Opposing Views

Deroy Murdock

Knoxville News Sentinel, March 4, 2002

The U.S. Supreme Court is considering oral arguments it heard recently on the constitutionality of Cleveland's school voucher program. As the nine justices deliberate, they should repeat this simple mantra: "School vouchers are just Pell Grants for kids."

Opponents of Cleveland's program—which gives some 4,200 low-income students up to $2,250 to help attend whatever schools they want—argue that it violates the separation of church and state, since most of the initiative's beneficiaries and their parents have chosen to use their vouchers at Catholic schools.

As it happens, Catholic campuses were ready, willing and able to accept these voucher-funded students. Others, admittedly fewer, have taken their vouchers elsewhere. This is the definition of school *choice.*

If these vouchers unconstitutionally entangle church and state, then so do Pell Grants. This popular voucher program gives up to $3,300 in federal money to help students attend colleges and universities that they and their parents choose.

As Joshua Hall, director of educational policy at the free-market Buckeye Institute in Columbus, Ohio, explained to me, Pell Grants can purchase course credits at government-run institutions such as Ohio State University. They also may be used at private, secular schools—such as Case Western Reserve University—and even the Methodists' Baldwin-Wallace College and the Jesuits' John Carroll University. Oddly enough, People for the American Way is not tying its knickers in knots to keep Pell Grants away from college students at these private schools, all in or near Cleveland.

And just listen to what Hillary Clinton told the 1996 California Democratic Party convention: "We also need to increase the number and maximum award of Pell Grants."

Defenders of the dreadful educational status quo quickly reply that college kids are old enough to decide whether they want God as their study partner. So, then, why do anti-voucher liberals support the $4.8 billion Child Care and Development Block Grant program? It provides federal funds for day care.

The vouchers can be used at government-run child-care facilities, at private, nonsectarian establishments and even at day-care centers run by religious institutions. The pre-school at the Rev. Floyd Flake's Allen AME Church in Queens, N.Y., accepts these vouchers. Its federally funded 3- to 5-year-old students actually memorize verses of the Holy Bible!

Indeed, Section 658-P of the federal Child Care and Development Fund law explicitly states: "Nothing in this subchapter shall preclude the use of such certificates for sectarian child-care services if freely chosen by the parent." Where is the outrage?

In fact, rather than denounce this program, which allows taxpayer dollars to flow from Washington to parents into the pockets of priests and ministers—liberals want even more money for the child-care program.

"The president has made a string of decisions with disturbing consequences for millions of children," Rep. Dick Gephardt, D-Mo., said at a press conference last March 21. Gephardt complained that President Bush's FY 2002 budget "reduces resources for existing Child Care Development Block Grant (CCDBG) projects by $285 million."

On April 3, 2001, Sen. Christopher Dodd, D-Conn., asked reporters, "Which children are they going to leave behind, when 60,000 families—60,000 kids—will lose the needed support under the Child Care Development Block Grant?"

Just last Jan. 30, the left-wing Children's Defense Fund released a statement declaring that President Bush "should put considerable investment in the Child Care and Develop-

ment Block Grant this year so that 2 million more children in working families can have quality, affordable, safe child care and enter school ready to learn and succeed."

The anti-voucher crowd clicks its church-state angst on and off like a flashlight. Federal vouchers for church-based educational services? "We want more!" for pre-schoolers.

However, they're pure evil from kindergarten through high school. But give us more for college students. If day-care workers and university professors joined the National Educational Association in droves, the position of anti-voucher politicians beholden to the NEA finally might develop some consistency.

As it is, this hodgepodge reveals the moral Chapter 11 status of those who gleefully relegate young black kids in Cleveland and beyond to the back of the opportunity bus.

Chicken Little Calling Out, "Global Warming!"

Thomas Sowell

Knoxville News-Sentinel, June 8, 2002

The campaign to stampede the federal government into drastic action to counter global warming has never let honesty cramp its style. The most recent ploy has been the release of a study from the Environmental Protection Agency which concluded that human actions were responsible for rising temperatures and that government restrictions on those actions were necessary to prevent various disastrous scenarios from unfolding.

The problem is that all this hysteria was based on a computer model which had been shown to be incompatible with factual data.

Patrick Michaels, a professor of environmental sciences at the University of Virginia, had already exposed the inability of that

computer model to account for existing temperature changes before its release to the public was allowed to suggest that it was able to predict future temperature changes.

This is by no means the first time that a supposedly scientific report turned out to be a political report wrapping itself in the mantle of science. Last year, the National Academy of Sciences issued a report, garnished with the names of numerous eminent scientists, which was widely hailed in the media as proving the dangers of global warming.

The problem with that particular report was that the scientists whose names were put on display had not written the report nor even seen it before it was released.

One of those eminent scientists, Massachusetts Institute of Technology professor

Richard S. Lindzen, publicly repudiated the conclusions of the study on which his name had been displayed. As Lindzen, a meteorologist, pointed out, "The climate is always changing. Innumerable factors go into temperature changes and many of these factors, such as the changing amounts of heat put out by the sun during different eras, are beyond the control of human beings."

The same kind of ploy was used by a United Nations report on climate in 1996. After the scientists had reviewed the report, the following sentence was added without their knowledge: "The balance of evidence suggests a discernible human influence on global climate." But that is not what the scientists said.

What are all these ploys about? There are people in the environmental cult and in the media who are determined to have the United States and other countries sign the Kyoto treaty that would drastically restrict how our economy works and what kind of life the average American could lead.

Anything that allows them to impose their superior wisdom and virtue on the rest of us gets a sympathetic hearing. Moral melodrama also has great appeal to some. As Eric Hoffer said, "Intellectuals cannot operate at room temperature."

Every record hot day is trumpeted in the media as showing global warming. But record cold days are mentioned only as isolated curiosities, if they are mentioned at all.

Environmental cults have already stampeded us into recycling programs that studies have shown to be counterproductive—except for appeasing shrill zealots and allowing them to feel like they are saving the planet.

In the 1970s, the big scare was global cooling—a new ice age. And, of course, drastic government action was needed to head it off. There has to be moral melodrama.

The real question is not whether human beings have any effect on temperature. The question is: How much? And how much can we change the temperature—and at what price? And what if we do nothing? What will happen? And how dire will it be?

Professor Michaels estimates that most of the global warming over the past century has been due to the sun's getting hotter. If we do everything the Kyoto treaty calls for, it would not lower the average temperature in the world by half a degree over the next 50 years. But it could wreck some economies.

And what if we do nothing? Actually there are benefits to global warming, such as a longer growing season, but we are not likely to see a lot of those benefits because there is not likely to be a lot of warming. Moreover, it is mostly the very cold places that are getting warmer.

As Michaels points out, "Siberia has warmed from minus 40 to minus 28 in January." Is anyone complaining—other than professional complainers and professional doomsayers?

Closing the Wealth Gap

P. J. O'Rourke

Cato Speeches and Transcripts, 1999

P.J. O'Rourke is the Cato Institute's Mancken research fellow. He delivered these remarks at a June 1997 conference in Shanghai, China.

It's important to remember that this is not a technocratic conference. We are not here primarily to discuss the "hows" and "whys" and "ifs" of Chinese economic development.

On those subjects, more powerful people than we will have more important discussions than this. We are here to discuss ideas.

And the most important idea we are discussing is collectivism. I do not mean collectivism as it specifically applies to Chinese socialism. I mean collectivism as a general premise of almost all political systems in the world.

The foundation of collectivism is simple: There should be no important economic differences among people. No one should be too rich. No should be too poor. We should "close the wealth gap."

This is a very powerful idea.

This is a very common idea.

This is a very bad idea.

"Gaps"—differences—are innate to mankind. Do we want to close the "beauty gap" and make every woman look like Margaret Thatcher? Do we want to close the "talent gap" and field a World Cup football team starring, for example, the people on this panel?

In a world without gaps we'd all be the same. We'd all be the same sex. Who'd get pregnant? We'd all know the same things. What would we talk about? We'd all have the same work. Some job that would be. We'd all get the same vacation. Five point seven billion people playing a game of volleyball—2.85 billion to a side. The idea of a world where all people are alike—in wealth or in anything else—is a fantasy for the stupid.

But proposing to close the "wealth gap" is worse than silly. It entails a lie. The notion of economic equality is based on an ancient and ugly falsehood central to bad economic thinking. There's a fixed amount of wealth. Wealth is zero-sum. If I have too many cups of tea, you have to lick the tea pot. But wealth is based on productivity. Productivity is expandable. Otherwise there wouldn't be any economic thinking, good or bad, or any tea or tea pots either.

Since the beginning of the industrial revolution human productivity has proven to be fabulously expandable. The economist Angus Maddison has been studying economic growth since the 1950's. In 1995, under the auspices of the Organization for Economic Co-Operation and Development, he published a book, Monitoring the World Economy 1820–1992. The earth had fewer natural resources and no more farm land in 1992 than it had in 1820 and in that period the earth's population multiplied by five. But, in 1990 U.S. dollars, the value of everything produced in the world grew from $695 billion in 1820 to almost $28 trillion in 1992 and the amount of that production per person went from $651 to $5,145.

A collectivist can hear these figures and claim they are just averages, claim they don't show who actually got that money. The collectivist can recite the old saying: "The rich get richer and the poor get poorer." But there is no statistical evidence of this. The United Nations Population Division's "World Population Prospects: 1996 Revision" contains past and present statistics on infant mortality and life expectancy at birth. And these figures don't present the same averaging problems as per capita world product. No matter how rich the elite of a country is, its members aren't going to live to be 250 and distort the averages. And if the few rich babies in a country live and the mass of poor babies in a country die, that country will not have a "normal" infant mortality rate but a very bad one. Infant mortality and life expectancy are reasonable indicators of general well-being in a society.

Besides giving figures for individual countries, the U.N. consolidates averages into three groups: "More Developed Regions," "Less Developed Regions," and "Least Developed Regions." The last meaning countries that are damn poor—Laos, Madagascar, Chad. In the early 1950's the richer countries in the world had an average of 58 deaths per 1,000 live births. They now have an average of 11. Over the same period the poorest countries went from 194 deaths per 1,000 to 109. The "gap" was 136 dead babies 40 years ago and the "gap" is 98 dead babies now. This is still too many dead babies, of course, but the difference isn't increasing. The rich are getting richer but the poor aren't becoming worse off. They're becoming parents.

The same trend is seen in life expectancy. In the early 1950's people in rich countries had a life expectancy of 66.5 years. Now they live 74.2 years. In the poorest countries average lifespans have increased from 35.5 years to 49.7 years. The difference in life expectancy between the world's rich and poor has decreased by 6 1/2 years. The rich are getting richer. The poor are getting richer. And we're all getting older.

So, if wealth is not theft, if the thing that makes you rich doesn't make me poor, why don't collectivists concentrate on the question, "How do we make everyone wealthy?" Or better, "How have we been managing to do this so brilliantly since 1820?"

Why, instead, do collectivists concentrate on the question, "How do we redistribute wealth?"

And it is especially the collectivists in the non-socialist West who do this. Bill Clinton is more concerned with redistribution than anyone in the Chinese government.

Such collectivism is, I think, not only silly and untruthful but immoral.

The Ten Commandments in the Old Testament of the Bible are very clear about this.

Now the Bible might seem to be a strange place to do economic research—particularly for a person who is not very religious and here in a country that is not predominately Jewish or Christian.

However, I have been thinking—from a political economy point of view—about the Tenth Commandment.

The first nine commandments concern theological principles and social law: thou shalt not commit adultery, steal, kill, etc. All religions contain such rules. But then there's the tenth commandment: "Thou shalt not covet they neighbor's house, thou shalt not covet thy neighbor's wife, nor his manservant, nor his maidservant, nor his ox, nor his ass, nor anything that is thy neighbor's."

Here are God's basic rules about how the Tribes of Israel should live, a very brief list of sacred obligations and solemn moral precepts, and right at the end of it is, "Don't envy your friend's cow."

What is that doing in there? Why would God, with just ten things to tell Moses, choose, as one of them, jealousy about the things the man next door has? And yet think about how important to the well-being of a community this commandment is. If you want a donkey, if you want a meal, if you want an employee, don't complain about what other people have, go get your own. The tenth commandment sends a message to collectivists, to people who believe wealth is best obtained by redistribution. And the message is clear and concise: Go to hell.

Collectivism is silly, deceitful, a sin. It's also cowardly. We fear the power others have over us. And wealth is power. So we fear the rich.

But how rational is this fear? Take a midnight stroll through a rich neighborhood then take a midnight stroll through the U.S. Capital. Yes, you can get in a lot of trouble in Monte Carlo. You can lose at roulette. But you're more likely to get robbed in the slums of Washington.

Not that we should begrudge the crimes of those poor people. They're just practicing a little "free-lance collectivism." They're doing what the U.S. Government does, in their own small way. Because the real alternative to the power of the rich is not the power of the poor but plain, simple power. If we don't want the world's wealth to be controlled by people with money then the alternative is to have the world's wealth controlled by people with guns. Governments have plenty of guns.

The theory of this is quite good. The robber puts down his pistol, picks up the ballot box and steals from rich people instead of from you. But the reality is different. Witness the track record of collectivism in this century. The holocaust, Stalin's purges, the suffering caused by the Great Leap Forward here.

We should quit thinking about the "wealth gap" and start thinking about wealth. Wealth is good. Everybody knows that about his own wealth. If you got rich it would be a great thing. You'd improve your life. You'd improve your family's life. You'd purchase education, travel, knowledge about the world. You'd invest in wise and worthwhile things. You'd give money to noble causes. You'd help your friends and neighbors. Your life would be better if you got rich. The lives of the people around you would be better if you got rich. Your wealth is good. So why isn't everybody else's wealth good, too?

Wealth is good when many people have it. It's good when few people have it. This is because money is a tool, nothing more. You can't eat money or drink money or wear money. And wealth—an accumulation of money—is a lot of tools.

Tools can be used to do harm. You can hit somebody over the head with a shovel. But tools are still good. When a carpenter has a lot of tools we don't say to him, "You have too many tools. You should give some of your saws and planes and nails and chisels to the man who's cooking omelettes." We don't try to close the "tool gap."

Wealth brings great benefits to the world. Rich people are heroes. They don't usually mean to be but that's their moral problem not ours. Most of the world now admits that free enterprise works. Economic liberty makes people rich. But in our residual collectivism and our infatuation with equality we keep trying to get rid of rich people.

There's a joke President Reagan told about the way collectivist politicians treat rich people. A traveling salesman stays overnight with a farm family. When the family gathers to eat there's a pig seated at the table. And the pig has three medals hanging around his neck and a peg leg. The salesman says, "Um, I see you have a pig having dinner with you."

"Yes," says the former. "That's because he's a very special pig. You see those medals around his neck? Well, the first medal is from when our youngest son fell in the pond, and he was drowning, and that pig swam out and saved his life. The second medal, that's from when the barn caught fire and our little daughter was trapped in there and the pig ran inside, carried her out and saved her life. And the third medal, that's from when our oldest boy was cornered in the stock yard by a mean bull, and that pig ran under the fence and bit the bull on the tail and saved the boy's life."

"Yes," says the salesman, "I can see why you let that pig sit right at the table and have dinner with you. And I can see why you awarded him the medals. But how did he get the peg leg?"

"Well," says, the farmer, "a pig like that—you don't eat him all at once."

Topics for Discussion and Writing

1. Review Naomi Wolf's "The Beauty Myth" and Christina Hoff Sommers's "The Backlash Myth" as well as the student discussion of them in chapter 5. How **Rogerian** are both Wolf and Sommers in representing the opposing position fairly and sympathetically, and how closely do they follow the above "Ground Rules for Polemicists"? How effectively do both combine scholarly style with a polemical tone?

2. The three readings here are all conservative rebuttals to liberal or leftist arguments, including several made in other readings throughout the book. They make use of statistical arguments and analogies, and they are all more or less polemical, although they vary from one another in tone. Evaluate them by the criteria suggested in this chapter. Also refer to the "Guide to Political Terms and Positions" and "Predictable Patterns of Political Rhetoric" in chapter 13 to help identify the conservative lines of argument in each. The pieces by Sowell and Murdock are short op-ed columns; O'Rourke's is a transcript of a speech, somewhat longer (but as typical of speeches, containing little documentation). Compare and evaluate the authors' use of facts and figures within the space and style limitations of these forms.

3. P. J. O'Rourke is a conservative humorist, and the **tone** of this talk is semifacetious. The talk was delivered, however, at a conference in China sponsored by

the Cato Institute, the most prominent libertarian think tank, and he is addressing serious economic issues. Can you distinguish here between purely humorous points and serious arguments—for example, his citation of the Ten Commandments? Of the several **analogies** throughout the talk, which do you think are to be taken seriously, and how valid are they by the criteria in this chapter? Most prominently, O'Rourke equates "the wealth gap" with "the beauty gap" or "the talent gap." How significant a difference is it that beauty and talent are inborn qualities beyond the influence of public policies, while differences in wealth can be controlled by government legislation concerning tax rates, minimum wage laws, regulation of corporate practices, and so on? To what extent do his arguments against reducing economic inequality substantively refute the arguments by Jonathan Kozol in chapter 11, Steve Brouwer in chapter 13, and Holly Sklar and Jonathan Chait in chapter 16? Does O'Rourke **draw the line** about what extreme of economic inequality would become intolerable? Can you push the implications in his arguments to extremes to reduce it to absurdity?

4. O'Rourke concludes his talk with a joke. In such cases, jokes serve as a form of **analogy** for the arguments being made. Evaluate this joke as an analogy.

5. Find some liberal sources on climate change that defend the positions Sowell refutes in "Chicken Little Calling Out, 'Global Warming.'" Also do research on what **special interests** fund research on opposing sides of this issue, and what corporate profits would be at risk through curtailment of industrial emissions allegedly harmful to the ozone layer and contributing to global warming. (Sowell is employed by the Hoover Institution, a prominent conservative think tank funded by corporate foundations—a possible cause for **special pleading**, as defined in chapter 15.) Sowell calls liberal environmentalists "shrill zealots." How legitimate would it be to use a **tu quoque** line of argument against him to suggest that his tone and that of some other climate change deniers is equally that of shrill zealotry? Would his columns like this one and "Look Behind Statistics" in chapter 4 be more or less persuasive if he used less invective, name-calling, and sarcastic put-downs of his opponents?

6. In "Vouchers, Choice: Opposing Views," Deroy Murdock makes an **analogy** equating school vouchers with Pell Grants and federal child-care support, in order to point out a **double standard** on the part of liberals who support the latter programs but oppose vouchers. How well does he support this analogy? Can you think of any significant differences between the programs he equates that would make the analogy false? Murdock and Sowell are both conservative blacks who criticize policies like affirmative action, welfare, and opposition to vouchers that are favored by liberal blacks. Compare Murdock's versus Sowell's reasoning and tone. Also compare Murdock's line of argument on vouchers with the Mallard Fillmore cartoon in chapter 2. For a tacit liberal argument against vouchers, see Jonathan Kozol's "Other People's Children" and the topics for discussion following it in chapter 11.

CHAPTER 10

Logical and Rhetorical Fallacies

Sometimes after students have started to study fallacies, they are inclined to approach arguments searching just for fallacies in them, only looking for points to pick apart, rather than also looking for good, fallacy-free arguments or those that effectively point out fallacies in someone else's argument. The latter approach should be part of your goal in studying this list of logical and rhetorical fallacies. ("Logical fallacies" is the usual term, referring mainly to unintentional flaws in reasoning. "Rhetorical fallacies" here refers to more devious motives in, and modes of, argument.)

Students sometimes also fret excessively over what is the proper label for a fallacious argument, rather than simply explaining in their own words how the argument is fallacious; pinning the label to the fallacy may be worthwhile, but it is secondary to showing your understanding of the argument's substantive flaws. Another source for fretting is which of several similar terms is the "right" one; several of these terms, however, are synonymous or closely enough related so that they may be interchangeable. Here are some clusters of related fallacies, gathered from the alphabetical glossary below.

- Presenting only one side of a story, or slanting an account to one side: propaganda, special pleading, stacking the deck, half-truth, double standard, selective vision, cleans and dirties, *tu quoque* (in the sense of pointing out legitimately the fallacy in opponents who are guilty of the same fault of which they accuse others).
- Oversimplification: overgeneralization, sweeping generalization, either-or, false dilemma, false dichotomy, reductive fallacy, not accounting for all factors or variables.
- Hasty conclusion or non sequitur: inadequate evidence, unrepresentative sample, argument from the exception.
- Inconsistency: compartmentalized thinking, self-contradiction, doublethink, shifting ground, equivocation, "I Won't, but I Will," "Heads I Win, Tails You Lose."
- Distraction: begging the question, evading the issue, shifting ground, red herring, irrelevance.
- Personal attacks: ad hominem, name-calling, straw man, poisoning the well, smearing, character assassination, tu quoque, guilt by association, derision, distortion.
- Appeals to widespread opinion or common practice: *ad populum,* bandwagon, plain folks, appeal to the past or resistance to change, common practice, two wrongs make a right.

- Emotional appeal: appeals to pity or fear, demagogy, scare tactics, sentimentality, religiosity, flag-waving, jingoism.

GLOSSARY OF LOGICAL AND RHETORICAL FALLACIES

ad hominem. Latin for argument "against the man." The rhetorical fallacy of attacking the character or motives of an opponent as a means of discrediting or evading the substance of his or her arguments. Variants include *name-calling, poisoning the well, smearing,* and *character assassination*. What is or is not *ad hominem* can be a difficult judgment call. Certainly the character and motives of writers are relevant factors in evaluating their arguments (the term **ethos** in classical rhetoric refers to determining the credibility of speakers' character and to the positive image they try to establish with their audience), although evaluation of these factors should never be a substitute for judging arguments on their own grounds. In calculating sources' possible biases, we need to become aware of **special interests** that they or those for whom they speak may represent, and whether they are political **partisans**, paid propagandists, public relations or advertising agents—in which case their arguments are likely to be **special pleading** and subject to more skeptical scrutiny than those made by independent journalists or scholars. And we need to inform ourselves of their record of credibility in the past. Presenting negative evidence against a source on these counts is a perfectly valid line of argument, *but it must be adequately documented* to avoid *ad hominem,* and it still needs to be supplemented with substantive evaluation of the arguments. A **predictable pattern of political rhetoric** is that those whose character or motives have been legitimately discredited will charge that they are the victims of character assassination.

ad ignoratiam. Latin, "argument to what is not known." The logical fallacy of arguing that because we do not know that something is not true, or that because something cannot be disproved, therefore it *is* true—arguing, for example, that because it cannot be proved that God does not exist, therefore God *does* exist.

ad populum. Latin, appeal "to the people." The logical fallacy of arguing that something is true because many or most people believe it is, or that a policy is valid because many or most agree with it. The fallacy lies in the fact that mass opinion is not always well informed, accurate, or morally just (see Michael Kinsley's example of misinformed public opinion about U.S. foreign aid, in "The Intellectual Free Lunch" in chapter 2). Appeal to popular opinion is one of the most frequent lines of public argument, and here again it can be a tough judgment call to determine when it is valid and when fallacious. Democracy itself is based on majority rule, as expressed in elections and opinion polls, so all sides seek to gain majority approval; we all want to believe, and want our audience to believe, that our position has wide support. However, we are all inclined to a **double standard** or **selective vision** in invoking popular opinion when it supports our side but seeing the *ad populum* fallacy when it supports the opposition. (For example, President Bush's administration played up majority support for waging war in Iraq, but when that support dwindled to a minority, they then **shifted ground** to charge that the public had lost the moral fortitude to "stay the course.")

When is it valid to cite majority opinion in the general population, or within any particular group, to support your position? When you can present evidence that the majority is well informed and/or has benefited from the policy you advocate.

appeal to authority or **transfer of authority**. This logical fallacy takes three common forms. One is citing as a source on a particular subject someone who is an authority on *some* subject but not the one at issue, or even someone who is only, in Daniel Boorstin's phrase, "well-known for being well-known." (The celebrity endorsement ad is the most frequent occasion for this form.) Another form is citing the opinion of a source who is an authority on the issue as sufficient in itself, without presenting the evidence on which that opinion is based. The opinions of those who are authorities on a subject are likely to be supported with better evidence than those of nonexperts, but their evidence still needs to be documented. The third form is when a genuine authority is cited, but the authority's opinion diverges from the opinions of other authorities or is otherwise suspect. This might happen when the cited authority has a conflict of interest or holds an opinion about an issue that differs from the consensus of other authorities in a field. To avoid this third form of the fallacy, you should acknowledge the difference and present a case for why this authority's word should prevail over others' if you think it should.

appeal to fear or **scare tactics**. Along with its flip side, **appeal to pity**, the most common form of **emotional appeal**—most prominently in calls for war or, more recently, protection against terrorism. This is another case where a judgment call is always necessary to determine whether such an appeal has legitimate grounds, when it is a perfectly valid line of argument, or whether it is deliberately fabricated or exaggerated to frighten people into compliance with those in power, or to attract a profitable media audience.

appeal to the past or **tradition**, or **resistance to change**. The logical fallacy of arguing for a policy only because it has been followed in the past or is a tradition in one's culture, regardless of whether it might be outdated.

appeal to pity. A common variety of **sentimentality**. The judgment call here is whether the people being defended truly deserve pity or whether the audience's heartstrings are being tugged on fraudulently. For example, in law courts, attorneys will often attempt to elicit the jury's pity for their clients to help their clients' case. But pitying someone is not a good justification for thinking that he or she did or did not commit a crime or that his or her legal claims have any warrant. Evidence is needed for that.

argument from the converse. The logical fallacy of starting with a statement whose truth has been established, in the form of "All (or most) Xs are Y," then jumping to the converse conclusion, "All (or most) Ys are X," which is a form of **non sequitur**. This fallacy can usually be explained in terms of logical classes and subclasses or sets and subsets, as in mathematics, and illustrated through circle diagrams (see chapter 11).

argument from the exception. The logical fallacy of supporting an argument with a case that is an exception to the rule, contrary to the larger body of evidence supporting the opposing side; synonymous with an **unrepresentative sample**.

bandwagon. A variety of **ad populum**, attempting to lure you to get on the bandwagon, to agree with a policy or take an action because "everybody's doing it." Extremely common in advertising.

begging the question. A fallacy in deductive logic in which a conclusion depends on prior acceptance of a premise whose truth has not been established or is disputable. Often used synonymously with **circular argument**.

changing the subject or **shifting ground**. This rhetorical fallacy occurs when people have no effective response to a refutation of an argument they have made, so they bring up a different line of argument on the same subject while hoping no one notices that they are **evading the issue**.

circular argument. A logical fallacy in which a reason given in support of a conclusion presupposes the truth of the conclusion, or in which the conclusion depends on prior acceptance of a premise that is believed only because the conclusion is already believed. "I believe the president is telling the truth." "How do you know that?" "Because he's a God-fearing man." "How do you know that?" "Because he says so, and he tells the truth." Another form is the attempt to support a premise with words that simply repeat the premise in slightly different language; for example, "Capitalism is desirable because it promotes free enterprise." Free enterprise is just another name for capitalism, so the argument does not give a reason why capitalism, or free enterprise, is desirable.

cleans and dirties. The rhetorical fallacy of using **connotatively** loaded language applying all positive words to your side and all negative ones to your opponents', purely for **emotional appeal**, without sufficient evidence that the words are accurate. Using loaded language like this is not fallacious, however, if it *is* supported by evidence.

common practice. The rhetorical fallacy of justifying a shady ethical practice because "everybody does it." Also see **tu quoque** and **two wrongs make a right**.

compartmentalization or **compartmentalized thinking**. Logical self-contradiction or inconsistency. In its extreme form it results in Orwellian **doublethink**. The concept can also apply to saying one thing but doing another.

demagogy or **demagoguery**. The use of **emotional appeal** by unscrupulous politicians or other public figures to manipulate the ethnocentric beliefs or prejudices of a mass audience for their own benefit.

derision. A form of **ad hominem** in which the opponent's ideas or character are just ridiculed or sneered at without any substantive refutation.

distortion. The rhetorical fallacy of misrepresenting an opponent's ideas, whether unintentionally or intentionally. Related to **straw man**.

double standard. The rhetorical fallacy, or mode of deception, in which a variety of critical standards are applied to opponents but are not applied consistently, not applied as strongly, or not applied at all to one's own views or to the views of people on one's side. See "A Semantic Calculator for Bias in Rhetoric" in chapter 5, as well as **selective vision** and **stacking the deck**.

doublethink. Coined by George Orwell in his novel *1984* to describe the logical or rhetorical fallacy of being induced by propaganda to believe self-contradictory ideas like "war is peace," "slavery is freedom," "ignorance is strength." Also applicable to abrupt reversals or deceptions in political policies without recognition of an inconsistency. In *1984*, a government reduction in the chocolate ration is announced as an increase, but the people swallow it unquestioningly.

either-or. Also known as *false dilemma* or *false dichotomy*. The fallacy of setting two positions in opposition to each other when they might be mutually compatible, or of suggesting that there are only two feasible alternatives when there are in fact others.

emotional appeal. The rhetorical fallacy of invalid appeal to the audience's emotions at the expense of reason. Appeals to emotion are fallacious generally when they appeal to feeling about something *as evidence* for it. For example, fearing that global warming is now happening cannot serve as evidence that it is happening. However, if there is firm evidence that global warming really is happening, our fear of the consequences can be used as a good reason supporting a call to action. For distinctions between valid and fallacious appeals to emotion, see chapter 12.

equal and opposite extreme. The logical fallacy of rejecting an irrational, extreme position, but then failing to **draw the line** in lurching to an opposite extreme that is equally irrational, as in critics of the prejudices in white or male-dominated culture who end up proclaiming the innate superiority of blacks or women, in "reverse racism" or "reverse sexism."

equivocation. The rhetorical fallacy of changing the sense in which a word is used, in the middle of an argument, or of using a definition of it that is not applicable in the context. A mode of **shifting ground**. For example, when people defending capital punishment because they believe it deters potential murderers are confronted with **empirical**

evidence to the contrary, they sometimes respond, "Well, it deters the executed criminal from killing again."

evading the issue. There are several fallacious means of trying to squirm out of acknowledging that one's opponent has made a point that one cannot logically refute, including **begging the question, changing the subject**, introducing a **red herring, shifting ground,** *ad hominem*, **name-calling**, and *tu quoque* attacks on the opponent.

false analogy or **false equation**. The logical fallacy of arguing that two situations are similar to one another or exactly the same, so that what we accept as true about one should also be accepted about the other, when there are significant differences between them. For distinctions between valid and false analogies, see chapter 9.

faulty causation. See the following causal fallacies in chapter 11: *post hoc, ergo propter hoc*; **reductive fallacy; slippery slope; blaming the victim; too much or too little?; giving your side credit for positive results, blaming the other side for negative results; confusion of cause and effect.**

flag-waving, jingoism. The rhetorical fallacy of emotional appeal deceptively manipulating patriotism and fear of a foreign enemy.

guilt by association. The rhetorical fallacy of smearing opponents by falsely associating them with a disreputable person or organization. It is not fallacious to criticize opponents for their actual, admitted association with disreputable forces.

half-truth. The rhetorical fallacy of **stacking the deck** by **playing up** only those portions of a truth that favor one's own side, while suppressing mention of other portions that discredit it, as in ads that boast of a certain feature of a brand without mentioning that every other brand of the product has the same feature.

hasty conclusion. The logical fallacy of jumping to a conclusion based on inadequate evidence, an **unrepresentative sample**, or an **overgeneralization**.

heads I win, tails you lose, or **damned if you do, damned if you don't**, or **you can't win**. A variety of **stacking the deck** or **shifting ground** in which opponents are criticized for one reason if they take a particular position but criticized for another reason if they take the opposite position.

inadequate evidence or **unrepresentative sampling**. In inductive reasoning, the fallacy of drawing a conclusion or making a generalization based on a sampling of evidence, or set of examples, too small to generalize from or unrepresentative of a larger sampling.

inconsistency or **self-contradiction**. The logical fallacy of an argument some of whose parts are inconsistent with, or contradict, others in the same argument or an earlier one by the same author.

inductive leap. A form of **non sequitur** or **hasty conclusion** in which one jumps to an extreme conclusion based on skimpy **empirical evidence**.

irrelevance. An argument that is not relevant to the point at issue. Whether intentional or unintentional, it is a form of **evading the issue**.

I won't ... but I will. A common form of **compartmentalized thinking**. This was a favorite during the Cold War, when politicians routinely used phrases like, "I won't say my opponent is a Communist, but ...."

let's you and him fight. The rhetorical fallacy of people provoking conflicts between others, on a personal, social, or international level, while avoiding risk themselves. Especially common in people advocating war ("We've got to fight them or else ..."), when they themselves, and often their family members, have no intention of risking their own lives in battle or even joining the armed forces. A form of **What do you mean, "we"**?

lip service. The rhetorical fallacy of making a public show of belief in a popular cause, such as religion or patriotism, while not practicing what one preaches.

name-calling. The most common variety of ***ad hominem***, substituting nasty words describing opponents for reasoned refutation of their arguments. As with other forms of **emotional appeal**, name-calling can be a valid rhetorical method *if you support the name you call someone by sufficient evidence,* or if such evidence has been historically established beyond much dispute—such as, "Hitler, Stalin, and Saddam Hussein were insane, murderous tyrants."

non sequitur. Latin, "it does not follow," that is, one statement does not follow logically from the previous one. The many kinds of non sequitur include **syllogisms** or **enthymemes** in which the conclusion does not follow from a premise, **evading the issue**, **circular argument**, **hasty conclusion, inductive leap, faulty causation,** and **argument from the converse**. Also a general term for an abrupt change of subject in which the second subject is asserted to be related to the first but isn't.

overgeneralization or **sweeping generalization**. The logical fallacy of making a generalization that is so vague or vast as to be practically useless, or that jumps to a conclusion about a large class of people or things based on an **inadequate** or **unrepresentative sampling**.

oversimplification. The broadest category of the many logical and rhetorical fallacies that reduce a complex set of realities to an overly simplistic, black-and-white explanation.

plain folks. The rhetorical fallacy of a politician or other public figure who in wealth, power, or education is an **elitist** but who pretends to be a **populist**, speaking like, and claiming to represent the interests of, the masses of ordinary citizens, often for the purpose of **demagogic** manipulation.

propaganda. A deliberately one-sided view of any issue, usually produced by governments, political parties and candidates, **special interests**, and professional agents in their service. Propaganda employs the whole range of rhetorical methods of **stacking the deck**. See chapter 15.

quotation out of context. The rhetorical fallacy of quoting a few words or sentences from a source text in a manner that makes them appear to have a different meaning than they have within the context of the complete text. This is a common tactic in writers of **invective** who deliberately distort their opponents' ideas in this manner. It is also used by advertisers of cultural productions to put the most favorable spin on journalistic reviews, as when an ad quotes a review of a movie calling it "spectacular," when the full text reads, "This film is the most spectacular disaster in years."

red herring. The rhetorical fallacy of **changing the subject** by jumping from addressing an issue to dragging in another one, usually strong in **emotional appeal**, to distract attention from the first.

religiosity. The rhetorical fallacy of an insincere, exaggerated, or sentimentalized posture of religious belief, without evidence of any theological or moral substance, as when politicians profess their deep religious faith in order to court votes, or adamantly defend "under God" in the Pledge of Allegiance, but don't practice their faith. Popular films and TV series about guardian angels and charming nuns, without any real religious substance, are another example, such as *The Sound of Music,* with its pseudoreligious organ swells and lines such as "like a lark that is learning to pray." (Can you visualize a lark learning to pray?)

selective vision. The rhetorical fallacy of seeing, or discussing, only your opponents' bad policies and behavior, while turning a blind eye to your own side's similar faults. Synonymous with **double standard**.

sentimentality. The rhetorical fallacy of using excessive or manipulative evocation of positive **emotional appeal**. Words commonly applied to sentimental appeals are "tear-jerking," "corny," and "sappy." Staples of sentimentality are **religiosity**, flag-waving, images of Mom and apple pie, cute little children and puppy dogs, soap-opera-like **appeal to pity** (as in celebrity journalism's accounts of the tragedies of the rich and famous), and so on. Also used in public relations to fabricate a cosmeticized, saintly image of some public figure or organization (see chapter 12). Like other forms of emotional appeal, sentimentality is often employed with **selective vision**, by which one tries to gain sympathy for a favored individual or group while ignoring the fact that an opponent or some other social group might deserve as much or more sympathy. In politics and war, sentimentality is evident in selective emotional appeals for one's own side's causes or forces while the opponents' are demonized.

shifting ground. The logical or rhetorical fallacy of changing your position or line of argument—especially in a contradictory manner—without justification, resulting in **compartmentalized thinking** or **doublethink**. In the 2000 presidential election, when the Florida Supreme Court was overruled by the U.S. Supreme Court to give George W. Bush the victory, Democrats, who usually support the primacy of federal government over state governments, shifted ground in denouncing the U.S. Supreme Court action, while Republicans did the opposite shift.

special pleading. The rhetorical fallacy of claiming to be an objective, neutral analyst in order to conceal the reality that one is an advocate for **special interests** or one side of an issue, or of arguing that some extenuating circumstances apply—"I'm special" "This case is special"—when in fact the circumstances are not very special (and if we granted an exception in this case, we would have to grant far too many exceptions). In other words, an argument that tries to establish an exception where there is no real warrant for it, as when students ask to be allowed to take a class when they haven't fulfilled the prerequisites, without giving sufficient reasons why the prerequisites should not be applied in their case.

stacking the deck. General term for the whole repertory of rhetorical fallacies—including **double standard** and **selective vision**—used to present a **propagandistically** one-sided view, through **playing up**, or **"cherry picking,"** all arguments and evidence in favor of one side while **downplaying** or suppressing altogether all arguments and evidence against that side and in favor of the other side. See "A Semantic Calculator for Bias in Rhetoric" in chapter 4.

straw man. The rhetorical fallacy of depicting an image of opponents that bears no real resemblance to them or that distorts or oversimplifies their ideas and then claiming that you have disposed of their ideas by refuting the false version of them.

tokenism. A form of **lip service** in which one complies minimally or halfheartedly with a required policy, such as equal-opportunity hiring, with "a token woman" or "a token minority."

tu quoque. Latin, "you too." The rhetorical fallacy of defending your side against an accusation by saying the other side is guilty of the same abuse. A form of **two wrongs make a right**. *Tu quoque* can be a valid, effective line of argument if it is not used to excuse your side from fault but to point out the other side's hypocrisy in not practicing what they preach to others.

two wrongs make a right. The logical fallacy of rationalizing one's bad behavior on the grounds of **common practice**, *tu quoque*, or "getting even." That is, it's okay for me/us to do this, because you/our opponents have done the same thing. This is frequently practiced with a **double standard**, by which one side—in war, for example—will justify its atrocities or desire to get even, while denying any such justification to the other side.

what do you mean, "we"? The rhetorical fallacy of a falsely all-encompassing "we," as when a teacher says, "We'll have an exam next week," or a wealthy government official says, "We all need to make sacrifices in this time of war," or a corporate polluter says, "We're all concerned about the environment."

wishful thinking. The form of **rationalization** in which people believe what they want to believe, or what benefits them or their allies, rather than drawing reasoned conclusions. See chapter 8.

Topics for Discussion and Writing

What possible fallacies are found in the following arguments, or which ones are being alleged by the writers in the people they criticize? In the latter cases, how persuasive are their allegations?

1. A letter in the *San Antonio Express-News* in 2004:

   Your editorial "Scalia makes a bad call in Cheney energy case" chastised Supreme Court Justice Antonin Scalia for refusing to recuse himself from a case involving the vice president [Richard Cheney].

   However, I noted a March 19 article in the Los Angeles Times reported that 13 congressmen asked Supreme Court Justice Ruth Bader Ginsberg to withdraw from abortion cases "because of her affiliation with the National Organization of Women Legal Defense and Education Fund." Since you were quick to criticize Scalia for going on a duck hunt with the vice president, I wonder how you feel about Ginsburg's activities on behalf of the abortion industry.

2. "I don't believe these statistics showing that economic opportunity for most Americans has declined since the 1970s. My parents worked their way out of poverty into the middle class, so anybody can."

3. The book *The Myth of Separation*, by David Barton, a spokesperson for the Christian Coalition, argues that the "founding fathers" intended the First Amendment only to protect the practice of religion from government, not also to protect individuals from government imposition of religion. (The main object of his criticism is the 1962 Supreme Court decision declaring officially sponsored and organized prayer in public schools unconstitutional.) Barton quotes Thomas Jefferson's 1802 letter to the Danville Baptist Association, the best-known statement of the notion of a wall of separation between church and state, as saying, "'I contemplate with sovereign reverence that act of the whole American people which declared that their legislature should "make no law respecting an establishment of religion, or prohibiting the free exercise thereof," thus building a wall of separation between church and state'" (41). However, Barton leaves out the first part of the same sentence: "Believing with you that religion is a matter which lies solely between man and his God, that he owes account to none other for his faith or his worship, that the legislative powers of government reach actions only, and not opinions" (*Thomas Jefferson: Writings* 510).

4. Barton also writes in *The Myth of Separation*:

   As a note of interest, while the phrase "separation of church and state" is not found in the United States Constitution, it is found in another prominent document—the Constitution of the Soviet Union:

   Article 124: In order to ensure citizens freedom of conscience, the church in the U.S.S.R. is separated from the State, and the school from the church.

   It seems that, because of the current Court's rulings, we have more similarities with the Soviet Union than we might have thought. (45)

5. In the 2004 presidential election, Democrats charged that Vice President Richard Cheney had **conflicts of interest** in large Defense Department contracts for the war in Iraq with Halliburton Industries, of which Cheney had previously been CEO and from which he was still receiving deferred payments. Republicans replied that these charges were just ad hominem and character assassination. What arguments and evidence might be produced to support the opposing sides?

6. A columnist in a campus newspaper sides with liberals, who, the writer says, consider national health care a right, against conservatives, who consider it a privilege, then comments, "Let's set aside the ironies of how privileged those that subscribe to the latter notion of health care are."

7. *New York Times* columnist Maureen Dowd in July 2004 quoted President George W. Bush saying in defense of attacking Iraq, "So I had a choice to make: either take the word of a madman or defend America." He also said of the terrorists, "We will confront them overseas so we do not have to confront them here at home." Dowd commented, "That's nonsense. Just because terrorists are attacking Americans abroad doesn't mean terrorists are poised to also attack us at home. . . . It's just like the president's other false dichotomies: You're either with us, or you're with the terrorists. If we don't stop gays from marrying, it will destroy the institution of marriage."

8. "I've seen a lot more lawn signs and bumper stickers for Candidate X than for Candidate Y, so I guess I'll vote for X."

9. "People in nearly every other democratic country except the United States have enacted legislation for national health insurance. So maybe we should consider their models as a possible alternative to ours."

10. In his syndicated column (June 26, 2004), Thomas Sowell, who is black, wrote (with no further support): "People sometimes ask if I have tried to convince black leaders to take a different view on racial issues. Of course not. I wouldn't spend my time trying to persuade the mafia to give up crime. Why should I spend time trying to convince race hustlers to give up victimhood? It's their bread and butter."

11. Al Franken's book *Lies and the Lying Liars Who Tell Them* contains a chapter documenting the factual errors and criticizing the **ad hominem** name-calling in Ann Coulter's *Slander: Liberal Lies about the American Right*. The chapter is titled "Ann Coulter: Nutcase," and among Franken's comments on Coulter's misquotations of sources is, "Coulter pulls this wild distortion, like so very, very many, directly out of her ass" (14).

12. "No conclusive evidence has been found that Saddam Hussein had weapons of mass destruction. But there's no conclusive evidence that he *didn't,* so I think he did."

13. A radio talk show host defended tax cuts for the rich on the grounds that they are paying an increasingly larger share of taxes. In response to a caller who pointed out that this is because they have gained an increasingly larger share of income, he said, "And they *deserve* to have higher income because they work hard for it."

14. In their book *The Hammer: Tom DeLay—God, Money, and the Rise of the Republican Congress,* Lou Dubose and Jan Reid describe House of Representatives majority leader Tom DeLay as a man with a "petty and vindictive mean streak" whose coming to Christ they characterize as being "born again into Republican electoral politics." They add, "This is not to suggest that his motives were anything less than spiritual, but the result was political."

15. Bill O'Reilly, commenting on Fox News about critics of the Iraq war in 2003: "This is just fair warning to Barbra Streisand and others who see the world the way you do. We don't want to demonize you, but those of you who hurt the country at a time like this, let's just say you will be spotlighted."

16. In a critical review of Michael Moore's film *Fahrenheit 9/11* posted on Salon .com, June 21, 2004, Christopher Hitchens wrote: "The same 'let's have it

both ways' opportunism infects his treatment of another very serious subject, namely domestic counterterrorist policy. From being accused of overlooking too many warnings—not exactly an original point—the administration is now lavishly taunted for issuing too many."

17. In "A World Without Public Schools" in *The Weekly Standard* of June 4, 2007, David Gelernter, a prominent conservative professor of Computer Science at Yale, denounces *The Official SAT Study Guide* (2005 edition) in the course of a sweeping condemnation of liberal domination of American public education. He cites the guide as one of "many ways to see the school establishment's bias." As evidence, he writes, "Here's a sentence from a passage that students are quizzed on. 'The First World War is a classic case of the dissonance between official, male-centered history and unofficial female history.' You might object that the idea of 'official history' is a sham and a crock, unless you refer specifically to accounts commissioned by the combatant governments themselves. But this silly assertion is presented as if it were fact." Gelernter next quotes a passage criticizing " 'the Eurocentric conviction that the West holds a monopoly on science, logic, and clear thinking.' " After a long paragraph condemning this "breathtakingly absurd, breathtakingly offensive" passage, he asks, "What kind of imbecile could write such a passage?—and offer it to unwitting high school students as *fact*?" [Gelernter's italics]

However, the study guide clearly does not present either of these passages as "fact" or as the opinion of its authors. The first is quoted directly (on p. 544) from one of two contrasted books on World War I. The second (on p. 392) is introduced, "The following passage appeared in an essay written in 1987, in which the author, who is of Native American descent, examines the representation of Native Americans during the course of United States history." Furthermore, both texts are quoted simply as a basis for reading comprehension tests. The sample test questions following the texts are aimed solely at interpretation of what particular words and phrases mean (and in the first, of how the two commentaries differ)—without any implication that they are factual or that students are asked to agree or disagree with them.

18. In a column for the *Springfield (Mo.) News-Leader*, June 9, 2004, Joan Collins wrote:

[Our National Security Strategy policy statement] claims to have human dignity at its core. The policy devotes an entire chapter to saying the United States 'will stand firmly for the non-negotiable demand of human dignity.'

This conflict between the principle of human dignity and the action of our soldiers arrogantly ordering Iraqi prisoners to engage in humiliating indignities symbolizes the arrogance of a policy that says we will dominate the world and are immune from its judgment. How does 'human dignity' square with imperial designs?

19. From "Radio Waves: Invisible Danger," by Arthur Firstenberg, *Earth Island Journal*, Winter 2000–2001:

World health authorities have been puzzled by recent sharp increases in asthma, sleep disorders, hypertension, tinnitus, and memory-loss. Influenza and flu-like illnesses also have become more severe and more frequent. In the US, this sharp increase began in November 1996, the same time that digital cell phone service first became available in many cities. In the last four years, RF [radio frequency] and microwave radiation levels have increased tenfold around the world.

20. In the 2004 presidential election debates, Democratic candidates John Kerry and John Edwards raised the subject of Vice President Cheney's daughter being

an open lesbian, ostensibly in order to praise the Cheneys' tolerance of homosexuality. Republicans charged that this was a stealth ploy to flaunt the fact in order to alienate homophobic Republicans from Cheney. In the 2008 election, Barack Obama said, "I have never suggested that Sen. McCain picks his positions on national security based on politics or personal ambition." Discuss these as variants of "I won't (attack my opponents on these points) . . . but I will."

21. After September 11, 2001, Ann Coulter wrote on her Web site about Islamic fundamentalists, "We should invade their countries, kill their leaders, and convert them to Christianity." Coulter has never been in military service.

22. Conservative commentator Laura Ingraham, in defining "liberal elitists," writes, "Their core belief is that they are superior to We the People. They think we're stupid. They think where we live is stupid. They think our SUVs are stupid. They think our guns are stupid." Ingraham grew up in a middle-class Connecticut suburb, is a graduate of Dartmouth College and University of Virginia law school, and lives in Washington.

CHAPTER 11

Causal Analysis

Was the crisis in the financial industry in 2007–08 the result of too little government regulation or too much?

Do sex education and condom distribution in high schools lead to increased sexual activity by students?

Does capital punishment deter murderers?

Is constantly putting more criminals in prison an effective solution to the high crime rate, or is it merely a Band-aid approach that treats the symptoms without doing anything to cure the root causes of crime, and does it perhaps, ironically, *increase* crime by breeding future criminal behavior in prisoners?

Does gun control reduce crime? Does having a gun in your house make you safer?

Does violence on television or in movies provoke violent behavior in viewers? Does pornography provoke sexual crimes?

Did President Reagan's military buildup win the Cold War?

Does smoking cause cancer?

Does welfare destroy incentive to work and promote illegitimate births?

Why haven't women achieved parity with men in jobs and income?

Is affirmative action a solution to, or a cause of, racial divisiveness?

What is the origin of the breakdown in family values?

Does raising the minimum wage increase unemployment?

Have Reaganomics and Bushonomics had a beneficial or a harmful effect on the American economy? Does reducing tax rates stimulate the economy? Does everyone benefit equally from across-the-board tax cuts?

Has the War on Terrorism made Americans more or less safe?

Causal analyses are probably the most common and controversial variety of argument in social and economic issues. They are mainly forms of **inductive reasoning**, depending on **empirical evidence** for adequate support. Causal analysis can be highly eloquent and powerful; its skillful practitioners typically draw from a repository of **cultural literacy**, marshaling historical or socioeconomic data and assuming the ability of readers or listeners to follow an **extended line of argument** that develops a sequence of historical or social causes and effects. **Irony** and **paradox** also often characterize skillful causal arguments, as illustrated in chapter 10, and they are intrinsic to variations such as **vicious circle** or **self-fulfilling prophecy** lines.

Here is an example of a two-step vicious circle argument. First Step: Since the 1970s, most analysts agree, the number of well-paying jobs in the United States has decreased; the increasing competition for a smaller share of jobs has pressured many high school and college students to follow an exclusively vocational curriculum at the expense of general education. The general-education curriculum, however, includes the civic literacy and critical thinking skills necessary to try to understand the causes for the declining job market and possible courses of political action to reverse it, so by restricting themselves to the vocational curriculum, students are caught in the vicious circle of never having access to the information they need to understand or challenge the socioeconomic forces constricting their options. Second Step: Once those same students graduate to become taxpayers and parents, because they have never learned the value of general education for their life choices, they are apt to vote for tax cuts that reduce funds for general education in public secondary schools and colleges, thus creating another vicious circle, as they now further deprive their children, or themselves as adult students, of the same value.

Causal analyses are often highly politicized; opposing forces devote sizable economic and rhetorical resources trying to persuade us that their causal analysis is the correct one; on each of the issues listed at the head of this chapter and many more, conservative and leftist sources come up with "irrefutable evidence" proving that the historical or socioeconomic facts support their side. Moreover, causal analysis is susceptible to an entire, distinct repertory of fallacious and deceptive reasoning, as will be surveyed here. So as a critical reader, listener, and writer, you need to learn to make well-reasoned judgments about which causal arguments are logical and which are fallacious.

The remainder of this chapter is devoted to an examination of some common causal fallacies you may encounter.

Post Hoc, Ergo Propter Hoc. Latin for "After this, therefore because of this" ("post hoc" for short). Arguing, without adequate evidence, that because one thing followed another chronologically, or because the two occur simultaneously, or because they are correlated in some other way, the first caused the second. It has been found that most male sex offenders view pornography, but is it logical to conclude that the pornography caused them to commit sexual offenses? Contrary evidence would be that many men view pornography who never commit a sexual offense, or that countries where pornography is legal tend to have low rates of sexual crimes. (Note that the latter argument does not **imply** the converse post hoc argument, that an abundance of pornography causes a low sexual crime rate—it only suggests that there is no verifiable causal relation between pornography and sex crimes one way or the other; the low sex crime rate might be attributable to other cultural factors.)

Variants on post hoc include **wishful** or magical **thinking** (also forms of **rationalization**), in which we convince ourselves, without adequate evidence, of the truth of what we want to believe, or what serves our own interests to believe, about the cause of favorable events. A whimsical example is provided by the joke about the man who every day passes on the sidewalk of his city another man who constantly and frenetically snaps his fingers. Finally, curiosity gets the better of the first man and he stops the other to ask him, "Why do you always snap your fingers like that?"

"It keeps away elephants."

"Keeps away elephants? That's the craziest thing I ever heard of."

"Oh, yeah? You may think it's crazy, but I've been doing this all my life and I've never been trampled by an elephant."

Reductive Fallacy. Reducing a probable multiplicity of causes to one; a common variety of **oversimplification**. In contrast to post hoc, in which a causal relation between two events is claimed where there is none provable, in the reductive fallacy there might be such a relation, but there are probably other significant causes as well. To claim "All the problems of African Americans today are attributable to slavery" may be true in a broad historical sense, but it is reductive to disregard the multiple, complex probable factors that postdated slavery (see "A Historical-Causal Analysis of 'The White Problem'" in chapter 2).

Slippery Slope. Arguing that if one particular thing occurs, it will lead inevitably to another particular thing, then to another and another, on down a slippery slope of consequences that are more and more remote and unverifiable. Post hoc and reductive fallacy usually refer to events that have already occurred, while slippery slope arguments are usually a prediction that a present situation or one proposed by your opponents will have dire future consequences.

Be careful not to label every argument based on a prediction or **hypothesis** a slippery slope; judge each on its own plausibility. In *The Way Things Ought to Be,* Rush Limbaugh argued that Democrats and liberal civil rights leaders opposed Republican Clarence Thomas's nomination to the Supreme Court because he stood for attitudes contrary to theirs in racial matters. "As a result [of his appointment], blacks inevitably will be drawn away from the traditional civil rights leaders.... Once that happens, a certain percentage of minority votes will likely abandon the Democratic party" (119). This hypothesis has a respectable degree of plausibility; it is quite possible that some blacks have changed parties as a result of Thomas's appointment and of other recent efforts by the Republican Party to attract more black voters. The prediction can also be verified empirically by studying the demographics of voters since Thomas has been on the Court; this is, in fact, an excellent research project. On the other hand, elsewhere in the same book Limbaugh argues, "No one can convince me that the point of [multiculturalism] is not to discredit all that America stands for—and the ultimate goal, I firmly believe, is the destruction of the capitalist way of life, the destruction of free enterprise, and the establishment of socialism" (213). This is classic slippery slope, beginning with a key term, "multiculturalism," whose definition is ambiguous, and continuing with a string of dire consequences that have no apparent connection (certainly none established by Limbaugh) to what many advocates of multiculturalism claim to believe; in other words, Limbaugh is attacking a **straw-man** multiculturalist.

A con artist in Meredith Willson's musical comedy *The Music Man* devises the famous slippery slope patter song, "Ya Got Trouble" to gull the citizens of River City, Iowa, around 1900, into believing that the arrival of a pool hall in their community poses a flood of dangers that only the nonexistent band instruments and uniforms he claims to be selling can avert.

"Ya Got Trouble"

Meredith Willson

from *The Music Man*
G. P. Putnam and Sons, 1959

HAROLD
Ya got trouble, my friend, right here,
I say, trouble right here in River City....
I say that any *boob* kin take
And shove a ball in a pocket.
And I call that sloth!
The first big step on the road
To the depths of deg-ra-day—
I say, first, medicinal wine from a teaspoon,
Then beer from a bottle.
An' the next thing ya know,
Your son is playin' for money
In a pinch-back suit.
And list'nin to some big out-a-town Jasper
Hearin' him tell about horse-race gamblin'.
Not a wholesome trottin' race, no!
But a race where they set down right on the horse!
Like to see some stuck-up jockey-boy

Sittin' on Dan Patch? Make your blood boil?
Well, I should say.

PEOPLE

Trouble, oh we got trouble,
Right here in River City!
With a capital "T"
That rhymes with "P"
And that stands for Pool,
That stands for pool.
We've surely got trouble!
Right here in River City,
Right here!
Gotta figger out a way
To keep the young ones moral after school!

Blaming the Victim. A frequent form of rationalization involves explaining the misfortune of those below us on the social scale, for which we might be actively or passively responsible, as the result of their own inadequacies. Blaming the victim has been a historical constant in prejudice against women and African Americans (see "A Historical-Causal Analysis of 'The White Problem'" in chapter 2). Another example, previously mentioned here, would be teachers or older citizens who get angry at today's students for being poorly informed about history or current events, when most of these students are simply victims of schools that have failed to teach these subjects adequately. Teachers are also frequently blamed for these shortcomings, but again, if communities do not care enough about good teaching to provide tax funding for adequate training, testing, payment, and classroom conditions for teachers, then the community is blaming the victims of its own indifference—both the teachers and the students. [*Reader Advisory:* **I might be special pleading here.**]

This example of blaming the victim also illustrates the related term **scapegoating,** as teachers are made the scapegoat for the community's failures. It is not only victims who are scapegoated, however. In the Salem witch trials of the late seventeenth century, innocent members of that Massachusetts community were arbitrarily accused of being agents of the devil, as scapegoats for the disintegration of the earlier, close-knit Puritan community. Likewise, Hitler singled out the Jews to use as scapegoats for Germany's economic troubles in the 1930s. The irony of both the cases of Salem and Germany is that, although they were not originally cases of blaming the victim, the accused "witches" and Jews became victims through a self-fulfilling prophecy; naming a group as a scapegoat results in their becoming victimized.

Too Much or Too Little? When someone argues that a course of action has been unsuccessful because it has been pushed too far, is the reverse possibly true, that it has not been pushed far enough to have a fair chance to succeed? Thus conservatives point to all the government money that has been spent on public education or welfare without visible results, as evidence that the effort has been misguided from the beginning, while liberals counter by claiming that this amount has merely been **tokenism,** inadequate to meet the real needs of schools or poor people. Liberals say that tax cuts instituted by Presidents Ronald Reagan and George W. Bush were misguided because they led to massive increases in federal deficit spending and the national debt, while conservatives protest that liberal opposition prevented the even greater cuts that would have been necessary for the policy to have positive results. In the face of such arguments, you need to resist being swayed just by assertions on either side and to evaluate the supporting evidence.

Giving Your Side Credit for Positive Results, Blaming the Other Side for Negative Results. This is a staple of campaign rhetoric. When economic conditions are good, the incumbent party can be predicted to take credit for them, whether they are verifiably the result of that party's policies, the late-appearing results of the other party's previous term in office, or sheer coincidence. When present conditions are bad, expect the opposition party to blame them on the incumbents—with the same likelihood of unverifiability. At best, such analyses usually commit the reductive fallacy, though in some cases one side may actually have valid evidence for its claims; so, as always, compare the dueling evidence with an open mind.

Confusion of Cause and Effect, or Addressing Effects, or Symptoms, or Reactions, Rather than Causes or Actions. One of President Bush's justifications for the war on Iraq in 2003 was that Iraq was harboring terrorists. When the American forces occupying Iraq came under attack by terrorists, conservatives said, "See, we told you so. This proves we were right." But liberals said, "There was not a substantial number of terrorists in Iraq under Saddam Hussein, who was not closely allied with the Islamic fundamentalists who were the main source of terrorism. But when he was overthrown and American forces moved in, a power vacuum was created, and Islamic fundamentalists and other terrorists swarmed into the country from adjoining Arab states, eager to attack Americans who were now easy prey. So attacking Iraq caused the widespread presence of terrorists there." These opposing analyses are likely to be debated for years to come.

This is also an extremely common pattern of fallacy in arguments about issues such as crime, poverty, and welfare, and it is often used in tandem with blaming the victim. This fallacy, or the possibility of it, often comes out in disagreements about whether affirmative action is a cause of racial and gender discrimination or a reaction against them (though it is also possible that, in a **vicious circle**, it is both). In another constant public dispute, conservatives argue that welfare causes poverty, through destroying the incentive to work, and also causes illegitimate births, through the increased financial support welfare mothers receive for additional children; liberals **refute** this argument by claiming that most able-bodied recipients of welfare turn to it because there are no jobs available or because they are working at jobs whose wages are below the poverty level, and that poverty itself, for various cultural and psychological reasons, is the main cause of illegitimate births among the poor and that the meager additional welfare benefits are a minor motivation at best. These disagreements in turn lead into policy disputes about whether reducing welfare will cause more people to find jobs, and whether cutting off welfare benefits for additional children will dissuade women from having further children.

Yet another related causal dispute between conservatives and liberals is whether granting welfare benefits to women with children results in their independence from men, to the point that the women throw men out or deprive them of their sense of family responsibility—or whether this is a reversal of the more common causality, that a growing number of men have lost a sense of paternal responsibility for other reasons and have abandoned their women and children, forcing the women to turn to welfare.

These are all issues in which you should be wary of **deductive** arguments that simply posit a hypothetical scenario that concurs with one side's ideological biases. In such issues you should look for sound inductive arguments based on empirical studies.

Other People's Children: North Lawndale and the South Side of Chicago

Jonathan Kozol

From Savage Inequalities *(Crown, 1992). The following chapter from* Savage Inequalities, *about Chicago inner-city schools, begins with a transition from the previous chapter, about East St. Louis, Illinois, "which is 98% black, has no obstetric services, no regular trash collection, and few jobs. Nearly a third of its families live on less than $7,500 a year" (7). Schoolchildren there suffer from numerous illnesses caused by toxic waste from Pfizer and Monsanto chemical plants.*

Almost anyone who visits in the schools of East St. Louis, even for a short time, comes away profoundly shaken. These are innocent children, after all. They have done nothing wrong. They have committed no crime. They are too young to have offended us in any way at all. One searches for some way to understand why a society as rich and, frequently, as generous as ours would leave these children in their penury and squalor for so long—and with so little public indignation. Is this just a strange mistake of history? Is it unusual? Is it an American anomaly? Even, if the destitution and the racial segregation and the toxic dangers of the air and soil cannot be immediately addressed, why is it that we can't at least pour vast amounts of money, ingenuity and talent into public education for these children?

Admittedly, the soil cannot be de-leaded overnight, and the ruined spirits of the men who camp out in the mud and shacks close to the wire fencing of Monsanto can't be instantly restored to life, nor can the many illnesses these children suffer suddenly be cured, nor can their asthma be immediately relieved. Why not, at least, give children in this city something so spectacular, so wonderful and special in their public schools that hundreds of them, maybe thousands, might be able somehow to soar up above the hopelessness, the clouds of smoke and sense of degradation all around them?

Every child, every mother, in this city is, to a degree, in the position of a supplicant for someone else's help. The city turns repeatedly to outside agencies—the federal Department of Housing and Urban Development, the federal and Illinois EPA, the U.S. Congress, the Illinois State Board of Education, religious charities, health organizations, medical schools and educational foundations—soliciting help in much the way that African and Latin American nations beg for grants from agencies like AID. And yet we stop to tell ourselves: *These are Americans.* Why do we reduce them to this beggary—and why, particularly, in public education? Why not spend on children here at least what we would be investing in their education if they lived within a wealthy district like Winnetka, Illinois, or Cherry Hill, New Jersey, or Manhasset, Rye, or Great Neck in New York? Wouldn't this be natural behavior in an affluent society that seems to value fairness in so many other areas of life? Is fairness less important to Americans today than in some earlier times? Is it viewed as slightly tiresome and incompatible with hardnosed values? What do Americans believe about equality?

"Drive west on the Eisenhower Expressway," writes the *Chicago Tribune,* "out past the hospital complex, and look south." Before your eyes are block after block of old, abandoned, gaping factories. "The overwhelming sensation is emptiness.... What's left is, literally, nothing."

This emptiness—"an industrial slum without the industry," a local resident calls it—is North Lawndale. The neighborhood, according to the *Tribune,* "has one bank, one supermarket, 48 state lottery agents ... and 99 licensed bars and liquor stores." With only a single supermarket, food is of poor quality and overpriced. Martin Luther King, who lived in this neighborhood in 1966, said there was a 10-to-20-percent "color tax" on produce, an estimate that still holds true today. With only a single bank, there are few loans available for home repair; private housing therefore has deteriorated quickly.

According to the 1980 census, 58 percent of men and women 17 and older in North Lawndale had no jobs. The 1990 census is expected to show no improvement. Between 1960 and 1970, as the last white families left the neighborhood, North Lawndale lost three quarters of its businesses, one quarter of its jobs. In the next ten years, 80 percent of the remaining jobs in manufacturing were lost.

"People carry a lot of crosses here," says Reverend Jim Wolff, who directs a mission church not far from one of the deserted factories. "God's beautiful people live here in the midst of hell."

As the factories have moved out, he says, the street gangs have moved in. Driving with me past a sprawling red-brick complex that was once the world headquarters of Sears, Roebuck, he speaks of the increasing economic isolation of the neighborhood:

"Sears is gone. International Harvester is gone. Sunbeam is gone. Western Electric has moved out. The Vice Lords, the Disciples and the Latin Kings have, in a sense, replaced them.

"With the arrival of the gangs there is, of course, more violence and death. I buried a young man 21 years old a week ago. Most of the people that I bury are between the ages of 18 and 30."

He stops the car next to a weed-choked lot close to the corner of Sixteenth and Hamlin. "Dr. King," he says, "lived on this corner." There is no memorial. The city, I later learn, flattened the building after Dr. King moved out. A broken truck now occupies the place where Dr. King resided. From an open side door of the truck a very old man is selling pizza slices. Next door is a store called Jumbo Liquors. A menacing group of teen-age boys is standing on the corner of the lot where Dr. King lived with his family. "Kids like these will kill each other over nothing—for a warm-up jacket," says the pastor.

"There are good people in this neighborhood," he says, "determined and persistent and strong-minded people who have character and virtues you do not see everywhere. You say to yourself, 'There's something here that's being purified by pain.' All the veneers, all the facades, are burnt away and you see something genuine and beautiful that isn't often found among the affluent. I see it in children—in the youngest children sometimes. Beautiful sweet natures. It's as if they are refined by their adversity. But you cannot sentimentalize. The odds they face are hellish and, for many, many people that I know, life here is simply unendurable.

"Dr. King once said that he had met his match here in Chicago. He said that he faced more bigotry and hatred here than anywhere he'd been in the Deep South. Now he's gone. The weeds have overgrown his memory. I sometimes wonder if the kids who spend their lives out on that corner would be shocked, or even interested, to know that he had lived there once. If you told them, I suspect you'd get a shrug at most...."

On a clear October day in 1990, the voices of children in the first-floor hallway of the Mary McLeod Bethune School in North Lawndale are as bright and optimistic as the voices of small children anywhere. The school, whose students are among the poorest in the city, serves one of the neighborhoods in which the infant death rate is particularly high. Nearly 1,000 infants die within these very poor Chicago neighborhoods each year. An additional 3,000 infants are delivered with brain damage or with other forms of neurological impairment. But, entering a kindergarten classroom on this autumn morning, one would have no sense that anything was wrong. Kindergarten classes almost anywhere are cheerful places, and whatever damage may already have been done to children here is not initially apparent to a visitor.

When the children lie down on the floor to have their naps, I sit and watch their movements and their breathing. A few of them fall asleep at once, but others are restless and three little boys keep poking one another when the teacher looks away. Many tiny coughs and whispers interrupt the silence for a while.

The teacher is not particularly gentle. She snaps at the ones who squirm around— "Relax!" and "Sleep!"—and forces down their arms and knees.

A little boy lying with his head close to my feet looks up, with his eyes wide open, at the ceiling. Another, lying on his stomach, squints at me with one eye while the other remains closed. Two little girls, one in blue jeans, one in purple tights, are sound asleep.

The room is sparse: a large and clean but rather cheerless space. There are very few of those manipulable objects and bright-colored shelves and boxes that adorn suburban kindergarten classrooms. The only decorations on the walls are posters supplied by companies that market school materials: "Winter," "Spring," "Summer," "Autumn," "Zoo Animals," "Community Helpers." Nothing the children or teacher made themselves.

As the minutes pass, most of the children seem to sleep, some of them with their arms flung out above their heads, others with their hands beneath their cheeks, though four or five are wide awake and stare with boredom at the ceiling.

On the door is a classroom chart ("Watch us grow!" it says) that measures every child's size and weight. Nakisha, according to the chart, is 38 inches tall and weighs 40 pounds. Lashonda, is 42 inches and weighs 45. Seneca is only 36 inches tall. He weighs only 38.

After 30 minutes pass, the teacher tells the children to sit up. Five of the boys who were most restless suddenly are sound asleep. The others sit up. The teacher tells them, "Folded hands!" They fold their hands. "Wiggle your toes!" They wiggle their toes. "Touch your nose!" They touch their noses.

The teacher questions them about a trip they made the week before. "Where did we go?" The children answer, "Farm!" "What did we see?" The children answer, "Sheep!" "What did we feed them?" A child yells out, "Soup!" The teacher reproves him: "You weren't there! What is the right answer?" The other children answer, "Corn!"

In a somewhat mechanical way, the teacher lifts a picture book of Mother Goose and flips the pages as the children sit before her on the rug.

"Mary had a little lamb, its fleece was white as snow.... Old Mother Hubbard went to the cupboard to fetch her poor dog a bone.... Jack and Jill went up the hill.... This little piggy went to market...."

The children recite the verses with her as she turns the pages of the book. She's not very warm or animated as she does it, but the children are obedient and seem to like the fun of showing that they know the words. The book looks worn and old, as if the teacher's used it many, many years, and it shows no signs of adaptation to the race of the black children in the school. Mary is white. Old Mother Hubbard is white. Jack is white. Jill is white. Little Jack Horner is white. Mother Goose is white. Only Mother Hubbard's dog is black.

"Baa, baa, black sheep," the teacher read, "have you any wool?" The children answer: "Yessir, yessir, three bags full. One for my master...." The master is white. The sheep are black.

Four little boys are still asleep on the green rug an hour later when I leave the room. I stand at the door and look at the children, most of whom are sitting at a table now to have their milk. Nine years from now, most of these children will go on to Manley High School, an enormous, ugly building just a block away that has a graduation rate of only 38 percent. Twelve years from now, by junior year of high school, if the neighborhood statistics hold true for these children, 14 of these 23 boys and girls will have dropped out of school. Fourteen years from now, four of these kids, at most, will go to college. Eighteen years from now, one of those four may graduate from college, but three of the 12 boys in this kindergarten will already have spent time in prison.

If one stands here in this kindergarten room and does not know these things, the moment seems auspicious. But if one knows the future that awaits them, it is terrible to see their eyes look up at you with friendliness and trust—to see this and to know what is in store for them.

In a fifth grade classroom on the third floor of the school, the American flag is coated with chalk and bunched around a pole above a blackboard with no writing on it. There are a couple of pictures of leaves against the windowpanes but nothing like the richness and the novelty and fullness of expression of the children's creativity that one would see in better schools where principals insist that teachers fill their rooms with art and writing by the children. The teacher is an elderly white woman with a solid bun of sensible gray hair and a depleted grayish mood about her. Among the 30 children in the room, the teacher says that several, all of whom are black, are classified "learning disabled."

The children are doing a handwriting lesson when I enter. On a board at the back of the room the teacher has written a line of letters in the standard cursive script. The children sit at their desks and fill entire pages with these letters. It is the kind of lesson that is generally done in second grade in a suburban school. The teacher seems bored by the lesson, and the children seem to feel this and compound her boredom with their own. Next she does a social studies lesson on the Bering Strait and spends some time in getting the class to give a definition of a "strait." About half of the children pay attention. The others don't talk or interrupt or fidget. They are well enough behaved but seem sedated by the teacher's voice.

Another fifth grade teacher stops me in the corridor to ask me what I'm doing in the building. He's 50 years old, he tells me, and grew up here in North Lawndale when it was a middle-class white neighborhood but now lives in the suburbs. "I have a low fifth grade," he says without enthusiasm, then—although he scarcely knows me—launches into an attack upon the principal, the neighborhood and the school.

"It's all a game," he says. "Keep them in class for seven years and give them a diploma if they make it to eighth grade. They can't read, but give them the diploma. The parents don't know what's going on. They're satisfied."

When I ask him if the lack of money and resources is a problem in the school, he looks amused by this. "Money would be helpful but it's not the major factor," he replies. "The parents are the problem."

The principal, Warren Franczyk, later tells me this: "Teachers are being dumped from high school jobs because of low enrollment. But if they've got tenure they cannot be fired so we get them here. I've got two of them as subs right now and one as a permanent teacher. He's not used to children of this age and can't control them. But I have no choice."

The city runs a parallel system of selective schools—some of which are known as "magnet" schools—and these schools, the principal tells me, do not have the staffing problems that he faces. "They can select their teachers and their pupils. So it represents a drain on us. They attract the more sophisticated families, and it leaves us with less motivated children."

Chicago, he tells me, does not have a junior high school system. Students begin Bethune in kindergarten and remain here through eighth grade. Eighth grade graduation, here as elsewhere in Chicago, is regarded as a time for celebration, much as twelfth grade graduation would be celebrated in the suburbs. So there are parties, ball gowns and tuxedos, everything that other kids would have at high school graduation. "For more than half our children," says the principal, "this is the last thing they will have to celebrate."

Even in the most unhappy schools there are certain classes that stand out like little islands of excitement, energy and hope. One of these classes is a combination fifth and sixth grade at Bethune, taught by a woman, maybe 40 years of age, named Corla Hawkins. . . .

There are wonderful teachers such as Corla Hawkins almost everywhere in urban schools, and sometimes a number of such teachers in a single school. It is tempting to focus on these teachers and, by doing this, to paint a hopeful portrait of the good things that go on under adverse conditions. There is, indeed, a growing body of such writing; and these books are sometimes very popular, because they are consoling.

The rationale behind much of this writing is that pedagogic problems in our cities are not chiefly matters of injustice, inequality or segregation, but of insufficient information about teaching strategies: If we could simply learn "what works" in Corla Hawkins's room, we'd then be in a position to repeat this all over Chicago and in every other system.

But what is unique in Mrs. Hawkins's classroom is not what she does but who she is. Warmth and humor and contagious energy cannot be replicated and cannot be written into any standardized curriculum. If they could, it would have happened long ago; for wonderful teachers have been heroized in books and movies for at least three decades. And the problems of Chicago are, in any case, not those of insufficient information. If Mrs. Hawkins's fellow fifth grade teachers simply needed information, they could get it easily by walking 20 steps across the hall and visiting her room. The problems are systemic: The number of teachers over 60 years of age in the Chicago system is twice that of the teachers under 30. The salary scale, too low to keep exciting, youthful teachers in the system, leads the city to rely on low-paid subs, who represent more than a quarter of Chicago's teaching force. "We have teachers," Mrs. Hawkins says, "who only bother to come in three days a week. One of these teachers comes in usually around nine-thirty. You ask her how she can expect the kids to care about their education if the teacher doesn't even come until nine-thirty. She answers you, 'It makes no difference. Kids like these aren't going anywhere.' The school board thinks it's saving money on the subs. I tell them, 'Pay now or pay later.'"

But even substitute teachers in Chicago are quite frequently in short supply. On an average morning in Chicago, 5,700 children in 190 classrooms come to school to find they have no teacher. The number of children who have no teachers on a given morning in Chicago's public schools is nearly twice the student population of New Trier High School in nearby Winnetka.

"We have been in this class a whole semester," says a 15-year-old at Du Sable High, one of Chicago's poorest secondary schools, "and they still can't find us a teacher."

A student in auto mechanics at Du Sable says he'd been in class for 16 weeks before he learned to change a tire. His first teacher quit at the beginning of the year. Another teacher slept through most of the semester. He would come in, the student says, and tell the students, "You can talk. Just keep it down." Soon he would be asleep.

"Let's be real," the student says. "Most of us ain't going to college.... We could have used a class like this."

The shortage of teachers finds its parallel in a shortage of supplies. A chemistry teacher at the school reports that he does not have beakers, water, bunsen burners. He uses a popcorn popper as a substitute for a bunsen burner, and he cuts down plastic soda bottles to make laboratory dishes.

Many of these schools make little effort to instruct their failing students. "If a kid comes in not reading," says an English teacher at Chicago's South Shore High, "he goes out not reading."

Another teacher at the school, where only 170 of 800 freshmen graduate with their

class, indicates that the dropout rate makes teaching easier. "We lose all the dregs by the second year," he says.

"We're a general high school," says the head of counseling at Chicago's Calumet High School. "We have second- and third-grade readers.... We hope to do better, but we won't die if we don't."

At Bowen High School, on the South Side of Chicago, students have two or three "study halls" a day, in part to save the cost of teachers. "Not much studying goes on in study hall," a supervising teacher says. "I let the students play cards.... I figure they might get some math skills out of it."

At the Lathrop Elementary School, a short walk from the corner lot where Dr. King resided in North Lawndale, there are no hoops on the basketball court and no swings in the playground. For 21 years, according to the *Chicago Tribune*, the school has been without a library. Library books, which have been piled and abandoned in the lunch room of the school, have "sprouted mold," the paper says. Some years ago the school received the standard reading textbooks out of sequence: The second workbook in the reading program came to the school before the first. The principal, uncertain what to do with the wrong workbook, was told by school officials it was "all right to work backwards...."

This degree of equanimity in failure, critics note, has led most affluent parents in Chicago to avoid the public system altogether. The school board president in 1989, although a teacher and administrator in the system for three decades, did not send his children to the public schools. Nor does Mayor Richard Daley, Jr., nor did any of the previous four mayors who had school-age children.

"Nobody in his right mind," says one of the city's aldermen, "would send [his] kids to public school."

Many suburban legislators representing affluent school districts use terms such as "sinkhole" when opposing funding for Chicago's children. "We can't keep throwing money," said Governor Thompson in 1988, "into a black hole."

The *Chicago Tribune* notes that, when this phrase is used, people hasten to explain that it is not intended as a slur against the race of many of Chicago's children. "But race," says the *Tribune,* "never is far from the surface...."

As spring comes to Chicago, the scarcity of substitutes grows more acute. On Mondays and Fridays in early May, nearly 18,000 children—the equivalent of all the elementary students in suburban Glencoe, Wilmette, Glenview, Kenilworth, Winnetka, Deerfield, Highland Park and Evanston—are assigned to classes with no teacher.

In this report, the city's dropout rate of nearly 50 percent is regarded by some people as a blessing. If over 200,000 of Chicago's total student population of 440,000 did not disappear during their secondary years, it is not clear who would teach them.

In 1989, Chicago spent some $5,500 for each student in its secondary schools. This may be compared to an investment of some $8,500 to $9,000 in each high school student in the highest-spending suburbs to the north. Stated in the simplest terms, this means that any high school class of 30 children in Chicago received approximately $90,000 less each year than would have been spent on them if they were pupils of a school such as New Trier High.

The difference in spending between very wealthy suburbs and poor cities is not always as extreme as this in Illinois. When relative student needs, however, have been factored into the discussion, the disparities in funding are enormous. Equity, after all, does not mean simply equal funding. Equal funding for unequal need is not equality. The need is greater in Chicago, and its children, if they are to have approximately equal opportunities, need more than the children who attend New Trier. Seen in this light, the $90,000 annual difference is quite startling.

Lack of money is not the only problem in Chicago, but the gulf in funding we have seen is so remarkable and seems so blatantly unfair that it strikes many thoughtful citizens at first as inexplicable. How can it be that inequalities as great as these exist in neighboring school districts?

The answer is found, at least in part, in the arcane machinery by which we finance public education. Most public schools in the United States depend for their initial funding on a tax on local property. There are also state and federal funding sources, and we will discuss them later, but the property tax is the decisive force in shaping inequality. The property tax depends, of course, upon the taxable value of one's home and that of local industries. A typical wealthy suburb in which homes are often worth more than $400,000 draws upon a larger tax base in proportion to its student population than a city occupied by thousands of poor people. Typically, in the United States, very poor communities place high priority on education, and they often tax themselves at higher rates than do the very affluent communities. But, even if they tax themselves at several times the rate of an extremely wealthy district, they are likely to end up with far less money for each child in their schools.

Because the property tax is counted as a tax deduction by the federal government, home-owners in a wealthy suburb get back a substantial portion of the money that they spend to fund their children's schools—effectively, a federal subsidy for an unequal education. Home-owners in poor districts get this subsidy as well, but, because their total tax is less, the subsidy is less. The mortgage interest that homeowners pay is also treated as a tax deduction—in effect, a second federal subsidy. These subsidies, as I have termed them, are considerably larger than most people understand. In 1984, for instance, property-tax deductions granted by the federal government were $9 billion. An additional $23 billion in mortgage-interest deductions were provided to home-owners: a total of some $32 billion. Federal grants to local schools, in contrast, totaled only $7 billion, and only part of this was earmarked for low-income districts. Federal policy, in this respect, increases the existing gulf between the richest and the poorest schools.

All of these disparities are also heightened, in the case of larger cities like Chicago, by the disproportionate number of entirely tax-free institutions—colleges and hospitals and art museums, for instance—that are sited in such cities. In some cities, according to Jonathan Wilson, former chairman of the Council of Urban Boards of Education, 30 percent or more of the potential tax base is exempt from taxes, compared to as little as 3 percent in the adjacent suburbs. Suburbanites, of course, enjoy the use of these nonprofit, tax-free institutions; and, in the case of private colleges and universities, they are far *more* likely to enjoy their use than are the residents of inner cities.

Cities like Chicago face the added problem that an overly large portion of their limited tax revenues must be diverted to meet nonschool costs that wealthy suburbs do not face, or only on a far more modest scale. Police expenditures are higher in crime-ridden cities than in most suburban towns. Fire department costs are also higher where dilapidated housing, often with substandard wiring, and arson-for-profit are familiar problems. Public health expenditures are also higher where poor people cannot pay for private hospitals. All of these expenditures compete with those for public schools. So the districts that face the toughest challenges are also likely to be those that have the fewest funds to meet their children's needs.

Many people, even those who view themselves as liberals on other issues, tend to grow indignant, even rather agitated, if invited to look closely at these inequalities. "Life isn't fair," one parent in Winnetka answered flatly when I pressed the matter. "Wealthy children also go to summer camp. All summer. Poor kids maybe not at all. Or maybe, if they're lucky, for two weeks. Wealthy children have the chance to go to Europe and they have the access to good libraries, encyclopedias, computers, better doctors, nicer homes. Some of my neighbors send their kids to schools like Exeter and Groton. Is government supposed to equalize these things as well?"

But government, of course, does not assign us to our homes, our summer camps, our doctors—or to Exeter. it does assign us to our public schools. Indeed, it forces us

to go to them. Unless we have the wealth to pay for private education, we are compelled by law to go to public school—and to the public school in our district. Thus the state, by requiring attendance but refusing to require equity, effectively requires inequality. Compulsory inequity, perpetuated by state law, too frequently condemns our children to unequal lives.

In Illinois, as elsewhere in America, local funds for education raised from property taxes are supplemented by state contributions and by federal funds, although the federal contribution is extremely small, constituting only 6 percent of total school expenditures. State contributions represent approximately half of local school expenditures in the United States; although intended to make up for local wealth disparities, they have seldom been sufficient to achieve this goal. Total yearly spending—local funds combined with state assistance and the small amount that comes from Washington—ranges today in Illinois from $2,100 on a child in the poorest district to above $10,000 in the richest. The system, writes John Coons, a professor of law at Berkeley University, "bears the appearance of calculated unfairness."

There is a belief advanced today, and in some cases by conservative black authors, that poor children and particularly black children should not be allowed to hear too much about these matters. If they learn how much less they are getting than rich children, we are told, this knowledge may induce them to regard themselves as "victims," and such "victim-thinking," it is argued, may then undermine their capability to profit from whatever opportunities may actually exist. But this is a matter of psychology—or strategy—and not reality. The matter, in any case, is academic since most adolescents in the poorest neighborhoods learn very soon that they are getting less than children in the wealthier school districts. They see suburban schools on television and they see them when they travel for athletic competitions. It is a waste of time to worry whether we should tell them something they could tell to us. About injustice, most poor children in America cannot be fooled.

Table 11.1. School Funding in the Chicago Area (Figures for the 1988–1989 School Year)

School or District	Spending Per Pupil
Niles Township High School	$9,371
New Trier High School	$8,823
Glencoe (elementary and junior high schools)	$7,363
Winnetka (elementary and junior high schools)	$7,059
Wilmette (elementary and junior high schools)	$6,009
Chicago (average of all grade levels)	$5,265

Source: Chicago Panel on School Policy and Finance.

Table 11.2. School Funding in New Jersey (Figures for the 1988–1989 School Year)

District	Spending Per Pupil
Princeton	$7,725
Summit	$7,275
West Orange	$6,505
Cherry Hill	$5,981
Jersey City	$4,566
East Orange	$4,457
Paterson	$4,422
Camden	$3,538

Source: Educational Law Center, Newark, New Jersey.

Table 11.3. School Funding in the New York City Area (Figures for the 1986–1987 School Year)

District	Spending Per Pupil
Manhasset	$11,372
Jericho	$11,325
Great Neck	$11,265
Bronxville	$10,113
Rye	$9,092
Yonkers	$7,399
Levittown	$6,899
Mount Vernon	$6,433
Roosevelt	$6,339
New York City	$5,585

Source: "Statistical Profiles of School Districts" (New York State Board of Education).

Table 11.4. The Widening Gap (School Funding in Six Districts in the New York City Area: Changes in a Three-Year Period)

District	1986–1987 School Year	1989–1990 School Year
Manhasset	$11,372	$15,084
Jericho	$11,325	$14,355
Great Neck	$11,265	$15,594
Mount Vernon	$6,433	$9,112
Roosevelt	$6,339	$8,349
New York City	$5,585	$7,299

Source: "Statistical Profiles of School Districts" (New York State Board of Education) and *New York Times.*

Crisis in American Education

William J. Bennett

From *The De-Valuing of America: The Fight for Our Children and Our Culture,* Simon & Schuster, 1992

There's a Chuck Berry song that goes in part, "I got a chance, I oughta take it." Well, I got my chance when President Reagan asked me to be Secretary of Education in 1985, and I was going to take it. I didn't want to leave that job and say to myself, "Boy, when I was Secretary, I wish I had said such and such." I've always tried to say what I really thought while I held a post, not later; to speak truthfully and not to leave with a lot of "I should have saids." I hate it when you don't find out what government officials really think until after they leave office and write a "revealing" memoir. "Retirement candor" cheapens the currency; it makes people suspicious of what people say when they are in the job. At least I can say that when I had my chance I took it.

"How can anyone who [cares] about children not feel terrible about Chicago schools?" This was the question I put to the city during a November 1987 visit while I was Secretary of Education. For about $4,000 per student per year, Chicagoans were supporting a public school system in which nearly half of the children who entered the public school system dropped out before graduating from high school, many to become involved in lives of welfare dependency, drugs, or violent crime. When the scores of the American College Testing (ACT) Program (a standard college-entrance exam) were disclosed, more than *half* of the city's public schools reported high school senior scores in the *bottom 1 percent* of schools nationwide.

The Chicago public school system—the nation's third largest after Los Angeles and New York—was "the worst in the nation," I said. "You have an educational meltdown." (An employee of the Chicago public school system later insisted, "We are not the worst public school system in America. Detroit is worse." I told him that he was guilty of what Justice Holmes called "low aspirations.")

And practically everyone in Chicago—parents, employers, other teachers, and the schoolchildren themselves—knew it. In recent years we've seen some efforts at improvement, but the seventies and eighties in Chicago saw countless thousands of young lives ruined, and still today, tens of thousands of children are not being educated. According to the *Chicago Tribune* (in a full-page editorial written at the end of a tough, unflinching investigative series in 1988), "The Chicago public schools are so bad, they are hurting so many thousands of children so terribly, they are jeopardizing the future of the city so much that drastic solutions must be found."

The *Tribune* series charged school administrators with "institutional child neglect."

Here are but a few of the many horror stories documented:

- All 22 students in Grace Currin's 4th-grade class were supposed to attend summer school in 1988 because, their principal said, Currin did not teach the children enough to pass to the next grade. Currin did not hand in a lesson plan all year. Four principals tried unsuccessfully to have Currin fired. "It's a terrible shame," said Dyanne Dandridger-Alexander, a principal.

"Those children have suffered because they have a totally inept teacher that no one has been able to fire." Parents who sat in on her classes said they were at a point where they thought it was hopeless. Currin said she did not deserve the negative ratings. "I still think they did not really get to know me as a teacher," she said. "I am part of the problem, but remember, you can't expect miracles when you have low achievers." Currin told the *Tribune* that her career goal was "to retire at full pension."

- Deborah Harris was suspended from Chicago's Shoop Elementary School after she consistently refused to go to her 7th-grade classroom. Each day she gave the principal a doctor's note saying that she should be given "light duties." Harris was told daily, in writing, by the principal and the district superintendent, to report to class. She hid in the boiler room, according to testimony. The hearing officer ordered Harris reinstated because the board had not given her written notice that she would be fired if she did not go to class. Harris took a leave of absence the day she was reinstated to Curtis Elementary School and never returned. The board appealed the ruling but lost. "We were shocked," one attorney said. "Hearing officers view this as a man's or woman's livelihood. The hearing officer barely mentioned the children."

- In 1987, ten weeks into the first semester, typing students at Du Sable High School had gone through four substitutes, none of them trained to teach typing or certified in any business subject. During the 11th week, a certified typing teacher arrived, and only then did the students learn where to place their hands on the keyboard. Four weeks later, she took a job in private industry. "It's a shame that we have been in this class a whole semester and they still can't find us a teacher," according to one fifteen-year-old, who spent most of one teacherless class putting on makeup and fixing her hair. "We'll probably have to take it over again." Chicago School Superintendent Manford Byrd, Jr., was surprised that such a situation existed. "I'm not aware of that kind of imbalance," he told the *Tribune.* "Our aim is to get regular certified teachers in all the openings. But I don't know if we've ever been in a better shape than we are now."

- The Chicago Board of Education headquarters, called "Pershing Gardens" by school critics, is in a former warehouse that was renovated at a cost of $22 million. The nearly 3,000 people who worked at the offices on the South Side listened to piped-in music, walked on thick carpets, and enjoyed a panoramic view of the city from their 5th-floor cafeteria.

The late Harold Washington, then mayor of Chicago, was outraged by my criticisms of the city's public school system. "Mr. Bennett has a lot of gall to be criticizing Chicago public schools—or any other school system," he said. Chicago Board of Education president Frank Gardner added, "We hope the impact of his statements do [sic] not further demoralize teachers, who are doing an excellent job."

Jacqueline Vaughn, president of the Chicago Teachers Union (CTU), one of the most powerful teacher unions in the country, told a group of teachers, "I resent your efforts being taken for granted and [people] saying we are responsible for the ills in education because, without us, they would have none.

"We are tired of being given mandates, dictates, instructions and directions from everybody when we are not asked to give our input," she said. "We don't tell them [parents and others] what to do in their kitchens, so why should they tell us what to do in our classrooms?" Vaughn elicited frenzied applause from the assembled school employees.

During a joint press conference with Vaughn, I said I'd be more impressed with her union if it made some effort, any effort, to get rid of its bad teachers while rewarding its good ones.

Her reply was Chicago didn't have *any* bad teachers. . . .

In 1983 the National Commission on Excellence in Education released the landmark report *A Nation at Risk,* the closest thing we have had to a national education grievance list. It cited, among other problems, poor performance by American students on a variety of international education tests; a decline in scores on most standardized tests; and a decline in student knowledge in crucial subjects such as English and physics. It gave voice to the growing public sense of crisis about our children and their schools. "The educational foundations of our society are presently being eroded by a rising tide of mediocrity that threatens our very future as a nation and a people," the report said. "We have, in effect, been committing an act of unthinking, unilateral educational disarmament." Countless reports since 1983—some issued by me—have further documented a performance that can only charitably be described as mediocre. "American education is to education what the Soviet economy is to the economy," according to Chester E. Finn, Jr., one of the most insightful commentators on American education.

Our students score last in math and science in comparison with students of other industrialized nations. A 1989 international comparison of mathematics and science skills showed American students scoring at the bottom and South Korean students scoring at the top (South Korean students perform at high levels in math at *four times* the rate of U.S. students). Ironically, when asked if they are good at math, 68 percent of American students thought they were (the highest percentage of any country) compared to 23 percent of South Korean students (the lowest percentage of any country), which demonstrates that this country is a lot better at teaching self-esteem than it is at teaching math.

According to the 1991 National Assessment of Educational Progress (NAEP) study, 72 percent of our fourth-graders can do third-grade math, only 14 percent of our eighth-graders can do seventh-grade math, and only 5 percent of our high school seniors "showed an understanding of geometry and algebra that suggested preparedness for the study of relatively advanced mathematics," i.e., for college-level math.

Math and science aren't the only subjects where American students are left in the backwaters of education. Finn and Dianne Ravitch, authors of *What Do Our Seventeen Year Olds Know?,* have shown that 43 percent of our high school seniors could not place World War I between 1900 and 1950. More than two-thirds of them did not know even the half-century in which the Civil War took place. And more than 75 percent were unable to say within twenty years when Abraham Lincoln was President.

One-third of high school students tested in 1986 did not know that the Declaration of Independence marked the American colonists' break from England. Sixty percent did not know that *The Federalist Papers* was written to urge ratification of the Constitution, and 40 percent could not say even approximately when the Constitution was written and ratified. Only three students in five were able to recognize a definition of the system of checks and balances that divides power among the three branches of our federal government.

According to an NAEP [National Assessment of Educational Progress] -based survey of 21- to 25-year-olds conducted in 1986, fewer than 40 percent were able to interpret an article by a newspaper columnist. And the situation is worse among minorities; just one in ten black young adults and two in ten Hispanic young adults can satisfactorily interpret the same newspaper column. In 1989, *National Geographic* did a survey of geography knowledge. Americans aged eighteen to twenty-four finished *last* among ten countries, including Mexico.

Yet in Chicago and in cities and state capitals all across America, instead of rolling up their sleeves and beginning the hard task of improving education, the education establishment—that wide array of professional organizations putatively representing teachers, administrators, and other educators—by and large offers a steady stream of defenses, denials, ultimatums, and repeated calls

for more money. Many of these education bureaucrats, or "educrats," have abdicated their responsibility; they should abdicate their authority as well. The few who occasionally break rank and point to problems in the system are usually quickly brought back into line or punished. Too often this education establishment itself is the single greatest obstacle to sound education reform.

When I was in Chicago, I said it was time to challenge the unions, and to "explode the 'blob'"—the bloated education bureaucracy, that ever-increasing population of nonteaching personnel. Whether enrollment declines or increases, the blob always grows—setting new guidelines, rules, procedures, and thereby helping to destroy the capacity of schools and communities to run their own schools free of interference. All school districts have a blob, and together they make the American Education Blob. It may be staffed by fine, well-intentioned people, but when they act together, it is a powerful obstacle to educational achievement and school and parental autonomy.

Unfortunately, much of the education establishment, which includes the unions and other "professional" educational organizations, opposes every common-sense reform measure: competency testing for teachers, opening the teaching profession to knowledgeable individuals who have not graduated from "schools of education," performance-based pay, holding educators accountable for how much children learn, an end to tenure, a national examination to find out exactly how much our children know, and parental choice of schools. These are reforms most Americans endorse and are all initiatives that I endorsed or proposed legislatively while I was Secretary of Education. It should come as no surprise, then, that I found myself in constant friction with the education establishment. If you cut through all of the cant and self-justifying rhetoric, you will confront this hard reality: the education establishment opposes reform because it is interested in maintaining *power.* It will fight to expand that power, and it will fight ferociously any attempt to rein it in. In the end, our children pay the highest price. That

I would clash with these special interests was thus inevitable. Our clashes became a major feature of my tenure.

So it went. For three and a half years, my efforts to challenge American education met well-organized institutional resistance, most often from the educational establishment: teacher unions, education lobbyists, and bureaucrats—all groups skilled at the exercise of narrow, self-interested political power. Early on, their opposition appeared as a form of denial—the schools were not so bad as they seemed. A little later, the opposition took a different tack, admitting that things might be bad, but insisting that they could not be fixed in or by the schools—that first "society" or "the system" must be altered. More recently we heard what might be called opposition by extortion, the false claim that fixing our schools would require a fortune in new funding.

But the fundamental problem with American education today is not lack of money; we do not underspend, we underproduce. A review of some 150 studies shows no correlation between spending and educational achievement. The American people have been remarkably generous in their contributions to our schools. In 1990 we spent $414 billion on education, roughly $140 billion more than on national defense. In the international competition on education spending, the United States wins the gold medal. In absolute terms we spend more on education than any other nation in the world. And expenditures keep climbing. In 1950, we spent (in 1989 dollars) $1,333 per student. In 1989, we spent $4,931. As John Silber, the president of Boston University, has written, "It is troubling that this nearly fourfold increase in real spending has brought no improvement. It is scandalous that it has not prevented substantial decline." During that period we probably experienced the *worst* educational decline in our history. Between 1963 and 1980, for example, combined average Scholastic Aptitude Test (SAT) scores—scores which test students' verbal and math abilities—fell 90 points, from 980 to 890. . . .

The more I visited schools the more I deviated from the Washington/education establishment orthodoxy. Seeing outstanding schools in action makes it clear why they succeed: *local people, leadership, community commitment,* and *shared values,* not federal tutelage.

From time to time we provided the media with lists of schools that work. Those who wished to find out the possibilities of American education, or who thought it couldn't be done, needed only to visit these schools and see for themselves. You can't learn it, you can't know it, simply by the aggregate numbers or the studies. To the doubters, to cynics, to the no-can-doers, you need to repeat what I once heard a parent say to her child about a school: "You go there and then you *will* learn."

In my trips I came across men and women who deserve to be regarded as true American heroes. They are for the most part quiet, unsung heroes. But for the work they do and the lives they change, we can all be grateful. Thankfully, many of their communities already are. There's no exact "blueprint" of what makes for an outstanding teacher; great teaching and great leadership come in all styles. But these teachers and principals are people of good character, committed to academic excellence, and have a genuine regard for the well-being of children.

Ted Yanak, an eighth-grade teacher of American history and government at Miller Junior High in West San Jose, California, had a classroom covered, plastered, and overwhelmed with clippings, posters, and campaign paraphernalia—buttons, hats, and bumper stickers. At a meeting with students, parents, and teachers, he was singled out by the principal to thunderous applause. He frequently appeared at these events dressed in a bright red jacket, blue pants, red-white-and-blue shoes, a flag-print tie, and a tricolor hat. He gives his heart to his students and he works them hard. They learn their history, and they repay him with their affection, appreciation, and achievement born of effort equal to his.

Carolyn Oubray, a self-composed young professional, teaches English the old-fashioned way to young black women at Xavier High School in New Orleans. In her senior class on

Edgar Allan Poe, Elayne and I witnessed her stress "disciplined thinking and disciplined analysis" to her students. They responded with thoughtful, disciplined answers. Xavier has a traditional curriculum, heavy on the basic disciplines. Later, Mrs. Oubray and her principal proudly explained to us that the uniformed, well-educated students of Xavier made something good of their lives.

"You won't find many Xavier girls on welfare, and you won't find them having babies as teen-agers because they have nothing else to do," she told us. Elayne was pleased to hear that. She directs a program in Washington, D.C., called "Best Friends," aimed at encouraging young women to remain abstinent while in school. Her program works and so does the regime at Xavier, and with the same effect. "Our girls have plenty to do," Oubray told us, "and they graduate from here and make good lives for themselves. And when they get married and have children, they send their daughters here."

In the end, it is people like this—the individual principal, teacher, superintendent, parent, and citizen—who make all the difference in our schools. "In every case there was someone who took a personal interest in children and their future," I once told a group of business leaders. "Not a government, but a *face*. Such people are like guardian angels we used to hear about in school—close by, watching, helping you and expecting you to do your best."

I told the audience about businessman Eugene Lang, who spoke at the sixth-grade graduation in his old Harlem elementary school and promised each child $2,000 toward college tuition. Most of the children who remained in that district stayed in school to accept the offer, thwarting a 40 percent dropout rate. The $2,000 that each youngster received was roughly the amount of a federal Pell Grant. "But our Pell Grants don't motivate like Eugene Lang motivates," I told them. The difference was personal encouragement and support.

This, then, is the iron law of education: the "system" doesn't educate anyone. Individuals do. Yeats wrote, "All the drop-scenes drop at once / Upon a hundred thousand stages," and it is on those individual stages that the educational dream fails or succeeds. In our time there are a few well-known giants on the school stage. I went to their classrooms to see what all the excitement was about and whether the accolades were merited. They were.

Topics for Discussion and Writing

1. Outline Kozol's and Bennett's causal analyses of the problems of inner-city schools in Chicago and elsewhere, and what you see as their main points of disagreement. With reference to "A Semantic Calculator for Bias in Rhetoric," what significant arguments on the opposing side does each **downplay** or ignore altogether?

2. With reference to "Predictable Patterns of Political Rhetoric" in chapter 13, what left-versus-right oppositions do these two articles illustrate, and how well do they support these lines of argument?

3. Bennett asserts "The fundamental problem with American education today is not lack of money," and argues that a large increase in national spending on education—to $4,931 per student in 1989—was followed by a drastic decline in test scores. Might this be a **reductive fallacy** ignoring other possible causes? Kozol's figures, moreover, suggest that this *average* does not factor in the large funding discrepancies between wealthy, mostly white school districts and poor, mostly minority ones. Bennett also does not say whether his figures on "national spending" include private as well as public schools or spending on higher education; nor does he address the historical and current socioeconomic conditions

that, according to Kozol and "A Historical-Causal Analysis of 'The White Problem,'" are the main causes of these discrepancies. (Bennett's book contains no documentation for these statistics, so for a research project you might search for studies that provide data on these subjects, at the time he was writing in 1991 and up to the present.) What do you think Bennett would see as the relationship, and relative importance, of these problems and "the education establishment"? Does Kozol perhaps ignore the negative influence of the groups Bennett criticizes in the inner-city schools he discusses? How much power would they seem to have, positively or negatively, in dealing with the financial and socioeconomic injustices Kozol describes?

4. Bennett's two **anecdotes** about successful schools are among several he presents as examples of inner-city schools in which skilled, enthusiastic teachers and principals overcome negative circumstances. (Bennett fails to identify Xavier High in New Orleans as a private, Catholic school, receiving funding from the Church, charging tuition, being selective in admitting and dismissing students, and not allowing teachers' unions. Might this omission cast a different light on his use of it as a positive example for public schools?) Kozol presents a similar case about teacher Corla Hawkins, but he argues that such cases represent an **inadequate sampling** or **argument from the exception**, because "the problems are systemic" and cannot be overcome systemically or reliably by individual effort; nor should the burden be put on individual teachers to prevail against a system in which the deck is stacked economically against them and their students, and in favor of those in wealthy, white school districts. (The primacy of individual effort or of systemic injustices is a recurrent, general point of opposition between conservatives and liberals in addressing socioeconomic problems; in the outlines of arguments at the end of chapter 16, see Conservative #5 and Leftist #3.) Compare the evidence Kozol presents here with Bennett's throughout the rest of *The De-Valuing of America* to judge which of their generalizations on this point are better argued. [*Irony Alert:* Kozol's paragraph beginning "The rationale behind ..." summarizes conservative arguments like Bennett's, and many students are predisposed to read this as Kozol's opinion. How do Kozol's following paragraphs **refute** these arguments?]

5. Bennett sees the main source of opposition to educational reform as "the education establishment—that wide array of professional organizations putatively representing teachers, administrators, and other educators," including "the unions" and "the bloated education bureaucracy, that ever-increasing population of nonteaching personnel." Speculate, in terms of the opposing lines of causal analysis, on why the same forces don't seem to present a large problem in the high-achieving, better-funded suburban schools Kozol describes. Does Bennett imply that teachers or their unions and administrators and other nonteaching personnel form part of a homogeneous "blob"? How does this equation account for the fact that teachers are employees while administrators are management (hence tending to be more conservative), so that the two groups are often in conflict, with unions representing teachers against management? Do some research on the extent to which these groups are united or opposed, and on which are most influential in determining educational policy.

6. The reforms advocated by Bennett and other conservative leaders include "competency testing for teachers, opening the teaching profession to knowledgeable individuals who have not graduated from 'schools of education,' performance-based pay, holding educators accountable for how much children learn, an end to

tenure, a national examination to find out exactly how much our children know, and parental choice of schools." What effect do you see the implementation of these policies—along with a voucher system facilitating parental choice of private schools (like Xavier High), which Bennett has actively promoted—having on the inner-city schools and neighborhoods Kozol describes? (Read more conservative sources to see what they say about incentives for private schools—especially for-profit ones, which Bennett has also promoted—to locate in inner cities.) None of these policies involve a substantial general increase in funding for schools of the kind Kozol advocates. Is Bennett's implication that these measures would negate any need to change the financial discrepancies between wealthy and poor districts? Can you defend this position?

7. Bennett **plays up** the negative influence of liberal **special interest** groups in education. What conservative special interests might be involved in issues like vouchers and systems of for-profit private schools?

8. Conservatives like Bennett point to polls showing that many parents in inner cities support vouchers for private schools because they would prefer to take their children out of failing public schools. Liberals respond that this reasoning involves several causal fallacies: treating symptoms without providing a cure for the root problem (inadequately funded schools), blaming the victim, and a vicious circle in which the flight of better-motivated students out of failing public schools will contribute to their further failure. Debate the pros and cons of these opposing positions.

9. To what extent do Kozol's and Bennett's analyses present **either-or thinking**? Write a paper, perhaps drawing on **Rogerian argument**, that imagines solutions combining elements from both sides and rejecting none from either. See the chapter on education in Barack Obama's book *The Audacity of Hope* for an analysis that does combine both viewpoints, without direct reference to Kozol or Bennett.

CHAPTER **12**

Uses and
Misuses of
Emotional Appeal

The term **emotional appeal** is sometimes used in rhetoric textbooks with a negative **connotation**, as a form of fallacy, but that is misleading. Emotional appeal is by no means always, or even usually, incompatible with logical reasoning in argumentation. The most eloquent expressions of humanity throughout history have appealed to feeling as well as to reason: "Give me liberty, or give me death," "We have nothing to fear but fear itself," "I have a dream." Emotional appeal is acceptable and even admirable when it is fully warranted by the facts (either as generally agreed on or as established through evidence) and reasoned analysis of the situation; it only becomes fallacious when it becomes a *substitute* for a well-supported argument and distracts attention from the weakness of a poorly supported one, as a form of **evading the issue**. It is often a tricky judgment call, however, to determine when an emotional appeal is justified and when it isn't, and the **ESBYODS principle** comes strongly into play here, inclining us all to judge that such an appeal is justified whenever it is on our own side and fallacious whenever it is on the other.

APPEALS TO "CLEANS" AND "DIRTIES"

Emotional appeals are sometimes categorized as either "appeal to pity" or "appeal to fear," but this oversimplifies the range of emotions in both categories; a broader way of dividing them might be to separate them into semantic **"cleans,"** words connoting positive emotions, and **"dirties,"** those connoting negative emotions. "Clean" appeals evoke not only pity but also patriotism, religion, children and family, the elderly and disabled, romantic love, cute animals, "America, Mom, and apple pie." **Sentimentality** is a word applied to an appeal to such emotions that we sense is manipulative or out of proportion to reality, laid on too heavily, to the point of being "corny" or "sappy." Again, however, we constantly need to judge when an appeal to such emotions is warranted by the situation and when it goes over the edge into sentimentality. In Martin Luther King's 1963 "Letter from a Birmingham Jail" protesting segregated public facilities in Alabama, King describes one among the many personal effects of segregation on African Americans:

242

You suddenly find your tongue twisted and your speech stammering as you seek to explain to your six-year-old daughter why she can't go to the public amusement park that has just been advertised on television, and see tears welling up in her little eyes when she is told that Funtown is closed to colored children, and see the depressing clouds of inferiority begin to form in her little mental sky. (King, *Why We Can't Wait,* 22)

Is this passage overly sentimental? It can plausibly be argued that everything in it was warranted by the facts of the situation and that describing the devastating emotional effects of segregation constituted logically powerful evidence. On the other hand, it might be argued that King laid the emotion on a bit more than was necessary, as in twice using the adjective "little," and that his case would have been just as effective without the use of "little." What do you think?

"Dirty" appeals evoke "fear and loathing" of people who are evil, or "other"; such appeals are heavy on **name-calling**, frequently along with the whole range of logical fallacies and modes of deceptive reasoning surveyed throughout this book that serve to demonize opponents. Once again, however, name-calling in itself is not necessarily fallacious. Is it name-calling to say that Hitler, Stalin, Saddam Hussein, and Osama bin Laden were vicious, murderous tyrants? Yes, but it is almost universally agreed that these names are accurate. Name-calling only becomes fallacious, then, when it is applied to an opponent who does not manifestly deserve a "dirty" label, when it is not supported by adequate evidence, when it serves only as a smear instead of being part of a reasoned argument.

PUFF PIECES AND HATCHET JOBS

A stock form of journalistic article or book known in the trade as a "puff piece" is an uncritical promotion for the public figure it is written about, making him or her appear unrealistically virtuous or glamorous. Puff pieces are either designed by public relations (PR) agencies hired by the subject, with the cooperation of editors, or written at the initiative of the editors themselves to make the subject look good for one reason or another—political sympathies, possible advertising revenue if the subject is a businessperson, cronyism with the medium's executives, and so on. Puff pieces are the verbal counterpart to, and are often accompanied by, photos or sketches touched up to make the subject look unrealistically attractive and benevolent, like the official portraits of Communist dictators—rosy-cheeked, twinkly-eyed "Uncle Joe" Stalin, Chairman Mao, or "Comrade Fidel" kissing babies.

A similar portrait of investor Bunker Hunt for the cover story in the *Saturday Evening Post,* written by Holly G. Miller, included in this chapter, depicts Hunt as younger than his years, thinner than his 250 pounds, and uncharacteristically healthy complexioned and smiling. Hunt and his brother Lamar inherited a multibillion-dollar fortune from their father, H. L. Hunt, an oil wildcatter and commodities speculator whose eccentricities included bigamy. (The Texas Hunts were the model for the Ewings on *Dallas,* though the television show's characters were depicted, with typical media sentimentality, as considerably better looking and more glamorous than the stodgy Hunts.) In 1979 the Hunt brothers illegally tried to corner the silver market—that is, to buy up the major share of the world's silver supply—so that the scarcity of the commodity would cause its value to skyrocket, at once benefiting from the inflation that was at a peak then and also causing further inflation. Early in 1980, silver prices reached their peak, increasing to nine times their level a year before, but then the market collapsed, drastically reducing the Hunts' net worth, estimated to be in the range of $7 billion to $14 billion. The Hunts were convicted of racketeering, fined $10 million for fraudulent trading by the Commodities Futures Trading Commission and $130 million in a civil lawsuit for defrauding the Peruvian government's mineral marketing company, and required by the Internal Revenue Service to pay multimillion-dollar back taxes. However, the *Saturday Evening Post* article, which appeared in 1985 after most of these events, contains no hint of this history, which is strikingly conspicuous by its absence. Without knowing exactly how the article came to be published in this form, we can recognize in it the classic traits of a puff piece, presenting Bunker Hunt as little less than a saint, and it resembles the kind of article typically initiated by a public relations agency hired by wealthy figures to polish up a tarnished public image.

The opposite of a puff piece is a "hatchet job" or a "hit piece," an article or book calculated to smear and **play up** everything unfavorable to its subject and **downplay** or suppress anything favorable, often with malicious and deceptive intent. (Another word for speech or writing that employs the insulting, abusive style of the hatchet job is **invective**, discussed further in chapter 15.) In *Blinded by the Right,* David Brock, recanting his earlier journalistic efforts as a conservative, explicitly describes his books and articles on Anita Hill and Bill and Hillary Clinton as hit pieces and asserts that this kind of malicious invective is deliberately encouraged in conservative journalistic circles, more so than in liberal ones.

Bunker Hunt's Greatest Investment

Holly G. Miller

Saturday Evening Post, January–February 1985

In rumpled pin stripes and disheveled dress shirt, Nelson Bunker Hunt takes a pool-side seat among the bronzed and briefed sun worshipers of southern Arizona. He nods when someone inquires, from across a gin and tonic, if his three-piece suit feels comfortable under the desert rays.

"These are my resort clothes," he deadpans.

If the jacket looks oversized, it's because Hunt recently embarked on a trim-down-shape-up program that calls for time on a treadmill and slow jogs around his sprawling Texas ranch. Shoehorning an exercise regimen into his jammed work schedule wasn't easy. As one of America's richest men, Hunt has never placed leisure activity at the top of his priority list—at least not when the phone is ringing, a meeting has to be chaired or a decision needs to be made.

But at age 58, he's doing better. Although he expertly side-steps the question of retirement, he explains his workday is shorter now—6 a.m. to 6 p.m.—and more and more details are being delegated to his lieutenants.

"Really, I don't work as hard as I should," he insists. "There are some things I don't en-

joy doing, businesswise, so I'm directing my attention to what I like to do and less to the drudgery part. In that respect, I'm probably looking for the easier life."

For Hunt, that translates into football—brother Lamar owns the Kansas City Chiefs—his classical-art collection and his thoroughbred horses. He is respected around the world as a breeder and owner of race horses and trains them in Kentucky, France, Ireland, Australia, New Zealand and Texas. Thoroughbreds in the Hunt stable have won 100 major stakes races in seven countries, and his prize filly, Dahlia, has earned more than $1.5 million in five years.

"He's very sports-minded," says his secretary, Jo Gilmore. "I'm amazed that after a grueling day at the office, rather than go home and watch television, he's ready to attend a sports event. He's so curious about everything—especially people. He's the kind of person who passes a box on a table and is compelled to open it."

The combination of investment savvy, curiosity and appreciation for fine antiques has led him to acquire enviable collections of rare painted vases and gold, silver and bronze coins that date back to early Egypt, Rome and Greece. More contemporary *objets d'art,* particularly equestrian sculpture and paintings, decorate his plush offices on the 24th floor of the Thanksgiving Tower.

In spite of the valuable trappings around him Hunt describes himself as "a man of little vanity," and seems to have no idea of the influence he commands. His demeanor is the comfortable-as-an-old-shoe variety, hardly smacking of the spit-and-shine discipline he struggled with as a student at Culver Military Academy. He spent three years at the venerable Indiana institution, cringes at memories of his attempts to conform to the strict rules—yet those memories are fond enough that he was shocked when his alma mater went coed several years ago.

"I liked it," he insists. "But I wasn't a very good military person. I didn't shine my shoes too well or keep my clothes as spotless as they should be. Culver was so strict that later, when I joined the Navy, it seemed like a picnic in comparison. The staff at military school used to write to parents every few weeks to tell them how their sons were doing. I don't think my letters were all that complimentary. My mother got tired of reading about my problems."

He credits his mother with being a key influence in his life. Not only did she help mold his personality first by exposing him to (and then rescuing him from) the rigors of Culver's field artillery troop, but she instilled in him her own concern and appreciation for people. She guided his education from the disciplined Hoosier military setting to Pennsylvania's very proper Hill School, to the University of Texas, to Southern Methodist University. Along the way he mingled with a smorgasbord of people and learned, by his mother's example, to blend with every mix.

"In a way, my mother was the most democratic person I ever knew," he says of Lyda Bunker Hunt. "It didn't matter to her if a person were the king of England, a cabdriver or a waiter. She treated them all in the same polite manner. To this day I'll have people I don't even know come up to me and say they never met a lady with a finer personality and more kindly manner. I think that's

remarkable because she's been gone since 1955. That's almost 30 years now.

In their mother's memory, Bunker and his six brothers and sisters donated $3.5 million to underwrite a new building for the Dallas Highland Park Presbyterian Church's expansion program.

Oil wildcatter H. L. Hunt was the richest man in America when he died in 1974. He left $2 billion to his offspring. That legacy has mushroomed, thanks in part to Bunker's business acumen. His success is reflected in his various titles: chairman, Hunt Energy Corporation, Hunt International Resources Corporation and Hunt Electronics Corporation; president/director of numerous companies in countries where Hunt interests actively pursue searches for oil, gas, coal and geothermal energy; past chairman, Texas Bible Society; past chairman, executive committee, Here's Life campaign, Campus Crusade for Christ; past president, Council for National Policy.

If business titles can be traced to his father, his zeal for good works is a result of his mother's influence. He is an outspoken Christian, a longtime member of the Presbyterian Church, who quietly investigates and then invests generously in evangelical causes. He recalls no dramatic conversion experience as a child, but claims what he learned in conventional Sunday School classes in Tyler, Texas, always underscored at home by his mother.

"She was probably more instrumental in my Christian commitments than my father was, although in the latter 20 years of his life my father was a strong believer," said Bunker. "My mother's best friend in Tyler was a wonderful Christian lady named Mrs. Wilcox. Her sons were grown and off to college, so she used to invite me to spend time at her house. She knew the Bible better than any preacher I ever remember; she really got me interested in spiritual things."

He approaches religion almost academically, claiming the bible is "the finest historical document" available. Although he occasionally makes reference to a Biblical passage in conversation, he downplays his knowledge by apologizing for his loose

paraphrase which, more often than not, is King James verbatim. He prefers to live his faith rather than to talk about it, never smokes and rarely drinks—"I think I'm a little allergic to it," he confides—and leaves any evangelizing to the brethren with the theological degrees.

"I don't know that I'd be a very good one-on-one witnesser, although I occasionally talk to a friend," he says. "Maybe I do my witnessing through helping some organizations. That could be the easy way out, and I don't now if it's Biblical or not, but if it helps bring a few people to the Kingdom, so much the better."

His favorite causes run the gamut from the STEP Foundation (Strategies to Elevate People), which is geared to helping urban minorities, to Campus Crusade, the fundamentalist effort to strengthen Christian principles in college-age students. He's been an advocate of the Campus Crusade ministry for 20 years and has watched the organization grow from its founding on eight or ten campuses to its current presence in more than 100 countries and on every major campus in the United States. His belief in the campus ministry led him to provide $5.5 million to underwrite the Film *Jesus,* released in 1979 and distributed by Warner Brothers.

"The Campus Crusade and Here's Life people felt it would be a tremendous evangelical tool, that no comparable film could do what this movie could do," he says. "I kept hearing about it and finally decided I'd help them make it. I think now it's available in 60 or 80 languages and is being shown all over the world. I've heard of places where 5,000 see the film and afterward, 2,500 accept Christ. I'm glad it's worked out so well. If I don't do anything else, maybe that's something worthwhile that I've done."

While he prefers to maintain a low profile himself, he keeps in close contact with highly visible evangelists such as Pat Robertson and Jerry Falwell. He tracks their efforts and boasts of their accomplishments.

"I'm no great church historian but the pendulum swings, and right now there's a tremendous acceptance for the gospel. Jerry Falwell told me the other day that his theological school is producing 250 graduates a year and each graduate will go out and start a church or school. Of course organizations like Pat Robertson's are doing so much good and reaching so many people on television. In this country we had gone so far toward the agnostic and atheistic side that we had to experience a revulsion. I think a lot of politicians are surprised at the depth of religious interest and beliefs. If America survives it will be because of its return to Christian beliefs."

He hopes the trend toward religious evangelism and political conservatism will eliminate legal abortion and curb the government's welfare program. He's a vocal opponent of both and expresses disbelief at one and dismay at the other. His fondness for children colors these feelings: "How can anyone justify taking a baby's life?" he asks; and, "Sure, a lot of worthy people—children in particular—need assistance, but I think America would be better off if the churches and individuals supplied the help."

To support his beliefs he cites examples from personal experience. He recalls, as a boy growing up in Arkansas and Texas, watching as neighbors pitched in to help a member of the community who was in financial difficulty. To underscore the need to trim welfare, he tells of owning a ranch adjacent to an Indian reservation. He claims many Indians have lost their initiative because of too many government giveaways of too much cash. Again, he advocates less federal aid and more involvement by the private sector.

Such comments, often quoted in the media, evoke a deluge of requests for donations. Hunt admits to being solicited by more good causes than he can afford, and he's devised some loose guidelines to help him pick the recipients of his contributions.

"Basically, I don't give to 'individual situations,'" he explains. "I'm very sympathetic, I hear heart-rendering stories, but there's no way I can help them. So, I give to a few organizations; that's the best I can do, and I hope the organizations will do well with my donations."

He refutes the notion that wealthy industrialists like Bunker Hunt have a social responsibility to give away a certain portion of their earnings. No one tells Bunker Hunt when, why and how much he's going to give in support of worthy charities. He makes his own decisions and is not influenced by persons advocating that he has an obligation to share his fortune.

"I suspect I've contributed as much or more than anyone around," he says. "I enjoy giving to causes I believe in, but I certainly don't give to them because I think it's my social responsibility. Of course there are liberal folks who imply such an obligation exists, but most of them won't contribute any of their own money. They want the government to do it. They try to give a guilt complex to anyone who works hard to produce something that's valuable. Well, I think that's a phony situation. I'm probably overly generous to a lot of causes, but I don't think that makes me any better, and I don't think I do it because I feel any sort of obligation."

His candor borders on outspokenness and when taken out of context by media interviewers results in a less-than-accurate portrayal of the man. He is neither materialistic nor pompous. His modest wardrobe is purchased off the rack, he drives his own car and when he travels by air he specifies coach rather than first-class. Unlike many colleagues in his income bracket, he prefers to mingle with the crowd at large social gatherings rather than seal himself off with a phalanx of security guards. But if his image has suffered at the hands of magazine and newspaper biographers who attempt to "capture" him in 2,000 words or less and emphasize his vast holdings, he harbors no grudges. Even when offered the opportnity to counter the misconceptions, he shrugs and declines.

Nelson Bunker Hunt testifying in Congressional hearings on his illegal activities in trying to corner the world silver market. (Photo: *Time*)

"I really don't care. I accept the media for what they are, as they are ... which is not very favorable where I'm concerned. I don't expect a good press; in fact, I have a saying I think is accurate: The press can make a heel out of a hero or a hero out of a heel. We see this happen every day. That may be overstated or oversimplified, but journalists have the power to paint any picture they desire."

More important to him than building a positive public image is maintaining the solid personal rapport he and his wife, Caroline, enjoy with their son, 3 daughters and 12 grandchildren. Although Bunker jokingly accuses Caroline of being an "overzealous grandmother," he credits her with adding softness to his strict child-rearing philosophy. Among the results has been a mutual respect on the part of parents and children. This relationship Hunt has every intention of exploring and savoring.

"I'd say my priorities right now are to enjoy life, my children, my grandchildren, my friends, and to stay healthy," he stresses.

Interestingly, he doesn't mention acquiring more money. Or oil. Or silver. Or real estate.

"Being financially rich or financially poor can't be compared with being happy," he says. "Some of the happiest people you'll meet are some of the poorest. I've observed that most groups of wealthy people are sort of miserable. They sit around and worry about their money and the problems it causes. Me? I've never been much of a worrier."

Neither has he been one to sit around. In spite of his efforts to shorten his workday, delegate authority and schedule more leisure time with his family, he can't be expected to retire to a neutral corner of his mammoth Texas ranch now that the causes he champions are coming into vogue. He greets society's swing back to basics with what his friends in the news media might label "cautious optimism."

"I'm encouraged about the increased spiritual awareness because if we have a good spiritual atmosphere in the world, the political situation will improve too. When the people are good, we have good government. Yes, we're getting better ... at least I hope so."

Does he expect, as a longtime proponent of conservatism, to enjoy new clout in his spiritually aware atmosphere? Will he, for instance, command the ear of the President 24 hours a day? The questions bring a slow smile and spark his quick wit: "I've never seen fit to talk to the President … or vice versa," he quips.

Which is the more social version of another favorite response, usually reserved for his pals, the media: No comment.

Topics for Discussion and Writing

1. How does the author, Holly Miller, attempt by **implication** and hints **between the lines** to gloss over (1) Hunt's fraudulent activities in silver trading, (2) his weight, (3) his father's bigamy, (4) the fact that Hunt is so wealthy that he has no need to "work" as working is usually conceived?

2. The article emphasizes Hunt's ownership of thoroughbred horses, rare art, and rare coins. These happen to be three kinds of investment favored by the very wealthy because **special interest** legislation has provided tax advantages for them and because their appreciation in resale value has far outstripped the rate of inflation (i.e., they are good "hedges against inflation"). How does the article put a favorable spin on these investments by Hunt?

3. Enumerate some of the many examples of how the article downplays the immense wealth and power of Hunt and his family, depicting them as **plain folks**.

4. To what extent would you argue that Hunt's charitable activities, support of the Campus Crusade for Christ, and other religious commitments offset his devious financial dealings? What arguments can be made for and against the consistency of those financial dealings with the teachings of the New Testament about wealth and poverty? Might this be a case of **compartmentalized thinking** and **rationalization**?

5. Read the "Guide to Political Terms and Positions" in chapter 13 and note the ways in which Hunt's views about government policies on wealth and poverty exemplify the conservative positions outlined there. What evidence do he and Miller provide that would be useful to cite as source material in support of the conservative position? Does the fact that he was born a billionaire enhance or diminish his qualifications to speak as an authority on the behavior of poor people? Could his views on these topics be interpreted as **special pleading**? Likewise, in the outlines at the end of chapter 16 do you think what he says about his charitable activities provides better support for the Conservative Position (#8, 11, and 12) or the Liberal Position (19, 20)?

6. "Pictures don't lie." Analyze the two pictures of Bunker Hunt, one a photo, the other a sketch, as examples of the subjectivity of **viewpoint** in the use of pictures in journalism: their selection by an editor to create a favorable or unfavorable image, the particular details that contribute to that image, and so on. Can you judge which picture of Hunt is more accurate?

PREDICTABLE PATTERNS OF WARTIME RHETORIC: APPEALS TO FEAR AND PITY

> Naturally, the common people do not want war … but after all, it is the leaders of a country who determine policy, and it is always a simple matter to drag the people along, whether it is a democracy, or a fascist dictatorship, or a parliament, or a communist dictatorship. All you have to do is tell them they are being attacked, and denounce the pacifists for lack of patriotism and exposing the country to danger. It works the same in every country.
> —*Hermann Goering, Minister of War in Nazi Germany*

> Patriotism is the last refuge of a scoundrel.
> —*Samuel Johnson, eighteenth-century English essayist and poet*

> We're in a bigger, better war for our patriotic pastime.
> We don't know what we're fighting for, but we didn't know the last time.
> —*George and Ira Gershwin, "Strike Up the Band" (1937)*

> Where have all the soldiers gone, long time passing, where have all the soldiers gone, long time ago?

> Where have all the soldiers gone? Gone to graveyards every one. When will they ever learn? When will they ever learn?
> —*Pete Seeger, "Where Have All the Flowers Gone?" (1961)*

Since September 11, 2001, appeal to fear has been the dominant tone of American public discourse. Fear of another terrorist attack was George W. Bush's administration's major justification for the war on Iraq and the major theme of his reelection campaign in 2004. The sheer, indisputable evil of Al Qaeda's attacks on America, and the fear that they would be repeated, understandably made Americans long for strong, resolute leadership, an effective retaliation for 9/11, and assurance against further attacks. So the Bush administration benefited from a great deal of public suspension of skeptical doubt stemming from wishful thinking that the president had the "war on terror" under control. In any such situation, however, blind, wishful trust accorded to the leader presents the danger that a less than wholly virtuous administration might manipulate both the fear and the trust for its own, partisan advantage. Likewise, the Iraq war was presented as a retaliation for 9/11 and preventative action against recurrence of terrorist attacks and was justified by claims about Saddam Hussein's weapons of mass destruction and ties to Al Qaeda. Whether the war was in fact an effective deterrent or an act prompted by emotional wishful thinking and faulty intelligence information leading to a fiasco with the **ironic** consequence of increasing the likelihood of terrorism is a matter of fierce disagreement at this writing, in the midst of the 2008 election campaign, and it undoubtedly will continue to be well into the future. So the rhetorical issue is the extent to which the Bush administration's appeals to fear, to pity for the victims of 9/11 and the American troops fighting in Iraq, and to patriotism were justified by the realities or were devices to keep that administration and the Republican Party in office and to intimidate their opponents or critics. The larger question is the extent to which, in the light of past history, political leaders can be expected to use appeals to fear and pity to wage, or respond to, wars honestly or dishonestly. This section will explore that and related issues.

War Destroys Truth and Memory

A familiar saying is that the first casualty in every war is truth. The selling of wars nearly always depends on lies about the true nature of war. Wars throughout history, even the most justifiable ones like World War II, have brought out subhuman behavior in many individuals in every country that takes part in them—side by side with acts of great heroism and self-sacrifice, to be sure. The gruesome flesh-and-blood realities of war belie the high-minded, flag-waving ideals that tend to blind the masses who rally to "support our troops," a point made eloquently in Mark Twain's "The War Prayer."

To begin with, war destroys historical memory. The intensity of emotion provoked by every war is so great that the natural human inclination is for individuals to perceive each war as unique and unprecedented, and that is invariably the way it is presented by every warring country's government and media. In the manner Mark Twain depicts in "The War Prayer" (prompted by the Spanish-American War), later in this chapter, when people get caught up in "war fever," they lose all perspective. The consequence is that the same tragic mistakes can be repeated over and over again with each new war, and all too often, as Goering noted, unscrupulous rulers are able to manipulate the populace into uncritically supporting a war, just or not, while anyone who critically questions the war or tries to provide some historical perspective is denounced as unpatriotic or even treasonous. Historically, it has often been writers, artists, scholars, and other intellectuals who have raised critical questions about impending wars; they are invariably reviled at the time, yet history has often proved them to be in the right.

The agonizing problem here is precisely that in historical perspective some wars have been judged to be just and others unjust. In American history the Revolutionary War, the Civil War, World War II, the Korean War, and the war in Afghanistan have been almost unanimously regarded as just, but the Mexican-American and Spanish-American wars, World War I, the Vietnam War, the Persian Gulf War, and the Iraq war have all been strongly disputed at the time they occurred and subsequently. But whether a war is right or wrong, in America or in other countries, governments resort to the same emotional appeals and propagandistic rhetoric, as indicated by the quotation from Hermann Goering describing Hitler's incitement of the Germans to war. In Boswell's *Life of Johnson* in 1791, James Boswell famously quoted Samuel Johnson as saying, "Patriotism is the last refuge of a scoundrel." However, in an example of the fallacy of **quotation out of context**, Boswell's explanatory follow-up is rarely quoted: "But let it be considered, that he did not mean a real and generous love of our country, but that pretended patriotism which so many, in all ages and countries, have made a cloak for self-interest" (251). In other words, the cynical manipulation of appeals to patriotism (along with appeals to religion) is one of the most frequent tools of **demagogues**.

Every government in every war can be predicted to lie, or at least to resort to one-sided propaganda and semantic slanting that oversimplifies the issues in dispute, attributing totally virtuous motives to our side and totally evil ones to the enemy. The home country's armed forces will be called "our boys" and "our brave, patriotic troops." The other side's soldiers will never be referred to as "their boys" but labeled with depersonalizing phrases like "enemy forces." Nor can it ever be suggested that they might be equally brave and patriotic, that they have loved ones who grieve their deaths.

As George Orwell says in his essay "Politics and the English Language," the realities of war "are too brutal for most people to face, and ... do not square with the professed aims of political parties. Thus political language has to consist largely of euphemism, question-begging, and sheer cloudy vagueness" (256). So our news media suppress photos or footage of enemy bodies and, even more so, American bodies; nor are the bodies of civilian "collateral damage" shown. Whenever a gruesomely realistic photo does leak through the censorship screen into the mass media, people scream about this outrage to "decency." The section from Paul Fussell's book *The Real War 1939–1945* included in this chapter describes graphically the ghastly realities of war that governments and media euphemize, in a similar manner to Twain's "The War Prayer" nearly a century earlier.

In a column about the Iraq war in the *Chronicle of Higher Education* (April 16, 2004, online edition), titled "War Rhetoric's Toll on Democracy," Bruce A. Williams, a communications professor at the University of Illinois, discussed Harold Lasswell, the founder of the modern public relations industry in early twentieth-century America and an advocate of governmental propaganda:

> Lasswell argued that mobilizing public opinion through propaganda was a prerequisite for modern war, since conflict had become total, requiring conscript armies and the marshaling of a nation's entire resources. The justification for war had to be widely understandable and capable of fostering total popular commitment to the conflict. Since it's difficult to communicate to a mass audience the inevitably complex and usually debatable reasons for one nation's use of force against another, the leader of the enemy state must be used to stand for the entire nation and then demonized. Lasswell meant the term quite literally: The enemy leader must be portrayed as the incarnation of evil, the devil himself. Sound familiar? Just as Saddam Hussein became the personification of both Iraq and evil, so too was Kaiser Wilhelm used by Allied propagandists in World War I.

In every war there is profiteering by the corporations who provide weapons and other military matériel as well as contracting for reconstruction, and their lobbies often have close ties to government officials, to the point where they sometimes become the tail wagging the dog in determining military policy. And yet, no government will admit that profiteering is taking place or is influencing policy. (See "Government Public Relations; the Military-Industrial Media Complex" in chapter 15.) A presidential administration might exploit the public's psychological need to believe in its trustworthiness in order to push its partisan political agendas, having little or nothing to do with the war effort, through a Congress whose members are afraid to be branded unpatriotic if they vote against the president, and without critical scrutiny by news media, which are similarly intimidated.

Another predictable pattern in every side in every war is that the government will attempt to censor news of defeats suffered and blunders or atrocities committed by our military. It is always tempting to rationalize government lying, or at least secrecy, in war. We think, "Well, our leaders have secret information that we don't, and revealing the truth might tip our hand to the enemy." Or, alternately, we want to believe that we can trust our leaders to act in our interests because they have that secret information. Or, we believe that making unfavorable events public gives aid and comfort to the enemy. (So when in the Iraq war stories and photos came out showing gross American abuse of prisoners at Abu Ghraib prison, some conservatives complained that this news should have been suppressed.) All of these justifications might be true in any given case—but they also might *not* be true in any given case and leaders may simply be using them to cover up lies, blunders, criminal acts, or financial corruption. So none of these arguments should be accepted uncritically, without skeptically checking out the facts.

The History of War

Throughout all the centuries of history previous to our own age, wars were a constant in most societies, going back to prehistoric battles for survival, wars between adherents of opposing religious beliefs and denominations, fights for imperial conquest and booty, for extension of land in the formation of nations, or for corporate control of foreign natural resources and labor. Emperors, kings, and aristocrats waged wars for their personal vanity and machismo, forcing masses of their subjects into bloodbaths against the masses of their rivals' states, while the rulers usually stayed on the sidelines but got all the glory for victory. In these cases, wars played much the same role as sports do in our day; spectators held parties like today's tailgate parties while watching the battles of the American Civil War.

In every one of those wars, the masses have been incited by patriotic propaganda and high ideals about the glories of fighting for one's country, by demonization of the enemy, and by claims that God is on their side. Most of those wars have also been started by wealthy old men who personally benefited from them but who themselves often have been exempt from risking their lives in them, as have been their children. (Prominent exceptions to this rule have arguably included, in America, the Revolutionary War, the Civil War, and World War II, in which George Herbert Walker Bush and John F. Kennedy volunteered for combat—as did Kennedy's older brother, who died—along with several wealthy movie and sports stars. In the Vietnam War, John Kerry volunteered for combat, Al Gore was a frontline army journalist, and John McCain was a naval officer held captive by the North Vietnamese.) Those wars have been fought mainly by poor young men with few other options in life, usually drafted or in earlier ages kidnapped and forced into fighting, who have had nothing to gain personally from the war and have generally been regarded contemptuously by the rulers as "cannon fodder."

In America's most recent war at this writing, that in Iraq beginning in 2003, much has been made by political leaders and the media of our volunteer armed forces fighting out of patriotic motives. This was unquestionably true in many cases. But wouldn't a less sentimentalized view be that many, if not most, young people who joined the peacetime army did so primarily because they were poor and lacked many other opportunities, so military service offered them an education and job skills? (There were very few instances in this war of volunteers who were politically connected, wealthy, or prominent in show business and sports.) How many of them expected to find themselves in the Middle Eastern desert wearing combat gear in 110-degree heat, fighting an enemy whose very identity was unclear, and confronting a culture, language, and religion largely unknown to them, with a great deal of hostility toward America directed at them personally? The abuses at Abu Ghraib prison by American forces in 2003 reflected, to some extent, the lack of preparation of many rank-and-file personnel for dealing with war prisoners or with captives of such a different culture, most of whom turned out to have no connection to terrorism or Saddam Hussein. How many of those who volunteered for service would have done so if they had known what awaited them in Iraq?

Regardless of the grim, suppressed realities that have marked past wars and that persisted at some level in the Iraq war, it cannot be denied that September 11 confronted the United States with a warlike situation and a very real enemy, in Al Qaeda, different from any in our history, which created a legitimate cause for fear and demanded some kind of military response. The question then becomes whether the Bush administration's antiterrorism policies, in Iraq and elsewhere, were sincerely motivated and effective or were opportunistic and ineffective, which at this writing remains open to debate.

The Position of the Soldier

Emotional appeals in support of every war are keyed to sympathy for the members of our military forces, and they are frequently shown in interviews voicing their belief in the justice of the cause for which they have been called to fight. There is no denying the sacrifices that troops are called on to make, or the bravery and patriotism that many show. But are those fighting in a war objective sources of judgment on its justness? What is the situation of the typical combat soldier? (I will refer to "he" here for brevity, with the understanding that women are increasingly present on the front lines.) From the moment he begins training, generally speaking, he is not presented with a multiperspectival education on the complexities of right and wrong in the present war but is indoctrinated with one-sided propaganda about the rectitude of our country's cause and the villainy of our enemies, along with rigid requirements to follow orders and accept the hierarchy of command. (It was this reduction of soldiers to unthinking conformity that Thoreau criticized in "Civil Disobedience," studied in chapter 8.) Soldiers who might question these oversimplifications after what they see in combat are generally coerced into keeping quiet.

Moreover, soldiers and their families almost inevitably have an overwhelming emotional need to believe that the cause for which they are killing and dying is just. For them, as for citizens in general, the possibility that young men and women are being asked to die "in vain," in the cause of some political ruler's vanity, greed, or political advantage, is understandably unbearable. So an element of psychological denial of that possibility is almost certain to be the result, and anyone who publicly voices that possibility is almost certain to be fiercely resented.

The soldier is trained for combat by being turned into a brutal killer, with attitudes similar to those that characterize sociopathic criminals in civilian life. When stories come out about atrocities or torture by our forces, we pretend to be shocked at such "un-American" conduct, without acknowledging that such behavior may be the not-too-surprising extension of the brutality that is necessarily bred into fighting forces. The soldier has to be conditioned to dehumanize the soldiers on the opposing side into "dirty" animals who will kill him if he doesn't kill them. (In the musical comedy *Bye Bye Birdie,* a dimwitted rock star satirically modeled on Elvis Presley is drafted into the peacetime army in the 1950s. His managers exploit the occasion for publicity, and at a press conference he declares, "Gee, I can't wait to go over there and get me one of those dirty Jerries [Germans]—or whoever's dirty this time.") The soldier is not encouraged to understand that the soldiers on the other side are likely to have been conditioned in exactly the same way toward "those dirty Americans." So one soldier meets the other on the battlefield and, sure enough, there's that dirty enemy trying to kill him. They are intent on killing each other, perhaps without ever understanding that both are just following their orders and conditioning, with no personal cause for hatred toward one another.

Now, all of the above attitudes into which soldiers are indoctrinated might well be necessary in even the most honorable war. The point here is how many emotional forces can blind them, and the rest of us, and how difficult—though necessary—it is to resist those forces and try to form a more detached judgment on whether *this* war is just or unjust.

"We Support Our Troops"

Another pressure against critical thinking is "support our troops" slogans. The argument goes something like, "We could debate about whether this war was justified or not before it began, but now that our troops are in battle, we have to support them by showing a united front because dissension at home undermines troop morale and gives aid and comfort to the enemy." The problem with this thinking is that it can be exploited—and repeatedly has been throughout history—by unscrupulous rulers who know that once they start the war, they can use it to extort compliance and silence dissent.

A similar mind-set was attacked by Mark Twain in one of several of his criticisms of the Spanish-American War and the American military occupation of the Philippines from 1900 to 1906. In a situation that had possible parallels with the Iraq war, the United States supported Philippine independence from Spain, but American military forces aiding the rebels there stayed on after the Philippines gained independence and turned the country into an *American* colony. The American politicians and public, with wishful ethnocentrism, believed that the Filipinos would be grateful for our bringing them what Twain sarcastically called "The Blessings of Civilization Trust" ("trust" meaning a business monopoly), in much the same way the Bush administration predicted the Iraqis would be grateful for our overthrow of Saddam Hussein. However, the Filipinos rose up in resistance to the American occupation, and (in one of the more suppressed episodes in our history) American troops massacred upward of twenty thousand insurgents. In a fragment from an unfinished work titled "Glances at History" or "The Papers of the Adam Family," Twain writes, in terms reminiscent of Thoreau's "Civil Disobedience" half a century earlier:

> Against our traditions we are now entering upon an unjust and trivial war, a war against a helpless people, and for a base object—robbery. At first our citizens spoke out against this thing, by an impulse natural to their training. Today they have turned, and their voice is the other way. What caused the change? Merely a politician's trick—a high-sounding phrase, a blood-stirring phrase which turned their uncritical heads: *Our Country, right or wrong!* An empty phrase, a silly phrase. It was shouted by every newspaper, it was thundered from the pulpit, the Superintendent of Public Instruction placarded it in every schoolhouse in the land, the War Department inscribed it upon the flag. And every man who failed to shout it or who was silent, was proclaimed a traitor—none but those others were patriots. To be a patriot, one had to say, and keep on saying, "Our Country, right or wrong," and urge on the little war. Have you not perceived that that phrase is an insult to the nation?
>
> For in a republic, who *is* "the Country"? Is it the Government which is for the moment in the saddle? Why, the Government is merely a *servant*—merely a temporary servant; it cannot be its prerogative to determine what is right and what is wrong, and decide who is a patriot and who isn't. Its function is to obey orders, not originate them. Who, then, is "the Country"? Is it the newspaper? is it the pulpit? is it the school superintendent? Why, these are mere parts of the country, not the whole of it.... They are but one in the thousand; it is in the thousand that command is lodged; *they* must determine what is right and what is wrong; they must decide who is a patriot and who isn't....
>
> Each must for himself alone decide what is right and what is wrong, and which course patriotic and which isn't. You cannot shirk this and be a man. To decide it against your convictions is to be an unqualified, inexcusable traitor, both to yourself and to your country; men label you as they may. If you alone of all the nation decide one way, and that way be the right way according to your convictions of the right, you have done your duty by yourself and by your country—hold up your head! You have nothing to be ashamed of.
>
> The stupid phrase needed help, and it got another one: "Even if the war be wrong we are in it and must fight it out: *we cannot retire from it without dishonor.*" Why, not even a burglar could have said it better. We cannot withdraw from this sordid raid because to grant peace to those little people upon their terms—independence—would dishonor us. You have flung away Adam's phrase—you should take it up and examine it again. He said, *"An inglorious peace is better than a dishonorable war."* (108–109)

As Twain asked, if the motives of the government that starts a war are devious or if its tactics are a disaster, is it really a sign of patriotism or support of our troops not to question the government that has forced them into pointless slaughter, and not to try to stop the slaughter before it gets worse? Recent revelations about the Vietnam War indicate that both Presidents Lyndon Johnson and Richard Nixon (as well as Johnson's secretary of defense Robert McNamara, as revealed in his memoirs) realized that it had been a fatal mistake to get into it, but they were afraid they would lose face—and reelection—if they admitted as much publicly and withdrew. So they continued to send tens of thousands of American troops to their death and continue the death of hundreds of thousands of Vietnamese, just because they couldn't admit they were wrong. Furthermore, the war policies of incumbent presidents are frequently influenced by upcoming elections; so whether soldiers and civilians live or die may be determined by cynical calculations of what will get the incumbent reelected.

"God Is on Our Side"

One of the most extreme instances of ethnocentrism is the belief by virtually every country or faction in every war throughout history that God is on its side. The Protestant Reformation in the sixteenth century was followed by some two hundred years of bloody wars between

Catholic and Protestant countries, and of civil wars between those religions, and even denominations within them, in the same countries. Both the Union and the Confederacy in the Civil War prayed to the same God for victory. Nazi Germany's slogan was *Gott Ist Mit Uns*–(God is with us) as they murdered six million Jews in the name of upholding Christian civilization. The Israelis believe the Jewish God is on their side, and the Palestinians believe that Allah is on theirs. The 9/11 hijackers and Osama Bin Laden praised Allah and believed that they would get into heaven by killing the Western infidels.

The compartmentalized thinking of Christians, whose key beliefs include loving your neighbor as yourself, loving your enemies, and turning the other cheek but who have invoked God or Jesus Christ in wars from the medieval crusades up to the American war on Iraq, has long been a favorite topic for literary satirists. Jonathan Swift in book 4 of *Gulliver's Travels* (1726) gives a long list of ridiculous reasons for which Christian countries in Europe had gone to war, foremost among which were the most petty differences in theological beliefs. Another famous eighteenth-century satirist, Voltaire, described in his novel *Candide* (1759) a battle between the armies of two Christian monarchs, in which ten thousand men were killed and no one won, after which "the two kings in their respective camps celebrated the victory by having *Te Deums* sung" (322.) (The Te Deum is a Christian hymn of praise to God.) As noted in chapter 6, Mark Twain wrote around 1900, "Man is the Religious Animal. He is the only Religious Animal. He is the only animal that has the True Religion–several of them. He is the only animal that loves his neighbor as himself, and cuts his throat if his theology isn't straight." If God loves all his children, does it seem likely that he looks down approvingly on any of them hating others and tearing them to shreds? Or that he "blesses" the armies of one nation-state, ruled by all-too-human political and economic elites, over all others?

The Role of the Media

News media are always caught in a bind during the buildup to and fighting of wars. On the one hand, they like to see themselves as independent, neutral investigators and reporters of the facts. On the other hand, they are afraid they will be perceived by the government and the public as unpatriotic if they report facts that are unfavorable to the war effort. The result is that, over and over again, the pattern is repeated of news media being pressured into taking the government's case for war at face value. The media's—and public's—credulity is reminiscent of the comic strip "Peanuts," in which every fall, Lucy tells Charlie Brown she'll hold the football on the ground while he kicks it. Every year she pulls the ball away at the last second and he falls on his butt. But every year he ardently believes her assurances that *this* year she won't. We always want to believe that *this* time the government is telling the truth, in defiance of all past evidence to the contrary. We might think that this history would teach the media to be extra skeptical and scrupulous *next* time, but it never seems to.

In the early stages of the Vietnam War, most major media went along unquestioningly with the justifications presented by Presidents Kennedy and Johnson. Years later, those media acknowledged that they had been taken in. During the Gulf War in 1991, the media accepted military officials' claims about the effectiveness of the Patriot missile, claims that subsequently proved to be false (see "The Military-Industrial Media Complex" in chapter 15). And yet again during the buildup to the Iraq war in 2002 and 2003, most media accepted the Bush administration's claims about Saddam Hussein's weapons of mass destruction, his ties to Al Qaeda, and others. By 2004, however, the *New York Times*, the *Washington Post,* and other major news sources published editorial statements admitting that they had been insufficiently skeptical and had allowed themselves to be misled on these issues. The Iraq war brought the innovation of "embedded reporters," journalists accompanying American forces into action, with the promise that their reports could produce unprecedented accuracy.

After the fact, however, several of these reporters and their news agencies admitted that the pressure on them to suppress unfavorable reports in the perceived cause of patriotism was just too strong to resist.

"When will they ever learn? When will they ever learn?"

Conclusion

To reiterate, this has been a survey of some reasons to be skeptical about emotional appeals by government and media in support of war. None of these reasons are sufficient cause to conclude that President Bush's justifications for the Iraq war were false, or that any such future justifications will be. They might quite conceivably have *been* true at that particular time and be confirmed as such in the future. In any given situation like this, however, opposing accounts of the facts must be weighed open-mindedly and evenhandedly, according to all of the guidelines presented throughout this book. The point here is, yet again, not to let yourself be swayed by listening only to what you would *like* to believe, on one side or the other, not to be swayed by the emotional appeal and semantic slanting that always accompany war—particularly the appeals to fear following 9/11 that could conceivably stampede us into military "quick fixes" that might just increase the dangers facing us—rather than demanding reasoned argument from leaders, the media, and ourselves.

The War Prayer

Mark Twain

From *Europe and Elsewhere*, Harper 1923

It was a time of great and exalting excitement. The country was up in arms, the war was on, in every breast burned the holy fire of patriotism; the drums were beating, the bands playing, the toy pistols popping, the bunched firecrackers hissing and spluttering; on every hand and far down the receding and facing spread of roofs and balconies a fluttering wilderness of flags flashed in the sun; daily the young volunteers marched down the wide avenue gay and fine in their new uniforms, the proud fathers and mothers and sisters and sweethearts cheering them with voices choked with happy emotion as they swung by; nightly the packed mass meetings listened, panting, to patriot oratory which stirred the deepest deeps of their hearts, and which they interrupted at briefest intervals with cyclones of applause, the tears running down their cheeks the while; in the churches the pastors preached devotion to flag and country, and invoked the God of Battles, beseeching His aid in our good cause in outpouring of fervid eloquence which moved every listener. It was indeed a glad and gracious time, and the half dozen rash spirits that ventured to disapprove of the war and cast a doubt upon its righteousness straightway got such a stern and angry warning that for their personal safety's sake they quickly shrank out of sight and offended no more in that way.

Sunday morning came—next day the battalions would leave for the front; the church was filled; the volunteers were there, their young faces alight with martial dreams—visions of the stern advance, the gathering momentum, the rushing charge, the flashing sabers, the flight of the foe, the tumult, the enveloping smoke, the fierce pursuit, the surrender!—then home from the war, bronzed heroes, welcomed, adored, submerged in golden seas of glory! With the volunteers sat their dear ones, proud, happy, and envied by the neighbors and friends who had no sons and brothers to send forth to the field of honor, there to win for the flag, or, failing, die the noblest of noble deaths. The service proceeded; a war chapter from the Old Testament was read; the first prayer was said; it was followed by an organ burst that shook the building, and with one impulse the house rose, with glowing eyes and beating hearts, and poured out that tremendous invocation—

"God the all-terrible! Thou who ordainest, Thunder thy clarion and lightning thy sword!"

Then came the "long" prayer. None could remember the like of it for passionate pleading and moving and beautiful language. The burden of its supplication was, that an ever-merciful and benignant Father of us all would watch over our noble young soldiers, and aid, comfort, and encourage them in their patriotic work; bless them, shield them in the day of battle and the hour of peril, bear them in His mighty hand, make them strong and confident, invincible in the bloody onset; help them to crush the foe, grant to them and to their flag and country imperishable honor and glory—

An aged stranger entered and moved with slow and noiseless step up the main aisle, his eyes fixed upon the minister, his long body clothed in a robe that reached to his feet, head bare, his white hair descending in a frothy cataract to his shoulders, his seamy face unnaturally pale, pale even to ghastliness. With all eyes following him and wondering, he made his silent way; without pausing, he ascended to the preacher's side and stood there, waiting. With shut lids the preacher, unconscious of his presence, continued his moving prayer, and at last finished it with the words, uttered in fervent appeal, "Bless our arms, grant us the victory, O Lord our God, Father and Protector of our land and flag!"

The stranger touched his arm, motioned him to step aside—which the startled minister did—and took his place. During some moments he surveyed the spellbound audience with solemn eyes, in which burned an uncanny light; then in a deep voice he said:

"I come from the Throne—bearing a message from Almighty God!" The words smote the house with a shock; if the stranger perceived it he gave no attention. "He has heard the prayer of His servant your shepherd, and will grant it if such shall be your desire after I, His messenger, shall have explained to you its import—that is to say, its full import. For it is like unto many of the prayers of men, in that it asks for more than he who utters it is aware of—except he pause and think.

"God's servant and yours has prayed his prayer. Has he paused and taken thought? Is it one prayer? No, it is two—one uttered, the other not. Both have reached the ear of Him Who heareth all supplications, the spoken and the unspoken. Ponder this—keep it in mind. If you would beseech a blessing upon yourself, beware! lest without intent you invite a curse upon a neighbor at the same time. If you pray for the blessing of rain upon your crop which needs it, by that act you are possibly praying for a curse upon some neighbor's crop which may not need rain and can be injured by it.

"You have heard your servant's prayer— the uttered part of it. I am commissioned of God to put into words the other part of it—that part which the pastor—and also you in your hearts—fervently prayed silently. And ignorantly and unthinkingly? God grant that it was so! You heard these words: 'Grant us the victory, O Lord our God!' That is sufficient. The *whole* of the uttered prayer is compact into those pregnant words. Elaborations were not necessary. When you have prayed for victory you have prayed for many unmentioned results which follow victory—*must* follow it, cannot help but follow it. Upon the listening spirit of God the Father fell also the unspoken part of the prayer. He commandeth me to put it into words. Listen!

"O Lord our Father, our young patriots, idols of our hearts, go forth to battle—be Thou near them! With them—in spirit—we also go forth from the sweet peace of our beloved firesides to smite the foe. O Lord our

God, help us to tear their soldiers to bloody shreds with our shells; help us to cover their smiling fields with the pale forms of their patriot dead; help us to drown the thunder of the guns with the shrieks of their wounded, writhing in pain; help us to lay waste their humble homes with a hurricane of fire; help us to wring the hearts of their unoffending widows with unavailing grief; help us to turn them out roofless with their little children to wander unfriended the wastes of their desolated land in rags and hunger and thirst, sports of the sun flames of summer and the icy winds of winter, broken in spirit, worn with travail, imploring Thee for the refuge of the grave and denied it—for our sakes who adore Thee, Lord, blast their hopes, blight their lives, protract their bitter pilgrimage, make heavy their steps, water their way with their tears, stain the white snow with the blood of their wounded feet! We ask it, in the spirit of love, of Him Who is the Source of Love, and Who is the ever-faithful refuge and friend of all that are sore beset and seek His aid with humble and contrite hearts. Amen."

(*After a pause.*) "Ye have prayed it; if ye still desire it, speak! The messenger of the Most High waits."

It was believed afterward that the man was a lunatic, because there was no sense in what he said.

The Real War 1939–1945

Paul Fussell

From *Wartime: Understanding and Behavior in the Second World War*, Oxford University Press, 1989

The peruser (reader would be the wrong word) of the picture collection *Life Goes to War* (1977), a volume so popular and widely distributed as to constitute virtually a definitive and official anthology of Second World War photographs, will find even in its starkest images no depiction of bodies dismembered. There are three separated heads shown, but all, significantly, are Asian—one the head of a Chinese soldier hacked off by the Japanese at Nanking; one a Japanese soldier's badly burnt head (complete with helmet), mounted as a trophy on an American tank at Guadalcanal; and one a former Japanese head, now a skull sent home as a souvenir to a girlfriend by her navy beau in the Pacific. No American dismemberings were registered, even in the photographs of Tarawa and Iwo Jima. American bodies (decently clothed) are occasionally in evidence, but they are notably intact. The same is true in other popular collections of photographs, like *Collier's Photographic History of World War II*, Ronald Heiferman's *World War II*, A.J.P. Taylor's *History of World War II*, and Charles Herridge's *Pictorial History of World War II*. In these, no matter how severely wounded, Allied soldiers are never shown suffering what in the Vietnam War was termed traumatic amputation: everyone has all his limbs, his hands and feet and digits, not to mention an expression of courage and cheer. And recalling Shakespeare and Goya, it would be a mistake to assume that dismembering was more common when warfare was largely a matter of cutting weapons, like swords and sabers. Their results are nothing compared with the work of bombs, machine guns, pieces of shell, and high explosives in general. The difference between the two traditions of representation is not a difference in military technique. It is a difference in sensibility, especially in the ability of a pap-fed public to face unpleasant facts, like the actualities apparent at the site of a major airplane accident.

What annoyed the troops and augmented their sardonic, contemptuous attitude toward those who viewed them from afar was in large part this public innocence about the bizarre damage suffered by the human body in modern war. The troops could not contemplate without anger the lack of public knowledge of the Graves Registration form used by the U.S. Army Quartermaster Corps, with its space for indicating "Members Missing." You would expect frontline soldiers to be struck and hurt by bullets and shell fragments, but such is the popular insulation from the facts that you would not expect them to be hurt, sometimes killed, by being struck by parts of their friends' bodies violently detached. If you asked a wounded soldier or Marine what hit him, you'd hardly be ready for the answer "My buddy's head," or his sergeant's heel or his hand, or a Japanese leg, complete with shoe and puttees, or the West Point ring on his captain's severed hand. What drove the troops to fury was the complacent, unimaginative innocence of their home fronts and rear echelons about such an experience as the following, repeated in essence tens of thousands of times. Captain Peter Royle, a British artillery forward observer, was moving up a hill in a night attack in North Africa. "I was following about twenty paces behind," he wrote in a memoir,

> when there was a blinding flash a few yards in front of me. I had no idea what it was and fell flat on my face. I found out soon enough: a number of the infantry were carrying mines strapped to the small of their backs, and either a rifle or machine gun bullet had struck one, which had exploded, blowing the man into three pieces—two legs and head and chest. His inside was strewn

on the hillside and I crawled into it in the darkness.

In war, as in air accidents, insides are much more visible than it is normally well to imagine. And there's an indication of what can be found on the ground after an air crash in one soldier's memories of the morning after an artillery exchange in North Africa. Neil McCallum and his friend "S." came upon the body of a man who had been lying on his back when a shell, landing at his feet, had eviscerated him:

> "Good God," said S., shocked, "here's one of his fingers." S. stubbed with his toe at the ground some feet from the corpse. There is more horror in a severed digit than in a man dying: it savors of mutilation. "Christ," went on S. in a very low voice, "look, it's not his finger."

In the face of such horror, the distinction between friend and enemy vanishes, and the violent dismemberment of any human being becomes traumatic. After the disastrous Canadian raid at Dieppe, German soldiers observed: "The dead on the beach—I've never seen such obscenities before." "There were pieces of human beings littering the beach. There were headless bodies, there were legs, there were arms." There were even shoes "with feet in them." The soldiers on one side know what the soldiers on the other side understand about dismemberment and evisceration, even if that knowledge is hardly shared by the civilians behind them.

War Is the Supreme Drug

An Interview with Author Chris Hedges

TomPaine.com, October 30, 2002

Chris Hedges has been a war reporter for the past 15 years, most recently for the New York Times, *and earlier for the* Dallas Morning News, *the* Christian Science Monitor, *and* NPR. *His book,* War Is a Force That Gives Us Meaning *(Anchor Books, 2003), a finalist for the National Book Critics Award, is one of the most striking analyses and critiques of what happens to people and societies as they go to war to be published in many years. Writing with a clarity and tone reminiscent of Albert Camus, Hedges unravels the myths and dysfunctional nationalism that grip nations head-*

ing to war; the intoxicating effect of these causes and rhetoric; and the terrible costs that soldiers, victims and societies pay—when the realities of war—not the rhetoric—are experienced. He spoke to TomPaine.com's *Steven Rosenfeld.*

TomPaine.com: When a country prepares for war and goes to war, there are changes in that country's politics and culture. You write that a myth emerges—a seductive myth as leaders spin out a cause. You write that a patriotism, a "thinly veiled form of self-worship appears." What do you mean by this myth, this cause, this patriotism and what you then say is an intoxicating result?

Chris Hedges: Well myth is always part of the way we understand war within a society. It's always there. But I think in a peacetime society we are at least open to other ways of looking at war. Just as patriotism is always part of the society, in wartime, the myth becomes ascendant. Patriotism, national self-glorification, infects everything, including culture. That's why you would go to symphony events and people wave flags and play the "Star Spangled Banner." In essence, it's the destruction of culture, which is always a prerequisite in wartime. Wartime always begins with the destruction of your own culture. Once you enter a conflict, or at the inception of a conflict, you are given a language by which you speak. The state gives you a language to speak and you can't speak outside that language or it becomes very difficult. There is no communication outside of the clichés and the jingos, "The War on Terror," "Showdown With Iraq," "The Axis of Evil," all of this stuff. So that whatever disquiet we feel, we no longer have the words in which to express it. The myth predominates. The myth, which is a lie, of course, built around glory, heroism, heroic self-sacrifice, the nobility of the nation. And it is a kind of intoxication. People lose individual conscience for this huge communal enterprise.

TP.c: You write there are different war myths—myths that fuel conflicts. What type of myth do you see animating the discussion today in the United States as it looks at Iraq?

Hedges: Well I think the myth is remarkably similar from war zone to war zone. At least, as it pertains to how the nation that prosecutes a war looks at itself. We become the embodiment of light and goodness. We become the defenders of civilization, of all that is decent. We are more noble than others. We are braver than others. We are kinder and more compassionate than others—that the enemy at our gate is perfidious, dark, somewhat inhuman. We turn them into two-dimensional figures. I think that's part of the process of linguistically dehumanizing them. And in wartime, we always turn the other into an object, and often, quite literally, in the form of a corpse.

TP.c: Where are we in the United States, now, in this progression?

Hedges: Well, we've come frighteningly far in this process. And this has been a long progression. It began at the end of the Vietnam war. The defeat in Vietnam made us a better nation and a better people. We were forced to step outside our own borders and see how other people saw us. We were forced to accept very unpleasant truths about ourselves—our own capacity for evil. I think that that process, especially during the Reagan years, or at least that state, began to disintegrate. War once again became fun: Grenada; Panama, culminating in the Persian Gulf War. So that we're now at a process—Freud argues that all of life, both for the individual and within human society, is a battle between Eros, or love, and Thanatos, or the death instinct. And that one of these instincts is always ascendant, at one time or another. I think after the Vietnam war, because of the terrible costs that we paid, because of the tragedy that Vietnam was, Eros was ascendant. I think after the Persian Gulf war, where we fell in love with war—and what is war, war is death—Thanatos is ascendant. It will, unfortunately, take that grim harvest of dead, that ultimately those that are intoxicated with war must always swallow, for us to wake up again.

TP.c: When you say the rush to war is like a drug, how is it addictive? What void does it fill? What needs are fulfilled by this kind of rhetoric and this kind of myth-making, and this kind of political discourse, that are not otherwise accomplished in a peacetime political environment?

Hedges: Well, I think war is probably the supreme drug. War—first of all, it is a narcotic. You can easily become addicted to it. And that's why it's often so hard for people who spend prolonged times in combat to return to peacetime society. There's a huge alienation, a huge disconnection, often a longing to go back to the subculture of war. War has a very dark beauty, a kind of fascination with the grotesque. The Bible called it "the lust of the eye" and warned believers against it. War has a rush. It has a hallucinogenic quality. It has that sort of stoned-out sense of—that zombie-like quality that comes with not enough sleep, sort of being shelled too long. I think, in many ways, there is no drug, or there are no combination of drugs that are as potent as war, and one could argue as addictive. It certainly is as addictive as any narcotic.

TomPaine.com: For people who haven't read your reports in the *New York Times,* or don't know what actually goes behind the reporting that's gone into them, where have you been that has brought you on this course to write about this topic?

Chris Hedges: Well, I went to Seminary—I didn't go to journalism school. So this stretches way back to my own education, my own theological education, my study of ethics. I went to war, not because I was a gun nut, or wanted adventure, although to be honest, that was part of it. I did have a longing for that kind of epic battle that could define my life. I grew up reading everything on the Holocaust and on the Spanish Civil War, but I went as an idealist. I went to Latin America in the early '80s when most of these countries were ruled by pretty heinous military dictatorships. And I thought this was as

close as I was going to come in my lifetime to fighting fascism. I wanted that. Unfortunately, I didn't understand what war was. And I got caught up in the subculture, and to be honest, the addiction that war was. And I ended up over the next 15 years traveling from war zone to war zone to war zone with that fraternity of dysfunctional war correspondents who became my friends—some of whom were killed, including my closest friend who was killed in Sierra Leone in May of 2000. So I got sucked into the kind of whirlpool that war is—into the death instinct.

TP.c: For people here, in the states, who have never been in a war zone, can you just talk about some of the situations you put yourself into and what you saw about war that is completely counterpoint to the rhetoric about the cause.

Hedges: Well, the cause is ... is always a lie. If people understood, or individuals or societies understood in a sensory way what war was, they'd never do it. War is organized industrial slaughter. The good example is the Vietnam War. It began as a mythic war against communism and this kind of stuff, and—especially when the middle class began finding their sons coming home in body bags—people began to look at war in a very different light. It no longer was mythic. It became sensory war, i.e., we began to see war without that film, that mythic film that I think colors our vision of all violent conflicts. And then the war became impossible to prosecute. So the cause, the myth, the notion of glory—those are lies. They're always lies. And nations need them. Empires need them especially in order to get a populace to support a war. But they're untrue.

TP.c: So, you'd be sent into the field to cover different conflicts, what would you see that would be fundamentally at odds with this— what you're describing as the lie?

Hedges: Well, it takes anyone in combat about 30 seconds to realize that they've been lied to. War, combat is nothing like it's presented— not only by the entertainment industry, by Hollywood, but by the press, by writers such as Cornelius Ryan or Stephen Ambrose, who just died. These are myth-makers. The press is guilty of this. The press in wartime is always part of the problem. But when you get into combat, it's venal. It's dirty. It's confusing. It's humiliating, because you feel powerless. The noise is deafening. But, most importantly, you feel fear in a way that you've probably never felt fear before. And anyone who spends a lot of time in combat struggles always with this terrible, terrible fear—this deep, instinctual desire for self-preservation. And there are always times when fear rules you. In wartime, you learn you're not the person you want to be—or think you were. You don't dash out under fire to save your wounded comrade. Occasionally, this happens, but most of the time you're terrified. And that's very, very sobering. And it's a huge wake-up call. It shows you that the images that you've been fed, both about war, and that you have created for yourself, are wrong.

TP.c: Well, what do you think reporters can or should be doing that's different?

Hedges: Well, I think the big thing is you can't accept the language the state gives you. I mean, this is not a war in any conventional sense—I'm talking about the "War on Terror"—nor is it a war on terror. I think we have to dissect the clichés. Clichés are the enemy of bad writing, but also the enemy of clear thought, as George Orwell wrote. I think that's the first thing, we have to not speak in the language in which the state gives us. Secondly, I think we have to ask the hard questions. And I think the *New York Times* hasn't been bad on this. I think the *Times* has been pretty good, by looking at "what is it?" There was an editorial, I think in yesterday's *Times*, that said, "You know, there is no hard intelligence that he [Saddam Hussein] has anything that he's going to use against us, and before we go to war you have to show us." That is the proper response, and I laud the paper for printing that editorial.

TP.c: What's so interesting is, it doesn't get much stronger than that. Yet, on the other hand, what you write about in the book, is that a lot of people in the country who aren't privy to details at that level, or aren't as politically tuned in—they want to believe that this cause is good. They trust what the president says. And there's an appeal, as you say, in society's march toward war that fills certain needs.

Hedges: Well, I think that's the problem. There's a lot that we just don't really feel like seeing because we're having too much fun exulting in our own military prowess and our ability to mold and shape the world in ways that we want. There is a kind of suspension of self-criticism, both as a nation and as a person that takes place in wartime. And that's part of what removes the anxiety of normal daily living. We're no longer required to make moral choice. Moral choice has been made for us by the state. And to question the decisions of the state is to be branded, not only a traitor, but to be pushed outside that kind of communal entity within a society that war always creates. And that's a very difficult, lonely and painful experience. So most people, not necessarily because they're bad people in any way, but most people find it emotionally far more convenient, but also far more pleasurable just to go along. The problem is, under poor leadership, or wandering into a war where we shouldn't be, we can find ourselves in heaps of trouble.

Topics for Discussion and Writing

1. What **semantic** themes surveyed in chapter 4 are reiterated in the readings by Twain, Fussell, and Hedges?
2. Do you think Samuel Johnson's "Patriotism is the last refuge of a scoundrel" is a reckless over-generalization, or just literary hyperbole for shock effect? How could the wording be qualified to be more generally acceptable?

3. Could you reasonably draw the **inductive inference** from the text or any of the readings in this section that no war is justified? If this is not their implication, what *is*? To put it another way, they all suggest that many people in the United States and other countries who rush to support wars on the basis of abstract appeals to fear and pity by their government are apt not to understand the flesh-and-blood realities of war. Hedges says, "If people understood, or individuals or societies understood in a sensory way what war was, they'd never do it." Is it conceivable that people *could* understand these realities but still reasonably support a particular war? How might this line of reasoning apply to military action in Afghanistan, Iraq, or elsewhere in reaction to September 11? For example, the September 11 hijackers were indifferent to shedding blood. Can such people be opposed without bloodshed, on the individual level or through war? Try to write a paragraph or more that expresses possible reasoning on opposing sides here.

4. If governments and news media are unwilling to tell the truth about the goriness of war, about blunders and atrocities on our side, for fear that their people would not support even a just war if they knew the full truth, what does this suggest about the relation between government and the governed in democracy today, and between the media and their audience? See chapter 14 for more on the question of whether media "give the people what they want."

5. Do you think Chris Hedges's credentials qualify him as an authoritative source in writing about war? How do his having studied in a religious seminary and his stated affinity with writers like Orwell, Camus, and Freud inform his viewpoint and the way he articulates issues? Do you find this literary dimension rhetorically effective or not? This interview with him appeared some six months before the war in Iraq began, but he expressed skepticism about slogans like "the War on Terror" and "Showdown with Iraq." You might do an Internet search to see what he had to say about the war after the fact. Conservatives might argue that Hedges has a liberal bias. What arguments might they present in **rebuttal** to his?

6. Debate with classmates the following **hypotheses**:

a. Anyone who advocates a particular war should be willing, in principle, to die in it. It is hypocritical to say, in effect, "Let's you and him fight," especially when the "you" has no personal relationship to the speaker.

b. If rank-and-file military troops are dying in a war, should corporations be allowed to profit from military contracts? Should their profits be surtaxed to help pay for the costs of war? How can we know that the tail of corporate profits is not wagging the dog of war policy?

c. During a war, everyone in a country should be expected to make sacrifices. Wars are hugely expensive, and the Iraq war added billions of dollars to deficit spending, which was already at record heights. Shouldn't everyone be willing to pay higher taxes in wartime? How many Americans who supported the Iraq war would have been willing to have their taxes increased, and by how much, to pay for it? Were President Bush's continued attempts to cut taxes during wartime an example of telling voters that they could have their cake and eat it too, by entering into an expensive war without having to sacrifice anything for it?

Part IV

Thinking Critically About the Rhetoric of Politics and Mass Media

CHAPTER 13

Thinking Critically About Political Rhetoric

POLITICAL SEMANTICS

To begin with, *liberal, conservative,* and other terms like those in the prestudy exercises are constantly used by American politicians, mass media, and individuals as though they had a fixed, universally agreed-upon definition; yet, as these exercises have probably indicated to you, such terms are almost infinitely ambiguous, especially when writers and speakers fail to indicate the exact sense or context in which they are using the words. Politicians and other public figures sometimes deliberately exploit the ambiguity of these terms by using them simply as **cleans** and **dirties**, strong on **connotative** slanting but weak in **denotative** meaning. Much similar confusion is caused in argumentation when two opponents deliberately

267

or unconsciously use different definitions of these terms as underlying assumptions—that is, they **stack the deck** by using the definitions favorable to their own side and unfavorable to the opponent's. Thus, the conservative is apt to assume a definition of *conservative* something like "cautious, responsible, moral" and of *liberal* something like "wasteful, permissive, immoral," while the liberal uses *liberal* to mean "open-minded, humane, progressive" and *conservative* to mean "bigoted, greedy, and hypocritically self-righteous." (Remember a key axiom of semantics and rhetoric: whoever defines the terms gains the upper hand in argumentation.)

How much help are dictionary definitions of these terms? Here are the pertinent definitions in *Random House Webster's College Dictionary* (2001 edition):

> **liberal.** Favorable to progress or reform, as in political or religious affairs. Pertaining to, based on, or having views or policies advocating individual freedom of action and expression. Of or pertaining to representational forms of government rather than aristocracies and monarchies. Free from prejudice or bigotry; tolerant. Free of or not bound by traditional or conventional ideas, values, etc.; open-minded.

> **conservative.** Disposed to preserve existing conditions, institutions, etc., or to restore traditional ones, and to limit change. Cautiously moderate. Traditional in style or manner; avoiding novelty or showiness. Having the power or tendency to conserve.

Now, in some of these senses—such as attitudes toward reform or change—the two ideologies are clearly opposed. But in other senses, the two are incomparable, like apples and oranges. Nothing in the definitions of *conservative,* or in most contemporary American conservatives' professed beliefs, suggests that conservatives want to restore aristocracies and monarchies, that they oppose progress, that they are intolerant or opposed to individual freedom (indeed, many conservatives believe *they* are the defenders of individual freedom against encroachments by liberals). Likewise, few liberals consider themselves incautious or absolutely opposed to tradition and conservation (indeed, contemporary American liberals tend to be more committed to environmental conservation than most conservatives). Moreover, each side regularly accuses the other of **compartmentalized thinking** in pursuing behavior or policies that are just the opposite of their professed ideals.

So not even the largest unabridged dictionary provides an adequate explanation of the **context** of oppositions between liberals and conservatives, or leftists and rightists, at any particular historical time or place, including present-day America. Fully understanding those oppositions necessitates a far more complex, multidimensional study in semantics. What are some of these dimensions?

Reader Advisory: The following sections lead rather deeply into subject matter that would normally be expected in a political science or contemporary history textbook, and some students or teachers might question its appropriateness in an English text and course. Please try to keep in mind that the essential context here is semantic: the necessity for you as a writer to have a clear conception in your own mind of the exact sense in which you use any of these political terms and to convey that conception to your reader either by explicit definition or by the context of the passage in which they appear. As a critical reader, you also need to hold professional writers whose work you are analyzing, or citing as sources, accountable for the same clear usage. Another semantic issue here is the incredible ambiguity of political terms, especially as they are used in the discourse of government and mass media, and the oversimplification that results in their public usage. While the following discussion addresses that problem and tries to indicate the process needed to overcome it as much as possible within the confines of space here, a large degree of oversimplification is unavoidable, as it would be in any text short of a book-length treatment. The map is not the territory.

LIBERALISM, CONSERVATISM, DEMOCRAT, REPUBLICAN

Furthermore, within any single ideological belief, there are usually many different varieties, degrees, and factions, all of whom disagree, often heatedly, among themselves, although they are generally united in opposition to broader ideological adversaries. Contemporary American conservatives are divided among numerous factions, paleoconservatives (i.e., longtime, old-fashioned ones) versus neoconservatives (converts from liberalism, maintaining vestiges of liberal ideas), the religious right versus libertarians (there is also, however, a Libertarian Party opposing both Republicans and Democrats), blue-collar and middle-class conservatives (the "Joe Lunchpail" stereotype) versus upper-class ones ("country club conservatives"), small businesspeople versus multinational corporate executives and inheritors of fortunes, and so on. Those who call themselves conservative run the gamut from Ku Klux Klanners and American Nazis to upholders of an earlier, patrician notion of conservatism defending hereditary aristocracy, a united church and state, and the elite, high culture of Western civilization.

American liberals likewise are divided among factions, which include, among others, organized labor, the majority of poor people and racial minorities, teachers and scholars in humanistic subjects, liberally inclined members of the upper classes ("limousine liberals"), feminists, environmentalists, consumer advocates, and "neoliberal" centrists like Bill and Hillary Clinton and John Kerry. (At this writing, just before the 2008 election, it was uncertain whether Barack Obama was more liberal or centrist.) This mix is further complicated by the fact that the Democratic Party, which most liberals support, was throughout the twentieth century the party of very conservative big-city political machines, Southern white segregationists, "Reagan Democrats" (former rank-and-file Democrats who in the 1960s and 1970s became more conservative and in many cases started voting Republican), and circles of large corporate campaign contributors and lobbyists similar to those who support the Republicans—in many cases the same ones contribute to and lobby *both* parties. Because of the influence of the conservative factions in the Democratic Party, many people who consider themselves left-of-liberal (most prominently, members of the New Left movements that arose in the 1960s) dissociate themselves from the Democratic Party or would like to see it move much further to the left than it has been since at least the time of Roosevelt's New Deal in the 1930s and 1940s. So it is a semantic fallacy, which you should avoid, to use *Democrat* and *liberal* synonymously. In other words, an **argument from the converse** must be avoided here: most liberals are Democrats, but most Democrats are not necessarily liberals.

If many Democrats are conservatives, are there also liberal Republicans? Yes, though fewer than conservative Democrats. Before about 1968, there was a sizable liberal wing of the Republican Party, represented by leaders like Nelson Rockefeller and the young George H. W. Bush. The presidencies of Richard Nixon and Ronald Reagan, however, have led to domination of the party by its conservative wing up to the present. There are still some relatively liberal Republicans like John McCain, although in the 2008 presidential election he adopted more conservative positions. Nevertheless, you should avoid equating *conservative* with *Republican* in opposition to *Democrat*, mainly because of the large numbers of conservative Democrats.

The diversity of interests within both major American parties suggests the semantic problems presented by the **culturally conditioned assumption** of a two-party system, in contrast to the multiparty system of most other contemporary democracies. One wit has observed that if the Democratic Party were in any Western European country, it would be five different parties. The multiplicity of constituencies in both parties, the overlap of some similar constituencies in both parties, and the widespread influence of corporate wealth in both—all diminishing the differences between the two—frequently result in an **either-or**

fallacy: many voters, disillusioned with one party, turn toward the other for a while, then when they get disillusioned with that one, turn back toward the first again, without understanding that both are too diffuse and compromised to provide any significant alternative to one another. There *are* other parties on the ballot in many states, such as the Reform Party, the Libertarian Party, the American Independent Party (more consistently conservative than the Republicans), the New Party, Peace and Freedom, and Socialist parties (all pro-labor and democratic socialist), and the Green Party (environmentalist); there is no law preventing voters from turning to them, or to independent candidates like Ralph Nader and Ross Perot. Many political analysts believe that breaking the monopoly of the two-party system, or at least establishing proportional representation in legislatures, which would enable other parties to gain seats in proportion to their votes, would be a progressive step for American politics and clear public discourse.

> *Grammatical Note: In the context of U.S. politics,* Democrat *and* Republican *are the names of parties, and as such must always be capitalized;* liberal *and* conservative *are names of ideologies—that is, systems of political or philosophical beliefs—so they and other ideological terms discussed here subsequently should never be capitalized except at the beginning of sentences. In the United States there is no such thing as "the Liberal Party" or "the Conservative Party."* Democratic *is the adjective form of the party's name;* democratic *is the adjective form for the ideology of democracy. Likewise for* Republican *and* republican. *In other words, most Republicans are democrats and most Democrats are republicans. Although we cannot hear these distinctions in speaking (we have to make them through the context of surrounding words), it can be very confusing for readers if you do not use the correct capitalization in writing.*

SOCIALISM, COMMUNISM, MARXISM

Yet another set of terms that are widely used in a confusing manner includes *socialism, communism,* and *Marxism.* Here again, each of these ideologies contains many opposing variations and factions among its adherents. *Socialism* is the broadest term; *communism* and *Marxism* are two of many varieties, or subsets, of socialism. (See "A Guide to Political Terms and Positions" for further explanation.) Capitalization usage for these terms varies widely among writers and publishers; most commonly, *Socialist* and *Communist* are used in reference to particular political parties, *socialist* and *communist* in reference to the ideologies, the usage I follow in this book.

Marxism can denote either the theoretical views of Karl Marx and his followers or the political doctrines applied by Communist parties and governments claiming to base their practices on Marxist ideology. The complications here begin with the infinity of disagreements among the intellectual followers of Marxist ideology—the varying degrees of their acceptance of Marx's original views and of revisions of them adjusted to changing historical circumstances from Marx's time, their emphasis on different facets of Marxism, including Marxist philosophy, economics, history, sociology, anthropology, cultural criticism, and so on. Most contemporary Marxist theorists interpret Marxism as a democratic ideology, but the political practice of self-styled Marxist parties and governments (sometimes designated Marxist-Leninist) has most often been undemocratic and totalitarian—causing many theoretical Marxists to denounce Communist parties for exploiting Marx's concept of communism (lower case *c*) to institute perverse distortions of his ideals. Marxist or neo-Marxist theory has continued to exert a strong influence in the contemporary intellectual and academic world; many scholars who are not doctrinaire Marxists, including myself, have found valid-

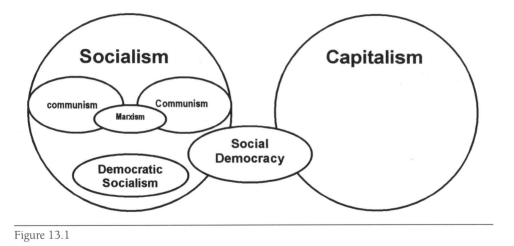

Figure 13.1

ity in one form and degree or another of Marxist ideas (again, in support of democracy and freedom); in fact, several of the aspects of critical thinking in this book and chapter reflect Marxist concepts. A common rhetorical tactic of political rightists, however, has been to try to discredit theoretical Marxist scholars and their ideas through red-baiting **guilt by association** with Communist dictatorships. (The circle diagrams, figure 13.1, may help to clarify the relations among these terms.)

THE WORLD POLITICAL SPECTRUM

Terms like *liberal* and *conservative, leftist* and *rightist* are ambiguous not only because they have a vast number of denotations and connotations but also because they cannot be accurately understood in isolation but only within a larger context, framework, or schema of beliefs and relative positions on a spectrum. The writer seeking accuracy of definition needs to key these political terms to a spectrum of positions from far right to far left in the United States and the rest of the world (see table 13.1).

Table 13.1 is based on the world alignment from the time of World War II to around 1985. Much has changed since 1985, rendering some of the schema obsolete; it is also a very broad sketch and does not purport to be all-inclusive. However, this model retains value as a map of the alignments that shaped our concepts of the left and right in world and American politics over most of the twentieth century and that in some important ways persist in the twenty-first. (See the more extensive notes on table 13.1 at the end of this chapter for some of the modifications in the twenty-first century.) Upheavals in the Communist world since the 1980s have especially compounded semantic complexities: the adjective "left-wing" has been historically equated with communism as a political and economic ideology opposed to capitalism, but if left-wing is defined as opposition to the status quo, does that make those who have overturned the status quo in Communist countries leftists or rightists? In post–Cold War Eastern Europe, supporters of the old Communist regime are now generally designated "right-wing" and "conservative," while those working for democratic government and a capitalist economy are designated "liberal."

Several further explanations and qualifications are also necessary regarding table 13.1. "Social democratic" is the term applied to the mixed economy in Canada and Western European democracies, which maintain a basically capitalist economy but with considerably more government regulation of business; more progressively structured taxes (i.e., increasing

Table 13.1. Twentieth-Century Political Spectrum

Dictatorship	Left Wing		Right Wing		Dictatorship
	Political Democracy, Freedom				
Communism	Socialism		Capitalism	Plutocracy	Fascism
USSR	Nicaragua (Sandinista)	Sweden	France		Chile (Pinochet)
China	Chile (Allende)	Denmark	Italy		Philippines (Marcos)
Cuba		Norway	Germany		South Africa (Apartheid)
North Vietnam			Spain		El Salvador (1980s)
Cambodia			Canada		Nicaragua (Somosa)
North Korea			England		South Vietnam
Zimbabwe			USA		South Korea
			Japan		Taiwan
					Indonesia
					Nazi Germany
					Fascist Italy
					Franco Spain
					Fascist Japan

American Parties

Green   Democratic   Republican

Libertarian

percentage of tax on higher-level incomes); and more government-subsidized health care, higher education, and family benefits. (See Steve Brouwer's "If We Decided to Tax the Rich" later in this chapter as an argument for the benefits of European-style social democracy over American capitalism.) Since the 1980s, Western European countries have moved toward somewhat more privatization in these fields, but still not to the extent of the United States. So a politician or position labeled "moderate" in the United States is considered right-wing from today's European or Canadian perspective, while many American "radicals" would be "moderates" in Europe or Canada. Similarly, many "ultraconservatives" in American terminology appear "moderate" in comparison to fascistic countries. The practical significance is that, to expose themselves to a fuller range of ideological viewpoints, students need to seek out sources, mainly left-of-liberal and libertarian, excluded from the mainstream of American discourse, though such sources may be hard to find in many communities.

Another semantic confusion in American public discourse results from our tendency to equate terms referring to governmental systems, such as *democracy, freedom,* and *dictatorship,* with words referring to economic systems—*capitalism* or *free enterprise* and *socialism.* As indicated in the bracketed terms in table 13.1 and in the Guide to Political Terms below, in dictionary definitions and in actual historical practice, both a capitalist and a socialist economy can exist under either a democratic or dictatorial government. To oversimplify a complex point, capitalism under a political dictatorship is plutocracy, socialism under a political dictatorship is (capital C) Communism, while fascism consists of a combination of socialist and capitalist economies in the service of militaristic nationalism, as opposed to the internationalistic essence of socialism in general (**Nazi** is an acronym of **National Socialist**), under an all-powerful political dictatorship.

One must again go beyond dictionary definitions to address the relation between these political and economic systems in actual practice, for partisans of varying ideologies assume different connections between, say, freedom and democracy on one hand and capitalism and socialism on the other. Conservatives argue that capitalistic free enterprise is the economic system that best contributes to political freedom and democracy, but leftists argue (as in the socialist position described in the Guide to Political Terms below) that free enterprise in practice tends to destroy democracy and freedom because capitalists gain excessive political power. (This is Robert Jensen's argument in "Anti-Capitalism in Five Minutes or Less" in chapter 6.) To the extent that in American usage "capitalism" is commonly used synonymously with political democracy and freedom—in disregard of the dictionary definitions—conservatives have managed to control the semantic agenda, excluding from public discourse widespread arguments for democratic socialism or social democracy. If conservatives say, for example, "Post-Communist Russia is moving toward democracy," when the fact is that Russia is moving toward a capitalist economy, this argument is based on the underlying assumption that capitalism necessarily leads to democracy. Leftists would **refute** this argument somewhat as follows: "Russia's turn toward capitalism does not necessarily mean a turn toward democracy; a political dictatorship of the Communist Party is simply being replaced by a political dictatorship of capitalists." More generally, leftists argue, "Sweden, Norway, and Denmark—with semisocialistic economies—certainly have more democratic politics than many capitalist countries like pre-Castro Cuba, El Salvador in the 1980s, South Africa before free elections there, the Philippines under Marcos, or Indonesia and Saudi Arabia today—all dictatorships supported by the United States because they were friendly to American business and military interests. Furthermore, the United States has befriended China, not because it has changed into a democracy, but because it has changed from a Communist dictatorship into a capitalist dictatorship, which provides cheap labor for American corporations and trillions of dollars in American government and business loans. (Ironically, the American left press, like *The Nation* and Pacifica Radio, was more vocally critical of the 2008 Olympics being held in Beijing, more harsh on suppression of human rights in China, than the conservative press and 'mainstream media,' which reaped high audience ratings and advertising revenues from their saturation coverage.) The United States usually gets along fine with dictatorships, so long as they are capitalist and do business with American corporations."

THE AMERICAN POLITICAL SPECTRUM

Looking at the placement of American Parties in the worldwide left-to-right spectrum in table 13.1 calls attention to the **ethnocentrically** limited span of ideology represented by the poles of the Republican and Democratic parties and of "conservatism" and "liberalism" that define the boundaries of most American political, journalistic, scholarly, and cultural discourse. Political forces that are considered liberal in the United States, for example, usually stay well within the limits of capitalist ideology, and thus are considerably to the right of the labor, social-democratic, and Communist parties with large constituencies in most other democratic countries today. We need to keep this limitation in mind when we consider controversies over political viewpoints in American communications media. (Chapter 14 further develops the complexities of this topic.)

As with American political figures, the whole range of American news media—along with individual journalists and scholars, and even figures or shows in popular entertainment like Mel Gibson and George Clooney, Doonesbury and Mallard Fillmore, *The Apprentice* and *The Simpsons*—can be placed on a spectrum from left to right in such a precise way that their political identity can be agreed on to a large extent by those of every ideological persuasion. In both sections of table 13.2, even the division into columns is an arbitrary semantic oversimplification of what could be broken down into several more columns or even a continuous, linear spectrum from left to right. Rather than speaking of "the liberal *New York Times*," one should explain and document the sense and degree of liberalism referred to. "Liberal" in relation to what other media? One might clarify the label by placing the *Times* to the left of *Time* but to the right of *The Nation*. (Many of these placements are disputable, to be sure, and subject to revision as different media and individuals periodically shift their positions. The placement of libertarians is especially problematic; here they are placed between liberal and conservative, but for more refinement, see the following Guide to Political Terms and Positions.)

A GUIDE TO POLITICAL TERMS AND POSITIONS

Left Wing, Right Wing, Capitalism, Communism, Socialism

After we establish a spectrum of positions from far left to far right, we still need to concretize the notions of left and right in terms of specific ideological beliefs, as follows.

Left wing and right wing (also see table 13.1). The *left wing* (adjective: *left-wing* or *leftist*) is a broad term that includes a diversity of parties and ideologies (which often disagree among themselves but usually agree in their opposition to the right wing) including liberals, nearest the center of the spectrum, and—progressively toward the left—socialists and communists (the latter two are also sometimes called "radical"). *Progressive* is a word that is sometimes used synonymously with *liberal* but is sometimes a **euphemism** for more radical leftism.

The *right wing* (adjective: *right-wing* or *rightist*) is a broad term that includes a diversity of parties and ideologies (which often disagree among themselves but usually agree in their opposition to the left wing) including libertarians, nearest the center of the spectrum, and—progressively toward the right—conservatives, ultraconservatives, plutocrats, and fascists.

Table 13.2. American Media, Journalists, and Commentators from Left to Right

A. Media

1. Left	2. Liberal	3. Liberal-to-Conservative	4. Conservative
The Nation	*NY Review*	*Time*	*Readers Digest*
In These Times	*Harper's*	*Newsweek*	*Weekly Standard*
Mother Jones	*New Yorker*	CNN	*Wall St. Journal*
Extra!	PBS Documentaries	*Washington Post*	*Commentary*
The Progressive	*60 Minutes*	*Atlantic*	*American Spectator*
Z Magazine	*New York Times*	*New Republic*	*National Review*
Media Matters		*Reason*	Fox News
Pacifica Radio	MSNBC	CBS news	*Washington Times*
Air America Radio		NBC, ABC news	*Insight*
		Lehrer News Hour	Most local newspapers, TV & radio

B. Journalists and Commentators

1. Left	2. Liberal	3. Libertarian	4. Conservative
Alexander Cockburn	Dan Rather	Virginia Postrel	Rush Limbaugh
Molly Ivins	Tom Brokaw	Stephen Moore	Pat Buchanan
Noam Chomsky	Ted Koppel	Doug Bandow	Jerry Falwell
Edward Herman	Jim Lehrer	Debra Saunders	Pat Robertson
Katrina vanden Heuvel	Larry King	Nat Hentoff	David Brooks
Barbara Ehrenreich	Cokie Roberts	James Pinkerton	Paul Harvey
Robert Scheer	Oprah Winfrey	Jesse Ventura	Sam Donaldson
Jonathan Kozol	Rosie O'Donnell	Ron Paul	George Will
Todd Gitlin	Bob Woodward	Bob Barr	John McLaughlin
Jim Hightower	Mark Shields	Nick Gillespie	Fred Barnes
Bob Herbert	Paul Krugman	P.J. O'Rourke	Paul Gigot
Jeff Cohen	Stephen Colbert		Charles Krauthammer
Norman Solomon	Michael Kinsley		Jonah Goldberg
Gore Vidal	Frank Rich		Robert Novak
Julianne Malveaux	Gloria Steinem		Phyllis Schlafly
Victor Navasky	Seymour Hersh		John Leo
Roger Wilkins	David Halberstam		Cal Thomas
Cornel West	Carl Bernstein		Thomas Sowell
Betty Friedan	Donald Barlett		Gordon Liddy
Ralph Nader	James Steele		Bob Grant
Katha Pollit	Naomi Wolf		Don Imus
Jesse Jackson	Jon Stewart		R. Emmett Tyrrell
Bernie Sanders	James Carville		Laura Ingraham
Michael Moore	George Stephanopolous		Mona Charen
Eric Alterman	Cynthia Tucker		William Kristol
Michael Lerner	Al Franken		Sean Hannity
Lewis Lapham	Martha Nussbaum		Rich Lowry
William Greider	Bill Maher		Norman Podhoretz
Susan Sontag	Keith Olbermann		John Podhoretz
Barbara Kingsolver	Eugene Robinson		Matt Drudge
Arundhati Roy	Arianna Huffington*		Henry Kissinger
Bill Moyers	David Brock*		Dinesh D'Souza
Holly Sklar	Michael Lind*		Lynne Cheney
Amy Goodman			Florence King
Adolph Reed	*Former conservative		Mary Matalin
Howard Zinn			Christina Sommers
Thomas Frank			Ann Coulter
			Jeff Jacoby
			Tucker Carlson
			Bill O'Reilly
			Bernard Goldberg
			Michael Savage
			David Horowitz*
			Christopher Hitchens*
			*Former leftist

Leftists tend to support:	*Rightists tend to support:*
The poor and working class	Middle and upper class
Labor (employees), consumers, environmental and other regulation of business	Management (employers), business, unregulated enterprise
More equality (economic, racial, sexual) than at present	The present state of equality, or return to earlier states
Civil and personal liberties; government control over economic liberty	Economic liberty; controls on personal liberties (e.g., abortion, prayer in schools, sexual conduct)
Cooperation	Competition
Internationalism	Nationalism (primary loyalty to one's own country)
Pacifism (exception: Communists)	Strong military and willingness to go to war
Questioning of authority—skepticism (exception: Communism is authoritarian)	Acceptance of authority, especially in military, police, and strong "law and order" policies
Government spending for public services like education, welfare, health care, unemployment insurance, broadcasting	Government spending for military, subsidies to business as incentive for growth and competition against public sector
Progressive taxes, i.e., greatest burden on wealthy individuals and corporations	Low taxes for wealthy individuals and corporations as incentive for investment ("supply-side economics" or "trickle-down theory")
Religious pluralism, skepticism, or atheism	Religious orthodoxy

Capitalism. Capitalism is an economic system based on private investment for profit. Jobs and public services are provided, and public needs met, to the extent that investment in them will predictably result in a return of capital outlay. In its principles capitalism does not provide any restrictions on extremes of wealth and poverty or on social power, but its advocates (especially pure, libertarian capitalists) believe that the workings of a free-market economy, unrestricted by government controls or regulation, will minimize social inequity.

Capitalism is not a political system; in principle, a capitalist economy can operate under either a democratic government or a dictatorship, as in plutocracy or fascism (see table 13.1).

Socialism. An economic system based on public investment to meet public needs, provide full employment, and reduce socioeconomic inequality. Socialism does not allow great extremes of wealth and poverty, though most forms allow for some range of differences in salary. In various models of socialism, investment and industrial management are controlled either by the federal government or by local governments, workers' and consumers' cooperatives, a variety of community groups, and so on. Socialism is not a political system; in principle, a socialist economy can operate under either a democratic government or a dictatorship, as in Communism (see table 13.1).

Communism. With lower-case c, communism refers to Marx's ideal of the ultimate, future form of pure democratic socialism, with virtually no need for centralized government. With upper-case C as in present-day Communist parties, Communism is a socialist economy under undemocratic government. Historically, Communists have manipulated appeals to left-wing values like socioeconomic equality and worldwide cooperation in order to impose police-state dictatorship and military aggression.

Plutocracy. Rule by the rich; a capitalist economy under undemocratic government.

Fascism. A combination of capitalist and socialist economies under an undemocratic government. Historically, fascists have manipulated appeals to conservative values like patriotism, religion, competitiveness, anticommunism, respect for authority and law and order, traditional morality and the family, in order to impose police-state dictatorship. Fascism typically is aggressively militaristic and imperialistic and promotes racial hatred based on theories of white (or "pure Aryan") supremacy and religious persecution of non-Christians. It glorifies strong authority figures with absolute power.

Conservatives, Liberals, Socialists, Libertarians

Conservatives. In the American context, most conservatives are pro-capitalist, believing that a capitalist economy best promotes political democracy. In other words, they believe what's profitable for big business also serves the interests of good government, labor, consumers, the environment, and the public in general—"What's good for General Motors is good for America." As David Horowitz asserts in "The Intellectual Class War" here, "Entrepreneurs generally want a better-educated, better-paid, more diverse working force, because that means better employees, better marketers, and better consumers of the company product. That is why, historically, everywhere capitalism has been embraced, labor conditions have improved and inequalities have diminished whether there has been a strong trade union presence or not." Because mainstream conservatives believe a major function of government is to help business maximize profits, they justify low taxes and government subsidies, protections, and bailouts for big business such as those for the mortgage industry in the late 2000s (although libertarian conservatives preferred to let the free market sort out the problems of individuals losing their houses to foreclosures, and irresponsible mortgage lenders bankrupting their companies and causing bond markets to plunge when the housing "bubble" of previous decades burst). They believe that the capitalistic, or free-enterprise, system is the best guarantee of equal social opportunity for everyone and that a large diversity of private enterprises is the best guarantee against excessive concentration of power in government (the main danger of socialism). They believe that abuses by businesses can and should be best policed or regulated by business itself, and when conservatives control government they routinely appoint businesspeople to public administrative positions and regulatory agencies because of their managerial expertise (a practice that liberals view as often leading to **conflicts of interest**). Mainstream conservatives tend, however, to want government to control *personal* conduct in areas like abortion, censorship, sexual behavior, and religion, with the exception that they oppose gun control.

Liberals. Most American liberals, like conservatives, basically believe in capitalism. But they also believe that the interests of big business are frequently contrary to those of democratic government and of employees, consumers, the environment, and the public in general. They think that capitalism tends to lead to excessive concentration of wealth in a few corporations and individuals, leading in turn toward plutocratic government—dictatorship of the rich. So they think that capitalism needs to be saved from its own self-destructive tendencies and kept on an even keel by policing business abuses through government regulation, by limiting extremes of wealth and poverty through progressive taxation and through welfare, unemployment insurance, Social Security, public education, and other free or low-cost public services. Though they are not "anti-business," as conservatives charge, liberals support labor unions as a counterbalance to the power of big business, and they believe that excessive cutbacks in regulatory agencies pushed through by corporate lobbies beginning with President Reagan's administration have resulted in a drastically accelerating "wealth gap" and several waves of financial scandals and crises. These include the collapse of savings and loan banks in the eighties and of Enron and several other giant corporations in the early 2000s, as well as the crisis in the banking and loan industries, in which top executives pocketed millions while their companies went bankrupt, along with uncontrolled executive salaries and speculative fortunes on Wall Street from arcane investments like hedge funds and derivatives. As noted above, these are the classic positions of the Democratic Party, though that party has moved more in the direction of conservatism in many ways through the last three or four decades. Liberals generally think, however, that government should *not* control personal conduct (except for gun control, which they tend to favor); in this area, they are much the same as libertarians.

Socialists. While liberals (and Democrats) want to save capitalism by regulating it, socialists want to replace it altogether. And while American liberals support the Democratic Party, socialists see both Democrats and Republicans as procapitalist, plutocratic parties, so they favor forming separate socialist or labor parties. American socialists, or radicals, believe more strongly than liberals that the interests of big business are contrary to democracy and the public interest; they believe that capitalism is basically an irrational, corrupt system (see "Questioning Capitalism" in chapter 6); that the profit motive is destructive of the natural environment, public health and safety, and traditional morality; and that wealthy business interests inevitably gain control over government, foreign and military policy, the media, and education and use the power of employment to keep the workforce and electorate under their control. They believe it is in the nature of capitalism for many (not all) owners of businesses to maximize profits by charging customers "whatever the traffic will bear" and by getting the most work out of employees for the lowest wages and cheapest working conditions possible. Socialists view globalization as a strategy by businesses to exploit slave labor abroad and drive down wages for American workers who are in a weakened position to bargain. They think liberal government reforms and attempts to regulate business are usually squashed by the power of business lobbies and that even sincere liberal reformers in government offices usually come from or eventually adopt the ethnocentric viewpoint of the upper classes. The socialist economic alternative is to operate on a nonprofit basis at least the biggest national and international corporations, as well as the defense industry, thereby preventing at the source the excessive accumulation of wealth and power through profits gained by capitalist investors. Socialists also go beyond liberal support of labor unions; they would have most businesses owned and managed democratically by their workers. In other words, socialism is an extension of the principles of democratic government into control of *economic* institutions. On the principle that there are many more workers than capitalists, and that it is the workers whose labor produces the profits that go into capitalists' pockets, a government and economy controlled by the totality of workers would be far more democratic than our present plutocracy. Short of the distant goal of full socialism, they tend (as in Europe and elsewhere) to form "social democratic" parties implementing a "mixed economy" of capitalism and socialism under democratic government, but they move further toward socialism than American liberals and Democrats. Socialists tend to side with liberals and libertarians in not wanting government to control personal conduct (though Communist governments tend to be highly "conservative" in legislating morality).

Libertarians. Libertarians agree with democratic leftists in supporting civil liberties and personal freedom in moral conduct, and with democratic rightists in supporting economic free enterprise with no or minimal government interference, and they accuse both leftists and conservatives of compartmentalized thinking or inconsistencies between the two realms. Thus, while libertarianism is one form of conservatism, libertarians criticize mainstream conservatives for inconsistency when they support government subsidies or bailouts for business or protectionist policies supposedly in the national interest. They are neither nationalistic and militaristic (like mainstream conservatives) nor for international cooperation (like leftists); they believe in unrestricted economic competition and free trade internationally as the best road to world peace. They oppose military drafts and favor minimal government spending on defense. They tend to oppose big defense spending as a racket for **special interests** and agree with leftists that arms races and wars result from excessive influence of the military and the defense industry on the government and economy of each opposing country.

NOTES ON THE GUIDE TO POLITICAL TERMS AND POSITIONS

I have attempted here to arrive at definitions that are acceptable to leftists and rightists alike— or at least to arrive at agreement between leftists and rightists on what they disagree about. This is a fiendishly difficult enterprise, since it is nearly inevitable that anyone attempting to do this, even with the best intentions, will stack the deck to some extent by projecting her or his own biases into the definitions. The best way to deal with this difficulty is to get suggestions for improvements from people on the other side, as I have done in modifying this schema over several years. The whole schema is best understood as an exercise in semantic open-endedness, open to constant, dialogic revision; you should use it that way too, adding your own and your classmates' suggestions for improvement.

A Note on Leftists and Rightists

The topics under "Leftists tend to support" and "Rightists tend to support" need some qualification. Note the phrasing "tend to"; that is to say, these oppositions and other general categories in this section are not asserted as absolute or total but only indicate the sympathies of the majority of people in each group, taking account of many exceptions and historical changes of allegiance. As for the list of issues on which leftists and rightists are opposed, there is bound to be dispute over the very way these oppositions are set up. For example, as the summary of the conservative position above indicates, conservatives (such as David Horowitz in the reading in this chapter) will argue that the interests of the wealthy, business, management, and unregulated enterprise are not opposed to the interests of the poor, working class, employees, consumers, or the environment. Their arguments may be persuasive, yet the neutral fact remains that leftists and rightists constantly argue over whether these sets of interests are opposed or not.

   The issues of economic, racial, and sexual equality are among the most heated sources of contemporary disputes. My initial wording here was that leftists tend to support equality and rightists inequality in these areas. My justification was that throughout most of Western history, conservatives have defended undemocratic, established hierarchies of class, race, and gender, while the eighteenth-century movement for democracy that culminated in the American Revolution and the credo that "all men are created equal" (with the significant exception of women and slaves) was the basis of modern liberalism.

   Even in contemporary America, some conservatives continue to defend certain forms of inequality within a democracy. For example, in *Giants and Dwarfs,* a sequel to his controversial 1987 book *The Closing of the American Mind,* Allan Bloom argues against the excessive democratization of higher education: "The university is, willy-nilly, in some sense aristocratic in both the conventional and natural senses of the term. It cannot, within broad limits, avoid being somewhat more accessible to the children of parents of means than to the children of the poor" (291). And he asserts that the liberal campaign for affirmative action "will brook no vestige of differentiation in qualities between men and women.... It would more willingly accept a totalitarian regime than a free one in which the advantages of money, position, education, and even talent are unevenly distributed" (367). Another way of putting Bloom's argument is that excessive liberal demands for greater equality will have the **ironic** opposite effect of establishing a new, worse hierarchy of inequality with bureaucratic administrators at its top. Economic inequality is defended in this book's readings by other conservatives, such as P. J. O'Rourke, "Closing the Wealth Gap," in chapter 9, and others discussed in chapter 16.

Not all contemporary conservatives go so far in defense of inequality as Bloom and O'Rourke, however. A more typical current conservative, or libertarian, line of argument is that unrestricted free enterprise is a more effective means of reducing all forms of inequality than liberal government legislation for affirmative action or progressive taxation, minimum-wage laws, and other attempts at more equitable income distribution. Another line used by conservatives is that they believe in equality of opportunity, as opposed to leftists' belief in equality of outcome, as in affirmative action. Many leftists, however, consider this a **false dichotomy**, since their position is that minorities, women, and the poor do *not* have equality of opportunity at present, so that affirmative action and other liberal policies are aimed at overcoming *this* inequality, not at attaining rigid equality of outcome. These are the reasons I have revised my wording to define the opposition as one between liberal calls for greater equality than at present versus conservative defenses of our present system as the best guarantor of equality. I hope, again, that this wording allows leftists and rightists to agree on what they disagree on. Do *you* agree, and if not, how can you improve on the definition?

On controversies like abortion, sexual conduct, pornography, legalization of drugs, and prayer in schools, leftists try to control the agenda by defining these issues in terms of civil and personal liberties, while rightists try to define them in terms of conservative morality versus liberal immorality or permissiveness. On morality in general, conservatives accuse leftists of favoring total relativism, hedonism, and rewarding of laziness, in opposition to conservative restraint and industriousness. Leftists claim this is another false dichotomy and **oversimplification**, misrepresenting what they actually believe and involving **selective vision** in ignoring comparable immoral behavior on the part of many conservatives who do not practice what they preach. Since neither side accepts the premises of the other on these issues, no common ground may be attainable here beyond agreement on what the disagreements are.

Another approach to these issues involves the possibility of compartmentalized thinking on both sides. Leftists tend to justify a permissive position on issues of personal morality as a defense of individual liberties against intrusive government control, but on economic issues they favor government control to curb immoral business practices or economic policies that result in excessive wealth and power for the corporate elite. Rightists tend to favor just the opposite: government control over personal morality but not over business morality. Similarly, conservatives say that they oppose big government spending and fostering of individual dependency on government handouts; yet liberals respond that conservatives are all for big government spending and handouts as long as they go to favored conservative constituencies like the military and corporate subsidies or bailouts. Libertarians believe that theirs is the only consistent position on all these issues. Do you agree with them, or can you find statements by either leftists or rightists that reconcile their apparent inconsistencies?

Concerning views on religion, some refinement is needed of the suggestion that leftists favor pluralism, skepticism, or atheism, while rightists favor religious orthodoxy. Certainly it is true that historically liberals, socialists, and communists have tended strongly toward religious skepticism, and consequently toward tolerance of diverse beliefs and even of atheism; at the extreme left, to be sure, Communist governments have been intolerant of religion. But these tendencies on the right and left must be qualified by noting that Protestants, Catholics, Jews, Muslims, and others are all internally divided between conservative and liberal factions; many Catholic "liberation theologians" even have Marxist social sympathies, in spite of Marxism's historical hostility toward religion as "the opiate of the masses." Also, leftists frequently are less opposed to religion itself than to the hypocrisy they claim to find in conservatives who do not practice the religious values they preach. As for conservatives, they might say the word *orthodoxy* has a negative **connotation** and prefer to replace it with something like "traditional religious beliefs and moral values." Religious conservatives too are divided between orthodox groups like Pat Robertson's Christian Coalition and more ecumenical or pluralistic ones.

A Note on Fascism

As a consequence of some forty-five years of Cold War anti-Communism (1945–1990), most Americans are probably familiar with the notion that if leftist or even liberal values are pushed to extremes, they can lead toward Communism. Far fewer Americans understand that if conservative values are pushed to extremes, they can lead toward fascism. Our concept of fascism is generally limited to movies about Nazi military atrocities in World War II, which convey little sense of the ideology of fascism. In fact, it might be said that the greatest danger of fascism is that so few people understand what it really is, so many might be attracted to its publicly stated beliefs without comprehending its evils. Several of my students have said, in effect, "Gee, fascism values strong patriotism, military strength, and leadership, as well as religious orthodoxy, family values, and law and order. Sounds pretty good to me." What they do not understand is that historically, fascists have manipulated these appeals to gain power and then abolished democracy and imposed brutal dictatorships. Nor did fascism disappear after World War II, as is widely believed; quasi-fascist dictatorships have thrived all around the world up to the present, as indicated in the "Right Wing" column of table 13.1, and the United States has had an embarrassing record of supporting them, partly because they were strongly anti-Communistic but also partly because they tended to do business with American corporations and the military.

Fascism is the ultimate manifestation of the human tendency toward authoritarianism and conformity studied in chapter 8. The "good German" soldiers and civilians under Hitler **rationalized** going along with Nazi atrocities because "Our leader must know what he's doing" and they had been culturally conditioned to obey those in authority. The appeal of fascism is especially strong in periods of national danger, when **appeals to fear** can be manipulated by those in power, as indicated in "Predictable Patterns of Wartime Rhetoric" in chapter 12. Lawrence Britt's "Fascism Anyone" in the readings here suggests sobering parallels between past fascist societies and certain tendencies in the United States following September 11, 2001. Britt's article presents a provocative subject for class debate.

Notes on Social Class and Political Attitudes

The table on what leftists and rightists tend to support includes "the poor and working class" on the left and "middle and upper class" on the right. These class labels are among the most ambiguous in political usage in this country, where nearly all people tend to describe themselves as middle class and where the even vaguer term "working Americans" serves to blur any distinction between the working and middle class. Up until the mid-twentieth century, "working class" generally meant poor people, blue-collar workers, and those with a high school or lower level of education. The Democratic Party was known as the party of the working class, and the Republicans as the party of the middle class, the rich and big business. For various historical reasons, these identifications have changed since the 1950s, with the Republicans gaining the allegiance of many at the lower socioeconomic levels and trying to tar the Democrats as the party of "elitism." In the 2008 election campaign, the

Table 13.3. Social Class and Political Attitudes, Left to Right

(These are very general approximations, indicating simply the tendencies of the majority of people in each group, with exceptions, and open to dispute)

LIBERAL   CONSERVATIVE

UPPER CLASS
Income Over $200,000, Net Worth over $5 Million

Limousine Liberals:
    Some Democratic politicians, bureaucrats
    Some executives and "stars" in media
    A few labor union officials

Country Club Conservatives:
    Big business executives and major
        stockholders, corporate lawyers and
        lobbyists
Media owners and advertisers
Top Republican and many Democratic
    politicians
Military top ranks
Top university administrators and trustees

MIDDLE CLASS
Income $30,000-$200,000, Net Worth $100,000-$5 Million

Professors and teachers in liberal arts
Rank and file public employees
Journalists & media employees
Artists
Middle-class minorities
College liberal arts students and graduates

Teachers in business and vocational ed
Independent businesspeople and professionals
White collar employees in the private sector

Vocational college students and grads

WORKING CLASS
Income under $10,000-$30,000, Net worth: Zero to $100,000

Left-wing populists:
    Labor union members
    "Underclass" whites and minorities
        (Income under $15,000, net worth
        under $50,000)

Right-wing populists:
    White race, blue collar, and some white
        collar workers,
    Military rank and file

declining economic situation of most Americans except for the rich prompted Democrats to renew their avowed support for "the working class"—used as a blanket term for everyone in the middle class and below.

Also, the class people *support* is not always the same class to which they *belong*. Many working-class Americans staunchly defend the rich and are driven by the conservative dream of someday becoming rich themselves. Conversely, conservative pundits ridicule upper-class "limousine liberals" who express concern for the poor and working class. Table 13.3 suggests a very rough, unscientific approximation of the makeup of American social classes and how the classes relate to political attitudes. You can test this schema against your own impressions. The totality of citizens who are termed "liberals" or "conservatives" is a coalition of the very different constituencies belonging to the three socioeconomic classes in the two columns. Most published sources (politicians, journalists, scholars) that you will encounter belong to the upper-middle or upper classes on either the left or right; typically, however, they will claim to be speaking and acting as **populists**, in support of the lower classes, who lack access to media of public opinion. In predictable rhetorical patterns, those at the upper levels on one side will say that they are true populists, having the interests of the lower levels on their side at heart, while partisans of the other side will accuse those on the first side of being **elitists** who hypocritically pretend to be populists, manipulating the lower-class masses for their own benefit. So you need to make a judgment call about which side is sincere.

The line suggesting an S-curve from bottom to top indicates the following. In America and other societies, people at the poorest level, left-wing populism (*populism* being defined as what represents, or is to the benefit of, the majority, or the common people, as opposed to the socioeconomic or cultural *elite*) tend to be liberal or leftist, as do those a step above them economically who are unionized workers—labor unions being the prime constituency of the liberal wing of the Democratic Party. (This group also tends to include first-generation immigrants and city dwellers.) People reaching a higher level within the working class, and in sectors like the military, tend more to be conservative Republicans, the constituency of right-wing populism. (This group also includes many rural and small-town dwellers and second-generation immigrants.) These are some of the divisions that after the 2000 presidential election came to identify "Blue States" as Democratic and "Red States" as Republican, although liberal versus conservative attitudes on religion and other "social issues" within this broad socioeconomic range are another complicating variable.

As working-class people, or their children, move up into the middle class and go to college, those who follow business-oriented majors tend to stay on the right through life, while general-education majors are more inclined to become liberals, remaining so if they go to work in the public, nonprofit sector (especially teachers and professors) or in media, the arts, and other intellectual fields. If they advance toward upper-class status, those who remain liberal as labor union or Democratic Party officials, media executives, or "stars" are often termed "limousine liberals" (think Sean Penn, Rosie O'Donnell, and Oprah Winfrey), implying a compartmentalization between class status and political attitudes. It is, however, less common for those who attain this level to remain liberal (which is why the concept of the limousine liberal is something of a **paradox**) than to swing back toward the right, the natural tendency, almost by definition, of people who attain status, wealth, and power—as, for example, teachers or college faculty who become administrators, journalists who become editors, and performers who become executives.

PREDICTABLE PATTERNS OF POLITICAL RHETORIC

The following list of predictable patterns, like the "Semantic Calculator for Bias in Rhetoric," is intended mainly to enable you to recognize a particular line of argument when you see it, not automatically to dismiss it as biased. It is a necessary and perfectly legitimate part of argumentation to make the strongest case you can for your own cause and to point out the faults in opponents' positions. Once you recognize these patterns, the more important task is to evaluate whether the points being played up and downplayed are well-reasoned and supported, or whether they are just appealing one-sidedly to knee-jerk emotional response.

Leftists will play up:	*Rightists will play up:*
Right-wing bias in media and education; power of business interests and administrators	Left-wing bias in media and education; power of employees and unions
Crimes and fraud by the rich; luxury, waste, selfish interests	Crimes and fraud by the poor; luxury and waste by

and control of government by private industry and the military	government bureaucrats; selfish interests and control over government by labor unions, teachers, environmentalist and civil rights organizations
Conservative ethnocentrism and sentimentality toward the middle and upper classes and America abroad	Leftist "negative thinking," "sour grapes," anti-Americanism, and sentimentality toward the lower classes and Third World peoples
U.S. military strengths, right-wing "hawks'" scare tactics about foreign adversaries' strengths and menace	Foreign adversaries' strengths, menace, and manipulation of left-wing "doves"; left-wing scare tactics about negative consequences of American military actions
Conservative rationalization of right-wing extremism and foreign dictatorships allied with U.S. (e.g., South Vietnam in Vietnam War, El Salvador in the 1980s, Saudi Arabia)	Liberal rationalization of left-wing extremism and Communist dictatorships or guerillas (e.g., Cuba, Sandinista Nicaragua, North Vietnam, Aristide in Haiti, Mugabe in Zimbabwe)

A NOTE ON TWENTY-FIRST CENTURY MODIFICATIONS TO TABLE 13.1

The worldwide, political spectrum in table 13.1, which goes back to the twentieth-century foundation for the left-to-right spectrum, has undergone considerable change, and as noted earlier, does not aim to be all-inclusive. The major change in the 1990s was the collapse of the Soviet Union and its satellite Communist governments in Eastern Europe. At this writing, there still exist some Communist dictatorships on the far left (most prominently Cuba, North Korea, Vietnam, and China, though the latter two have moved toward a capitalist economy while remaining political dictatorships) and some plutocratic dictatorships on the far right such as Saudi Arabia, Indonesia, and Guatemala, or military dictatorships like Pakistan and Myanmar (Burma). However, the extreme poles of Communism on the left and Fascism on the right no longer dominate world politics as they did through much of the twentieth century. The United States still remains to the right of Europe, Canada, and Japan on the spectrum of socialist-to-capitalist democracies. However, Western Europe in recent decades has seen a resurgence of an extreme right-wing, prompted mainly by opposition to swelling ranks of immigrant labor, mostly Arab, which is perceived as a threat to native employment and culture and as a possible source of terrorism. Anti-Semitism is also prevalent in the European right, a phenomenon of compartmentalized thinking, in light of the right's equal anti-Arab bias and of the antagonism between Arabs and Jews in Israel.

Two primary complications have made the worldwide left-right polarity somewhat obsolete, although it remains viable in the American spectrum in table 13.2. One is economic globalization, which has to a large extent eclipsed national identities and conflicts. Advocates of the global economy tend to be conservatives in the sense that they support multinational corporations, although they are sometimes termed "neoliberals" because they emphasize its progressive, democratizing effects on governments and economies in previously undeveloped countries. Opponents of globalization, generally leftists, say neoliberalism is a code word for allowing corporations free reign to impose a new form of worldwide colonialism and plutocracy calculated to drive down wages, worsen working conditions, and undermine unionized labor.

The other recent complication is the prominence of worldwide religious and ethnic conflicts, especially between, and within, the Western and Muslim worlds. Here distinguishing between left and right gets extremely complicated. Islamic terrorism is an outgrowth of Muslim countries that are internally conflicted between two different forms of conservative politics: either secular, plutocratic (mainly oil-rich) forces—some allied with America and Western Europe, like Saudi Arabia and Kuwait, some hostile, like Iraq under Saddam Hussein—or the fundamentalist Islamic movements in countries like Afghanistan and Iran. (Islamic fundamentalists are considered conservative in their own countries in the sense of opposing secular society and Westernization.) Almost no figures in American public life endorse terrorism or supported Saddam Hussein, but most conservatives are "hawks" and most liberals "doves" in their degree of support for military and domestic antiterrorist policies. (Liberals tend to favor more international diplomacy and policies that address underlying causes of Muslim antagonism toward the United States, while conservatives tend to favor primarily military action.) The Israeli-Palestinian conflict is primarily a struggle over land, not ideology, although it also involves religion and colonialism. Israel is a leftist social democracy internally, but it is periodically dominated by governments that are right-wing (and closely allied to American conservatives) in their hard-line policy toward the Palestinian Arabs, in contrast to the Israeli left, which seeks compromise with the Palestinians. For these reasons and others, American conservatives generally support Israel, while leftists generally support the Palestinians.

POLITICAL VIEWPOINTS IN SOURCES

Many sources that you will use for college papers have an explicit or implicit political viewpoint. Consider the following lists and discussion of American periodicals, book publishers, and research institutes identified by political position.

General Circulation Periodicals

This is a partial list, mainly of journals of opinion, intended to supplement, not replace, the more accessible, mass-circulation newspapers and magazines, most of which have a center-conservative to center-liberal orientation. (These hyphenated terms reflect the discussion of table 13.2 above, suggesting that identifying points on a continuous spectrum from left to right would be more accurate than labels like "liberal" and "conservative." A rough approximation can be achieved by sets of terms like "left-liberal," "center-liberal," "right-liberal," and so on.) For links to their online versions, see chapter 18.

American Enterprise	Monthly	Center-to-right conservative
American Prospect	Monthly	Left-Liberal
American Spectator	Monthly	Right-conservative
Atlantic Monthly	Monthly	Right-liberal
Chronicles	Monthly	Left-conservative Christian
Commonweal	Biweekly	Left-liberal Catholic
Dissent	Bimonthly	Socialist-to-liberal
Extra!	Bimonthly	Socialist
Harper's	Monthly	Left-liberal
Human Events	Weekly	Right conservative
Insight (Washington Times)	Weekly	Right conservative
In These Times	Monthly	Socialist
Modern Age	Quarterly	Center-conservative

Mother Jones	Monthly	Left-liberal
Ms.	Monthly	Center-to-left-liberal
The Nation	Weekly	Socialist-to left-liberal
National Review	Biweekly	Center-conservative
New Politics	Quarterly	Socialist
New Republic	Weekly	Right-liberal to left-conservative
New York Review of Books	Biweekly	Center-to-left liberal
Sunday New York Times	Weekly	Center liberal to left conservative
New Yorker	Weekly	Center-to-left liberal
Policy Review	Monthly	Center-to-right conservative
Progressive	Monthly	Socialist
Public Interest	Quarterly	Left-to-center-conservative
Public Opinion	Monthly	Center-conservative
Reason	Monthly	Conservative libertarian
Rolling Stone	Biweekly	Center-liberal
Tikkun	Bimonthly	Left-liberal
Utne Reader	Monthly	Digest of liberal journals
Village Voice	Weekly	Left-liberal
Washington Monthly	Monthly	Center-liberal
Weekly Standard	Weekly	Center-conservative
World Press Review	Monthly	Digest of foreign views
Z Magazine	Monthly	Socialist

Most of the influential national newspapers—such as the *New York Times,* the *Washington Post,* and the *Los Angeles Times*—attempt to strike a balance between liberal and conservative in their reporting, editorial and op-ed pages, and cultural reviews, although they are generally considered predominantly liberal (except by comparison to the smaller journals of opinion to their left, which delight in trashing the big papers for their relative conservatism). The *Wall Street Journal,* however, is openly conservative, especially in its editorial and op-ed sections. The *Washington Times* was founded in the 1980s by the Reverend Sun Myung Moon as a conservative daily counterpart to the *Washington Post.* Most other newspapers around the country—along with TV and radio stations—tend either to be owned by large local business interests and consequently to represent their conservative politics and that of their corporate advertisers and community peers, or, more recently, to have been bought up by conservative national chains, as documented by Ben H. Bagdikian in *The New Media Monopoly.* In reading newspaper or newsmagazine reviews of books on controversial topics, you should be aware that reviews are likely to be colored by the reviewer's own political viewpoint as well as that of the authors reviewed, and that editors' biases sometimes influence whether they assign a book to a reviewer who is on the same side as the author reviewed or to one on the opposing side. In both reviews and other articles written by either staffers or freelance authors (and sometimes even in letters to the editor), editors are also free to demand revisions and even to rewrite the author's text substantially, with or without permission, so much of what we read, watch, or hear may be filtered through editors' biases.

Journals of opinion in America and other countries have served, throughout their centuries-long history, largely as a voice for the particular political viewpoint of their owners (typically a single individual or family), although that viewpoint might change over the years with changes in owners or in the original owners' views. Two of the best-known for over a century have been *The Nation* and the *New Republic;* the early history of both was radical leftist—until the 1950s they were sometimes aligned with the Communist Party of America. *The Nation* has remained the best-known left-of-liberal journal (anti-Communistic under publisher Victor Navasky, though its critics still claim to find vestiges of its earlier history), while the *New Republic* under the ownership of Martin Peretz since the 1960s has become conservative on some issues, liberal on others. Other accessible journals on the left-of-liberal side include *Progressive, In These Times, Dissent, Mother Jones, Z Magazine,* and *Extra!* (published by FAIR, or Fairness and Accuracy in Reporting). The *New Yorker* has wide circulation and its scope is broader than politics, but insofar as it is partially a journal of opinion and reportage, in recent decades it has been consistently mainstream liberal. Two magazines well established in American history back to the mid-nineteenth century are *Harper's* and the *Atlantic Monthly;* like the *New Yorker,* they have semi-mass circulation and contain a wide variety of articles and fiction, but they have been generally liberal in their politics, though this has shifted with changes in owners and editors. For example, in the last decade or so *Harper's,* under the editorship of Lewis Lapham, has been decidedly more liberal than *Atlantic Monthly.*

The best-known conservative journals of opinion since the 1950s have been *Commentary* (which under the editorship of Norman Podhoretz shifted sharply from left to right in the late 1960s) and *National Review,* long owned and edited by William F. Buckley, who also was a prominent spokesperson for the right on public television. With the rise of the conservative "counterintelligentsia" since the 1970s has come a profusion of other conservative journals, including *American Spectator* (which began as a semischolarly, conservative counterpart to the *New York Review,* but which now aims at a broader audience and contains more political exposés, opinion, and invective) and the *Weekly Standard,* funded by Rupert Murdoch and edited by William Kristol (who was chief of staff to Vice President Dan Quayle), which serves as the unofficial voice of the Republican Party intelligentsia. *Insight,* the weekly magazine of the *Washington Times,* is available at some newsstands nationally, and a *Washington Times* weekly edition also has national circulation, as does the *Washington Post* weekly. Several publications of the conservative research institutes discussed below began as scholarly journals but are now aimed at a general audience: *American Enterprise* (American Enterprise Institute), *Policy Review* (Heritage Foundation), and the *Cato Journal* (Cato Institute). *Reason* is a widely available libertarian journal.

Publishers of Books and Reports

Liberal or Socialist	*Conservative or Libertarian*
Pantheon Press	Arlington House
Monthly Review Press	Freedom House
South End Press	Brandon Books
Praeger	Reader's Digest Books
Beacon Press	Basic Books
Seabury/Continuum Books	Laissez-Faire Books (libertarian)
Routledge	Regnery Books
Methuen	Simon & Schuster
Bergin & Garvey	Free Press
New Press	Spence Publishing
Metropolitan Books	
Common Courage Press	
Paradigm Publishers	

Most of the major publishers of serious nonfiction and fiction books have no fixed political viewpoint, so they publish a mix of conservative and liberal works. Some of them, however, are predominantly, though not exclusively, conservative—Simon & Schuster, Free Press, Basic Books—and others are predominantly liberal, most notably Random House and its Pantheon division, though changes in corporate ownership have cut back on Pantheon's leftist offerings, and its editor André Schiffren left several years ago and started the New Press as an alternative. Several smaller presses publish almost exclusively conservative books and others almost exclusively liberal to left-of-liberal ones, as listed in the table of books.

Research Institutes and Foundations ("Think Tanks")

Institute for Policy Studies	American Enterprise Institute
Center for Responsive Law (*Public Citizen*)	(*American Enterprise*)
Public Interest Research Groups	Center for Strategic and International Studies
Common Cause (*Common Cause*)	Hoover Institution (Stanford University)
Brookings Institution	Media Institute
Institute for Democratic Socialism	Hudson Institute
(*Democratic Left, Socialist Forum*)	Heritage Foundation (*Policy Review*)
Economic Policy Institute	Olin Foundation
Rockridge Institute	Scaife Foundation
Progressive Policy Institute	Cato Institute (libertarian)
Center for American Progress	Harry and Lynde Bradley Foundation
Demos	Manhattan Institute

Most of the American public is not very familiar with the workings of research institutes, also known as think tanks, or the foundations that fund them, but they have become increasingly influential in the formation of public opinion in the past few decades, along **partisan** political lines. Throughout the twentieth century and into the twenty-first, large American universities have housed a variety of research institutes where faculty members work virtually full-time rather than teach; teaching faculties also conduct research projects with funding from government agencies, corporations, nonprofit foundations, and occasionally labor or consumer organizations. In both universities and the more recent private research institutes, projects dealing directly or indirectly with socioeconomic or environmental issues may have a liberal or conservative bias according to the researchers' and funders' own ideological inclinations. The best way to find out whether a book you use as a source has been sponsored by a foundation or think tank, liberal or conservative, is to look in the acknowledgments section at the beginning or end of most journalistic and scholarly books, where the author will thank such-and-such a foundation or institute for financial support. Similar affiliations of writers of op-ed columns are typically indicated in a biographical note.

In the early 1970s, a group of national conservative leaders sought a solution to what they saw as the overall liberal or left-of-liberal bias of American universities, at least in the humanities and social sciences, and of the media, foundations, and intellectual life generally. They set out to build up a conservative counterintelligentsia by persuading several large corporations and corporate-aligned foundations to pour millions of dollars into the creation of think tanks mostly independent of universities. These institutions would conduct research supporting conservative causes and would publish books and reports, magazines and newspaper articles and lobby the media, as well as provide policy analyses and proposals for conservative politicians. These foundations have also endowed professorships in many universities in an attempt to increase conservative influence within them. Thus the Heritage Foundation and the American Enterprise Institute in Washington, D.C., and the Hoover Institution at Stanford University have been in direct service to Republican presidential administrations, members of Congress, and judges. From the eighties to the present, the Republican-allied Olin, Scaife, and Bradley foundations have sponsored many books, magazines, and public television programs as platforms for conservative journalists and scholars on education and "the culture wars." Books sponsored by these organizations include Allan Bloom's *Closing of the American Mind*, Christina Hoff Sommers's *Who Stole*

Feminism? and David Brock's *Real Anita Hill* and *The Seduction of Hillary Clinton* (portions of both had been published in *The American Spectator,* a flamboyantly conservative journal of opinion funded by billionaire Richard Mellon Scaife, who also funds the Scaife Foundation).[1] (As noted in "Setting the Agenda" in chapter 9, several of the same sponsors and foundations fund conservative college student organizations such as Young America's Foundation.) Although many other think tanks and foundations have a liberal orientation, the only ones with a direct link to the Democratic Party are the Progressive Policy Institute, a branch of the centrist Democratic Leadership Council, with which Bill Clinton and Al Gore were affiliated, and more recently, the left-liberal Center for American Progress.

Conservatives, typified by David Horowitz in "The Intellectual Class War" here, argue that their foundations and think tanks serve as a legitimate counterforce to more lavishly funded foundations like Ford, Rockefeller, Carnegie, and MacArthur, which support mainly liberal causes. Liberals argue that this is a **false analogy** on several points: unlike the conservative ones, these foundations are not exclusively involved with political issues, they do not have an overt political agenda or party affiliation, they do not act as agents of the corporations sponsoring them (indeed, some of the projects they fund are highly critical of such corporations), and they fund some conservative projects along with a majority of liberal ones whose nature makes them unlikely to receive corporate funding.

The rise of these conservative institutes has provoked a great deal of controversy, with liberals questioning the integrity of their research and charging them with conflict of interest and **special pleading**. Their defenders' rebuttal is that their overt partisanship serves legitimately to counterbalance the covert liberal partisanship of most university faculties (at least in the humanities and social sciences), journalists, and foundations. And the liberal counterrebuttal is that liberal bias in these groups is a legitimate counterbalance to all the realms of American public discourse that are dominated by corporations—political lobbies, advertising and public relations, corporate-owned media, business-oriented academic departments, university trusteeships and administrations, and so on—and that most liberal scholars or journalists are not beholden to special interests funding them. Be that as it may, for our purposes here it is useful for you just to know that you are likely to get a liberal viewpoint in the courses and writing of university or research-institute scholars in the humanities or social sciences and that you should compare it with the viewpoint of professors in business-oriented courses and information originating with the conservative think tanks.[2]

The somewhat absurd nature of this recent politicization of research institutes was captured in a satirical column by Jon Carroll (*San Francisco Chronicle,* December 4, 1998, C20), "Thinking about Think Tanks":

> There are your right-wing think tanks and your left-wing think tanks. They are funded by people with agendas; they are stocked like trout streams with people of a particular ideological bent who produce papers that discover reasons why it Makes Sense to believe tweedle or, contrariwise, twaddle.
> The people in the think tanks are often described as "respected" or "distinguished." They are "scholars." They just sit and think and think, and when they are done thinking, they believe whatever the person who's paying them to think also believes.

Notes

1. In a 1997 article for *Esquire* and in his 2002 book *Blinded by the Right: The Conscience of an Ex-Conservative,* Brock tells of how he was dropped as a reporter by the *American Spectator* when that publication and Scaife found his book on Hillary Clinton insufficiently negative toward the Clintons. Scaife also withdrew his financial support from *American Spectator* when it did not pursue his personal campaign against President Clinton to his satisfaction.

2. Several books have been written on the history of these conservative think tanks, including Sidney Blumenthal, *The Rise of the Counter-Establishment: From Conservative Ideology to Political Power* and Jean Stefancic and Richard Delgado, *No Mercy: How Conservative Think Tanks and Foundations Changed America's Social Agenda*. For personal accounts by former insiders in these circles who now criticize them for being **propaganda** organs of the Republican Party, see Michael Lind, *Up from Conservatism* and David Brock, *Blinded by the Right* and *The Republican Noise Machine*.

If We Decided to Tax the Rich

Steve Brouwer

From *Sharing the Pie*, Henry Holt, 1998. A full version of this article, including the works cited that provide substantive support for Brouwer's arguments, can be found online at http://www.paradigmpublishers.com/Books/BookDetail.aspx?productID=208952.

The very rich are different from you and me.—F. SCOTT FITZGERALD

Yes ... *they have more money.*—ERNEST HEMINGWAY

Can the people of the United States retake control, once again taxing the richest citizens at a progressive rate and creating a fair society for all? If we had a Congress and a president who were willing to promote the interests of the vast majority of Americans, we could recapture some of the accumulated wealth that has been transferred to the rich over the last two decades. A reallocation of our resources could serve working people in the following ways:

- by creating full employment, with a higher minimum wage and shorter workweek
- by supporting quality day care for all who need it
- by providing for federally funded health care that serves everyone
- by rebuilding the nation's schools, roads, bridges, sewers, and parks
- by offering free higher education and other training to all citizens

Measures such as this will certainly cost hundreds of billions of dollars. Where can we get this kind of money while keeping the budget deficit reasonably low? There are several places to start:

- We must reestablish upper-bracket federal income tax rates comparable to those imposed during the prosperous decades of the 1950s and 1960s. The current effective rate on the richest 1 percent, whose income is at least $900 billion per year, is about 25 percent. An effective tax rate of 50 percent on the very richest 1 percent of Americans would raise an extra $225 billion.

- Raise the effective tax rate on corporate profits to 50 percent, the approximate rate of the 1950s. Profits have risen dramatically, to over $600 billion per year, while taxes have remained at an effective rate of about 25 percent, so this increase would yield another $150 billion.

- Institute an annual wealth tax of 3 percent on the richest 1 percent of Americans; this will yield $250 billion per year.

- Cut defense spending on new weaponry by $100 billion to stay in line with the diminished military budgets of the rest of the world.

These proposals, and the $725 billion they would raise, might outrage the corporations and the rich, as well as the politicians whom they have so carefully cultivated; but it would hardly be a case of impoverishing the well-to-do. The $625 billion in increased taxation would simply restore the more equitable (but hardly equal) distribution of income and wealth enjoyed by Americans three decades ago. The exact fiscal measures used to achieve more egalitarian economic outcomes are not all that important; the ones listed above could be modified or partially replaced by others. (For instance, Social Security taxes could be made less regressive by assessing them on the highest salaries, and on all forms of property and financial income as well. Other worthy forms of taxation could be reestablished, such as the once progressive but now largely eviscerated inheritance tax.)

A class war, waged by the rich with very little opposition from the working class, has already taken place. The size of economic transfers recommended here would enable us to redress the imbalance of power in appropriate proportion to the inequality that has been imposed over the past twenty years. The money is there, and its redistribution back to working people would establish the balance that exists in most of the other highly industrialized countries.

Righting the imbalance between the rich and the working class is not just a matter of tinkering with budget deficit rules or massaging the Consumer Price Index or the measures of productivity. It is a battle for political and economic power, a matter of control over the political economy. Sharing our economic resources more equitably again will require ordinary citizens to exercise their democratic rights in a determined and unified manner. This fundamental shift cannot be accomplished by a quick swing of voters in one election, but only through a lengthy process of education and organization that convinces the American people that major changes are both desirable and possible.

Even though labor unions in the United States threw $35 million into targeted congressional races in 1996, there is little merit in the conservative claim that organized labor has the same kind of power in the Democratic Party as big business interests have in the Republican Party. Unions have resources that are minuscule compared with those of business interests: in 1996, all labor associations together collected $6 billion in dues, as compared with the $4 trillion in revenues and $360 billion in profits gathered by corporations. Labor can gain politically only when millions of working people, unionized and nonunionized, are engaged in the political process.

There are reasons for optimism. Despite the fact that the percentage of organized workers has been more than cut in half in the past forty years, from 35 percent to less than 15 percent, unions have made recent gains in organizing women, Hispanics, and African-Americans as members. In making an effort to organize the working poor and to alleviate the exploitation of part-time and contingent workers, unions are reviving the universal goals that once gave life to the labor movement. The emphasis on raising the wages of those at the bottom is crucial in two ways: it stresses the equal status due to all those who are willing to work, and it protects the wages and benefits of those already organized.

A distinct turnaround in public perceptions of the labor movement became evident in August of 1997 during the strike by drivers and package handlers at United Parcel Service. Opinion polls showed that Americans backed the Teamsters over UPS management by a margin of 2 to 1. This was a bit surprising given the Teamsters' well-publicized history of corruption and the fact that UPS was generally regarded as a good company. Two beliefs seemed most compelling to average Americans: first, that a company making billions in profits should be able to share them with hardworking employees; and second, that a company which had increased its number of part-timers to over 60 percent of its workforce, then paid them only half the wages of full-time workers, was trying to screw people over. This resonated with many average Americans who had either experienced downsizing themselves or who clearly understood that many companies felt free to throw loyal and competent workers aside.

The shift in public attitudes was having an effect on some voices emanating from the business press. *Business Week,* which had celebrated corporate CEOs as "stars" who deserved the 30 percent raises they received in 1995, did an about-face in April of 1997 when it reviewed the 54 percent increase in CEO compensation for 1996: "Call it Executive Over-Compensation," read the headline of their editorial, which concluded, "Compensation is running riot in many corner offices of corporate America. This simply has to stop." More surprising still was the magazine's reaction when it uncovered a tiny increase in wages of working Americans (about 1 percent) that had occurred between the summer of 1996 and the summer of 1997: "The prosperity of recent years is finally being shared by those in the lower tier of the economy—and that is cause for celebration, not despair." While *Business Week* was obviously premature in announcing that prosperity was being shared, its sentiments suggested that American concerns with inequality were finally being heard.

While the destruction of the social safety net has been a defeat for labor, welfare itself can be redefined by a progressive, labor-backed political program. Welfare should represent part of a universal social contract that can be extended to anyone who meets with severe economic hardships. The contract would make only one demand: that every capable citizen be willing to work. In return each citizen would receive good wages, quality education, and job training, with the added benefits of universal health care and day care. This kind of practical social democracy, grounded in the culture of working people, would quickly deflate the false claims of the right, that the poor are "lazy," "shiftless," and worse. The vast majority of the unemployed and underemployed poor, of whatever race, would be happy to claim membership in a newly dignified working class.

The power of labor has been unfairly curtailed in recent decades, so it is necessary to fight the legal restrictions and management policies that prevent union activity among the poorly paid and unorganized. But this alone is not sufficient. The more challenging task is convincing a good portion of the middle class that it too benefits from working-class mobilization. New kinds of political and social organizations must be formed—not necessarily traditional labor

unions—to articulate the goals that middle-class employees share with lower-paid workers. Political solutions will require a very broad solidarity among working Americans, a solidarity that can bridge class, racial, and ethnic lines. This should not be too difficult at a time when working conditions, benefits, and job security are deteriorating even among privileged salaried workers, and when many in the so-called middle class are being subjected to "working-class" treatment by senior management.

This short book is filled with facts and numbers and analyses that some will consider negative, depressing, and downright un-American. My purpose in drawing this picture of the political economy is to plant the seeds of understanding in the minds of working Americans. Not all of our economic and social problems began the last two decades of the twentieth century, but the policies pursued during the Reagan-Bush-Clinton era have made things considerably worse. Working people have suffered so that a small elite could enlarge its fortunes. In turn, this accumulated money has been wasted on speculative trading, widespread fraud, and nonproductive sectors of the economy, as well as corporate investment in countries where labor is provided by desperately poor people.

The old structures of capital accumulation have brought us regular cycles of poverty and depression in the past. Today things are worse, for capital has lost whatever productive drive and capability it once possessed; the glorification of entrepreneurship in the 1980s brought on the destruction, not the multiplication, of our national assets. The upper class tried to regenerate itself through money games that were far removed from real economic production: the plunder of the banking system, the privatization of public savings, and the paper trade in corporate assets.

It seemed, only a few years back, that if the United States failed to break these habits we would keep sinking in relation to other highly industrialized countries. The ascent of the economies of Japan, Germany, and the rest of Western Europe from 1950 to 1990 was remarkable. They seemed poised to leave us behind precisely because they were taking much better care of their people at the same time that their societies were becoming more productive.

Today something more frightening is happening. The United States, in concert with the corporate engines of globalization, may well bring the rest of the industrialized world down to its level. Once that has happened, the forces unleashed by international finance capital will keep pushing living standards downward. It is uncertain whether the kinds of social democracy set up in Western Europe can survive the current trends that have internationalized capital. Now, as capital moves quickly from continent to continent, often searching for cheap labor disciplined by authoritarian regimes, the capitalists are becoming more internationalized, too (whether they know it or not). They cannot possibly show loyalty, whether feigned or real, to the working and middle classes in their own countries.

Without a sharp turnaround toward democracy and equality in the United States, Europe will be virtually alone in its commitment to social democracy. The pressures of low-wage immigrant labor, cheap imports from Eastern Europe and Asia, and free-market practices of governments are already threatening once secure areas of employment and causing right-wing populism to pop up in various Western European countries. Surprising numbers of middle-class and working-class voters have supported ultranationalist, neofacsist parties throughout Europe because, like white male workers in the United States, they see their status slipping.

Europe's weakened remnants of social democracy may survive for a while, but are unlikely to do very well if the American, Japanese, and other international investors (including Europeans) keep filling the world's markets with cheaper products produced by mainland Chinese, Indonesians, Thais, Vietnamese, Filipinos, and others in the vast new workhouse of Asia. In this chaotic world mess, the authoritarian/austerity regimes based on the Taiwanese and South Korean experience will be the model for modern development; their kinds of management teams are exportable, as are their long hours and brutal working conditions. These factors are rapidly turning China, the ultimate labor resource, into a giant replica of the Asian Tiger economy.

In the United States few mainstream commentators are paying attention to the ways that "free-trade" ideology is undermining real freedom. They have failed, for instance, to see the dark portents behind President Clinton's willingness to seek campaign contributions from Indonesian billionaires and Chinese corporations. Conservative columnist and former Nixon speechwriter William Safire was one of the few to see the situation clearly when he described "the central point of the ideo-economic struggle going on in today's world. On one side are governments that put 'order' above all, and offer an under-the-table partnership to managers who like arranged outcomes and a docile work force."

If Arkansas, which looks suspiciously like a center of Third World development within the United States, is the economic and political model stuck inside our President's head, then we are already in trouble. And if Singapore is the model state for globalizing high-tech development in the eyes of the world's investing class, then we are drifting toward something worse: an illusion of democracy called "authoritarian democracy."

Nearly one hundred and seventy years ago, Alexis de Tocqueville wrote that "the manufacturing aristocracy which is growing up before our eyes is one of the harshest that ever existed in the world.... If ever a permanent inequality of conditions and aristocracy again penetrate the world, it may be predicted that this is the gate by which they will enter." The new corporate aristocracy—controlling not just transnational manufacturing but also worldwide finance and services—is more powerful than anything de Tocqueville could have imagined, and it has diminished the prospects for democracy in America.

The citizens of the United States need to restrain the single-minded accumulation of private capital, invest in strong public institutions, and give human values some room to thrive. Real democracy requires that the people find ways to share wealth and power. As the repositories of immense wealth and technical expertise, the rich nations of the North ought to promote peaceful and fair development rather than unleash free-market chaos throughout the rest of the world. At home, the productive forces of the United States and the other advanced industrialized countries are easily sufficient to enhance equality and democratic values, as well as provide a comfortable standard of living for all.

The Intellectual Class War

David Horowitz

From *The Art of Political War,* Spence Publishing, 2000

A few years after the fall of the marxist utopias, I found myself in Beverly Hills sitting next to a man who was worth half a billion dollars. His name was Stanley Gold, and he was chairman of a holding company that was the largest shareholder in Disney, at the time the largest media corporation in the world. Since I was engaged in a conservative project in the entertainment community and the occasion was a cocktail reception for a Republican senator, I quickly turned the conversation into a pitch for support. But I was only able to run through a few bars of my routine before Gold put a fatherly hand on my arm and said, "Save your breath, David. I'm a socialist."

I am reminded of this story every time a leftist critic assaults me (which is often) and deploys the marxist cliché that I have "sold out" my ideals, or suggests that an opinion I have expressed can be explained by the "fact" that somewhere a wealthy puppetmaster is pulling my strings. I am not alone, of course, in being the target of such ad hominem slanders, which are familiar to every conservative who has ever engaged in a political debate.

Of course, those who traffic in socially-conscious abuse have a ready answer for anecdotes like mine, namely, that it is an aberration. Even if it is true, therefore, it is false because there is a larger marxist "truth" that trumps little facts like this. This truth is that conservative ideas express the views of corporate America, serve the status quo,

defend the rich and powerful, and legitimize the oppression of the poor. Whereas leftist views, however well paid for, are noble because they oppose all the injustice that corporate America, the status quo, and the rich represent. The "truth" is that conservative views *must* be paid for because they could not possibly be the genuine views of any decent human being with a grain of integrity or compassion.

In the fantasy world of the left, the figure of Stanley Gold can only be understood as a human oxymoron: a good-hearted capitalist who is a friend to humanity and a traitor to his class. But, then, so are such famous left-wing moguls as Ted Turner, David Geffen, Oprah Winfrey, Steven Spielberg, Michael Eisner, and a hundred others less famous (but equally wealthy) that one could easily name.

In fact, Stanley Gold is exceptional only in his wit and candor—and his ideological frame of mind. For, unlike the self-identified progressives named above, the CEOs of most major corporations studiously avoid ideological politics, left or right, because such politics are not in the corporate interest. To become identified with a hard political position is to become a target for opponents who control the machinery of regulation and taxation and exert life-and-death power over business. Moreover, from a business point of view most politicians are fungible: the kind of favors businesses require can be performed by one politician as easily as another. It is safer to stay above the fray and buy politicians when necessary, Republicans as well as Democrats, conservatives and liberals. Money, not ideological passion, is the currency of corporate interest, power rather than ideas its political agenda. Therefore, politicians rather than intellectuals are the normal objects of its attention.

There are two exceptions to this rule of political neutrality. First, when an administration, for whatever reason, chooses to declare war on a wealthy individual, corporation, or even an entire industry, embracing the political opposition may seem the best option in an already bad situation. Big Tobacco, Microsoft, and Michael Milken, for example, when assaulted by government, adopted this defensive strategy (Tobacco and Microsoft went strongly Republican; Milken became a Democrat). Second, when political activists shake down a large corporation, a tactic almost exclusively of the left, the corporation will choose to underwrite their group. Under attack from radical Greens, for example, major companies like ARCO have become large subsidizers of the environmental movement. Through similar extortionist efforts, Jesse Jackson's Rainbow/Push coalition has received more corporate underwriting than any dozen conservative groups put together.

Nevertheless, the norm for corporate interests remains the removal of themselves and their assets from ideological politics. The same applies to individuals who are serious financial players. I have had very conservative billionaires tell me that whatever their personal views, they cannot afford to be political (in my sense) at all.

A consequence of this standoff is that most of the contributions available to ideological activists of the left or right are either small individual donations solicited through direct mail campaigns or large institutional donations from tax-exempt foundations. In this area, too, the fevered imaginations of the left have created a wildly distorted picture in which well-funded goliaths of the right, Olin, Scaife, and Bradley, overwhelm the penurious Davids of the left. Edward Said, for example,

used the platform of the once distinguished Reith lectures to attack Peter Collier and myself over the "second thoughts" movement we launched years ago as a critique of the left: "In a matter of months during the late 1980s, Second Thoughts aspired to become a movement, alarmingly well funded by right-wing Maecenases like the Bradley and Olin Foundations...."

Some years later, a report appeared, "The Strategic Philanthropy of Conservative Foundations," documenting the annual disbursements of what were deemed to be the key conservative grant-giving institutions. The annual sum of the subsidies from twelve conservative foundations was seventy million dollars. This amount may seem large until one looks at the Ford Foundation, which dispenses all by itself more than five hundred million dollars each year—more than seven times as much—mainly to liberal and left-wing causes. Ford is the principal founder, for example, of the hard-left Mexican American Legal Defense Fund (MALDEF), which lacks any visible base in the Mexican American community, but has been the principal promoter of illegal immigration and the driving force behind the failed multibillion-dollar bilingual education programs. Ford created MALDEF and has provided it with more than twenty-five million dollars over the years. Ford has also been the leading funder of left-wing feminism and black separatism on American campuses, and of the radical effort to balkanize our national identity through multicultural university curricula.

Ford is typical. The biggest and most prestigious foundations, bearing the names of the most venerable captains of American capitalism—Ford, Rockefeller, Mellon, Carnegie, and Pew—are all biased to the left, as are many newer but also well-endowed institutions like the MacArthur, Markle, and Schumann foundations. MacArthur alone is three times the size of the "big three" conservative foundations—Olin, Bradley, and Scaife—combined.

Moreover, these foundations do not represent the most important support the corporate "ruling class" and its social elites provide to the left. That laurel goes to the private and public universities that have traditionally been the preserve of the American aristocracy and now, as Richard Rorty has happily pointed out, are the "political base of the left." With its multibillion-dollar endowment and unmatched intellectual prestige, Harvard provides an exemplary case, its relevant faculties and curricula reflecting the absolute hegemony of left-wing ideas. The Kennedy School of Government at Harvard is arguably the most prestigious and important reservoir of intellectual talent and policy counsel available to the political establishment. Cabinet officials are regularly drawn from its ranks. Of its more than 150 faculty members, only five are identifiable Republicans, a ratio that is extraordinary given the spectrum of political opinion in the nation at large. Yet it is the rule in the university system.

The institutional and financial support for the left—through its dominance in the universities, the book publishing industry, the press, television news, and the arts—is so overwhelming it is hardly contested. There are no prestigious universities where the faculty ratio in the liberal arts and social sciences is 150 Republicans to five Democrats. There is not a single major American newspaper whose features and news sections are written by conservatives rather than liberals—and this includes such conservative-owned institutions as the *Wall Street Journal,* the *Los Angeles Times,* whose editorial pages are left wing as well, the *Orange County Register,* and the *San Diego Union.*

Some will object to my definition of what is "left" as a way of avoiding the irrefutable reality it describes. They will argue that because Noam Chomsky is regarded as a fringe intellectual by segments of the media, the media cannot be dominated by the ideas of the left. But this supposes that Chomsky's exclusion is ideological rather than idiosyncratic. After all, Peter Jennings is a fan of Cornel West who is a fan of Noam Chomsky's. Christopher Hitchens is a fan of Noam Chomsky and ubiquitous on television and in print. Regardless, the fact remains that an America-loathing crank like Chomsky is an incomparably more influential figure in

the left-wing culture of American universities than any conservative one could name.

The left, it can hardly be disputed, is funded and supported by the very "ruling class" it asserts is the puppetmaster of the right and the oppressor of minorities, the working class, and the poor. Institutional support and funds provided to the intellectual left by the "ruling class" far exceed any sums it provides to the intellectual right, as anyone with a pocket calculator will grasp. Why is this so? Could it be that the marxist model itself is nonsense?

It is hardly evident, for example, that the interest of the corporate rich lies in preserving the status quo. If the Clinton years did nothing else, they should certainly have served to put this canard to rest. The Clinton Administration's most important left wing projects were the comprehensive government-controlled healthcare plan, which failed, and the effort to preserve racial preferences, which succeeded. Both agendas received the enthusiastic support of corporate America—the healthcare plan from the nation's largest health insurance companies and racial preferences from Fortune 500 corporations across the board.

Or try another measure: in the 1999 presidential primary campaign, Bill Bradley was the Democratic candidate running from the left. The chief points of Bradley's platform were a revival of the comprehensive Clinton healthcare scheme and the pursuit of left wing racial grievances. Bradley's most recently acquired African American friend is the anti-Semitic racist Al Sharpton, the black leader of choice for Democratic Party candidates. But despite these radical agendas, as everyone knows, "Dollar Bill's" thirty-plus-million-dollar campaign war chest was largely filled by Wall Street, where he himself has made millions as a stockbroker over the years.

The explanation for the paradox is this: Unless one is seduced by the discredited poppycock of leftist intellectuals, there is no reason the rich should be adversaries of the poor or oppose their interests. Not in a dynamic market society like ours. Only if the market is a zero-sum game as marxists and their clones believe—"exploited labor" for the worker, "surplus value" for the capitalist—would leftist clichés make any sense. But they do not. The real-world relation between labor and capital is quite the opposite of what the left proposes. Entrepreneurs generally want a better-educated, better-paid, more diverse working force, because that means better employees, better marketers, and better consumers of the company product. That is why, historically, everywhere capitalism has been embraced, labor conditions have improved and inequalities have diminished whether there has been a strong trade union presence or not. That is why the capitalist helmsmen of the World Trade Organization are better friends of the world's poor than any of the Luddite demonstrators against them in Seattle.

The twenty-first century political argument is not about whether to help the poor, or whether to include all Americans in the social contract. Republicans embrace these objectives as firmly as Democrats, conservatives as well as liberals. The issue is how best to help the poor, how best to integrate the many cultures of the American mosaic into a common culture that works. Twenty years after the welfare system was already a proven disaster for America's inner city poor, Democrats and leftists were still demanding more welfare and opposing significant reforms. Clinton himself vetoed the Republican reform bill twice and only signed it when he was told he would not be reelected if he did not. Welfare reform has liberated hundreds of thousands of poor people from dead-end dependency and given them a taste of the self-esteem that comes from earning one's keep.

If the left were serious about its interest in the poor, it would pay homage to the man who made welfare reform possible, the despised former Speaker Newt Gingrich. If hypocrisy were not their stock-in-trade, self-styled champions of the downtrodden like Cornel West and Marian Wright Edelman would be writing testimonials to Newt Gingrich as a hero to America's poor. But that will not happen. Instead, the left will go on tarring Gingrich and his political allies as the grinches who stole Christmas, as "enemies of the poor" and lackeys of the rich. Such witch-hunting is indispensable to the left's intellectual class war. The dehumanization of its opponents is the next best option to developing an argument to refute them.

In fact, there is no conservative party in America. Certainly not Republicans, who are responsible for the major reforms of the Clinton years. The mantle of reaction is better worn by the left, given its resistance to change and its rearguard battles against the market and free trade. But the left controls the culture, and with it the political language. Therefore, in America, reactionaries will continue to be called "progressives" and reformers "conservatives."

Fascism Anyone?

Laurence W. Britt

Free Inquiry magazine, Volume 23, Number 2, 2003

We are two-and-a-half generations removed from the horrors of Nazi Germany, although constant reminders jog the consciousness. German and Italian fascism form the historical models that define this twisted political worldview. Although they no longer exist, this worldview and the characteristics of these models have been imitated by protofascist regimes at various times in the twentieth century. Both the original German and Italian models and the later protofascist regimes show remarkably similar characteristics. Although many scholars question any direct connection among these regimes, few can dispute their visual similarities.

Beyond the visual, even a cursory study of these fascist and protofascist regimes reveals the absolutely striking convergence of their *modus operandi*. This, of course, is not a revelation to the informed political observer, but it is sometimes useful in the interests of perspective to restate obvious facts and in so doing shed needed light on current circumstances.

For the purpose of this perspective, I will consider the following regimes: Nazi Germany, Fascist Italy, Franco's Spain, Salazar's Portugal, Papadopoulos's Greece, Pinochet's Chile, and Suharto's Indonesia. To be sure, they constitute a mixed bag of national identities, cultures, developmental levels, and history. But they all followed the fascist or protofascist model in obtaining, expanding, and maintaining power. Further, all these regimes have been overthrown, so a more or less complete picture of their basic characteristics and abuses is possible.

Analysis of these seven regimes reveals fourteen common threads that link them in recognizable patterns of national behavior and abuse of power. These basic characteristics are more prevalent and intense in some regimes than in others, but they all share at least some level of similarity.

1. *Powerful and continuing expressions of nationalism.* From the prominent displays of flags and bunting to the ubiquitous lapel pins, the fervor to show patriotic nationalism, both on the part of the regime itself and of citizens caught up in its frenzy, was always obvious. Catchy slogans, pride in the military, and demands for unity were common themes in expressing this nationalism. It was usually coupled with a suspicion of things foreign that often bordered on xenophobia.

2. *Disdain for the importance of human rights.* The regimes themselves viewed human rights as of little value and a hindrance to realizing the objectives of the ruling elite. Through clever use of propaganda, the population was brought to accept these human rights abuses by marginalizing, even demonizing, those being targeted. When abuse was egregious, the tactic was to use secrecy, denial, and disinformation.

3. *Identification of enemies/scapegoats as a unifying cause.* The most significant common thread among these regimes was the use of scapegoating as a means to divert the people's attention from other problems, to shift blame for failures, and to channel frustration in controlled directions. The methods of choice—relentless propaganda and disinformation—were usually effective. Often the regimes would incite "spontaneous" acts against the target scapegoats, usually communists, socialists, liberals, Jews, ethnic and racial minorities, traditional national enemies, members of other religions, secularists, homosexuals, and "terrorists." Active opponents of these regimes were inevitably labeled as terrorists and dealt with accordingly.

4. *The supremacy of the military/avid militarism.* Ruling elites always identified closely with the military and the industrial infrastructure that supported it. A disproportionate share of national resources was allocated to the military, even when domestic needs were acute. The military was seen as an expression of nationalism, and was used whenever possible to assert national goals, intimidate other nations, and increase the power and prestige of the ruling elite.

5. *Rampant sexism.* Beyond the simple fact that the political elite and the national culture were male-dominated, these regimes inevitably viewed women as second-class citizens. They were adamantly anti-abortion and also homophobic. These attitudes were usually codified in Draconian laws that enjoyed strong support by the orthodox religion of the country, thus lending the regime cover for its abuses.

6. *A controlled mass media.* Under some of the regimes, the mass media were under strict direct control and could be relied upon never to stray from the party line. Other regimes exercised more subtle power to ensure media orthodoxy. Methods included the control of licensing and access to resources, economic pressure, appeals to patriotism, and implied threats. The leaders of the mass media were often politically compatible with

the power elite. The result was usually success in keeping the general public unaware of the regimes' excesses.

7. *Obsession with national security.* Inevitably, a national security apparatus was under direct control of the ruling elite. It was usually an instrument of oppression, operating in secret and beyond any constraints. Its actions were justified under the rubric of protecting "national security," and questioning its activities was portrayed as unpatriotic or even treasonous.

8. *Religion and ruling elite tied together.* Unlike communist regimes, the fascist and protofascist regimes were never proclaimed as godless by their opponents. In fact, most of the regimes attached themselves to the predominant religion of the country and chose to portray themselves as militant defenders of that religion. The fact that the ruling elite's behavior was incompatible with the precepts of the religion was generally swept under the rug. Propaganda kept up the illusion that the ruling elites were defenders of the faith and opponents of the "godless." A perception was manufactured that opposing the power elite was tantamount to an attack on religion.

9. *Power of corporations protected.* Although the personal life of ordinary citizens was under strict control, the ability of large corporations to operate in relative freedom was not compromised. The ruling elite saw the corporate structure as a way to not only ensure military production (in developed states), but also as an additional means of social control. Members of the economic elite were often pampered by the political elite to ensure a continued mutuality of interests, especially in the repression of "have-not" citizens.

10. *Power of labor suppressed or eliminated.* Since organized labor was seen as the one power center that could challenge the political hegemony of the ruling elite and its corporate allies, it was inevitably crushed or made powerless. The poor formed an underclass, viewed with suspicion or outright contempt. Under some regimes, being poor was considered akin to a vice.

11. *Disdain and suppression of intellectuals and the arts.* Intellectuals and the inherent freedom of ideas and expression associated with them were anathema to these regimes. Intellectual and academic freedom were considered subversive to national security and the patriotic ideal. Universities were tightly controlled; politically unreliable faculty harassed or eliminated. Unorthodox ideas or expressions of dissent were strongly attacked, silenced, or crushed. To these regimes, art and literature should serve the national interest or they had no right to exist.

12. *Obsession with crime and punishment.* Most of these regimes maintained Draconian systems of criminal justice with huge prison populations. The police were often glorified and had almost unchecked power, leading to rampant abuse. "Normal" and political crime were often merged into trumped-up criminal charges and sometimes used against political opponents of the regime. Fear, and hatred, of criminals or "traitors" was often promoted among the population as an excuse for more police power.

13. *Rampant cronyism and corruption.* Those in business circles and close to the power elite often used their position to enrich themselves. This corruption worked both ways; the power elite would receive financial gifts and property from the economic elite, who in turn would gain the benefit of government favoritism. Members of the power elite were in a position to obtain vast wealth from other sources as well: for example, by stealing national resources. With the national security apparatus under control and the media muzzled, this corruption was largely unconstrained and not well understood by the general population.

14. *Fraudulent elections.* Elections in the form of plebiscites or public opinion polls were usually bogus. When actual elections with candidates were held, they would usually be perverted by the power elite to get the desired result. Common methods included maintaining control of the election machinery, intimidating and disenfranchising opposition voters, destroying or disallowing legal votes, and, as a last resort, turning to a judiciary beholden to the power elite.

Does any of this ring alarm bells? Of course not. After all, this is America, officially a democracy with the rule of law, a constitution, a free press, honest elections, and a well-informed public constantly being put on guard against evils. Historical comparisons like these are just exercises in verbal gymnastics. Maybe, maybe not.

References

Andrews, Kevin. *Greece in the Dark*. Amsterdam: Hakkert, 1980.

Chabod, Frederico. *A History of Italian Fascism*. London: Weidenfeld, 1963.

Cooper, Marc. *Pinochet and Me*. New York: Verso, 2001.

Cornwell, John. *Hitler as Pope*. New York: Viking, 1999.

de Figuerio, Antonio. *Portugal—Fifty Years of Dictatorship*. New York: Holmes & Meier, 1976.

Eatwell, Roger. *Fascism, A History*. New York: Penguin, 1995.

Fest, Joachim C. *The Face of the Third Reich*. New York: Pantheon, 1970.

Gallo, Max. *Mussolini's Italy*. New York: MacMillan, 1973.

Kershaw, Ian. *Hitler* (two volumes). New York: Norton, 1999.

Laqueur, Walter. *Fascism, Past, Present, and Future*. New York: Oxford, 1996.

Papandreau, Andreas. *Democracy at Gunpoint*. New York: Penguin Books, 1971.

Phillips, Peter. *Censored 2001: 25 Years of Censored News*. New York: Seven Stories. 2001.

Sharp, M.E. *Indonesia Beyond Suharto*. Armonk, 1999.

Verdugo, Patricia. *Chile, Pinochet, and the Caravan of Death*. Coral Gables, Florida: North-South Center Press, 2001.

Yglesias, Jose. *The Franco Years*. Indianapolis: Bobbs-Merrill, 1977.

Topics for Discussion and Writing

1. Regarding table 13.3, "Social Class and Political Attitudes, Left to Right," and the notes following it, discuss in groups or write about how closely this **hypothesis** matches your sense of these realities. Do some research on the sociology and economics of social class, or on social class and political affiliations, to test against this model.

2. On what points do Brouwer and Horowitz exemplify "A Semantic Calculator," the oppositions in this chapter described under "Leftists/Rightists Tend to Support" and "Predictable Patterns of Political Rhetoric," and the points of opposition outlined at the end of chapter 16? How do they differ on (1) the importance of labor unions? (2) President Clinton's welfare reform legislation? (3) economic globalization? (See Horowitz's references to "everywhere capitalism has been embraced," "free trade," and "the World Trade Organization," whose meeting in Seattle was protested by anti-globalization demonstrators.) Evaluate the relative quality of reasoning and supporting evidence in Brouwer and Horowitz, and compare their **tone** in the use of **invective** and **name-calling**.

3. *Irony Alert:* Horowitz's paragraph beginning "Of course, those who traffic . . ." is a sarcastic account of the "truth" that he claims is falsely promoted by his leftist opponents. Translate what he is saying ironically into its literal opposite, which it really means. Also explain his use of semantic **paradox** in his last paragraph.

4. Brouwer's viewpoint in "If We Decided to Tax the Rich" is left-of-liberal, or radical left, to the extent that he is arguing for the benefits of European social democracy over American capitalism. On what points does he criticize the Democrats and President Clinton from the left, and how does his criticism differ from Horowitz's criticism from the right? What different lines of argument might he make if he were advocating pure socialism or Communism rather than social democracy?

5. The book in which Horowitz's "The Intellectual Class War" appeared, *The Art of Political War,* was published by Spence Publishing Company, an explicitly conservative publishing house. According to David Brock's *The Republican Noise Machine,* Horowitz was an advisor in the 2000 presidential election to George W. Bush, who took the theme of "compassionate conservatism" from Horowitz's "playbook" in *The Art* (Brock 103). Although Horowitz does not mention it in this chapter, which defends "the 'big three' conservative foundations— Olin, Bradley, and Scaife," elsewhere he acknowledges that he has received considerable financial support from all three for his books, his think tank David Horowitz Freedom Center, the organization Students for Academic Freedom (which monitors alleged cases of liberal and leftist college faculty bias), and other projects including his Web site, frontpage.com. With reference to the discussion of **conflict of interest** in chapter 15, judge whether Horowitz seems to be engaging in **special pleading** here or makes a well-reasoned argument in defense of funding by these foundations' Republican-aligned corporate sponsors.

6. The book in which Brouwer's "If We Decided to Tax the Rich" appeared, *Sharing the Pie: A Citizen's Guide to Wealth and Power in America,* was published by Henry Holt, a mainstream house with no clear political viewpoint. He has published other books with leftist presses, and a publisher's biographical note says he "organized and built housing cooperatives, founded a worker-owned construction company, and developed a community-owned housing program." No apparent partisan affiliations or conflicts of interest here, but you might "Google" him to see if you can find any.

7. Horowitz **refutes** a central leftist line of argument, that large corporations and wealthy individuals have strongly conservative, and most often Republican, political affiliations. He begins with an **anecdote** about multimillionaire Stanley Gold, who claims he is a socialist, and argues that this is not a case of **arguing from the exception**. Does he provide an adequate **causal analysis** for the **paradox** of why wealthy corporations and individuals should ever support political forces that would divest them of their wealth and power? How clear is the sense of "socialism" as Horowitz discusses it here? Do you think Horowitz would say it extends to government or worker ownership of corporations and control of their policies concerning labor unions, wages, working conditions, and environmentalism?

8. As in "A Semantic Calculator," Brouwer and Horowitz play up the other side's sources of wealth and power while downplaying their own side's. As an individual or class research paper project, survey **empirical** studies objectively comparing: (a) corporations, (b) the *Fortune* 500 largest corporations and the *Forbes* 400 wealthiest individuals (or comparable corporations and individuals in your own state and locality), and (c) labor unions, in their support of conservative versus liberal or leftist causes, or of the Republican versus the Democratic Party (or other parties), and the amount of money they spend in that support. Similarly compare relative conservative versus liberal or leftist political and financial backing of lobbies (including documented cases of bribing politicians), political action committees, campaign contributions, media ownership, advertising and public relations agencies, foundations and think tanks, university administrators and faculties, and student organizations.

9. In the first paragraph, Horowitz describes his own fund-raising effort as "a pitch for support." He later says, without supporting evidence, that liberal activist

groups "shake down a corporation" using "extortionist efforts." Discuss as an example of **cleans** and **dirties**. What reasons for supporting these liberal causes might corporations have other than extortion? Do you suppose that Horowitz had documentation for his claim that Jesse Jackson's group "has received more corporate support than any dozen conservative groups put together," or is it meant as **hyperbole**? (Horowitz's chapter and the book in which it appeared contain no documentation beyond what is in the text.)

10. Debate in class the feasibility of the **implication** in Lawrence Britt's "Fascism Anyone?" that conservative tendencies in the United States today could lead toward fascism.

11. Relate the subject and viewpoint of the cartoon at the beginning of chapter 14 to the topics of these two chapters. Tom Tomorrow's cartoons appear in left-liberal journals like *Z Magazine* and *American Prospect*.

CHAPTER 14

Thinking Critically About Mass Media

20   Z MAGAZINE JANUARY 1997

Do news, entertainment, and advertising media give the people what they want, or *tell* the people what they want? Can the media be objective, and *should* they be? How can it be that conservatives are convinced that the media have a left-wing bias while leftists are equally convinced the media have a right-wing bias? These issues are endlessly, heatedly debated by political partisans, media critics, and scholars. Once again, we must recognize the rhetorical and semantic ambiguities involved in addressing these questions in their full complexity. (The present chapter develops some of the topics in chapter 13 in specific reference to media, and the issues here parallel those about whether political elections and legislation truly represent the people, so it would be useful to review the concepts and definitions in that chapter. As in chapter 13, this chapter attempts to arrive at definitions and judgments that are acceptable to leftists and rightists alike, while recognizing the extreme difficulty in doing so, and it is likewise open to refinement and revision at readers' suggestions.)

DO THE MEDIA GIVE PEOPLE WHAT THEY WANT?

In a chapter entitled "Masscult and Midcult" in his book *Against the American Grain* (New York: Vintage, 1962), Dwight Macdonald writes:

> The masses are in historical time what a crowd is in space: a large quantity of people unable to express their human qualities because they are related to each other neither as individuals nor as members of a community. In fact, they are not related to *each other* at all.... Yet this collective monstrosity, "the masses," "the public" is taken as a human norm by the technicians of Masscult [mass culture]. They at once degrade the public by treating it as an object, to be

handled with the lack of ceremony of medical students dissecting a corpse, and at the same time flatter it and pander to its taste and ideas by taking them as the criterion of reality. . . .

Whenever a Lord of Masscult is reproached for the low quality of his products, he automatically ripostes, "But that's what the public wants, what can I do?" A simple and conclusive defense, at first glance. But a second look reveals that (1) to the extent the public "wants" it, the public has been conditioned to some extent by his products, and (2) his efforts have taken this direction because (a) he himself also "wants" it—never underestimate the ignorance and vulgarity of publishers, movie producers, network executives and other architects of Masscult—and (b) the technology of producing mass "entertainment" (again, the quotes are advised) imposes a simplistic, repetitive pattern so that it is easier to say the public wants this than to say the truth which is that the public gets this and so wants it. . . .

For some reason, objections to the giving-the-public-what-it-wants line are often attacked as undemocratic and snobbish. But it is precisely because I do believe in the potentialities of ordinary people that I criticize Masscult. (9–11)

Do—and *should*—mass news and entertainment media "give the people what they want"? Both sides of this question are equally complex. Do those running commercial media really know what the people want, in the sense that large numbers of people actively make known to media representatives what they would like to read, hear, and see? Or are the people mainly providing passive feedback to what they are offered, in the form of random surveys and ratings polls that are impersonal and imprecise at best? Macdonald suggests that there is a **vicious circle** or **self-fulfilling prophecy** here: the people are conditioned, to some extent, to want what they get, or at least to take what they get in the absence of any preferable alternatives. Have audiences asked for the constantly increasing number and length of commercials on TV and radio? Have pro sports fans asked for constantly longer seasons and multiplying numbers of teams and league divisions, or have they simply failed to resist the TV broadcasters' drive to increase coverage, and thus advertising revenue? Defenders of the media say no one is forced to watch or listen to anything, and everyone is free to take it or leave it. But critics like Macdonald ask, if we are all conditioned from the time we are infants to consume and accept media messages, are we really free to choose? (All these questions about the media parallel the questions about the whole, larger economic system of "free enterprise," of which the media form a key part, and the conservative assumption that consumers are free to take or leave the products the system produces, as in the discussion of "the beauty myth" in chapter 5.)

Furthermore, if "the people" are considered to be the largest segment of the audience numerically, that means those at the literacy level of high school graduates or lower—and they are indeed defined by many media marketers as the target audience. This is the presumed audience for supermarket tabloids like the *National Enquirer,* for action movies filled with shoot-outs and explosions, for pro wrestling, hate radio shows, and TV and radio programs like those of Jerry Springer and Howard Stern that parade outrageous sexual practices. Political **demagogues**, on the right or left, also give the people what they want, by appealing to the most uninformed and prejudiced segments of the population to win their support. This notion of "the people" as a mass of illiterates to be both pandered to and exploited by media and politicians, then, is quite removed from Thomas Jefferson's and J. Hector St. John de Crèvecoeur's ideal of a nation of critical citizens who "will carefully read the newspapers, enter into every political disquisition, freely blame or censure governors and others," and whose education will have "raised the mass of the people to the high ground of moral respectability necessary to their own safety, and to orderly government."

The argument can be made that, instead of appealing to the lowest common denominator in the public, at least some media should give the more informed and critical segment of the people what *it* wants. Certain media, which are not exclusively concerned with "bottom-line" profitability, do in fact appeal to that segment—such as journals of opinion, public broadcasting, C-SPAN, and influential national newspapers like the *New York Times* and *Wall*

Street Journal. In other words, if the media were considered as a profession comparable to education, law, or medicine, wouldn't it be reasonable to expect its practitioners to be more knowledgeable about world and national events, culture and the arts, than the mass audience, and therefore to have a responsibility to inform, even to educate their audience, in the manner of teachers, rather than descending to the level of the lowest common denominator? (In this **analogy**, few people would say that teachers should gear their classes to the level of the least informed or most prejudiced students.) This responsibility to inform was in fact the original intention of the chartering of the public airwaves by the federal government in the 1920s, and the takeover of broadcasting (first radio, then television) by advertising was strongly opposed by large segments of public opinion, led by then Secretary of Commerce Herbert Hoover, who by the standards of that time was considered a conservative Republican. Hoover said that it was "inconceivable that we should allow so great a possibility for service . . . to be drowned in advertising chatter," and that if a presidential message ever became "the meat in a sandwich of two patent medicine advertisements," it would destroy broadcasting (quoted in Eric Barnouw, *The Sponsor* 15).

Traditionally, news divisions of national and local TV companies were not expected to garner high ratings or advertising revenue, and their losses were "carried" by owners out of some vestige of the public service concept at the origin of American broadcasting. This has changed in the past few decades, however, as news broadcasters have devised more profitable formats for what is now termed "infotainment," including "happy-talk" and "top-forty stories" featuring "If it bleeds, it leads" sensationalism. One professional consultant who pioneered these formats justified them by claiming, "People who watch television the most are unread, uneducated, untraveled and unable to concentrate on single subjects more than a minute or two."

Other recent influences in the sensationalizing of newscasts include the proliferation of twenty-four-hour-a-day cable TV networks and the concentration of media ownership by megacorporations like Disney, Time-Warner, ABC–Capital Cities–Paramount, and Rupert Murdoch's News Corporation—which most recently has acquired the *Wall Street Journal*. (For recent surveys of media concentration that update Edward Herman's "The Illiberal Media" here, see *The Nation*'s biennial chart "The National Entertainment State" [http://www.thenation.com/doc/20060703/mediachart] or Eric Alterman's book *What Liberal Media?*) These megacorporations typically have imposed demands that newspapers and broadcast news meet a profit quota comparable to that of their more profitable divisions, with the result of drastic cutbacks in editorial staff, news coverage, in-depth reporting, commentary, and cultural pages. These cutbacks have been compounded by the shift of readership to the Internet, where online versions of news media do not have comparable advertising revenue and so cannot afford to maintain full editorial staffs. The same process has changed the book publishing industry, where corporate conglomerates have bought up relatively small, low-profit publishers and textbook companies, resulting in demands for higher profits. These demands in turn have led to "dumbing down" of content, increased prices, and more frequent new editions of the same textbooks to abort used-book resales. This trend has also been compounded by the monopolization of bookstores by big chains like Barnes and Noble and Borders.

These, then, are some of the complexities and dangers of "giving the people what they want" mainly in terms of maximizing audiences, and these are some implicit arguments in favor of media producers instead exercising their own professional judgment and tastes in setting the media agenda. This alternative, however, can lead to the danger at the **equal and opposite extreme**—of the producers manipulating audiences into compliance with their own biases or special interests. As Dwight Macdonald put it in an earlier version of "Masscult and Midcult," comparing mass culture in capitalist and Communist countries, "The Lords of *kitsch* [a German term for mass culture], in short, exploit the cultural needs of the masses in order to make a profit and/or to maintain their class rule—in communist countries, only the second purpose prevails." In the readings included in this chapter, leftists like Edward Herman point to instances of corporate owners and advertisers doing so to impose capitalist ideology, social conformity, trivial pursuits, and consumption of commodities as a "bread and circuses" distraction from critical political awareness, while conservatives like Bernard Goldberg point to instances of liberal media elites imposing their own self-interested politics in the manner Macdonald ascribes to Communists. Both sides here are apt to fall into the **heads I win, tails you lose** fallacy: when media bias favors their own side, they say the media are just giving the people what they want, but when bias favors the other side, they accuse the "media elite" of manipulating, and being contemptuous of, the people.

One final variable that needs to be factored in here (and that has received a lot of attention in recent media scholarship) is the extent to which audiences are capable of seeing through and resisting the ideological messages sent out by the media or of re-appropriating those messages to their own purposes, and how much they do so in daily practice. This is a trickier question than it may first appear. You might firmly believe that you are not "taken in" by advertising or political slanting in media, but can you be certain that you do not unconsciously absorb many **culturally conditioned assumptions** through the media? For example, a review by John Cassidy in the *New Yorker* (January 25, 1999) of Juliet Schor's 1998 book *The Overspent American* discusses Schor's thesis that media images of upscale characters have prompted many Americans to go into debt to emulate their lifestyle. In contrast to earlier decades in which most Americans tried to keep up with the Joneses next door,

> [T]hese days, according to Schor, they are more likely to judge themselves against the affluent yuppies who proliferate in shows like "Ally McBeal" and "Frasier." Schor claims that every additional hour of television a person watches each week increases that person's annual spending by about two hundred dollars. "The likely explanation is that what we see on television inflates our sense of what is normal," she writes. "With a few exceptions, TV characters are upper-middle-class, or even rich." (90)

Topics for Discussion and Writing

1. Explain why you agree or disagree with Macdonald that the media do not treat audience members as individuals but as "masses."
2. Do you think that the media give you personally what you want? That you are completely free to "take it or leave it"? Or do you think your wants may have been conditioned by the media? How can you know? Consider as test cases the influence of the media on your views of one of the following: fashions in clothes and grooming; brand names; the most popular magazines; ideals of female or male mates; sports; popular music; news and politics; performers or dramatic characters on TV and in other media as role models for spending money, as described by Juliet Schor above.
3. Macdonald says, "For some reason, objections to the giving-the-public-what-it-wants line are often attacked as undemocratic and snobbish." In other words, people tend to confuse criticisms like Macdonald's of the media for looking down on and manipulating the common people with criticisms of the people themselves. Try to explain Macdonald's distinction in your own terms, then explain why you agree or disagree with it.
4. In group discussions, see what examples various students come up with of people *not* being taken in by media manipulation but of having skeptical distance from

media productions or turning them to their own personal, multicultural, or political purposes.

5. In connection with the discussion here of the dumbing down of news and other media under the influence of concentration of ownership and demands for increased profit margins, to what extent do you think these trends call into question (1) the operation of communication media for the purpose of corporate profit, (2) a broader fault in the ideology of "free enterprise" and the profit motive, in the tendency to aim at the lowest common denominator of taste or literacy in markets, and (3) the claims of conservatives to support moral principles in social issues while in economics they to tend to subordinate those principles to the defense of maximizing profits?

6. With regard to the quotation at the end of this section from Juliet Schor about the social classes depicted in sitcoms and other media, monitor several popular TV programs or current movies to research the extent to which "upper-middle-class, or even rich" people are the norm.

7. The analogy was suggested above that at least some media should have an obligation to inform and educate the audience in the same way that teachers do. Discuss and write about the extent to which you find this analogy valid.

ARE NEWS MEDIA OBJECTIVE? WHAT ARE THEIR BIASES?

The directors of news media often insist that they are committed to objectivity in their news pages or newscasts and that they limit subjective viewpoints to their editorial and opinion pages or broadcast commentaries. Scholars of the media, however, have pointed out dozens of subjective variables that color selection and presentation of the news in both print and broadcast media. A partial list of these factors includes ownership of media companies; hiring of editors and reporters, and assignment of stories to particular writers and editors; selection of what stories to cover and books to review, of sources interviewed and letters to the editor published, of prominence in space or time accorded different sources, and of headlines (written by editors, not writers); editing, sequencing, and abridging of writers' copy or camera footage; the institutional structure and conventions of news operations; and, of course, all of the rhetorical and semantic choices in every piece of writing or speaking that are discussed throughout this book.

Here is just one of an infinite number of possible illustrations of how journalists' subjective judgments, political and otherwise, come out in every day's news. During the 1998 senatorial election in New York, Rupert Murdoch's *New York Post,* which editorially endorsed the Republican incumbent Al D'Amato against the Democratic challenger Charles Schumer, at one point ran a front-page headline "Al Storms Ahead," followed by a story showing D'Amato leading in a poll by 1.3 percent. Shortly thereafter, a report that Schumer had gone ahead in the same poll by 4.2 percent was carried on an inside page with a smaller headline, "Chuck Squeaks Ahead of Al." Schumer won by 9 percent.

A conceivable alternative to our present conventions of print and broadcast news being presented in the form of a monologue, with no questioning of the reporter's or editor's bias, might be to present the news in a more self-reflexive, multi-perspectival format, in which several reporters and analysts with a variety of ideological viewpoints collaborate on the same story and take part in a dialogue on the problems presented by their own subjectivity on each issue. One program that successfully applied this approach was a former nightly feature on PBS station KQED-TV in San Francisco, *Newsroom of the Air.* There are vestiges of it in the current PBS *NewsHour,* which features nightly counterpoints by pairs or panels of commentators, though their ideological range is restricted to near-centrist liberals and conservatives. In the current absence of widely available media like this, your best alternative as a critical consumer of the news is to gain regular access to the widest possible range of media and to learn to compare their viewpoints on a day-to-day basis.

Topics for Discussion and Writing

1. Read a current newspaper or view a TV newscast or background report looking for ways in which reporters have injected their opinion into ostensibly neutral reports. Also look for examples of reports in which a successful effort has been made toward neutrality or balancing of opposed views.
2. As a group project with your classmates, prepare a mock broadcast on yesterday's news with a panel of students representing a conservative, liberal, libertarian, socialist, feminist, and ethnic viewpoint on the day's events.
3. In group discussions with classmates, brainstorm what alternative systems of communications (or means of diversifying our present one) might be feasible. For example, what about national and local print media or Internet equivalents to public broadcasting? Research existing alternative media in America and systems in other countries that differ significantly from ours.

THE DEBATE OVER POLITICAL BIAS IN MEDIA

An attempt toward an evenhanded overview of this debate needs to be approached through further consideration of several of the complex rhetorical and semantic dimensions of the issue.

First Dimension: Ambiguity of Definitions

Once again, terms like *left, right, liberal, conservative, centrist, moderate, mainstream, middle of the road, radical,* and *extreme* have no fixed, universally agreed-on definitions but can only be accurately referred to in some specified context. Most people like to consider themselves moderate and mainstream, and few describe their views as radical or extremist. (An exception would be leftists who accept the designation of radical in the sense of the word related etymologically to "root" from the Latin *radix,* meaning that they believe in going to the root causes of social problems—e.g., the structure of capitalism—in contrast to what they perceive as the superficial policies of liberals who only deal with symptoms or effects while ignoring structural causes.) Often, "radical" and "extremist" are used merely as name-calling **"dirties"** against one's opponents; so if you want to use those labels legitimately, you need to provide concrete support for them.

Another ambiguity in *moderate, centrist,* and *middle of the road* is that, although such words usually carry a favorable connotation, positions described with these labels may sometimes just be vague, muddled, and noncommittal. It is possible for such positions to be adhered to (say, by news media or scholars) in a dogmatic manner that excludes a hearing for any positions outside a narrow range near the center—in which case, it is conceivable to speak of "the radical middle," "extremism of the center," or "immoderate moderation." Left-of-liberal Texas humorist Jim Hightower titled a recent book of his essays *There's Nothing in the Middle of the Road but Yellow Stripes and Dead Armadillos.*

Finally, we must always ask about "centrist" and "middle of the road" positions, what are they the center *of,* and what road are they the middle of? For example, in a worldwide perspective, both American politics and news media are to the right of the many democracies that have large socialist, Communist, and labor parties and presses. Some views that are considered radical left here are considered centrist in the social democracies of Western Europe, Canada, and Japan, while those called centrist would be considered rightist from those countries' perspectives. This is a very good reason to familiarize yourself, to the extent possible, with political views and media in countries that are not bound by American ethnocentrism.

A sarcastic commentary on this point was made in the *Los Angeles Times* Column Left/ Column Right section by socialist journalist Alexander Cockburn after the election of Democrat Gray Davis as governor of California in 1998:

> "I am a moderate and a pragmatist by nature," Davis declared. "I will govern neither from the right nor the left, but from the center, propelled not by ideology but by common sense." This same common sense had prompted Davis earlier that day to meet with a platoon of lobbyists for the state's energy, agriculture and real estate sectors at which time the incoming governor assured them of his profound concern for their interests. If there were equivalent encounters that day with farm workers, nurses and others from kindred walks of life, they escaped the attention of the press. As with Bill Clinton, centrism on Davis' terms means uncritical acceptance of the most abrasive of all ideologies: the belief that the role of government is to promote the corporate agenda. ("Gray Davis's Real Agenda: Corporatism," Jan. 7, 1999, B9)

Another consequence of the skewing of the American balance to the right in a worldwide and historical context is that "radical leftists," that is, democratic socialists, in American politics and media are sometimes equated with "the radical right" of the Ku Klux Klan, American Nazis, racist or homophobic murderers, abortion-clinic bombers, violent militias, and right-wing death squads elsewhere in the world. Even many conservatives, however, would probably agree that this degree of extremism would characterize few current American leftists, although it might have applied in earlier decades to the Communist Party or violent groups that emerged briefly in the 1960s like revolutionary Marxist-Leninist sects. (This is not to imply that most conservative politicians or media figures, such as Rush Limbaugh and Pat Robertson, endorse right-wing extremism; the criticism they are open to is selective vision in **downplaying** denunciation of right-wing extremists while they disproportionately **play up** every fault they find in leftists.) Perhaps the Nation of Islam would fit the "extreme left" category today, though some of its social and religious doctrines, such as male supremacy, are quite conservative.

To reiterate yet another important semantic distinction from chapter 13, debates between *liberalism* and *conservatism* concern both economic and social (or moral) issues, and media are not always consistent on their positions in these two realms. For example, corporate media like Disney or the Fox network, which generally support the conservative economic interests of their owners and advertisers, present some productions that are widely perceived as liberal in *moral* issues, like *Pulp Fiction, Ellen* (a sitcom in which Ellen DeGeneres revealed she was gay)*, Desperate Housewives,* and *South Park*—thereby convincing social conservatives of their liberal bias and providing leftists evidence of the hypocrisy of conservative business interests that preach morality but practice whatever is profitable. Partisans of one side often **stack the deck** by playing up alleged bias in their opponents in media on the basis of the opponents' position on, say, moral issues like these while playing down their conflicting position on economic issues.

In their book *Watching America: What Television Tells Us about Our Lives,* S. Robert Lichter, Linda S. Lichter, and Stanley Rothman, whose research was funded by the conservative American Enterprise Institute and Olin and Scaife foundations, nevertheless admirably avoid this kind of selective vision by presenting clearly qualified distinctions between the economic and moral realms, and between liberals and radical leftists, in summarizing the findings of their research on the backgrounds and attitudes of the creators of current television entertainment. (Their results parallel similar findings by these and other conservatives about those who dominate news media.) About those creators' "alienation" from mainstream American opinion, the authors say, "These findings suggest that the Hollywood community's political alienation is rooted in social rather than economic issues. In fact, it is their social liberalism that most clearly distinguishes them from the general public" (16). And, "Television preaches a kind of Porsche populism that reflects Hollywood's socially liberal and cosmopolitan sensibility.... This is not to say that TV entertainment has followed this agenda unreservedly or has engaged in anything like a radical critique of American society" (290).

Topics for Discussion and Writing

1. If you can find World Link, oneworld, the *Economist*, BBC News, or Al Jazeera on cable TV or the Internet, compare their reports on a day's news with coverage on the American networks.
2. Read several left-of-liberal journals of opinion like *The Nation, In These Times,* the *Progressive, Z Magazine,* and *Extra!* to see if their viewpoint strikes you as "radical" or "extreme." Read some conservative journals of opinion like *American Spectator,* the *Weekly Standard,* and *National Review,* or listen to Rush Limbaugh, Gordon Liddy, and Pat Robertson to see if they are as critical of right-wing extremists as they are of all liberals.
3. In an individual or group research project, monitor TV news and magazines, dramatic and entertainment shows, or current films to see if you find a distinction between liberal or conservative viewpoints on social (or moral) issues—for example, religion, abortion, drugs, sexual promiscuity, obscenity, homosexuality—versus economic ones such as depictions of different socioeconomic classes (the rich, the poor, and the middle class; professionals versus blue-collar workers; employers versus employees).
4. In the quoted column by Alexander Cockburn, explain his use of irony in the phrase "this same common sense" and his **between-the-lines** refutation of Governor Davis's claim that he is "propelled not by ideology."
5. Lichter, Lichter, and Rothman coined the phrase "Porsche populism." This is a figure of speech called an *oxymoron,* a form of paradox in which two words generally considered opposites are linked. What is your understanding of what they mean by this phrase? Is it essentially the same as "limousine liberalism"?

Second Dimension: Relativity of Viewpoint

For an explanation of why conservatives see only left-wing bias in the media and leftists see only right-wing bias, let's come back to the spectrum of American media and commentators from left to right, reproduced from chapter 13 (see table 14.1 on page 314).

In the table, the division of sections A and B into four columns is an arbitrary semantic oversimplification of what could be broken down into several more columns or even a continuous, linear spectrum from left to right. Many of these placements are also disputable, to be sure, and subject to revision as different media and individuals periodically shift their positions.

Table 14.1. American Media, Journalists, and Commentators from Left to Right

A. Media

1. Left	2. Liberal	3. Liberal-to-Conservative	4. Conservative
The Nation	*NY Review*	*Time*	*Readers Digest*
In These Times	*Harper's*	*Newsweek*	*Weekly Standard*
Mother Jones	*New Yorker*	CNN	*Wall St. Journal*
Extra!	PBS Documentaries	*Washington Post*	*Commentary*
The Progressive	*60 Minutes*	*Atlantic*	*American Spectator*
Z Magazine	*New York Times*	*New Republic*	*National Review*
Media Matters		*Reason*	Fox News
Pacifica Radio	MSNBC	CBS news	*Washington Times*
Air America Radio		NBC, ABC news	*Insight*
		Lehrer News Hour	Most local newspapers, TV & radio

B. Journalists and Commentators

1. Left	2. Liberal	3. Libertarian	4. Conservative
Alexander Cockburn	Dan Rather	Virginia Postrel	Rush Limbaugh
Molly Ivins	Tom Brokaw	Stephen Moore	Pat Buchanan
Noam Chomsky	Ted Koppel	Doug Bandow	Jerry Falwell
Edward Herman	Jim Lehrer	Debra Saunders	Pat Robertson
Katrina vanden Heuvel	Larry King	Nat Hentoff	David Brooks
Barbara Ehrenreich	Cokie Roberts	James Pinkerton	Paul Harvey
Robert Scheer	Oprah Winfrey	Jesse Ventura	Sam Donaldson
Jonathan Kozol	Rosie O'Donnell	Ron Paul	George Will
Todd Gitlin	Bob Woodward	Bob Barr	John McLaughlin
Jim Hightower	Mark Shields	Nick Gillespie	Fred Barnes
Bob Herbert	Paul Krugman	P.J. O'Rourke	Paul Gigot
Jeff Cohen	Stephen Colbert		Charles Krauthammer
Norman Solomon	Michael Kinsley		Jonah Goldberg
Gore Vidal	Frank Rich		Robert Novak
Julianne Malveaux	Gloria Steinem		Phyllis Schlafly
Victor Navasky	Seymour Hersh		John Leo
Roger Wilkins	David Halberstam		Cal Thomas
Cornel West	Carl Bernstein		Thomas Sowell
Betty Friedan	Donald Barlett		Gordon Liddy
Ralph Nader	James Steele		Bob Grant
Katha Pollit	Naomi Wolf		Don Imus
Jesse Jackson	Jon Stewart		R. Emmett Tyrrell
Bernie Sanders	James Carville		Laura Ingraham
Michael Moore	George Stephanopolous		Mona Charen
Eric Alterman	Cynthia Tucker		William Kristol
Michael Lerner	Al Franken		Sean Hannity
Lewis Lapham	Martha Nussbaum		Rich Lowry
William Greider	Bill Maher		Norman Podhoretz
Susan Sontag	Keith Olbermann		John Podhoretz
Barbara Kingsolver	Eugene Robinson		Matt Drudge
Arundhati Roy	Arianna Huffington*		Henry Kissinger
Bill Moyers	David Brock*		Dinesh D'Souza
Holly Sklar	Michael Lind*		Lynne Cheney
Amy Goodman			Florence King
Adolph Reed	*Former conservative		Mary Matalin
Howard Zinn			Christina Sommers
Thomas Frank			Ann Coulter
			Jeff Jacoby
			Tucker Carlson
			Bill O'Reilly
			Bernard Goldberg
			Michael Savage
			David Horowitz*
			Christopher Hitchens*

*Former leftist

If your viewpoint is that of the far right, you are obviously going to consider all the other points on the spectrum biased toward the left, while if your viewpoint is far left, you will consider all the others biased toward the right. This is not to say that the views from either end of the spectrum are inaccurate or eccentric. In section A, the media in columns 1 and 4 are more overtly partisan than those in columns 2 and 3. Most of those in column 4 overtly support conservatism and the Republican Party (although they disagree among themselves over the degree and nature of conservatism the Republicans should stand for; see the discussion of differences among conservatives in chapter 13). Most in column 1 in both sections A and B are to the left of the mainstream of the Democratic Party and of the media in A-2 and A-3, and of the individuals in B-2. Whether overtly socialistic or not, they are more critical than liberals of the Democratic Party, capitalism, and nationalism; more strongly pro-labor, multicultural, and feminist; and inclined to support leftist third parties, such as (most recently) the New Party, the Labor Party, and the Green Party. Fairness and Accuracy in Reporting (FAIR), *The Nation,* Edward Herman, and Noam Chomsky criticize the true conservatism of the "liberal" media more than they do the overtly conservative media; when the "liberal" media acknowledge such criticisms at all, it is usually to dismiss the "radical" left with contempt.

By contrast to columns 1 and 4 in section A and columns 1 and 3 in section B, the media in section A-2 and A-3, and the individuals in section B, column 2, are not overtly affiliated with one political party or ideology, and they insist on their commitment to neutrality or objectivity. In practice, however, many in section A-2, column 2, and section B-2, lean toward the liberal wing of the Democratic Party and its policies, although their support of Democrats, capitalism, and American nationalism clearly positions them to the right of those in column 1. Some in section A-3, however, and in section B-2, tend toward the more conservative wing of the Democratic Party (Clinton-Gore-Kerry) and the more liberal wing of the Republican Party—for example, John McCain, who in the 2000 primaries positioned himself to the left of George W. Bush, though he moved to the right in the 2008 election. (So when Republicans make the case that the media in section A-3, have a liberal or left bias, they could perhaps more accurately argue that the bias is liberal-centrist, to the left of conservative Republicans but to the right of those in columns 1 and 2.)

Moreover, the media in table section A-2, and even more so in section A-3, attempt to maintain a degree of balance between liberal and conservative views, especially in their commentators and columnists; the *New York Times* op-ed page, for example, currently has regular columns by liberals Bob Herbert, Paul Krugman, and Maureen Dowd and by conservatives David Brooks, William Kristol, and Thomas Friedman (a liberal on some issues but conservative as an influential advocate of globalization, as in his book *The World Is Flat*). (Frank Rich, a former op-ed page liberal, currently is writing a column in the Sunday News of the Week section.) Sections A-2 and A-3 are only occasionally open to either libertarian or left-of-liberal views. The *Los Angeles Times*'s former "Column Left/Column Right" was one of the few major op-ed sections in the country that regularly featured radical leftists like Alexander Cockburn, Robert Scheer, and feminist Ruth Rosen—all of whom lost their positions when the paper was taken over by more conservative, bottom-line-oriented owners. Few of the conservative media in A-4 grant any regular time or space at all to liberal or left authors, though they do sometimes include libertarians, and the *Wall Street Journal* op-ed page, generally the staunchest supporter of the Republican Party line, recently added left-liberal Thomas Frank, author of *The Wrecking Crew: How Conservatives Rule*, to its columnists for some balance.

These refinements indicate that there may be good reason for those on the far right to consider all the media to the left of them to be biased against their clearly articulated conservative position, and for those on the far left to feel the same way about all the other positions opposed to their own clear-cut position. (All of which is to reiterate the value of having regular exposure to sources on the far left and far right, to gain understanding of their clear-cut viewpoints in contrast to the frequent muddle of opinions in the mainstream media.) Those on the far left and far right do, however, tend to ignore all the degrees of difference among and within the positions other than far left or far right. (Another axiom of rhetorical ethnocentrism is that we are all inclined to play up significant differences among those we are most familiar with, but to downplay differences among our opponents and to consider them a monolithic bloc.)

Topics for Discussion and Writing

1. As a collective exercise, conduct a survey within your class based on table 14.1-B. Have every student add up the number of people in each of the four columns whom (1) they have heard of, (2) they remember seeing on TV, hearing on radio, or reading in newspapers, magazines, and the Internet. Collate the results and see if any inferences are warranted about which points on the spectrum are most favored by the media.
2. Discuss in class how valid everyone finds the placement of media figures in the four columns of table 14.1-B as well as the breakdown of the columns themselves. Suggest alternatives, perhaps for more columns providing for finer distinctions among positions on the left or right.

Third Dimension: Diverse Influences in Media

Every day, media "watchdog" organizations on the right like Accuracy in Media (aim. org), FrontPage Magazine (frontpagemag.com), and others cited below by Bernard Goldberg, "cherry pick" every example of liberal bias, and those on the left like Media Matters (mediamatters.org) and FAIR (fair.org) do the opposite. When we read conservative views like Goldberg's, the evidence they present of liberal bias in media seems overwhelming; yet when we read articles by leftists like Edward Herman on the same topic, their evidence for conservative bias seems equally persuasive. What, then, can we conclude from a comparative reading of the opposing sides? Perhaps that each side is using **selective vision, stacking the deck** by playing up every cause and instance of bias on the other side while downplaying every one of bias on its own? (This is a classic case of the "Predictable Patterns of Political Rhetoric" in chapter 13.) Thus the most plausible answer to the question of whether the media have a liberal or a conservative bias is "both"—the bias is sometimes and in some ways liberal (though almost never explicitly socialist) and at other times and in other ways conservative. This is not necessarily to imply that there is a 50–50 balance, only that we need to take an evenhanded overview of partisan viewpoints supporting the opposing camps, carefully weigh the evidence presented by opposing sources, and recognize more complexities in the issue than acknowledged by partisans on either side, in order to arrive at our own judgment of what the actual balance might be.

As anyone who has worked in commercial media (including myself) will attest, "the media" aren't a monolithic entity but are organizations in which several opposing forces are jockeying for dominance every day. These forces include at least the following, in no fixed order of influence:

1. Employees: editors and writers in print media; producers, directors, newscasters, and performers in television, films, radio, concerts, and recordings

2. Owners and executives of media corporations ("management" as opposed to employees or "labor")
3. Advertisers
4. Pressure groups, public relations agencies, and lobbyists, including those of government, public-policy foundations, and research institutes
5. Audiences

Among these groups, at both the national and local level, most individual or corporate owners of media corporations, their appointed top executives, and major advertisers are in the wealthiest stratum, and thus by definition most can be expected to be conservative, in the sense of supporting capitalism and a corporate social order; their party affiliation is more often Republican than Democratic. (David Horowitz's article "The Intellectual Class War" in chapter 13 takes issue with this general point.) Ted Turner, a liberal Democrat who founded CNN, would be a prominent exception to this rule, although multimillionaire Turner is far from an opponent of capitalism, and CNN is now owned by Time-Warner. Another partial exception here is newspapers like the *New York Times*, *Washington Post*, and *Los Angeles Times* (when it was owned by the Chandler family), which are owned by families with long-established wealth and dedication to public service, and who thus are willing to subordinate direct editorial control and maximizing of profit to maintain their papers' reputations for the independence of their journalist employees. But here again, leftists like Herman and Chomsky argue that these media are still ultimately organs of corporate capitalism, albeit self-styled "responsible capitalism."

Most public relations agencies, lobbies, foundations, and research institutes that represent big business are conservative, while those that represent labor unions and citizen-advocacy groups like Common Cause, Public Citizen, and the Sierra Club are liberal. (See the readings in chapter 15.) Various segments of government also employ public relations agents and researchers, and their politics will vary according to whether the particular agency employing them tends to be conservative (such as the Defense Department—see chapter 15) or liberal (such as the Environmental Protection Agency), and according to the ideology of the party currently in office. As for audiences, they obviously contain the same proportion of liberals and conservatives that the electorate does at any particular time. To the extent that the media attempt to "give the people what they want," some media try to target either the liberal or the conservative audience, while others try to work both sides of the street, with vague or mixed political messages.

The politics of the various kinds of media employees in number 1 is more complicated. Media scholars generally agree that this group includes the most liberals, at least relatively, in comparison to groups 2, 3, and 4. Those select media employees who are "stars" tend be an exception to the rule equating wealth with conservatism, their politics often being that of the Hollywood Democrat, limousine liberal, or Porsche populist variety, retaining the affiliation of most artists and intellectuals with the Democratic Party—see table 13.3, "Social Class and Political Attitudes." Nevertheless, when those in this group become multimillionaires as performers, news anchors, analysts, or talk show hosts, and when they become social peers and associates of political leaders and wealthy executives, many experience the conservatizing force of wealth, status, and power. (See David Sirota's "Matthews vs. McNulty" below.) And few media liberals come close to the $38 million a year that staunch conservative Rush Limbaugh is currently paid. (Comparing liberal and conservative media figures' wealth would be a good research project.)

All of the above forces try to impose their own viewpoint in the daily workings of the media; when the conservative forces prevail, we get a conservative bias, and when the liberal ones prevail, we get the opposite. None of these forces prevail all the time or without conflict and accommodation. (Sometimes the conflicting forces result in self-contradiction or **compartmentalization**, as when the *New York Times*'s and the *New Yorker*'s liberal editorial content, sympathizing with the poor and opposing a growing wealth gap, is juxtaposed with advertisements for $10,000 Cartier jewelry, $700 Gucci shoes, and multimillion-dollar homes aimed at a limousine-liberal audience.) Liberals argue that owners have ultimate control over media content through the power of the pocketbook, including the power to hire and fire employees, but conservatives point to many examples in which the employees' views prevail over the owners'. Liberals also argue that owners and advertisers attempt to control content in a manner calculated to maximize profits and create a pro-corporate and nationalistic agenda, while conservatives respond that if a leftist media production, writer, or performer, is popular enough, and if the liberal or left-of-liberal audience is large or affluent enough, owners and advertisers at least sometimes will subordinate their ideological preferences to the propagation of an opposing but more profitable message. So conservatives point to Michael Moore's films as evidence that leftists can become wealthy through appealing to a progressive/populist audience, and they consider him a hypocrite for attacking corporations and the wealthy while enriching himself by doing so. Moore's *Fahrenheit 9/11* was dropped for distribution by Disney, allegedly under political pressure, but was picked up by Miramax and became very profitable. Leftists point to other instances where corporate ideology trumps popularity, such as that of Moore's *TV Nation,* a documentary series satirically criticizing corporations, which had high ratings on Fox but was canceled by right-wing billionaire Rupert Murdoch when he bought that network, or Jim Hightower's talk radio show, which was dropped by ABC when it bought up the network that was carrying it. So leftists see a **vicious circle**, in which prior restraint on leftist views precludes the theoretical possibility of their gaining a profitable audience.

Noncommercial public television and radio in America through most of the last half of the twentieth century presented many more leftist views than did commercial broadcasting, from which it can plausibly be inferred that commercial ownership and advertising do indeed tend to impose conservative economic views, and that funding by government and other noncorporate sources (e.g., audience contributors, colleges) does not necessarily lead to government control or censorship of content, which conservatives use as an **appeal to fear** against public broadcasting. ("Bill Moyers' Journal" on PBS is probably the most liberal program on TV, and also the most intellectual. A Republican chair of the Corporation for Public Broadcasting, Kenneth Tomlinson, pressured PBS to cancel Moyers' show, but after Tomlinson himself was forced to resign for excessive interference in what is chartered as an independent agency, it was brought back. So in this case, the attempt at government control was a conservative one.) Likewise for C-SPAN, which is noncommercial though funded as a public service by commercial broadcasters, and which presents congressional hearings, political speeches, extensive panels on public affairs, academic conferences, and book discussions, with a balance of liberal and conservative sources. (Most other democracies today have much more publicly funded broadcasting and some print media, and likewise tend to be more liberal than American commercial media.) In the past few decades, however, conservative politicians have tried to eliminate or drastically reduce government funding for public television and radio and to replace government support with corporate "underwriting" (often a euphemism for direct sponsorship and control of content in production), with the direct result of an increase in conservative views—for example, *Suze Orman: The Courage to Be Rich.*

Topics for Discussion and Writing

1. Look at the reading in chapter 15, the *60 Minutes* transcript "Confessions of a Tobacco Lobbyist." Here is a report that clearly has a liberal viewpoint critical of the big business of tobacco. Although tobacco advertising is now banned on TV, the major tobacco companies form part of larger conglomerates, such as RJR-Nabisco, that are large TV advertisers and are quite possibly represented on the networks' boards of directors (you might research this). To what extent, then, does this report provide evidence for the conservative argument that media content is controlled by liberal producers rather than advertisers or corporate management? In your memory of TV news reports and magazine shows like *60 Minutes*, would you judge that such strong criticism of the tobacco industry, big business in general, and its lobbying of politicians is the rule or the exception? Research stories about efforts by the tobacco industry to suppress negative media reports about it, including another *60 Minutes* report on a cover-up by the tobacco industry of the addictive effects of nicotine. The popular Hollywood film *The Insider* was a thinly fictionalized account of this broadcast; study that film to analyze its viewpoint and possible bias.
2. Monitor print and broadcast coverage of strikes, protests against globalization of the economy and sweatshop labor, and other labor-management conflicts to see whether the coverage sympathizes with one side or the other. Look for positive or negative images of business executives and labor unions projected in both news and entertainment media. How much do you think ownership of media by unions rather than corporations would alter such coverage?
3. Monitor programming on PBS television or NPR radio for a week and compare it to programming on the commercial networks and local stations. What differences and similarities do you find, and what is their ideological significance? Note who "underwrote" programs and whether the underwriter's influence is obvious. Discuss the positive and negative effects of the decline in public funding and increasing influence of corporate underwriters, and the question of how public broadcasting *should* differ from commercial media.

Fourth Dimension: Political Viewpoints and Levels of Education

A comparison of columns 1 and 4 in both sections A and B of table 14.1 reveals a peculiarity of American media. Many of the media and personalities in column 4 are among the most widely circulated in the country—for example, *Reader's Digest*, the *Wall Street Journal*, *The McLaughlin Group*, Rush Limbaugh, Pat Robertson, and Pat Buchanan, along with most regional newspapers, TV, and radio, which serve for the most part as boosters of local business interests and have less of a "wall" between editorial and ownership and advertising divisions than the national media. However, none of the media in table A-1 and few of the personalities in B-1 have circulation anywhere comparable to those in A and B, column 4. One reason for the large circulation of these media and individuals in column 4 (and of most other mass-circulation print and broadcast media) is that their rhetoric is aimed at the widest possible audience—that is, the majority of the public, with an average high-school-graduate literacy level. At the other end of the spectrum, all of the left-of-liberal media and most of the individuals in column 1 of tables A and B address a more limited audience, mainly at a college-graduate level and advanced stage of cognitive development and critical thinking;

their editors and writers tend to have strong academic credentials in liberal education (many hold PhDs) and are clearly identifiable as intellectuals.

A major historical irony here is that leftism in the last few centuries was the politics of the proletarian masses and conservatism was that of upper-class elites, but over the course of the twentieth century, at least in the United States, the masses have moved toward the right and tended to align with the wealthy, so that conservative interests have preempted the **ethos** of populism, while the American left has shrunk to a constituency largely characterized by intellectuals (with exceptions including the remnants of militant labor unions, the poor, racial minorities, and immigrants), with the result that conservatives like Bernard Goldberg, David Horowitz, and William J. Bennett now stigmatize the left as the realm of "the cultural elite," entrenched in liberal arts departments of universities, small-circulation journals of opinion, public television and radio, and other intellectual media and out of touch with the mainstream of American opinion. It is significant that PBS previously was the main TV and radio outlet for classical music, ballet, opera, and Broadway theater, but as it has been taken over by corporate underwriters and producers, it has added more "lowbrow" music—pop, country, and rock—while NPR has added commentary on sports as well as pop music.

To be sure, some of the conservative media and individuals in column 4 are comparable to those in column 1 in their intellectual level. Journals of opinion like *Commentary,* the *Weekly Standard,* and *National Review,* as well as scholarly journals like *American Enterprise* and *Policy Review* are edited and written by individuals, and are addressed to an audience, at the same, postcollegiate level. (To reiterate, that is why these journals make more credible conservative sources for college-level papers than mass-media conservatives like Rush Limbaugh.) So while there are intellectual media and spokespeople addressing an educated audience on the American right as well as the left, the *mass* media provide little voice for either the intellectual right or left, mainly because they limit expression to "sound bites" and oversimplifications, excluding the kind of extended, complex discourse that characterizes university-level teaching and writing. This contrast is clear in the exceptions like C-SPAN, which regularly broadcasts university and research-institute conferences from both left and conservative sources, or what still remains of educational television and radio programming on public broadcasting stations.

Although the mass media tend to exclude intellectuals on both the right and the far left, leftists argue that the positions of the intellectual right do not differ as much from mainstream conservatism as those of the intellectual far left do from mainstream liberalism (intellectual leftists generally being more critical of the Democratic Party than intellectual rightists are of the Republicans). As a result, the far left is the one position on the American political spectrum with least access to mass media (other than the extreme right of neo-Nazis, white supremacists, and militias, which has few intellectually reputable representatives). The more fair-minded conservatives acknowledge this fact, though they tend to downplay the difference between leftists and liberals, or else they speculate that in recent decades, ideas from the intellectual left have "trickled down" little by little into mainstream media, as Lichter, Lichter, and Rothman argue in *Watching America:*

> Television thus stands at the end of a long chain of popularization that begins with the creation of ideas and issues in universities, think tanks, "public interest" groups, and the like. The process continues with their entry into what Herbert Gans calls "upper middle" popular culture via the prestige press and "quality" magazines like *Atlantic* and *The New Yorker.* The most simplified version reaches the mass public in TV movies, "realist" dramatic series, and socially conscious sitcoms. (297)

Be that as it may, the practical implication of this analysis is that to get a full range of informed opinions, you should familiarize yourself with the ideas of intellectual leftists on university faculties and in books and journals of opinion, because you are unlikely to see or hear much of their ideas *at first hand*, without their being watered down through the "chain of popularization," in mass media.

Leftists argue that another reason their viewpoints do not receive an equal hearing in mass media is that most conservative ideas—such as patriotism, orthodox religion, family values, free enterprise, low taxes, commodity consumption, and strong support of the military, police, the right to bear arms, and "getting tough on criminals"—are not only more easily simplified and instinctively appealing to the mass audience but also are more congenial to wealthy media owners and advertisers with an interest in maximizing their profits and maintaining the status quo of consumer society. Leftists have long argued that "mass culture" in general has a conservative bias because it appeals to the lowest common denominator of cognitive development and to all the "conservative" blocks to critical thinking surveyed here previously—nationalistic ethnocentrism, authoritarianism and conformity, prejudice and stereotyping, rationalization of the status quo, and so on. (For a comprehensive survey of this line of argument, see *American Media and Mass Culture: Left Perspectives,* Donald Lazere, ed.) Another significant difference between left and right journals of opinion, which you can easily verify for yourself, is that the ones on the right have far more advertisers and funding (billionaires Rupert Murdoch and Richard Mellon Scaife funded the *Weekly Standard* and *American Spectator* respectively, and the Olin, Scaife, and Bradley foundations have funded others), and are more slickly produced, while most left journals barely survive on low advertising and sales, supplemented by donations from subscribers and occasional wealthy "angels" acting out of conscience against their own class interests in supporting journals critical of the wealthy (although they may receive charitable tax deductions, as do the funders of conservative journals). Leftists argue that this creates **conflicts of interest** for the conservative journals.

A few of the individuals in section B-1, such as Michael Moore, Ralph Nader, the late Molly Ivins, Jim Hightower, Will Durst, and Paula Poundstone, do attempt to attain a populist appeal in their style and intended audience; Barbara Ehrenreich's columns sometimes appear in *Time* and the *New York Times,* but few of these commentators are allowed on the major TV discussion shows or have prominent roles in the Democratic Party (from which Nader has separated himself as an independent candidate for president), and none have reached the mass audience of *Reader's Digest,* Limbaugh, Robertson, or Buchanan (both Robertson and Buchanan have run for president as Republicans). In the last few years, as liberalism in general has been on the incline and conservatism on the decline, Keith Olbermann on MSNBC, Jon Stewart and Stephen Colbert on Comedy Central, and Bill Maher on HBO—all liberal Democrats, not socialistic leftists—have been catching up with Bill O'Reilly's popularity on Fox News.

CONCLUSION

This has been a sketchy survey of some of the issues to keep in mind as you read through the following selections (or other critiques from the left or right) and evaluate the authors' rhetoric. Pay close attention, then, to the extent to which the various authors take all these variables into account, their evenhandedness in weighing evidence on both sides, and the strength of their own support for the case that either conservative or leftist bias is prevalent on balance.

The Illiberal Media

Edward S. Herman

Z Magazine, January 1997

Claims of a pervasive "liberal" or "left" media bias are heard repeatedly in the allegedly liberal/left media, but counterclaims of exceptional "illiberal" or "conservative" bias and power in the media are exceedingly rare. This is hardly a reflection of reality: there is a huge right-wing Christian radio and TV system; the right-wing Rupert Murdoch owns a TV network, movie studio, 132 newspapers, book publishers (including HarperCollins), and 25 magazines, among other holdings; Rush Limbaugh admirer John Malone's Tele-Communications Inc. is the largest cable system in the United States (14 million subscribers) and has interests in 91 U.S. cable content services; the editorial page of the largest circulation national newspaper, the *Wall Street Journal,* is aggressively reactionary; the talk show on radio and TV is dominated by the likes of Robert Novak, "CrossFire," the "McLaughlin Group," and Rush Limbaugh. Even PBS is saturated with right-wing regulars, going back to William F. Buckley *[Editor's note: more recently David Brooks, Paul Gigot, Rich Lowry, Tucker Carlson].*

Fairness and Accuracy in Reporting (FAIR) recently listed 52 national media figures of the right, from Roger Ailes to Walter Williams, most of whom have proclaimed the media's liberal bias while occupying positions of access and power vastly more extensive than liberals could ever hope to attain. Leftists are an extinct species in the mainstream media; the firing of Jim Hightower by ABC, immediately following the Disney acquisition, was like the passing of the last carrier pigeon. This doesn't prevent the pundits, and even the media moguls, from making bitter complaints about the power of the "left." Rupert Murdoch started Fox News in order to combat the "left bias" of the media. The right-wing Canadian mogul Conrad Black, who owns more than half the daily newspa-

pers in Canada and over 100 in this country (including the *Chicago Sun Times*) also whines about the liberal-left bias of the press.

The reason we only hear complaints of a "liberal" media is that the right-wing is so well entrenched and aggressive that its members can pretend that their own potent selves don't exist. Just as power allowed the right-wing and a complicit "liberal media" to label university dissidents a PC threat, while ignoring the massive right-wing attempt to impose its own political agenda on the university, so in the case of the media, views disapproved by the powerful are "liberal" or "left"—the views of the numerous right-wing moguls and pundits are implicitly unbiased or merely countering those of the omnipresent, subversive, but elusive "liberals." We can call this the "pitiful giant syndrome," harking back to Nixon era claims that the poor U.S. was a pitiful giant being pushed around by Third World upstarts.

The pitiful moguls are, of course, in the supremely privileged position of being able to create their own right-wing news and commentary operations and exclude those that don't meet their political standards. Murdoch personally funded the new conservative magazine *The Weekly Standard,* and he has placed Roger Ailes in charge of his new cable news services—Ailes is the Republican specialist in media dirty tactics (famous for his role in the Willie Horton ploy in 1988), who came to the Murdoch news operation after a stint as Rush Limbaugh's producer. John Malone recently created his own talk-commentary program, "Damn Right!" hosted by David Asman, the *Wall Street Journal* editorial page's noted apologist for state terrorism in Central America, along with another "citizen education" show, "The Race for the Presidency," under partisan Republican management. He has also welcomed to TCI cable Pat Robertson's Family Channel and the new, exclusively right-wing, Empowerment Channel. At the same time, Malone succeeded in killing the 90s Channel, that rare (and now approaching the extinct) entity called a "liberal" channel, by raising its entry rates to his cable system to prohibitive levels. The pitiful giant was exercising raw economic power in pursuit of his political agenda, but the liberal media didn't notice or complain. (The Clinton FCC, while sanctioning one giant monopoly power enhancing merger after another, refused to intervene.

In the real world, the resurgent power of corporate and financial interests, an increasingly concentrated media ever more closely integrated with advertisers (now spending on the media over $75 billion a year), the proliferation of corporate-funded think tanks and the corporate "leasing the ivory tower," has shifted political power and media opinion sharply to the right. At this point, "left" in the media is conservative, centrist, and in a defensive mode, accepting without question the premises of corporate capitalism and the imperial state, but weakly supporting the preservation of an eroding welfare state. The strong liberalism of L. T. Hobhouse (*Liberalism*), Louis Brandeis (*The Curse of Bigness*), and John Dewey (*Reconstruction in Philosophy*), with its powerful strain of equalitarianism and opposition to concentrated economic power, is still deeply rooted in the public, but is hard to find in mainstream politics or the media. The centrist-conservative media "left" is epitomized by David Broder, although Mark Shields, Roger Rosenblatt, or Jack Germond would do just as well. In the late 1980s, when a Central American activist asked the editor of the *Philadelphia Inquirer* to identify his left columnist who offset Charles Krauthammer and George Will, the editor answered: David Broder. But Broder's views are pure establishment; he evades tough issues, joins almost every establishment crusade (NAFTA, Persian Gulf war, Soviet Threat and military buildup, welfare and entitlements out of control), and devotes maximum attention to election horse-racing. He also never fights for principles against strong establishment opposition—thus, while disliking Reagan's Central America

wars, he simply abandoned the subject, giving the floor to Will, Krauthammer, and the administration. So Broder never bothers anybody important, adapts beautifully to class and imperial warfare, and is the ideal liberal for an era of counterrevolution.

Meanwhile, the right-wing opposition to Broder and company—Will, Krauthammer, Robert Bartley, Fred Barnes, Mona Charren, the Kristols, John Leo, and dozens more—are not conservatives, they are reactionary servants of the corporate community, which has been on the offensive for over 20 years, striving to remove all obstacles to its growth and profitability. These obstacles include the welfare state, regulation of corporate practices, and an organized labor movement. Removing these, and returning us to 19th century socio-economic conditions, is not a "conservative" project, it is reactionary. So is the support of the "strong state" in the Pinochet-Reagan-Thatcher modes, featuring ruthless law and order regimes, imperial aggressiveness, and military-industrial and prison-industrial complexes riding high

With centrists like Broder as the left, and even these in small numbers, the large array of aggressive right-wing pundits and editors like Robert Bartley (*Wall Street Journal*) can engineer agendas. In order to fix agendas, themes must be repeated, with passion, to make them seem important. The right wingers are sufficiently numerous to be able to constitute an "echo chamber," in which the charges are repeated, each small elaboration used to keep the subject on the agenda, and the agenda pushed relentlessly....

The spineless political and media liberals not only don't set agendas, they often get on the right-wing bandwagons themselves. They quickly swallowed the line of a Sandinista threat, and in the phony MIG crisis of 1984 competed with one another in urging an aggressive U.S. response. Liberal congressperson Lee Hamilton was notorious for caving in during the Iran-Contra investigation, in the interest of a "national unity" that the right-wing regularly ignores in attacking their enemies. David Broder followed Hamilton and his fellow Democrats in failing to press the attack on North, Reagan, and Bush despite their carrying out covert terrorist operations in violation of law and constitutional principles. Clinton refused to pursue the Bush administration's involvement in the Banco Lavoro case and indirect funding of Saddam Hussein, and the media liberals followed in his wake. The 1995 testimony by former Reagan official Howard Teicher that the Reagan administration had "authorized, approved and assisted" delivery of cluster bombs to Iraq, among other massive arms support, was of no interest to the liberal media. . . .

While the right-wing echo chamber has been important in pushing numerous nasty policy trends, it should be recognized that this echo chamber is underwritten by big money and would not work without "liberal media" cooperation. The "McLaughlin Group" is funded by General Electric, many of the other right wingers are or have been supported by corporate funded think tanks, and a majority of them are carried as columnists by the liberal media. The liberal media have also regularly joined in right-wing propaganda campaigns—*Newsweek* and the *New York Times* were major participants in the PC propaganda wave; they all gave prominence to *The Bell Curve,* and supported the Reaganite arms race and wars of the 1980s; and they are virtually all now in the Concord Coalition camp elevating the threat of entitlement costs into a crisis and setting the stage for the further erosion of the welfare state.

Just as money and power allow the dominant illiberals to call the media liberal and left, so money and power allow them to study and "prove" media bias. S. Robert Lichter, Linda Lichter, and Stanley Rothman have been the most prominent rightists who have engaged in this "scientific" effort. The Lichters organized their Center for Media and Public Affairs in 1985, with accolades from Reagan and Pat Buchanan; Rothman has had a chair at Smith College and generous right-wing foundation support. In a 1981 article on "Media and Business Elites" (*Public Opinion*), Lichter and Rothman (hereafter referred to as LR) tried to prove the liberal bias of the media by showing that the "media elite" votes Democratic and has opinions more liberal than those of mainstream America.

The LR study violated every scientific standard you could name. They claimed to be studying a "media elite," but actually sampled media personnel who had anything to do with media "content," so most of them may be ordinary reporters (they failed to disclose the composition of their sample). LR compared their "media elite" with a sample of middle and upper levels of corporate management, not with comparable professionals like teachers, let alone non-professional "middle Americans." Their questions were ambiguous and loaded (for a good analysis, see Herbert Gans, "Are U.S. Journalists Dangerously Liberal?," *Columbia Journalism Review,* November-December 1985), making one wonder why anyone would participate in this survey. Ben Bradlee, the top editor of the *Washington Post*—one of the papers allegedly sampled by LR—claimed that he couldn't locate a single employee who had participated in the LR survey.

One key technique of right-wing proofs of liberal bias is to focus on social issues, as the affluent and urban media journalists and editors tend to be more liberal than blue collar workers on issues like abortion/choice, gay rights, and the handling of drug problems, as are urban professionals across the board. On the other hand, on matters like government regulation, distrust of big business, income distribution, and jobs policies, "middle America" is to the left of the business and media elite. Right-wingers like LR handle this by bypassing the problematic areas and focusing on social issues, where they can score points.

Right-wing proofs of a liberal media also focus on voting patterns. The 1981 LR piece featured the pro-Democrat voting records of the media elite in the four elections between 1964 and 1976. In April 1996 a similar finding was published by the Roper Center and Gannett Freedom Forum; 89 percent of a sample of 139 Washington journalists allegedly voted for Clinton in 1992. The inference quickly drawn from this, as from the LR study, was that the media has a liberal bias. But the true media elite is the owners, who have legal control of the media companies, can hire, promote, and fire their employees, and can shape policy a la Malone and Murdoch. LR and their allies never poll owners.

There are other questions to be asked in regard to these conservative polls. Why don't they compare the media elite's views on NAFTA with the views of middle America? How can we explain the mainstream media's failure to focus on the declining economic position and insecurity of middle Americans as an election issue? How can we explain the fact that a majority of newspapers came out editorially for Bob Dole with the "liberals" controlling the media? How can we explain the steady attacks on Clinton's character and focus on Whitewater, and more cursory treatment of Iran-Contra and the Banco Lavoro case, in terms of a pro-Democrat bias? In what sense is Clinton a "liberal" anyway?

These and other questions can be answered by media analyses that focus on the control, funding, structure, and performance of the media, rather than reporter opinions and voting patterns. For example, the "propaganda model," spelled out in my book *Manufacturing Consent* (co-authored with Noam Chomsky), describes the working of the mainstream media in terms of underlying structural factors and "filters" that define the parameters within which media underlings work. These constraints and filters include ownership and the financial pressures for bottom line performance; the need to adapt to the interests of advertisers, who pay the media bills; sourcing processes which cause journalists to depend heavily on government and business newsmakers; the threat of flak, which keeps the journalists under pressure and in line; and anticommunist and market-supportive premises that journalists internalize. The right-wing pundits and their echo chamber fit into this model quite nicely, which is why General Electric and the advertising community give them generous support.

It should be noted the FAIR, in its bimonthly publication *EXTRA!*, has provided numerous studies with compelling evidence of conservative domination of talk shows and public broadcasting. With the exception of their study of the huge bias in the selection of guests on "Nightline," their efforts have been given much less attention in the mainstream media than right-wing "proofs" of liberal media bias as pronounced by Lichter and Rothman and the recent Roper-Gannett study. This is a reflection of genuine media bias, with the right-wing network always able to push congenial findings into the echo chamber, giving themselves and their principals a boost. But this publicity and neglect of the FAIR offerings are living proof that the claim of "liberal bias" is a lie and that the reality is one of illiberal domination.

Networks Need a Reality Check

Bernard Goldberg

From *Bias: A CBS Insider Exposes How the Media Distort the News*, Regnery, 2001

There are a lot of reasons fewer people are watching network news, and one of them, I'm more convinced than ever, is that our viewers simply don't trust us. And for good reason.

The old argument that the networks and other "media elites" have a liberal bias is so blatantly true that it's hardly worth discussing anymore. No, we don't sit around in dark corners and plan strategies on how we're going to slant the news. We don't have to. It comes naturally to most reporters.

Which brings us to a recent "Reality Check" on the *CBS Evening News*, reported by Eric Engberg, a longtime friend. His subject was Steve Forbes's flat tax. It's not just

Democrats and some Republican presidential candidates who don't like the flat tax—it's also a lot of big-time reporters. The flat tax rubs them the wrong way. Which is fair enough—until their bias makes its way into their reporting. And Mr. Engberg's report set new standards for bias.

He starts out saying: "Steve Forbes pitches his flat-tax scheme as an economic elixir, good for everything that ails us." Sure, the words "scheme" and "elixir" are loaded, conjuring up images of Doctor Feelgood selling worthless junk out of the back of his wagon. But this is nothing more than a prelude—warm-up material to get us into the right frame of mind.

The report shows Mr. Forbes saying the U.S. economy can grow twice as fast if we remove "obstacles, starting with the tax code." Mr. Forbes may be right or wrong about this, so Mr. Engberg lets us know which it is. "Time out" he shouts in his signature style. "Economists say nothing like that has ever actually happened."

He then introduces us to William Gale of the Brookings Institution, who says "It doesn't seem plausible to think that we're going to have a whole new economy or economic Renaissance Age due to tax reform."

CBS News instructs its reporters and producers to identify people in a way that will help the audience understand any political bias they might have. We are told, for example, to identify the Heritage Foundation as "a conservative think tank." I have done this on more than one occasion, myself. It's a good policy.

But where was the identification of the Brookings Institution as "a liberal think tank"? Might that influence Mr. Gale's take on the flat tax? Instead, Mr. Gale was presented to America simply as an expert with no tax ax to grind.

Mr. Engberg then shows Mr. Forbes saying: "A flat tax would enable this economy to grow. That would mean more revenues for Washington." To this, Mr. Engberg tells the audience: "That was called supply-side economics under President Reagan: Less taxes equal more revenue. It didn't work out

that way." Immediately after this we hear Mr. Engberg ask this question of Mr. Gale: "Is it fair to say the last time we tried something like this, we ended up with these hideous deficits?" To which Gale obediently replies, "It's perfectly fair to say that."

Mr. Engberg continues: "And if we try it again, your fear is ... " And Mr. Gale replies: " ... that we end up with the same problem again."

But haven't other experts argued that we would up with "hideous deficits," not because of the tax cut but because of increased spending? And to the best of my knowledge, neither Mr. Forbes nor any other flat-tax proponent is suggesting we increase spending.

(Part of the problem is that most reporters and editors—television and print—are total dunces when it comes to the economy. Most don't know a capital gain from a mutual fund. This, as much as bias, in some cases leads to the kind of reporting we see on the flat tax and a lot of other economic issues.)

One thing to remember about network news is that it steals just about everything from print. So if the *New York Times* is against the flat tax, and the *Washington Post* is against the flat tax, the networks can't, and won't be far behind.

Mr. Engberg concludes his piece à la David Letterman by saying that "Forbes's Number One Wackiest Flat-Tax Promise" is the candidate's belief that it would give parents "more time to spend with their children and each other."

Can you imagine, in your wildest dreams, a network news reporter calling Hillary Clinton's health care plan "wacky"? Can you imagine any editor allowing it?

Finally, Mr. Engberg says: "The fact remains: the flat tax is a giant, untested theory. One economist suggested, before we put it in, we should test it out someplace—like Albania."

"Reality Check" suggests the viewers are going to get the facts. And then they can make up their mind. As Mr. Engberg might put it: "Time out." You'd have a better chance of getting the facts someplace else—like Albania.

Liberal Hate-Speech

Bernard Goldberg

From *Bias: A CBS Insider Exposes How the Media Distort the News*, Regnery, 2001

If arrogance were a crime, there wouldn't be enough jail cells in the entire United States to hold all the people in TV news.

A network correspondent told me that once, but when he found out I was writing a book he got amnesia. Not only couldn't he remember ever saying such a subversive thing, but if by some insane chance he had—which he hadn't, of course—he didn't want any credit for it.

No problem.

Except that when network news correspondents are afraid to say even something as harmless as that out loud, there's not much chance they'll take on more serious problems, which then leaves the field wide open to idiots like me or, more ominously, to the real pros ... the conservative media watchdogs that monitor every second of network news in order to document every single example of liberal bias, real or imagined.

Such an organization is the Media Research Center, based in Alexandria, Virginia, right outside Washington, D.C. Every month or so MRC mails a newsletter to reporters and anchors and other sages in the big-time national media. "Notable Quotables," they call it, is chock-full of "the latest outrageous, sometimes humorous, quotes in the liberal media." They also put out a daily report online called CyberAlert, which MRC says tracks media bias.

You'd think this exposure, before your own colleagues no less, might cause a certain amount of embarrassment, especially when the example of bias is especially egregious. Dream on. Network correspondents don't embarrass easily.

It's easy to dismiss "Notable Quotables," because professional liberal bashers compile it. But the right-wing scoundrels at the Media Research Center have come up with some good stuff. What follows are some of the more noteworthy examples, from the last ten years or so, of how journalists on the Left see the world.

- "Some thoughts on those angry voters. Ask parents of any two-year-old and they can tell you about those temper tantrums: the stomping feet, the rolling eyes, the screaming.... Imagine a nation full of uncontrolled two-year-old rage. The voters had a temper tantrum last week.... Parenting and governing don't have to be dirty words: the nation can't be run by an angry two-year-old."—*ABC anchorman Peter Jennings in his radio commentary after the GOP won the House, November 14, 1994*

- "It's short of soap, so there are lice in the hospitals. It's short of pantyhose, women's legs go bare. It's short of snowsuits, so babies stay home in the winter. Sometimes it's short of cigarettes so millions of people stop smoking, involuntarily. It drives everybody crazy. The problem isn't communism; no one even talked about communism this week. The problem is shortages."—*NBC Nightly News commentator John Chancellor on the Soviet Union, August 21, 1991*

- "I would be happy to give him [Clinton] a blow job just to thank him for keeping abortion legal. I think American women should be lining up with their presidential kneepads on to show their gratitude for keeping the theocracy off our backs."—*Time contributor and former reporter Nina Burleigh recalling what she told the* Washington Post's *Howard Kurtz about her feeling toward Bill Clinton, as recounted by Burleigh in the July 20, 1998, New York Observer*

- "The man is on the Court. You know, I hope his wife feeds him lots of eggs and butter and he dies early like many black men do, of heart disease. Well, that's how I feel. He is an absolutely reprehensible person."—USA Today *columnist and Pacifica Radio talk show host Julianne Malveaux on Justice Clarence Thomas, November 4, 1994, PBS,* To the Contrary

- Inside Washington (TV) host Tina Gulland: "I don't think I have any Jesse Helms defenders here, Nina?"

Nina Totenberg: "Not me. I think he ought to be worried about what's going on in the Good Lord's mind, because if there is retributive justice, he'll get AIDS from a transfusion, or one of his grandchildren will get it."—*National Public Radio and ABC News reporter Nina Totenberg reacting to Senator Jesse Helms's claim that the government spends too much on AIDS research, July 8, 1995*

- "Yes, the case is being fomented by right-wing nuts and yes, she is not a very credible witness, and it's really not a law case at all. But Clinton has got a problem here. He has a history of womanizing that most people believe is a problem. . . . It leads to things like this, some sleazy woman with big hair coming out of the trailer parks."—Newsweek *Washington bureau chief Evan Thomas on Paula Jones, May 7, 1994,* Inside Washington

- "In the plague years of the 1980s—that low decade of denial, indifference, hostility, opportunism, and idiocy—government fiddled and medicine diddled and the media were silent or hysterical. A gerontocratic Ronald Reagan took this [AIDS] plague less seriously than Gerald Ford had taken swine flu. After all, he didn't need the ghettos and he didn't want the gays."—CBS Sunday Morning *TV critic John Leonard, September 5, 1993*

- ". . . Toni Morrison wrote in the *New Yorker* that Clinton was our first 'black President,' and I think, in a way, Clinton may be our first 'woman President.' And I think that may be one of the reasons why women identify, because he does have a lot of feminine qualities about him: The softness, the sensitivity, the vulnerability, that kind of thing."—*the* Washington Post's *Sally Quinn on CNN's* Larry King Live, *March 10, 1999*

- "He [Ted Kaczynski] wasn't a hypocrite. He lives as he wrote. His manifesto, and there are a lot of things in it that I would agree with and a lot of other people would, that industrialization and pollution are terrible things, but he carried it to an extreme, and obviously murder is something that is far beyond any political philosophy, but he had a bike. He didn't have any plumbing, he didn't have any electricity."—Time *Washington reporter Elaine Shannon talking about the Unabomber, April 7, 1996,* Sunday Journal

- "I think liberalism lives—the notion that we don't have to stay where we are as a society, we have promises to keep, and it is liberalism, whether people like it or not, which has animated all the years of my life. What on earth did conservatism accomplish for our country?—*Charles Kuralt talking with Morley Safer on the CBS special* One for the Road with Charles Kuralt, *May 4, 1994*

- Linda Chavez, Center for Equal Opportunity: "If you're someone like me, who lives out in a rural area—if someone breaks into my house and wants to murder or rape me or steal off of my property, it'll take a half an hour for a policeman to get to me. . . . Thousands of lives are saved by people being able to protect themselves."

Bonnie Erbe, host and former NBC Radio/Mutual reporter: "And if you look at the statistics, I would bet that you have a greater chance of being struck by lightning, Linda, than living where you live, and at your age,

being raped. Sorry."—*PBS, To the Contrary,*
May 13, 2000

- "I'm all news all the time. Full power,
  tall tower. I want to break in when
  news breaks out. That's my agenda.
  Now respectfully, when you start talking about a liberal agenda and all the,
  quote, 'liberal bias' in the media, I quite
  frankly, and I say this respectfully but
  candidly to you, I don't know what
  you're talking about."—*Dan Rather to
  Denver KOA Radio's Mike Rosen, November 28, 1995*

In fairness to the media elites, these aren't
really examples of *unethical* liberal bias. Dan
Rather was giving his opinion on a radio talk
show. Peter Jennings didn't liken the American
voter to an angry two-year-old on the *World
News Tonight.* He did it in a radio commentary,
a place he's allowed to give his opinions. John
Chancellor wasn't *reporting* the news when he
made his absurd observation that the problem
in the old Soviet Union wasn't communism,
but shortages. He was doing *commentary.*

Liberals have as much right to be downright silly as anyone else. But I doubt Peter
would have gone on a rant if liberal Democrats had been swept into office instead of
conservative Republicans. I doubt he would
have compared American voters to a bunch
of babies having temper tantrums had they
voted for people more to Peter's liking and
the liking of his Manhattan pals.

But there is something interesting about
how liberals in the media can get away with
making certain observations that conservatives never could.

Nina Totenberg says, "[I]f there's retributive justice, he'll [Jesse Helms] get AIDS from
a transfusion, or one of his grandchildren will
get it," and she remains a member in good
standing of the liberal media elites.

What if a conservative journalist such
as Fred Barnes of the *Weekly Standard* had
said, *"If there's any justice in this world, Teddy
Kennedy will drive off a bridge late at night and
kill himself. Or one or two of his kids."*

He would rightly be considered a con-
temptible hatemonger whose every word

on every subsequent subject would be scrutinized for traces of venom, and it wouldn't
be long before other journalists would mar-
ginalize him.

USA Today columnist Julianne Malveaux
says of Clarence Thomas, "I hope his wife
feeds him lots of eggs and butter and he
dies early like many black men do, of heart
disease," and she gets invited back on TV talk
shows all the time.

If Robert Novak, the conservative columnist and CNN commentator, had said, "I
hope Jesse Jackson's wife feeds him lots of
eggs and butter and he dies early like many
black men do, of heart disease," he'd rightly
be seen as a nasty right-wing nut and compared to the Grand Wizard of the KKK.

Newsweek's Evan Thomas cavalierly calls
Paula Jones "some sleazy woman with big
hair coming out of the trailer parks," and
he's seen as a pundit instead of a liberal elitist snob.

Can anyone in his right mind really
imagine a conservative journalist of Evan
Thomas's stature ridiculing a not-too-sophis-
ticated, not-too-educated, young black or
Hispanic woman, as someone *"with big hair
coming out of the ghetto"*?

Bonnie Erbe tells Linda Chavez on PBS
that she's got a greater chance of being struck
by lightning than being raped—*at her age.*

If Brit Hume had said something so
incredibly insensitive and so downright stupid (which I know he never would), NOW
would have screamed that, like so many
men, he just doesn't get it, that rape is *not*
about sex, but about *power and control,* and
then, just to set an example, the president of
NOW would have led a contingent to hang
Brit Hume in effigy, or maybe in the flesh.
They would have thrown a million pickets
into the crusade to get him off the air, and
they'd all be marching around Fox headquarters in New York and Washington chanting
"Brit's a Twit and He's Got to Go." Quicker
than you can say "male chauvinist pig" Brit
Hume would become an embarrassment to
Fox and a pariah in the world of big-time
journalism.

But when a liberal says it on PBS, no big
deal. Chavez is a conservative after all—and

the sin of all sins, she says things Hispanic women aren't supposed to say. White liberals hate it when minorities do that. So, ipso facto, she's fair game.

Why is it that when liberal media stars say nasty things they're merely sharing their thoughts with us and (even more important) their feelings, but when the same sentiment comes out of a conservative's mouth, it's seen as mean-spirited?

After Bill Clinton was impeached, *Newsweek's* Eleanor Clift ("Eleanor Rodham Clift," in some circles) said, "That herd of managers from the House, I mean, frankly, all they were missing was white sheets."

Likewise, the *Arkansas Times* editorialized that "Kenneth Starr is cunning, ruthless, and about as well-mannered as Heinrich Himmler."

On January 15, 1999—Martin Luther King's birthday—the *Los Angeles Times* published an op-ed by "frequent contributor" Karen Grigsby Bates who spewed the following:

"It is a totally visceral reaction, but whenever I hear [Republican Senate majority leader] Trent Lott speak, I immediately think of nooses decorating trees. Big trees, with black bodies swinging from the business end of the nooses."

This is vile. Maybe it went over big with what they like to call the "creative community" in Los Angeles, but it is vile hate speech no matter how you cut it.

And what of the *Los Angeles Times,* the newspaper that published it? The *Times* is nothing if not a monument to political correctness, so much so that an op-ed page editor yanked a line from a syndicated George Will column that said, "I think it is reasonable to believe that [Bill Clinton] was a rapist." This offended the sensibilities of the *Times* editor. Linking a United States senator to the likes of Ku Klux Klan murderers, however, apparently falls into the category of nothing to get worked up over.

The media elites, at the *Los Angeles Times* and everyplace else, can hear, even when the whispers of what they consider hate speech is fifty miles away—whether they imagine that it's coming from conservative talk show hosts or right-wing religious fundamentalists or just about anyone opposed to affirmative action. But they can't hear it dripping off their own nasty tongues … and probably think "liberal hate-speech" is an oxymoron.

It's a good thing arrogance isn't a crime.

Matthews vs. McNulty

David Sirota

Creators Syndicate, April 24, 2008

If television is the nation's mirror, then no two TV characters reflect the intensifying "two Americas" gap better than Chris Matthews and Jimmy McNulty.

A recent New York Times profile of Matthews describes a name-dropping dilettante floating between television studios and cocktail parties. The article documents the MSNBC host's $5 million salary, three Mercedes and house in lavish Chevy Chase, Md. Yet Matthews said, "Am I part of the winner's circle in American life? I don't think so."

That stupefying comment sums up a pervasive worldview in Washington that is hostile to any discussion of class divides. Call it Matthews-ism—an ideology most recently seen in the brouhaha over Barack Obama's statement about economic dislocation.

The Illinois senator said that when folks feel economically shafted, they get "bitter." Matthews-ism spun the truism into a scandal.

The Washington Post labeled Obama's statements "Bittergate." Tim Russert invited affluent political consultants on "Meet the

Press" to analyze the "controversy," with millionaire James Carville saying, "I'm hardly bitter about things." Hillary Clinton called Obama "elitist," ignoring her mansions in Washington and Chappaqua, $109 million income, career as a Wal-Mart board member, and legacy pushing job-killing policies like NAFTA.

This sickening episode was topped off by ABC's Charles Gibson, who only months ago humiliated himself by insinuating that typical middle-class families make $200,000 a year (95 percent make less). Last week, while moderating a debate, Gibson segued from the "bitter" comment into a tirade against rescinding capital gains tax breaks, implying the proposal would hurt most Americans. This, even though the tax cuts in question delivered the vast majority of their benefits to the richest 1 percent.

By downplaying inequality and couching royalism in middle-class arguments, the Beltway elite pretend there are not two Americas but only one: theirs.

Matthews routinely turns discussions of economic issues into debates about tactics, and then heads home to Chevy Chase telling himself he isn't "part of the winner's circle." Tim Russert asks millionaires to explain working-class struggles, and then reminds viewers he roots for the Buffalo Bills—as if that proves he speaks for blue-collar America.

Hillary Clinton makes a career out of speaking for powerful corporations, and then shows up at an Indiana bar to decry "elitism." Gibson suggests six-figure salaries are common, and then says the masses should worry about rich people like him having to pay slightly higher taxes.

In sum, economic blindness, sports symbols, beery photo-ops and uninformed idiocy have become the iconography of working-class solidarity that disguises the ongoing class war.

How could this happen, you ask? How could it not?

Pop culture tells us "The Cosby Show's" economically privileged family represents the ordinary black experience, politics tells us a money-controlled electoral system is "democratic," and pundits tell us that aristocrat George Bush is a "regular guy." Propaganda is ubiquitous—and it results in Jimmy McNulty.

He is the cop from HBO's "The Wire"— the quintessential everyman. For a time, he tries to understand politics by watching vapid Matthews-style talk shows, but quickly becomes frustrated. "It doesn't matter who you've got [running for office], none of them has a clue what's really going on," he says, lamenting that politics treats him "like a [expletive] doormat"—as if the day-to-day challenges he faces are "some stupid game with stupid penny ante stakes."

McNulty may be fictional, but McNulty-ism is a very real reaction to Matthews-ism. When the media responsible for explaining our world deny the existence of the world most of us inhabit, they breed—yes— bitterness. And the more the Matthewses treat us McNultys like reality is just "stupid games with stupid penny ante stakes," the wider the gulf between the two Americas will become.

Outfoxed *Tweaks Rupert Murdoch's Mayhem-isphere*

Susan Gerhard

San Francisco Guardian, August 4, 2004

If the United States took a survey of the TV habits of its visitors to emergency rooms, you have to wonder, what kind of patterns might emerge? How many bleeding ulcers and broken limbs have been triggered by viewing a segment of The O'Reilly Factor? Sean Hannity takes on a guest and how many eyeballs are pulled from their sockets? Somewhere in TV land's pixelated global theater—where a tap on the remote can bring you Amish in the City or Wildboyz fondling a giant dead squid—lives a 24-hour news channel that, in its zeal to reinvent the news in the image of its creator, has merged all the credibility of professional wrestling with the subtlety of a New York Post headline. With no wink and no nod, but huge three-dimensional graphics sewn together by Betsy Ross, it markets itself under the slogan "fair and balanced."

So abused, the phrase "fair and balanced"—like the words "justice system"—is, by now, its own warning. We know enough to avoid it. But Robert Greenwald, director of the new documentary Outfoxed, does what no other informed American would even consider: he takes Fox News at its word. As in his journey back to one sad day in the land of "fair," when O'Reilly Factor host Bill O'Reilly brought on Jeremy Glick, the son of a man who died in one of the World Trade Center towers on Sept. 11. Glick was on the show because he'd signed the Not in Our Name petition against the war in Iraq. Unfortunately for O'Reilly, Glick had done his homework; he'd actually timed with a stopwatch just how long it generally took O'Reilly to shut down his uncooperative guests. He'd practiced his delivery with the hope of getting out a message: a full subject-predicate sentence. That he managed to clearly enunciate through O'Reilly's repeated interruptions sent the host into a full volcanic fury, which ended in all manner of "shut ups" and even one unfortunate reference to Glick's grieving, widowed mother.

O'Reilly's tirade, it turns out, wasn't just for the cameras, as Glick relates to the makers of Outfoxed, who—in scrutinizing and tracking vast quantities of Fox News footage looking for patterns of behavior—closely paralleled Glick's strategy. Glick tells them the host called security to take him away, but as the Sept. 11 survivor attempted to drink one last sip of liquid in the green room, more handlers told him he'd better get out of the

building before O'Reilly did something that would land him in jail. When Glick turned on Factor the next day, he heard O'Reilly retell the story a whole different way, saying Glick was "out of control." O'Reilly repeated that and other false assertions so many times that Glick asked a lawyer whether he might be able to sue the host for libel. No, he was advised, everything O'Reilly says is so outrageous, it would be difficult to claim O'Reilly knew he was telling a lie.

The nature of Fox network's news reporting changed the course of history. Election night 2000, duly vilified in the more entertaining and trenchant political doc of the season, Fahrenheit 9/11, all came down to a call made by Fox News's election desk, which had Bush cousin John Ellis working on it—and he'd been in contact with his pals Jeb and George W. just that evening. Even though the Associated Press held out and said the election was too close to call, Fox News rushed to judgment and gave it to Bush. And the rest of the free TV press? In a kooky totalitarian reversal of the "Dewey Defeats Truman" gaffe or even the New York Post's "Dem picks Gephardt as VP candidate" one, they shamefully jumped on board within minutes. Fox News chair Roger Ailes, former media strategist for Nixon, Reagan, and Bush Sr., later testified to a nation that wasn't really listening anymore that "we gave our audience bad information. . . . It will not happen again."

There's no shortage of non-innovatively filmed talking heads in Outfoxed, including Walter Cronkite and the always on-point Robert McChesney, to explain the ongoing harm caused by Rupert Murdoch's ownership of a media empire, a collection of 9 TV satellites, 175 newspapers, 40 book imprints, 100 cable stations, 40 TV stations, and one movie studio, reaching a total 4.7 billion people, which is about three-fourths of the people on the Earth. And it's no surprise that the empire's flagship news channel supports the Republicans who help Murdoch stay on top of the dirt pile.

What is a surprise are the smoking guns Greenwald digs up to show just how it's done. Fox's firees and escapees—producers, contributors, and newscasters—speak, sometimes under duress, about tortured tenures in Murdoch's mad, mad media world. Greenwald savors the memos from the office of John Moody, a Fox News senior vice president—perhaps a little too heavy-handedly with a demonic-sounding voice-over reading—as they give the day's instructions on tone and even word choice. "Let's refer to the U.S. Marines we see in the foreground as 'sharpshooters' not 'snipers,' which carries a negative connotation," one such memo notes. A former contributor recalls the top-down instruction to rename "suicide bombings" as "homicide bombings." The film dissects some of the strategies for merging "news" and "opinion" and eliminating the middleman—sources—by, for example, using the phrase "some people say." And in its most entertaining sequences—and you have to admit, "entertainment" isn't a primary goal of this extremely sober doc—the film pastes together varieties of Fox News's worst habits, its echo-chamber repetition of the Republican message of the day, be it John Kerry's purported "flip-flop" voting record or Richard Clarke's supposed hopes of being part of the Kerry cabinet.

It's all so ridiculous, it calls out for the kind of domineering shaming only a Michael Moore can pull off. A back-them-into-a-corner-and-stab technique, or at the very least, a slightly hipper use of music than laying Don Henley's "Dirty Laundry" over the credits. I mean, kick 'em when they're up. But maybe it's unfortunate that this guerrilla-produced, grassroots-distributed sleeper doc hit is being compared with more theatrically minded projects of this supercharged election year. It is, itself, journalism—meant for the moment, not for the archives—and on those terms it succeeds. There are even some of the best comic scenes of the year, as it smacks down O'Reilly with a "shut up" montage. But as the film ridicules Fox News's use of aggressive graphics and short-attention-span crawls, you can't help noticing that *Outfoxed* is itself, in some way, being outFoxed—falling victim to the idea that images of reasonable people speaking about relevant political issues should be enough to carry a nonfiction essay. No sophisticated audiovisuals or artful, cinematic pre-thinking required.

Which brings up the obvious: why do TV viewers like Fox News? Probably the scariest, most important question the film could have answered remained unasked. Surveys conducted by the University of Maryland's Program on International Policy Attitudes and Knowledge Networks show viewers of Fox News are up to five times more ignorant about key political issues than audiences of PBS and NPR. Fox News, by keeping its audience misinformed and baiting anger from all sides, has extended TV news's reach from our minds into our guts. It doesn't gather facts; it collects emotion, then empties it safely into the trash.

Topics for Discussion and Writing on Readings

1. Synthesize the survey in this chapter of the multiple factors involved in media bias and write a comparative analysis and evaluation of the articles by Edward Herman and Bernard Goldberg. Drawing from Rogerian argument or Believers and Doubters, try to write the most evenhanded account you can, delineating aspects and examples of *both* liberal/left and conservative bias in media, as documented in these articles and other sources.
2. Herman's article appeared in *Z Magazine*, which has a left-of-liberal or socialist viewpoint, and Herman with his frequent coauthor Noam Chomsky is a prominent spokesperson for that viewpoint, most comprehensively developed in his and Chomsky's book *Manufacturing Consent: The Political Economy of the Mass Media*, the most recent edition of which was published in 2002. He and Chomsky

devote much of their writing to criticizing what they perceive as conservative bias in reputedly liberal media like the *New York Times* and PBS. The fact that they are rarely allowed to express themselves in mainstream print or broadcast media is itself cited by leftists as evidence of those media's conservative bias. Where in his article does Herman criticize mainstream Democrats and "liberal" media from the left, and how does his criticism of them differ from Goldberg's? Do you think Herman's viewpoint here deserves wider media circulation, or would you dismiss him, as David Horowitz does Chomsky in "The Intellectual Class War" in chapter 13, as "an America-loathing crank"? (Also see *The Anti-Chomsky Reader*, edited by Horowitz and Peter Collier.)

3. The two selections by Bernard Goldberg are from his best-selling book *Bias: A CBS Insider Exposes How the Media Distort the News*. See the review of this book by Jonathan Chait in the *New Republic*, March 18, 2002, which raises many of the same issues that this chapter does, while suggesting that Goldberg presents a one-sided viewpoint. Also see the exchange between Goldberg and Chait in the letters section of the *New Republic*, April 29, 2002. See also Geoffrey Nunberg, "Label Whores: Bernard Goldberg's *Bias* Points in the Wrong Direction," in the *American Prospect*, May 6, 2002, 32–35. Nunberg did an Internet search for news media labeling of conservatives and liberals, which led to the conclusion that liberals were in fact labeled more often than conservatives. He directs readers to his results at http://people.ischool.berkeley.edu/~nunberg/table.html.

4. Both Goldberg and David Sirota in "Matthews vs. McNulty" criticize TV commentators as elitists. Sirota singles out prominent Democrats like James Carville (a former consultant to President Clinton) and Hillary Clinton, along with Chris Matthews and the late Tim Russert, who are generally regarded as liberals and probably Democrats. (Charles Gibson is generally considered more conservative, though not an overt Republican.) On what grounds does Sirota's critique from the left of these figures differ from Goldberg's from their right? If one problem with media elites, whether considered as liberal or conservative, is that they are wealthy and powerful, to what extent is the very nature of commercial media as profit-driven corporations part of this problem? What alternatives can you and classmates envision to make the media more populist, more open both to journalists, commentators, and entertainers who are not wealthy, and to those who have expert opinions but are not wealthy? (C-SPAN would be a model here, in its presentations by scholars and authors of in-depth journalistic books.) Good topics for a research paper are the "blogosphere," Internet-based, non-profit political and media organizations, and various alternative media movements (e.g., FreePress.net) as counterforces to "the mainstream media."

5. Susan Gerhard's review of *Outfoxed*, a documentary film criticizing the conservative bias of Fox News, agrees with the film that Fox differs significantly from the "liberal" media that Fox claims it is merely counterbalancing. The charge is that, in contrast to other media whose owners are at least ostensibly dedicated to gathering and reporting news in a professional and independent manner, without political party affiliation—in spite of the biases that occur in their individual personnel, on individual occasions—the "news" and opinion on Fox (and in several other conservative media) are deliberately controlled and slanted to follow the line of the Republican Party, with which its owner, Rupert Murdoch, and its top editors and executives are overtly allied. In this respect, Fox is more like a print journal of opinion than a news medium, except that rather than admitting this, it claims to be "fair and balanced." Rent or buy *Outfoxed* in DVD to evaluate how

persuasively it supports this case. How do you think Bernard Goldberg would reply to this case?

ASSIGNMENT FOR A PAPER

Write a thousand-word (three or four typewritten pages) review of a recent issue of a left-wing journal of opinion and a right-wing one. Get these from the periodical room at your campus or public library, from the Internet, or from a newsstand or bookstore. Recommended right-wing journals: *Weekly Standard, National Review, American Spectator, Washington Times Weekly, Human Events, Reason* (libertarian); left-wing ones: *The Nation, In These Times,* the *Progressive, Z Magazine, Extra!, Mother Jones.*

Read through all the articles, ads, and cartoons in both journals and, in about half the paper, summarize the scope of articles (and ads) in both, indicating to what extent the general range of topics and viewpoints reflects the left or right positions and patterns of rhetoric in chapter 13, "Thinking Critically about Political Rhetoric." (Remark on any notable exceptions.) Then focus on one article in each that you find interesting and that expresses a left or right position particularly clearly or effectively, and summarize how it does so in as much detail as space allows. Also try to figure out whether the leftist magazine in general, and in your specific article, is liberal or socialist/left-of-liberal (i.e., does it criticize the Democrats from the left?), and whether the one on the right is mainstream Republican Party conservative or libertarian conservative (i.e., does it criticize the Republicans on libertarian terms?).

It might make it more interesting for you if you can find articles in the two journals on the same subject, so that you can note the opposing lines of argument. This is not essential, though, and do not try to get into a point-by-point comparison of the opposing lines, since this would make the paper too long.

The purpose of this assignment is to give you practice in understanding how the general rhetorical patterns of opposition between the left and right come out on particular current issues. Therefore, limit yourself to identifying these patterns objectively, *without expressing your opinions about the quality of the magazine or about particular articles and their arguments.* Do comment briefly, however, on whether either journal gave you a clearer understanding of the viewpoint it expresses than you had before, and in what way.

CHAPTER 15

Deception Detection: Varieties of Special Interests and Propaganda

SPECIAL INTERESTS, CONFLICT OF INTEREST, AND SPECIAL PLEADING

The significance of the terms *special interests, conflict of interest,* and *special pleading* in argumentative rhetoric hinges on definitions of both the words *interest* and *special* that differ from everyday usage. When we say that someone is "an interested party" in a dispute, that "it is in her interest to support this policy," or that "his argument is self-interested," we do not mean that the person simply is interested in the subject; "to have an interest" here refers to having an investment or stake (financial or otherwise) in the outcome, some personal benefit. The term *disinterested,* as in "disinterested research," refers approvingly to the neutral, objective rhetorical stance of a speaker or writer who has no personal stake in an issue. (Note that *disinterested* is not synonymous with *uninterested,* though it is often misused that way.)

Likewise, *special* here is synonymous with a private, often selfish motive for support of a public policy. *Merriam-Webster's Collegiate Dictionary* defines *special interest* as "a person or group having an interest [as in *investment*] in a particular part of the economy and receiving or seeking special advantages therein often to the detriment of the general public." Special pleading, then, refers to people arguing for a position that they present as being in the public's benefit when it is secretly for the benefit of special interests. So special pleading typically uses the one-sided tactics of **propaganda** and **stacking the deck** to conceal the fact that the speaker or writer is presenting only the side of an issue that favors the interests being served. Most advertising, public relations, and lobbying messages are obvious forms of special pleading.

Conflict of interest is a financial investment or some kind of affiliation that is likely to bias the views of a speaker or writer. (Note that this concept differs from the simple term *conflict* in the sense of a disagreement, so be careful not to confuse them in your usage.) The classic conflict of interest situation is that of a government official who either stands to benefit

334

personally from particular legislation or who is closely associated with someone who does, such as a campaign contributor. Conflict of interest becomes a rhetorical issue when it leads to special pleading, as when a legislator who has a personal financial investment benefited by pending legislation conceals that fact and makes a speech falsely arguing that the legislation is in the public interest. When you use statements by public officials as sources, you should try to find out what conflicts of interests might be biasing the views presented.

Other sources of information that you may draw on in researching papers are also subject to conflicts of interest. Journalistic sources may have conflicts involving owners', advertisers', or reporters' financial investments in issues reported on. The findings of journalists' or scholars' research might benefit or be harmful to special interests affiliated with the foundation or research institute subsidizing the research, in which case there might be explicit or tacit pressure on the researcher that taints the findings. Professors sometimes have investments in, or are paid consultants for, businesses that their research benefits—a situation that may also taint their teaching or published findings and conflict with university faculties' code of ethical disinterestedness. In one such case, according to the *Chronicle of Higher Education*, "Tobacco companies financed the work of several university scientists who published research and offered testimony that minimized the dangers of smoking" (http://chronicle. com, December 19, 1997). (Also see Mildred K. Cho, "Secrecy and Financial Conflicts of Interest in University-Industry Research Must Get Closer Scrutiny," *Chronicle of Higher Education*, August 1, 1997.) Teachers in public schools and universities have an obvious conflict of interest when they teach the pros and cons of increased taxes and spending for education, and if they belong to a teacher's union, they have a similar conflict in teaching about labor issues.

In recent decades, conservatives have defined teachers, media employees, and other professionals and intellectuals as members of a "new class" that allegedly advocate liberal policies primarily because they serve the selfish interests of that class. [*Reader Advisory*: In the interests of full disclosure, I am an employee of a public university and member of a teachers' union.]

There are several other forms of conflict of interest beyond financial ones. Nepotism (favor toward relatives) and cronyism (favor toward friends) are also possible sources of conflicts of interest in many areas of public life. Journalistic reviews of books, films, recordings and concerts, restaurants, and other cultural topics are susceptible to distinctive kinds of conflict of interest. Advertising in a journal is often a trade-off for a review of the product, especially a positive one. When the same corporation owns the medium in which the review appears as well as the book publisher or film or recording company producing the work reviewed, there may be pressure from management for a favorable review. Journalist John Podhoretz, writing in the *Weekly Standard* (December 8, 1997), used impudent humor to deal with such a situation. After praising a film produced by Rupert Murdoch's Twentieth Century Fox, he made this "obligatory disclosure: Twentieth Century Fox is owned by News Corporation, which owns the *Weekly Standard* as well as the *New York Post*, my current employer. Now drop dead" (39).

Reviewers of books are subject to a variety of possible conflicts of interest, and the choice of assignments to freelance reviewers presents a constant test of the fair-mindedness of the editors of supplements such as the Sunday *New York Times Book Review*, in terms of conflicts of interest as well as ideological bias and avoiding assignments to either friends or enemies of the author. Editors' own biases can be discerned if they consistently solicit reviewers who they know in advance will be either favorably or unfavorably disposed toward a certain book. When I was chosen to review an anthology of articles for one such Sunday supplement, the editor would not allow me to say anything about one article because it quoted approvingly from a book of mine. Under a different editor, though, the same supplement later allowed a writer to defend certain research institutes criticized for political bias in the book he was reviewing, even though his own research had been subsidized by those institutes. (If he had admitted to this conflict of interest in the review, he would have been less subject to criticism, but he did not.) The author of a review in the *New England Journal of Medicine* panning a book alleging that environmental chemicals are contributing to an epidemic of cancer was later revealed to be the medical director at chemical producer W. R. Grace & Co. This incident occurred in spite of the journal's stated policy that "rather than simply requiring authors to disclose potential conflicts of interest, it would not accept reviews or editorials from anyone connected to firms with a financial stake in the drug or device being discussed" (*San Francisco Chronicle*, December 27, 1997, A3).

Questions concerning special interests, special pleading, and conflict of interest can be highly complex and disputable. Just to determine in a given circumstance what does or does not constitute special pleading or conflict of interest can be a difficult judgment call. Nearly everyone is motivated to some extent by self-interest, and anyone who speaks or writes publicly is likely to have one degree or another of conflict of interest, so the degree of gravity in any particular conflict needs to be evaluated. As a general rule, people should not be criticized as being selfish for arguing in defense of their (or their group's) own right to life, liberty, pursuit of happiness, equality under the law, a living income, or reasonable profit. People *are* subject to criticism, however, (1) if the policy they are arguing for results in them or interests they are speaking for receiving a disproportionate, unfair benefit at the expense of others or of the public interest, or (2) if they cover up or play down their self-interest, pretending to be arguing *disinterestedly* or *impartially* for the public benefits of a policy from which they or their associates will personally benefit.

The ad hominem fallacy is a real danger in these matters; that is, you should be careful not to dismiss the substance of someone's arguments *only* because they may be self-interested. Most speakers and writers sincerely believe that what benefits their own group is also in the public interest and that their familiarity with the subject in question qualifies them as authorities; their arguments and evidence always need to be evaluated on their own merits. If special pleading or conflicts of interest are clearly present, however, that should alert you to being extra certain to check out the evidence carefully. It is perfectly legitimate in your writing to point out *possible* conflicts of interest and special pleading in your sources, as one factor among others in evaluating their arguments.

The most honest way of dealing with an unavoidable conflict of interest is to declare it openly and honestly—"full disclosure" is the conventional phrase—and to deal with it as scrupulously as possible. When President George H. W. Bush was making cabinet appointments, he urged nominees to be forthright in avoiding not just actual conflicts but also "any *appearance* of conflict of interest." Judges will sometimes "recuse," or excuse, themselves from sitting in a case in which they have a conflict; legislators will decline to debate or vote on bills involving their own interests; and government appointees will make a full financial disclosure statement. In a controversial case during the administration of President George W. Bush, the Supreme Court was considering a suit filed against Vice President Richard Cheney to make public the records of his private meetings with energy company and foreign oil executives for an energy task force. While this suit was pending, Justice Antonin Scalia flew in Cheney's private plane with him on a duck-hunting trip in Louisiana. However, Scalia refused to recuse himself, scoffing at the suggestion that this trip constituted a conflict of interest. The court ruled in favor of Cheney.

As in many semantic issues, even the definition of "special interests" is largely subjective and partisan. Historically, the term has been applied to a few wealthy individuals or businesses trying to buy government favoritism to increase their profits, or to "pork-barrel legislation" (more recently called "earmarks") designed only to benefit some local constituency. In recent years, the original meaning has been dissipated by application of the term (mainly by conservative business interests against their liberal opponents) to any constituency or lobby, no matter how large, and even if not motivated by financial investments. Many advocacy groups are concerned solely with the public good as they view it in principle, without selfish motives, whether on the conservative side like religious and right-to-life groups or on the liberal side like environmentalists, feminists, and pro-choice groups. A second category, including groups like AARP (the American Association of Retired Persons) and the NAACP (National Association for the Advancement of Colored People) certainly represent the special interests of their constituents, but they include millions of diverse members and can generally make a strong case that what is in their interest is also in the public interest.

Conservatives sometimes try to discredit the officials of liberal nonprofit organizations of environmentalists, feminists, consumer advocates, and civil rights activists by claiming that they are in it only for the money they receive in executive salary. However, this line of argument often comes across as ad hominem because those who make it rarely can present any concrete evidence to support it, and they also tend to apply it with **selective vision** that fails to make the same charges against conservative advocacy groups—such as the National Rifle Association, anti-abortion and religious organizations—or against corporate executives, lobbyists, advertising and PR agents, many of whom make a lot more money. (The tax reports of nonprofit organizations are on the public record, so you can research liberal and conservative ones to compare their executive salaries.)

Labor unions are a somewhat more ambiguous case; they undoubtedly lobby for their own financial interests, but they also represent millions of constituents. Critics of unions, though, often accuse their officials of acting in only their own interests, not those of their rank-and-file members, and there are certainly instances of officials defrauding their members. Conservative defenders of business lobbies argue that the owners and executives of corporations likewise represent all their stockholders and employees, as well as the public interest. The credibility of this line of argument was tarnished in the early years of this century with corporate scandals like Enron. In a famous episode of the 1950s, President Dwight Eisenhower's nominee for secretary of defense was the president of General Motors, Charles Wilson, whose confirmation was challenged because of conflicts of interest concerning GM as a major military contractor. He testified that there was no conflict because "What's good for General Motors is good for America."

Another kind of borderline case is the National Rifle Association (NRA), number one on the following list of most powerful lobbies in Washington. Officially it is a civil rights organization defending the perceived constitutional rights of its millions of rank-and-file members to bear arms, but it also receives a substantial part of its funding and administration from gun manufacturers and dealers. A skeptical view of NRA's opposition to gun control suggests that manufacturers' and dealers' profits may be a stronger motive than principled defense of Second Amendment rights.

LOBBYING AND PUBLIC RELATIONS

By the earlier definition of propaganda as one-sided information produced by paid professionals, much, if not most, political lobbying and professionally produced public relations are forms of propaganda, although of course there is a wide range in the legitimacy of the interests represented and the validity of the claims made. A vast number of organizations, internationally, nationally, and locally, hire lobbyists and PR representatives: individual corporations and industrial associations (like those representing oil (see the exercise about the American Petroleum Institute's advertising campaign at the end of chapter 16), energy and automobile producers, or more broadly the National Association of Manufacturers and the Chamber of Commerce), professional associations (like the American Medical Association, American Bar Association, and National Education Association), government agencies, foreign governments, trade and public employee unions, and advocacy groups across the political spectrum—environmentalists, the National Rifle Association, religious denominations, retirees, organizations for civil rights and women's rights, and groups for or against abortion, and so on.

In 2001 (May 28) *Fortune* magazine published what used to be an annual list of "the most powerful" lobbies in Washington (it was unclear how they measured power). That was the last year it was updated, but a more recent list of all major lobbyists is available at Fortune.com:

Washington Power 25			
National Rifle Association	1	Am. Hospital Association	13
AARP	2	Nat'l Education Association	14
Nat'l Fed. of Indep. Business	3	Am. Farm Bureau Federation	15
Am. Israel Pub. Affairs Comm.	4	Motion Picture Assoc. of Am.	16
Association of Trial Lawyers	5	Nat'l Assoc. of Broadcasters	17
AFL-CIO	6	Nat'l Right to Life Committee	18
Chamber of Commerce	7	Health Insurance Association	19
Nat'l Beer Wholesalers Assoc.	8	Nat'l Restaurant Association	20
Nat'l Assoc. of Realtors	9	Nat'l Governors' Association	21
Nat'l Assoc. of Manufacturers	10	Recording Industry Assoc.	22
Nat'l Assoc. of Home Bldrs.	11	Am. Bankers Association	23
Am. Medical Association	12	Pharmaceut. Rsrch. & Manuf.	24
		Int'l Brotherhood of Teamsters	25

The list includes three labor unions—AFL-CIO, National Education Association, and the Teamsters—as well as the nonprofit American Association of Retired Persons, National Governors' Association, and National Right to Life Committee, plus one foreign lobby, American Israel Public Affairs Committee (which is not an official representative of the Israeli government). Otherwise all of the top twenty-five represent corporate or professional special interests.

Making judgments about these diverse groups' motives, methods, and rhetoric calls for nuanced thought, as was indicated earlier with respect to the ambiguity of the definition of a "special interest group." In all corporate and industrial-association lobbies, however, the factor of the profit motive creates a different rhetorical situation from that of nonprofit groups. Both defenders and critics of capitalism agree that the primary purpose of capitalism and corporations is to return maximum profits to stockholders. If this is considered as the first **premise** in a **deductive argument**, and if the second premise is that the means of maximizing profits are sometimes contrary to the public interest (e.g., in effects on the environment, workers, consumers, health and safety, or public services like education and communication media), then the **conclusion** is that at least some corporations are apt to put the quest for profits ahead of the public interest. Corporate executives will rarely admit publicly that they are doing this, however; so much of the lobbying and PR efforts of corporations must consist of propagandistic disguising of selfish interests as public interests, as in the case of "Confessions of a Tobacco Lobbyist" below.

Another distinguishing factor of corporate lobbying and PR is that large corporations and individuals whose wealth has derived from corporations, whether on the local, national, or international level, generally have more disposable money to spend on PR and advertising than any other interest groups, both on ads for particular products and on advocacy ads promoting their ideological interests; in fact they far outspend all other interest or advocacy groups in this area as well as in political action committees' (PAC's) campaign contributions. The only comparable groups are the largest labor unions; however, according to Steve Brouwer's "If We Decided to Tax the Rich" in chapter 13, "In 1996, all labor associations together collected $6 billion in dues, as compared with the $4 trillion in revenues and $360 billion in profits gathered by corporations"—so their relative outlay for lobbying and PR is likely in proportion, though this is a good topic for research. Although the degree of generalization is difficult to call here ("all," "most," "some"?), the combination of the motive to put profits above the public welfare and the wealth to overwhelm opposing interest groups in hiring PR servants is sufficient cause to predict that *a substantial amount* of corporate rhetoric will be propagandistically slanted.

VARIETIES OF PROPAGANDA

"Propaganda" is one of those semantically ambiguous words, with multiple **denotations** and **connotations**. Although it usually has a strongly negative connotation, it has one definition that is connotatively neutral, which is simply the propagation of any ideology or viewpoint; in this sense, it is close in meaning to "rhetoric," in the broad sense of persuasion. So in this neutral sense, any individual or group that tries to persuade an audience to its views engages in propaganda, and cannot be faulted for doing do.

In the more common, negative sense of the word, propaganda is usually the product of a political or commercial organization that hires professionals to propagate its messages; sometimes one individual who is powerful or wealthy enough to hire others through media ownership or a political organization is the source. It is reasonable to assume that such professionals are not acting primarily out of their own convictions but are flacking for their employers, as a job. (A "flack" in insider slang is a public relations agent; the term connotes someone who will do anything for money.) When we are evaluating the arguments presented by hired propagandists, it is not necessarily an **ad hominem** or **poisoning the well** fallacy to point out that they are being paid for making the arguments they do, and therefore that we should be rather skeptical about their validity; at the very least, we need to carefully check out their data and reasoning. Sometimes, however, certain individuals known as **ideologues** freely choose to be propagandists for a cause or organization out of their own convictions rather than for pay. This situation constitutes a borderline case between the two definitions of propaganda; in such cases, the key question is whether or not these individuals show the other negative traits of propagandists.

These negative traits include those identified by Aldous Huxley in his essay "Propaganda under a Dictatorship," which speaks of "the slogans, the unqualified assertions and sweeping generalizations which are the propagandist's stock in trade."

> "All effective propaganda," Hitler wrote, "must be confined to a few bare necessities and then must be expressed in a few stereotyped formulas." These stereotyped formulas must be constantly repeated, for "only constant repetition will finally succeed in imprinting an idea upon the memory of a crowd." ... The demagogic propagandist must therefore be consistently dogmatic. All his statements are made without qualification. There are no grays in his picture of the world; everything is either diabolically black or celestially white. In Hitler's words, the propagandist should adopt "a systematically one-sided attitude towards every problem that has to be dealt with. He must never admit that he might be wrong or that people with a different point of view might be even partially right." (36)

Hitler was an extreme case, but his prescription for propaganda remains depressingly reminiscent of the quadrennial Democratic and Republican nominating conventions and other campaign rallies, TV spectacles stage-managed by entertainment professionals and featuring masses of the faithful chanting platitudinous slogans in much the same manner as Hitler's infamous Nazi Party mass rallies or the brainwashed crowds in Orwell's *1984*. Huxley, incidentally, notes that Hitler claimed to have modeled his rallies on the quasi-militaristic passions stirred up in the spectators at American football games.

One item in propagandists' stock in trade is a mode of **compartmentalization** and **selective vision** whereby they will predictably accuse their opponents or victims of employing all these traits of one-sided rhetoric that they themselves are employing (while denying that they themselves are using them), in an attempt to obscure the truth by reversing the roles of the honest truth seekers and the propagandists. Watch for examples of this trick in your reading, listening, and viewing of news and opinion media; when you find an example, you can legitimately fault its perpetrator for committing the **tu quoque** ("you too") fallacy—accusing someone else of doing what you yourself are also, or solely, doing.

INVECTIVE AND SMEARING

In chapter 9, a distinction was made between **polemics** and **invective**. A polemic is a heatedly **partisan** argument ("polemics" is the name for this genre of argument and is used as either a singular or plural noun); that is to say, it argues for one side in a dispute, with strong **emotional appeal**, usually appealing to, or expressing, fear of or anger against the other side. Polemics, then, are often propagandistically invective in tone, but as noted previously, they need not be, if they are responsibly reasoned and supported and if they follow the ground rules for polemicists in chapter 9. Disregard for such rules, however, is the mark of propagandistic motives and the invective tone—abusive and insulting, name-calling (without sufficient evidence for the names), **hyperbolically** indignant, simplistically one-sided, and ideologically dogmatic or even fanatic, seething with **primary certitude**. (A related adjective is "tendentious," referring to an argument that is presented as being nonpartisan and evenhanded but that is really pushing a one-sided case or ideological "tendency.") Think Al Franken, Michael Moore, and Keith Olbermann versus Ann Coulter, Bill O'Reilly, and Rush Limbaugh. Turning the positive ground rules into their negative forms produces the following characteristics of propaganda, invective, and tendentiousness.

- Not applying the same standards to yourself and your allies that you do to your opponents.
- Not identifying your ideological viewpoint and how it might bias your arguments. Approaching the other side's actions and writings with a closed mind and malice aforethought. Not conceding the other side's valid arguments, or tacking them on grudgingly in inconspicuous phrasing. Not acknowledging points on which you agree at least partially and might be able to cooperate.
- Not summarizing the other side's case fully and fairly, in an account that its proponents would accept, rather than refuting a **straw-man** version of it. Presenting it through the most outlandish statements of its lunatic fringe and through your own paraphrases rather than direct, documented quotations. Putting the worst light on opponents' statements rather than the most generous interpretation.
- Taking opponents' quotes out of context in a way that distorts the meaning or tone of the longer passages in which they appear.
- Repeating a second-hand account of events unfavorable to the opposing side as though you were there and can vouch for its accuracy. Not citing your source and taking account of its author's possible biases, especially if the author is your ally.
- In any account that you use to illustrate the opponents' misbehavior, not granting that there may be another side to the story and taking pains to find out what it is. If opponents claim that they have been misrepresented, not giving them their say and the benefit of the doubt.
- Being unwilling to acknowledge misconduct, errors, and fallacious arguments by your own allies, and not trying scrupulously to establish an accurate proportion and sense

of reciprocity between those faults and those you criticize in your opponents. Playing up the fields and extent of the other side's power while denying or downplaying your own side's.

- Not responding forthrightly to opponents' criticisms of your own or your side's previous arguments, and evading their strongest arguments. Not admitting it when they make criticisms that you cannot refute. Continuing to repeat the same claims over and over again, even after they have been refuted ("staying on message," in political consultants' jargon).
- Substituting derision and name-calling for reasoned argument and substantive evidence.
- Accusing the other side of committing all of these rhetorical abuses, without showing any evidence that they have done so.

The calculated use of such unscrupulous rhetorical methods by political or other organizations to discredit an opponent, often accompanied by outright malicious lies, is known as "smearing" or "a smear campaign." (A frequent, and ugly, variety of smearing in the twentieth century, and one still resorted to by some right-wing polemicists today, was known as "redbaiting"—lumping Democrats, liberals, democratic socialists, or social democrats together with Communists in **guilt by association**, or discrediting any leftist policy as "communistic." Rush Limbaugh in *The Way Things Ought to Be* asserted, "It is neither farfetched nor unfair to draw an analogy beween the [American] civil rights leadership and the Soviet Communist leadership, insofar as exploitation of their people is concerned" (118). But in the absence of any evidence comparable to the history of Soviet murders, imprisonments of millions, and suppression of free elections, isn't this analogy pretty farfetched? In the reading at the end of this chapter, "Confessions of a Tobacco Lobbyist," Victor Crawford reveals how he devised a smear campaign against opponents of smoking in which they were labeled "the health Nazis."

A form of smear campaign that has become increasingly prominent in recent decades is political campaign "attack ads," usually on TV and radio. These make malicious accusations, often falsehoods or **half-truths**, against the opposing candidate or position on an initiative and are most effectively timed just before the election, when it is too late for the attacked party to refute them. The political consultants who devise attack ads and other forms of negative campaigning frequently will work for candidates and issues of any party or ideological persuasion, and these consultants have become a class of celebrities in their own right, renowned for their "dirty tricks." They include the late Lee Atwater, who devised the infamous Willy Horton ads for George Bush against Michael Dukakis in the 1988 presidential campaign; Dick Morris, who has represented prominent Republicans as well as President Bill Clinton; and Mary Matalin and James Carville, she a Republican operative and he a Democratic one, married to each other. (See their book *All's Fair* for an entertaining account of political strategizing.)

GOVERNMENT PUBLIC RELATIONS; THE MILITARY-INDUSTRIAL-MEDIA COMPLEX

Various segments of the federal and local governments have researchers and public relations divisions, which are subsidized by our tax dollars. Much, perhaps most, of their activity is conducted in the public interest, simply to collect and convey useful information, and is free of propagandistic motives. In some cases this activity will have an ideological viewpoint that varies according to whether the particular agency tends to be conservative (such as the Defense Department) or liberal (such as the Environmental Protection Agency), and according to the ideology of the party currently in office.

In several ways, the U.S. Department of Defense (DOD), also known by the **metonym** the Pentagon, presents a unique case, along with those areas of the executive branch, primarily the presidency and the Department of State, and of Congress that are closely tied to the DOD. (George Orwell pointed out in his 1947 essay "Politics and the English Language" that the very term "Department of Defense" is a **euphemism**, since all major world powers, even the most militaristic, had recently adopted that **clean** name instead of the earlier **dirty** one, "Department of War.") On the one hand, nearly everyone agrees that strong military defense is in the public interest. On the other hand, military spending entails several potential **conflicts of interest** that no other major area of government spending does. First, the defense industry is one of the largest and most profitable in the American private sector, but virtually its only client is the federal government, so military manufacturers maintain well-financed lobbies to win government contracts and maintain their profit levels; this is a prime example of what critics call "corporate welfare" or "socialism for the rich." They are also major campaign contributors, and there is a "revolving door" for executives between the industry and the Defense Department, in what President Eisenhower, a conservative Republican, termed in 1960 (warning against the danger of its growing influence) "the military-industrial complex." Thus there have been periodic scandals concerning bribery in military contracts and grossly inflated DOD expenses, with taxpayers footing the padded bills for items like $900 toilet seats and $100 monkey wrenches. The Iraq war in 2003 was strongly advocated by Vice President Richard Cheney, who had previously been CEO of Halliburton Industries, which became one of the largest military contractors and beneficiaries in that war and which came under attack for gaining contracts with no competitive bidding and for cost overruns and other excess profiteering. Many foreign governments—such as Israel, Saudi Arabia, Kuwait, South Korea, and Taiwan—also have well-financed lobbies in Washington to acquire or maintain American military support, which in turn entails profits for the private companies supplying that support. (In *Fortune*'s 2001 list, the American-Israeli Public Affairs Committee—AIPAC—was the fourth most powerful lobby in Washington.)

Another source of potential conflict of interest lies in reporting on American military activity by commercial media that are part of corporate conglomerates whose owners and advertisers include major defense contractors. A prime example was when in the 1991 Gulf War, NBC broadcast glowing reports (subsequently revealed to be false) on the successes of the Patriot missile. Neither NBC nor any other major media mentioned that the electronic components of the missile were manufactured by General Electric, NBC's parent corporation.

One more area of potential conflict of interest has to do with the **paradox** that much military spending is necessarily invested in costly weapons and personnel that may never be used in a war; the weapons that are never used usually can serve no other purpose and rapidly become obsolete. To a certain extent, this paradox is a necessary evil in maintaining up-to-date weaponry, but a real danger is that the need for the military industry to maintain its profits through constant turnover in weapons, or "planned obsolescence," and for the armed forces to maintain their size and influence, may lead to "the tail wagging the dog," in **special pleading** by these interests for going to war or at least **appealing to fear** of war for self-serving motives; most of us are highly susceptible to this particular appeal to fear, because as lay people we are dependent on military and political authorities' word that their policies are effective in combating foreign threats. With the end of the Cold War, we might have expected to see a large reduction in American military spending; one possible reason that this did not occur was lobbying by the military industry and DOD to avert having their budgets and profits cut. A central plank in conservatives' ideological platform is opposition to excessive size, bureaucracy, cost, and corruption in federal government agencies. But conservatives are vulnerable to charges of a **double standard** and compartmentalized thinking in their tendency toward promoting constant growth in spending for the Department of

Defense without expressing concern about inefficiency there. The key to this inconsistency might be that defense spending also is beneficial to corporate profits—perhaps the highest priority on the conservative ideological agenda, dear to both Republicans and Democrats dependent on campaign contributions from military contractors.

These are all reasons for remaining aware of the danger that public relations and lobbying by the military-industrial complex may on occasion cross the line from disinterested advocacy in the public interest to propagandistic special pleading and deception. Most governments in most wars through history have tried to cover up their military blunders and atrocities or have fabricated accounts of ones by their enemies. The selling of the Vietnam War to Americans was a prominent example of deception by the government and military brass in our time. More recent examples are found in Joel Bleifuss's "Flack Attack." Bleifuss says, "By the time Reagan left office, 3,000 public relations officers were busy spending $100 million of taxpayers' money annually to manipulate the public's impressions of the military-industrial complex." A classic propaganda campaign described by Bleifuss concerns the Washington PR firm Hill and Knowlton, which in the 1991 Gulf War worked for both the Bush administration and the Kuwaiti royal family (lobbying for American military intervention against Iraq's invasion) to devise a fraudulent atrocity story about Iraqi soldiers pulling babies out of incubators in Kuwait hospitals. This story was highly effective in rallying Americans to war against Saddam Hussein, and when its falsity was revealed, long after the war, no action was taken against its perpetrators. An incident based on this one was depicted in the 1998 film *Wag the Dog,* which satirized a Clintonesque president who starts a phony war to distract public attention from a sex scandal. The film presented a not-very-exaggerated account of the sophistication with which PR consultants can now sell wars like advertisers do soap flakes, tugging on the public's heartstrings with fabricated tales of atrocities by the enemy and heroism by "our boys." Again, this is not to **imply** cynically that reports of American heroism and enemy atrocities are not sometimes truthful—just that they are not *always* true and that a dose of skepticism cannot hurt you.

Hill and Knowlton was again the PR agency of choice for George W. Bush's White House. Stories emerged about a proposed DOD "psychological operations" unit whose job would include disseminating false stories, a plan that was retracted when it became public. (Also see *Weapons of Mass Deception: The Uses of Propaganda in Bush's War on Iraq,* by Sheldon Rampton and John Stauber.) At least five prominent stories about propaganda in the Iraq war have come to light at this writing. In one, American news media all showed footage of jubilant Iraqis pulling down a statue of Saddam Hussein in April 2003. According to a report by David Zucchino in the *Los Angeles Times* (July 3, 2004), that episode was staged by American military officials for the benefit of TV coverage. "A Marine recovery vehicle toppled the statue with a chain, but the effort appeared to be Iraqi-inspired because the psychological team had managed to pack the vehicle with cheering Iraqi children."

A second story was generated by highly publicized news footage, immediately after the initial conquest of Baghdad in spring 2003, of President Bush, dressed in Navy flight gear, landing on an aircraft carrier beneath a banner reading "Mission Accomplished." Viewers might well have assumed the carrier was in the Persian Gulf, but in fact it was in San Diego. Few media pundits bothered to ask what purpose was achieved by the president flying from Washington to San Diego, other than a propaganda photo op. This episode turned into an embarrassment for Bush after militant resistance to the American occupation escalated.

The third episode concerned Private Jessica Lynch, whose unit in Iraq was ambushed and who was subsequently rescued by U.S. troops from an Iraqi hospital. Initial reports released by the Pentagon included claims that she had been stabbed and shot in hand-to-hand combat, that she was abused in the hospital, and that her rescuers shot their way in against armed resistance. Subsequent revelations cast doubt on all these claims. According to critics of the Pentagon's version, she had not been in combat and her wound resulted from falling from her vehicle, she was well cared for and treated in the hospital, and her rescue was staged as a photo op, with unnecessary gunfire against nonexistent enemy fire. (A BBC reporter called this "one of the most stunning pieces of news management ever conceived.") This was a classic case of "which side are you going to believe?" *People* magazine (June 16, 2003), the source of the BBC quotation, presented an unusually balanced report simply summarizing the opposing accounts. No one doubted the heroism and suffering of Private Lynch, but she herself, when she had recovered enough to speak publicly, was extremely modest and expressed embarrassment over the exaggerated, propagandistic uses that had been made of her ordeal.

In the fourth episode, Army Ranger Pat Tillman, a National Football League player who volunteered for combat duty in Afghanistan, died there in action in 2004. The Pentagon's official account claimed that he was killed by enemy forces, and it took several years for the truth to come out, that he died from our own troops' "friendly fire."

The fifth episode involved dozens of former high military officers who appear regularly in the media as expert analysts. The *New York Times* reported online, April 20, 2008, "To the public, these men are members of a familiar fraternity, presented tens of thousands of times on television and radio as 'military analysts' whose long service has equipped them to give authoritative and unfettered judgments about the most pressing issues of the post-Sept. 11 world. Hidden behind that appearance of objectivity, though, is a Pentagon information apparatus that has used those analysts in a campaign to generate favorable news coverage of the administration's wartime performance." Furthermore, it is not revealed to the public that these authorities "represent more than 150 military contractors either as lobbyists, senior executives, board members or consultants."

The Historic Power of Special Interests

Bruce J. Schulman

Los Angeles Times, June 27, 1999

The machinery of American democracy ground to a halt recently. Despite overwhelming public support for new restrictions on firearms, the National Rifle Assn. and its allies again stymied gun-control legislation on Capitol Hill. In the past, cataclysmic events and national crises allowed the nation to surmount organized interests and enact much-needed, much-demanded reform. But even after the school massacre in Littleton, Colorado and school shootings in Georgia, the majority appears powerless against the money and influence of the gun lobby. The stalemate has flummoxed even Vice President Al Gore; on the campaign trail he wondered how he might rouse "the 80% of the electorate" who favor safer gun laws.

Of course, the gun lobby is hardly the only special interest to squeeze Capitol Hill in a chokehold. Nor is it the first to paralyze Washington by diverting attention from effective reform onto other, vaguer issues like violent videos, creepy Internet chat rooms and schools that do not prominently display the Ten Commandments. But the lessons of history and the astonishing intractability of the current Congress, even in the face of national uproar over schoolyard violence, raise serious questions about the ability of cynical, well-heeled minorities to suffocate the will of the majority.

After World War II, President Harry S. Truman introduced a national health insurance plan. Truman's proposal, especially medical coverage for the elderly, enjoyed broad popular support in the United States. At that time, every other industrial democracy in the world was adopting a similar policy.

But fearing a loss of income and prestige for doctors, the American Medical Assn. launched a relentless effort to spike the plan. The AMA lobbied Congress and ran a vicious advertising campaign against the bill. It even fabricated a quotation from Vladimir I. Lenin, purporting that the architect of Soviet communism had called national health insurance "the keystone to the arch of the Soviet state." The AMA triumphed, and the United States remained the only Western democracy not to provide its citizens with guaranteed medical care.

A generation later, amid the double-digit inflation of the 1970s, the federal government maintained price supports and import quotas to protect Big Sugar. The program benefited a handful of sugar producers but pummeled millions of U.S. consumers already victimized by skyrocketing food prices. Asked to defend the sugar supports, President Jimmy Carter's inflation czar, economist Alfred E. Kahn, remained speechless. Although everyone understood, he could not confess before a congressional committee that the Carter administration dared not offend the sugar lobby. After a long, awkward pause, Kahn replied, "Let the record show an embarrassed silence." Sugar subsidies survived.

But not just economic interests have derailed popular reforms. Party organizations, religious groups and fraternal societies have also maintained strangleholds on the political process. They have subverted the general welfare to their narrow, parochial aims.

During the 1880s, Americans became increasingly disenchanted with corruption in public office. A decade of high-profile scandals, reminiscent of today's campaign-finance imbroglios, convinced many that the excesses of the spoils system needed to be tamed. The nation could no longer condone the rewarding of political supporters with sinecures and lucrative contracts or the practice of requiring public employees to kick back part of their salaries to the machines that had provided their jobs. Still, the party organiza-

tions, particularly the national Republican party, which controlled the White House and its rich stores of patronage, repeatedly blocked civil-service reform. The spoils system remained intact until a disappointed office seeker assassinated President James A. Garfield. Then clamor for action finally became irresistible and Congress passed the Pendleton Civil Service Act in 1883. This "Magna Carta of civil-service reform" forbade mandatory kickbacks and awarded many public offices by competitive examination rather than cronyism. Still, civil-service reform proved a rare and partial victory.

During the late 19th century, however, no issues so exercised the electorate as moral reform—temperance, Sabbatarianism, birth control. Most parts of the nation enacted Sunday "blue laws," closing shops and offices on the Sabbath, and enforced restrictions on the sale and use of contraceptives. However popular these measures were during the Gilded Age, they were outmoded by the 1960s. But while vast majorities of Americans opposed these restrictions, a committed vocal minority kept them on the books.

For example, when Massachusetts scientists conducted clinical tests for the birth-control pill, contraception was still illegal in that state. Legislators simply would not risk the wrath of churches and other religious organizations, despite the wishes of constituents. Only after the Supreme Court invalidated bans on contraceptives in 1965 and the cultural turmoil of the '60s eroded support for blue laws, did Congress and the state legislatures begin to retire these relics of the Gilded Age.

Half a century ago, Americans first surveyed the alarming rise of special interests like the NRA and the AMA. Analysts like John Kenneth Galbraith and David Reisman conceded the U.S. voters possessed little real influence on the political process. Policymaking had become so arcane and complex that ordinary citizens could barely keep track of deliberations in Washington, much less surmount the power of organized interests.

But 1950s observers remained confident about the resilience of American democracy. In their minds, the opposing interest groups seemed to counteract each other: Labor checked business, veterans groups balanced professional organizations, civil-rights lobbies monitored church groups. A democracy of interest groups flourished in the modern United States, even if citizen voices grew faint. In the last analysis, in times of crisis—a presidential assassination, an international incident, a cultural rebellion—Americans would break through the gridlock that stalled legislative action.

Recent events cast doubt on that sanguine view. The interests do not cancel each other out and produce a harmonious, functioning democracy. After the shooting rampage by two students at Littleton High School, it seems that even a national disaster cannot pry a congressional majority free from the tentacles of a well-financed, well-organized lobby.

The failure of gun control raises issues more fundamental than the fate of firearms restrictions or even the country's ability to prevent juvenile violence. It asks whether this nation can any longer find the resolve and the unity of purpose to cast aside the lobbyists, their slick ads and their fat checkbooks. It asks whether American democracy or any other so stymied and dominated by selfish interests can long endure. In the current crisis, the answers are by no means certain.

When Money Talks

John Brain

Baltimore Sun, March 6, 1997

MONEY TALKS, the saying goes, and most people think that in politics it talks out of turn. Influencing elections with campaign contributions is denounced as corrupting democracy, as PACs, corporations and pressure groups vie to influence elections and ultimately the votes of the candidates they support. We're shocked, shocked. Everywhere the cry goes up for campaign-finance reform.

But wait a minute.

The democratic ideal has always been just that, a pleasant fiction of popular government by the people for the people and of the people. In practice, democratic government has always been controlled by dominant elites occasionally subject to the consent of a carefully screened electorate. From a realistic perspective, democracy is largely a PR strategem for engineering the consent of the governed.

In America today the power elite is drawn not from a governing class of patrician aristocrats, as in the 18th century, but from a pool of ambitious leaders who own or manage the nation's mammoth organizations: corporations, trade and professional associations, unions, ethnic and religious groups, the PACs, and of course government itself at all levels. These are the real players on the political scene, and their power is expressed in terms of money.

Some see this process as a corruption of democracy, but only if we accept the democratic ideal in all its naivete. Those who urge campaign-finance reform would do well to ponder whether the government of a complex modern nation is best controlled by a majority of ignorant voters, or by an aristocratic elite, or by major business corporations, or by ethnic or religious groups, or by the defense establishment, or whatever.

Clearly all have a role to play as stakeholders, and maybe PAC contributions are as good a way as any to introduce reality into the democratic ideal.

A government sensitive to pressure groups is not "corrupt," but rather balanced and functional. We are naive if we believe that legislation springs from the creative imaginations of inspired legislators.

Most legislation results from the advocacy of pressure groups, and quite often is actually written by their lobbyists.

At the same time, it is often opposed by pressure groups and lobbyists on the other side of the issue, and the outcome is workable legislation.

In America today citizens can vote at infrequent intervals and do influence elections, but if they want to exercise hands-on influence, they must join and support organizations which mobilize voting blocs and raise money to lobby legislators.

Our current laws relating to the handicapped, the environment, endangered species, employment security, education and other subjects were spearheaded by citizens who organized, raised money and advocated change.

At the same time, industry groups had their own agendas, but legitimately represented the profit motive and the interests of corporations.

Pragmatically, this "corrupt democracy" produces a balance between the interests of ordinary citizens and their desire for clean air, clean water, pure food, a safe workplace and so on, and the interests of those who manage businesses and have to make a profit to survive, and all the other stakeholders in society.

We don't want to return to the bad old days of Boss Tweed and the Robber Barons. So we should admit that General Motors and Microsoft and Boeing, *et al.,* deserve a place at the table along with John Q. Citizen.

In theory, a system might be devised whereby all these players had blocks of votes to cast depending on their importance to society, but it would be unmanageable and no one would agree on the evaluation.

Instead, we allow organizations to have influence in proportion to the money they contribute to political parties—a rough and ready expedient, but better than outright bribery.

Powerful interest groups are going to make their influence felt in the political arena one way or another, whatever reforms are made. The best we can hope for is a working compromise, beginning with full disclosure. That will have to do, until genetic research enables us to come up with a breed of philosopher kings.

Flack Attack—Public Relations Is Shaping Public Life in Ways We're Not Supposed to Notice

Joel Bleifuss

In These Times, September 6–October 4, 1993

The Founding Fathers didn't have public relations (PR) firms to package their revolution. They wrote their own sound bites: "Give me liberty or give me death." Media events like the Boston Tea Party were carried off without the help of corporate sponsors like Celestial Seasonings.

Today, something as momentous as a national revolution could not happen without an army of corporate PR mercenaries churning out the information, telling the media how to interpret the events, and putting forward hired experts to shoot down opposing views.

The public relations industry is often overlooked as a force in contemporary U.S. politics. PR professionals, serving the needs of their corporate clients, define the subjects of public debate and then frame the limits of that debate. As media critic Morris Wolfe has observed, "It is easier and less costly to change the way people think about reality than it is to change reality."

Manipulating the public's perceptions of reality takes special skills. Younger professionals in the field of "communications" earn PR degrees from journalism schools. Others get their start in government service and then, contacts in hand, cash in their experience with a high-paying job in the PR industry. But what the best in the business have in common is that they have rotated through a revolving door of government, journalism, and PR until their identities and allegiances have been blurred beyond recognition.

One of the most successful broad-based PR efforts of the '80s accompanied the Reagan administration's budget-busting military buildup. The growth in Pentagon spending under President Reagan went hand in hand with a blossoming Defense Department PR staff. By the time Reagan left office, 3,000 public relations officers were busy spending $100 million of taxpayer money annually to manipulate the public's impressions of the military-industrial complex.

O'Dwyer's Public Relations Services Report, the PR industry's trade journal, observes, "Over the next few years the Pentagon will be asked to take major 'hits' in its budget due to the end of the Cold War, putting pressure on military spokespeople to justify the need for costly programs." But the Defense Department and the PR firms that represent military industries have come up with a program to deflect the "hits."

"A key weapon the military has in its arsenal," *O'Dwyer's* reports, "is an intern program in which top military PR people learn the tricks of the trade at leading PR firms." In other words, the Pentagon PR flacks will learn the most up-to-date techniques for congressional apple polishing and public propagandizing.

A number of firms are involved in the Pentagon's PR internship program, including the infamous Hill and Knowlton, which during the Gulf War operated as an annex of the Bush White House. (One of the company's greatest Gulf War coups was congressional testimony by a young Kuwaiti "war victim," later exposed as a Washington resident, the daughter of the Kuwaiti ambassador. For its efforts the company was paid $10 million by the Kuwaiti royal family.)

The man in charge of the sheik's fifth column was Hill and Knowlton CEO Craig Fuller, friend and former chief of staff of President Bush. Fuller was appointed to his new Hill and Knowlton post the day before Saddam Hussein invaded Kuwait. He is now the top flack at Philip Morris, where he is promoting the fortunes of a real killer—the tobacco industry.

Susan Trento, author of a book about Hill and Knowlton, *The Power House,* writes that in the Gulf War truth wasn't the only casualty. The integrity of constitutional government suffered too. "Something has changed in Washington. Boundaries no longer exist," writes Trento. "The triangle—the media, the government, and the lobbying and PR firms—protect each other."

Relations between points on this triangle are not always friendly, as is shown in the PR battle being waged over Bill Clinton's health care proposal. Last summer, *Jack O'Dwyer's Newsletter* (another O'Dwyer publication that tracks the industry) reported that the Health Insurance Association of America (HIAA), headed by former Ohio Republican representative Bill Gradison, was advertising for a PR firm that would tell the HIAA "how best to influence the debate on Capitol Hill." The job description included getting the proper spokespeople on morning network TV shows, *Crossfire, This Week with David Brinkley,* and *Larry King Live.* Further, the association wants to attend "editorial board meetings" at the *New York Times,* the *Wall Street Journal,* and the *Los Angeles Times.*

While the HIAA gets its act together, other corporate players in the health care debate have no doubt contracted to buy the cutting-edge tool of the PR industry, the video news release (VNR).

You've seen VNRs, but you just don't know it. Earlier this year, David Lieberman reported in *TV Guide* that a Nielson Media Research survey of 92 TV newsrooms revealed that all use these canned "news stories" in their broadcasts, often passing off the VNR as independent reporting and not packaged PR. This raises troubling questions about the integrity of television news reporting—the primary source of news for more than 90 percent of the U.S. public.

On VNRs, today's network news reporter can become tomorrow's flack. Martin A. Lee and Norman Solomon write in *Unreliable Sources*. "On one video news release [produced by the American Chemical Society and broadcast on ABC], Sam Donaldson was heard introducing a segment on airport security systems that featured a new chemical-sensing device for detecting plastic explosives."

To get a VNR on a news network like ABC, the PR professional needs to know the right people. Mary Ofiara, a former TV news producer who works at KEF Media Associates, told *O'Dwyer's*, "We're finding it easier to place client VNRs with the major news feeds and networks because we know who our friends are within the news decisionmaking process."

PR professionals also need to know who their enemies are, or rather who the enemies of their corporate clients are. To that end the industry has appropriated the covert arts of the intelligence community. On the cutting edge of this phenomenon of flack as political spy are the 14 PR professionals who work at the Washington firm Mongoven, Biscoe and Duchin (MBD).

MBD was founded in 1988 by the firm's current president, John Mongoven. From 1978 to 1981, Mongoven served as deputy director of communications for the Republican National Committee. From there, he went to work for Nestlé, defending the company's marketing of infant formula—a sales strategy that indirectly resulted in the death of an untold number of Third World babies.

MBD publicly describes itself as a company "specializing in the resolution of public policy conflicts between corporations and activist groups." MBD marketing literature, however, reveals that what the company really provides is "issue intelligence" for corporate America.

"We understand the role of activism in the public policy process," MBD boasts, adding that the company helps clients prepare "comprehensive strategic plans" to counter "organizations which seek policy changes in opposition to our client's interests." To that end, MBD "maintains extensive files on organizations and their leadership," paying particular attention to leaders who "would affect the client's interest adversely."

The company routinely "monitors" 66 subjects, including "the South African issue/all phases," "polystyrene," and "consumer groups." MBD's promotional package lists 20 tasks that the company performs. These include reviewing lists of those registered to attend annual stockholders' meetings, suggesting particular "individuals from the environmental community as candidates for corporate boards of directors" and "analyz[ing] grant proposals from public interest groups to corporate foundations." In short, MBD's PR professionals, files in hand, sort through the public policy community, cultivating those who pose no threat and weeding out those who "would affect [the client's] interests adversely."

MBD co-founder and vice president Ronald Duchin is particularly concerned about the adverse effects of the more than 11,000 grassroots environmental organizations that he says operate in the United States. According to Duchin, many of these groups have a "commitment to a radical change in the way America governs itself."

In 1991 Duchin gave a speech to the National Cattleman's Association convention titled "Take an Activist Apart and What Do You Have?" In Duchin's world there are four kinds of activists: opportunists, idealists, realists, and radicals.

Opportunists "exploit for their own personal agenda," he explained. *Idealists* "apply an ethical and moral standard" and are usually "naive." *Realists,* though, are "not interested in radical change" and are "willing to work within the system." The *radicals,* by contrast, "see multinational corporations as inherently evil" and "want to change the system." The best way to deal with radicals, Duchin contended, is to form an alliance with the realists and co-opt the idealists. Then the opportunists will jump on board, leaving the radicals isolated. This tactic works best between the time that "a radical group begins to push an issue and when the issue becomes accepted by credible groups." If corporations wait too long, Duchin warned, they will lose control over how the issue is framed and wind up facing legislation they do not like.

MBD spent last summer trying to "control" public policy decisions regarding the biotech drug bovine growth hormone, which is administered to dairy cows to pump up milk production. The chemical company Monsanto and the tobacco-food conglomerate Philip Morris/Kraft General Foods have both hired MBD to help ensure that the Food and Drug Administration (FDA) puts its stamp of approval on this controversial drug, whose safety to consumers is being questioned by health professionals, animal rights activists, and farmers. FDA approval of bovine growth hormone would mean higher profits for Monsanto, which has spent untold millions developing the drug. The use of the hormone would also greatly increase the supply of milk, thereby leading to lower milk prices that would benefit Philip Morris/Kraft, which buys or sells about half the cheese produced in the United States. These lower milk prices would force many small-scale family dairy farms out of business.

MBD memos, leaked by industry sources, include an eight-page intelligence report about a May 8 FDA hearing on bovine growth hormone, in which an MBD spy quoted from conversations between FDA panelists that had been "overheard." In one such exchange, panel members who favored labeling milk that had been treated with bovine growth hormone alluded to their chief worry, the legal hassles surrounding labeling. Awareness of such concerns allows MBD and other PR

firms to pinpoint opponents' vulnerabilities when crafting counterattacks.

MBD staffer Kara Zeigler talked about the growth hormone issue with Francis Goodman, a Wisconsin dairy farmer activist (who was under the impression that Zeigler was a writer for *Z Magazine*), Michael Hansen, a scientist at Consumers Union (who thought she was a friend of Goodman), and an aide to U.S. Sen. Russ Feingold (who didn't know whom Zeigler was representing). MBD was concerned about Feingold's successful attempts to add language to the 1994 budget bill that would mandate a moratorium on bovine growth hormone sales during a 90–day period that would begin upon FDA approval of the drug.

Sometimes a PR campaign tries to influence lawmakers covertly, by manufacturing and packaging "grassroots" expressions of civic outrage and then delivering those messages from the public to elected officials. Flacks have adopted the tactics of grassroots organizers, but use them to benefit their corporate clients. This is known as astroturf organizing.

William Greider, *Rolling Stone* political affairs columnist, has detailed, in his book *Who Will Tell the People,* how the auto industry hired a PR firm to put a halt on clean-air legislation that would have mandated that Detroit build cars with better fuel efficiency.

The brakeman for this effort was Jack Bonner of Bonner and Associates, a Washington-based PR firm that has perfected the technique of fishing through computerized membership lists of special interest organizations to target citizens sympathetic to a client's cause. They then phone and coach that person on the finer points of the issue, and then put the call through to a congressional office. The legislator's staff has no way of knowing that the call is not a spontaneous expression of concern.

Bonner told Greider how he puts together a corporate political campaign: "We sit down with the lobbyists and ask: How much heat do you want on these guys? Do you want 10 local groups or 200 groups? Do you want 100 phone calls from constituents or 1,000 calls? Obviously, you target senators inclined to go your way but who need some additional cover. They need to be able to say they've heard from people back home on this issue."

He also told Greider, "On the clean-air bill, we bring to the table a third party—'white hat' groups who have no financial interest. It's not the auto industry trying to protect its financial stake. Now it's senior citizens worried about getting out of small cars with walkers. Easter Seal, Multiple Sclerosis—a lot of these people have braces, wheelchairs, walkers. It's farm groups worrying about small trucks. It's people who need station wagons to drive kids to Little League games. There are groups with political juice and they're white hat."

Peter Stone reports in the *National Journal* that in addition to manufacturing grassroots mail and phone campaigns, the company engages in the more upscale form of astroturf organizing known as "grass-tops." For a price of $350 to $500 dollars per letter, Bonner and Associates will get "community leaders" or friends of members of Congress to write letters to any member of Congress. For $5,000 to $9,000, Bonner will arrange a personal meeting between supportive community leaders and a lawmaker.

Corporate-sponsored grassroots campaigns are known to have helped defeat a range of legislative and administrative policy proposals, including President Bush's proposed tax on profits from life insurance annuities and President Clinton's proposed energy tax. The success of Bonner and Associates is shown on an office wall adorned with framed letters of appreciation from the Pharmaceutical Manufacturers Association, the Smokeless Tobacco Council, and the American Bankers Association.

Among those who have helped me recognize the dangers posed by an out-of-control PR industry is John Stauber of Madison, Wisconsin. Stauber is the editor and publisher of *PR Watch,* a new quarterly devoted to exposing the machinations of the PR industry. "Bonner is on the cutting edge," Stauber says. "It is critical that people fighting for change realize that this is not 1970, when you are up against a corporation and its PR spokesperson. This is 1993 and we're up against a coalition of the most powerful and well-funded international PR firms in existence. Typically, a Fortune 500 firm will employ half a dozen PR firms at any one time. And the growing trend is one-stop shopping—lobbying, public relations, political consulting, a legal team and a counteractivism grassroots campaign all under one roof."

PR firms like Bonner and Associates are changing the nature of politics. The full effect of this corporate propaganda apparatus will never be fully known. It is most successful when the PR professionals leave no tracks near the scene of a winning campaign. The losers in this charade are citizens who still hold on to the notion that they can make a difference—in other words, to the democratic process.

Confessions of a Tobacco Lobbyist

60 Minutes, March 19, 1995

LESLEY STAHL, co-host: Despite court decisions that individuals can sue tobacco companies for their smoking addiction and states can sue for rising health costs, cigarettes are still a $50 billion a year industry. It's been 30 years since the US surgeon general first linked smoking with cancer, and for a while smoking rates did drop. But now they're on the rise again and so, it seems, is the influence of tobacco lobbyists who work the halls of Congress and every state legislature to head off anti-smoking laws. Now, for the first time, one of them, a former state legislator-turned-lobbyist for The Tobacco Institute, goes public. His name: Victor Crawford.

You yourself said it wasn't addictive when you were smoking and knew it was addictive.

MR. VICTOR CRAWFORD (*Former Tobacco Lobbyist*): Sure it's not a crime because I wasn't under oath. It wasn't perjury. And it was what I was being paid to do.

STAHL: (*Voiceover*) Victor Crawford was paid to make smoking seem OK.

MR. CRAWFORD: Was I lying? Yes.

STAHL: Yes.

MR. CRAWFORD: Yes.

STAHL: You took my question right out ...

MR. CRAWFORD: Yes. Yeah.

STAHL: And you knew it?

MR. CRAWFORD: Of course.

STAHL: And there were no tugs on your conscience, no second-guessing yourself? No going to bed saying ...

MR. CRAWFORD: Mm-mm.

STAHL: ... "I hate what I'm doing. I feel dirty"?

MR. CRAWFORD: Mm-mm. My job was to win.

STAHL: Even if you're going out there and lying about a product that could hurt kids?

MR. CRAWFORD: Even if you're going out lying about a product that's going to hurt kids. Your job is to win.

(*Footage of Crawford*)

STAHL: (*Voiceover*) Crawford says the tobacco lobbyists, often lawyers from the top firms, call themselves 'the black hats.' So you took on a black hat. Why did you ...

MR. CRAWFORD: Money.

STAHL: ... do that?

MR. CRAWFORD: Big money.

STAHL: You ...

MR. CRAWFORD: The big money—unfortunately, the—the other groups are not in a position to pay—to pay the big bucks, which is necessary to hire the best people.

(*Footage of Crawford on the phone*)

STAHL: (*Voiceover*) To lobby the state Legislature in Maryland, who better than a former state senator?

MR. CRAWFORD: I could make a phone call and get the speaker of the House of Delegates out of his bathtub at home to come to the phone.

STAHL: So you were ...

MR. CRAWFORD: Not many people could ...

STAHL: ... a plum?

MR. CRAWFORD: Of course. My job was to defeat legislation that was going to hurt the industry. If I couldn't defeat it, then the job was to wound it to the point where it wouldn't fly.

STAHL: (*Voiceover*) And how would he do that? Well, Crawford says he would use evidence he didn't even believe in.

MR. CRAWFORD: We used to bring a scientist out of the woodwork and have this particular lab do this, and we'd have a poll pulled by some cockamamy pollster saying this, that or the other.

STAHL: You're walking around with a study, and you're thinking to yourself. "This study's totally bull ...

MR. CRAWFORD: Oh. sure.

STAHL: ... but I'm going to give it to this guy anyway"?

MR. CRAWFORD: Oh, sure. Just to show them that the jury's still out, that you shouldn't take away anybody's civil rights until you're absolutely sure what you're doing. How can you be absolutely sure when this—this X-Y-Z laboratory, world-famous laboratory—why ...

STAHL: I ...

MR. CRAWFORD: ... is it world famous? Because I said it is, and nobody's checked.

STAHL: I have to tell you, it's shameful.

MR. CRAWFORD: It happens. It happens every day. It happens in every—in every legislature.

STAHL: It's what's going on with—with the lobbyists out there today?

MR. CRAWFORD: Oh, sure.

(*Footage from the Tobacco Institute, people smoking, group of demonstrators*)

STAHL: (*Voiceover*) One of Crawford's first assignments as a lobbyist for the Tobacco Institute was to head off a local ordinance in Maryland to ban smoking in bars, taverns and restaurants. He thought a rally for smokers' rights would be a good idea. And how do you arrange a pro-smoking rally? Well, the name of just about every smoker who's ever filled out a cigarette coupon or questionnaire goes right into some computer somewhere.

MR. CRAWFORD: And in some cases, even the brands they smoke. And no ...

STAHL: Every smoker?

MR. CRAWFORD: ... how they—of course.

STAHL: "Of course"?

MR. CRAWFORD: They send out the ...

STAHL: Well, wait.

MR. CRAWFORD: ... cards and ...

STAHL: People are going to be surprised to know that if they're a smoker—just because they're a smoker, their name's on some computer.

MR. CRAWFORD: Oh, sure. How do you think—how do you think all of a sudden, in 24 hours' notice, I was able to turn out a big display, 'Smokers for equal rights,' waving signs? Where do you think that—all that information comes from?

STAHL: Well, how ...

MR. CRAWFORD: You pick up a phone ...

STAHL: How did you get those people ...

MR. CRAWFORD: Pick up a phone, call down, say, 'Hey, I need a demonstration; you'd better get all the troops alerted.' And next thing you know, most of them show up.

(*Footage of Crawford and Stahl*)

STAHL: (*Voiceover*) But the demonstration against the proposed ban didn't work, so Crawford tried a new tactic. He denounced the ban's backers as 'health Nazis,' a term he coined. What did you mean when you first used it?

MR. CRAWFORD: I attacked the messenger on the grounds that they were trying to destroy civil liberties; that what they were trying to do was put their values upon the general public and try to impose it upon the working man, who wants a glass of beer and a pack of cigarettes, and destroys his freedom of choice.

STAHL: I've heard that argument myself.

MR. CRAWFORD: That's right. If you've got good people arguing for you, you can turn the issue away from the message. That's what I'm saying. Get them away from the focus—because you can't ...

STAHL: You know, you are describing ...

MR. CRAWFORD: ... defend it—and attack the messenger.

STAHL: ... the most cold-hearted, cynical, destructive set of values—I'm sorry—because these were your values:

MR. CRAWFORD: They were.

STAHL: And you're just telling it to us as if 'Sure.'

MR. CRAWFORD: It's the American way.

(*Footage of Stahl and Crawford*)

STAHL: (*Voiceover*) Why is Victor Crawford turning on his former tobacco teammates? After a lifetime of smoking—he started when he was 13—he got throat cancer, which spread first to his lungs and now to his hip.

You don't smoke anymore?

MR. CRAWFORD: Oh, God, no.

STAHL: But ...

MR. CRAWFORD: I still miss it.

STAHL: You still miss it?

MR. CRAWFORD: Yeah. Oh yeah.

STAHL: Come on.

MR. CRAWFORD: I can still remember how great it was in the morning with that cup of coffee and a cigarette. I mean, I—even now.

STAHL: You have a look of—close to ecstasy on your face.

MR. CRAWFORD: If—if it wasn't for this—the cancer, I'd be smoking. I'm an addict. If you can—statistically, if you can hook people like me in their teens, they always stay hooked.

(*Footage of teen smoking: meeting*)

STAHL: (*Voiceover*) And that may be the great hope of the cigarette makers: teen-agers. Former chief of the Federal Trade Commission Michael Pertschuk now heads the anti-smoking Advocacy Institute.

MR. MICHAEL PERTSCHUK (*Advocacy Institute*): The most serious problem in smoking in this country today is the increasing numbers of young girls who are taking up smoking.

STAHL: Because they want to be thin.

MR. PERTSCHUK: If you poll young girls, the single most important reason many of them will give for smoking is that it keeps them thin, and being thin is something they want desperately to be. So that—you let—you tell me. If you've designed a cigarette called Virginia Slims and the models are slim, what are you saying to—what are you saying to young girls?

(*Footage of Marlboro exhibit*)

STAHL: (*Voiceover*) What about this Marlboro Miles? Have you heard about this?

MR. PERTSCHUK: (*Voiceover*) One of the things that's happened with the industry is they've moved into promotion, into sponsoring events, into sponsoring things like the Marlboro Miles, where you get premiums, where you get T-shirts, where you get gear.

STAHL: (*Voiceover*) The tobacco industry insists it's not targeting teenagers. Makes you wonder when you see the Marlboro gear and who likes it.

(*Footage of Marlboro race car; baseball park; tennis match*)

Announcer #1: (*Voiceover*) Here's Al Unser Jr. in the pit lane ...

STAHL: (*Voiceover*) Despite the television ban on cigarette advertising, whether it's auto racing or baseball or tennis, there is no shortage of cigarette brand names on TV.

(*Footage from auto races with close-ups of Marlboro logos*)

Announcer #2: (*Voiceover*) Sit down and strap in. The Indy car season is about to begin.

STAHL: (*Voiceover*) So who needs ads anyway?

I mean, they are on television in every major sports event. Now how is this possible?

MR. PERTSCHUK: One thing you learn about the tobacco industry is that no matter how clever anyone is in developing a regulation or legislation, they will get around it.

(Excerpts from "Die Hard", "Pulp Fiction")

STAHL: (*Voiceover*) Tobacco keeps winning.

MR. BRUCE WILLIS (*Actor*): (*From movie*) Do you smoke?

STAHL: (*Voiceover*) If you doubt it, consider Bruce Willis in "Die Hard" or almost anyone in "Pulp Fiction" ...

Unidentified Actress: (*From movie*) So dance good.

MR. JOHN TRAVOLTA (*Actor*): (*From movie*) All right (*Footage from "True Romance"*)

STAHL: ... or take a look at hip Hollywood stars like Patricia Arquette and Christian Slater in "True Romance."

MS. PATRICIA ARQUETTE (*Actress*): (*From movie*) You mind if I smoke?

STAHL: (*Voiceover*) In the movies, it's cool again to smoke. It's dangerous and rebellious.

Would you say that we are in an era where we're seeing the comeback of the tobacco lobby?

MR. PERTSCHUK: Well, I'm afraid that's true. I mean, I think that up until this last election, the tobacco lobby was really on the run.

(*Footage from congressional hearings*)

STAHL: (*Voiceover*) Last spring, the tobacco industry was facing an investigation by a hostile Congress. But that was before the Republicans swept Capitol Hill. Now Richmond, Virginia, Congressman Tom Bliley is in charge of the committee, where tobacco company executives were accused of manipulating or spiking their cigarettes with nicotine to make them addictive. And what did Chairman Bliley think of that? He told our CBS affiliate in Richmond.

Representative TOM BLILEY (*Republican, Virginia*): There was a-a kangaroo court-type operation in which the chairman brought them in and swore these executives in and treated them rather shabbily, and they testified and—under oath that they did not spike their cigarettes, and they don't

(*Footage of Philip Morris headquarters*)

STAHL: (*Voiceover*) Bliley, by the way, represents the Virginia district that includes the headquarters of Philip Morris, maker of Marlboro, the world's best-selling cigarette.

Rep. BLILEY: As far as I'm concerned, we have enough laws on the books regulating the sale of tobacco already.

MR. CRAWFORD: They have—the chairman of the committee makes no bones he's from Richmond; that—that he's financed by—by Philip Morris.

STAHL: Mr. Bliley?

MR. CRAWFORD: Yeah.

STAHL and MR. CRAWFORD: (*In unison*) He makes no bones.

MR. CRAWFORD: ... about—no. He makes no bones about it. There's no question about it. And he says no bill will ever get out of his committee.

STAHL: Are you saying he's owned by the tobacco lobby:

MR. CRAWFORD: I—owned? I—I would certainly say he's controlled by it. If he's—if he's going to stand up and say that 'No tobacco bill will ever pass my committee.'

That's a pretty clear indication where he's coming from and who's—who's pulling his strings.

MR. PERTSCHUK: And in every key congressional district, Philip Morris hires a particular lobbyist.

STAHL: Every single district?

MR. PERTSCHUK: Well, every single key district where they—where there's a key chairman or a key—key member of Congress that they need to get. They hire a lobbyist with one purpose: to lobby one member of Congress.

(*Footage of the Tobacco Institute; the Capitol*)

STAHL: (*Voiceover*) And now they're having more success than they've had in years. The tobacco companies have taken the lead in lobbying for legislation that would freeze government regulations and put a cap on product liability claims, bills that sailed through the House as part of the Republicans' Contract with America.

Are they different from other lobbies or . . .

MR. PERTSCHUK: Only.

STAHL: . . . is this just . . .

MR. PERTSCHUK: Well, they're different from other lobbies in two ways. First of all, they have more serious problems than any lobby in the country because they kill people. Their product kills hundreds of thousands of people, and—that's a great big elephant sitting there that they've got to make people not see. And secondly, they hire more people because they have more money than anybody else.

(*Footage of Pertschuk and Crawford*)

STAHL: (*Voiceover*) Victor Crawford once called Michael Pertschuk a 'health Nazi.' But then, 18 months ago, these two opponents in the battle over smoking met, fittingly, through the yin and yang of t'ai chi, the Chinese art of moving meditation.

(*Footage from Chinese meditation class*)

MR. PERTSCHUK: (*Voiceover*) Now I didn't know Victor. And I had seen this guy over the years. I mean, he was . . .

STAHL: (*Voiceover*) But you didn't know who he was.

MR. PERTSCHUK: No. Not only didn't I know who he was, but I didn't like him.

I mean, he did this t'ai chi in a way that was sort of—well, something of a show-off, is what I thought.

MR. CRAWFORD: I didn't know who he was, and we were sitting around having breakfast after my t'ai chi. I was still taking t'ai chi—I still am—for 30 years.

MR. PERTSCHUK: And we introduce ourselves around, and he says, 'My name is Victor Crawford. I used to be a tobacco lobbyist, and now I've got throat cancer. I guess I've got my just desserts.' Just like that

(*Footage of Pertschuk and Crawford, Crawford's treatment, at Maryland Statehouse*)

STAHL: (*Voiceover*) They became friends. Pertschuk was the one who convinced Crawford to speak out. Now, dying of cancer, Crawford goes to the hospital every day for radiation treatments. And a few weeks ago he went back to the Maryland Statehouse to lobby one last time. But on this occasion, he was fighting the tobacco industry.

MR. CRAWFORD: Governor, how are you doing?

Governor PARRIS GLENDENING (*Maryland*): Fine, Victor.

MR. CRAWFORD: Thank you very much for seeing me.

Gov. GLENDENING: Good to see you.

STAHL: (*Voiceover*) Two days later, Maryland Governor Parris Glendening announced the toughest ban on indoor smoking in the nation, thanks in large part to the lobbying of Victor Crawford.

MR. CRAWFORD: I didn't expect this.

STAHL: Right after the announcement, the tobacco lobby went into action, flooding the governor's office with protest calls.

And as far as you know, he's the first tobacco lobbyist to crack, to—to go public.

MR. PERTSCHUK: Nobody's been willing to be public.

(*Footage of Crawford*)

STAHL: (*Voiceover*) So why is Victor Crawford saying what he's saying?

MR. PERTSCHUK: (*Voiceover*) Victor really doesn't give a damn.

Victor's really thinking about how he can make some use of the rest of his life.

STAHL: Have you heard from your old colleagues?

MR. CRAWFORD: I have received word back by the grapevine that they—they feel I'm not exactly kosher to bite the hand that fed me, and they have a good point. That's exactly what I'm doing. There's nothing they can do to me. Like I told them—the person that called me, I said, 'What are you going to do? G—g—give me cancer?' Ha.

STAHL: You might ask, 'Where is the other side of this issue?' Well, no one on the other side would talk to us, not Congressman Bliley, not anyone from Philip Morris or RJR or American Brands or Lorillard or even Victor Crawford's former employer, The Tobacco Institute.

Topics for Discussion and Writing

1. Based on the readings, discuss what kind of conflicts of interest might bear on the topics you study in your major subject.
2. Monitor television or radio broadcasts and newspapers in your area for possible conflicts of interest stemming from ownership or advertising.
3. If your college or university has an office of research, interview the director and some faculty members conducting sponsored research, and ask them what their policy is for dealing with possible conflicts of interest.
4. If there are any non-university research institutes in your area, interview their administrators and researchers to pose the same question as in number 3.
5. In *Fortune*'s list of the top twenty lobbies, which are liberal and which conservative, and how large and democratic a constituency does each represent? Use this list as a point of reference for the readings throughout this book that argue that liberal or conservative special interests exert the most power. The two biggest lobbies are the NRA and the AARP. To what extent are these two **analogous** in terms of representing special interests, in the sense of direct financial profits at stake?
6. Do a close comparison of the arguments in Bruce Schulman's article "The Historic Power of Special Interests" and John Brain's "When Money Talks." For example:
   Brain: "Pragmatically, this 'corrupt democracy' produces a balance between the interests of ordinary citizens and their desire for clean air, clean water, pure food, a safe workplace and so on, and the interests of those who manage businesses and have to make a profit to survive, and all the other stakeholders in society."
   Schulman: "The interests do not cancel each other out and produce a harmonious, functioning democracy. After Littleton, it seems that even a national disaster cannot pry a congressional majority free from the tentacles of a well-financed, well-organized lobby [the NRA]."

   Does one writer or the other provide sufficient evidence to refute the other? Evaluate Schulman's "tentacles" metaphor in terms of connotation and denotative accuracy.
7. Brain says, "From a realistic perspective, democracy is largely a PR stratagem for engineering the consent of the governed." Would you describe this view as *skeptical* or *cynical*? Does Brain draw liberal or conservative conclusions from this **premise**? Do you think Brain's justification for the power of special interests outweighs the evidence of abuses by special interests elsewhere in this chapter? If so, defend this opinion.
8. Look for examples in the readings in this book—and in the author's text itself—or elsewhere of written or spoken arguments that display the negative traits listed here as characterizing propaganda and invective.

9. Did any of the specific examples in "Flack Attack" particularly surprise you or inform you of significant information of which you were unaware before? To what extent do you think the difficulty in gaining access to such information negates the concepts of "the free market of ideas" and the pluralistic exchange of views by opposing interests in an open society? Bleifuss says, "By the time Reagan left office, 3,000 public relations officers were busy spending $100 million of taxpayers' money annually to manipulate the public's impressions of the military-industrial complex." Research the uses of this Pentagon PR budget to determine the extent to which it is or is not a justifiable use of taxpayers' money.

10. "Flack Attack" appeared in *In These Times*, a small-circulation, left-of-liberal journal of opinion that appears on few newsstands. It was reprinted in the *Utne Reader*, a digest of left and liberal journals that has a slightly wider circulation. Neither journal has much advertising except for other liberal, nonprofit organizations, which limits financing for wider circulation. To what extent does the scarce coverage of stories like these in the mainstream, commercial media suggest that advertisers have the power to censor news that puts them in a bad light? And to what extent does this form of conservative bias refute conservative claims of liberal bias in mass media, such as those expressed by Bernard Goldberg in chapter 14?

11. In "Confessions of a Tobacco Lobbyist," what were some of the rhetorical tactics Victor Crawford devised to legitimate the tobacco industry and to smear liberal public interest groups opposing it? Compare his phrase "the health Nazis" to Rush Limbaugh's "feminazis" and other conservative invective against public interest groups.

Part V

Putting It All Together in a Long Paper

CHAPTER 16

A Case Study: Rhetoric and the Wealth Gap

This chapter and chapter 17 will do double duty. First, they apply rhetorical analysis of statistical arguments. Second, synthesizing **cumulatively** from previous chapters, they provide models for the process of extended study of a single subject into a term paper of fifteen to twenty pages, with emphasis on rhetorical analysis of opposing sources and arguments. (A sample of the preliminary stages for such a paper is included in chapter 17, and the complete paper is online at http://www.paradigmpublishers.com/Books/BookDetail .aspx?productID=208952.) The topic for study will be one of the most important debates in recent decades between conservatives and liberals or leftists—the extent to which economic inequalities, and especially the gap between the rich and the middle class and poor, have been increasing in the United States since the 1970s. This debate also involves the consequences for economic inequality of tax cuts and cutbacks in government regulation of business, which were justified by "supply-side economics," or "Reaganomics," during the presidential administration of Ronald Reagan (1980–1988) and again revived by President George W. Bush (2000–2008) and by John McCain as a presidential candidate in 2008. Conservative and liberal positions on these issues are more fully developed in "An Outline of Conservative and Leftist Arguments . . ." at the end of this chapter, and it would be helpful for you to read through them now as background for the following discussion of statistical evidence presented by the opposing sides in support of their general lines of argument.

Here are some preliminary points to keep in mind. First, these are not just abstract matters of economics but crucial facts of life for you and every individual, directly pertinent to your own financial future. These facts include the availability and cost to students of tax-funded, public secondary, college, and graduate education (and of student financial aid), what jobs will be available to you after graduation and how much they pay, what your tax burden will be in relation to that of wealthy people and corporations, how much government deficits resulting from tax shortfalls cost you in taxes, whether Social Security will still be funded when you are old enough to receive it, and whether national health insurance would be a possibility if priorities in taxation and areas of government spending were changed.

Also keep in mind the different levels of audience at which arguments on these issues, based largely on statistics, are pitched. The highest level is that of specialized economic analysis, which can get too advanced for nonspecialists like most of us to evaluate, and which is developed in scholarly or professional articles, reports, and books that are too long to include in a textbook like this. So why should we even dare to delve into issues whose resolution might only be found in texts that are over our head? One answer is that even at that level, there are fierce disagreements and polemical battles between conservative and liberal economists. Another answer is that scholarly discourse on these issues gets popularized at the level of mass media, in political speeches and in op-ed columns, which are presumably comprehensible to general readers or listeners. That is the level we will be studying here, with analysis of them that relies mainly on unspecialized, commonsense reasoning. The sound-bite length and lack of documentation in such articles limits their value, but they can be useful in introducing lines of argument and, at best, citing sources that we can pursue in research from there. Some citations and links will be included for longer, more scholarly versions of liberal versus conservative lines of argument.

Finally, keep in mind that the **polemics** on these issues are a classic case of how opposing forces try to control the rhetorical and semantic agenda. In that effort, liberals predictably accuse conservative spokespeople of being paid propagandists for the rich, while conservatives accuse liberal ones, especially academic ones like me, of **special pleading** in behalf of tax-funded government spending that provides their jobs, at least in public schools and colleges, and in behalf of the labor unions they belong to.

GOLDBERG VERSUS CHAIT ON TAXES

The Rich Aren't Made of Money

Jonah Goldberg

Los Angeles Times, November 13, 2007

"The question is: Should we be giving an extra $120 billion to people in the top 1%?"

So asked Gene Sperling, Hillary Clinton's chief economic advisor, at a recent National Press Club panel discussion. Translation: It's the government's money, and anything left over after Uncle Sam picks your pockets is a "gift."

Indeed, to hear leading Democrats talk about the "richest 1%"—a diverse cohort of investors, managers, entrepreneurs and, to be sure, some fat-cat heirs—one gets the impression that wealthy Americans are a natural resource, to be pumped for as much cash as we need.

Further, the Democrats don't think that well will ever run dry. "I no more believe that the hedge-fund managers are going to quit working at billion-dollar hedge funds because tax rates go up 5% than Alex Rodriguez will quit playing baseball because they

put in a salary cap," Austan Goolsbee, Barack Obama's economics guru, said last Friday.

This sort of thing used to be a staple of the hard left. "Look at the wealth of America, weigh its resources, feel its power," wrote *The Nation*'s editors back in 1988, endorsing presidential candidate Jesse Jackson's extravagant public spending plan. "There's enough money in this country to do everything Jackson asks, and more."

But now this vision simply defines liberal economics. John Edwards' unending campaign for president is based on the idea that there are two Americas and that everyone will be better off when unrich America mugs rich America. According to Democrats, it's greedy to want to keep your own money, but it's "justice" to demand someone else's.

Michael Boskin, Rudy Giuliani's economic advisor, said, "There is no—let me repeat—no example in the last quarter-century of a large, complex economy that has been successful with high taxes." He adds, "The Western Europeans have seen their standards of living decline by 30% in a little more than a generation because of their high taxes." The U.S., meanwhile, has outperformed the competition over the last quarter of a century.

I'm with Boskin. But I think there's a more pressing issue. What does it do to a democracy when people see government as something only other people should pay for?

Let's take seriously for a moment the notion that rich people are an inexhaustible army of Energizer bunnies that just keep going and going, no matter what taxes you throw in their path. You can see where Democrats get this idea, after all. The top 1% of wage earners already provide nearly 40% of federal income tax revenues. And the bottom half of taxpayers contribute only about 3%.

Taxes are a necessary evil. But their silver lining is that they foster a sense of accountability and reciprocity between the taxpayer and the tax collector. Indeed, democracy is usually born from this relationship. Widening prosperity brings a rising middle class, which in turn demands the rule of law, incorrupt bureaucracies and political representation in exchange for its hard-earned money. You might recall the phrase "no taxation without representation."

The one great exception is what development experts call the "oil curse." In countries "blessed" with oil wealth or similar resources, the relationship between the government and the governed gets distorted. These "trust-fund states" (a term coined by Newsweek International editor and columnist Fareed Zakaria) don't need taxes, so their rulers worry little about representation and accountability, opting instead for paternalism or authoritarianism. Worse, the people are less inclined to see government as their expensive servant and more as a source for goodies.

Today, our politics seems to be suffering from a "rich people curse." We treat the rich like a constantly regenerating piñata, as if they will never change their behavior no matter how many times they get whacked by taxes. And we think everyone can live well off the goodies that will fall to the ground forever.

Of course, typical wage earners pay plenty of taxes, but not in ways that foster a sense of reciprocity with the government in Washington. Their biggest federal payment is the regressive payroll tax intended to fund Social Security and Medicare. And even though as a matter of accounting these payments are no different from any other taxes, they're sold simply as retirement and health insurance programs.

Meanwhile, Democrats keep telling the bottom 95% of taxpayers that all of America's problems will be solved if only the rich people would pay "their fair share" of income taxes. Not only is this patently untrue and a siren song toward a welfare state, it amounts to covetousness as fiscal policy.

I don't know what the best tax rates are, for rich or poor.

But I'm pretty sure that it's unhealthy for a democracy when the majority of citizens don't see government as a service they're reluctant paying for but as an extortionist that cuts them in for a share of the loot.

A Very Special Kind of Math

Jonathan Chait

Los Angeles Times, April 29, 2005

The very rich are earning a larger and larger share of our national income. Therefore, fairness dictates that we must cut their taxes.

You might think that the above is an absurd piece of moral reasoning. And you'd be right. But it's exactly the argument that influential conservatives are making.

A *Wall Street Journal* editorial this week cites a recent IRS study detailing which income groups pay what level of taxes. The editors note with satisfaction that the highest-earning 0.1% of the population paid 5.06% of the federal tax burden in 1979, and was paying 9.52% as of a couple of years ago.

To the *Journal* editors, this proves that "the overall tax burden grew more progressive from 1979 to 1999." The editorial goes on to note that any move to raise taxes on the rich would be deeply unfair because those poor folks "already bear an outsized share of the American tax burden."

It is certainly true that the richest 0.1% are paying a higher share of the national tax burden. Is that because they're getting socked by the tax code? No, it's because the very rich are earning a far bigger proportion of the national income. In 1979, the highest-earning 0.1% took home about 3% of the national income, and paid about 5% of the taxes. In 1999, they earned about 10% of the national income and paid about 11% of the taxes.

In fact, the tax rate borne by the very rich has plummeted. In 1979, the top 0.1% paid, on average, 32% of their income in taxes. Today, they pay less than 23%. So what's happening is that the top 0.1% are paying a higher share of the tax burden because their share of the national income is rising faster than their tax rates are falling. The *Journal* editorial board sees this state of affairs as class warfare against the rich.

At this point, you may be wondering whether it's really possible that professional editorial writers at a first-rate newspaper—people who, after all, are paid to think seriously about issues like this—could make such a simple statistical mistake. Are they really so dishonest or so dumb as to think that you can measure the fairness of a tax code by looking at what share of the taxes various groups pay without considering how much they earn? I can tell you, as a regular reader of that page, that the answer is: Yes, they really, really are.

Indeed, of the many statistical butcherings the *Journal* employs to defend its various misguided beliefs, this particular device ranks among its favorites. It hauls out some form of this argument—the rich are being mistreated because they're paying a rising share of the tax burden—at least once a year.

In 2002, to take one example at random, a *Journal* editorial noted: "The top 1% of tax filers are also paying a much higher share than they used to."

So how progressive, or confiscatory, is our tax system? Federal taxes are progressive. According to calculations by Citizens for Tax Justice, workers in the middle of the income scale pay about 16% of their income in federal taxes, while those in the top 1% pay about 25%. But that's offset in part by state and local taxes, which hit the poor and middle class much harder.

Taking into account all taxes, the top 1% pay around 33% of their income in taxes, while the bottom 99% pay 29.7% of their income in taxes. The rich pay somewhat higher tax rates, but not that much higher. (President Bush's tax cuts, which disproportionately benefited the rich, narrowed that gap.)

Is this system confiscatory? Communist? Only if you're a complete economic illiterate.

*   *   *

Both of these columns appeared in the *Los Angeles Times*. Goldberg is an editor of the conservative *National Review* and author of *Liberal Fascism: The Secret History of the American Left, From Mussolini to the Politics of Meaning*. Chait is an editor of the liberal-to-conservative *New Republic* and author of *The Big Con: The True Story of How Washington Got Hoodwinked and Hijacked by Crackpot Economics*. The most obvious rhetorical point that emerges in comparing the two is that Goldberg seems to be applying the same **selective vision** that Chait finds in the *Wall Street Journal*, by claiming to "measure the fairness of a tax code by looking at what share of the taxes various groups pay without considering how much they earn." When President Reagan was elected in 1980, the rate for the top marginal income tax bracket was 70% (on income over some $250,000 a year, though the rate on any individual's income was lower on amounts up to that level). Under Reagan and succeeding presidents (especially George W. Bush) that rate has been cut currently by half, to 35%. Simply as a problem in deductive logic, how is it possible for the tax rate to have been cut in half for the upper bracket but for its individual members to be paying more tax dollars? Chait provides one obvious answer: "The top 0.1% are paying a higher share of the tax burden because their share of the national income is rising faster than their tax rates are falling." (The increasing number of rich people has also increased their tax share as a group—although analysts are sometimes ambiguous about whether they are discussing individual or collective gains.)

Conversely, Goldberg adds, "The top 1% of wage earners already provide nearly 40% of federal tax revenues. And the bottom half of taxpayers contribute only about 3%." Goldberg does not discuss how these percentages have changed since 1980, but most conservative and liberal economists agree that the tax share in dollars for the rich has steadily increased as that for the middle class and poor (who have received about the same percentage tax cuts as the rich) has decreased. If the income for the bottom 50% had also increased at anything like the rate of the top 1%, we can **deduce** that they too would be paying more in taxes even after tax-rate reductions. But since they are paying comparatively *less* as a group, isn't the logical **inference** that they must be *earning* less, or at least not substantially more? (Much empirical evidence presented by liberals indicates that the lower levels have indeed lost ground in income and net worth. See Holly Sklar's "Billionaires Up, America Down" in the readings here.)

In this perspective, it becomes apparent that arguments by Goldberg and many other conservatives contain a large element of statistical and semantic slanting, framing, or "spin." Conservatives typically use phrases like "the burden of taxation has shifted increasingly to the rich," with the **connotation** that the wealthy are suffering and have been forced to take over the cost of taxation from the slackers who don't pay their share (in reality, as noted above, because they *make* less). Another common line is that high taxes "penalize" the rich and rob them of their incentive. Elementary logic, however, would seem to dictate that under just about any democratic system or degree of taxation, the more money people make, the larger the share of taxes they will pay. This would hold true even under the flat tax system favored by many conservatives (where all income brackets pay at the same rate) or the "Fair Tax" system advocated by 2008 Republican presidential candidate Mike Huckabee, a form of flat-rate national sales tax. It is all the more true if the relative share of income gained by the rich is constantly increasing while that of the middle class and poor is decreasing. If Bill Gates made all the income in America, he'd also be paying all the income taxes. Would this be a "burden" and a "penalty"? Chait suggests that conservatives sometimes seem to insinuate—without making it explicit—that the more money people have, the less they should be expected to pay in taxes, while the less money people have, the more they should be expected to pay.

Goldberg downplays the escalation of wealth in the past few decades at the level Sklar discusses of *Forbes* 400 billionaires and $640-million-dollar CEO salaries. Nor does he acknowledge the simultaneous cutting of income taxes in half for this income level since 1980, or comparable reductions in corporate, capital gains, and estate taxes. (See, among others, Paul Cay Johnston, *Perfectly Legal: The Covert Campaign to Rig Our Tax System to Benefit the Super Rich—and Cheat Everybody Else*. Johnston also argues that some taxes that are hardest on the middle class and poor, especially payroll deductions for Social Security and Medicare, have stealthily been raised to offset cuts in income tax, as Goldberg also obliquely implies.) The issue that provokes Goldberg's column at the beginning is simply the opposition by Democrats to *further* cuts at this level and the statement by Obama's adviser that "multibillion-dollar hedge fund managers" can afford to have their tax cuts rolled back by 5% without pain. So is Goldberg perhaps being **hyperbolic** to characterize these modest proposals with **invective** like "pumped for as much cash as we [running the government] need," "when unrich America mugs rich America," and "we treat the rich like a constantly regenerating piñata"? (To be sure, Chait indulges in similar invective and ridicule of conservative thinkers here and more so in *The Big Con*, and once again, we should judge the worth of invective on either side on how well it is supported with reasoning and evidence.)

Goldberg and other conservatives like P. J. O'Rourke in chapter 9 might also be employing a **slippery slope** fallacy in which any effort by liberals to return tax levels for the rich closer to their level in America a mere three decades ago, or to stem the extreme increase in economic inequality, is demonized with slogans like "class warfare" and "confiscation" (*Wall Street Journal*) and regarded, like the pool table in *The Music Man*, as, "the first big step on the road to the depths of deg-ra-day . . . ." So O'Rourke makes a **straw-man** equation of these modest liberal proposals for "closing the wealth gap" with the collectivism of Communist China. "The foundation of collectivism is simple: There should be no important economic differences among people." First, ya reduce tax cuts on billionaires, and the next thing ya' know, you're being forced to live on a collective farm! O'Rourke attacks liberals like Bill Clinton, whom he claims was "more concerned with redistribution than anyone in the Chinese government" for supposedly asking, "How do we redistribute wealth?" O'Rourke opposes redistributing from the wealthy to the poor, but what do you think he or Goldberg would say in response to Holly Sklar's evidence that, "Wealth is being redistributed from poorer to richer"?

In a column titled "What's Behind Income Disparity?" (*Washington Post*, September 27, 1993), George Will wrote:

> A society that values individualism, enterprise and a market economy is neither surprised nor scandalized when the unequal distribution of marketable skills produces large disparities in the distribution of wealth. This does not mean that social justice must be defined as whatever distribution of wealth the market produces. But it does mean that there is a presumption in favor of respecting the market's version of distributive justice. Certainly there is today no prima facie case against the moral acceptability of increasingly large disparities of wealth.

By this he seems to assert, like O'Rourke, that increasing inequality is good for society. Would a logical **implication** of this assertion be that the more inequality increases, the better? Do either O'Rourke or Will give any indication of where they would **draw the line** at a point past which increasing inequality would be bad for American society? (You might read some of Will's more recent columns or books to see if he has clarified or modified his position.) It is fair play for conservatives to ask liberals where *they* would draw the line past which decreasing inequality would be bad for society. However, most of the liberal sources we have studied are pretty clear in advocating that tax rates, regulation of business, and real wages just be returned to their level in 1980 before the advent of Reaganomics. As a presidential candidate in 2008, Barack Obama advocated restoring taxes to their level in Bill Clinton's presidency, only slightly higher than at present. A letter in the *Knoxville News-Sentinel* in 2008 quoted Obama as saying, "'A strong government hand is needed to assure that income is distributed more equitably.' This is Marxist. Vote for Obama? No thank you." Does wanting government to reduce income inequality to its level in America thirty years ago, or prevent its further escalation, make one a Marxist—or is this just **red-baiting**?

Goldberg and other conservatives further attempt to "frame" the whole concept of taxation negatively, framing allegedly liberal beliefs about taxes with **dirties** like "anything left after Uncle Sam picks your pockets is a gift" "covetousness as social policy," "government as an extortionist," and "it's greedy [for conservatives] to want to keep your own money, but it's 'justice' [for liberals] to demand someone else's." Liberals, however, have quite a different conception of taxation, and (as George Lakoff suggests in chapter

4), if they were able to frame the public discussion of the issue, it would go something like the following:

First, taxes are not "extortion" by the government but simply the operating costs we should be happy to pay for all the benefits we expect from government. Conservatives resort to irrational **appeal to fear** of government that fails to recognize that in American democracy, government is supposed to serve the people, not vice versa. Government policies on taxation and other issues are ultimately subject to the people's will, and if the people fail to curb the government in excessive taxation, that is no one's fault but their own, so conservatives should be blaming the majority of voters instead of making government the **scapegoat**.

Second, in the liberal view, the justifications for progressive taxation are (1) that those in the highest bracket can afford to pay higher taxes because their after-tax, disposable income and net worth are still far above their basic living expenses, in contrast to the middle class and poor, for whom taxes come out of income that is barely, if at all, sufficient to meet basic expenses, (2) that progressive taxes also help to keep the gap in wealth—and, more importantly, power—between the rich and everyone else from growing ever wider, and (3) that it is the rich, not the lower-class recipients of welfare and other "entitlements," who benefit most from government spending, e.g., defense and aerospace contracts, "corporate welfare," bailouts of failing industries like banking and mortgages in the 2000s, and the millions spent by public agencies like schools and colleges providing jobs and purchasing private-sector equipment, construction, and services. When the government bailed out failing investment banks, mortgage lenders, and insurance companies in 2008, leftists said it proved that American capitalism really means socialism for the rich and free enterprise for the poor, and that corporate profits are privatized while losses are socialized.

Likewise for the services funded by taxes like public education, which trains the corporate workforce and enables workers to earn enough money to buy commodities, thus keeping up the level of corporate profits; services like law enforcement, which protects the wealthy from theft or physical attack and maintains the social stability that allows prosperity; and above all national defense, which protects the corporate and personal possessions of the wealthy from being destroyed or confiscated by foreign invaders. The "free market" economy would probably collapse if it were not for the employment, spending, and education provided by the public sector. These arguments tend to be suppressed by conservative polemicists, who for the past three decades have waged an unrelenting campaign against government spending (except for the military), which, according to liberal *New York Times* columnist Paul Krugman, they call "starve the beast." In *The Great Unraveling*, Krugman quotes Republican strategist Grover Norquist as saying he wants to shrink government "'down to the size where we can drown it in the bathtub'" (xxi–xxii)—leaving corporations and the rich in uncontested control of society.

Thomas Frank's 2008 book *The Wrecking Crew: How Conservatives Rule* more fully develops Krugman's claim about Norquist's and allied Republicans' **hidden agenda** of budget cuts as a strategem for defeating liberal constituencies that benefit from government funding and regulation. Frank quotes passages written by Norquist that reflect his express aim to "crush the structures of the left," including labor unions, public schools and universities, welfare, Social Security and Medicare (whose administration would be turned over to corporations for profit) and trial lawyers who defend plaintiffs in damage suits against corporations (258).

If conservatives want to refute these arguments, they need to address them directly instead of resorting to **straw man** distortions and **red herring** distractions.

So in researching conservative sources, see if you can find ones that do directly refute any of these arguments. Arthur Laffer, one of the original theoreticians of Reaganomics in the 1980s, wrote an extensive rebuttal to Chait's *The Big Con*, at the level of advanced economics, published in *National Review Online* at http://www.nationalreview.com/kudlow/laffer_onslaught_part1_10-31-07.pdf. Also see Chait's article "Feast of the Wingnuts" and responses from conservatives in *New Republic Online*, September 10, 2007.

In a corollary issue here, Goldberg writes: "Michael Boskin, Rudy Giuliani's economic advisor, said, 'There is no—let me repeat—no example in the last quarter-century of a large, complex economy that has been successful with high taxes.' He adds, 'The Western

Europeans have seen their standards of living decline by 30% in a little more than a genera-tion because of their high taxes.' The U.S., meanwhile, has outperformed the competition over the last quarter of a century." Boskin's statement, which was also a mainstay of John McCain's campaign rhetoric in 2008 (McCain even dropped the "in the last quarter-century" qualifier), has been strongly contradicted by liberal economists, who point to the economic prosperity after President Clinton raised taxes, or the earlier boom in the American economy under a 90% top income tax rate after World War II. (Of course, it is a **post hoc** or **reduc-tive fallacy** for either side to claim that tax rates are the only or primary cause of economic trends, which result from a complex combination of factors. But these two examples do seem to disprove Boskin's and McCain's assertions as they are worded.) Boskin's claim about the European economy is also contradicted by Steve Brouwer's "If We Decided to Tax the Rich" in chapter 13 here and by Paul Krugman in several books and articles. For a research paper project, you might compare the statistical evidence provided by well-documented sources on the opposing sides.

SKLAR VERSUS THE *WALL STREET JOURNAL*

Billionaires Up, America Down

Holly Sklar

McClatchy-Tribune News Service, October 27, 2007

When it comes to producing billionaires, America is doing great.

Until 2005, multimillionaires could still make the Forbes list of the 400 richest Americans. In 2006, the Forbes 400 went billionaires only.

This year, you'd need a Forbes 482 to fit all the billionaires.

A billion dollars is a lot of dough. Queen Elizabeth II, British monarch for five decades, would have to add $400 million to her $600 million fortune to reach $1 billion. And she'd need another $300 million to reach the Forbes 400 minimum of $1.3 billion. The average Forbes 400 member has $3.8 billion.

When the Forbes 400 began in 1982, it was dominated by oil and manufacturing fortunes. Today, says Forbes, "Wall Street is king."

Nearly half the 45 new members, says Forbes, "made their fortunes in hedge funds and private equity. Money manager John Paulson joins the list after pocketing more than $1 billion short-selling subprime credit this summer."

The 25th anniversary of the Forbes 400 isn't party time for America.

We have a record 482 billionaires—and record foreclosures.

We have a record 482 billionaires—and a record 47 million people without any health insurance.

Since 2000, we have added 184 billion-aires—and 5 million more people living below the poverty line.

The official poverty threshold for one person was a ridiculously low $10,294 in 2006. That won't get you two pounds of caviar ($9,800) and 25 cigars ($730) on the Forbes Cost of Living Extremely Well Index. The $20,614 family-of-four poverty threshold is lower than the cost of three months of home flower arrangements ($24,525).

Wealth is being redistributed from poorer to richer.

Between 1983 and 2004, the average wealth of the top 1 percent of households grew by 78 percent, reports Edward Wolff, profes-sor of economics at New York University. The bottom 40 percent lost 59 percent.

In 2004, one out of six households had zero or negative net worth. Nearly one out of three households had less than $10,000 in net worth, including home equity. That's before the mortgage crisis hit.

In 1982, when the Forbes 400 had just 13 billionaires, the highest paid CEO made $108 million and the average full-time worker made $34,199, adjusted for inflation in $2006. Last year, the highest paid hedge fund manager hauled in $1.7 billion, the highest paid CEO made $647 million, and the average worker made $34,861, with vanishing health and pension coverage. (Source: The U.S. Department of Labor Bureau of Labor Statistics, which defines "workers" as "production workers in natural resources and mining and manufacturing, construction workers in construction, and nonsupervisory workers in the service-providing industries. These groups account for approximately four-fifths of the total employment on private nonfarm payrolls.")

The Forbes 400 is even more of a rich men's club than when it began. The number of women has dropped from 75 in 1982 to 39 today.

The 400 richest Americans have a conservatively estimated $1.54 trillion in combined wealth. That amount is more than 11 percent of our $13.8 trillion Gross Domestic Product (GDP)—the total annual value of goods and services produced by our nation of 303 million people. In 1982, Forbes 400 wealth measured less than 3 percent of U.S. GDP.

And the rich, notes Fortune magazine, "give away a smaller share of their income than the rest of us."

Thanks to mega-tax cuts, the rich can afford more mega-yachts, accessorized with helicopters and mini-submarines. Meanwhile, the infrastructure of bridges, levees, mass transit, parks and other public assets inherited from earlier generations of taxpayers crumbles from neglect, and the holes in the safety net are growing.

The top 1 percent of households—average income $1.5 million—will save a collective $79.5 billion on their 2008 taxes, reports Citizens for Tax Justice. That's more than the combined budgets of the Transportation Department, Small Business Administration, Environmental Protection Agency and Consumer Product Safety Commission.

Tax cuts will save the top 1 percent a projected $715 billion between 2001 and 2010. And cost us $715 billion in mounting national debt plus interest.

The children and grandchildren of today's underpaid workers will pay for the partying of today's plutocrats and their retinue of lobbyists.

It's time for Congress to roll back tax cuts for the wealthy and close the loophole letting billionaire hedge fund speculators pay taxes at a lower rate than their secretaries.

Inequality has roared back to 1920s levels. It was bad for our nation then. It's bad for our nation now.

Movin' On Up: A Treasury Study Refutes Populist Hokum About "Income Inequality"

Wall Street Journal, November 13, 2007

If you've been listening to Mike Huckabee or John Edwards on the Presidential trail, you may have heard that the U.S. is becoming a nation of rising inequality and shrinking opportunity. We'd refer those campaigns to a new study of income mobility by the Treasury Department that exposes those claims as so much populist hokum.

OK, "hokum" is our word. The study, to be released today, is a careful, detailed piece of research by professional economists that avoids political judgments. But what it does do is show beyond doubt that the U.S. remains a dynamic society marked by rapid and mostly upward income mobility. Much as they always have, Americans on the bottom rungs of the economic ladder continue to climb into the middle and sometimes upper classes in remarkably short periods of time.

The Treasury study examined a huge sample of 96,700 income tax returns from 1996 and 2005 for Americans over the age of 25. The study tracks what happened to these tax filers over this 10-year period. One of the notable, and reassuring, findings is that nearly 58% of filers who were in the poorest income group in 1996 had moved into a higher income category by 2005. Nearly 25% jumped into the middle or upper-middle income groups, and 5.3% made it all the way to the highest quintile.

Of those in the second lowest income quintile, nearly 50% moved into the middle quintile or higher, and only 17% moved down. This is a stunning show of upward mobility, meaning that more than half of all lower-income Americans in 1996 had moved up the income scale in only 10 years.

Also encouraging is the fact that the after-inflation median income of all tax filers increased by an impressive 24% over the same period. Two of every three workers had a real income gain—which contradicts the Huckabee-Edwards-Lou Dobbs spin about stagnant incomes. This is even more impressive when you consider that "median" income and wage numbers are often skewed downward because the U.S. has had a huge influx of young workers and immigrants in the last 20 years. They start their work years with low wages, dragging down the averages.

Those who start at the bottom but hold full-time jobs nonetheless enjoyed steady income gains. The Treasury study found that those tax filers who were in the poorest income quintile in 1996 saw a near doubling of their incomes (90.5%) over the subsequent decade. Those in the highest quintile, on the other hand, saw only modest income gains (10%). The nearby table tells the story, which is that the poorer an individual or household was in 1996 the greater the percentage income gain after 10 years.

Only one income group experienced an absolute decline in real income—the richest 1% in 1996. Those households lost 25.8% of their income. Moreover, more than half (57.4%) of the richest 1% in 1996 had dropped to a lower income group by 2005. Some of these people might have been "rich" merely for one year, or perhaps for several, as they hit their peak earning years or had some capital gains windfall. Others may simply have not been able to keep up with new entrepreneurs and wealth creators.

The key point is that the study shows that income mobility in the U.S. works down as well as up—another sign that opportunity and merit continue to drive American success, not accidents of birth. The "rich" are not the same people over time.

The study is also valuable because it shows that income mobility remains little changed from what similar studies found in the 1970s and 1980s. Some journalists and academics have cited selective evidence to claim that income mobility has declined in recent years.

But the 58% of lowest-income earners who moved to a higher income quintile in this study is roughly comparable to the percentages that did so in several similar studies going back to the late 1960s. "The basic finding of this analysis," says the Treasury report, "is that relative income mobility is approximately the same in the last 10 years as it was in the previous decade."

All of this certainly helps to illuminate the current election-year debate about income "inequality" in the U.S. The political left and its media echoes are promoting the inequality story as a way to justify a huge tax increase. But inequality is only a problem if it reflects stagnant opportunity and a society stratified by more or less permanent income differences. That kind of society can breed class resentments and unrest. America isn't remotely such a society, thanks in large part to the incentives that exist for risk-taking and wealth creation.

The great irony is that, in the name of reducing inequality, some of our politicians want to raise taxes and other government obstacles to the kind of risk-taking and hard work that allow Americans to climb the income ladder so rapidly. As the Treasury data show, we shouldn't worry about inequality. We should worry about the people who use inequality as a political club to promote policies that reduce opportunity.

*　*　*

It would be hard to find a more mind-boggling contrast than between these two opinion pieces, with their dueling statistics such the *WSJ*'s claim that the richest 1% in 1996 lost 25.8% of their income by 2005, versus Sklar's claim about the vastly increasing wealth of the *Forbes* 400 and, "Between 1983 and 2004, the average wealth of the top 1 percent of households grew by 78%." Where can we begin to sort out what to believe? For background, Sklar writes a syndicated newspaper column and articles for small-circulation left journals like *Z Magazine*. As is typical of op-eds, this one is not thoroughly sourced, although she clearly draws from the conservative *Forbes* (whose annual survey of the 400 wealthiest Americans appears in its October issue) along with liberal sources like economist Edward Wolff, author of several scholarly books on economic inequality in America, and Citizens for Tax Justice—with their predictable possible biases—which can easily be researched further. (Her books like *Raise the Floor: Wages and Policies That Work for All of Us* and *Chaos and Community: Seeking Solutions, Not Scapegoats for Bad Economics* include full documentation.) She makes an **inductive** argument accumulating empirical data, structured through a series of contrasts between rich and poor, toward the opposite conclusion from the *WSJ*: "It's time for Congress to roll back tax cuts for the wealthy and close the loophole letting billionaire hedge fund speculators pay taxes at a lower rate than their secretaries." How well reasoned do you find the column? Do you find any possible fallacies or dubious assertions? A rebuttal to Sklar's earlier versions of these arguments appeared in "Why Try Holly Sklar's Socialist Plans for Economy When United States Is Doing Just Fine?" by Elizabeth Carnell, posted on LeftWatch.com, September 1, 1999, which follows much the same lines as the *WSJ*.

The *WSJ*'s source is a thickly documented, twenty-two page report, titled *Income Mobility in the U.S. from 1996 to 2005*, issued by the U.S. Department of the Treasury on November 13, 2007, at http://www.treas.gov/offices/tax-policy/library/incomemobilitystudy03-08revise .pdf. The report was heavily promoted in conservative circles, although it only claims to be an objective study of statistics without drawing **inferences** or editorializing about them as the *WSJ* does. However, liberal economists predictably weighed in with counterrefutations dismissing the report as propaganda from a Republican-stacked branch of the Bush administration, and tearing apart the fallacies they claimed to find in it. See, for example, Paul Krugman's blog http://krugman.blogs.nytimes.com/2007/11/28/zombie-ideas-about -income-mobility and "The Ladder of Lies, Damn Lies and Statistics—Let Me Count the Ways," by Patricia L. Johnson and Richard E. Walrath: searchwarp.com/swa271650.htm. You could do a further Google search for Treasury Department Income Mobility Report, and write an entire term paper just on opposing views of this report.

Part of the difficulty in comparing sources like Sklar versus *WSJ* is that different sources are often not discussing the same kind of data. Thus the Treasury Department only compares yearly income at different levels and their relative year-to-year changes, while Sklar discusses relative net worth, which the Treasury Department ignores. (Sklar does mention the growing income gap between CEO's and their employees, a topic the Treasury Department does not address.) The Treasury Department (like several previous conservative studies by conservative think tanks such as the Heritage Foundation) also is addressing changes in the income category of individuals over their lifetime, based on tax returns of those over 25, as well as changes over time in income of various percentiles of the population. Sklar and other liberal/leftist sources are more inclined to play up changes in the number of people in different categories in any particular period, rather than movement of individuals in and out of those categories. Each side argues that theirs is the more important measure. So in writing about these issues, you should think about which are the more significant measures, why, and why the opposing sides select the ones they do for rhetorical advantage.

Finally, these opposing sources present many examples of semantic "spin," or connotative **cleans** and **dirties**, as described in chapter 4. The *WSJ* says, "Of those in the second lowest income quintile, nearly 50% moved into the middle quintile or higher, and only 17% moved down. This is a stunning show of upward mobility, meaning that more than half of all lower-income Americans in 1996 had moved up the income scale in only 10 years." But liberal columnist Eugene Robinson in the *Washington Post* (November 23, 2007), looking at the same figures, wrote, "An incredible 42 percent of children born into that lowest quintile are still stuck at the bottom, having been unable to climb a single rung of the income ladder."

Another semantic topic from chapter 4, **unconcretized verbal abstractions**, is pertinent here. The *WSJ* condemns politicians who "want to raise taxes and other government obstacles to the kind of risk-taking and hard work that allow Americans to climb the income ladder so rapidly." George Will's "What's Behind Income Disparity?" similarly justified increasing concentration of wealth at the top because it is necessary to "a high rate of savings—the deferral of gratification that makes possible high rates of investment in capital, research and development and education," and he concludes, "That is why promoting more equal distribution of wealth might not be essential to, or even compatible with, promoting a more equitable society. And why increasingly unequal social rewards can conduce to a more truly egalitarian society, one that offers upward mobility equally to all who accept its rewarding disciplines." All this is at a rather high level of abstraction and prompts the questions in our Rhetoric Checklist #13, about theory versus practice: "Are the … abstract principles consistent with empirical (verifiable) facts and probabilities, and are they based on adequate firsthand witness to the situation in question?" The ideal conservative model is the entrepreneur who "defers gratification," scrimping and saving to risk her or his own capital and borrowed funds, to start a business introducing an innovative, socially beneficial product or service that also creates jobs, and who works hard building up and personally managing the business day by day, year after year, until it is profitable. There are unquestionably many such entrepreneurs.

But if we look at current lists of big financial winners and losers, we also see many who fit quite a different profile. Sklar says about the 2007 *Forbes* 400, "Nearly half of the 45 new members made their fortunes in hedge funds and private equity. Money manager John Pearson joins the list after pocketing more than $1 billion short-selling subprime credit." (Subprime credit involves bonds based on high-risk loans whose proliferation led to the mortgage meltdown of the late 2000s when the value of houses plunged. The *Knoxville News-Sentinel*, September 20, 2008, defined short-selling as "borrowing a company's shares, selling them at a higher price, buying them back after the stock falls to a lower price, and pocketing the difference.") Most of these people *started* with millions in capital and, however they may have originally acquired it, basically pyramided it through investment, often speculative—that is, seeking to make a fast profit buying and selling stocks and bonds (or whole corporations) on a gamble that the market would go up or down. One of the most common varieties of speculation is "leveraged" purchases. This refers to buying stock, real estate, or whole companies through a small down payment while borrowing the rest of the price, on the assumption that the value of the purchased property will increase enough to repay the loan and produce a net profit. A similar practice is "buying on margin," a major contributor to the stock market crash in 1929, in which brokers allow stockholders to use the current market value of their stock beyond its purchase price to buy further stock. These practices work as long as markets are going up, but when they drop, investors can be ruined by devalued holdings and unpayable loan or purchase debt. In the mortgage meltdown in 2007–08, this happened both to individual homeowners and to the mortgage companies and giant lenders like Fannie Mae and Freddie Mac, which "bundled" individual mortgages (many not adequately secured) into bonds, whose over-leveraged value estimate—used to justify multimillion-dollar executive salaries—plummeted when the real-estate market collapsed. (This is another case in which liberals argued that the root problem was "Reaganomics" legislation that had undone government regulation of limits on leveraged purchases and of adequate security for mortgage and other loans.)

Other members of the *Forbes* 400 in recent decades have included inheritors like the six heirs of Sam Walton and seven heirs of H. L. Hunt, including Bunker Hunt, studied in chapter 12, who have never had to work or take much risk at all as their inherited investment appreciated. (See the *Forbes* annual issue on the top 400 to survey how various ones made or augmented their fortunes, and what **generalizations** can be drawn.) To be sure, "work," "risk," and managerial skill are required in managing investment funds and playing the market—though rich people typically hire professional investment managers, who only earn a small percentage of what the owners do. But isn't there also an **equivocation** here in the definition of these terms from their description of risk and work in putting one's capital into and personally running a company for a long term, to a description of impersonally managing vast capital funds, buying and selling whole companies as an occupation, or making a quick killing on Wall Street, where the risk is essentially that of gambling—not generally regarded as a socially beneficial occupation, worthy of reward by low-tax incentives? Where is the "deferral of gratification"? And how much do these activities contribute to job creation or investment in "research and development and education"? Indeed, one of the most common current liberal lines of argument is that America's economy has stagnated precisely because of the drastic shift in investment from productive, high job-producing industries into financial speculation and profitable, but unproductive and low-employment, industries like gambling casinos and lotteries.

At the other end of the socioeconomic scale, read Jonathan Kozol's very concrete description, in "Other People's Children" in chapter 11, of the conditions of inner-city schools and neighborhoods and their causes in the flight of businesses and middle-class residents to the suburbs, taking with them jobs and tax revenue needed to fund schools. Do you think the *WSJ*, George Will, or you would be able to make a persuasive case that the problems of these people and the "5 million more people living below the poverty line" since 2006, at the official poverty threshold for one person of $10,294 (Sklar) are attributable primarily to poor individuals' lack of "risk-taking and hard work that allow Americans to climb the income ladder so rapidly" (*WJS*)? Or that American society "offers upward mobility equally to all who accept its rewarding disciplines" (Will)—inner-city children and suburban children of billionaires?

You can see, then, how conservatives attempt to set the agenda of public awareness on these issues by propagating the abstract case that allowing the rich to get richer will ultimately help everyone else more than would raising taxes and other restrictions on the rich in order to directly provide better education and jobs for the poor and middle class, as liberals argue in the concrete terms of Sklar and Kozol. So a more advanced conservative case would need to refute liberals' concrete evidence rather than evading it through abstractions, and in your research you should see if you can find such advanced conservative arguments. As previously mentioned, the Treasury Department Report is one example of a more advanced, statistically based rebuttal to liberals, as are various reports on poverty and income mobility from the Heritage Foundation—sources that prompt counterrebuttals from liberal economists and journalists, in an upwardly spiraling, unending progression of give-and-take.

ANALYZING STATISTICAL TRICKS

The following is a portion of a student paper pursuing these and related issues.

Conservative rhetoric on Reaganomics plays heavily on **plain folks** appeals attempting to persuade us that trickle-down economics have benefited the middle class and poor at least as much as the rich, and on **appeals to pity** for the virtuous rich, who are unfairly punished by high taxes and excess government regulation, to the detriment of all of us. So conservatives argue that there is no solid proof that Reaganomics policies created a large income disparity gap. In an article for the *Weekly Standard* (July 1, 1996, 19), "Wealth Gap Claptrap," John Weicher, senior fellow at the Hudson Institute and chief economist at the Office of Management and Budget during the Reagan administration, uses Federal Reserve Board statistics to show that "The total wealth of American households increased by over $4 trillion between 1983 and 1992.... Average wealth per household increased by about 11 percent." He claims that the liberal rhetoric just pushes the wealth gap myth in order to gain support for unneeded increased taxes, government spending, and regulation. He ends his argument, "Yes, the rich are getting richer. And the poor are getting richer. And they're doing it more or less equally."

A careful reading reveals several possible fallacies in Weicher's claim that all classes have gotten wealthier at about an equal rate. Let's say a family in the middle class, with net worth of $100,000, a family with $10 million, and a billionaire all gained 11%. That means a gain of $11,000 for the first family, but $1.10 million for the second, and $110 million for the third. Did all gain equally, in terms of purchasing power rather than percentage points? In addition, one of the things that those of us in the middle class, who are unable to save or invest much at all, have a hard time understanding about wealth is that rich people aren't just rich, but they are highly likely to keep getting richer all the time, because most of their money is in investments that normally appreciate and compound every year, so every million dollars compounding at, say 10% a year, will be worth over two million in ten years.

In several of his books and articles, liberal economist and *New York Times* columnist Paul Krugman provides further refutation of arguments like Weicher's that downplay the growing gap in income and wealth since the eighties. Krugman points out the difference between *total* or *average* (Weicher's terms) and *median*. Total income or wealth is calculated by adding up all the family incomes or net worths, and their average calculated by dividing the total by the number of families. (If you total or average Bill Gates's wealth and that of a homeless street person, it would look like the latter is a billionaire.) Median income or wealth, a much more meaningful measure, is the one at the middle, in the sense that there are the same number of families above and below it. Krugman has similar figures as Weicher's, that from 1979 to 1989 average family income rose 11 percent, but asserts, "70% of the rise in average family income went to the top 1%," while "the median family income rose only 4 percent" (137–38). In a later article, Krugman adds, "In 1998 the top 1 percent started at $230,000. In turn, 60 percent of the gains of that top 1 percent went to the top 0.1 percent, those with incomes of more than $790,000. And almost half of those gains went to a mere 13,000 taxpayers, the top 0.01 percent, who had an income of at least $3.6 million and an average income of $17 million" ("For Richer" 65). In light of Krugman's figures, Weicher's claim about the *total* national growth of wealth also means little, because the small percentage at the top accounted for most of the growth, just as it skewed average income and wealth upward, while the bottom 40% have seen their income and wealth go down.

In tax policy, liberals argue for highly progressive rates—which is to say that the percentage rate you are taxed goes up more sharply the more you make, while conservatives favor pretty much the same rate for all income levels, which they say is the most fair policy. The same differences apply in conservatives' call for lowering taxes by the same rate for all classes, versus liberals' call for lowering taxes for the middle class and poor but raising them on the rich.

Let's oversimplify and round off a bit just to illustrate the general principle. If a middle-class family earning, say, $30,000 a year, had their rate cut by 50%, from something like 26% to 13% (about the current rate), they'd save about $3,900 per year—which is fine with liberals, though their policies would save them more through taxing the rich more. After his first cuts, President George W. Bush appeared on TV with such a family proudly showing a blow-up of a check for their couple of thousand dollars refund. Have they benefited equally with the rich, whose taxes were cut by about the same rate? Well, yes and no.

Consider the example of Bill Gates, whose net worth was $59 billion in 2007—up from $53 billion in 2006—according Forbes Magazine's annual list of 400 richest Americans. Also simplifying to a round number of $60 billion—hey, what's a billion here or there?—and not taking account of adjustments to taxable income like deductions and many other ways rich people can avoid paying much income tax at all, let's modestly estimate an annual return on investments of that much at 10%, or $6 billion in taxable income.

This means the following, in very rough approximations. In 1980, before President Reagan started cutting income tax, the rate for the top bracket was 70% on income over about

$225,000 (though brackets have always been staggered so the rate is lower on the portion of income below that level). 1980 tax on $6 billion income @ 70% = $4.2 billion, leaving $1.8 billion income after taxes (without any dent in the original net worth.) 2007 tax on $6 billion income @ 35% = $2.1 billion, leaving $3.9 billion income after taxes—a saving of some $2.1 billion for one family for one year. So at the same percentage-rate cut, one family would save $3,900 and the other $2.1 billion. Both benefited equally, right? Did President Bush ask Gates to appear with him showing his refund check?

Next, just for fun, let's extend this hypothetical analysis to a flat tax system like that proposed by Steve Forbes. At the same rate on all brackets, like 12%, the above family earning $30,000 would save $4,200 over their 1980 rate of 28%, leaving them $22,500 after taxes. If Bill Gates's income is $6 billion, though, he would now pay only $720 million—$3.48 billion less than at the 1980 rate and $1.38 billion less than at the current rate! (Considering that Steve Forbes happens to be the publisher of *Forbes* magazine, as well as a regular among its 400 richest Americans, might his flat tax proposal have been a case of special pleading?) So the catch in flat-rate proposals is that they predictably will vastly benefit the rich over any progressive tax.

Columnist Holly Sklar writes, "Tax cuts will save the top 1 percent a projected $715 billion between 2001 and 2010. And cost us $715 billion in mounting national debt plus interest." Of course, the rich repay some of what they get back from tax cuts in additional taxes on their increased earnings, providing jobs, etc. However, defenders of supply-side economics would need to prove that these additional revenues exceed what the rich would have paid at a higher rate—sort of a hard sell in light of the record government deficits under both presidents Reagan and George W. Bush. It is also likely that as an increasing share of income goes to the rich, resulting in relatively declining income for the middle class and poor, tax revenue from the latter groups also declines, possibly resulting in a net loss of revenue—although this needs to be verified through empirical research.

The trouble with most of us mere middle class mortals is that we just can't wrap our minds around the meaning of wealth at that stratospheric level, so we project our own psychology to that level—a state of mind that conservative propagandists exploit with their appeals to fear of tax raises. In class discussion about this, when we heard that the top tax rate before 1980 was 70%, some students got indignant and argued that this rate was totally unfair. I think this was because they were imagining how that percentage would deprive them or their families of subsistence income. Conservative talking heads play on this middle-class mentality by charging that a rate like 70% is "confiscatory"—as though the government, as under Communism, is taking away 70% of everything a family owns. This thinking shows lack of imagination in several ways. First, because most of our families don't have much net worth beyond a mortgaged house and a financed car, we do not understand that the income taxes paid by the very rich do not cut into their total wealth at all. They do not in fact owe any income tax on that net worth or on annual compounding of it, even amounting to billions, that is plowed back into the principal, until and unless they sell off some profits (in which case they only have to pay a 15% capital gains tax); they just pay property taxes on business and residential property. So their income tax is based only on their actual income for the year, which usually is a small, easily affordable amount *relative to their net worth*. In fact, rich people often have their accountants arrange things so they report little or no yearly income, just to avoid paying taxes. (This indicates a flaw in conservative studies like the Treasury Department report based on income tax returns. See Johnston, *Perfectly Legal*.) In conclusion, the harshness of taxes should not be judged by how much we have to pay, but on how much we have left after taxes, both in income and net worth. In a class discussion, I asked my classmates, "Would you rather earn $30,000, pay only $3,900 tax on it at 13%, and have $26,100 left; or earn $6 billion, pay a "confiscatory" $4.2 billion in taxes at 70%—and have $1.8 billion left for the year, compounding a $60-billion-dollar net worth?"

There were no takers for the lower tax rate.

Another area where our middle-class imaginations are limited is understanding what the super-rich do with their surplus money. We're inclined to think in terms of just spending it all on personal luxuries and going on sprees. But most people at the multimillion-dollar level can't begin to spend all their money (they are pretty foolish if they do). The first thing most do, as noted earlier, is reinvest their surplus to keep compounding their net worth and corporate ownership, widening the gap between them and everyone else. Even more important are all the forms of *power* that money can buy—running for office; gaining governmental favoritism through campaign contributions to politicians and parties; hiring lobbying, public relations, and law firms; monopolizing ownership of corporations and media; being able to set prices and wages to their advantage; etc., etc. Maybe their most effective exercise of power is to hire publicists and control the media to persuade all of us peasants how wonderful the rich are and why they deserve ever-lower taxes and less government regulation. I have not been able to find any conservative sources that have a real rebuttal to this line of argument about the power that money can buy, the strongest one in support of the case that there has been a scarily increasing gap of wealth and power in America.

SUMMARY OF SUSPICIOUS STATISTICAL ARGUMENTS

In conclusion, we always need to keep in mind the implications of economic statistics for each individual, not just abstract social aggregates, and to be on guard against arguments that overwhelm us with compilations of statistics that may look impressive but that obscure individual realities. The following is a summary of some patterns of rhetorically suspicious statistical arguments of the kind we have surveyed here.

1. Arguments that play up the large amount of taxes paid by the wealthy (and the relatively small amount paid by the middle class or poor) in a single year, or a growing amount over a period of years, without also comparing actual dollar income and net worth among the classes being compared.
2. Arguments that play up a total or average (as opposed to median) increase in income or net worth in the entire society or within one broad bracket, without factoring in large increases at the very top of the society or bracket that might skew upward the total or average, and that consequently downplay relative losses for those in the middle and lower sectors. Similarly, arguments that play up the total amount spent by government in a field like education without factoring in large discrepancies in spending between wealthy and poor sectors (as in William J. Bennett's "Crisis in American Education" in chapter 11).
3. Arguments that play up the same percentage change in different brackets of income, net worth, or tax reductions as alleged evidence of equitable results in all groups, while downplaying the large differences in dollar amounts among the groups resulting from an equal percentage change in each.
4. Arguments that play up the benefits of one part of a policy change (e.g., reduction of income taxes) while downplaying the negative effects of another part of that change (e.g., increase in Social Security or other taxes); or conversely, arguments that play up the negative effects (e.g., more people becoming wealthy at other classes' expense under Reaganomics) while downplaying, as liberals do, the positive effects (closing of prior loopholes, resulting in more tax revenue).

AN OUTLINE OF CONSERVATIVE AND LEFTIST ARGUMENTS ON THE RICH, THE POOR, AND THE MIDDLE CLASS

The following is an outline of the broad points of opposition between conservatives and leftists on the topics in this chapter and throughout much of the rest of this book. In keeping with good semantic principles, the outline is meant to be open-ended. The facts that the leftist arguments get the last word here and are more numerous (a reflection of the weight of evidence accumulated throughout the book) should simply serve as a challenge to you and your classmates to use this as a point of departure, seeing what effective conservative rebuttals you can find. So "the last word" in this outline, this chapter, and this book is, "ETC., ETC., ETC."

The Conservative Position

The basic position of Presidents Reagan, both Presidents Bush, and their conservative supporters is that American government has been overloaded trying to provide for the public welfare in programs like education, Social Security, Medicare, welfare, unemployment insurance, minimum wage laws, and so on. Moreover, excessive taxation and bureaucratic government regulation of business (especially for environmental protection) have stifled the productive power of free enterprise. This overload on government has led to inflation, deficit spending, and dependency of beneficiaries of programs like welfare on "handouts." Therefore, if government spending on domestic programs is reduced and taxes cut by equal percentage rates across all income lines (with the largest savings going to wealthy individuals and corporations), private enterprise will be freed to function more effectively; it will be more efficient than government and the public sector of the economy in generating jobs, producing more tax revenue, and filling other public needs. The reason these beneficial "Reaganomic" policies haven't been fully effective is that they haven't been given an adequate chance to work, their full implementation having been blocked by Democrats in Congress and other leftist bureaucrats and special interest groups purely because of their partisan and selfish motives. Deficit spending has increased only because Democrats in Congress rejected every effort by President Reagan and both Presidents Bush to reduce the budget.

Conservatives also argue that:

1. Budget and tax cuts in the federal government under Reagan and both Bushes, and in states like California since Proposition 13, have just trimmed the fat, eliminating unnecessary programs and administrative waste and leaving intact essential programs and the "safety net" of support for the truly needy.
2. Flat-rate taxes and tax cuts are fairer than progressive taxes because all income levels pay and benefit from cuts at the same rate.
3. Government spending in many areas such as education and welfare can be more properly and efficiently handled by states and localities than by the federal government; the funding burden should be shifted to them.
4. Much of the overload on government has resulted from selfish, excessive demands for "entitlements" from special interests like welfare recipients, minorities, the elderly, veterans, teachers, and students. These groups have become dependent on handouts and have lost their incentive to work.
5. Individual initiative, not government programs, is the best solution to social problems. Conservatives believe in equality of opportunity, not an inaccessible equality of outcome as liberals do, and believe that all Americans *do* have equal opportunity to succeed. Everyone who tries hard enough can get a good job and be financially successful. It is usually a person's own fault if he or she is poor or unemployed. The poor should just try harder and be more virtuous.
6. Spending on national defense is an exception to the need to cut government because increases in the eighties were necessary to defeat Russia in the arms race (Communism's collapse vindicated Reagan's hard-line policies); a strong defense is still necessary because of terrorism and other potential threats, like Saddam Hussein, to American security.
7. The most effective way to reduce poverty and unemployment is to permit the rich to get richer—the trickle-down theory or supply-side economics—because their increased spending trickles down to benefit all other segments of society proportionately. The concentration of wealth at the top is not a zero-sum game, in which the gains of the rich come at the expense of the middle class or poor.

8. Wealthy individuals and corporate executives can be trusted to use their increased benefits for the public welfare because in order to attain and maintain their position they have to be exceptionally intelligent, hardworking, honest, and civic-minded.

9. Most rich people have worked hard for their money and have risked their investments, so they shouldn't be penalized by high taxes and government regulations that stifle their incentive to work and to invest. Executives' high salaries are proportionate to the profits they have produced for their companies.

10. Minimum-wage laws, high corporate or individual taxes, and excessive regulations—especially in environmental, safety, and health issues—force industries to move their operations to lower-cost locations in the United States or to other countries. Such increased expenses are also passed on to consumers in higher prices, so they are self-defeating.

11. The rich are generous in sharing their wealth; the more money they are allowed to keep, the more they give to charities.

12. Wealth is compatible with religious, and especially Christian, morality. Many wealthy people like Nelson Bunker Hunt use their wealth to support religious organizations and causes.

13. Leftist criticisms of Reagan, George W. Bush, and the rich often consist of "sour grapes" rationalizations by government bureaucrats, intellectuals, teachers, journalists, or public employees who are just unwilling or unable to make it themselves in the private sector and who are jealous of those who do. These "bleeding hearts" sentimentalize the poor.

14. Leftist teachers' and other public employees' arguments may reflect ethnocentric bias, conflict of interest, or special pleading, since members of these groups benefit personally from higher taxation and the resulting increases in government spending. Likewise, arguments by leftist intellectuals may be self-interested, concealing their drive to replace the rich as the new ruling class.

15. History has shown that, in spite of all its faults, capitalism or free enterprise is a more efficient and humane economic system than any form of socialism or mixed economy.

16. Statistically based arguments: Empirical evidence that Reaganomics worked includes the facts that the 1980s saw a reduction in inflation and the longest period of steady growth in the American economy since World War II; millions of new jobs were created; the rich paid higher dollar amounts and an increased percentage of tax revenues, and total tax revenues increased. Liberal-leftist claims of a growing gap between the rich and the middle class and poor are based on faulty statistical analyses. There has been much more socioeconomic mobility in recent decades than liberals want to admit, with many people moving out of poverty into the middle class, and many others dropping out of the upper income brackets.

The Leftist Position

Democracy in America is being destroyed and replaced by plutocracy—rule by and for the rich. Reagan and both Bushes have been agents of plutocratic special interests, as are most Republican and Democratic politicians, including Presidents Kennedy and Clinton. These politicians appeal to liberal constituencies to get elected but then sell them out on many if not most issues. Reaganomic policies have had the effect, intentionally or unintentionally, of entrenching plutocracy by making the rich richer and the middle class and the poor poorer and by eliminating needed welfare programs and productive areas of public spending and employment. Government spending primes the pump when the economy slumps and provides services not offered by the private sector, while progressive taxation serves to reduce the gap of wealth and power between the rich and the rest of the population (Keynesian economics). The conservative line of argument against Keynesian economics is largely a propaganda program engineered by wealthy special interests to rationalize their own greed. In fact, Reagan and both Bushes consistently proposed budgets that were higher (mainly because of defense increases) than those passed by Congress, but their budget increases amounted to "Keynesian" socialism for the rich, free enterprise for the poor.

Leftists also make the following arguments. The numbers in parentheses refer to refuted conservative arguments.

1. American cultural conditioning favors the rich by fostering common blocks to clear thinking like authoritarian awe and sentimentality toward the rich, the ethnocentrism and wishful thinking of middle-class people hoping to become rich, and favorable stereotypes of the rich and prejudiced ones of the working class and poor.

2. (9) There is often little correlation between how hard people work or how much risk they take and how much money they make. Many of those who make the most money don't make it through work at all but through investments (often inherited) and speculation, while many of those who work the hardest and at the greatest risk (e.g., farmworkers, coal miners, police, firefighters) make the least. Corporate executive salaries have gotten totally out of proportion to performance—in many cases, CEOs have received vastly increased income even when their companies have lost money—partly because of conflicts of interest between CEOs and boards of directors who determine their compensation.

3. (5) Conservative "try harder" arguments fail to recognize the basic inequities structured into a capitalist economy and the external economic forces—national and worldwide economic trends, inflation, recession, discrepancies in opportunity between different geographical areas or demographic groups, and so on—that often make individual effort futile. In a free-enterprise economy, there is no certainty of full employment, of a job being available for everyone who needs one, or of a minimum wage above poverty level. Conservatives have constructed a straw-man leftist who demands nothing less than total equality of outcome from social policies, but most liberals and leftists simply believe that present-day America is far from presenting equal opportunity for all, so that their policies are only aimed at bringing about that *opportunity*.

4. (7) There is no conclusive evidence that the trickle-down theory has ever worked in practice or ever will. Contrary to conservative claims that supply-side tax cuts would actually increase tax revenues, federal and local revenues have been lower than they would have been under previous progressive rates, and huge deficits have resulted at both the national and local levels. Much of what the rich get back in tax cuts is often invested not in job-producing enterprises but in personal luxuries, tax dodges, hedges against inflation, speculation, corporate takeovers resulting in monopoly and inflated prices for consumers and lost jobs for workers, or investments in foreign countries that exploit cheap labor there while taking jobs and money out of the United States.

5. (7, 8, 10) Outlandish corporate profits and gaps between executives and employees in recent decades belie conservatives' claims that the rich getting richer benefits everyone, as well as their appeals to pity for overtaxed, overregulated corporations. Businesses often use these appeals to pity and the appeal to fear of their relocating within the United States or abroad as blackmail to get their way. Globalization and outsourcing of jobs simply exploit the absence in poorer countries of minimum-wage laws, labor unions, and environmental, safety, and health regulations. Corporate relocation abroad, motivated by greed, has devastated American workers and contradicts conservative claims that capitalists are virtuous and patriotic.

6. While much money spent in the private sector does not trickle down to the rest of society, virtually all money spent in the public sector "trickles up" back into the private

sector. Spending on education, public health, welfare, and so on is a good investment by society that pays off in higher productivity. Spending by tax-funded public agencies (e.g., universities) creates jobs and subsidizes private-sector contractors for construction, equipment, and services. Corporate interests want (and depend on) these subsidies without wanting to pay the taxes needed to fund them.

7. The private sector is just as wasteful and inefficient as the public sector, and the most waste in both occurs at the executive levels, where spending is administered (primarily in administrators' own interests). Thus budget cuts resulting from laws like Proposition 13 in California have left governmental administrative "fat" intact while bankrupting local governments, causing layoffs of rank-and-file public employees and harmful cuts in essential services like education and law enforcement. The conservative belief that there is a vast amount of fat that can be trimmed from government agencies at the rank-and-file level is often just wishful thinking or rationalization of conservatives' politically motivated desire to squeeze out liberal constituencies served by government spending.

8. (3) As a result of local tax cuts like Proposition 13 in California, state and local governments are even more hard-pressed financially than the federal government, so conservative claims that funding responsibilities are better handled at the local level are simply rationalizations or passing the buck.

9. (9) Those who can afford to pay the most taxes and who benefit most from a prosperous society—that is, the rich—should be expected to pay the most. Flat-rate tax cuts disproportionately benefit the rich and widen the gap in wealth and ownership of income-producing holdings like stocks, bonds, real estate, and farms, enabling the rich to increase their power in all of the following ways.

10. The rich can buy political influence with both the Republican and Democratic parties and government officials, causing legislation to be passed in their interest and against that of the middle class and poor, particularly in tax policies, such as regressive cuts in income, corporation, inheritance, and property taxes that in recent decades have sharply reduced the burden on the rich.

11. As a result of 10, the tax burden has shifted increasingly from the rich to the middle class, especially in tax increases for Social Security and Medicare and, at the local and state levels, in sales taxes. As a further result, members of the overtaxed middle class vote to support cuts in public services that harm themselves and society as a whole but not the rich, who don't depend on these services, such as public education, Social Security, public health insurance, welfare, law enforcement, public libraries, and public transportation. Middle class people rationalize these cuts by turning the poor, "big government," and public employees into scapegoats, blaming them instead of the rich for the financial squeeze on themselves.

12. The rich can use the power of hiring and firing to force workers and students (as future workers) into compliance with prorich attitudes; because we have to cater to them to get or keep a job, we tend to fall into doublethink compartmentalized thinking to rationalize our servitude to them.

13. The rich are able to create a favorable public image of themselves through ownership or sponsorship of news and entertainment media, advertising, and public relations. They exert a large degree of control over education as donors or university trustees and by sponsoring research in both universities and private think tanks that supports their interests.

14. (8) Many rich people and corporations get away with criminal or unethical activity that causes relatively little public indignation or opposition from law enforcement agencies, compared to actions by lower-class criminals or "leeches." The middle class tends to have a double standard or selective vision in playing down misconduct by the rich and

playing up that by the poor. How can we expect poor people to respect the law or act morally when those at the top of society set such a poor example?

15. It is often affluent conservative businesspeople who benefit most from the government subsidies that conservatives claim they oppose (compartmentalized thinking): subsidies to farmers (including for food stamps); to insurance companies, doctors, pharmaceutical manufacturers, and sellers of health insurance; to bankers for student loans; to bondholders for government debts, and so on.

16. (6) Wealthy people and corporations control the defense industry, which receives the biggest government subsidy of all and whose only customer is the government. Spending on weapons that are only intended to be destroyed or replaced by more advanced ones is disastrous for the national economy. (But the defense industry is exempt from conservative attacks on government bureaucracy and waste, because it produces big corporate profits and campaign contributions.) More and more of our national income has been eaten up by this wasteful spending, which is a major cause of inflation and deficit spending and which has squeezed out spending on more productive domestic programs like education and employment for public works. During the Cold War, the military-industrial complex and its wealthy executives became the tail that wagged the dog of defense policy in their own self-interest, artificially perpetuating tensions with Russia to bolster their profits and power (mirroring the military establishment in Russia that was similarly self-interested). The main reason Communism collapsed was not the American arms buildup but the inept, dictatorial bureaucrats who were running the Soviet Union's government and economy. But because American conservatives are always partial to militarism, they tend to be blind to the military as a special interest and to fraud and waste in military spending, which has accelerated again after September 11 and the Iraq war, rationalized by appeals to fear of terrorism.

17. The rich can influence foreign policy to protect their foreign investments, markets, and sources of natural resources and cheap labor. International competition for markets has frequently been the cause of wars throughout history.

18. The wealthy profit from wars that are conducted in their class interests and that consume weapons that they produce, but they and their children rarely risk their own lives fighting in those wars. Any business interest that profits from a war should be expected to pay increased taxes to finance it.

19. (11) Rich people on the whole do not give a great amount to charity, relative to their income or net worth, and they benefit from what they give through tax deductions, trusteeships, and a favorable public image as philanthropists or supporters of religion.

20. (12) Attempts to reconcile wealth with Christianity amount to hypocritical rationalizations, since they are completely contrary to the teachings of Jesus Christ.

21. (15) Some semisocialist countries (e.g., Denmark, Sweden) have surpassed America in per capita income, quality of life, and well-functioning democracy, while some capitalist countries (e.g., Saudi Arabia, South Africa under apartheid, Chile under Pinochet, El Salvador under Duarte, the Philippines under Marcos) are plutocratic, right-wing dictatorships, and Americans' prosperity and freedom are paid for at the expense of poor people in those countries, which are in effect colonies of American corporations.

22. (16) Statistically based arguments: Since the 1980s, the income of the richest 1 percent of Americans has skyrocketed, and the gap between the rich, middle class, and poor has become greater than at any time since the 1920s. The rich obviously are paying more in taxes because their *income* is greater in relation to everyone else's, thanks to Reaganomic subsidies, and their after-tax savings have increasingly outstripped everyone else's. Inflation has been reduced mainly through reduction of real income for the majority of workers, largely through outsourcing of jobs to Third World sweatshops. Economic growth since the eighties has been slower than in previous decades, and

the jobs created have been mostly low-wage ones. The main reason more people are working is that two or more people in the same household have been forced to work in order to make the real income previously earned by one; most Americans now have to work more hours to make the same real income they did thirty years ago.

Topics for Discussion and Writing

1. A rebuttal to earlier versions of Sklar's arguments here can be found in "Why Try Holly Sklar's Socialist Plans for Economy When United States Is Doing Just Fine?" by Elizabeth Carnell, posted on LeftWatch.com, September 1, 1999, http://www.leftwatch.com/holly_sklar/sklar001.html. Among Carnell's arguments are, "The truth is Americans are much better off today than they were even 20 years ago, and the United States still enjoys the highest standard of living in the world." Consider whether Carnell might be committing a version of #2 in "Suspicious Statistical Arguments" in the above list—that is, are *all*, or even most, Americans better off and enjoying the highest standard of living? Is the "average American"? The "median-income American?" (She provides no supporting data here. You might check her data with the Bureau of Labor Statistics studies cited by Sklar for "the average worker.") Compare her statement about Americans' comparative standard of living with Brouwer's "If We Decided to Tax the Rich" in chapter 13. Look up Carnell's article to see how fully it refutes Sklar on other points.

2. In the late 2000s when gas prices escalated, along with record-setting oil company profits and executive income, the American Petroleum Institute, the industry trade association or lobby, sponsored a widespread campaign of television and print ads under the signature of EnergyTomorrow.org. The ads played up the industry's investment in developing alternative sources of energy, along with strong **plain folks** appeal—they are signed, "THE **PEOPLE** OF AMERICA'S OIL AND NATURAL GAS INDUSTRY." (Do you suppose "the people" commissioned or wrote these ads?) One shows a photo of a young, obviously middle-class couple with two children in their modest breakfast room, over the headline, "Do you own an oil company?" Another shows a pie chart indicating that only 1.5% of stock shareholders belong to "corporate management," while "the majority of oil and natural gas company shareholders are middle-class U.S. households with small portfolios, pension accounts or other retirement accounts and small portfolios." The conclusion is, "So when Congress starts talking about raising energy taxes or taking 'excess profits' from U.S. oil companies, look at the facts and ask yourself, 'who does that really hurt?'" How might their breakdown of stock ownership be a **half truth** in terms of what amount of stock is actually owned by the different categories collectively and individuals within them? And how would this reflect on whom would be most hurt by raising taxes on oil company profits, along the lines of the analysis of the effects of tax increases and cuts in this chapter? See if you find the answers at this Web site or elsewhere.

3. In his *New York Times* column (July 1, 2008), David Brooks wrote, "When he is swept up in rhetorical fervor, Obama occasionally says that his campaign is 90 percent funded by small donors. He has indeed had great success with small donors, but only about 45 percent of his money comes from donations of $200 or less." How might this argument by Obama be similarly fallacious to the API ads in #2?

4. Use "An Outline of Conservative and Leftist Arguments on the Rich, the Poor, and the Middle Class" as a point of departure for individual or group study toward a research paper, looking for conservative rebuttals of the liberal and leftist lines of argument.

CHAPTER 17

Collecting and Evaluating Opposing Sources: Writing the Research Paper

The foregoing study units might culminate in an assignment, for the preliminary stages of a term paper, of an annotated bibliography and working outline, described below and designed for you to locate and analyze articles and books with opposing partisan viewpoints on the chosen topic. These exercises are designed to help prevent you from simply picking off the Internet or the library shelf *The Weekly Standard* or *In These Times*, a book published by Regnery Publishing or South End Press, a report from American Enterprise Institute or the Institute for Policy Studies, to use as a source and quoting it as gospel, without a critical understanding of the sponsor's habitual viewpoint. Following this procedure should enable you to avoid assertions in your papers like, "Reaganomics was hugely successful" or "Reaganomics was a total disaster," and instead to use phrasing like, "Holly Sklar, writing in the leftist *Z Magazine*, presents a socialist argument that Reaganomics vastly widened the gap between the rich and poor in the United States"; or, "Ed Rubenstein, in the conservative *National Review*, refutes statistics presented by leftists like Ehrenreich claiming that Reaganomic policies have widened the gap between the rich and poor." You can then go on to explain how the source's general ideological viewpoint applies to the particular issue in question, to analyze the rhetorical/semantic patterns accordingly, and to evaluate the source's arguments against opposing ones. In this way you can get beyond the **parochial** mentality of those who read and listen only to sources that confirm their preconceptions while deluding themselves that these sources impartially present a full range of information.

Lest this approach be misconstrued as an invitation to total relativity or skepticism, in the conclusion to your term paper you should try not to make a final and absolute judgment on which side is right and wrong about the issue at hand, but to make a balanced summary of the strong and weak points made by each of the limited number of sources you have studied, and then to make—and support—your judgment about which sources have presented the best-reasoned case and the most thorough refutation of the other side's arguments. Your instructor should then be able to grade you for the paper and the course on the quality of your support for your conclusion—regardless of what that conclusion may be.

ASSIGNMENT FOR AN ANNOTATED BIBLIOGRAPHY AND WORKING OUTLINE

Turn in a set number of bibliographical entries, determined by your teacher, on an equal number of leftist and rightist sources, including at least one magazine article and one book or monograph report from the left-wing publishers and one article and book or report from the right-wing publishers in chapter 13. Then annotate them according to the following guidelines, and develop them into a detailed working outline keyed to citations of these entries.

1. Identify the author's political position, using clues from his/her affiliation with a particular research institute, book publisher, journal of opinion, party, or organization, and—more importantly—from arguments s/he presents that exemplify the glossary terms and the particular patterns of political rhetoric outlined in chapter 13; give enough quotes (or highlighted photocopies) to support your identification. In cases where the author is not arguing from an identifiable position, but is only reporting facts, indicate which position the reported facts support, and explain how. (Note: some newspapers, magazines, etc., have an identifiable political viewpoint in general, in their news and op-ed orientation, but also attempt to present other views at least some of the time; e.g., the *New York Times* is predominantly liberal, but often carries conservative op-ed columns, letters, etc. So you shouldn't assume that any article appearing in such a periodical will automatically have its predominant viewpoint; look for other identity clues.)
2. Apply to each source the "Semantic Calculator for Bias in Rhetoric" (chapter 4) and "Predictable Patterns of Political Rhetoric" (chapter 13) along with the more general principles of rhetorical analysis throughout this book.

SAMPLE ANNOTATED BIBLIOGRAPHY ENTRY

David Frum, "The Vanishing Republican Voter: Why Income Inequality is Destroying the G.O.P Base." *New York Times Magazine,* Sept 7, 2008, 48–51.

Who is he, and what is his viewpoint?

Prominent conservative journalist and one-time economics speechwriter for President George W. Bush. Resigned and became a critic of Bush administration. Author of *Comeback: Conservatism That Can Win Again* (2007). Resident Fellow at conservative bastion American Enterprise Institute.

Surprising article in upsetting expectations of "predictable patterns of political rhetoric" in light of demographic shifts in the past decade or so. He concedes a great deal to liberals about rising income inequality and how it is working electorally against Republicans who have been in denial about it. A significant twist, though, is that he argues that upper-income-earners and those with higher levels of education are becoming more Democratic. Quote: "7 out of America's 10 best-educated states are strongly 'blue' in national politics . . . . Of the 10 least-educated, only one (Nevada) is reliably Republican" (51). This contradicts the assumption of the equation of wealth with conservatism, but his explanation seems to be that those with higher educations now consider Democrats to be more competent managing government and the economy. Conversely, the Republicans constantly try to present themselves as the party of populism, against liberal elites, but under the Bush administration the middle and working classes have lost ground economically and lost faith that Republicans care about them. His conclusion: "Equality in itself never can or should be a conservative goal. But inequality taken to extremes can overwhelm conservative ideals of self-reliance, limited government, and national unity. . . . We must develop a positive agenda that integrates the right kind of egalitarianism with our conservative principles of liberty" (51).

So Frum contradicts other conservative sources who either deny that inequality is rising or deny that inequality is a bad thing. But he also implies that neither the Republican nor the Democratic elite really represents the interests of poor people, blue-collar workers, or the middle class.

SAMPLE WORKING OUTLINE

I. Introduction
   A. Bewildering nature of contradictions between conservative and liberal views on the wealth gap, taxation, regulation, college costs, etc., as surveyed in *Reading and Writing for Civic Literacy*, mainly chapter 16. This paper will take that survey as a point of departure for further exploration of sources beyond those in the textbook.
   B. Briefly explain points of opposition on economic issues between conservatives and liberals.
   C. My viewpoint and bias: conservative parents, upbringing, and major. Acknowledge validity of liberal arguments, but in transition to main body, note concentration here on Laffer and Frum as substantial conservative sources.
II. Main Body
   A. McCain's and Obama's positions in 2008 election.
   B. Definitions and justifications of Reaganomics; contrast to Keynesian economics.
   C. Arthur Laffer's "The Onslaught from the Left" as a substantial, scholarly defense of the conservative position against liberal critics. Rebuttal to Chait's *The Big Con*. L's background: Former professor of Economics at U of Chicago. Advisor to President Reagan. Currently an investment consultant. Known as inventor of "The Laffer Curve," a hypothesis that lowering taxes on the rich will increase tax revenue and trickle down to benefit all classes as increased productivity exceeds revenue from the initial higher rate.
      1. Strong points:
         a. President Kennedy cut top rates, with beneficial consequences. (P. 4)
         b. Cites (presumably) liberal Berkeley economists on negative effects of high taxes. (5)
         c. Social-democratic countries in recent decades have also cut taxes. (7)
         d. Data indicating rising income of lower 50% of taxpayers (similar to Treasury Department). He doesn't deny that inequality has increased. "The increasingly unequal distribution of income during the era of supply-side economics, however, has resulted from the poor increasing their incomes at a rate

that has not kept pace with the phenomenal gains in income the rich have experienced—not from the poor getting poorer." (5–6)

  e. "Income inequality is a global phenomenon. Both capitalistic and socialistic countries are facing increased income inequality.... The true cause of income inequality probably has much more to do with globalization and improvements in technology than with American tax cuts on the rich." (8)

  f. Median family income has sharply increased in America since 1982. (9)

  g. Female participation in the American economy has grown. (10)

2. Weak points:

  a. Possible reductive fallacy (by some liberals as well as conservatives) in causal analysis of correlation between tax rates and economic trends.

  b. Equivocates between tax incentives to "work" vs. to "invest," and in not distinguishing the differential benefits of tax cuts to middle-class wage-earners and investors gaining millions and billions in profits (plain folks fallacy).

  c. Plays up cuts in income taxes, which allegedly benefit the middle class and poor, but downplays increases on taxes that hit these groups hardest (Social Security, sales).

  d. Evades the issue of record government deficits under Presidents Reagan and George W. Bush's supply-side policies vs. surplus under Clinton.

  e. Doesn't address the arguments that deregulation of big business has led to widespread fraud, runaway wealth at the top, and instability in the American economy (e.g. mortgage and credit meltdown in late 2000s).

  f. Doesn't address the astronomically widening pay gap between executives and their employees.

  g. Doesn't address excesses of speculative investing, new domination of stock market by hedge funds, equity funds, and unproductive industries like gambling.

  h. Doesn't address the power of wealthy special interests to influence government tax and regulatory power, and to create loopholes in whatever taxes and regulations are legislated.

  i. Typical conservative semantic and rhetorical stacking the deck to claim that the middle class and poor gained ground at about the same rate as the rich, and that women gained ground on men (without noting that more women have been forced to work to offset declining real income). (Contrast to Sklar, Giroux.)

D. David Frum, "The Vanishing Republican Voter: Why Income Inequality is Destroying the G.O.P Base." Prominent conservative source contradicts other conservatives like Laffer and the Treasury Department in affirming that inequality has increased and that it is working against the Republicans on several levels, so he urges Republicans to address the problem forthrightly. Confirms conservative stereotype of liberals as elitists, but with a different twist: The rich, especially those who are highly educated and attuned to technological advances and the global economy, are tending Democratic—not because the Democrats are the party of elitism vs. populism, but because those in this class have perceived that the Democrats have a more realistic, flexible view of these economic and technological changes.

III. Conclusion. Who can we believe? What special interests and special pleading might bias arguments on the opposing sides?

A. Conservative: Rich individuals and corporations spend lots of money supporting politicians and lobbying government, hiring public relations and advertising agents, funding foundations and think tanks, and controlling media through ownership and advertising to push the conservative line. Many people (including a lot that I know) will do and say just about anything, whether it's honest or not, for money and favor by the rich.

B. Liberal and left: People and organizations that benefit from liberal government programs act as comparable special interests on the left, such as public employees including teachers at public schools and universities, and unions representing these groups. Liberal politicians, media, foundations, or professors might pander to these constituencies and others, like poor people, minorities, and feminists, to make money, get elected, or otherwise advance their own careers. Such pandering to these groups, however, would appear to be less easy to verify as a motivating force and less lucrative than conservative pandering to the rich and corporations.

C. This analysis is complicated somewhat by Frum's argument that more wealthy people have been shifting their allegiance to the Democratic Party, though not necessarily to liberal constituencies. That is, they might have simply decided that the Democrats more effectively serve their interests than do the Republicans—which leaves poorer liberal constituencies in the lurch. Example of Obama's support by wealthy interests.

SAMPLE RESEARCH PAPER

See "Rhetoric and the Wealth Gap," by Sarah Whelan, online at:
http://www.paradigmpublishers.com/Books/BookDetail.aspx?productID=208952.

CHAPTER **18**

Documentation and Research Resources

DOCUMENTATION

Citations in Your Text

The recommended documentation style for college papers varies among academic disciplines and instructors; however, the standard style for most English and other humanities courses is based on the Modern Language Association's *MLA Handbook for Writers of Research Papers* (2003). Instead of older, cumbersome styles of footnotes and bibliographies, the current MLA system uses streamlined, brief notes with page references in parentheses following citations, along with a "Works Cited" section at the end providing full bibliographical data.

The online student paper in chapter 17 by Sarah Whelan illustrates this style (see page 388).

The basic rule for documentation is to use common sense in providing readers whatever they need to know about who your sources are throughout the course of your paper, in providing enough bibliographical information in your list of works cited for them to look up the sources themselves, and in making perfectly clear which ideas in the paper are your own and which ones you are attributing to sources ("According to," "In so-and-so's opinion"). Failing to make the latter distinction at any point in your paper can amount to plagiarism.

Whenever you directly or indirectly cite outside sources, you should identify authors with full name and any pertinent identifying information in introducing the quotation, although after the first reference you can just use last names. You might also give the name of the work in introducing it if you think it is useful for readers, as this saves them time in having to look ahead to the works cited section, and you can abbreviate long titles to a word or two. If you discuss a work by one author at length, alternating quotations that have various page numbers and your own text, and it is clear that all quotations refer to the same work, you needn't repeat the author's name each time you give a page reference. If you come back to a previously cited work after others have intervened, put the author's last name in the parenthetical reference, for example, (Roberts 25). If you cite more than one source by an author, include a shortened version of the title of the work you're citing within the parenthetical reference, for example, (Krugman, *Peddling* 24). Readings from a textbook like this one should be cited in their original source publication when possible. Otherwise, the quotation should be cited in this form: (Morse, as quoted in Lazere 1). Lazere should then be included in the works cited, as indicated in that section below.

Style of Parenthetical References

Parenthetical page references are placed at the end of the last sentence quoted, after the quotation marks but before the final period or question mark, with spacing as follows:

> "... Italy's was four times larger" (29).

Page references need not use "p." or "pp." or be preceded by a comma—for example, (Barlett and Steele 11–36).

Dates for periodicals cited in your text can follow either the form (2 July 1999) or (July 2, 1999). If there is no day, there should be no comma between month and year (July 1999). The *MLA Handbook* recommends spelling out the full name of months in your text but abbreviating those with more than four letters in your works cited section.

Indented Quotations

Quotations longer than four lines should be introduced by a colon, set off from the introductory text with a double space, and indented ten spaces from the left margin and another five spaces for paragraph beginnings. Do not use quotation marks with indented quotations, since the setoff style itself signals a quotation. In this style, the parenthetical reference goes after the last sentence and after the period:

> ... the facts tell an entirely different story. (29)

WORKS CITED SECTION

In MLA style, all sources cited throughout the text are fully documented in a works cited section at the end. (If you want to include works that you have consulted without citing them in the paper, title this section "Works Cited and Consulted.") Sources are listed with last names first, in alphabetical order. Entries for which the author is not identified are alphabetized by title. Entries are double-spaced with no extra space between lines. If an entry runs longer than one line, additional lines are indented five spaces, using a "hanging indent" word-processing command. Main elements are separated by periods. Publication information is written in one sentence, in this order: New York: Basic Books, 1986.

Sample Entries

Books

Book by One Author. The author's last name is followed by a comma, the first name, and a period. The title comes next, italicized (underlined if the paper is handwritten or typed on a typewriter), followed by a period. Next is the city of publication, followed by a colon, then the name of the press, comma, and year of publication. If the city of publication is not one of the major publishing centers and its state is perhaps unknown to readers, include a standard abbreviation for the state after the city name.

> Schrag, Peter. *Paradise Lost: California's Experience, America's Future.* New York: New Press, 1998.
>
> Barton, David. *The Myth of Separation.* 4th Edition. Plano, TX: Wallbuilder Press, 1991.

Book by Two or Three Authors. List the names of all authors, reversing the first and last name of only the first author.

> Barlett, Donald, and James Steele. *America: What Went Wrong?* Kansas City: Andrews McNeel, 1992.

Book by Four or More Authors. List only the first author's name, followed by a comma and et al. (Latin, "and others").

> Belenky, Mary Field, et al. *Women's Ways of Knowing.* New York: Basic Books, 1986.

Two or More Works by the Same Author. Arrange the works alphabetically by title (not counting "The" or "A"). After giving the author's name in the first entry, begin subsequent entries with three hyphens and a period.

> Krugman, Paul. *The Great Unraveling.* New York: W. W. Norton, 2004.
> ———. *Peddling Prosperity.* New York: W. W. Norton, 1994.

Chapter in a Single-Author Book. Begin with author and chapter title (in quotation marks), followed by period, then book title. Page numbers for the selection follow the publication date after a period.

> Kozol, Jonathan. "Other People's Children." *Savage Inequalities.* New York: Crown, 1991. 40–82.

Book or Anthology with an Editor. Begin entry with author's name, followed by comma and "ed."

> Aufderheide, Patricia, ed. *Beyond PC: Toward a Politics of Understanding.* Saint Paul, MN: Graywolf, 1992.

Chapter in an Anthology. Begin with author and title of the selection (in quotation marks), followed by the anthology title, editor's name, publisher and date, followed after a period by page numbers of the article.

> D'Souza, Dinesh. "The Visigoths in Tweed." *Beyond PC: Toward a Politics of Understanding.* Ed. Patricia Aufderheide, Saint Paul, MN: Graywolf, 1992. 11–22.

Periodicals

For signed articles, start with author's name (alphabetized by last name), article title in quotation marks, periodical name italicized, and date (abbreviate months longer than four letters), followed by a colon and page number. For unsigned articles or editorials, alphabetize by title.

Article in a Newspaper.

> Ivins, Molly. "Tax Cut Redistributes Wealth in Wrong Direction." *Knoxville News-Sentinel,* 14 Feb. 2001: A12.

Article in a Weekly or Biweekly Magazine.

> Grossman, Jerome. "Blame Game." *The Nation,* 26 Oct. 1992: 457.

Article in a Monthly or Bimonthly Magazine.

> Roberts, Paul Craig. "What Everyone 'Knows' About Reaganomics." *Commentary,* Feb. 1991: 25–30.

Personal Interviews

> Hansley, Dr. Phillip, Associate Chancellor, University of Tennessee. Personal interview. 28 June 2002.

Sources on the World Wide Web

Carnell, Elizabeth. "Why Try Holly Sklar's Socialist Plans for the Economy When the United States Is Doing Just Fine?" Left Watch 1 Sept. 1999 <http://www.leftwatch.com/holly_sklar/sklar001.html>.

Include page numbers as in other entries if they are provided, though they are not in many Web sites and e-mail postings.

RESEARCH RESOURCES

In this edition, the lists of research resources, including partisan ones on the political left and right, which formed a separate chapter in the original edition, have been moved to the Web site at http://www.paradigmpublishers.com/Books/BookDetail.aspx?productID=208952.

Index

Abramoff, Jack, 158–59, 201
absolutism, 128
abstract language, 81, 84–5; 372–73
Abu Ghraib prison, 68, 179, 253
Accuracy in Media, 313
ad hominem fallacy: defined, 155; forms of, 214–16; propaganda, 339; self-interests and, 336
ad populum fallacy, 212–13
Adams, John, 14
advertising: conflicts of interests 335; corporate, 307; political attack ads, 341. *See also* media
advocacy groups, 337; categories of, 337; corporate, 338–39; lobbying by, 337–39; most powerful list, 338. *See also* special interests
Afrocentrism, 145, 161
Against the American Grain (Macdonald), 304
agenda setting, 199–202
Agnew, Spiro, 67
Aid to Families with Dependent Children (AFDC), 83
Air America Radio, 200
Al Qaeda, 31, 178, 250, 253, 256
Allport, Gordon, 155
allusions, 42
Alterman, Eric, 200, 306
American Association of Retired Persons (AARP), 337
American Bandstand, 8–9
American Enterprise Institute, 288
American Independent Party, 270
American Media and Mass Culture (Lazere), 319
American Revolution, 33
"American Scholar" (Emerson), 15, 57, 172
American Spectator, The, 287, 289, 319
American-Israeli Public Affairs Committee (AIPAC), 342
analogy, 85; arguments by, 73; false, 192; reasoning by, 38; symbolic, 73
analysis: critical thinking and, 58; modes of, 41; statistical

tricks, 372–76. *See also* causal analysis
Andersen, Arthur, 7, 158
anecdotes, 145
annotated bibliography, 385–86
anthropomorphism, 145–46
"Anti-Capitalism in Five Minutes or Less" (Jensen), 147–50
Antigone (Sophocles), 176
anti-Semitism, 284
Anzaldúa, Gloria, 87
Apology, The (Plato), 14, 66, 126–27, 176
appeal to authority, 212–13
appeal to fear, 213, 281, 316, 367
appeal to pity, 213, 373
appeal to tradition, 213
Apprentice, The, 157, 274
argumentation, 3; agenda setting, 199–202; by analogy, 180; analogies in, 192; analysis, synthesis, and judgments, 40–42; cogently reasoned, 38–42; connotation in, 80–3; construction, 38; deductive and inductive, 191–97; defined, 32; demagogic, 81; denotation in, 79; elements, 40; eloquence and moral force, 42–3; extended line of, 222; facts *vs.* opinions in, 33–35; glossary, 213; modes of analysis in, 41; phrasing, 100; public, 32; refutation of opposing arguments, 40; relevancy in, 39–40; researching, 33; Rogerian argument, 59, 130–31; style and tone, 42–3; synthesis in, 41–42; tone and style, 202; well balanced, fair-minded, and qualified, 40; writing, 33–4
argument from the converse, 195, 213, 269
argument from the exception, 161–62, 213
argument to authority, 132
argument to best explanation, 38
Aristotle, 13–14, 42
Aronowitz, Stanley, 58, 84

assertion, 38
assumptions. *See* culturally conditioned assumptions
Atlantic Monthly, 287
Atwater, Lee, 341
authoritarianism and conformity, 142, 171–74
authority: argument to, 132

Baker, Dean, 35
Baker, Russell, 144
Baldwin, James, 52–3, 68–71, 72, 161, 180–81
bandwagon, 213
Barlett, Donald, 159, 163
"Battle over Patriotism Curriculum" (Rohter), 136–38
Beauty Myth, The: How Images of Beauty Are Used Against Women (Wolf), 114, 116–120, 134, 143
Before the Fall (Safire), 8
begging the question, 213
Belenky, Mary Field, 128
"Believers and Doubters," 59
Bennett, William J., 30, 127, 239–41, 318, 376
Berkeley (University of California), v, xv, 7, 17–19, 28, 41, 42, 43, 60, 90, 91
Berkeley in the Sixties, 43
"Best and Worst in the National Heart" (Reeves), 132–33
bias, 126; anti-business, 160; in book reviewers, 335–36; ESBYODS principle, 128–29, 155, 179, 192; in media, 308–09; in rhetoric, 88–9
Bible, the 67
Big Con, The: The True Story of How Washington Got Hoodwinked and Hijacked by Crackpot Economics (Chait), 364, 367, 386
"Billionaires Up, America Down" (Sklar), 368–69
"Bill Moyers' Journal," 316
Bin Laden, Osama, 178
Black Muslims. *See* Nation of Islam
blaming the victim: causal analysis, 225; common patterns of, 226; fallacy of, 11; projection and, 180; sexism and, 134

Credits

A SEMANTIC CALCULATOR FOR BIAS IN RHETORIC

This is a guide that you can apply in writing papers about sources, with respect both to those sources' biases and to your own as a writer.

1. What is the author's vantage point, in terms of social class, wealth, occupation, gender, ethnic group, political ideology, educational level, age, and so on? Is that vantage point apt to color her/his attitudes on the issue under discussion? Does she/he have anything personally to gain from the position she/he is arguing for, any conflicts of interest or other reasons for special pleading? (See chapter 17.)
2. What organized financial, political, ethnic, or other interests are backing the advocated position? What groups or special interests stand to profit financially, politically, or otherwise from it? In the Latin phrase, cui bono, "Who benefits?" (See chapter 17.)
3. Once you have determined the author's vantage point and/or the special interests being favored, look for signs of ethnocentrism, rationalization or wishful thinking, sentimentality, one-sidedness, selective vision, or a double standard. (See chapter 8.)
4. Look for the following forms of setting the agenda and stacking the deck reflecting the biases in number 3:
   a. Playing up
      (1) arguments favorable to one's own side
      (2) arguments unfavorable to the other side
      (3) the other side's power, wealth, extremism, misdeeds ("a widespread pattern of abuses"), or unity ("a vast conspiracy," "a tightly coordinated machine")
   b. Downplaying (or suppressing altogether)
      (1) arguments unfavorable to one's own side
      (2) arguments favorable to the other side
      (3) one's own side's power, wealth, extremism, misdeeds ("a small number of isolated instances," "a few rotten apples"), or unity ("an uncoordinated collection of diverse, grassroots groups")
   c. Applying "clean" words (ones with positive connotations) to one's own side, without support
      Applying "dirty" words (ones with negative connotations) to the other side, without support
   d. Assuming that the representatives of one's own side are trustworthy, truthful, and have no selfish motives, while assuming the opposite of the other side's representatives
   e. Giving credit to one's own side for positive events
   f. Blaming the other side for negative events